MILITARY BIBLIOGRAPHY OF THE CIVIL WAR

VOLUME I

### Military Bibliography of the Civil War

Volume I (reprint edition 1971, clothbound) Arno Press and The New York Public Library

Originally published 1961–1962 by the Library as: Regimental Publications and Personal Narratives of the Civil War: Northern States

In 7 parts:

1. Illinois
2. New York
3. New England States
4. New Jersey and Pennsylvania
5. Indiana and Ohio
6. Iowa, Kansas, Michigan, Minnesota, and Wisconsin
7. Index of Names

Volume II (1967, paperbound) The New York Public Library

Regimental Publications and Personal Narratives: Southern Border, and Western States and Territories; Federal Troops

Union and Confederate Biographies

Volume III (*Forthcoming*) The New York Public Library

General References

Armed Forces

Campaigns and Battles

Volume IV (*Forthcoming*) The New York Public Library

Comprehensive Index

# Military Bibliography of the Civil War

*Compiled by* C. E. DORNBUSCH

Volume One

Regimental Publications and Personal Narratives: Northern States
(in seven parts)

1. Illinois    2. New York    3. New England States
4. New Jersey and Pennsylvania    5. Indiana and Ohio
6. Iowa, Kansas, Michigan, Minnesota, and Wisconsin
7. Index of Names

THE NEW YORK PUBLIC LIBRARY
ASTOR, LENOX AND TILDEN FOUNDATIONS

&

ARNO PRESS INC.
A PUBLISHING AND LIBRARY SERVICE OF THE NEW YORK TIMES
New York

Originally published 1961-1962 by The New York
Public Library in seven parts as *Regimental
Publications and Personal Narratives of the
Civil War*, Volume One: Northern States

(final preface appears in Part VI)

Reprint edition 1971

LC 72-137700
NYPL ISBN 0-87104-504-4
ARNO ISBN 0-405-01744-8

THIS VOLUME HAS BEEN PUBLISHED WITH HELP

FROM THE EMILY ELLSWORTH FORD SKEEL FUND

Manufactured in the United States of America

# Regimental Publications
# & Personal Narratives
# of the Civil War

## A Checklist

*Compiled by* C. E. DORNBUSCH

Volume One    Northern States
PART I    ILLINOIS

New York

The New York Public Library

1961

THIS VOLUME HAS BEEN PUBLISHED WITH HELP

FROM THE EMILY ELLSWORTH FORD SKEEL FUND

# Preface

THIS CHECKLIST of regimental histories, publications of regimental associations, and personal narratives of participants in the Civil War is a revision of and supplement to the section on "Military Organizations" in the third edition of the *Bibliography of State Participation in the Civil War*, prepared and published by the War Department Library, Washington, D. C. in 1913 as its Subject Catalogue No 6.*

The present checklist is to be published in seven Parts. The first six will cover the batteries and regiments of seventeen Northern states: I Illinois; II New York; III New England states; IV New Jersey and Pennsylvania; V Indiana and Ohio; and VI Iowa, Kansas, Michigan, Minnesota, and Wisconsin. A final section will provide an index of the publications listed for these seventeen states.

The compiler has followed the arrangement of the 1913 work. Within each state military units are arranged numerically by arm of service — Artillery, Cavalry, and Infantry. While the earlier work entered only units for which publications were known, the present compilation has recorded all units which were organized. Again, while rosters and compilations of regimental histories were reported in one section headed "State Publication" in *BSP*, the present work has indexed these publications under the individual military units.

The compiler has located and personally examined each work entered in this checklist. Some entries which were listed in *BSP* have been omitted — entries based on titles taken from bibliographies, correspondence, dealers' catalogues, and other sources but not in the War Department Library. Such "ghosts" as have remained have been omitted here. The present checklist also omits the *BSP* references to the *National Tribune*, and a group of articles by George L. Kilmer which are cited in *BSP* not by original publication but as mounted clippings in ten volumes in the War Department Library collections.

Although a monumental work, some errors found their way into the *BSP*. For instance, Douglas Putnam's *Recollections of the battle of Shiloh* was entered under the 92nd Ohio Regiment, the regiment to which he belonged. But that regiment was formed some months after the battle was fought, and Putnam could write of it not as a member but as a civilian observer. Similarly

---

* The Bibliography (hereafter referred to as *BSP*) was prepared as a catalogue and index of a major Civil War collection, now part of the National War College Library, Washington.

Eagan's *Battle of Birch Coolie* is entered under the 1st Minnesota Heavy Artillery, although that unit did not participate in the battle.

The seventeen states covered by this checklist had a total of 2,202 batteries and regiments which took part in the Civil War. Each of these units has been listed with a brief statement of its service, i. e. muster in and muster out dates. Where the same number has been assigned to two regiments, they have been distinguished by the term of original enlistments, i. e. three months or three years. Changes in a unit's designation or arm of service as well as amalgamations have been reported. Although some units mustered out before the close of the war and transferred their recruits and veterans to other units, the checklist has not reported this movement of personnel. Reference is made to regimental rosters and narratives of a unit's service where this information may be found.

The compiler has included any articles and publications which could be associated with a particular battery or regiment. The bulk of these are the regimental histories, reunion proceedings, and unit rosters. Publications of sermons preached at soldiers' funerals have been reported. Though their size did not lend to preservation, a surprising number of soldiers' memorials have been located. Broadsides of company rosters, often illustrated in color, were soldiers' souvenirs of the war. The inclusion of all these types of material has here resulted in the broadest possible bibliographical coverage of Civil War materials. All prison narratives have been entered under the regiment in which the author was serving at the time of his capture. Newspapers printed in the field by army units have not been included.

The value of this checklist is primarily in the listing of the personal narratives of Civil War participants, the rank and file as well as officers, from Lieutenant to Colonel. (By reason of the honorary Brevet rank, the Colonel of a regiment could be appointed Brigadier General at the close of the war, and in this case later reference to his rank is as General.) Usually the publication identifies the battery or regiment of the author. Occasionally, however, he may have served in two or more units, and the later service (often at a higher rank) is used on the title-page. Such items are entered in the checklist under the unit in which the author served at the time the events narrated took place.

Narratives which reflect service in two or more units are entered under the unit of first service, with cross reference to other units in which the author served. When an author's service crossed state lines or when it was with the United States Colored Troops, his narrative has been fully entered under each unit.

The compiler has made extensive search of American journals and periodicals published since the close of hostilities. The very magnitude of this undertaking precludes even the hope of a definitive checklist. One assumes that obscure imprints with limited distribution have tended to disappear. In many cases only single surviving copies have been located. The search is continuing while other sections of the list are in preparation, and it is hoped that publication will bring new additions to light.

Following the statement of unit service, entries' are given in two groups, anonymous publications followed by author entries. At least one location of each title is reported, except in the case of standard works such as the papers of the Military Order of the Loyal Legion of the United States, or periodical entries which may be located through the *Union List of Serials* and its supplements. Title-pages have been transcribed in full, including author statements which supply rank and unit. Distinction is made between illustrations which appear in the body of the text and illustrations which appear on unpaginated plates. Plates that are paged have been considered as text illustrations. The place of publication is not identified when within same state as checklist is describing. The collation of reunion proceedings has been limited to their numbering and date.

The very size of the compiler's undertaking has meant assistance from many sources. In his inspection of collections throughout the country, the compiler has been helped by many librarians, and their contributions have been acknowledged in the appropriate sections of the checklist. Above all the compiler is indebted to the administrators of The Emily E. F. Skeel Fund of The New York Public Library for making the compilation of this checklist possible and for freedom in developing it.

ILLINOIS

# Table of Contents

# Abbreviations

| | |
|---|---|
| *AGR* | Report of the Adjutant General of the State of Illinois for the years, 1861–66, Springfield, 1900–02. 8 v. |
| *BandL* | Battles and leaders, New York, 1887–88. 4 v. |
| *BandG* | Blue and Gray, Philadelphia |
| *Coulter* | Travels in the Confederate states, a bibliography. By E. Merton Coulter. 1948 |
| *JIHS* | Journal of the Illinois state historical [library] society |
| *JUSCA* | Journal of the United States cavalry association, Fort Leavenworth |
| *MOLLUS* | Military order of the loyal legion of the United States |
| *DC* | War papers District of Columbia commandery |
| *Ill* | Military essays and recollections Illinois commandery |
| *Iowa* | War sketches Iowa commandery |
| *Me* | War papers Maine commandery |
| *Mass* | Civil war papers Massachusetts commandery |
| *Mich* | War papers Michigan commandery |
| *Minn* | Glimpses of the Nation's struggles Minnesota commandery |
| *Mo* | War papers Missouri commandery |
| *Neb* | Civil war sketches Nebraska commandery |
| *Wis* | Civil war papers Wisconsin commandery |
| *PMHSM* | Papers of the Military historical society of Massachusetts |
| *PIHL* | Publications of the Illinois state historical [library] society |
| *US* | The united service, Philadelphia |

In the preparation of this section of the checklist, Miss Margaret A. Flint, Assistant State Historian, Springfield, Illinois, has been most helpful to the compiler.

# Reference Works

Dyer, Frederick Henry, 1849–1917.

A compendium of the War of the rebellion. 1908 (reprinted 1959).

"Regimental index" 117–31. "Regimental histories" 1021–1103. The same pagination is used in the 1959 reprint.

Illinois.   Adjutant General.

Report of the . . . containing Reports for the years 1861–66. Revised by Brigadier General J. N. Reece. Springfield, Phillips Bros., State printers, 1900–02. 8 v. 21cm.

*The Union army.*

"Record of Illinois regiments," III (1908) 244–368.

United States.   Adjutant General's Office.

Official army register of the volunteer force of the United States army for the years 1861, '62, '63, '64, '65. Part VI. Indiana, Illinois. Washington, 1865.

A roster of officers by regiments with an alphabetical index for the two states.

# ILLINOIS

## Artillery

### 1ST REGIMENT OF LIGHT ARTILLERY

#### Battery A

Entered State service as Smiths' Chicago light artillery: April 17, 1861.
Reorganized for three year's service: July 16, 1861.
Mustered out: July 3, 1865.
AGR VIII 598–605.

First re-union of Battery "A," First Ill. artillery, Chicago, Illinois, Feb. 16th, 1885. [Chicago, Franz Gindele print. co., 1885] 28, (1) p. 23cm.                                DLC NHi    1

Chaleron, J        A
Battle echoes from Shiloh. Southern historical society papers XXI (Richmond 1893) 215–24.                                                    2
Text signed: J. A. Chaleron, senior surviving officer, Fifth company, Battalion Washington artillery.

Dudley, Henry Walbridge, 1840–
Autobiography of Henry Walbridge Dudley. Menasha, Wis., George Banta pub. co. [1914] 189 p. 2 plans, 2 plates (ports.). 23½cm.
                                                    IHi    3

Kimbell, Charles Bill, 1839–
History of Battery "A," First Illinois light artillery volunteers [by] Charles B. Kimbell. Chicago, Cushing print. co., 1899. viii, [9]–320 p. illus., ports. 23½cm. DLC NHi NN    4
"Biographical sketches . . ." [90]–255. Coulter 279.
Unit roster [24]–34.

#### Battery B

Mustered in: May 2, 1861.
Mustered out: July 6, 1865.
AGR VIII 606–14.

Reunions of Taylor's battery, 18th anniversary of the battle of Fort Donelson, February 14, 1880, 25th anniversary of the battle of Belmont, November 6, 1886. Chicago, Craig press [1890] 129 p. plates (illus., ports.). 24cm.
                                    DLC IHi NHi    5
"Remarks, both explanatory and apologetic" signed: C. W. Pierce.
Unit roster [117–27]

White, Patrick H        1833–1915.
Civil war diary of Patrick H. White. Contributed by J. E. Boos. JIHS xv (1923) 640–63. plate (port.).                        6

#### Battery C

Mustered in: October 31, 1861.
Mustered out: June 14, 1865.
AGR VIII 614–8.

#### Battery D

Mustered in: July 30, 1861.
Mustered out: July 28, 1865.
AGR VIII 618–23.

Woodruff, George H
History of Battery D, First artillery, McAlister's battery. In his Fifteen years ago (1876) 397–422.                        7

#### Battery E

Mustered in: December 19, 1861.
Mustered out: July 15, 1865.
AGR VIII 623–8.

#### Battery F

Mustered in: February 25, 1862.
Consolidated with other batteries: March 7, 1865.
AGR VIII 628–32.

#### Battery G

Mustered in: February 28, 1862.
Mustered out: July 24, 1865.
AGR VIII 632–5.

Osborn, Joseph Esbjörn
Personal memories of Brig.-Gen. C. J. Stolbrand. Yearbook of the Swedish historical society XXXIII (Chicago 1910) 5–17.    8

#### Battery H

Mustered in: February 20, 1862.
Mustered out: June 14, 1865.
AGR VIII 635–9.

Anderson, John A
Civil war reminiscences. Yearbook of the Swedish historical society XXXIII (Chicago 1910) 17–22.                        9

#### Battery I

Mustered in: February 10, 1862.
Mustered out: July 26, 1865.
AGR VIII 639–44.

Bouton, Edward, 1834–
The battle of "Shiloh," a paper prepared and read before California commandery of the Mili-

*Battery I, continued*

tary order of the loyal legion of the United States, April 11, 1896, by Edward Bouton. 27 p. 23½cm.                    DLC    *10*
On cover: War paper no. 16....

—— Events of the Civil war, by General Edward Bouton, with sketch of the author. [Los Angeles, Kingsley, Moles & Collins co., printers, 1906] 115 p. front. (port.), 1 illus., ports. 25cm.                DLC NN    *11*

### Battery K

*Mustered in: January 9, 1862.*
*Mustered out: December 10, 1864. The Battery was reorganized in March 1865 and mustered out: July 15, 1865.*
AGR VIII 644–50.

### Battery L

*Mustered in: February 22, 1862.*
*Mustered out: July 10, 1865.*
AGR VIII 650–3.

### Battery M

*Mustered in: August 12, 1862.*
*Mustered out: July 24, 1865.*
AGR VIII 653–6.

History of the organization, marches, campings, general services and final muster out of Battery M, First regiment of Illinois light artillery. Together with detailed accounts of incidents both grave and facetious connected therewith. Compiled from the official records and from the diaries of the different members, by members of the Battery. Princeton, Mercer & Dean, 1892. viii, [11]–301 p. 24½cm.
                              DLC    *12*

## 2ND REGIMENT OF LIGHT ARTILLERY

### Battery A

*Entered State service: May 23, 1861; Federal service: August 17, 1861.*
*Mustered out: July 27, 1865.*
AGR VIII 669–73.

### Battery B

*Organized: June 20, 1861.*
*Mustered out: July 15, 1865.*
AGR VIII 674–7.

### Battery C

*Organized: August 5, 1861.*
*Mustered out: August 3, 1865.*
AGR VIII 677–82.

### Battery D

*Mustered in: December 17, 1861.*
*Mustered out: May 21, 1864.*
AGR VIII 682–4.

### Battery E

*Mustered in: August 20, 1861.*
*Mustered out: September 29, 1864.*
AGR VIII 684–7.

### Battery F

*Mustered in: December 11, 1861.*
*Mustered out: July 27, 1865.*
AGR VIII 687–91.

### Battery G

*Mustered in: December 31, 1861.*
*Mustered out: September 4, 1865.*
AGR VIII 691–6.

United States military record Battery G, 2d Ill. lt. art'y. Chicago, Lith. & printed by Chas. Shober [1865] col. illus. broadside, 54 x 40½cm.
c1864 by S. Madison Moore & Co.    IHi    *13*

### Battery H

*Mustered in: December 31, 1861.*
*Mustered out: July 29, 1865.*
AGR VIII 696–701.

### Battery I

*Mustered in: December 31, 1861.*
*Mustered out: June 14, 1865.*
AGR VIII 701–5.

Woodruff, George H
[History of] Battery I, Second artillery, Barnett's battery. In his Fifteen years ago (1876) 423–37.                    *14*

### Battery K

*Mustered in: December 31, 1861.*
*Mustered out: July 14, 1865.*
AGR VIII 705–9.

*Battery L*

Mustered in: February 28, 1862.
Mustered out: August 9, 1865.
AGR VIII 709–15.

*Battery M*

Mustered in: June 6, 1862.
Mustered out: April 11, 1864.
AGR VIII 715–6.

### INDEPENDENT BATTERIES

*Bridge's Battery of Light Artillery*

Organized: January 14, 1863, from Company G, 19th regiment of infantry. Transferred to 1st regiment of light artillery as Battery B, December 21, 1864.
AGR VIII 767.

Ducat, Arthur Charles, 1839–1896.
Speech of Gen. Arthur C. Ducat, delivered at Rosehill cemetery, May 31st, 1870, at the dedication of the monument erected to the soldiers of the Bridges battery of the Army of the Cumberland who fell during the War of the rebellion. 8 p. 22cm.          DLC   **15**
Caption title.

*Chicago Board of Trade Battery of Light Artillery*

Mustered in: August 1, 1862.
Mustered out: June 30, 1865.
AGR VIII 644–7.

Calvin Durand, Sarah Gould Downs Durand, a memorial. Privately printed. Chicago [Printed by R. R. Donnelley & Sons co.] 1912. 100 p. 3 plates (facs., 2 ports.). 23½cm.   IHi   **16**
Autobiographical sketch of Calvin Durand, 1840–1911, p. 41–100.

Historical sketch of the Chicago Board of trade battery, horse artillery, Illinois volunteers. Chicago [Henneberry co.] 1902. 90 p. illus., ports. 24½cm.          DLC IHi NN   **17**
Unit roster 67–80.
[Three letters dated in November, 1902, with reference to the Historical sketch] [3] p. inserted.

Robinson, George I
With Kilpatrick around Atlanta, by Capt. George I. Robinson. 1886. *MOLLUS-Wis* I 201–27.          **18**

*Chicago Mercantile Battery of Light Artillery*

Mustered in: August 29, 1862.
Mustered out: July 10, 1865.
AGR VIII 739–46.

Pitts, Florison D
The Civil war diary of Florison D. Pitts. *Mid-America* XL (Chicago 1958) 22–63.   **19**

*Cogswell's Battery of Light Artillery*

Mustered in: November 11, 1861.
Mustered out: August 14, 1865.
AGR VIII 752–7.

*Colvin's Battery of Light Artillery*

Organized: October 6, 1863.
Transferred to 1st regiment of light artillery as Battery K, March 23, 1865.
AGR VIII 768.

*Henshaw's Battery of Light Artillery*

Mustered in: December 3, 1862.
Mustered out: July 18, 1865.
AGR VIII 763–6.

*Renwick's Elgin Battery of Light Artillery*

Mustered in: November 15, 1862.
Mustered out: July 18, 1865.
AGR VIII 758–62.

Hannaford, George A
My first campaign (read Jan 25, 1887). *MOLLUS-Iowa* I 8–17.          **19A**

*Springfield Battery of Light Artillery*

Mustered in: August 21, 1862.
Mustered out: June 30, 1865.
AGR VIII 747–51.

## Cavalry

### 1ST CAVALRY

Mustered in: July 3, 1861.
Mustered out: July 15, 1862.
AGR VII 461–85.

### 2ND CAVALRY

Mustered in: August 12, 1861.
Mustered out: November 22, 1865.
AGR VII 486–542.

Fletcher, Samuel H
The history of Company A, Second cavalry, by Samuel H. Fletcher, a member of the Company, in collaboration with D. H. Fletcher. [Chicago, 1912] xii, 212, (9) p. 20½cm.
Unit roster (9) p.          IHi NN   **20**

*2nd Cavalry, continued*

Hicks, Henry G
Fort Donelson, by Brevet-Major Henry G.
Hicks. *MOLLUS-Minn* IV 437–53.     **21**

## 3RD CAVALRY

*Mustered in: August 27, 1861.*
*Mustered out: October 18, 1865.*
*AGR* VII 543–602.

## 4TH CAVALRY

*Mustered in: September 26, 1861.*
*Consolidated with 14th cavalry: June 14, 1865.*
*AGR* VII 603–52.

Avery, Phineas O            1838–
History of the Fourth Illinois cavalry regiment, by P. O. Avery of Company I, Fourth Illinois. Humboldt, Neb., Enterprise, 1903. 194 p. plates (ports.). 22½cm.
                    DLC IHi NN     **22**
Unit roster 3–42. "Errata" slip inserted.

Wilson, William
History and roster of the surviving members of the 4th Illinois cavalry with their residences. Compiled by William Wilson, Secretary of 4th Illinois cavalry association. Chicago, Straub & Hallott, printers, 1884. 12 p. 15cm.    IHi     **23**
Title and imprint from cover.

Young, Jesse Bowman, 1844–1914.
What a boy saw in the army, a story of sightseeing and adventure in the War for the Union, by Jesse Bowman Young. 100 original drawings by Frank Beard. New York, Hunt & Eaton [1894] 398 p. illus., ports. 25cm.    NN     **24**

## 5TH CAVALRY

*Organized: August 31–December 30, 1861.*
*Mustered out: October 27, 1865.*
*AGR* VII 653–94.

## 6TH CAVALRY

*Organized: November 19, 1861.*
*Mustered out: November 5, 1865.*
*AGR* VIII 3–52.

Woodward, Samuel Lippincott
Grierson's raid, April 17th to May 2d, 1863. *JUSCA* XIV (1904) 685–710; XV (1904) 94–123. illus., map, port.     **25**

## 7TH CAVALRY

*Mustered in: October 13, 1861.*
*Mustered out: October 20, 1865.*
*AGR* VIII 53–104.

Eby, Henry Harrison, 1841–
Observations of an Illinois boy in battle, camp and prisons, 1861 to 1865, by Henry H. Eby. Published by the author. Mendota, 1910. 284 p. illus., 2 maps, ports. 20cm. IHi NN     **26**
Coulter 143.

Forbes, Stephen Alfred
Grierson's cavalry raid. *PIHL* XII (1908) 99–130. plates (fold. map, ports.).     **27**

Surby, Richard W            1830–
Grierson's raids, and Hatch's sixty-four days march, with biographical sketches, and the life and adventures of Chickasaw, the scout, by R. W. Surby. Chicago, Rounds and James, printers, 1865. 396 p. plates (illus., ports.). 18½cm.                    IHi NN     **28**
Coulter 439.

Wills, Charles Wright, 1840–1883.
Army life of an Illinois soldier, including a day by record of Sherman's march to the sea, letters and diary of the late Charles W. Wills, Private and Sergeant 8th Illinois infantry, Lieutenant and Battalion Adjutant 7th Illinois cavalry, Captain, Major and Lieutenant-Colonel 103rd Illinois infantry. Compiled and published by his sister . . . Washington, Globe print. co., 1906. 383 p. front. (port.). 24cm.
                    IHi NN     **29**
Coulter 480. "Copyright by Mary E. Kellogg."

## 8TH CAVALRY

*Mustered in: September 18, 1861.*
*Mustered out: July 17, 1865.*
*AGR* VIII 105–56.

Biographical sketch of Major William H. Medill of the 8th Illinois cavalry, who fell in the pursuit after the battle of Gettysburg . . . Chicago, James Barnet, printer, 1864. 22, (2) p. front. (port.). 23cm.     InHi     **30**
"From the Martyrs and heroes of Illinois."

Minutes of the . . . annual reunion of the 8th Ill. vet. cav. association. XXIV (1889); XXVII (1892).     IHi     **31**

Roster of the Eighth Illinois veteran cavalry. Leavenworth, Kansas, Ketcheson & Reeves, printers, 1888. 31 p. 13½cm.    KFLGS     **32**

Forsyth, George Alexander, 1837–1915.
Thrilling days in army life, by General George A. Forsyth, U.S.A. With illustrations

by Rufus F. Zogbaum. New York, Harper &
Brothers, 1900. 196, (1) p. plates (illus.).
19½cm.                    DLC NN      32A
Partial contents: Sheridan's ride, 125–68; The closing scene at Appomattox court-house, 171–[97].

Hard, Abner
History of the Eighth cavalry regiment,
Illinois volunteers, during the great rebellion,
by Abner Hard, Surgeon of the Regiment.
Aurora, 1868. 368 p. plates (ports.). 22½cm.
                    DLC IHi NN      33
Unit roster [331–41]. Coulter 213.

Harter, Frederick A
Erinnerungen aus dem Amerikanischen Bürgerkriege, Ernstes und Heiteres aus bewegter
Zeit, von F. A. Harter, ehemaligen Mitgleide
des 8. Illinois Kavallerie-Regiments. Chicago,
Verlag von F. A. Harter, 1895. 288 p. front.
(illus.). 19½cm.                  WHi      34

Ingersoll, Chalmers, 1838–1908.
The unknown friends, a Civil war romance,
letters of my father and my mother, compiled
by Charlotte Ingersoll Morse. Chicago, A.
Kroch & Son, 1948. 110 p. plates (facs., 2
ports.). 23½cm.                   DLC      35

## 9TH CAVALRY

*Mustered in: November 30, 1861.*
*Mustered out: October 31, 1865.*
*AGR* viii 157–212.

. . . Re-union of the 9th Illinois volunteer cav-
alry veteran association ii–iii (1887–1888)
(IHi); iv (1889) (NHi); v–xi (1890–1896)
(IHi).                                    36

Roster 9th Ill. cavalry veteran association . . .
December 1, 1886. 8 p. 19cm.      IHi      37
Includes brief reference to the 1st reunion and or-
ganization of an association of survivors.

Roster of Ninth Illinois cavalry. [Menomonie,
Wis., 188–] [4] p. 18½cm.         IHi      38
Caption title: Signed: S. J. Bailey, late Sergeant
Co. G.

Abbott, Othman A            1842–
The last battle of Nashville, by Lieut. O. A.
Abbott. *MOLLUS-Neb* i 236–42.            39

—— Recollections of a pioneer lawyer . . .
Edited by Addison E. Sheldon. *Nebraska history magazine* xi (Lincoln 1929) 3–176. plates
(facs., illus., ports.).                  40

—— —— Lincoln, Neb., Nebraska State Historical Society, 1929. 176 p. plates (facs., illus.,
ports.). 24cm.                 IHi NN      41

Brackett, Albert Gallatin, 1829–1896.
The battles of Nashville. *US* xiii (1885)
257–63.                                   42

—— A cavalry raid [Mississippi, Febr. 1864]
*US* ns viii (1892) 519–26.               43

—— The evacuation of New Madrid by the
Federals. *US* ns v (1891) 182–7.         44

—— History of the United States cavalry
from the formation of the Federal government
to the 1st of June, 1863, to which is added a
list of all the cavalry regiments, with the names
of their commanders which have been in the
United States service since the breaking out
of the rebellion, by Albert G. Gallatin, Colonel Ninth Illinois volunteer cavalry. New
York, Harper & Brothers, 1865. xii, [13]–337 p.
front. (illus.), illus., 2 maps. 19½cm.
Civil war, 211–337.            NHi NN      45

—— A memorable march [Batesville to Helena, Ark., 1862] *US* ns iv (1890) 336–41.  46

—— Operations before, and fall of, Atlanta.
*US* ns iii (1890) 194–200.               47

Davenport, Edward Adolphus, 1834–
History of the Ninth regiment Illinois cavalry volunteers. Published under the auspices
of the Historical committee of the Regiment
. . . [eight names] Edited by Edward A. Davenport. Chicago [Donahue & Henneberry, print-
ers] 1888. xii, [13]–450, (1) p. plates (ports.).
23½cm.                 DLC IHi NHi NN      48
"Errata" (1) p. Unit roster 191–364.

Hawes, Jesse
Cahaba, a story of captive boys in Blue, by
Jesse Hawes, formerly of 9th Ill. Cav. New
York, Burr print. house [1888] xviii, 480 p.
plates (illus., plan, ports.). 24cm.
                       IHi NHi      49
"Addresses of all ex-Cahaba prisoners known," 478–
80. "Errata" slip inserted.

Tyler, William N
The dispatch carrier, by comrade Wm. N.
Tyler, Co. I, 9th Ill. cav., Co. B, 95th Ill. vol.
inf. A thrilling description of the adventures
of a dispatch carrier in the late war, the cap-
ture, imprisonment, escape and recapture of a
Union soldier, a complete narrative of a sol-
dier's individual experience in the Civil war,
from 1861 to 1865, as written by himself.
Second edition. Port Byron, Port Byron "Globe"
print., 1892. 89, 61 p. 17cm.     NHi      50
On cover: The dispatch carrier and memoirs of
Andersonville prison.
"Memoirs of Andersonville," 61 p.

## 10TH CAVALRY

*Mustered in: November 25, 1861.*
*Mustered out: November 22, 1865.*
*AGR* VIII 213–81.

Proceedings of the annual reunion of the Society of the 10th Illinois cavalry. . . . 1894–1899.         NHi   *51*
1897–1898 issued in one volume.

Duncan, William
The Army of the Tennessee under Major-General O. O. Howard, by Brevet-Major William Duncan. *MOLLUS-Minn* IV 164–75.  *52*

—— Through the Carolinas with the Army of the Tennessee. *MOLLUS-Minn* IV 329–36.  *53*

—— With the Army of the Tennessee through the Carolinas. *MOLLUS-Minn* IV 517–29.  *54*

## 11TH CAVALRY

*Mustered in: December 20, 1861.*
*Mustered out: September 30, 1865.*
*AGR* VIII 282–331.

## 12TH CAVALRY

*Mustered in: February 24, 1862.*
*Mustered out: May 29, 1866.*
*AGR* VIII 332–405.

Reunion of 12th Illinois cavalry, Springfield, Illinois, October 5, 6 and 7, 1918. Historical sketch of the command and dedication of Lincoln & Douglas statues. 24 p. front. (illus.), port. 25cm.           IHi  *55*

Allen, Winthrop Sargeant Gilman, 1837–1901.
Civil war letters of Winthrop S. G. Allen, by Harry E. Pratt. . . . [Springfield, Phillips Bros. print, 1932] 27 p. front. (port.). 23cm.          DLC IHi  *56*
Reprinted from *JISH* XXIV No 3 (Oct 1931).

Luff, William M
March of the cavalry from Harper's ferry, September 14, 1862. *MOLLUS-Ill* II 33–48. *57*

Mitchell, Frederick W
"A conundrum of the days of '64." 1890. 7 p. *MOLLUS-DC* no 5.               *58*

—— Fighting guerrillas on the La Fourche, La. 1904. 16 p. *MOLLUS-DC* no 56.  *59*

—— My three recruits. 1913. 9 p. *MOLLUS-DC* no 92.                 *60*

—— A personal episode of the first Stoneman raid. 1911. 10 p. *MOLLUS-DC* no 85.  *61*

White, Julius
The first sabre charge of the war [Martinsberg, W. Va., Sept. 3, 1862] *MOLLUS-Ill* III 25–35.                 *62*

## 13TH CAVALRY

*Organized: October 30, 1861–February 20, 1862.*
*Mustered out: August 31, 1865.*
*AGR* VIII 406–52.

Behlendorf, Frederick
The history of the Thirteenth Illinois cavalry regiment, volunteers U.S. army, from September, 1861, to September, 1865 . . . compiled from the journals of different members of said Regiment and from official reports, by Major Frederick Behlendorff. Grand Rapids, Mich., 1888. 40 p. front. (port.), ports. 23½cm.
Title and imprint from cover.     IHi  *63*

Field, Charles D
Three years in the saddle, from 1861 to 1865, memoirs of Charles D. Field. Thrilling stories of the war in camp and on the field of battle . . . by Charles D. Field. [Goldfield, Iowa, 1898] 74 p. front. (port.). 21cm.
Coulter 159.           DLC IHi  *64*

## 14TH CAVALRY

*Mustered in: January 7, February 6, 1863.*
*Mustered out: July 31, 1865.*
*AGR* VIII 453–87.

Capron, Albert Banfield
Stoneman raid to Macon, Georgia, in 1864 (read April 4, 1901). *MOLLUS-Ill* IV 404–15.                 *65*

Capron, Horace, 1804–1885.
General Capron's narrative of Stoneman's raid south of Atlanta, prepared by Lieutenant-Colonel Gilbert C. Kniffen. 1899. 39 p. *MOLLUS-DC* no 32.           *66*

Connelly, Henry C
Recollections of the War between the States. *JIHS* V (1913) 458–74; VI (1913) 72–111. plate (port.).                 *67*

Dorr, Henry Gustavus
Mowhawk Peter, legends of the Adirondacks and Civil war memories, by Henry G. Dorr. Illustrations by Nellie L. Thompson. Boston, Cornhill pub. co. [1921] 275 p. plates (illus.). 19cm.              NN  *67A*
The author served in the 14th Illinois cavalry, September 25, 1862, to December 9, 1863; 8th Tennesee cavalry, December 9, 1863, to February 12, 1864; 4th Massachusetts cavalry, April 21, 1864, to May 15, 1865.
"Civil war memories" 161–275.

Sanford, Washington L     1835–
    History of Fourteenth Illinois cavalry and the brigades to which it belonged, compiled from the manuscript history by Sanford, West and Featherson, and from notes of comrades, carefully compared with and corrected by government published official reports and statistics furnished by Union and Confederate officers, with biographies of officers and rolls of men . . . compiled and published by W. L. Sanford, late First Lieutenant Company I, Fourteenth reg. Illinois cavalry. Chicago, R. R. Donnelley & Sons co., 1898. 347 p. plates (ports.). 19½cm.     DLC IHi NHi NN    **68**
    Unit roster 305–47.

Starr, Merritt
    General Horace Capron, 1804–1885. *JIHS* xviii (1925) 259–349. 2 plates (ports.).    **68A**
    Civil War 272–6.

## 15TH CAVALRY

*Organized: December 25, 1862.*

*Consolidated with 10th cavalry regiment: January 22, 1865.*

AGR viii 488–527.

First re-union of the Fifteenth Illinois cavalry vols., held at St. Louis, Missouri, September 27th and 28th, 1887. Worthington, Minn., Advance book and job print. house, 1888. 24 p. 23½cm.     IHi    **69**

Second re-union of the Fifteenth Illinois cavalry volunteers, held at Milwaukee, Wis., August 26 to 30, 1889. Fulda, Minn., Republican print. house, 1889. 39 p. 18cm.    NHi    **70**

## 16TH CAVALRY

*Organized: January–April, 1863.*

*Mustered out: August 19, 1865.*

AGR viii 528–61.

Allee, Abraham
    The campaigns in East Tennessee, by Capt. Abraham Allee. *MOLLUS-Neb* i 243–52.    **71**

Fox, James D
    A true history of the reign of terror in Southern Illinois, a part of the campaign in Western Virginia, and fourteen months of prison life . . . by James D. Fox, late Second Lieutenant Co. H, 16 Ill. cav. vols. Aurora, J. D. Fox, 1884. 60 p. front. (illus.), 1 illus. 20½cm. DLC **72**
    On cover: Non-partisan recollections of the rebellion, as written by an ex-Union Officer, and an ex-prisoner of war.

McElroy, John, 1846–1929.
    Andersonville, a story of Rebel military prisons, fifteen months a guest of the so-called

Southern confederacy, a private soldier's experience in Richmond, Andersonville, Savannah, Millen, Blackshear and Florence, by John McElroy, late of Co. L, 16th Ill. cav. Toledo, D. R. Locke, 1879. xxx, [33]–654, (1) p. front. (illus.), illus., maps. 23cm.     IHi    **73**
    Coulter 308.

—— Si Klegg. The deacon's adventures at Chattanooga in caring for the boys, by John McElroy. Washington, D. C., National Tribune co. [1912] xi, 15–286 p. front. (illus.), illus. 19½cm.     NN    **73A**
    On cover: Book no. 5. "Second edition, enlarged and revised."

—— Si Klegg. Experiences of Si and Shorty on the great Tullahoma campaign, by John McElroy. Washington, D. C., National Tribune co. [1910] xii, [15]–267 p. front. (illus.), illus. 19½cm.     DLC NN    **73B**
    On cover: Book no. 4. "Second edition, enlarged and revised."

—— Si Klegg, his development from a raw recruit to a veteran, and other stories. c1897, by McElroy, Shoppell & Andrews. Washington, National Tribune, 1897. iv, [5]–319 p. illus. 21½cm.     WHi    **74**
    On spine: Old glory library, no. 1, Aug. 23, 1897.

—— Si Klegg. Si, Shorty and the boys are captured at Kenesaw and taken to Andersonville, by John McElroy. Washington, D. C., National Tribune co. [1916] 271 p. front. (illus.), illus. 19½cm.     DLC NN    **74A**
    On cover: Book no. 7. "Second edition, enlarged and revised."

—— Si Klegg, Si and Shorty with their boy recruits, enter on the Atlanta campaign, by John McElroy. Washington, National Tribune co. [1915] vii, [11]–271 p. illus. 19cm.     DLC NN    **75**
    "Second edition, enlarged and revised." "Book no. 6."

—— Si Klegg. Si and Shorty meet Mr. Rosenbaum, the spy, who relates his adventures, by John McElroy. Washington, National Tribune [1910] xiii, [15]–265 p. illus. 19cm.     DLC NN    **76**
    "Second edition, enlarged and revised." "Book no. 3."

—— Si Klegg thru the Stone river campaign and in winter quarters at Murfreesboro, by John McElroy. Washington, National Tribune co. [1910] xiii, [15]–271 p. illus. 20cm.     DLC NN    **77**
    "Second edition, revised and enlarged." "Book no. 2."

*16th Cavalry, continued*

—— Si and Shorty, third book of the series. Washington, National Tribune, 1899. 248 p. illus. 21½cm.                                    WHi    *78*
On cover: By John McElroy. On spine: Old glory library, no. 20, Dec. 15, 1898.

—— This was Andersonville, by John McElroy. Edited with an introduction by Roy Meredith. The true story of Andersonville military prison as told in the personal recollections of John McElroy, sometime Private, Co. L, 16th Illinois cavalry. Illustrated by Arthur C. Butts IV. New York, McDowell, Oblensky, 1957. xli, 355 p. illus., map, plates (illus., ports.). 27½cm.                    NN    *79*

## 17TH CAVALRY

*Mustered in: January 22, February 12, 1864.*

*Mustered out : November 23–December 22, 1865.*

*AGR* viii 562–83.

Beveridge, John L
The first gun at Gettysburg (read February 8, 1885). *MOLLUS-Ill* ii 79–98.    *80*

Carpenter, Edwin A
History of the 17th Illinois cavalry volunteers, by F. [sic] A. Carpenter, Private Company "K." [1886?] [40] p. 29cm.
                                        DLC IHi NHi    *81*
Printed in three columns. Caption title.

## *Infantry*

### 7TH INFANTRY

*Mustered in: April 25, 1861.* (3 months)
*Mustered out: July 25, 1861.*
*AGR* i 257–72.
*Organized: July 25, 1861.* (3 years)
*Mustered out: July 9, 1865.*
*AGR* i 353–87.

Proceedings of the reunion held in . . . by the Association of survivors Seventh regiment Illinois veteran infantry volunteers. . . . 1898–1899 (NHi); 1900–1901 (DLC); 1902–1904 (NHi); 1905–1907 (NN); 1908 (DLC); 1909–1910 (NHi); 1911–1916 (NN); 1917 (IHi).                                        *82*
1898–1899 issued in one volume.

Ambrose, Daniel Leib
History of the Seventh regiment Illinois volunteer infantry, from its first muster into the U.S. service, April 25, 1861, to its final muster out, July 9, 1865, by D. Leib Ambrose. Spring-field, Illinois Journal co., 1868. xii, 391, (1) p. 19cm.                                DLC IHi NHi NN    *83*
Coulter 5. "Errata" (1) p. Unit roster [317]–91.

Burton, Elijah P
Diary of E. P. Burton, Surgeon, 7th reg. Ill., 3rd brig., 2d div., 16th A.C. Prepared by the Historical records survey, Division of professional and service projects, Works projects administration. Des Moines, 1939. 92 folios. 27½cm. Mimeographed.            IHi NN    *84*
Coulter 61.

Chandler, Josephine Craven
An episode of the Civil war, a romance of coincidence. *JIHS* xvii (1924) 352–68. 2 plates (ports.).                                    *85*
Colonel Edward Roberts and Captain Edward P. Strickland. Strickland at the end of three month's service in the 7th re-enlisted in the 114th infantry.

### 8TH INFANTRY

*Organized: April 25, 1861.* (3 months)
*Mustered out: July 25, 1861.*
*AGR* i 273–87.
*Organized: July 25, 1861.* (3 years)
*Mustered out: May 4, 1866.*
*AGR* i 388–431.

McWilliams, John, 1832–
Recollections of John McWilliams, his youth, experiences in California and the Civil war. [Princeton, N. J., Princeton University press, 1921?] 186 p. front. (port.). 23½cm.
                                        IHi MnHi    *86*
The author also served in the 129th infantry.

Hawes, Henry C
Experiences of a Union soldier, by H. C. Hawes. [Atlanta] Crithfield Bros., printers, 1928. 45 p. 3 plates (ports.). 22½cm. IHi    *87*
The author served in the 8th and 17th Illinois infantry regiments.

Moore, James P
War's first rude alarm in 1861, by Captain James P. Moore. *MOLLUS-Minn* iv 7–23.    *88*

Trowbridge, Silas Thompson, 1826–
Autobiography of Silas Thompson Trowbridge, late Surgeon of the 8. reg. Ill. vol. inf. . . . Printed by the family of the author. Vera Cruz, Mexico, 1872. 288 p. 18½cm.
                                        IHi MiDB    *89*
See also Title 30.

### 9TH INFANTRY

*Mustered in: April 28, 1861.* (3 months)
*Mustered out: July 26, 1861.*
*AGR* i 288–303.

*Organized: July 26–August 31, 1861.* (3 years)

*Mustered out: July 9, 1865.*

*AGR* I 432–77.

Ninth Illinois infantry association proceedings of the . . . annual reunion. III–IV (1888–89); VIII (1894). IHi **90**

Morrison, Marion, 1821–
A history of the Ninth regiment Illinois volunteer infantry, by the Chaplain Marion Morrison. Monmouth, John S. Clark, printer, 1864. 95 p. 22cm. DLC IHi NHi **91**

Oates, James
A gallant regiment and the place it holds in national history [by] James Oates, Cincinnati, Arkansas, presented by a lady friend. [Belleville, Post and Zeitung pub. co., printers, 189–] [4] p. 24cm. IHi **92**
Caption title.

### 10TH INFANTRY

*Mustered in: April 28, 1861.* (3 months)

*Mustered out: July 29, 1861.*

*AGR* I 304–18.

*Organized: July 29, 1861.* (3 years)

*Mustered out: July 4, 1865.*

*AGR* I 478–511.

Tenth Illinois veteran volunteer infantry [roster of survivors] [1887] 20 p. 15cm. IHi **93**
Title from cover.

Jamison, Matthew H
Recollections of pioneer and army life, by Matthew H. Jamison, Lieutenant E company, Tenth regiment Illinois veteran volunteer infantry. . . . Kansas City, Mo., Hudson press [1911] iv, 7–363 p. front. (port.), illus. 23cm. DLC IHi **94**

Wilson, Ephraim A          1837–
Memoirs of the War, by Captain Ephraim A. Wilson of Co. "G," 10th Illinois veteran volunteer infantry. Cleveland, Ohio, W. M. Bayne print. co., 1893. xxi, [23]–435 p. 4 front. (ports.), illus. 19cm. DLC IHi NHi NN **95**
Unit roster Company G, xi–xvii.

### 11TH INFANTRY

*Mustered in: April 30, 1861.* (3 months)

*Mustered out: July 30, 1861.*

*AGR* I 319–35.

*Organized: July 30, 1861.* (3 years)

*Mustered out: July 14, 1865.*

*AGR* I 512–50.

1st re-union Co. A, 11th Ill. infantry, Freeport, Illinois, Sept. 3, 1885. [Freeport] Adrian Times print [1885] 32, (3) p. 17cm. IHi **96**
Title and imprint from cover.

Churchill, James O
Wounded at Fort Donelson, by Brevet Lieut.-Col. Jas. O. Churchill. *MOLLUS-Mo* I 146–68. **97**

Parker, Harvey M
Proceedings of the first reunion of the Eleventh regiment Illinois volunteer infantry, held at Ottawa, Ill., Oct. 27, 1875, including addresses, toasts, speeches, poem, &c., and a brief history of the Regiment, and personal sketches of Wallace, Nevins, Ransom and Coastes, its four Colonels. Written, compiled and prepared by H. M. Parker, Co. A. Ottawa, Osman & Hapeman, printers, 1875. 78 p. 23cm.
IHi NHi **98**

Swap, Andrew La Fayette, 1841–
A. L. Swap in the Civil war, by Izora De Wolf. [n. p., 191–] 46 p. ports. 23cm.
KFLGS **99**
"Introductory notes" signed: Izora De Wolf. "Memorial verses by Izora De Wolf, written for memorial services at the National cemetery, Seven Pines, Va.," [39]–46.
The author served in the 11th and 37th Illinois infantry regiments.

### 12TH INFANTRY

*Mustered in: May 2, 1861.* (3 months)

*Mustered out: August 1, 1861.*

*AGR* I 336–52.

*Organized: August 1, 1861.* (3 years)

*Mustered out: July 18, 1865.*

*AGR* I 551–83.

Andreas, Alfred T
The "ifs and buts" of Shiloh (read May 12, 1887). *MOLLUS-Ill* I 105–24. **100**

—— Woman and the rebellion (read January 8, 1891). *MOLLUS-Ill* II 423–41. **101**

Chetlain, Augustus Louis
The battle of Corinth, October 3 and 4, 1862 (read February 6, 1884). *MOLLUS-Ill* II 373–82. **102**

—— Recollections of seventy years, by Augustus L. Chetlain. Galena, Gazette pub. co., 1899. 304 p. front. (port.). 22cm. NN **103**
"Errata" slip inserted. "Civil war, Fort Donelson to Vicksburg, 1862–63," 87–99. The author was appointed Brigadier General, Dec. 18, 1863. "Civil war, 1863–65" 100–17.

Holaday, Clayton A
Joseph Kirkland's Company K. *JIHS* XLIX (1956) 295–307. plate (port.). **104**

*12th Infantry, continued*

Hunt, George
The Fort Donelson campaign, by Captain
George Hunt (read January 25, 1899). *MOL-
LUS-Ill* IV 61–82.                               **105**

Mason, George
Shiloh (read May 5, 1880). *MOLLUS-Ill* I
92–104.                                          **106**

Paddock, George L
The beginnings of an Illinois volunteer regi-
ment in 1861 (read December 7, 1881). *MOL-
LUS-Ill* II 253–67.                              **107**

Wardner, Horace
Reminiscences of a Surgeon (read April 12,
1894). *MOLLUS-Ill* III 173–91.                  **108**

## 13TH INFANTRY

*Mustered in: May 24, 1861.*

*Consolidated with 56th regiment: July 9,
1864.*

*AGR* I 584–606.

Military history and reminiscences of the Thirteenth regiment of Illinois volunteer infantry
in the Civil war in the United States, 1861–
1865. Prepared by a committee of the Regiment, 1891. Publication . . . [four
names] Historians: A. R. Munn, A. H. Miller
[and] W. O. Newton. Chicago, Woman's Temperance pub. association, 1892. viii, 672 p.
plates (illus., maps, ports.). 23½cm.
                              DLC IHi NN    **109**
Unit roster with histories of the individual companies 465–623.

## 14TH INFANTRY

*Mustered in: May 4, 25, 1861.*

*Mustered out: September 16, 1865.*

*AGR* I 607–53.

### Veteran Battalion of the 14th and 15th Infantry

*Organized: July 1, 1864.*

*Disbanded when both regiments were
brought to full strength, April 28, 1865.*

*AGR* I 700–12.

Bacon, Alvin Q                              –1863.
Thrilling adventures of a pioneer boy, (of
the John M. Palmer, 14th ill. regiment), while
a prisoner of war. Alvan [sic] Q. Bacon, his
capture at the battle of Shiloh and escape
from Macon, Ga., going six hundred miles in
canoes by night, got to a Union gun boat and
sailed by ocean to New York. Written by himself. Returning to his regiment was afterwards

killed at the siege of Vicksburg. [n.p., 186–]
32 p. 21½cm.                            NHi    **110**
Coulter 12.

——— ——— Sold for the benefit of his father.
[Galesburg, 186–] 31, (1) p. port. 21½cm.
Advertising matter (1) p.              WHi    **111**

Camm, William, 1837–1906.
Diary of Colonel William Camm, 1861 to
1865. *JIHS* XVIII (1926) 793–969. plate
(port.).                                       **112**

Cherry, Peterson H
Prisoner in Blue, memories of the Civil war
after 70 years, by Peterson H. Cherry. Los
Angeles, Wetzel pub. co. [1931] 70 p. front.
(illus.), 2 illus. 20cm.                MB    **113**

Dugan, James
History of Hurlbut's fighting Fourth division,
and especially the marches, toils, privations,
adventures, skirmishes, and battles of the Fourteenth Illinois infantry, together with camp-
scenes, anecdotes, battle incidents, also a description of the towns, cities, and countries
through which their marches have extended
since the commencement of the war, to which
is added the official reports of battles in which
they were engaged, by James Dugan, of Company B, Fourteenth Illinois. Cincinnati, E. Morgan & co., 1863. viii, [9]–265 p. plates (ports.).
20cm.                                    IHi   **114**
Coulter 135.

Littlefield, Milton Smith
Campaigning in the West in '61 and '62. In
War talks of Morristown veterans (Morristown,
N. J., 1887) 17–21.                            **115**

Smith, William B
On wheels and how I came there, a real
story for real boys and girls, giving the personal experiences and observations of a fifteen-
year old Yankee boy as soldier and prisoner
in the American Civil war, by Private W. B.
Smith of Company K, 14th Illinois. Edited by
Rev. Joseph Gatch Bonnell. New York, Hunt
and Eaton [1892] 338 p. front. (port.). 18cm.
Coulter 425.                             NN    **116**
IHI has a reprint dated 1893.

## 15TH INFANTRY

*Mustered in: May 24, 1861.*

*Consolidated with 14th regiment as a Vet-
eran battalion: July 1, 1864.*

*Regiments recruited to full strength and
resumed separate regimental organization:
April 28, 1865.*

*Mustered out: July 1, 1865.*

*AGR* I 654–99.

Fourth annual re-union of the Fifteenth regiment, Illinois volunteer infantry, held at Rockford, Ill., May 25, 1885. Aurora, Beacon print [1885] 8 p. 16cm.   IHi   **118**

Title and imprint from cover, p. [1]

Celebration at Polo, Ill., of the fiftieth anniversary of the beginning of the War between the States. *JIHS* IV (1911) 200–11.   **119**

Ogle guards, Co. H., 15th Illinois.

Barber, Lucius W   1839–1872.
Army memoirs of Lucius W. Barber, Company "D," 15th Illinois volunteer infantry, May 24, 1861, to Sept. 30, 1865. Chicago, J. M. W. Jones print. co., 1894. v, [9]–233 p. front. (port.). 23½cm.   DLC IHi   **120**

Unit roster Company D, 220–5. Coulter 15.

McEathron, Alexander
Letters and memoirs of Alexander McEathron during the Civil war. [1938?] 27 p. 20½cm.   IHi   **121**

Unit roster of Company G, 23–6.

Whipple, Alphonzo
The diary of Alphonzo Whipple, a soldier of Company A, Fifteenth regiment, Illinois volunteer infantry, transcribed at Saint Louis, Missouri, 1921. St. Louis, Skaer print. co., 1922. 64 p. front. (port.), plate (port.). 22cm.

Unit roster Company A, 9–10.   NN   **122**

## 16TH INFANTRY

*Mustered in: May 24, 1861.*
*Mustered out: July 8, 1865.*
*AGR* II 3–37.

Kerr, Charles D
An episode in the Kentucky campaign of Generals Buell and Bragg, by Lieutenant-Colonel Charles D. Kerr. *MOLLUS-Minn* IV 266–80.   **123**

—— From Atlanta to Raleigh. *MOLLUS-Minn* I 202–23.   **124**

## 17TH INFANTRY

*Mustered in: May 24, 1861.*
*Mustered out: July 4, 1864.*
*AGR* II 38–63.

Campbell, Robert W
Brief account of the 17th regiment Illinois volunteer infantry, 1861–1864. *PIHL* no 20 (1914) 184–90.   **125**

Lloyd, Frederick
General Leonard F. Ross. *Iowa historical record* IV (Iowa City 1888) 145–83.   **126**

Wells, Seth J   1842–1864.
The siege of Vicksburg, from the diary of Seth J. Wells, including weeks of preparation and of occupation after the surrender. Detroit, Mich., Wm. H. Rowe, 1915. 101 p. 19cm.   MiDB   **127**

"Foreword' signed: S[arah] E[well] K[rolik].

See also Title 87.

## 18TH INFANTRY

*Mustered in: May 16, 1861.*
*Mustered out: December 16, 1865.*
*AGR* II 64–117.

Dorris, Jonathan T
Michael Kelly Lawler, Mexican and Civil war officer. *JIHS* XLVIII (1955) 366–401. port.   **128**

## 19TH INFANTRY

*Mustered in: June 17, 1861.*
*Mustered out: July 9, 1864.*
*AGR* II 118–48.

Haynie, James Henry, 1841–1912.
The Nineteenth Illinois, a memoir of a regiment of volunteer infantry famous in the Civil war of fifty years ago for its drill, bravery, and distinguished services. Edited by J. Henry Haynie, of Company D. . . . [Chicago, M. A. Donahue & co., 1912] 396 p. plates (illus., ports.). 23cm.   DLC IHi NHi NN   **129**

On cover: The Nineteenth Illinois, a memoir. "Who'll save the left."

## 20TH INFANTRY

*Mustered in: June 13, 1861.*
*Mustered out: July 16, 1865.*
*AGR* II 149–85.

Regimental roster of 20th Illinois volunteer infantry, 1901. [Clinton, 1901] [16] p. 12½cm.   IHi   **130**

Title from cover. Introduction signed: John A. Edmiston, Cor. Sec'y.

Brown, Andrew
. . . Company K, Twentieth regiment, Illinois volunteer infantry roster and record, by Andrew Brown. Yorkville, Kendall County Record print, 1894. 64 p. 17½cm.   IHi   **131**

At head of title: April 24, 1861. July 16, 1865.

## 21ST INFANTRY

*Mustered in: May 15, June 28, 1861.*
*Mustered out: December 16, 1865.*
*AGR* II 186–217.

Constitution and by-laws of the Society of the 21st Ills. vet. vol. infantry, with roll of honor, and roll call of surviving members, at their 8th annual re-union at Terre-Haute, September 19 and 20, 1882. [Paris] J. M. Sheets, printer, 1882. 24 p. 20½cm.                    IHi   *132*

Proceedings of the twenty-third annual reunion of the Society of the 21st Illinois veteran vol. infantry, held at Salem, Illinois, October 31, 1897, with roll call of surviving members. Neoga [1897] [9] p. 21cm.            IHi   *133*
Title and imprint from cover.

Bainum, Noah C
General Grant's first day's march. *JIHS* xv (1922) 664–9. plates (illus., ports.).          *134*

Boggs, Samuel S
Eighteen months a prisoner under the Rebel flag, a condensed pen-picture of Belle isle, Danville, Andersonville, Charleston, Florence and Libby prisons . . . [by] S. S. Boggs, late Sergeant 21st Illinois infantry, author and publisher. Lovington, 1887. 69 p. illus. 21cm.
                                         DLC NN   *135*

—— —— Lovington, 1887. 76 p. illus. 21cm.
                                              NN *135A*
A reprinting with additional material contributed by other authors, p. 70–6. NHi has a reprinting 1889. Coulter 42.

Crane, James L
Grant as a Colonel. Conversations between Grant and his Chaplain, reminiscences and anecdotes, by James L. Crane, late Chaplain of the Twenty-first Illinois U.S.V. *McClure's magazine* VII (1896) 40–5. port.          *135B*

Moore, Ensley
Grant's first march. *PIHL* xv (1912) 55–62. plates (illus.).                          *135C*

Welshimer, Philip
A brief sketch of the prison life of Capt. Philip Welshimer, as delivered by him to Neoga post no. 202 G.A.R. Published in loving memory by his daughter, Mrs. Alice Welshimer Young. 1908. 23, (1) p. front. (port.), facs. 24½cm.                                MnHi   *136*
On cover: Prison life.

## 22ND INFANTRY

*Mustered in: June 25, 1861.*
*Mustered out: July 7, 1864.*
*AGR* II 218–43.

Seaton, John
The battle of Belmont, November 7, 1861, a paper prepared and read before the Kansas commandery of the Military order of the loyal legion of the United States, by John Seaton, Captain 22d Illinois. [1902] 16 p. 22cm.
                                            DLC   *137*
On cover: War paper no. 22. Also published as War talks in Kansas, a series of papers read before the Kansas commandery of the MOLLUS, 305–19.

## 23RD INFANTRY

*Mustered in: June 15, 1861.*
*Mustered out: July 24, 1865.*
*AGR* II 244–99.

Allendorfer, Frederic von
The Western Irish brigade (23rd Illinois regiment). *Irish sword* II (Dublin 1955) 177–83.                                      *138*

Doyle, James M          1839–1909.
The diary of James M. Doyle. *Mid-America* xx (Chicago 1938) 273–83.          *139*

Mulligan, James Adelbert
The siege of Lexington, Mo. *BandL* I 307.
                                              *140*

## 24TH INFANTRY

*Mustered in: July 8, 1861.*
*Mustered out: August 6, 1864. Veterans and recruits consolidated in a company and mustered out: July 31, 1865.*
*AGR* II 300–27.

Kune, Julian
Reminiscences of an octogenarian Hungarian exile, by Julian Kune. Chicago, Published by the author, 1911. viii, 216 p. plates (facs., illus., ports.). 20cm.            DLC   *141*
Civil war, 92–124.

Vocke, William, 1839–
Der deutsche Soldat im amerikanischen Bürgerkriege. Vortrag gehalten von William Vocke vor der Northwestern university in Evanston am 5. December 1895. [Chicago, Verlag von Kölling & Klappenbach, 1896] 43 p. 24½cm.                            IHi NN   *142*

—— The military achievements of Major-General Ormsby MacKnight Mitchell, by Captain William Vocke (read March 1, 1900). *MOLLUS-Ill* IV 83–104.          *143*

—— Our German soldiers . . . April 9, 1896. *MOLLUS-Ill* III 341–71.          *144*
Also appeared as an offprint.

Wagner, William
History of the 24th Illinois volunteer infantry regiment (old Hecker regiment), by Dr. William Wagner, Surgeon of the Regiment. . . . [Chicago, 1911] 46 p. 23cm.      IHi   *145*
Includes the German text published 1864 in the *Illinois Staatszeitung* and an English translation.

## 25TH INFANTRY

*Mustered in: August 4, 1861.*
*Mustered out: September 5, 1864.*
AGR II 328–53.

## 26TH INFANTRY

*Mustered in: August 31, 1861.*
*Mustered out: July 20, 1865.*
AGR II 354–88.

Phillips, Martin V          B
Life and death in Andersonville; or, what I saw and experienced during seven months in Rebel prisons, by Rev. M. V. B. Phillips. Chicago, T. B. Arnold, 1887. 70, (2) p. front. (port.). 21½cm.      KHi   *146*
"Finale" (2) p.

## 27TH INFANTRY

*Organized: August 10, 1861.*
*Mustered out: September 20, 1864.*
AGR II 389–416.

Crippen, Edward W          –1863.
The diary of Edward W. Crippen, Private 27th Illinois vounteers, War of the rebellion, August 7, 1861, to September 19, 1863. Edited, with introduction and notes, by Robert J. Kerner. *PIHL* no 14 (1911) 220–82.      *147*

Heaps, Israel G
The battle of Mission ridge. The Fourth corps led in the grand assault. In *National Tribune Scrap Book* I 34–42.      *147A*

—— Oration delivered at the reunion of the 27th Illinois infantry at Quincy, Illinois, October 18th, 1894, by Capt. I. G. Heaps, on the life and public services of Dr. E. H. Bowman, Surgeon of the 27th regiment. Winchester, Standard print [1894] 18 p. 19cm. DNW *148*

Schmitt, William Andrew
History of the Twenty-seventh Illinois volunteers, with a roster of the surviving members. . . . Winchester, Standard print. house [1892] 27 p. 14cm.      IHi   *149*
On cover: History of the Twenty-seventh Illinois volunteers as written by Col. W. A. Schmitt.

## 28TH INFANTRY

*Mustered in: August 15, 1861.*
*Mustered out: March 15, 1866.*
AGR II 417–66.

Hobart, Edwin Lucius
Semi-history of a boy-veteran of the Twenty-eighth regiment Illinois infantry volunteers, in a black regiment. A diary of 28th Ill. from organization to veteranizing. History of the Fifty-eighth regiment, U.S. colored infantry, with some closing reminiscences with the former, and a rounding out of my long service with the later regiment . . . by Edwin L. Hobart, late Corporal Company D, 28th Illinois and . . . First Lieutenant 58th regiment United States colored infantry. [Denver? 1909] 41, 54 p. plates (ports.). 22cm.      NN   *150*
"Diary, by George W. Reese, of Company H" 4–17.
"Original addenda" 54 p.

## 29TH INFANTRY

*Mustered in: August 19, 1861.*
*Mustered out: November 6, 1865.*
AGR II 467–502.

## 30TH INFANTRY

*Mustered in: August 28, 1861.*
*Mustered out: July 17, 1865.*
AGR II 503–38.

The battle flag of the Thirtieth Illinois infantry after half a century, tattered and torn, comes to Memorial hall, Springfield. *JIHS* IV (1912) 493–6.      *151*

Goodnoh, Edward C
The famous tunnel escape from Libby prison. "From rat hell to liberty." By E. C. Goodnoh. Chicago, Lane & McBreen [n.d.] 32 p. illus., ports. 23cm.      OHi *152*

McDonald, Granville B
A history of the 30th Illinois volunteer regiment of infantry. [Sparta, Printed by Sparta News, 1916] 128 p. plates (ports.). 20cm.
IHi   *153*

## 31ST INFANTRY

*Mustered in: September 18, 1861.*
*Mustered out: July 19, 1865.*
AGR II 539–77.

Minutes of the annual reunion of the Thirty-first Illinois veteran volunteer infantry. . . . 1889, 1893–1897.      IHi   *154*
1893–1894 issued in one volume.

*31st Infantry, continued*

Morris, William S
   History 31st regiment volunteers, organized
by John A. Logan. [Evansville, Ind., Keller
print. and pub. co., 1902] 236, (1) p. plates
(illus., ports.). 23½cm.          IHi WHi    **155**
   "Introductory" signed: W. S. Morris, L. D. Hartwell
[and] J. B. Kuykendall, Committee. Unit roster [177]–
216.

Ozburn, Lindorf, 1823–1864.
   Letters from two wars, by Barbara Burr.
*JIHS* xxx (1937) 135–58.          **156**

## 32ND INFANTRY

*Mustered in: December 31, 1861.*

*Mustered out: September 16, 1865.*

*AGR* ii 578–611.

Hedley, Fenwick Y
   Marching through Georgia, pen pictures of
every-day life in General Sherman's army, from
the beginning of the Atlanta campaign until
the close of the war, by F. Y. Hedley, Adjutant
Thirty second Illinois infantry. Chicago, R. R.
Donnelley & Sons, 1885. 490 p. facs., illus.,
plan, ports. 19½cm.                  NN    **157**
   Coulter 225.
   NHi has an 1890 reprinting.

## 33RD INFANTRY

*Mustered in: September 3, 1861.*

*Mustered out: November 24, 1865.*

*AGR* ii 612–53.

Record of the burials of members of the 33rd
Illinois infantry in the National cemeteries.
Published by the Secretary of the Regimental
association and compiler of the Regimental history, Virgil G. Way. Procter, 1912. [4] p.
26½cm.                            IHi    **158**
   Caption title.

Reunion of the 33d Illinois regiment, at Bloomington, Oct. 21, 1875. (Anniversary of Freder-
icktown battle). Report of proceedings. Bloomington, Pantograph Book establishment, 1875.
16 p. 22½cm.                  DLC NHi    **159**
   "Historical sketch of the Thirty-third Illinois regiment, read by E. J. Lewis, Capt. Co. C . . . ," 10–16.

Report of the 33rd Illinois infantry veteran
association. iii–vi 1881–1882, 1884, 1887
(IHi); vii 1890 (DLC); 1908, 1915, 1917,
1921–1928 (IHi).                          **160**
   1926–1927 were not published.

Burnham, John Howard, 1834–1917.
   The Thirty-third regiment Illinois infantry
in the Civil war, 1861–1865, prepared by Capt.
J. H. Burnham, at the request of the Directors
of the Illinois historical society for the 1912
annual meeting of that Society [Springfield,
1912] [6] p. 26cm.                  DLC    **161**
   Caption title.
   "The Regimental association at its annual meeting,
Oct. 9th, 1912, approved it as a part of the Regimental history."

—— The Thirty-third regiment Illinois infantry in the War between the States. *PIHL* no 17
(1912) 77–85.                              **162**

Fortney, John F          M
   The wreck of the James Watson [Mississippi
steamer, March 6, 1865] a Civil war disaster.
*JIHS* xxxvii (1944) 213–28.              **163**

Marshall, Albert O
   Army life, from a soldier's journals, by Albert
O. Marshall. Incidents, sketches and record of
a Union soldier's army life, in camp and field,
1861–64. Second edition. Printed for the
author. Joliet [Chicago, Printed by the Chicago Legal News co.] 1884. 410 p. 19cm.
                                    NN    **164**

—— Army life, from a soldier's journal (copyrighted), by Albert O. Marshall. Incidents,
sketches and record of a Union soldier's army
life, in camp and field, 1861–64. Special edition. Printed for the author. Joliet, 1886.
[100] p. 20cm.                  DLC    **165**
   On cover: Extracts from Army life, by Albert O.
Marshall. Presented with the author's compliments.
Reprinted from the original plates, pagination un-
changed.

Way, Virgil Gilman, 1847–
   History of the Thirty-third regiment Illinois
veteran volunteer infantry in the Civil war,
22nd August, 1861, to 7th December, 1865,
by General Isaac H. Elliott, with Company and
personal sketches by other comrades, also complete historical rosters, compiled by Virgil G.
Way, Secretary and Treasurer of the Regimental association, by whom the work has been
prepared for publication. Gibson, Published by
the Association [Press of the Gibson Courier]
1902. 288 p. plan, ports. 27½cm.
                          DLC NHi NN    **166**
   Includes unit roster. On spine: Way. On cover: "It
is the voice of the years that are gone." Contributions
are signed by their authors.

Wilcox, Charles Edwards, 1839–1931.
   Hunting for cotton in Dixie, from the Civil
war diary of Captain Charles E. Wilcox. Edited
by Edgar L. Erickson. *Journal of Southern history* iv (Baton Rouge 1938) 493–513.    **167**

—— With Grant at Vicksburg, from the Civil
war diary of Captain Charles E. Wilcox. Edited
by Edgar L. Erickson. *JIHS* xxx (1938) 440–
503.                                      ***168***

## 34TH INFANTRY

*Mustered in: September 7, 1861.*
*Mustered out: July 12, 1865.*
*AGR* ii 654–90.

Payne, Edwin Waters, 1837–
History of the Thirty-fourth regiment of Illinois infantry, September 7, 1861—July 12, 1865 [by] Edwin W. Payne, Sergeant Company A, Regimental historian. [Clinton, Iowa, Allen print. co., 1902] viii, 370 p. illus., maps, ports., plates (fold. maps). 23cm.
           DLC NHi NN    *169*
Coulter 367. Unit roster 256–333.

## 35TH INFANTRY

*Mustered in: August 28, 1861.*
*Mustered out: September 27, 1864.*
*AGR* ii 691–715.

## 36TH INFANTRY

*Mustered in: September 23, 1861.*
*Mustered out: October 8, 1865.*
*AGR* iii 3–37.

Bennett, Lyman G
History of the Thirty-sixth regiment Illinois volunteers during the War of the rebellion, by L. G. Bennett and Wm. M. Haigh. Aurora, Knickerbocker & Hodder, printers, 1876. viii, [9]–808 p. plates (ports.). 22½cm.
           DLC NHi NN    *170*
"The first twenty and last seven chapters as well as the appendix were prepared by Mr. Bennett, while Mr. Haigh wrote the remainder."

Benson, Wallace P
A soldier's diary, diary of Wallace P. Benson of Company H, 36th Illinois volunteers. Printed by his sons, F. Raymond Benson and Ernest L. Benson. [Algonquin] 1919. 31 p. 21cm.
           WHi    *171*

Clark, Leach
The battle of Pea ridge. *Bivouac* ii (Boston 1884) 362–6.    *172*

—— Dreams that come to pass, a Thirty-sixth Illinois soldier's dream and its strange fulfillment. *Bivouac* ii (Boston 1884) 330–2.    *173*

Johnson, Ole H
Gamle Amerikabrev, av Jakob Jakobsson. *Aett og heim* (Stavanger, Norway 1956) 132–48.    *174*

Kelley, Leverett M
Battle of Nashville, by Captain Leverett M. Kelley. 1908. 13 p. *MOLLUS-DC* no 72. *175*

McBarron, Hugh Charles
36th Illinois infantry regiment, 1863. *Military collector & historian* ix (Washington 1957) 39–40. col. plate (illus.).    *176*

## 37TH INFANTRY

*Mustered in: September 18, 1861.*
*Mustered out: May 15, 1866.*
*AGR* iii 38–73.

Constitution, proceedings and roster of the 37th Ill. volunteer infantry veteran association, organized March 6th, 1885. . . . Chicago, Printed by Skeen & Stuart Stationery co., 1885. 21, (1) p. 15cm.    IHi    *177*

Black, John C
Our boys in the war (read June 9, 1892). *MOLLUS-Ill* ii 443–56.    *178*

Heer, George Washington, 1844–
History of Thirty-seventh Illinois infantry. In his Episodes of the Civil war (1890) 398–405.    *179*

Payne, Eugene Beauharnois, 1835–1910.
Prairie Grove, by Brevet-Brigadier General Eugene B. Payne. 1904. 22 p. *MOLLUS-DC* no 52.    *180*

—— The 37th Illinois veteran volunteer infantry and the battle of Pea Ridge, Arkansas. 1903. 15 p. *MOLLUS-DC* no 48.    *181*

White, Julius
Burnside's occupation of East Tennessee, by General Julius White (read April 4, 1883). *MOLLUS-Ill* iv 301–17.    *182*

## 38TH INFANTRY

*Mustered in: August 15, 1861.*
*Mustered out: December 31, 1865.*
*AGR* iii 74–103.

## 39TH INFANTRY

*Mustered in: August 15, 1861.*
*Mustered out: December 31, 1865.*
*AGR* iii 74–103.

. . . First reunion of the Thirty-ninth Illinois veteran volunteers, held at Bloomington, Ill., December 19, 1866. Oration, by Major-General Thomas O. Osborn. Poem, by Surgeon Charles M. Clark. Chicago, S. Emerson, printer [1867] 32 p. 22½cm.    IHi    *183*
At head of title: Yates phalanx.

*39th Infantry, continued*

Proceedings of the . . . annual reunion Yates phalanx 39th regiment Illinois infantry. . . . III 1884 (IHi); IV 1885 (WHi); VI 1886 (NHi); VIII–XXIII 1888–1903 (NHi); XXXVII–XXXVIII 1917–1918 (IHi). **184**

1895–1896 issued in one volume.

Clark, Charles M        1834–
The history of the Thirty-ninth regiment Illinois volunteer veteran infantry (Yates phalanx) in the War of the rebellion, 1861–1865, by Charles M. Clark (late Surgeon). Published under the auspices of the Veteran association of the Regiment. Chicago, 1889. xx, 554, (3) p. illus., 2 maps, plates (illus., ports.). 22½cm.

DLC NHi NN    **185**

Unit roster with biographies and casualties, 368–548.

Jenkins, William H
The Thirty-ninth Illinois volunteers, Yates phalanx. *PIHL* no 20 (1914) 130–6. 2 plates (ports.). **186**

Linton, Johnathan F
A bit of unrecorded history of the Army of the Potomac, by J. F. Linton, R.Q.M., 39th Illinois volunteer infantry. [n. p., 190–] 8 p. 20cm.    NN    **186A**

Caption title.

Woodruff, George H
History of the Thirty-ninth regt.; or, Yates phalanx. In his Fifteen years ago (1876) 143–79. **187**

## 40TH INFANTRY

*Mustered in: August 10, 1861.*
*Mustered out: July 24, 1865.*
*AGR III 144–72.*

George, G        Jasper
William Newby, alias "Dan Benton," alias "Rickety Dan," alias "Crazy Jack"; or, the soldier's return, a true and wonderful story of mistaken identity, a narrative full of strange paradoxes . . . by G. J. George, Lieutenant Company D, 40th Illinois infantry. Cincinnati, Press of C. J. Krebbiel & co., 1893. xii, 289 p. 2 maps (1 double, 1 fold.), ports. 20cm.

DLC NHi    **188**

Hart, Ephraim J
History of the Fortieth Illinois inf. (volunteers), by Sergeant E. J. Hart, Company E. Cincinnati, H. S. Bosworth, 1864. 198 p. 19½cm.    DLC NHi    **189**

Coulter 218. Unit roster [173]–98.

## 41ST INFANTRY

*Mustered in: August 5, 1861.*
*Consolidated with 53rd regiment: December 23, 1864.*
*AGR III 173–99.*

Sketch of the Forty-first Illinois veteran volunteer infantry with constitution and by-laws and roll call of surviving members. Monticello, Piatt Independent print, 1888. 28 p. 22cm.

MnHi    **190**

"Sketch . . . ," [3]–9 signed: E. T. Lee, Secretary.

Roberts, Job M
The experience of a Private in the Civil war, written January, 1904, by J. M. Roberts, Sylvan Beach, N. Y. [Oxford, N. Y., c1924] 51, (1) p. 20cm.    DLC    **191**

## 42ND INFANTRY

*Organized: July 22, 1861.*
*Mustered out: December 16, 1865.*
*AGR III 200–41.*

Hobart, Francis Rogers, 1850–
Desparate battles survived by youth. Edited by Emory H. English. *Annals of Iowa* s3 XXVI (Des Moines 1945) 198–204. **192**

Stevenson, Alexander F
The battle of Stone's river, near Murfreesboro', Tenn., December 30, 1862, to January 3, 1863, by Alexander F. Stevenson. Boston, James R. Osgood and co., 1884. vii, 197 p. 2 fold. plates (maps). 23½cm.    NHi    **193**

## 43RD INFANTRY

*Mustered in: October 12, 1861.*
*Mustered out: November 30, 1865.*
*AGR III 242–95.*

Nelson, Nels
Swedish-American boys in Blue, reminiscences from the Civil war. In *Prärieblöman kalendar* (Rock Island 1908) 170–87. **194**

## 44TH INFANTRY

*Mustered in: September 13, 1861.*
*Mustered out: September 25, 1865.*
*AGR III 296–328.*

[Bliss, Jesse C        ]
Letters from a veteran of Pea Ridge. Edited by Paul R. Cooper and Ted R. Worley. *Arkansas historical quarterly* VI (Fayetteville 1947) 462–71.    **195**

"Written by an officer of the Forty-fourth Illinois volunteers." The owner of the original requests "that the name of the writer of the letters and the names of the persons to whom the letters were addressed be withheld." Author identified by Margaret A. Flint, Ass't State historian, Springfield, Ill.

## 45TH INFANTRY

*Mustered in: December 25, 1861.*

*Mustered out: July 12, 1865.*

*AGR* III 329–62.

Adair, John M
Historical sketch of the Forty-fifth Illinois regiment, with a complete list of the officers and privates and an individual record of each man in the Regiment, by Capt. John M. Adair. Lanark, Carroll County Gazette print, 1869. 40 p. 22½cm.                  DLC NHi    **196**
On cover: "45th" Illinois, its war record and private history.
Unit roster [17]–40. "Read at the second annual re-union of the Regiment at Freeport, September 28th, 1869."

Crummer, Wilbur Fisk, 1843–
With Grant at Fort Donelson, Shiloh and Vicksburg, and an appreciation of General U. S. Grant, by Wilbur F. Crummer of the 45th regt. Ill. vols. Oak Park, E. C. Crummer & co., 1915. 190 p. plates (illus., ports.). 20cm.
NN    **197**

Fish, Daniel, 1848–
The Forty-fifth Illinois, a souvenir of the re-union held at Rockford on the fortieth anniversary of its march in the grand review, being the remarks of Daniel Fish of Co. G, to which is appended the substance of the Regiment's history as preserved in official records. Minneapolis, Byron & Willard, 1905. 31 p. 23cm.
DLC NN    **198**

## 46TH INFANTRY

*Organized: December 28, 1861.*

*Mustered out: February 1, 1866.*

*AGR* III 363–404.

Complete history of the 46th Illinois veteran infantry, from the date of its organization in 1861, to its final discharge, February 1st, 1866, containing a full and authentic account of the participation of the Regiment in the battles, sieges, skirmishes and expeditions in which it has been engaged, showing the promotions, commissioned and non-commissioned, deaths, discharges and desertions. Freeport, Bailey and Ankeny, printers, 1866. 76 p. 22cm.
Unit roster [3]–36.                  DLC NN    **199**

Jones, Thomas B          1841–
Complete history of the 46th regiment Illinois volunteer infantry, a full and authentic

account of the participation of the Regiment in the battles, sieges, skirmishes and expeditions in which it was engaged. Also a complete roster of the Regiment, together with biographical sketches. . . . [Freeport, Wm. H. Wagner & Sons, 1907?] 379, (4) p. plates (fold. map, ports.). 23½cm.                  DLC NN    **200**
"Introductory" signed: Thomas B. Jones, Lieut. Company B, Historian. Unit roster 101–45.

## 47TH INFANTRY

*Mustered in: August 16, 1861.*

*Mustered out: January 21, 1866.*

*AGR* III 405–53.

Bryner, Byron Cloyd, 1849–
Bugle echoes, the story of Illinois 47th, by Cloyd Bryner. [Springfield, Phillips Bros., printers, 1905] ix, [11]–262 p. plates (ports.). 23½cm.                  DLC NHi NN    **201**
Coulter 58. Unit roster [177]–262.

Burdette, Robert Jones, 1844–
The drums of the 47th, by Robert J. Burdette. Indianapolis, Bobbs-Merrill co. [1914] 211, (1) p. 19½cm.    DLC IHi NN    **201A**
Coulter 59.

McClay, John H
Defense of Robinette, by Lieut. J. H. M'Clay. *MOLLUS-Neb* I 167–72.    **202**

## 48TH INFANTRY

*Organized: September 12, 1861.*

*Mustered out: August 15, 1865.*

*AGR* III 454–91.

## 49TH INFANTRY

*Mustered in: December 31, 1861.*

*Mustered out: September 9, 1865.*

*AGR* III 492–521.

## 50TH INFANTRY

*Mustered in: September 12, 1861.*

*Mustered out: July 3, 1865.*

*AGR* III 522–55.

Report of . . . annual reunion of the 50th Ills. inf. reunion association. . . . x–xII 1896–1898 (NHi); xIII–xv 1899–1901 (IHi); xvI–xvIII 1902–1904 (NHi); xIx 1905 (IHi); xx–xxIII 1906–1909 (NHi); xxIv 1910 (DLC); xxxvII–xxxvIII 1923–1924 (DLC).    **203**
1899–1901 issued in one volume.

*50th Infantry, continued*

Roster of survivors of the Fiftieth regt. Ills. infantry reunion ass'n C. F. Hubert, Adjutant. Fowler [1904] 13 p. 16 x 8½cm.    IHi    *204*

Title and imprint from cover. "Officers of the Association, elected Oct. 16, 1904" [in IHi's copy corrected in ms. to 1903] p 2 of cover. "The Fiftieth Illinois infantry in the war," p 3 of cover.

Historical memorial from the members of the 50th regiment Illinois veteran volunteer infantry reunion association in behalf of the comrades of the 50th Illinois veteran volunteer infantry to Brevet Brigadier General William Hanna. Nineteenth annual reunion, Camp Point, Ill., Sept. 26–27, 1905. [Quincy, Monarch print. co., 1905] [44] p. illus., plates (illus., ports.) 7½ x 16cm.    DLC    *205*

"Edition is limited and numbered up to 300." Some leaves were distributed for insertion after the volume was completed.

Souvenier soldiers and sailors of all wars reunion banquet and campfire, October 4–5, 1922, hotel Quincy. 36th annual reunion 50th regiment, Illinois veteran volunteer infantry reunion association, Quincy, Illinois. 23 p. illus., ports. 15½cm.    DLC    *206*

Title from cover. "Origin of our prize drill banner."

Hubert, Charles F    1843–

History of the Fiftieth regiment Illinois volunteer infantry in the War of the Union, by Charles F. Hubert, assisted by members of the Regiment. Kansas City, Mo., Western Veteran pub. co., 1894. 630 p. illus., ports., plates (double map, ports.). 23cm.    NHi DLC    *207*

Unit roster 585–626.

## 51ST INFANTRY

*Mustered in: December 24, 1861.*
*Mustered out: September 25, 1865.*
*AGR* iii 556–87.

Davis, Charles W

New Madrid and Island no. 10 (read March 5, 1884). *MOLLUS-Ill* i 75–92. plan.    *208*

Fox, Thomas Bailey

Memorial of Henry Ware Hall, Adjutant 51st regiment Illinois infantry volunteers, an address delivered in the First church, Dorchester, Mass., Sunday, July 17, 1864, by Thomas B. Fox. With an appendix. Printed by request for private circulation. Boston, Printed by John Wilson and Son, 1864. 35 p. 22½cm.    DLC    *209*

Gardner, William

Decoration, some footprints of the Army of the Cumberland from the Private's standpoint. Third edition. By William Gardner, late Co. D,

51st [Ill.] V. V. infantry. Washington, Herald, 1883. 15, (1) p. 22cm.    WHi    *210*

## 52ND INFANTRY

*Mustered in: November 19, 1861.*
*Mustered out: July 5, 1865.*
*AGR* iii 588–617.

Historical memoranda of the 52nd regiment Illinois infantry volunteers, from its organization, Nov. 19th, 1861, to its muster out, by reason of expiration of service, on the 6th day of July, 1865. Elgin, Gilbert and Post, printers, 1868. 47 p. 23½cm.    IHi NHi    *211*

Nineteen hundred and eight membership roll of the Fifty-second Illinois veteran volunteer association. . . . [Elgin, Courier print, 1908] 12 p. 14½cm.    IHi    *212*

Title from cover.

Compton, James

The Second division of the 16th army corps in the Atlantic campaign, by Captain James Compton. *MOLLUS-Minn* v 103–23.    *213*

—— Some incidents not recorded in the Rebellion records. *MOLLUS-Minn* vi 251–8.    *214*

Wilcox, John S

Our commanders (read September 14, 1893). *MOLLUS-Minn* iii 385–96.    *215*

Wolcott, Laurens W

The battle of Corinth, by Laurens W. Wolcott, 1st Lieut. (read May 5, 1898). *MOLLUS-Mich* ii 264–76.    *216*

## 53RD INFANTRY

*Organized: January 1862.*
*Mustered out: July 22, 1865.*
*AGR* iii 618–55.

. . . Semi-centennial roster. Cushman's brigade souvenir . . . 53rd reg. Ill. vet. vol. infantry, Ford's cavalry co., Cogwell's battery artillery. [1915] [24] p. ports. 13½ x 16½cm.    IHi    *217*

At head of title: 1865. 1915. "We have held our annual reunions together as Cushman's brigade." Title from cover.

Harris, Joanis O

Recollections of an army surgeon. *BandG* iii (1894) 137–42.    *218*

Haskell, Orson S

Memorandum of the Fifty-third regiment Illinois vet. volunteer infantry, by Orson S. Haskell. . . . Louisville, Ky., Hanna & Duncan, printers, 1865. 8 p. 14½cm.    IHi    *219*

Ranstead, Herbert E

A true story and history of the Fifty-third regiment Illinois veteran volunteer infantry, its campaigns and marches, incidents that occurred on marches and in camp. What happened to some of its members and what became of others. Short stories of marches and how the army lived, by E. E. Ranstead, a member of Company D, Fifty-third regiment. 1910. 104 p. front. (port.). 21cm.　　DNW　220

## 54TH INFANTRY

*Mustered in: February 18, 1862.*

*Mustered out: October 15, 1865.*

*AGR* III 656–85.

Coleman, Charles H.　　and Paul H. Spence

The Charleston riot, March 28, 1864. *JIHS* XXXIII (1940) 7–56. 2 plates (illus., fold, plan).　　221

## 55TH INFANTRY

*Mustered in: October 31, 1861.*

*Mustered out: August 14, 1865.*

*AGR* III 686–714.

Report of the proceedings of the Association of the Fifty-fifth Illinois vet. vol. infantry. . . . I–V 1884–1892 (NHi); VII–IX 1896–1900 (IHi).　　222

Biennial meetings.

The story of the Fifty-fifth regiment Illinois volunteer infantry in the Civil war, 1861–1865. By a Committee of the Regiment. [Clinton, Mass., Printed by W. J. Coulter] 1887. 519 p. 23cm.　　DLC NHi NN　223

Unit roster [465]–517. Authors: Chapters I–IV, Captain Lucien B. Crooker; V–IX, Captain Henry S. Nourse; Chapters X–XIII, Sergeant-Major John G. Brown; XIV, Chaplain Milton L. Haney.

Capron, Thaddeus Hurlbut,　　　　–1890.

War diary of . . . 1861–1865. *JIHS* XII (1919) 330–406. plate (port.).　　224

Crooker, Lucien B

Episodes and character in an Illinois regiment (read November 10, 1887). *MOLLUS-Ill* I 33–49.　　225

—— A section of a battle, observations upon the conduct of the 55th Illinois infantry in the first day's battle of Shiloh, a missing link supplied. Prepared for the first reunion of that Regiment, held at Canton, Illinois, October 30th and 31st, 1884. By Lucian B. Crooker, Captain, 55th Illinois. 12 folios. 21cm.

Title from cover.　　WHi　226

Lawrence, Elijah C

Stuart's brigade at Shiloh, by Lieutenant Elijah C. Lawrence. *MOLLUS-Mass* II 489–96.　　227

McAuley, John T

Fort Donelson and its surrender (read March 3, 1880). *MOLLUS-Ill* I 69–74.　　228

Nourse, Henry Stedman, 1831–1903.

The burning of Columbia, S. C., February 17, 1865, by Henry S. Nourse, Captain. *PMHSM* IX 417–47.　　229

Stuart, David　　　　　　–1868.

A record of facts, by David Stuart, late Brigadier General of volunteers. Chicago, Evening Journal print, 1863. 16 p. 21cm.　　DLC　230

## 56TH INFANTRY

*Mustered in: February 27, 1862.*

*Mustered out: August 12, 1865.*

*AGR* IV 3–34.

Raum, Green Berry

Hazen's night expedition to Brown's ferry, by General Green B. Raum (read April 6, 1889). *MOLLUS-Ill* IV 276–83.　　231

Wilson, John　　　　　　–1910.

An Illinois soldier in North Mississippi: diary of John Wilson, February 15 — December 30, 1862. Edited by J. V. Frederick, *Journal of Mississippi history* I (Jackson 1939) 182–94.　　232

## 57TH INFANTRY

*Mustered in: December 26, 1861.*

*Mustered out: July 7, 1865.*

*AGR* IV 35–73.

Cluett, William W

History of the 57th regiment Illinois volunteer infantry, from muster in, Dec. 26, 1861, to muster out, July 7, 1865, by William W. Cluett. Princeton, T. P. Streeter, printer, 1886. 146 p. front. (illus.), plates (ports.). 22cm.

Unit roster [111]–46.　　DLC NN　233

Collins, Nathan G

. . . The prospect, the speech of Rev. N. G. Collins, Chaplain of the 57th Illinois, at Corinth, Miss., on the day of National thanksgiving, Aug. 3, '63, to the officers and men of Col. Bane's brigade. Chicago, Church, Goodman & Cushing, 1863. 16 p. 22½cm.

NN WHi　234

At head of title: Published by special request. Title and imprint from cover.

*57th Infantry, continued*

*Collins, Nathan G., continued*

—— Sermon by Rev. N. G. Collins, Chaplain of the 57th Illinois, delivered to the regiment of Western sharpshooters, 66th Ill. vol. infantry, Sunday, Nov. 22, 1863, at Pulaski, Tennessee. Reported phonographically by Serg't Frank E. Nevins, 66th Ill. Chicago, Church, Goodman & Cushing, print [1863] 14 p. 18cm.
WHi  **235**

Gross, Luelja Zearing
A sketch of the life of Major James Roberts Zearing. . . . *PIHS* no 28 (1922) 139–202. 2 plates (illus., port.).  **236**

"Letters written by Dr. James R. Zearing to his wife Lucinda Helmer Zearing during the Civil war, 1861–1865," 150–203.

## 58TH INFANTRY

*Organized: February 11, 1862.*

*Mustered out: April 1, 1866.*

*AGR* IV 74–133.

Second annual reunion of the 58th regiment Ills. vol. infantry, held at Scott's hall, Naperville, Ills., July 31st and August 1st, 1891. Cincinnati, Ohio, H. Watkins, printer [1891] 20 p. 23cm.  IHi  **237**
Title and imprint from cover.

## 59TH INFANTRY

*Organized as 9th Missouri infantry: September 1861.*

*Designated 59th Illinois infantry: February 12, 1862.*

*Mustered out: December 8, 1865.*

*AGR* IV 134–73.

Proceedings of the annual reunion of the Society of the 59th Ill. vet. vol. inf. reg't, held at . . . Springfield, Illinois, Tuesday, Sept. 29th, 1896. Springfield, Talbott & Hamann, printers [1896] 16 p. 14½cm.  IHi  **238**
Title and imprint from cover.

Proceedings of the tenth meeting of the 59th regt. Illinois veteran volunteer association, held in the Grand army hall at Kansas, Ill., August 10th, 1899. broadside, 26½ x 14½cm.
IHi  **239**

A roster of the survivors of the 59th regiment Illinois volunteer infantry. . . . [1900] 20 p. 10½ x 14½cm.  IHi  **240**

"Proceedings of the eleventh meeting of the 59th regt. Ill. vol. . . . August 30th, 1900," 3–6.

Ellet, Alfred Washington,           –1895.
Ellet and his steam-rams at Memphis. *BandL* I 453–9.  **241**

Heer, George Washington, 1844–
Episodes of the Civil war, nine campaigns in nine States, Fremont in Missouri, Curtis in Missouri and Arkansas, Halleck's siege of Corinth, Buell in Kentucky, Rosecrans in Kentucky and Tennessee, Grant at the battle of Chattanooga, Sherman from Chattanooga to Atlanta, Thomas in Tennessee and North Carolina, Stanley in Texas. In which is comprised the history of the Fifty-ninth regiment Illinois veteran volunteer infantry, together with special mention of the various regiments with which it was brigaded from 1861 to 1865, by Corporal Geo. W. Heer, late Company C, 59th Ill. San Francisco, Bancroft co., 1890. xiv, 461, xxx p. ports., plates (illus.). 25½cm.
Unit roster xxx p.  DLC NHi  **242**

Lathrop, David
The history of the Fifty-ninth regiment Illinois volunteers; or, a three years' campaign through Missouri, Arkansas, Mississippi, Tennessee and Kentucky, with a description of the country, towns, skirmishes and battles, incidents, casualties and anecdotes met with on the way . . . by Dr. D. Lathrop. Indianapolis, Ind., Hall & Hutchinson, 1865. 243 p. 3 plates (24 ports.). 20½cm.
Coulter 285.  DLC NHi NN  **243**

Mosman, Chesley A
Mosman's diary . . . kept by C. A. Mosman, late Lieutenant Company D, Fifty-ninth Illinois infantry, it recounts the movements of the Regiment, from January 24, 1862, to December 25, 1862. In Episodes of the Civil war, by G. W. Heer (1890) 361–97.  **244**

## 60TH INFANTRY

*Mustered in: February 17, 1862.*

*Mustered out: July 31, 1865.*

*AGR* IV 174–208.

## 61ST INFANTRY

*Mustered in: February 5, 1862.*

*Mustered out: September 8, 1865.*

*AGR* IV 209–43.

Stillwell, Leander, 1843–
In the ranks at Shiloh. *JIHS* xv (1922) 460–76.  **245**

—— Personal recollections of the battle of Shiloh, a paper prepared and read before the Kansas commandery of the M.O.L.L.U.S., March 2nd, 1892, by Leander Stillwell, First Lieutenant 61st Illinois. 19 p. 19½cm.  **246**

On cover: War paper no. 3. With title In the ranks at Shiloh, also published as War talks in Kansas, a series of papers read before the Kansas commandery of the MOLLUS, 109–26. Also appeared in the *Transactions of the Kansas state historical society* xi (1910) 296–305.

—— The story of a common soldier of army life in the Civil war, Erie, Kansas, Press of the Erie record, 1917. 154 p. 2 plates (ports.). 22cm.                                    WHi   **247**
"Only 100 copies printed, distributed to army friends," ms. note in WHi's copy.

—— The story of a common soldier of army life in the Civil war, 1861–1865. Second edition. [Erie, Kansas] Franklin Hudson pub. co., 1920. 278 p. plates (ports.). 19½cm.
DLC NHi NN   **248**

### 62ND INFANTRY

*Organized: April 10, 1862.*
*Mustered out: March 6, 1866.*
*AGR* iv 244–89.

### 63RD INFANTRY

*Mustered in: April 10, 1862.*
*Mustered out: July 13, 1865.*
*AGR* iv 290–314.

### 64TH INFANTRY

*Mustered in: December 16, 31, 1861.*
*Mustered out: July 11, 1865.*
*AGR* iv 315–47.

A list of living members as far as known. Also a list of those killed in battle or died of their wounds during the Civil war, 1861 to 1865. Also a record of the proceedings of their 49th reunion held at Walnut, Bureau county, Illinois, September 22nd and 23rd, 1915. 16 p. 16cm.
IHi   **249**
Sharland, George
Knapsack notes of Gen. Sherman's grand campaign through the empire state of the South, by George Sharland, Private Co. B, 64th reg't. Ill. . . . Springfield, Johnson & Bradford, printers, 1865. 68 p. 21½cm. NHi   **250**
Woodruff, George H
History of the Sixty-fourth regiment; or, Yates sharpshooters. In his *Fifteen years ago* (1876) 180–223.   **251**

### 65TH INFANTRY

*Mustered in: May 1, 1862.*
*Mustered out: July 13, 1865.*
*AGR* iv 348–96.

Milchrist, Thomas E
Reflections of a subaltern on the Hood-Thomas campaign in Tennessee, by Captain

Thomas E. Milchrist (read May 4, 1905). *MOLLUS-Ill* iv 451–65.   **252**

### 66TH INFANTRY

*Mustered in as 14th Missouri infantry: November 23, 1861.*
*Designated 66th Illinois infantry: November 20, 1862.*
*Mustered out: July 7, 1865.*
*AGR* iv 397–430.

Proceedings of the 9th annual reunion of the 66th Illinois, Western sharpshooters, held at Veedersburg, Ind., Aug. 24, 25, and 26, 1892. Paris, J. M. Sheets, printer, 1892. 9 p. 18cm.
NHi   **253**
Barker, Lorenzo A
Military history (Michigan boys) Company "D," 66th Illinois, Birge's Western sharpshooters in the Civil war, 1861–1865. [Reed City, Mich., 1905] 113 p. illus., map, ports. 23½cm.
NHi   **254**
Personal reminiscences, a complete roster of officers and privates of Company D," 48–110. "Preface" signed: "Ren" Barker.

McCord, William B
Battle of Corinth, the campaigns preceeding and leading up to this battle, and its results, by Lieutenant-Colonel William B. McCord. *MOLLUS-Minn* iv 567–84.   **255**
See also Title 235.

### 67TH INFANTRY

*Organized: June 13, 1862.*
*Mustered out: October 6, 1862.*
*AGR* iv 431–49.

### 68TH INFANTRY

*Organized: June 16, 1862.*
*Mustered out: September 27, 1862.*
*AGR* iv 450–69.

### 69TH INFANTRY

*Mustered in: June 14, 1862.*
*Mustered out: September 27, 1862.*
*AGR* iv 470–88.

### 70TH INFANTRY

*Mustered in: July 4, 1862.*
*Mustered out: October 23, 1862.*
*AGR* iv 489–506.

## 71ST INFANTRY

*Organized: July 26, 1862.*
*Mustered out: October 29, 1862.*
AGR IV 507–24.

## 72ND INFANTRY

*Mustered in: August 23, 1862.*
*Mustered out: August 6, 1865.*
AGR IV 525–55.

Harris, Luther William, 1843–
Soldiering on foot and on horseback during the Civil war, interesting experiences during the War of rebellion, by Luther William Harris. Augusta [n.d.] [8] leaves. port. 22cm.
                                             IHi    **256**
"Written by his daughter, Nellie G. Harris."

Heafford, George H
The army of the Tennessee, by Brevet Major George H. Heafford. *MOLLUS-Wis* I 308–23.
                                                    **257**
—— Chevrons and shoulder straps. [Chicago, Poole Bros., 189–] 16 p. 22½cm.    IHi    **258**
Caption title. Text signed: Geo H. Heafford.

Lord, John, 1846–
Frontier dust, by John Lord. Edited, with an introduction, by Natalie Shipman. Hartford, Conn., Edwin Valentine Mitchell, 1926. x, 198 p. 22cm.          MnHi NN    **259**
"With Thomas at Nashville," 1–21; "The Sixteenth corps," 63–71.

Sexton, James Andrew
The observations and experiences of a Captain of infantry at the battle of Franklin, November 30, 1864 (read November 8, 1904). *MOLLUS-Ill* IV 446–84.    **260**

Stockton, Joseph, 1833–1907.
War diary (1862–5) of Brevet Brigadier General Joseph Stockton. . . . Chicago, Printed by John T. Stockton, 1910. 35 p. 23cm.
                                             IHi    **261**
Title from cover. 2 ports., group port., and route of march map on p. 1–4 of cover. A brief biography of Joseph Stockton, folder, [6] p., laid in.

## 73RD INFANTRY

*Mustered in: August 21, 1862.*
*Mustered out: June 12, 1865.*
AGR IV 556–78.

Minutes of proceedings of the . . . annual reunion survivors of Seventy-third Illinois volunteer infantry. . . . II 1888 (IHi); v–VI 1891–1892 (WHi); VII 1893 (IHi); VIII 1894 (WHi); IX 1895 (NHi); x–XXXVII 1896–1923 (NN); XXXVIII 1924 (IHi).    **262**

Gilmore, James Roberts
Our visit to Richmond. *Atlantic monthly* XIV (1864) 372–83.    **263**
—— Our last day in Dixie. *Atlantic monthly* XIV (1864) 715–26.    **264**

Jaquess, James Frazier
Address to the 73rd regiment Illinois volunteer infantry, by Colonel James F. Jaquess, at a reunion held in Springfield, Illinois, October 8th–10th, 1890. 42 p. 21½cm.    NHi    **265**

Keeley, Charles W
The battle of Adairsville, Ga., May 17, 1864, Sherman's Georgia campaign, from the war diary of. . . . *JIHS* v (1912) 104–6.    **266**

Lawrence, William R
Address delivered in the Supreme court room, State capitol, Springfield, Illinois, on the occasion of the tenth annual reunion of survivors, 73d regt. Ill. vol. inft., Tuesday, September 29, 1896, by William R. Lawrence, late Lieut. Co. C. 7, (1) p. 24cm.    NHi    **267**
Caption title.

Newlin, William Henry
Annual address by W. H. Newlin delivered at the sixteenth annual reunion survivors Seventy-third regiment Illinois volunteer infantry, Springfield, Illinois, September 30, 1902. 15, (1) p. 21cm.    DLC NHi    **268**
Caption title. Cover title: Address, cherished memories, Illinois leadership in war and peace . . . talks on observance of Memorial day. . . .

—— A history of the Seventy-third regiment of Illinois infantry volunteers, its services and experiences in camp, on the march, on the picket and skirmish lines, and in many battles of the war, 1861–65 . . . Published by authority of the Regimental reunion association of survivors of the 73d Illinois infantry volunteers. [Springfield, 1890] 682 p. front. (port.), illus., ports. 22½cm.    DLC NHi NN    **269**
On cover: The preacher regiment, 1862–65. On spine: Persimmon regiment. Unit roster 24–66. "Introduction" signed: The Committee, W. H. Newlin, D. F. Lawler [and] J. W. Sherrick. Advertising circular inserted in NN's copy signed: W. H. Newlin, Historian, 73rd Illinois volunteers.

—— An account of the escape of six Federal soldiers from Danville prison at Danville, Va., their travels by night through the enemy's country to the Union pickets at Gauley's bridge, West Virginia, in the winter of 1863–64, by W. H. Newlin. Cincinnati, Western Methodist Book concern, 1888. 136 p. illus., plates (illus.). 22½cm.    **270**
On cover: Narrative of prison escape, by W. H. Newlin, late First Lieutenant, Seventy-third Illinois volunteers . . . also, memoranda of three years' service of Company "C," Seventy-third Ill. vol. infantry, embracing sketch of part borne by Opdycke's brigade in

battle of Franklin, Tennessee, November 30, 1864.
NN has an 1889 reprint with added leaf including
"corrections."

## 74TH INFANTRY

*Mustered in: September 4, 1862.*

*Mustered out: June 10, 1865.*

*AGR* iv 579–604.

Society of the Seventy-fourth Illinois volunteer
infantry. Reunion proceedings and history of
the Regiment. Rockford, W. P. Lamb, printer,
1903. 245 p. 24cm.          DLC NHi    **271**
  On cover: Campaigns of 74th Ills. vols. infantry.
"History of Seventy-fourth Illinois, by Hosmer P.
Holland," 7–36.

Freeman, Henry V
  Some battle recollections of Stone's river
(read January 10, 1895). *MOLLUS-Ill* iii 227–
46.                                            **272**

## 75TH INFANTRY

*Mustered in: September 2, 1862.*

*Mustered out: June 12, 1865.*

*AGR* iv 605–27.

Dodge, William Sumner
  A waif of the war; or, the history of the
Seventy-fifth Illinois infantry, embracing the
entire campaigns of the Army of the Cumber-
land, by Wm. Sumner Dodge. . . . Chicago,
Church and Goodman, 1866. vii, [17]–241,
(1) p. 22cm.             DLC NN    **273**
  "Errata" (1) p. Coulter 127.

## 76TH INFANTRY

*Mustered in: August 22, 1862.*

*Mustered out: July 22, 1865.*

*AGR* iv 628–53.

## 77TH INFANTRY

*Mustered in: September 3, 1862.*

*Mustered out: July 10, 1865.*

*AGR* iv 654–85.

Regimental record, Knoxville, Ill., 1885, the
tenth biennial reunion of the 77th Illinois volunteer infantry will be held at Knoxville, Ill.,
Sept. 2, 1885. . . . 14 p. 23cm.    NHi    **274**
  Advertising matter included. Title from cover.

Bentley, William H
  History of the 77th Illinois volunteer infantry, Sept. 2, 1862–July 10, 1865, by Lieut.
W. H. Bentley, with an introduction by General D. F. Grier. Peoria, Edward Hine, printer,
1883. 396 p. 20cm.          DLC NN    **275**
  Muster in roll, 28–92. Recruits, 221–33. Coulter 27.

Kennedy, John, 1835–1909.
  Diary of John Kennedy . . . copied by Ruth
Genevieve Hanneman . . . in March, 1959. . . .
[Rossville, Mich., 1959] 13 folios. 28cm.
  Mimeographed              MiDB    **276**

McCulloch, John Scouller, 1829–1910.
  Reminiscences of life in the army and as a
prisoner of war. 1 vol. front. (port.). 28cm.
                                   NN    **277**
  A facsimile reproduction on [32] pages of a manuscript dated: Knoxville college societies, Jan. 13th,
1888. A one page foreword is printed. Title from
cover.

## 78TH INFANTRY

*Mustered in: September 1, 1862.*

*Mustered out: June 7, 1865.*

*AGR* v 3–27.

Robbins, Edward Mott
  Civil war experiences, 1862–1865 . . . by Dr.
Edward M. Robbins. Carthage, 1919. [16] p.
front. (port.). 24cm.           IHi    **278**

## 79TH INFANTRY

*Mustered in: August 28, 1862.*

*Mustered out: June 12, 1865.*

*AGR* v 28–49.

Reunion of 79th Illinois at Charleston, Illinois,
Sept. 14 and 15, 1911. . . . 28 p. 2 ports. 15cm.
                                   IHi    **279**
  "Reminiscences . . . November 28th, 29th and 30th,
1864," by Peter Greggers, 16–28. Title from cover.

## 80TH INFANTRY

*Mustered in: August 25, 1862.*

*Mustered out: June 10, 1865.*

*AGR* v 50–71.

## 81ST INFANTRY

*Mustered in: August 26, 1862.*

*Mustered out: August 5, 1865.*

*AGR* v 72–99.

Newsome, Edmund
  Experience in the War of the great rebellion, by a soldier of the Eighty-first regiment
Illinois volunteer infantry, from August 1862,
to August 1865. Including nearly nine months
of life in Southern prisons at Macon, Savannah,
Charleston, Columbia and other places. Carbondale, Printed by E. Newsome, 1879. 137,
(3) p. 15cm.             DLC NHi    **280**
  Unit roster Company B, (3) p. Coulter 340.

—— —— Second edition, revised. Carbondale, Edmund Newsome, publisher, 1880.
297 p. 15cm.               NHi    **281**
  Unit roster [279]–97.

## 82ND INFANTRY

*Mustered in: October 23, 1862.*
*Mustered out: June 9, 1865.*
AGR v 100–24.

Salomon, Edward Selig, 1836–1913.
"Gettysburg," by Edward S. Salomon, Lt.
Col. 82d Illinois infantry, read before the California commandery of the Military order of the loyal legion of the United States at a banquet at San Francisco, California, January seventeenth, nineteen hundred and twelve. San Francisco, Shannon-Conmy print. co., 1913. 19 p. 23cm.                DLC  **282**
On cover: War paper no. 24. . . .

## 83RD INFANTRY

*Mustered in: August 21, 1862.*
*Mustered out: June 26, 1865.*
AGR v 125–50.

## 84TH INFANTRY

*Mustered in: September 1, 1862.*
*Mustered out: June 8, 1865.*
AGR v 151–71.

Roster of survivors of field and staff, 84th regiment Illinois volunteer infantry, by L. M. Dort and W. H. Tillson. Quincy, McMein print. co., 1906. 12 p. 14½cm.                IHi  **283**
Title and imprint from cover.

Simmons, Louis A
The history of the 84th reg't Ill. vols., by L. A. Simmons. Macomb, Hampton Brothers, 1866. 345, (1) p. 19½cm.      DLC NN  **284**
Coulter 417. "A table accounting for every man...," (1) p. Unit roster [281]–345.

## 85TH INFANTRY

*Mustered in: August 27, 1862.*
*Mustered out: June 5, 1865.*
AGR v 172–94.

. . . Reunion of the twins, Eighty-fifth and Eighty-sixth regiments Illinois vol. infantry, Peoria, Ill., Aug. 27–28, 1906. [24] p. plates (ports.). 22cm.                IHi  **285**
At head of title: Forty-fourth anniversary.

Aten, Henry J        1841–
History of the Eighty-fifth regiment Illinois volunteer infantry. Compiled and published under the auspices of the Regimental association, by Henry J. Aten, First Sergeant Company G. Hiawatha, Kansas, 1901. xi, [13]– 506 p. ports. 20½cm   DLC NHi NN  **286**

On cover: The story of a regiment and the campaigns of a brigade in the Army of the Cumberland. Unit roster 332–497. Coulter 11.

## 86TH INFANTRY

*Mustered in: August 27, 1862.*
*Mustered out: June 6, 1865.*
AGR v 195–217.

. . . Reunion of the Eighty-sixth regiment Illinois volunteer infantry. . . . i–xvii 1887–1903 (NHi); xviii 1904 (IHi); xxi–xxx 1907–1916 (IHi); xxxi–xxxv 1917–1921 (In); xtxvii 1923 (In).                **287**
For 1906 see Title 285.

Kinnear, John R
History of the Eighty-sixth regiment Illinois volunteer infantry, during its term of service, by J. R. Kinnear. Chicago, Tribune Company's book and job print. office, 1866. viii, [9]–139 p. 19cm.                DLC NHi NN  **288**
Coulter 280.

## 87TH INFANTRY

*Mustered in: October 3, 1862.*
*Mustered out: June 16, 1865.*
AGR v 218–39.

## 88TH INFANTRY

*Mustered in: September 4, 1862.*
*Mustered out: June 9, 1865.*
AGR v 240–60.

Francis, Charles Lewis
Narrative of a private soldier in the volunteer army of the United States, during a portion of the period covered by the great War of the rebellion of 1861, by Charles Lewis Francis, (Private Company B, Eighty-eighth Illinois volunteers). Brooklyn, N. Y., William Jenkins and co., 1879. viii, [7]–185 p. 18½cm.
DLC  **289**

Lammey, Ambrose
Roster of the Eighty-eighth Illinois volunteer infantry (or second Board of trade regiment). Organized in Chicago, August, 1862. Mustered into U. S. service, August 27, 1862. Left Chicago for Louisville, Ky., September 4, 1862. Participated in the battles of Perryville, Stone river, Chickamauga, Mission Ridge, the Atlanta campaign, Franklin and Nashville. Mustered out at Nashville, June 9, 1865, and disbanded at Chicago, June 23, 1865. [Chicago, 1892?] 40 p. 15 x 24cm.                DLC  **290**
"History of the Eighty-eighth infantry" 3–4.

## 89TH INFANTRY

*Mustered in: August 27, 1862.*
*Mustered out: June 10, 1865.*
AGR v 261–88.

Geographical history of the Railroad regiment, 89th regiment of Illinois vols. infantry. Chicago, Lithographed by Chas. Shober [1865] broadside. 100½ x 75cm.                    IHi    **291**
Route of march map. Text includes: Brief history of the Regiment, Chronological record of engagements, Summary of casualties, and Roster of officers.

Organization of the Eighty-ninth Illinois volunteer infantry reunion association, together with a register of membership, and reports of first primary meeting, held at Yorkville, Ill., Sept. 4, 1884, and first annual reunion . . . January 22, 1885. [Aurora, J. H. Hodder & co., printers, 1886] 18 p. 22½cm.
Title from cover.           DLC NHi    **292**

Wells, Ebenezer Tracy
The campaign and battle of Chickamauga. *US* ns xvi (1896) 205–33.          **293**

## 90TH INFANTRY

*Mustered in: September 7, 1862.*
*Mustered out: June 6, 1865.*
AGR v 289–311.

Woodruff, George H
History of the Ninetieth regiment; or, Irish legion. In his Fifteen years ago (1876) 361–96.          **294**

## 91ST INFANTRY

*Mustered in: September 8, 1862.*
*Mustered out: July 12, 1865.*
AGR v 312–32.

Beverly, James M          1843–
A history of the Ninety-first regiment Illinois volunteer infantry, 1862–1865, by James M. Beverly, Corporal Company H. White Hall, Pearce print. co. [1913] 59 p. plates (1 illus., ports.). 23cm.          DLC    **295**
"Roster of Greene county companies, 91st Illinois," 51–6.

## 92ND INFANTRY

*Mustered in: September 4, 1862.*
*Mustered out: June 21, 1865.*
AGR v 334–60.

Triennial reunion of the Ninety-second Illinois mounted infantry volunteers. . . . 4, 1876 (NHi); 5–7, 1879–1885 (MnHi); 8, 1888

(IHi); 9, 1891 (NN); 10, 1894 (MnHi); 11, 1897 (IHi); 12, 1900 (MnHi).          **296**

Ninety-second Illinois volunteers. . . . Freeport, Journal pub. house and bookbindery, 1875. 390 p. 20cm.          DLC NHi NN    **297**
Unit roster 254–305. "Published by the Ninety-second Illinois reunion association, under the supervision of a Committee. . . ."

Roster. [1930] [4] p. 20½cm.          IHi    **298**
Caption title. Cover text, an invitation to the 22nd triennial reunion, Polo, Aug. 14, 1930.

Atkins, Smith Dykins, 1836–1913.
Chickamauga, useless, disastrous battle, talk by Smith D. Atkins, Opera house, Mendota, Illinois, February 22, 1907, at invitation of Woman's reliefs corps, G.A.R. 13 p. 23cm.
Title from cover p [1].          IU    **299**

—— Wilder's brigade reunion, Effingham, Ill., Sept. 17, 1909. Remarks by Smith D. Atkins, late Colonel of the 92nd Illinois. 12 p. 22½cm.
Title from cover.          WHi    **300**

—— With Sherman's cavalry (read October 9, 1890). *MOLLUS-Ill* II 383–98.          **301**

## 93RD INFANTRY

*Mustered in: October 13, 1862.*
*Mustered out: June 23, 1865.*
AGR v 361–83.

Byers, Frederick W
Battle of Franklin, by Asst. Surg. Fred W. Byers. *MOLLUS-Wis* I 228–40.          **302**

Hicks, Henry G
The campaign and capture of Vicksburg, by Brevet-Major Henry G. Hicks. *MOLLUS-Minn* VI 82–107.          **303**

Trimble, Harvey Marion, 1842–
History of the Ninety-third regiment Illinois volunteer infantry, from orgaization to muster out. Statistics compiled by Aaron Dunbar. Revised and edited by Harvey M. Trimble, Adjutant. Chicago, Blakely print. co., 1898. 441 p. illus., maps, fold. plate (map). 23cm.
Unit roster included.          DLC NHi NN    **305**

## 94TH INFANTRY

*Mustered in: August 20, 1862.*
*Mustered out: July 17, 1865.*
AGR v 384–407.

Macy, William Madison, 1833–1926.
The Civil war diary of. . . . *Indiana magazine of history* xxx (Bloomington 1934) 181–97.          **306**

*94th Infantry, continued*

Orme, William Ward, 1832–1866.
Civil war letters of Brigadier General William Ward Orme, 1862–1866. Springfield, Schnepp & Barnes, printers, 1930. 72 p. 22½cm.                                        DLC  *307*
Reprinted from *JIHS* xxiii no 2 (1930).

## 95TH INFANTRY

*Mustered in: September 4, 1862.*
*Mustered out: August 18, 1865.*
*AGR* v 408–36.

Andrus, Onley, 1835–1881.
The Civil war letters of Sergeant Onley Andrus, edited by Fred Albert Shannon. Urbana, University of Illinois press, 1947. 147 p. map, 2 plates (facs.). 27cm.        NN  *308*
Half-title: Illinois studies in the Social sciences, volume XXVIII, number 4. . . .

Tyler, William N
Memoirs of Andersonville, by Mr. William N. Tyler, of Co. B, 95th Ill. infantry. . . . [Coal Valley, 1886] 32 p. 17cm.          IHi  *309*

Wood, Wales W
A history of the Ninety-fifth regiment Illinois infantry volunteers from its organization in the Fall of 1862, until its final discharge from the United States service, in 1865, by Wales W. Wood (former Adjutant of the Regiment). Chicago, Tribune co.'s book and job print. office, 1865. xii, [13]–240 p. 18½cm.
Unit roster 211–39.        DLC NHi NN  *310*

See also Title 50.

## 96TH INFANTRY

*Mustered in: September 6, 1862.*
*Mustered out: June 10, 1865.*
*AGR* v 437–65.

Reception to the Ninety-sixth regiment Illinois infantry volunteers, at the residence of their old commander, General John C. Smith, on the twenty-fifth anniversary of the battle of Nashville, Tenn., December 16, 1889. Chicago, Knight & Leonard co., printers, 1890. 81 p. plates (1 illus., ports.). 23½cm.
                                        DLC NHi  *311*
Reception to the members of the Ninety-sixth regiment, Illinois infantry volunteers, at the residence of their old commander, General John C. Smith, on the anniversary of the battle of Peach Tree creek, Georgia, July 20, 1893. Chicago, Knight, Leonard & co., printers, 1893. 75 p. plates (illus., ports.). 23½cm.
                                        DLC NHi  *312*

Blodgett, Edward A
The Army of the Southwest and the battle of Pea Ridge (read December 10, 1891). *MOLLUS-Ill* ii 289–312.               *313*

Earle, Charles Warrington
In and out of Libby prison (read November 11, 1886). *MOLLUS-Ill* i 247–92. plans.  *314*

—— Libby prison life and escape. *Maine bugle*, campaign III (Rockland 1896) 128–53.               *315*

Partridge, Charles Addison, 1843–
History of the Ninety-sixth regiment Illinois volunteer infantry. Published under the auspices of the Historical society of the Regiment . . . [six names] Edited by Charles A. Partridge. Chicago [Brown, Pettibone & co., printers] 1887. xv, [17]–938, (2) p. plates (illus., maps, ports.). 24cm.                         NN  *316*
Includes unit roster. "Memoranda. (For the future note here the date, place and cause of death of all comrades.)," blank pages, (2) p.

—— The Ninety-sixth Illinois at Chickamauga. *PIHL* no 15 (1912) 72–80.        *317*

## 97TH INFANTRY

*Mustered in: September 16, 1862.*
*Mustered out: July 29, 1865.*
*AGR* v 466–92.

## 98TH INFANTRY

*Mustered in: September 3, 1862.*
*Mustered out: June 27, 1865.*
*AGR* v 493–517.

## 99TH INFANTRY

*Mustered in: August 23, 1862.*
*Mustered out: July 31, 1865.*
*AGR* v 518–47.

Hobbs, Charles Albert
Vicksburg, a poem [by] C. A. Hobbs, First Sergeant Company B, Ninety-ninth Illinois infantry. Chicago, J. Fairbanks & co., 1880. 299 p. front. (port.), illus. 20½cm.
                                        CSmH NN  *317A*

## 100TH INFANTRY

*Mustered in: August 30, 1862.*
*Mustered out: June 12, 1865.*
*AGR* v 548–70.

Second annual reunion of the 100th regiment, Illinois volunteer infantry, held in Joliet, Illinois, September 16, 1886. Joliet, Press co., printers, 1886. 22 p. 23cm.          IHi  *318*

Bartleson, Frederick A      1833–1864.

Letters from Libby prison, being the authentic letters written while in Confederate captivity in the notorious Libby prison, at Richmond, by the gallant Union officer, Frederick A. Bartleson, Colonel of the 100th Illinois volunteers, captured at Chickamauga and, after his release, fated to die gloriously at Kenesaw mountain, as preserved and edited by his grand-niece, Margaret W. Peelle. New York, Greenwich Book pub., 1956. 95 p. front. (facs.). 21cm.      NN    **319**

Waterman, Arba N

The battle of Chickamauga (read June 4, 1884). *MOLLUS-Ill* I 231–45.      **320**

Woodruff, George H

History of the One hundredth; or, Will county regiment. In his Fifteen years ago (1876) 224–360.      **321**

## 101ST INFANTRY

*Mustered in: September 2, 1862.*
*Mustered out: June 7, 1865.*
AGR v 571–92.

Potter, John

Reminiscences of the Civil war in the United States, by Rev. John Potter. Including also an account of a visit to the battle grounds of Tennessee and Georgia in 1895, and a memorial sermon preached at Montezuma, Iowa, May 26th, 1895. [Oskaloosa, Iowa, Globe presses, 1897] 196 p. front. (port.). 20cm.
     DLC NHi NN    **322**

"Copyright 1897 by John Potter" rubber-stamped on title page. On spine: Personal memoirs of the war.

## 102ND INFANTRY

*Mustered in: September 1–2, 1862.*
*Mustered out: June 6, 1865.*
AGR v 593–615.

Roster of the living members of the 102d regt. Ill vols. [Galesburg?] 1911. 27 p. 17½cm.
     IU    **323**

Conger, Edwin H

The private, by Major E. H. Conger. *MOLLUS-Iowa* II 57–64.      **324**

Fleharty, Stephen F

Our regiment, a history of the 102d Illinois infantry volunteers, with sketches of the Atlanta campaign, the Georgia raid, and the campaign of the Carolinas, by S. F. Fleharty. Chicago, Brewster & Hanscom, printers, 1865. 192, xxiv p. 19½cm.      DLC NN    **325**

Unit roster xxiv p. Coulter 163.

## 103RD INFANTRY

*Mustered in: October 2, 1862.*
*Mustered out: June 21, 1865.*
AGR v 616–40.

Reminiscences of the Civil war from diaries of members of 103d Illinois volunteer infantry. Compiled by the following committee . . . [seven names] Chicago, J. F. Leaming & co., 1904. 293 p. plates (ports.). 20½cm.
Muster in roll 261–83.      DLC NN    **326**

See also Title 29.

## 104TH INFANTRY

*Mustered in: August 27, 1862.*
*Mustered out: June 27, 1865.*
AGR v 641–64.

Reunion of the 104th Illinois volunteers, held in Ottawa, Ill., Wednesday, Sept. 16, 1891. [4] p. 25cm.      IHi    **327**

Caption title.
"From the Daily republican-times, Sept. 16–17, 1891."

Calkins, William Wirt, 1842–

The history of the One hundred and fourth regiment of Illinois volunteer infantry, War of the great rebellion, 1862–1865, by William Wirt Calkins, First Lieutenant of Company E, One hundred and fourth regiment, and Aide de camp staff of General John Beatty. Historical committee . . . [four names] Chicago, Donohue & Henneberry, printers, 1895. 539 p. plates (illus., ports.). 22cm.
     DLC NHi NN    **328**

## 105TH INFANTRY

*Mustered in: September 2, 1862.*
*Mustered out: June 7, 1865.*
AGR v 665–88.

Pierce, Thomas Jefferson, 1836–1864.

Letters home, by Sgt. Thomas Jefferson Pierce who enlisted 13 August 1862, Wyoming, Illinois, Company E, 105 regiment, of the Illinois volunteers of the Union army of the United States of America, came to his death in line of duty, 3 March 1864, hospital # 11, Nashville, Tenn. Also, a roster of descendants of Charles and Catharine Pierce, compiled by Ellen K. Korbitz. [Burlington, Iowa, Weyher Advertising, 1957] 33 p. port. 21½cm.
     DLC    **329**

Romeyn, Henry

Scouting in Tennessee, by Major Henry Romeyn. 1905. 24 p. *MOLLUS-DC* no 59. **330**

**106TH INFANTRY**

*Mustered in: September 18, 1862.*
*Mustered out: July 12, 1865.*
AGR vi 3–25.

**107TH INFANTRY**

*Mustered in: September 4, 1862.*
*Mustered out: June 21, 1865.*
AGR vi 26–49.

**108TH INFANTRY**

*Mustered in: August 28, 1862.*
*Mustered out: August 5, 1865.*
AGR vi 50–74.

Bumstead, Samuel J
A Western volunteer. *US* xiii (1885) 674–83; xiv (1886) 27–36, 148–55.  *331*
"To be continued."

**109TH INFANTRY**

*Mustered in: September 11, 1862.*
*Transferred to 11th regiment: April 10, 1863.*
AGR vi 75–93.

**110TH INFANTRY**

*Mustered in: September 11, 1862.*
*Mustered out: June 8, 1865.*
AGR vi 94–122.

**111TH INFANTRY**

*Mustered in: September 18, 1862.*
*Mustered out: June 7, 1865.*
AGR vi 123–48.

**112TH INFANTRY**

*Mustered in: September 20, 22, 1862.*
*Mustered out: June 20, 1865.*
AGR vi 149–74.

Catalogue of the officers and members of the Henry county regiment, being the 112th regiment Illinois volunteers. Geneseo, Union Advocate print. establishment, 1862. 16, (4) p.
MnHi  *332*
Advertising matter included. Includes History of the Regiment and Biographical sketches of the commissioned officers. Roster of Company K, Recapitulation, and advertising matter (4) p.

Thompson, Bradford F
History of the 112th regiment of Illinois volunteer infantry, in the great War of the rebel-

lion, 1862–1865, by B. F. Thompson, late Captain in the Regiment. Toulon, Stark County News office, 1885. 480 p. 23cm.
DLC NHi NN  *333*
Unit roster [334]–430. Contributed articles: Saunders raid into East Tennessee, by Capt. James McCartney, 433–52; Escape of Charles T. Goss from the prison at Andersonville, compiled by B. F. Thompson from a letter written by Goss, 453–5; Capture, prison life and escape of George W. Nicholas, written by himself, 456–71; Belle Isle and Andersonville [by] F. J. Liggett, 471–7.

**113TH INFANTRY**

*Mustered in: October 1, 1862.*
*Mustered out: June 20, 1865.*
AGR vi 175–201.

Kellogg, John Jackson, 1837–
War experiences and the story of the Vicksburg campaign from "Milliken's Bend" to July 4, 1863, being an accurate and graphic account of campaign events taken from the diary of Capt. J. J. Kellogg of Co. B, 113th Illinois. [Washington, Iowa, Evening Journal, 1913] 64 p. front. (port.). 17½cm.  DLC NN  *334*
Coulter 271.

Woolworth, Solomon
Experiences in the Civil war, by Solomon Woolworth. Newark, N. J., 1903. 79, (1) p. front. (port.). 17½cm.  DLC  *335*
NHi has reprintings, 1904 and 1905.

**114TH INFANTRY**

*Mustered in: September 18, 1862.*
*Mustered out: August 3, 1865.*
AGR vi 202–23.

French, Alvin S
Civil war letters. *JIHS* xv (1922) 531–8.
*336*
See also Title 85.

**115TH INFANTRY**

*Mustered in: September 13, 1862.*
*Mustered out: June 11, 1865.*
AGR vi 224–47.

Royse, Isaac Henry Clay
History of the 115th regiment Illinois volunteer infantry, by Isaac Henry Clay Royse, late Second Lieutenant Company E. Published by the author with authority of the Regimental association. Terre Haute, Ind. [Chicago, Wind-

sor & Kenfield pub. co.] 1900. vi, 404, (1) p.
illus., maps, plates (ports.). 24cm.
DLC NN    **337**

<small>Unit roster [288]–404. "Buried in National cemetery, Nashville, Tenn." [Chattanooga, Tenn.; Andersonville, Ga.] (1) p.</small>

### 116TH INFANTRY

*Mustered in: September 30, 1862.*
*Mustered out: June 7, 1865.*
*AGR* vi 248–71.

### 117TH INFANTRY

*Mustered in: September 19, 1862.*
*Mustered out: August 5, 1865.*
*AGR* vi 272–91.

Proceedings of the Reunion association One
hundred seventeenth Illinois infantry volunteers. . . . 1909, 1915–1917, 1919–1920.

<small>1919–1920 issued in one volume.</small>    IHi    **338**

### 118TH INFANTRY

*Mustered in: November 7, 1862.*
*Mustered out: October 1, 1865.*
*AGR* vi 292–318.

### 119TH INFANTRY

*Mustered in: October 10, 1862.*
*Mustered out: August 26, 1865.*
*AGR* vi 319–43.

### 120TH INFANTRY

*Mustered in: October 29, 1862.*
*Mustered out: September 10, 1865.*
*AGR* vi 344–69.

Blackman, William S
The boy of Battle ford and the man. Marion,
Egyptian press print. co., 1906. 192 p. ports.
21½cm.      IHi NN    **339**
<small>Civil war 57–123.</small>

### 121ST INFANTRY

*Failed to complete organization.*

### 122ND INFANTRY

*Mustered in: September 4, 1862.*
*Mustered out: July 15, 1865.*
*AGR* vi 370–94.

Ibbetson, William H    H      –1883.
[Diary, Oct. 8, 1862 — Aug. 8, 1864] *PIHL*
no 37 (1930) 236–73.      **340**
<small>Unit roster Co. D, 122nd Ill., 270–3.</small>

### 123RD INFANTRY

*Mustered in: September 6, 1862.*
*Mustered out: June 27, 1865.*
*AGR* vi 395–421.

Connolly, James Austin, 1840–1914.
Three years in the Army of the Cumberland,
the letters and diary of Major James A. Connolly. Edited by Paul M. Angle. Bloomington,
Indiana University press [1959] 399 p. maps.
21cm.      NN    **341**
<small>"Civil war centennial series."</small>

—— —— *PIHL* no 35 (1928) 215–438. **342**

Crowder, James H
Before and after Vicksburg, by Rev. J. H.
Crowder. . . . Dayton, Ohio, Otterbein press
[1924] 112 p. front. (port.). 19cm.
IHi    **343**

### 124TH INFANTRY

*Mustered in: September 10, 1862.*
*Mustered out: August 15, 1865.*
*AGR* vi 422–48.

Beck, Stephen C      1842–
A true sketch of his army life, by S. C. Beck.
[Edgar, Neb., 1914] 51 p. 22cm.   DLC   **344**
<small>Title from cover.</small>

Howard, Richard L
History of the 124th regiment Illinois infantry volunteers otherwise known as the "Hundred and two dozen," from August, 1862, to
August, 1865, by R. L. Howard, Chaplain.
Springfield, Printed by H. W. Rokker, 1880.
ix, 519 p. 20½cm.    DLC NHi NN    **345**
<small>Coulter 244.</small>
<small>Unit roster 496–519.</small>

—— The Vicksburg campaign. *MOLLUS-Me*
ii 28–40.      **346**

—— The Vicksburg campaign, a personal experience. *Maine bugle*, campaign IV (Rockland
1897) 1–10.      **347**

### 125TH INFANTRY

*Mustered in: September 3, 1862.*
*Mustered out: June 9, 1865.*
*AGR* vi 449–70.

Harmon, Oscar Fitzalan, 1827–1864.
Life and letters of Oscar Fitzalan Harmon,
Colonel of the 125th regiment Illinois volunteers. Written and edited by his daughter, Lucy
Harmon McPherson. Trenton, N. J., MacCrellish & Quigley co., printers, 1914. 157 p. plates
(illus., 2 ports.). 23cm.      MnHi    **348**

*125th Infantry, continued*

Rogers, Robert M

The 125th regiment Illinois volunteer infantry. Attention battalion! By Robert M. Rogers, late Second Sergeant Co. B. Champaign, Gazette print, 1882. ix, [10]–226 p. front. (port.). 21½cm.                                    DLC   *349*
Unit roster [183]–202.

## 126TH INFANTRY

*Mustered in: September 4, 1862.*
*Mustered out: July 12, 1865.*
*AGR vi 471–91.*

Marshall, Henry, 1822–1864.
Civil war letters of. . . . *North Dakota historical quarterly* ix (1941) 35–57.    *349A*

## 127TH INFANTRY

*Mustered in: September 6, 1862.*
*Mustered out: June 4, 1865.*
*AGR vi 492–515.*

## 128TH INFANTRY

*Mustered in: November 4, 1862.*
*Disbanded: April 1, 1863.*
*AGR vi 516–32.*

## 129TH INFANTRY

*Mustered in: September 8, 1862.*
*Mustered out: June 8, 1865.*
*AGR vi 533–54.*

Ayers, James T                    1805–1865.
The diary of James T. Ayers, Civil war recruiter. Edited with an introduction by John Hope Franklin. Occasional publication [no. 50] of the Illinois state historical society. . . . Springfield, 1947. xxv, 138 p. 3 plates (facs., illus., port.). 23cm.                    NN   *350*
On spine: Publication no. 50.

Blakeslee, George H
"In foro conscientiae." *BandG* iii (1894) 42–4.                                           *351*

—— A day with John Morgan. *BandG* v (1895) 105–6.                                  *352*

Franklin, John Hope
James T. Ayers, Civil war recruiter. *JIHS* xl (1947) 267–97.                            *353*

Grunert, William
History of the One hundred and twenty-ninth regiment Illinois volunteer infantry, containing the marches, events and battles of the

army commanded by Gen. Sherman, from the commencement of the campaign against Atlanta, Georgia, to the arrival at Washington . . . by William Grunert. Winchester, Printed by R. B. Dedman, 1866. 383 p. 19½cm.
                              IHi WHi    *354*

Newton, George A
Battle of Peach Tree creek. *G.A.R. war papers* (papers read before Fred C. Jones post, no 401, Department of Ohio, G.A.R., Youngstown, 1891) 148–63.                    *355*

See also Title 86.

## 130TH INFANTRY

*Mustered in: October 25, 1862.*
*Mustered out: August 15, 1865.*
*AGR vi 555–88.*

History and roster 130th Illinois. [1889?] 12 p. 19½cm.                              IHi   *356*
Title from cover.

History and roster One hundred and thirtieth Illinois. Greenville, Advocate print [1892] 15 p. 18cm.                          DLC NHi   *357*
Title from cover.

History and roster of the 130th infantry regiment, Illinois volunteers. Greenville, Advocate print, 1893. 16 p. 20cm.          IHi   *358*

Johnson, Charles Beneulyn, 1843–
Muskets and medicine; or, army life in the sixties, by Charles Beneulyn Johnson. . . . Philadelphia, F. A. Davis co., 1917. 276 p. plates (illus., ports.). 21½cm.      NN   *359*
Coulter 258.

Wilkin, Jacob W
Personal reminiscences of General U. S. Grant. *PIHL* no 12 (1908) 131–40.    *360*

—— Vicksburg, by Captain Jacob W. Wilkin, (read April 14, 1898). *MOLLUS-Ill* iv 215–37.
                                        *361*

## 131ST INFANTRY

*Mustered in: November 13, 1862.*
*Consolidated with 129th regiment: November 15, 1863.*
*AGR vi 589–616.*

## 132ND INFANTRY

*Mustered in: June 1, 1864.*
*Mustered out: October 17, 1864.*
*AGR vii 4–21.*

### 133RD INFANTRY

*Mustered in: May 31, 1864.*
*Mustered out: September 24, 1864.*
*AGR* VII 22–37.

### 134TH INFANTRY

*Mustered in: May 31, 1864.*
*Mustered out: October 25, 1864.*
*AGR* VII 38–54.

Danforth, Willis         –1891.
How I came to be in the army and General
E. A. Paine's plan of Federal salvation, by
Surgeon Willis Danforth. *MOLLUS-Wis* I 324–
39.                                              **362**

### 135TH INFANTRY

*Mustered in: June 6, 1864.*
*Mustered out: September 28, 1864.*
*AGR* VII 55–72.

### 136TH INFANTRY

*Mustered in: June 1, 1864.*
*Mustered out: October 22, 1864.*
*AGR* VII 73–89.

### 137TH INFANTRY

*Mustered in: June 5, 1864.*
*Mustered out: September 4, 1864.*
*AGR* VII 90–107.

Castle, Henry Anson, 1851–1916.
The army mule. *MOLLUS-Minn* II 338–
66.                                              **363**
—— The army mule and other war sketches,
by Henry A. Castle, Private, Sergeant-Major
and Captain Illinois volunteers. With illustra-
tions by J. W. Vawter. Indianapolis, Bowen-
Merrill co., 1898. 269 p. plates (illus.). 19cm.
NHi    **364**
—— The boys in Blue grown gray. *MOLLUS-
Minn* IV 454–77.                                **365**
—— Dress parade. *MOLLUS-Minn* IV 227–
65.                                              **366**
—— General W. T. Sherman, a memorial.
*MOLLUS-Minn* III 495–502.                      **367**
—— Opdycke's brigade at the battle of Frank-
lin. *MOLLUS-Minn* VI 385–404.                  **368**
—— The shelter tent. *MOLLUS-Minn* III 440–
53.                                              **369**
—— Sheridan with the Army of the Cumber-
land. 1900. 25 p. *MOLLUS-DC* no 34.    **370**

—— Some of the army mules esteemed con-
temporaries. *MOLLUS-Minn* VI 462–78.   **371**
—— Some experiences of an enlisted man.
*MOLLUS-Minn* I 107–34.                         **372**
—— The sutler. *MOLLUS-Minn* IV 58–65.
**373**

### 138TH INFANTRY

*Mustered in: June 21, 1864.*
*Mustered out: October 14, 1864.*
*AGR* VII 108–23.

### 139TH INFANTRY

*Mustered in: June 1, 1864.*
*Mustered out: October 25, 1864.*
*AGR* VII 124–40.

### 140TH INFANTRY

*Mustered in: June 18, 1864.*
*Mustered out: October 29, 1864.*
*AGR* VII 141–57.

### 141ST INFANTRY

*Mustered in: June 16, 1864.*
*Mustered out: October 10, 1864.*
*AGR* VII 158–74.

Fuller, Ezra Bond
Who fired the first shot at the battle of
Gettysburg? *JUSCA* XXIV (1914) 784–96.
illus., 1 port.                                 **374**

### 142ND INFANTRY

*Mustered in: June 18, 1864.*
*Mustered out: October 27, 1864.*
*AGR* VII 175–90.

### 143RD INFANTRY

*Mustered in: June 11, 1864.*
*Mustered out: September 26, 1864.*
*AGR* VII 191–207.

### 144TH INFANTRY

*Mustered in: October 21, 1864.*
*Mustered out: July 14, 1865.*
*AGR* VII 208–29.

### 145TH INFANTRY

*Mustered in: June 9, 1864.*
*Mustered out: September 23, 1864.*
*AGR* VII 230–50.

## 146TH INFANTRY

*Mustered in: September 1864.*
*Mustered out: July 5, 1865.*
AGR vii 252–70.

## 147TH INFANTRY

*Mustered in: February 18–19, 1865.*
*Mustered out: January 20, 1866.*
AGR vii 271–91.

## 148TH INFANTRY

*Mustered in: February 21, 1865.*
*Mustered out: September 5, 1865.*
AGR vii 292–309.

## 149TH INFANTRY

*Mustered in: February 11, 1865.*
*Mustered out: January 27, 1866.*
AGR vii 310–28.

## 150TH INFANTRY

*Mustered in: February 14, 1865.*
*Mustered out: January 16, 1866.*
AGR vii 329–46.

## 151ST INFANTRY

*Mustered in: February 23, 1865.*
*Mustered out: January 24, 1866.*
AGR vii 347–65.

Reunion 55th anniversary of the 151st Illinois volunteer infantry held at Indianapolis, Indiana, September 20–25, 1920. [Leavenworth, Kansas, R. E. Davis, 1920] 44 p. 3 ports. (1 on cover). 20½cm.                                NN  **375**
Title from cover.

## 152ND INFANTRY

*Mustered in: February 18, 1865.*
*Mustered out: September 11, 1865.*
AGR vii 366–83.

## 153RD INFANTRY

*Mustered in: February 27, 1865.*
*Mustered out: September 15, 1865.*
AGR vii 384–402.

## 154TH INFANTRY

*Mustered in: February 21, 1865.*
*Mustered out: September 18, 1865.*
AGR vii 403–22.

## 155TH INFANTRY

*Mustered in: February 28, 1865.*
*Mustered out: September 4, 1865.*
AGR vii 423–40.

## 156TH INFANTRY

*Organized: February 16, 1865.*
*Mustered out: September 20, 1865.*
AGR vii 441–58.

# Regimental Publications
# & Personal Narratives
# of the Civil War

## A Checklist

Compiled by C. E. DORNBUSCH

Volume One    Northern States

PART II    NEW YORK

New York

The New York Public Library

1961

THIS VOLUME HAS BEEN PUBLISHED WITH HELP
FROM THE EMILY ELLSWORTH FORD SKEEL FUND

# Table of Contents

# Acknowledgments

Though their Civil War collections contributed substantially to the entire checklist, mention of two New York institutions is appropriate here. Dr James J. Heslin, Director, and Miss Geraldine Beard and Miss Rachel Minick of the New-York Historical Society have been most helpful to the compiler. At the Brooklyn Public Library, the assistance of Miss Louise M. Turpin is acknowledged.

# Abbreviations

| | |
|---|---|
| *BandL* | Battles and leaders, New York, 1887–88. 4 v. |
| *BandG* | Blue and Gray, Philadelphia |
| *Coulter* | Travels in the Confederate states, a bibliography. By E. Merle Coulter. 1948 |
| *JMSIUS* | Journal of the Military service institution of the United States |
| *MOLLUS* | Military order of the loyal legion of the United States |
| *DC* | War papers District of Columbia commandery |
| *Ill* | Military essays and recollections Illinois commandery |
| *Ind* | War papers Indiana commandery |
| *Kan* | War papers Kansas commandery |
| *Me* | War papers Maine commandery |
| *Mass* | Civil war papers Massachusetts commandery |
| *Mich* | War papers Michigan commandery |
| *Minn* | Glimpses of the Nation's struggles Minnesota commandery |
| *Mo* | War papers Missouri commandery |
| *Neb* | Civil war sketches Nebraska commandery |
| *NY* | Personal recollections of the War of the rebellion New York |
| *Wis* | War papers Wisconsin commandery |
| *NYH* | New York history, Cooperstown |
| *PMHSM* | Papers of the Military historical society of Massachusetts |
| *PNRISSHS* | Personal narratives Rhode Island soldiers and sailors historical society |
| *Pfisterer* | New York in the War of the rebellion, 1861 to 1865. Compiled by Frederick Pfisterer. Third edition. 1912 |
| *Register* | [Registers of New York regiments in the War of the rebellion] Serial no. [1]–43, 1894–1906 |
| *US* | The united service, Philadelphia |

*Location symbols are those of National Union Catalogue.*

# Reference Works

Dyer, Frederick Henry, 1849–1917.

A compendium of the War of the rebellion, 1908 (reprinted 1959).

"Regimental index" 179–99; "Regimental histories" 1367–1471. The same pagination is used in the 1959 reprint.

New York. Adjutant-General.

[Registers of New York regiments in the War of the rebellion] Serial no [1]–43. Albany, 1894–1906. 43 v. 23cm.

Issued as supplementary volumes to the Annual report of the Adjutant-General for 1893–1905.

Pfisterer, Frederick, 1836–1909.

New York in the War of the rebellion, 1861 to 1865. Compiled by Frederick Pfisterer. Third edition. Albany, J. B. Lyon co., State printers, 1912. 5 v. plates (col. illus., 3 maps, 1 double). 28½cm.

The five volumes are continuously paged.

—— Index. Third edition. Albany, J. B. Lyon co., State printers, 1912. 376 p. 28½cm.

*The Union army.*

"Record of New York regiments," II (1908) 50–248.

United States. Adjutant General's Office.

Official army register of the volunteer force of the United States army for the years 1861, '62, '63, '64, '65. Part II. New York and New Jersey. Washington, 1865.

A roster of officers by regiments with an alphabetical index for the two states.

## ARTILLERY

## Regiments

### 1ST ARTILLERY, MARINE

*Mustered in: November 12, 1861, to August 18, 1862.*
*Regiment disbanded: March 31, 1863.*
*Pfisterer 1541-8.*
*Register serial no 15, 1-160.*

Proceedings of citizens of Chicago, in relation to the so-called "Marine artillery." [Chicago, 1862] 16 p. 20½cm.                    DLC    **1**

Avery, William B
The Marine artillery with the Burnside expedition and the battle of Camden, N. C., by William Avery, late Captain. 1880. 28 p. *PNRISSHS* 2d ser, no 4.                    **2**

Waples, E                    Harris
The youngest "boy in Blue." *BandG* IV (1894) 176.                    **3**

White, Oliver
Pencil sketches of service in the Marine artillery, with some incidental reflections on the use and abuse of "shoulderstraps, and things," by Oliver White. Toulon, Ill., Printed at the office of the "Stark County News," 1863. 86 p. 22½cm.                    DLC    **4**

### 1ST ARTILLERY (LIGHT)

*For muster in and out dates, see individual batteries.*
*Pfisterer 1208-34.*
*Register serial no 8, 1-472.*

A threnody, sta viator, heroem calcas! In remembrance of Brevet Colonel U.S. & N.Y. vol. John Watts de Peyster, Junior, died 12th April, 1873, at 4:55 a.m. New York, J. R. Huth, printer, 1874. xxii p. 25cm.        NHi    **5**
Title and imprint from cover. "In memoriam ! Brief words at the funeral of Brev. Col. John Watts de Peyster, Jr . . . by Rev. G. Lewis Platt," [i]–iv.

### Battery A

*Mustered in: September 12, 1861.*
*Mustered out: June 28, 1865.*

### Battery B

*Mustered in: August 31, 1861.*
*Mustered out: June 18, 1865.*

### Battery C

*Mustered in: September 6, 1861.*
*Mustered out: June 17, 1865.*

Cutler, Cyrus Morton, 1841–1870?
Letters from the front, from October, 1861, to September, 1864, by Cyrus Morton Cutler, while a member of Co. F 22nd Massachusetts volunteer infantry regiment and Battery C 1st New York (light) artillery regiment. [San Francisco, 1892] 39 p. front. (port.). 26cm.
Preface signed: A. D. Cutler.        MHi    **6**

### Battery D

*Mustered in: September 6, 1861.*
*Mustered out: June 16, 1865.*

### Battery E

*Mustered in: September 13, 1861.*
*Mustered out: June 16, 1865.*

### Battery F

*Mustered in: September 14, 1861.*
*Mustered out: June 17, 1865.*

### Battery G

*Mustered in: September 24, 1861.*
*Mustered out: June 19, 1865.*

Ames, Nelson
History of Battery G, First regiment, New York light artillery, by Capt. Nelson Ames. Marshalltown, Iowa, Marshall print. co., 1900. 151 p. front. (illus.), illus., plates (1 illus., ports.). 20cm.        NN    **7**
"Correction" slip inserted. On cover: Battery G, First N.Y.L.A., Second corps, Army of the Potomac. Unit roster [135]–42.

### Battery H

*Mustered in: October 10, 1861.*
*Mustered out: June 19, 1865.*

### Battery I

*Mustered in: October 1, 1861.*
*Mustered out: June 23, 1865.*

Remington, Cyrus Kingsbury
A record of Battery I, First N.Y. light artillery vols., otherwise known as Wiedrich's battery, during the War of the rebellion, 1861–'65 . . . compiled from reliable sources, by Cyrus Kingsbury Remington. Buffalo, Courier co., 1891. 156 p. plates (1 illus., ports.). 23½cm.
Unit roster [121–33]        NN    **8**

*1st Artillery (Light), continued*

### Battery K

*Mustered in: November 20, 1861.*

*Mustered out: June 20, 1865.*

Dudley, Edgar Swartwout

A reminiscence of Washington and Early's attack in 1864, read before the Ohio commandery of the Loyal legion of the United States, by Edgar S. Dudley. Cincinnati, Peter G. Thomson, printer, 1884. 22 p. 21½cm.

NHi      9

Also published as *MOLLUS-Ohio* I 107–27. plate (map).

### Battery L

*Mustered in: November 17, 1861.*

*Mustered out: June 17, 1865.*

Breck, George, 1833–1925.

George Breck's Civil war letters from "Reynold's battery." *Rochester historical society publications* XXII (1944) 91–149.      10

Shelton, William H

A hard road to travel out of Dixie. *Century magazine* XL (1890) 931–49. illus.      11

### Battery M

*Mustered in: October 14, 1861.*

*Mustered out: June 23, 1865.*

## 2ND ARTILLERY (HEAVY)

*Mustered in by companies: August 23 to December 12, 1861.*

*Mustered out: September 29, 1865.*

*Pfisterer 1235–64.*

*Register serial no 8, 473–1085.*

Roster of the Second New York artillery, a list of the survivors together with their post office addresses, by W. Hector Gale, Secretary, Second New York artillery association. . . . Oneida, Free Press print, 1887. 28 p. 23½cm.

NHi      12

"Comrades should always examine annual supplementary pages."

Armes, George Augustus, 1844–1919.

Ups and downs of an army officer, by Col. George A. Armes. Washington, D. C., 1900. xix, 784 p. facs., illus., ports. 22½cm.

NHi NN      12A

Mustered in as Captain 2nd N. Y. Artillery, November 17, 1864.

Irving, Theodore, 1809–1880.

"More than conqueror;" or, memorials of Col. J. Howard Kitching, Sixth New York artillery,

by the author of "The conquest of Florida." . . . New York, Hurd and Houghton, 1873. viii, 239 p. front. (port.). 18cm.      NN      13

Mustered in 2nd New York heavy artillery, September 18, 1861; discharged, July 6, 1862; mustered in 135th infantry (subsequently 6th artillery), September 6, 1862; died of wounds, January 10, 1865.

Miller, Delavan S           1849–

Drum taps in Dixie, memories of a drummer boy, 1861–1865, by Delavan S. Miller. Watertown, Hungerford-Holbrook co., 1905. vii, [9]–256 p. plates (ports.). 19½cm.

DLC NN      14

Roback, Henry

The veteran volunteers of Herkimer and Otsego counties in the War of the rebellion, being a history of the 152d N.Y.V., with scenes, incidents, etc., which occured in the ranks of the 34th N.Y., 97th N.Y., 121st N.Y., 2d N.Y. heavy artillery, and 1st and 2d N.Y. mounted rifles. Also the active part performed by the boys in Blue who were associated with the 152d N.Y.V. in Gen. Hancock's Second army corps, during Grant's campaign, from the Wilderness to the surrender of Gen. Lee at Appomattox court house, Va. Compiled and edited by Henry Roback. Little Falls [Utica, Press of L. C. Childs & Son, 1888] 196 p. 23cm.

NN      15

Roster of survivors, killed in action and wounded, 152nd, [172]–85.

Roemer, Jacob, 1818–1896.

Reminiscences of the War of the rebellion, 1861–1865, by Bvt.-Maj. Jacob Roemer, Battery L, Second N.Y. artillery, and Thirty-fourth N.Y.V.V. ind. 1t. battery. Edited by L. A. Furney. Published by the estate of Jacob Roemer. Flushing [Press of the Flushing Journal] 1897. 316, (1) p. front. (port.). 21cm.

On spine: The Flushing battery. DLC NN      16

## 3RD ARTILLERY (LIGHT)

*Mustered in as the 19th regiment of infantry: May 22, 1861.*

*Designated 3rd regiment of artillery (light): December 11, 1862.*

*Mustered out: June 23 to July 24, 1865.*

*Pfisterer 1264–92.*

*Register serial no 9, 1–579.*

Survivors of the 19th N.Y. volunteers and 3d N.Y. light artillery. Auburn, Wm. J. Moses, printer, 1892. 27 p. 15½cm.      DLC      17

Title and imprint from cover.

Hall, Henry, 1845–

Cayuga in the field, a record of the 19th N.Y. volunteers, all the batteries of the 3d New York artillery and 75th New York volunteers, comprising an account of their organization, camp life, marches, battles, losses, toils and triumphs in the War for the Union, with complete rolls of their members, by Henry Hall and James Hall. Auburn [Syracuse, Truair, Smith & co., printers] 1873. 316, [9]–269 p. 21cm.                                      DLC NN    *18*

Each section of the volume has separate title page. Their titles are: A record of the 19th N. Y. volunteers and 3d New York artillery . . . by Henry Hall; A record of the 75th N. Y. volunteers . . . by James Hall. Includes unit rosters.

Hamilton, John Cornelius Leon, 1842–
Personal reminiscences. In Historical sketches of the Roemer, Van Tassel and allied families, by John L. Roemer, 1917, p 122–7. port.
                                                *19*

#### 4TH ARTILLERY (HEAVY)

*Mustered in: November 1861 to February 1862.*
*Mustered out: September 26, 1865.*
*Pfisterer 1293–1323.*
*Roster serial no 9, 580–1215.*

Brown, Augustus Cleveland, 1839–
The diary of a line officer, by Captain Augustus C. Brown, Company H, Fourth New York Heavy Artillery. [New York, 1906] 117 p. front. (port.). 19cm.              NN    *20*

Kirk, Hyland Clare, 1846–1917.
Heavy guns and light, history of the 4th New York heavy artillery, by Hyland C. Kirk, assisted by a committee appointed by the Regiment. New York, C. T. Dillingham [1890] iv, viii, [9]–661 p. illus., maps, ports. 24½cm.
                                 DLC NHi NN    *21*
"Sketches of officers and men," unit roster [435]–655.

Lee, Henry Thomas, 1840–1912.
The last campaign of the Army of the Potomac from a "mudcrusher's" point of view, a paper prepared and read before the California commandery of the Military order of the loyal legion of the United States, March 23, 1893, by Henry T. Lee, Maj. 4th N.Y. heavy art. [San Francisco, Co-operative print. co., 1893] 10 p. 22½cm.                    DLC NN    *22*
On cover: War paper no. 10. . . .

Lockwood, James D
Life and adventures of a drummer-boy; or, seven years a soldier, by James D. Lockwood, a true story. . . . Albany, John Skinner, 1893. 191 p. front. (port.). 20½cm.      NN    *23*
Civil war 13–110.

Thompson, Joseph Parrish, 1819–1879.
Bryant Gray, the student, the Christian, the soldier, by Joseph P. Thompson. New York,

Anson D. F. Randolph, 1864. 148 p. front. (port.). 16cm.                    NHi NN    *24*

Tidball, John Coldwell, 1825–1906.
The artillery service in the War of the rebellion, 1861–65. *JMSIUS* xii (1891) 697–733, 952–79; xiii (1892) 276–305, 466–90, 677–704, 876–902, 1085–1109; xiv (1893) 307–39. maps.                                          *25*
Author mustered in as a Colonel, August 28, 1863; mustered out with the Regiment.

#### *4th Artillery (National Guard)*

*Ordered into service: June 18, 1863.*
*Mustered out: July 24, 1863.*
*Pfisterer 529–31.*

The regiment served as infantry.

#### 5TH ARTILLERY (HEAVY)

*Mustered in: April 1862.*
*Mustered out: July 19, 1865.*
*Pfisterer 1324–48.*
*Register serial no 10, 1–683.*

Circulars, reports and history, also commemorative exercises at the thirteenth annual re-union of the veteran association Fifth New York heavy artillery regiment, veteran volunteers, held on Monday, October 19th, 1891, Lyric hall, New York. . . . [New York, Gazlay Brothers, printers, 1891] 30 p. 22½cm.    NHi    *26*
"History of the Regiment . . . by Bvt. Lieut.-Col. John H. Graham," [15]–28.

Smith, Henry Bascom, 1841–
Between the lines, secret service stories told fifty years after, by Bvt. Major H. B. Smith. New York, Booz Brothers [1911] 343 p. plan, plates (illus., fold. map, ports.). 19cm.
                                                NHi NN    *27*

#### 6TH ARTILLERY (HEAVY)

*Mustered in as the 130th regiment of infantry: September 2, 1862.*
*Designated 6th regiment of heavy artillery: October 3, 1862.*
*Mustered out: August 24, 1865.*
*Pfisterer 1348–75.*
*Register serial no 10, 684–1286.*

Atkins, Thomas Astley, 1839–
Yonkers in the rebellion of 1861–1865, including a history of the monument to honor the men of Yonkers who fought to save the Union, by Thomas Astley Atkins and John Wise Oliver. [Yonkers] Yonkers Soldiers' and Sailors' Monument Association [New York, De Vinne

*6th Artillery (Heavy), continued*

press] 1892. 262, (1) p. front. (port.), illus., port. 24½cm. NN **28**

Partial contents: Company A, Seventeenth regiment, 27–32; Sixth New-York volunteer artillery, 33–45; The thirty-days men, 51–4; The home guards, 55–61; Brevet Brigadier-General John Howard Kitching, 83–104; Some personal records of the war, 105–37.

See also Title 13.

### 7TH ARTILLERY (HEAVY)

*Mustered in as 113th regiment of infantry: August 18, 1862.*

*Designated 7th regiment of artillery (heavy): December 19, 1862.*

*Mustered out: August 1, 1865.*

*Pfisterer 1375–96.*

*Register serial no 11, 1–407.*

Lockley, Frederick E
Letters of Fred Lockley, Union soldier, 1864–65. Edited by John E. Pomfret. *Huntington library quarterly* xvi (1952/53) 75–112. **29**

### 8TH ARTILLERY (HEAVY)

*Mustered in as the 129th regiment of infantry: August 22, 1862.*

*Designated 8th regiment of artillery (heavy): December 19, 1862.*

*Mustered out: June 5, 1865.*

*Pfisterer 1396–1419.*

*Register serial no 11, 408–828.*

Proceedings of the second annual meeting of the Association of the surviving officers of Col. Peter A. Porter's reg't, (Eighth N.Y.H.Art'y,) at Batavia, N.Y., August 22, 1866. Rochester, Stump & Southworth, printers, 1866. 24 p. 23½cm. NN **30**

"Annals of our Regiment, a poem read . . . by Capt. R. Baldwin," [8]–24.

Armstrong, Nelson
Nuggets of experience, narratives of the sixties and other days, with graphic descriptions of thrilling personal adventures, by Dr. Nelson Armstrong, V.S., late of the Eighth New York heavy artillery. . . . [Los Angeles] Times-Mirror, 1906. 257 p. front. (port.), illus., ports. 21cm. NN **31**

Civil war [29]–102.

Century Association, New York.
Proceedings of the Century association in honor of the memory of Brig.-Gen. James S. Wadsworth and Colonel Peter A. Porter, with eulogies read by William J. Hoppin and Fred-

eric S. Cozzens, December 3, 1864. New York, D. Van Nostrand, 1865. 88 p. 23cm.
NN **32**

"Mr. Cozzen's eulogy on Colonel Porter," [37]–88.

Cozzens, Frederic Swartwout, 1818–1869.
Colonel Peter A. Porter, a memorial delivered before the Century, in December, 1864, by Frederic S. Cozzens. . . . New York, D. Van Nostrand, 1865. 54 p. 21½cm. NN **33**

On cover: Eulogy on Colonel Porter. "The Century." This portion of Title 32 was printed from the same plates.

Hudnut, James Monroe, 1844–
Casualties by battles and by names of the Eighth New York heavy artillery, August 22, 1862 — June 5, 1865, together with a review of the service of the Regiment fifty years after muster-in, by James M. Hudnut, late Quartermaster Sergeant of Company D. New York, 1913. 56 p. 2 plates (ports.). 22½cm.
DLC NN **34**

―――― Historical roll of Company D, 8th regiment, New-York heavy artillery, originally 129th N.Y. infantry. Edited by James M. Hudnut. Revised edition. New York, De Vinne press, 1887. 17, (2) p. 23cm.
DLC NHi **35**

Title and imprint from cover. Text continued on p 3 of cover.

―――― Losses of the Eighth New-York heavy artillery, 2d brigade, 2d division, 2d corps, compiled by William F. Fox . . . printed as a supplement to "Historical roll of Co. D, 8th New-York heavy artillery. . . . [1887] [3] p. 23cm. DLC **36**

Caption title.

### 9TH ARTILLERY (HEAVY)

*Mustered in as 138th regiment of infantry: September 8–9, 1862.*

*Designated 9th regiment of artillery (heavy): December 19, 1862.*

*Mustered out: July 6, 1865.*

*Pfisterer 1419–41.*

*Register serial no 12, 1–426.*

Roe, Alfred Seelye, 1844–1917.
From Monocacy to Danville, a trip with the Confederates, by Alfred S. Roe, late Private, Company A, Ninth New York heavy artillery. 1889. 41 p. *PNRISSHS* 4th ser, no 1. **37**

―――― In a Rebel prison; or, experiences in Danville. 1891. 42 p. *PNRISSHS* 4th ser, no 16. **38**

―――― Monocacy, a sketch of the battle of Monocacy, Md., July 9th, 1864, by Alfred S. Roe, read before the Regimental reunion Oct. 19,

1894, in Weedsport, N. Y. . . . . Worcester [F. S. Blanchard & co.] 1894. 32 p. 24cm.   NHi **39**

—— The Ninth New York heavy artillery, a history of its organization, services in the defenses of Washington, marches, camps, battles, and muster-out, with accounts of life in a Rebel prison, personal experiences, names and addresses of surviving members, personal sketches, and a complete roster of the Regiment, by Alfred Seelye Roe. Worcester, Mass., Published by the author [F. S. Blanchard & co.] 1899. 615 p. illus., maps, plates (illus., ports.). 24½cm.   DLC NN **40**
Unit roster 453–598. Coulter 395.

—— Recollections of Monocacy. 1885. 32 p. *PNRISSHS* 3d ser, no 10. **41**

—— Richmond, Annapolis, and home. 1892. 41 p. *PNRISSHS* 4th ser, no 17. **42**

—— The youth in the rebelliion, address given before Geo. H. Ward post 10, G.A.R. in Mechanics hall, Worcester, Mass., June 3, 1883, by Alfred S. Roe. Worcester, Press of Charles Hamilton, 1883. 27 p. 24½cm.   NHi **43**

Snyder, Charles M
A teen-age G.I. in the Civil war. *NYH* xxxv (1954) 14–31. **44**

### 10TH ARTILLERY (HEAVY)

*Organized by consolidation of existing units, the 4th, 5th, and 7th battalions of artillery: December 31, 1862.*

*Mustered out: June 23, 1865.*

*Pfisterer 1142–60.*

*Register serial no 12, 427–812.*

Webb, Edward P
History of the 10th regiment N.Y. heavy artillery, from Madison barracks to Appomattox, with reminiscences, &c., by E. P. Webb, late Cap't 10th artillery. Watertown, Post Book and job print., 1887. 80 p. 22cm. DLC N **45**
Unit roster 20–61.

### 11TH ARTILLERY (HEAVY)

*Organization not completed.*

*Pfisterer 1460–2.*

### 12TH ARTILLERY (HEAVY)

*Organization not completed.*

*Pfisterer 1462.*

### 13TH ARTILLERY (HEAVY)

*Mustered in by companies: August 4, 1863 to June 11, 1864.*

*Men whose service would expire before*

*October 1, 1865, mustered out: June 28, 1865. Remaining men transferred to the 6th regiment of artillery.*

*Pfisterer 1463–76.*

*Register serial no 13, 1–334.*

Dawson, Henry Barton, 1821–1889.
The colors of the United States first raised over the Capitol of the Confederate states, April 3, 1865. Morrisania, 1866. 17 p. 25cm.
NHi **46**
"Introductory" signed: H.B.D. "Twenty-six copies printed for private circulation only."

Ryder, Richard H
The village color-bearer, together with a story of a U.S. life-saving service keeper, by Capt. Richard H. Ryder. Brooklyn, George S. Patton, 1891. 200 p. front. (port.), 2 illus. 20½cm.   DLC **47**
"Names of those who enlisted from Canarsie," 81–5. Mustered in 87th infantry, October 15, 1861; transferred to 40th infantry, September 6, 1862; mustered out, June 5, 1863; mustered in 13th artillery, July 16, 1863; transferred to 6th artillery, July 18, 1865; mustered out, August 24, 1865.

Wallace, William Miller
The battle of Shiloh. *JMSIUS* xxvi (1900) 14–25. **48**

### 14TH ARTILLERY (HEAVY)

*Mustered in by companies: August 29, 1863, to January 17, 1864.*

*Mustered out: August 26, 1865.*

*Pfisterer 1476–98.*

*Register serial no 13, 335–831.*

Houghton, Charles
In the Crater. *BandL* iv 561–2.

Kilmer, George Langdon
Boys in the Union army. *Century magazine* lxx (1905) 269–75. **50**

—— Gordon's attack on Fort Stedman. *BandL* iv 579–83. **51**

Shaw, Charles A
A history of the 14th regiment N.Y. heavy artillery in the Civil war from 1863 to 1865, compiled by Charles A. Shaw, of Co. I, principally from official record. Published by the Regimental veteran association. Mt. Kisco, North Westchester pub. co., 1918. 59 p. 22½cm.   CtY **51A**

### 15TH ARTILLERY (HEAVY)

*Received by transfer the 3rd battalion of artillery. Other companies mustered in: June 19, 1863, to January 30, 1864.*

*Mustered out: August 22, 1865.*

*Pfisterer 1498–1522.*

*Register serial no 14, 1–421.*

*15th Artillery (Heavy), continued*

Riddle, Albert Gallatin, 1816–1902.

Arguments for defence in the case of the United States vs. Colonel Louis Schirmer, 15th New York heavy artillery, tried before General court-martial . . . at the City of Washington, commencing March 20, and terminating May 31. A. G. Riddle and S. Wolf, counsel for defendant. Washington, D. C., 1865. 71 p. 22½cm.         DLC  **52**

## 16TH ARTILLERY (HEAVY)

*Mustered in by companies: September 1863 to February 2, 1864.*

*Mustered out: August 21, 1865.*

*Pfisterer 1523–41.*

*Register serial no 14, 422–926.*

Re-union of the Sixteenth regiment New York heavy artillery [Dolgeville, September 13–14, 1893] [4] p. 16½cm.     DNW  **53**

Pearce, Charles E

The expedition against Fort Fisher, by Major Charles E. Pearce. *MOLLUS-Mo* I 354–81. fold. map.     **54**

## *Battalions*

## 1ST BATTALION (HEAVY)

*Mustered in by companies: August 12 to September 20, 1861.*

*Disbanded, March 5, 1863. Men transferred to other units.*

*Pfisterer 1548–52.*

### *National Guard (Light)*

*Volunteered, August 2, 1864, to serve 100 days.*

*Mustered out: November 22, 1864.*

*Pfisterer 528–9.*

## 2ND BATTALION (LIGHT)

*Mustered in: December 9, 1861.*

*Disbanded, October, 1862. Companies were designated the 14th and 15th batteries of light artillery.*

*Pfisterer 1553–4.*

## 3RD BATTALION (HEAVY)

*Mustered in: October 14 to December 19, 1861.*

*Consolidated with the 15th regiment of artillery: September 30, 1863.*

*Pfisterer 1554–7.*

## 4TH BATTALION (HEAVY)

*Received its numerical designation: September 16, 1862.*

*Disbanded, December 31, 1862. Men transferred to the 10th regiment of artillery.*

*Pfisterer 1557.*

## 5TH BATTALION (HEAVY)

*Received its numerical designation, September 16, 1862.*

*Disbanded, December 31, 1862. Men transferred to the 10th regiment of artillery.*

*Pfisterer 1557–8.*

## 6TH BATTALION (HEAVY)

*Receieved its numerical designation, September 16, 1862.*

*Disbanded, December 31, 1862. Men transferred to the 5th regiment of artillery.*

*Pfisterer 1558.*

## 7TH BATTALION (HEAVY)

*Received its numerical designation, September 16, 1862.*

*Disbanded, December 31, 1862. Men transferred to the 10th regiment of artillery.*

*Pfisterer 1558.*

## ANTHON'S BATTALION, LATER WILLARD'S

*Organization not completed.*

*Pfisterer 1559.*

## ROCKET BATTALION

*Mustered in: December 6–7, 1861.*

*Disbanded: February 11, 1863. The companies were designated the 23rd and 24th batteries.*

*Pfisterer 1558–9.*

## *Independent Batteries of Light Artillery*

### *1st Battery*

*Mustered in: November 23, 1861.*

*Mustered out: June 23, 1865.*

*Pfisterer 1559–62.*

*Register serial no 15, 161–208.*

The re-union of Cowan's battery on the battlefield of Gettysburg, July 3rd, 1886. The twenty-third anniversary of the battle, with a sketch of the Battery, from 1861 to 1865. 49 p. 24½cm.                NHi    **55**

### 2nd Battery

*Mustered in: August 16, 1861.*
*Mustered out: June 13, 1863.*
*Pfisterer 1562–5.*
*Register serial no 5, 209–48.*

### 3rd Battery

*Battery originally Company D of the 2nd militia, later 82nd regiment of infantry. It served detached from its regiment and was known as Battery B, until December 7, 1861, when it received it numerical designation.*
*Mustered out: June 24, 1865.*
*Pfisterer 1565–8.*
*Register serial no 15, 249–305.*

### 4th Battery

*Mustered in: October 24, 1861.*
*Disbanded, December 4, 1863. Men transferred to other units.*
*Pfisterer 1569–71.*
*Register serial no 15, 306–30.*

Smith, James E
A famous battery and its campaigns, 1861–'64. The career of Corporal James Tanner in war and in peace. Early days in the Black hills, with some account of Capt. Jack Crawford, the poet scout. By Captain James E. Smith, 4th N.Y. independent battery. Washington, D.C., W. H. Lowdermilk & co., 1892. vii, 237 p. plates (plans, ports.). 19cm.    DLC NN    **56**

### 5th Battery

*Mustered in: November 8, 1861.*
*Mustered out: July 6, 1865.*
*Pfisterer 1571–4.*
*Register serial no 15, 331–83.*

### 6th Battery

*Mustered in June 15, 1861, as Company K of the 9th militia, later 83rd regiment of infantry. Company K served with its regiment until August 25, 1861, when de-*tached. Designated 6th battery: December 7, 1861.
*Mustered out: July 8, 1865.*
*Pfisterer 1574–6.*
*Register serial no 15, 384–424.*

### 7th Battery

*Mustered in, October 30, 1861, as an artillery company of the 56th regiment of infantry. Designated 7th battery, June 7, 1862.*
*Mustered out: July 22, 1865.*
*Pfisterer 1577–9.*
*Register serial no 15, 425–71.*

### 8th Battery

*Mustered in, October 30, 1861, as a part of the 56th regiment of infantry.*
*Designated 8th battery: December 7, 1861.*
*Mustered out: June 30, 1865.*
*Pfisterer 1579–82.*
*Register serial no 15, 472–512.*

### 9th Battery

*Mustered in, June 6, 1861, as Company F, 41st regiment of infantry. Company F detached from the regiment and became an independent battery, November 7, 1861. Designated 9th battery, December 7, 1861.*
*Mustered out: June 13, 1864.*
*Pfisterer 1582–3.*
*Register serial no 15, 513–28.*

### 10th Battery

*Mustered in: April 9, 1862.*
*Transferred to the 6th battery: June 21, 1864.*
*Pfisterer 1583–4.*
*Register serial no 15, 529–56.*

### 11th Battery

*Left State: January 17, 1862.*
*Mustered out: June 13, 1865.*
*Pfisterer 1585–7.*
*Register serial no 15, 557–95.*

Hollis correspondence. *Indiana magazine of history* xxxvi (1940) 275–94.    **57**

Wilkeson, Frank, 1845–
Recollections of a private soldier in the Army of the Potomac, by Frank Wilkeson. New

## 11th Battery, continued

York, G. P. Putnam's Sons, 1887, ix, 246 p.
16½cm.                      DLC NN    **58**
Mustered in 11th New York battery, March 29,
1864; discharged, June 2, 1864, to accept commission
in 4th U. S. artillery.

## 12th Battery

Mustered in: January 14, 1862.
Mustered out: June 14, 1865.
Pfisterer 1588–90.
Register serial no 15,632–66.

Dauchy, George K
The battle of Ream's station (read May 8,
1890). MOLLUS-Ill III 125–40.          **59**

## 13th Battery

Mustered in: October 15, 1861.
Mustered out: July 28, 1865.
Pfisterer 1590–4.
Register serial no 15, 632–66.

Dwight, Timothy, 1828–1916.
A discourse on the life and character of
Captain William Wheeler, delivered in the
Third Congregational church, New Haven,
July 17th, 1864, by Rev. Timothy Dwight. New
Haven, Press of Tuttle, Morehouse & Taylor,
1864. 23 p. 23cm.          CSmH NN    **59A**

Wheeler, William, 1836–1864.
. . . Letters of William Wheeler of the Class
of 1855, Y.C. Printed for private distribution.
[Cambridge, Printed by H. O. Houghton and
co.] 1875. v, 468 p. front. (mounted port.).
22½cm.                  CtY DLC NHi    **59B**
The author served also in the 7th New York
National Guard regiment.
At head of title: In memoriam. "Letters of army
life and service, 1861–1864." [279]–468.
Coulter 471.

## 14th Battery

Organized about December 21, 1861, by
the consolidation of Companies B and D,
2nd battalion of artillery. It was then
known as Company A of that battalion
until October 1862, when it was designated the 4th battery.
Disbanded: September 7, 1863.
Pfisterer 1594–5.
Register serial no 15, 667–91.

## 15th Battery

Organized about December 21, 1861, by
the consolidation of Companies A and C,
2d battalion of artillery. It was then known
as Battery B of that battalion until October 1862, when it was designated the
15th battery.
Transferred to the 32nd battery: February
4, 1865.
Pfisterer 1596–8.
Register serial no 15, 692–726.

## 16th Battery

Mustered in: March 27, 1862.
Mustered out: July 6, 1865.
Pfisterer 1598–1600.
Register serial no 15, 727–68.

## 17th Battery

Mustered in: August 26, 1862.
Mustered out: June 12, 1865.
Pfisterer 1601–02.
Register serial no 15, 769–96.

Eliot, Charles D
Port Hudson. Historic leaves (published by
the Somerville historical society) VII (1908)
49–61.                                **60**

## 18th Battery

Mustered in: September 13, 1862.
Mustered out: July 20, 1865.
Pfisterer 1602–03.
Register serial no 15, 797–843.

## 19th Battery

Mustered in: October 27, 1862.
Mustered out: June 13, 1865.
Pfisterer 1604–06.
Register serial no 15, 844–73.

## 20th Battery

Mustered in: September to December
1862.
Mustered out: July 31, 1865.
Pfisterer 1606–08.
Register serial no 15, 874–941.

## 21st Battery

Mustered in: December 12, 1862.
Mustered out: September 8, 1865.
Pfisterer 1608–09.
Register serial no 15, 942–73.

## 22nd Battery

Mustered in: October 28, 1862.
Assigned to the 9th regiment of artillery
as Company M: February 5, 1863.
Pfisterer 1609–10.
Register serial no 15, 974–92.

### 23rd Battery

*Originally Battery A, Rocket battalion of artillery, became the 23rd battery, November 1, 1862. The order making the change was, however, not approved until February 11, 1863.*

*Mustered out: July 14, 1865.*

*Pfisterer 1610–12.*

*Register serial no 15, 993–1043.*

### 24th Battery

*Originally Battery B, Rocket battalion of artillery, became the 24th battery, November 1, 1862. The order making the change was, however, not approved until February 11, 1863.*

*Transferred to 3rd regiment of artillery, March 8, 1865.*

*Pfisterer 1612–14.*

*Register serial no 15, 1044–74.*

Merrill, Julian Whedon
Records of the 24th independent battery, N.Y. light artillery, U.S.V., compiled by J. W. Merrill. Published for the Ladies' cemetery association of Perry, N.Y. [New York, J. O. Seymour, Kennard & Hay, printers] 1870. 280, 22 p. 2 plates (illus.). 22½cm.
DLC NHi NN **61**
Unit roster [8]–10. "Appendix. Document 1 [–13]" 22 p are concerned with Andersonville prison.

### 25th Battery

*Mustered in: December 12, 1862.*

*Mustered out: August 1, 1865.*

*Pfisterer 1615–16.*

*Register serial no 15, 1075–1107.*

### 26th Battery

*Mustered in: February 25, 1863.*

*Mustered out: September 12, 1865.*

*Pfisterer 1616–18.*

*Register serial no 15, 1108–43.*

### 27th Battery

*Mustered in: December 17, 1862.*

*Mustered out: June 22, 1865.*

*Pfisterer 1618–19.*

*Register serial no 15, 1144–79.*

### 28th Battery

*Mustered in: December 27, 1862.*

*Mustered out: July 31, 1865.*

*Pfisterer 1620–1.*

*Register serial no 15, 1180–1224.*

### 29th Battery

*Battery A, 1st battalion artillery designated 29th battery: March 16, 1863.*

*Mustered out: August 15, 1864.*

*Pfisterer 1621–2.*

*Register serial no 15, 1225–51.*

### 30th Battery

*Battery B, 1st battalion artillery designated 30th battery: March 16, 1863.*

*Mustered out: June 23, 1865.*

*Pfisterer 1622–4.*

*Register serial no 15, 1252–90.*

### 31st Battery

*Battery C, 1st battalion artillery designated 31st battery: March 16, 1863.*

*Mustered out: October 25, 1864.*

*Pfisterer 1624–6.*

*Register serial no 15, 1291–1314.*

### 32nd Battery

*Battery D, 1st battalion artillery designated 32nd battery: March 16, 1863.*

*Mustered out: July 12, 1865.*

*Pfisterer 1626–8.*

*Register serial no 15, 1315–58.*

### 33rd Battery

*Mustered in: September 4, 1862.*

*Mustered out: June 25, 1865.*

*Pfisterer 1628–30.*

*Register serial no 15, 1359–93.*

### 34th Battery

*Battery L, 2nd regiment of artillery designated 34th independent battery: November 19, 1863.*

*Mustered out: June 21, 1865.*

*Pfisterer 1630–3.*

*Register serial no 15, 1394–1431.*

Kennedy, Daniel F
Famous men of Flushing, Major Jacob Roemer, Commander, Flushing battery of artillery during the Civil war, by Major Daniel F. Kennedy. [Flushing, 1943?] [4] p. 22cm.
NN **62**
Eighth in a series of biographies issued by the Flushing historical society.

See also Title 16.

### 35th and 36th Batteries

*Organization not completed.*

*Varian's Battery (Light)*

Left State: April 19, 1861.
Mustered out: August 2, 1861.
Pfisterer 527–8.

See Title 56.

# CAVALRY

## Regiments

### 1ST DRAGOONS

Mustered in as 130th regiment of infantry:
September 2, 1862.
Converted to cavalry: July 28, 1863.
Designated 19th regiment of cavalry: August 11, 1863.
Designated 1st regiment of dragoons: September 10, 1863.
Mustered out: June 30, 1865.
Pfisterer 1147–62.
Register serial no 6, 1–192.

Regimental history of the First New York dragoons, with list of names, post-office addresses, casualties of officers and men, and number of prisoners, trophies, &c. captured, from organization to muster-out. Washington, D. C., Gibson Brothers, printers, 1865. 59 p. 18cm.
Unit roster [23]–59.        DLC N      **63**

Abbott, Allen O
Prison life in the South, at Richmond, Macon, Savannah, Charleston, Columbia, Charlotte, Raleigh, Goldsborough, and Andersonville, during the years 1864 and 1865, by A. O. Abbott, late Lieutenant First New York dragoons. New York, Harper & Brothers, 1865. x, [13]–374 p. illus. 19½cm.   DLC NN   **64**
"The name, rank, regiment, date, place of capture, and post-office address of the 1500 officers who were confined at Columbia, South Carolina, 1864 and 1865," [317]–74.
Coulter 1.

Bowen, James Riley, 1834–
Regimental history of the First New York dragoons (originally the 130th N.Y. vol. infantry), during three years of active service in the great Civil war, by Rev. J. R. Bowen. Published by the author. [Lyons, Mich.] 1900. x, [7]–464 p. plates (ports.). 20½cm.
Unit roster 324–460.        DLC NN      **65**

Lewis, Charles Edward
War sketches, by Capt. Charles E. Lewis, No. 1. With the First dragoons in Virginia. . . . [London, Simmons & Botten, printers, 1897] 87 p. 18½cm.        NN      **66**

# New York Cavalry Regiments

### 1ST CAVALRY

Mustered in: July 16 to August 31, 1861.
Mustered out: June 27, 1865.
Pfisterer 727–50.
Register serial no 1, 1–313.

Adams, Francis Colburn
The story of a trooper, with much of interest concerning the campaign on the Peninsula, not before written, by F. Colburn Adams. . . . Washington, D. C. McGill & Witherow, printers, 1864. 127 p. 19cm.        DLC      **67**
"Book first." On cover: New York, Dick & Fitzgerald, publishers.

—— —— New York, Dick & Fitzgerald, 1865. 616 p. plates (illus.). 19½cm.
Coulter 2.        DLC NHi      **68**

—— A troopers adventures in the War for the Union, a thrilling history of the campaigns, battles, exploits, marches, victories and defeats of the Army of the Potomac, being a complete and graphic narrative of the Peninsular campaign under McClellan, by a cavalryman. New York, Hurst & co. [n. d.] xv, (1), 616 p. front. (illus.). 19cm.        DLC NN      **69**
On cover: Arlington edition. Printed from the plates of Title 74 with "Index to contents." xv, (1) p., added.

Beach, William Harrison, 1835–
The First New York (Lincoln) cavalry, from April 19, 1861, to July 7, 1865, by William H. Beach. New York, The Lincoln Cavalry Association [Milwaukee, Burdick & Allen] 1902. vii, 579 p. plates (illus., ports.). 23½cm.
Unit roster 545–79.        DLC NN      **70**

—— Some reminiscences of the First New York (Lincoln) cavalry, by Lieut. W. H. Beach. *MOLLUS-Wis* i 276–302.      **71**

—— A visit to the battlefields of Virginia. *MOLLUS-Wis* iii 317–34.      **72**

Stevenson, James Hunter, 1833–
"Boots and saddles," a history of the First volunteer cavalry of the war, known as the First New York (Lincoln) cavalry, and also as the Sabre regiment. Its organization, campaigns, and battles, by Jas. H. Stevenson. Harrisburg, Penn., Patriot pub. co., 1879. xviii, 388 p. front. (port.), plates (illus.). 20cm.
Unit roster 363–88.        NN      **73**

—— The First cavalry, by Captain James H. Stevenson. *Annals of the war* (1879) 634–41.      **74**

### 1ST VETERAN CAVALRY

Left the State in detachments: July to November 19, 1863.
Mustered out: July 20, 1865.
Pfisterer 1162–73.
Register serial no 7, 1–250.

. . . Annual reunion proceedings of the Survivors' association 27th regiment N.Y. vols. and 1st N.Y. veteran cavalry, held at Rochester, N.Y., on Wednesday, July 21, 1886, and at Geneva, N. Y., Sept. 18,, 1886. Binghamton, Carl & Matthews, printers [1886] 59 p. 22cm.
At head of title: 1861, 1865.                   IHi  75

Annual reunion proceedings of the Survivors' association 27th regiment N.Y. vols., 1st N.Y. veteran cavalry, and 33d regiment N.Y. vols., held at Mount Morris, Livingston county, N.Y., on Thursday and Friday, Oct. 20th and 21st, 1887. Binghamton, Carl & Matthews, printers [1888] 90 p. 22cm.                 WHi  76

. . . Seventh and eighth annual reunion proceedings of the Survivors' association 27th regiment N.Y. volunteers, 1st N.Y., veteran cavalry, 33d regiment N.Y. volunteers, held at Binghamton, N. Y., Wednesday and Thursday, Sept. 24th and 25th, 1890, and at Rochester, N. Y., Wednesday and Thursday, Sept. 23d and 24th, 1891. [New York, Street Railway Journal press, 1891] 125 p. 21½cm.            MBLL  77
At head of title: 1861. 1865.

Eleventh, twelfth, thirteenth and fourteenth annual re-union proceedings of the Survivors' association 27th regiment N.Y. volunteers. 1st New York veteran cavalry. 33d regiment N.Y. volunteers. Held at Portage, N.Y., August 28th and 29th, 1894; Binghamton, N.Y., August 13th and 14th, 1895; Elmira, N.Y., November 10th and 11th, 1896; Buffalo, N.Y., August 23d and 24th, 1897. [Nunda, Printed at the office of the "News," 1898] 154 p. 3 plates (ports.). 23cm.                        WHi  78

Freeman, John C
Address on the civil and military career of General William Tecumseh Sherman, by John C. Freeman, Captain 1st New York veteran cavalry. MOLLUS-NY III 296–316.        79

*1st Provisional Regiment of Cavalry*

*Formed by consolidation of the 10th and 24th regiments of cavalry: June 17, 1865.*
*Mustered out: July 19, 1865.*
*Pfisterer 1188–93.*
*Register serial no 6, 220–468.*

## 2ND CAVALRY

*Mustered in: August 9 to October 8, 1861.*
*Mustered out: June 5, 1865.*
*Pfisterer 751–79.*
*Register serial no 1, 314–717.*

Glazier, Willard Worcester, 1841–1905.
Battles for the Union, comprising descriptions of many of the most stubbornly contested battles in the War of the great rebellion, together with incidents and reminiscences of the camp, the march, and the skirmish line. Embracing a record of the privations, heroic deeds, and glorious triumphs of the soldiers of the Republic, by Willard Glazier. Hartford, Dustin, Gilman & co., 1875. xix, 21–407 p. front. (port.), plates (illus.). 18½cm.    NN  80

——— ——— Hartford, Gilman & co., 1878. xix, 21–417 p. front. (port.), plates (illus.). 19½cm.                                NN  81
Printed from the plates of Title 80. Additional pages are "Testimonials."

——— The capture, the prison pen and the escape, giving an account of prison life in the South, principally at Richmond, Danville, Macon, Savannah, Charleston, Columbia, Millin, Salisbury and Andersonville, describing the arrival of prisoners, plans of escape, with incidents and anecdotes of prison life. Embracing, also, the adventures of an escape from Columbia, S. C., recapture, trial as a spy, and final escape from Sylvania, Georgia, by Willard W. Glazier, late Lieutenant, Harris light cavalry. Albany, J. Munsell, 1866. 352 p. front. (illus.), illus. 21½cm.           NN  82

——— The capture, the prison pen, and the escape, giving a complete history of prison life in the South, principally at Richmond, Danville, Macon, Savannah, Charleston, Columbia, Belle isle, Millin, Salisbury, and Andersonville, describing the arrival of prisoners, plans of escape, with numerous and varied incidents and anecdotes of the author's escape from Columbia, S. C., recapture, subsequent escape, recapture, trial as a spy, and final escape from Sylvania, Georgia, by Willard G. Glazier. Hartford, H. E. Goodwin, 1868. xiv, [19]–400 p. front. (port.), illus. 18cm.     NN  83

——— The capture, the prison pen, and the escape, giving a complete history of prison life in the South, principally at Richmond, Danville, Macon, Savannah, Charleston, Columbia, Belle isle, Millin, Salisbury, and Andersonville, describing the arrival of prisoners, and plans of escape, together with numerous and varied incidents and anecdotes of prison life. Embracing, also, the adventures of the author's escape from Columbia, South Carolina, his recapture, subsequent escape, recapture, trial as a spy, and his final and successful escape from Sylvania, Georgia, by Captain Willard Worcester Glazier. To which is added an Appendix, containing the name, rank, regiment, and post-office address of prisoners. New York, R. H. Ferguson, & co., 1870. xiv, [19]–446, (3) p. front. (port.), illus. 18½cm.     NN  84
"Testimonials," "Agents wanted! This book is sold principally by subscription!" (3) p. Coulter 190.

2nd Cavalry, continued

—— Three years in the Federal cavalry, by Willard Glazier. New York, R. H. Ferguson & co., 1870. xvi, [19]–339 p. plates (illus., ports.). 18½cm.                                NN      85

—— —— New York, R. H. Ferguson & co., 1874. xvi, [19]–356 p. plates (illus., ports.). 20cm.                                          NN      86

The plates of Title 85 have been used through p 298. Some of the additional material is "Testimonials," [349]–56. Coulter 191.

Meyer, Henry Codington, 1844–
[Autobiographical sketch of Henry C. Meyer. New York, 1896] [2] p. 24cm.      NN      87

Title and imprint from ms. note in NN's copy and continues "privately printed and but a few copies."

—— Civil war experiences under Bayard, Gregg, Kilpatrick, Custer, Raulston, and Newberry, 1862, 1863, 1864, by Henry C. Meyer, Captain 24th New York cavalry. New York, Privately printed [Knickerbocker press] 1911. ix, 119 p. plates (ports.). 22½cm.    NN      88

Mustered in 2nd New York cavalry, July 21, 1862; discharged to accept promotion, January 1864; mustered in 24th New York cavalry, February 21, 1864.

Owens, John Algernon
Sword and pen; or, ventures and adventures of Willard Glazier (the soldier-author), in war and literature. Philadelphia, P. W. Ziegler & co., 1881. xvi, 21–516 p. front. (port.), plates (illus., map). 19½cm.        DLC      89

Coulter 358. NN has 1883 reprint.

Randol, Alanson Merwin, 1837–1887.
Last days of the rebellion. The Second New York cavalry (Harris' light) at Appomattox station and Appomattox Court House, April 8 and 9, 1865, by Alanson M. Randol. Presidio of San Francisco, Cal., 1883. 12 p. 18cm.
                                            CSmH      90

—— —— Alcatraz Island, Cal., 1886. 11 p. 17½cm.                                CSmH      91

**2ND VETERAN CAVALRY**

Left the State in detachments: October to December 1863.

Mustered out: November 8, 1865.

Pfisterer 1173–86.

Register serial no 7, 251–483.

*2nd Provisional Regiment of Cavalry*

Formed by consolidation of the 6th and 15th regiments of cavalry: June 17, 1865.

Mustered out: August 9, 1865.

Pfisterer 1193–7.

Register serial no 6, 469–708.

**3RD CAVALRY**

Mustered in: July 17 to August 21, 1861.

Consolidated with 1st regiment of mounted rifles and designated 4th provisional regiment of cavalry: September 6, 1865.

Pfisterer 779–803.

Register serial no 1, 718–1026.

Roe, Edward Payson, 1838–1888.
Taken alive and other stories, with an autobiography, by Edward P. Roe. New York, Dodd, Mead & co. [1889] 375 p. front. (port.). 18cm.                            92

Mustered in as Chaplain 2nd New York cavalry, September 1, 1862; resigned, December 14, 1862; again mustered in as Chaplain 2nd New York cavalry, July 20, 1863; discharged March 8, 1864, to accept appointment as hospital Chaplain. Civil war 2–18.

Sprole, William Thomas, 1808?–1883.
The costly sacrifice, a memorial discourse occasioned by the death of Col. Charles Townsend, of the Army of the Potomac, by Rev. W. T. Sprole, delivered in the First Presbyterian church, Newburgh, N.Y., June 18, 1865. Printed for private distribution. 1866. 36 p. 18½cm.                          CSmH NN    92A

Townsend served in the 3rd New York cavalry, June 25, 1861; 106th New York infantry, August 29, 1862, killed in action, June 1, 1864.

Stahler, Enoch, 1836–
Enoch Stahler, miller and soldier, First Lieutenant Third New York cavalry. Washington, D. C., c1909. 30 p. front. (port.), 1 illus., 2 ports. 22½cm.       DLC      93

"Or of the author, Enoch Stahler."

Tucker, James Marion.
"Kautz raiding around Petersburg," by Lieutenant James Marion Tucker. MOLLUS-Minn v 124–35.                                       94

Wall, Edward, 1825–1915.
The first assault on Petersburg. Proceedings of the New Jersey historical society ns III (1918) 193–204.                            94A

—— Raids in Southeastern Virginia fifty years ago. Proceedings of the New Jersey historical society ns III (1918) 65–82, 147–61.      94B

*3rd Provisional Regiment of Cavalry*

Formed by consolidation of the 13th and 16th regiments of cavalry: June 23, 1865.

Mustered out: September 21, 1865.

Pfisterer 1197–1202.

Register serial no 6, 709–898.

## 4TH CAVALRY

*Mustered in: August 10 to November 15, 1861.*

*Transferred to 9th regiment of cavalry, February 27, 1865.*

*Pfisterer 803–22.*

*Register serial no 1, 1027–1266.*

The story of a Regiment [Fourth New York state volunteer cavalry] *United States army and navy journal* II (1864/65) 84.          **94C**

Cesnola, Luigi Palmi di, 1832–1904.
Ten months in Libby prison, by Louis Palma di Cesnola, late Colonel 4th N.Y. cavalry. [n. p., 186–] 7 p. 22½cm.     CSmH NN   **95**
Caption title.

Duganne, Augustine Joseph Hickey, 1823–1884.
The fighting Quakers, a true story of the war for our Union, by A. J. H. Duganne, with letters from the brothers to their mother and a funeral sermon, by Rev. O. B. Frothingham. By authority of the Bureau of military record. New York, J. P. Robens, 1866. 116 p. front. (illus.). 18½cm.          NN   **96**
John Townsend Ketcham mustered in 4th New York cavalry, February 13, 1863; captured, September 13, 1863; died, October 9, 1863. Edward Halleck Ketcham mustered in 120th New York infantry, August 19, 1862; killed in action, July 2, 1863.

—— The Quaker soldiers, a true story of the War for the Union, by A. J. H. Duganne. . . . New York, 1869. 116 p. front. (illus.). 18½cm.
Printed from the plates of Title 96.    NHi   **97**

Parnell, William Russell
Recollections of 1861. US XIII (1885) 264–70.          **97A**

*4th Provisional Regiment of Cavalry*

*Formed by consolidation of the 3rd regiment of cavalry and the 1st regiment of mounted rifles, July 21, 1865.*

*Mustered out: November 29, 1865.*

*Pfisterer 1202–07.*

*Register serial no 6, 899–1077.*

## 5TH CAVALRY

*Left the State: November 18, 1861.*

*Mustered out: July 19, 1865.*

*Pfisterer 822–46.*

*Register serial no 2, 1–373.*

John Hammond, died May 28, 1889, at his home, Crown Point, N.Y., born August 17, 1827. . . . Chicago, P. F. Pettibone & co., printers, 1890. 90 p. 2 plates (ports.). 23cm.
"Letters, 1861-4," 47–90.          NHi   **98**

Beaudry, Louis Napoleon, 1833–1892.
Historic records of the Fifth New York cavalry, First Ira Harris guard, its organization, marches, raids, scouts, engagements, and general services during the rebellion of 1861–1865, with observations of the author by the way, giving sketches of the Armies of the Potomac and of the Shenandoah. Also, interesting accounts of prison life and of the secret service. Complete lists of its officers and men. By Rev. Louis N. Boudry, Chaplain of the Regiment. Albany, S. R. Gray, 1865. xv, [17]–358 p. illus., ports. 18½cm.     NN   **99**
"Selections from the files of the weekly journal [The Libby chronicle] which I published or read, to the prisoners, while confined in Libby prison," [335]–58. Unit roster [310]–33.

—— Second edition. Albany, S. R. Gray, 1865. xv, [17]–358 p. illus., ports. 18½cm.
                                NHi   **100**

—— Third edition, enlarged. Albany, J. Munsell, 1868. xv, [17]–385 p. illus., ports. 21cm.
                                DLC   **101**

—— Fourth edition, enlarged. Albany, J. Munsell, 1874. xv, [17]–385, (3) p. illus., ports. 19½cm.          NN   **102**
J. Munsell was the printer of Titles 99–100. Titles 99–102 are printed from the same plates. In Titles 101–102 the Libby prison chronicle has been extended, p 359–89, and in Title 102 "Testimonials," (3) p, has been added.

—— The Libby Chronicle, devoted to facts and fun, a true copy of the Libby chronicle as written by the prisoners of Libby in 1863. Published by Louis N. Beaudry. Albany [C. F. Williams print. co., 1889] 46 p. front. (port.), illus. 23½cm.          NHi   **103**
"Editor-in-chief, Louis N. Beaudry, Chaplain Fifth N. Y. vol. cavalry." Nos 1–7; August 21 – October 2, 1863.

Dickenson, Foster S
The Fifth New York cavalry. . . . *Maine bugle* campaign I (Rockland, 1894) 147–61, 239–49; II (1895) 11–18, 221–34.          **104**

## 6TH CAVALRY

*Mustered in: September 12 to December 19, 1861.*

*Consolidated with the 15th regiment of cavalry and designated 2nd provisional regiment of cavalry, June 17, 1865.*

*Pfisterer 846–66.*

*Register serial no 2, 374–657.*

History of the Sixth New York cavalry (Second Ira Harris guard), Second brigade, First division, Cavalry corps, Army of the Potomac, 1861–1865. Compiled from letters, diaries, recollections and official records by Committee on

*6th Cavalry, continued*

regimental history, Major Hillman A. Hall, Chairman; Regt. Qr. Mr. Sgt. W. B. Besley, Treasurer; Sgt. Gilbert G. Wood, Historian. Worcester, Mass., Blanchard press, 1908. 575 p. plates (illus., maps, ports.). 23cm.
   Unit roster [279]–326.      DLC NN   **105**

. . . Reunion veteran association 6th New York cavalry. . . . II, 1888 (NHi); VI/VII, 1892/1893 (NHi); XIV–XV, 1905–1906 (DLC); XXII, 1913 (DLC)      **106**

Veteran association of the Sixth New York cavalry, organized Sept. 8, 1887, with the names and addresses of the surviving members. New York, C. D. Wynkoop, printer, 1887. 20 p. 19cm.      NHi   **107**

Clarke, Augustus P
   A cavalry surgeon's experiences in the battle of the Wilderness. *US* ns XI (1894) 138–64.
      **108**

—— The Sixth New York cavalry, its movements and service at the battle of Gettysburg. *US* ns XVI (1896) 411–15.   **109**

Foster, Alonzo, 1841–
   Reminiscences and record of the 6th New York v.v. cavalry, by Alonzo Foster, late Sergeant Co. F. [Brooklyn, 1892] 148 p. 18cm.
      DLC NN   **110**
   Roster of officers, [139]–46. First published in the Long Island traveler.

Heermance, William Laing
   The cavalry at Chancellorsville, May, 1863. *JUSCA* IV (1891) 107–13.   **111**

—— —— *MOLLUS-NY* II 223–30.   **112**

—— The cavalry at Gettysburg. *MOLLUS-NY* III 196–206.   **113**

—— Oration of Col. W. L. Heermance, at dedication of monument, Sixth New York cavalry, at Gettysburg, Pa., July 11th, 1889. New York, G. H. Burton, printer [1889] 9 p. 21cm.
      NHi   **114**

McKinney, Edward Pascal
   Life in tent and field, 1861–1865, by E. P. McKinney. Boston, Richard G. Badger [1922] 16 p. plates (ports.). 21cm.   DLC   **116**

### 7TH CAVALRY *

*Left State: November 23, 1861.*

*Mustered out: March 31, 1862.*

*Pfisterer 866–71.*

*Register serial no 2, 658–757.*

Cronin, David Edward, 1839–
   The evolution of a life, described in the memoirs of Major Seth Eyland, late of the mounted rifles. New York, S. W. Green's Son, 1884. 336 p. 19½cm.   NN   **117**
   Civil war 140–273. NN's copy inscribed by the author: David E. Cronin "Seth Eyland." Coulter 100.
   Mustered in 7th New York cavalry, September 9, 1861; mustered out, March 31, 1862; mustered in 1st New York mounted rifles, July 11, 1862; resigned, January 28, 1863; mustered in same regiment, May 27, 1863; mustered out, November 29, 1865.

Hamilton, Edgar A
   Personal reminiscences. In Historical sketches of the Roemer, Van Tassel and allied families, by John L. Roemer (1917) 109–21. port.
      **118**

### 8TH CAVALRY

*Left the State: November 29, 1861.*

*Mustered out: June 27, 1865.*

*Pfisterer 872–96.*

*Register serial no 2, 758–1148.*

Bell, Thomas
   At Harper's ferry, Va., September 14, 1862. How the cavalry escaped out of the toils. A swift night march . . . including a brief history of the Regiment, from its organization to this thrilling night's work, by Thomas Bell, Brevet Major, Eighth New York cavalry. [Brooklyn, 1900] 16 p. 23½cm.   NN   **119**
   Title from cover.

Norton, Henry
   Deeds of daring; or, history of the Eighth N.Y. volunteer cavalry, containing a complete record of the battles, skirmishes, marches, etc., that the gallant Eighth New York cavalry participated in, from its organization in November, 1861, to the close of the rebellion in 1865. Compiled and edited by Henry Norton. Norwich, Chenango Telegraph print. house, 1889. viii, [9]–184, (1) p. front. (port.). 20cm.
      DLC NN   **120**
   "Errata" (1) p. Unit roster 151–8.

—— A sketch of the 8th cavalry, unwritten history of the rebellion, by Henry Norton, a member of Company H, 8th N.Y. cavalry. 1888. 29 p. port. on cover. 21cm.
   Title from cover.   DLC NHi NN   **121**

Pope, Edmund Mann
   Personal experience, a side light on the Wilson raid, June, 1864, by Brevet-Brigadier-General Edmund M. Pope. *MOLLUS-NY* IV 585–604.   **122**

---

* First mounted rifles was also designated at times, and especially by the War department, as the 7th N. Y. cavalry.

## 9TH CAVALRY

*Left the State: November 26, 1861.*

*Mustered out: July 17, 1865.*

*Pfisterer 896–920.*

*Register serial no 3, 1–365.*

Bentley, Wilber Gorton, 1835–
Address delivered at the dedication of monument of the Ninth New York cavalry regiment, by Col. W. G. Bentley, July 2d, 1883. 15 p. illus. cover. 23cm.                   NHi   **123**

—— Under the searchlight, address delivered March 5, 1914, before the Commandery of the State of Illinois Military order of the loyal legion of the United States, by Wilber Gorton Bentley. [Chicago, Libby co., printers, 1914] 23, (1) p. 23½cm.           DLC WHi   **124**

—— "A vindictive peace and reconstruction, a peace of vengeance," a letter of protest, read as a paper, January 6, 1921, before the Commandery of the State of Illinois, Military order of the loyal legion of the United States. 8 p. 21½cm.                   DLC WHi   **125**
Title from cover.

Bradley, Samuel Henry, 1843–1909.
Samuel Henry Bradley recollections of army life. Genealogical data. [Olean, 1912] 27 p. front. (port.). 21½cm.          DLC   **126**
Contents: Samuel Henry Bradley, by Kate E. Bradley, 3–5; Recollections of army life as narrated by S. H. Bradley, 1889, 7–26; Ancestral genealogical data, 27.

Cheney, Newel
History of the Ninth regiment, New York volunteer cavalry, War of 1861 to 1865. Compiled from letters, diaries, recollections and official records, by Newel Cheney, Poland Center, N.Y. Jamestown, Martin Merz & Son, 1901. 416 p. 2 front. (illus., port.), illus. 23cm.
Unit roster 293–416.       DLC NN   **127**

—— —— Supplement. [417]–23, (1).   **127A**
"Those who have procured copies of the History can paste this supplement in their books."

## 10TH CAVALRY

*Left the State: December 24, 1861.*

*Consolidated with the 24th regiment of cavalry and designated 1st provisional regiment of cavalry, July 10, 1865.*

*Pfisterer 920–43.*

*Register serial no 3, 366–664.*

. . . Anniversary and reunion of the Tenth New York cavalry association. . . . xxv–xxxii, 1886–1893 (N); xxxiii–xxxiv, 1894–1895 (DLC); xxxv–xxxvi, 1896–1897 (MnHi);

xLvi, 1907 (DLC); L, 1911 (DLC); LII, 1913 (DLC)                   **128**
1888 has title: Dedication of the battle monument and annual re-union. 1907 numbered 56.

Kempster, Walter
The army of 1898 and the army of 1861, a comparison, by Walter Kempster, First Lieutenant Company D, 10th New York cavalry. *MOLLUS-Wis* III 353–71.          **129**

—— The cavalry at Cedar creek, remarks on Anson's paper, written by the unanimous request of the Commandery. *MOLLUS-Wis* IV 369–75.                   **130**

—— The cavalry at Gettysburg. *MOLLUS-Wis* IV 397–432. fold. map.          **131**

—— The early days of our cavalry, in the Army of the Potomac. *MOLLUS-Wis* III 60–89.                   **131A**

—— Major General Gouverneur K. Warren, an appreciation. *MOLLUS-Wis* IV 329–53. **132**

—— The volunteer soldier in relation to the progress of civilization. *MOLLUS-Wis* I 72–84.                   **133**

Porter, Burton B          1832–
One of the people, his own story, by Burton B. Porter. [Colton, Cal.] Published by the author [1907] v, (1), 382 p. front. (port.). 19cm.                   DLC NN   **134**
Civil war 109–235.

Preston, Noble Delance
History of the Tenth regiment of cavalry, New York state volunteers, August, 1861, to August, 1865, by N. D. Preston, with an introduction by Gen. McM. Gregg. Published by the Tenth New York cavalry association. New York, D. Appleton and co., 1892. xix, 710 p. illus., plates (4 maps, 3 fold.; ports.). 24½cm.
Unit roster [269]–506.       DLC NN   **135**

Tremain, Lyman, 1819–1878.
Memorial of Frederick Lyman Tremain, late Lieut. Col. of the 10th N.Y. cavalry, who was mortally wounded at the battle of Hatcher's run, Va., February 6th, and died at City Point hospital, February 8th, 1865, by his father. Albany, Van Benthuysen's print. house, 1865. 86 p. front. (port.). 23½cm.   NHi NN   **136**

Vinter, Thomas H
Memoirs of Thomas H. Vinter. Philadelphia, Walter H. Jenkins, 1926. 97 p. front. (port.), plate (port.). 24cm.          NN   **137**
A narrative and diary of the author's service. "Introduction" signed: Emma Vinter Jenkins.

Wiles, Clifton W
A skirmish at Little Auburn, Va. *First Maine bugle* campaign II (Rockland 1892) call 10, 71–4.                   **138**

## 11TH CAVALRY

*Left the State: May 5, 1862.*
*Mustered out: September 30, 1865.*
*Pfisterer 943–59.*
*Register serial no 3, 665–1009.*

Calvert, Henry Murray
Reminiscences of a boy in Blue, 1862–1865, by Henry Murray Calvert. New York, G. P. Putnam's Sons, 1920. vii, 347 p. 20½cm.
Coulter 68.  NN  *139*

Gammel, Charles, 1845–1906.
Carl the cavalry boy, his recollections of the rebellion. Utica, 1907. Utica [Clinton, H. Platt Osborne, printer] 1907. 184 p. front. (port.), plate (port.). 23cm.  CtY NUt  *140*
"This edition 'in memoriam' of Charles Gammel . . . is limited to fifty copies," colophon signed in ms.: Geo. W. Gammel. On spine: Gammel.

Smith, Thomas West
The story of a cavalry regiment, "Scott's 900," Eleventh New York cavalry, from the St. Lawrence river to the Gulf of Mexico, 1861–1865, by Thomas West Smith, Private of Troop F. Published by the Veteran association of the Regiment. [Chicago, W. B. Conkey co., 1897] viii, 344, (33) p. illus., ports, plates (illus., ports.). 26cm.  DLC NN  *141*
Unit roster (33) p.

Woodbridge, George
11th New York volunteer cavalry regiment (Scott's 900), 1862–1865. *Military collector & historian* ix (Washington 1960) 114. col. plate (illus.).  *142*

## 12TH CAVALRY

*Left the State by detachments: May to December 1863.*
*Mustered out: July 19, 1865.*
*Pfisterer 959–73.*
*Register serial no 3, 1010–1324.*

Budington, William Ives, 1815–1879.
A memorial of Giles F. Ward, Jr., late First Lieut. Twelfth N.Y. cavalry, by William Ives Budington. New York, Anson D. F. Randolph, 1866. 99 p. front. (port.). 18½cm.
NHi NN  *143*

Cooper, Alonzo
In and out of Rebel prisons, by Lieut. A. Cooper, 12th N.Y. cavalry. Oswego, R. J. Oliphant, printer, 1888. vii, [10]–335 p. front. (port.), illus., port. 23½cm.  MiDB NN  *144*
"List of officers confined in Macon, Ga.," [295]–330. Coulter 90.

Savage, James Woodruff, 1826–
The loyal element of North Carolina during the war, a paper read before the Nebraska commandery of the Military order of the loyal legion of the United States, May 5, 1886, by James W. Savage, late Colonel 12th N.Y. cavalry. Omaha [Omaha Republican print] 1886. 8 p. 23cm.  NHi  *145*
Also published as *MOLLUS-Neb* i 1–5.

## 13TH CAVALRY

*Formed by consolidation of the Davies light cavalry, the Horatio Seymour cavalry and the Tompkins cavalry, June 20, 1863.*

*Consolidated with the 16th regiment of cavalry and designated 3rd provisional regiment of cavalry: August 17, 1865.*

*Pfisterer 973–86.*

*Register serial no 4, 1–268.*

Hernbaker, Henry
True history. Jefferson Davis answered. The horrors of Andersonville prison pen. The personal experience of Henry Hernbaker, Jr. and John Lynch. Philadelphia, Merihew & Son, printers, 1876. 14 p. 22cm.  DLC  *146*
Contents: Statement of Henry Hernbaker, Jr., late of the 107th regiment, Penn'a vols., [3]–6; Statement of John Lynch, late Company F, 13th New York cavalry, [7]–14.

Hoadley, John Chipman, 1818–1886.
Memorial of Henry Gansevoort, Captain Fifth artillery, and Lieutenant-Colonel by brevet, U.S.A.; Colonel Thirteenth New York state volunteer cavalry, and Brigadier-General of volunteers by brevet. Edited by J. C. Hoadley. Printed for private distribution. Boston, Franklin press: Rand, Avery & co., 1875. 335 p. plates (facs., illus., 2 maps, ports.). 26cm.
DLC NHi NN  *147*

—— —— [Second edition] Boston, Franklin press: Rand, Avery & co., 1875. 335 p. 21½cm.  NN  *148*
"Preface to second edition" signed: Catharine Gansevoort Lansing. Though NN's copy has "List of illustrations," there are none.

## 14TH CAVALRY

*Left the State by detachments: February, April, and October, 1863.*
*Transferred to the 18th regiment of cavalry, June 12, 1865.*
*Pfisterer 987–98.*
*Register serial no 4, 269–506.*

## 15TH CAVALRY

*Left the State in detachments: September 1863 to January 1864.*

*Consolidated with 6th regiment of cavalry and designated 2nd provisional regiment of cavalry, June 17, 1865.*

*Pfisterer 998–1010.*

*Register serial no 4, 507–760.*

Hampton, Charles G
Twelve months in Rebel prisons, by Charles G. Hampton, Captain 15th N.Y. cavalry (read March 3, 1898). *MOLLUS-Mich* II 229–48.
**149**

Norton, Chauncey S
"The red neck ties;" or, history of the Fifteenth New York volunteer cavalry, containing a record of the battles, skirmishes, marches, etc., that the Regiment participated in from its organization in August, 1863, to the time of its discharge in August, 1865. Compiled and edited by Chauncey S. Norton. Ithaca, Journal book and job print. house, 1891. vii, [9]– 152 p. front. (port.), 2 illus., port. 20½cm.
Muster in roll 146–52.    DLC NN   **150**

## 16TH CAVALRY

*Left the State in detachments: June 19 to October 23, 1863.*

*Consolidated with the 13th regiment of cavalry and designated 3rd provisional regiment of cavalry: August 17, 1865.*

*Pfisterer 1010–24.*

*Register serial no 4, 761–1049.*

## 17TH CAVALRY

*Organization not completed.*
*Pfisterer 1024–5.*

## 18TH CAVALRY

*Left the State in detachments: September 26, 1863 to January 1864.*

*Mustered out: May 31, 1866.*

*Pfisterer 1025–39.*

*Register serial no 4, 1050–1369.*

## 19TH CAVALRY

*130th regiment of infantry was designated 19th regiment of cavalry: August 11, 1863.*

*19th regiment of cavalry designated 1st regiment of dragoons: September 10, 1863.*

*Pfisterer 1039.*

## 20TH CAVALRY

*Left the State: September 30, 1863.*

*Mustered out: July 31, 1865.*

*Pfisterer 1039–53.*

*Register serial no 5, 1–233.*

## 21ST CAVALRY

*Left the State in detachments: September 4, 1863 to February 1864.*

*Mustered out by companies: June 23 – August 31, 1865.*

*Pfisterer 1053–65.*

*Register serial no 5, 234–470.*

FitzSimmons, Charles
The Hunter raid, by General Charles Fitz-Simmons (read November 4, 1885). *MOLLUS-Ill* IV 392–403.   **151**

—— Sigel's fight at New Market (read January 4, 1882). *MOLLUS-Ill* III 61–7.   **152**

## 22ND CAVALRY

*Left the State: March 8, 1864.*

*Mustered out: August 1, 1865.*

*Pfisterer 1065–78.*

*Register serial no 5, 470–720.*

The 22nd cavalry: The statement that those who enlist in the new 22d cavalry regiment will not receive all the bounties . . . is entirely untrue. . . . Oneida, Union print [1864] broadside, 21 × 30½cm.    NN   **153**
D. F. Taft, recruiting officer.

Crumb, DeWitt, 1845–1908.
. . . Historical address, delivered by DeWitt Crumb, late Corporal Co. G., at the annual re-union held at Syracuse, N.Y., on the 2d day of August, 1887. South Otselic, N.Y., W. M. Reynolds, 1887. 22 p. 17½cm.   NN   **153A**
At head of title: 22d regiment, N. Y. vol. cav. "My recollections of the acts of our gallant old Regiment from June 29th 1864, to Aug. 9th 1865."

Lloyd, Harlan Page
The battle of Waynesboro, by Harlan Page Lloyd, late Captain Twenty-second New York cavalry. *MOLLUS-Ohio* IV 194–213.   **154**

## 23RD CAVALRY

*Left the State: May 1863.*

*Mustered out: July 22, 1865.*

*Pfisterer 1079–80.*

*Register serial no 5, 721–53.*

*Only two companies were organized.*

## 24TH CAVALRY

*Left the State: February 23, 1864.*
*Consolidated with the 10th regiment of*
*cavalry and designated 1st provisional*
*regiment of cavalry, July 10, 1865.*
*Pfisterer 1080–96.*
*Register serial no 5, 754–1006.*

Kelley, Daniel George, 1845–1868.
What I saw and suffered in Rebel prisons,
by Daniel G. Kelley, late Sergeant Company K,
Twenty-fourth New York cavalry. With an in-
troduction by Major Anson G. Chester. Buffalo,
Print. house of Matthews & Warren, 1866.
86 p. 18cm.                         DLC OU     **155**
—— —— Buffalo, Thomas, Howard & John-
son, 1868. 86 p. front. (port.). 18cm.
Coulter 269.                              NN     **156**

Newberry, Walter C
The Petersburg mine (read November 13,
1880). *MOLLUS-Ill* III 111–24.        **156A**

See also Titles 87–88.

## 25TH CAVALRY

*Left the State in detachments: 1864.*
*Mustered out: June 27, 1865.*
*Pfisterer 1096–1105.*
*Register serial no 5, 1007–1199.*

## 26TH CAVALRY

*Mustered in: February 1865.*
*Mustered out by companies: June 29 to*
*July 7, 1865.*
*Pfisterer 1106–09.*
*Register serial no 5, 1200–69.*

Organized in the States of Massachusetts, New York and Vermont for service
on the Northern frontier. The New York
companies were G, H, I, K and L. For
information and rosters of the other companies of the 26th cavalry see: Massachusetts. 1st battalion of cavalry; Vermont. Frontier Cavalry.

## *Companies*

### CAPTAIN DEVIN'S COMPANY

*Left the State: July 3, 1861.*
*Mustered in: July 14, 1861.*
*Mustered out: October 23, 1861.*
*Pfisterer 526–7.*

Recruited from the 1st cavalry National
Guard.

## ONEIDA CAVALRY

*Mustered in: September 4, 1861.*
*Mustered out: June 13, 1865.*
*Pfisterer 1187–8.*
*Register serial no 6, 193–219.*

# ENGINEERS

## 1ST ENGINEERS

*Mustered in by companies: October 11,*
*1861 to February 19, 1862.*
*Mustered out: June 30, 1865.*
*Pfisterer 1634–49.*
*Register serial no 16, 1–361.*

Harry Chapman's last battle. Victory, July 10,
1890. Newark, N.J., Geo. H. Wilson, printer,
1890. 32 p. 15cm.                      WHi     **157**
A pension claim.

Roster of the First regiment N.Y. veteran vol.
engineers, mustered into the U.S. service, Oct.
10th, 1861, mustered out of the U.S. service,
June 30th, 1865. New York, George F. Nesbit
& co., printers, 1865. 16 p. 17½cm.
                                    N NHi     **158**

Dalrymaple, Henry M
Capture of Fort Pulaski. In War talks of
Morristown veterans, Morristown, N.J., 1887,
35–8.                                           **159**

[Butler, Benjamin Franklin] 1818–1893.
Official documents relating to a "Chaplain's
campaign (not) with General Butler," but in
New York. Audi alteram partem. Lowell,
Mass., Charles Hunt, printer, 1865. 48 p.
22½cm.                               DLC     **160**
Embodies a report to General Butler by his former
Assistant Provost-marshal, John L. Davenport, on the
facts in the case of Chaplain Henry N. Hudson.

Hudson, Henry Norman, 1814–1886.
A Chaplain's campaign with Gen. Butler.
Printed for the author. New York, 1865. 66 p.
22cm.                               NHi NN     **161**
Text signed: N. H. Hudson.

—— General Butler's campaign on the Hudson. Second edition. With an appendix. Boston,
Printed by J. S. Cushing & co., 1883. 62 p.
18½cm.                            DLC NN     **162**

## 2ND ENGINEERS

*Organization not completed.*
*Pfisterer 1650.*

## 15TH ENGINEERS

*Mustered in as the 15th regiment of infantry: June 17, 1861.*

*Designated 15th regiment of engineers: October 25, 1861.*

*Mustered out by companies: June 13 to July 2, 1865.*

*Pfisterer 1650–69.*

*Register serial no 16, 362–799.*

Roster of 50th and 15th regiments, New York state volunteer engineers, Army of the Potomac. Compliments of the Secretary, Sam B. Williams. Rochester, Union and Advertiser press, 1894. 39 p. 14½cm.     DNW     **163**

Reminisco, Don Pedro Quarendo, pseud.
Life in the Union army; or, notings and reminiscences of a two years' volunteer. A rhythmical history of the Fifteenth N.Y. volunteer engineers, Colonel John McLeod Murphy, during its recent two years' campaign in and about Washington, and in the State of Virginia, by Don Pedro Quaerendo Reminisco, a private in the ranks. [New York] H. Dexter, Hamilton & co. [1863] 147 p. 21½cm.
     c1863 by Sinclair Tousey.     DLC NN     **164**

## 50TH ENGINEERS

*Mustered in by companies as the 50th regiment of infantry: August 26 to September 20, 1861.*

*Designated 50th regiment of engineers: October 22, 1861.*

*Mustered out: June 13–14, 1865.*

*Pfisterer 1669–88.*

*Register serial no 16, 800–1211.*

Brainerd, Wesley
The pontoniers at Fredericksburg. *BandL* III 121–2.     **165**

See also Title 163.

## INFANTRY

## *Irish Brigade* *

*63rd, 69th, and 88th New York infantry regiments.*
*28th Massachusetts infantry regiment.*
*116th Pennsylvania infantry regiment.*

Cavanagh, Michael
Memoirs of Gen. Thomas Francis Meagher, comprising the leading events of his career . . . by Michael Cavanagh. Worcester, Mass.,

Messenger press, 1892. iv, [5]–496, 38 p. 1 illus., plates (2 illus., port.). 23½cm.
     Civil war 367–494.     NN     **166**

Conyngham, David Power, 1840–1883.
The Irish brigade and its campaigns, with some account of the Corcoran legion, and sketches of the principal officers, by Capt. D. P. Conyngham. . . . New York, William McSorley & co., 1867. 599 p. 20½cm.
     DLC NHi NN     **167**

—— —— Boston, Patrick Donahoe, 1869. 599 p. 20cm.     DLC     **168**

Meagher, Thomas Francis, 1823–1867.
Full report of the great mass meeting and splendid speech at the armory of the National guard, by Thomas Francis Meagher, in support of the war and the Irish brigade, July 25th, 1862. [New York, 1862] 10 p. 21cm.
     DLC NN     **169**
"(From the corrected report of the Irish American.)"

## *Regiments*

## 1ST INFANTRY

*Mustered in: April 22, 1861.*

*Mustered out: May 25, 1863.*

*Pfisterer 1694–1707.*

*Register serial no 17, 1–158.*

## 2ND INFANTRY

*Mustered in: May 14, 1861.*

*Mustered out: May 26, 1863.*

*Pfisterer 1707–19.*

*Register serial no 17, 159–313.*

Carr, Joseph Bradford, 1828–1895.
Operations of 1861 about Fort Monroe. *BandL* II 144–52.     **170**

*2nd Infantry (National Guard)*
*see 82nd Infantry*

## 3RD INFANTRY

*Mustered in: May 14, 1861.*

*Mustered out: August 28, 1865.*

*Pfisterer 1719–38.*

*Register serial no 17, 314–636.*

Spears, Catherine S     B
The living story of a Union soldier as related by himself and family, by C. S. B. S. Passaic, N. J., J. F. Morris & co., printers, 1888. 18 p. 14½cm.     NHi     **171**
On cover: Story of a Union soldier. William A. Tompkins, 3rd New York infantry.

* For other references on the Irish brigade, see entries under the regiments that formed the Brigade.

## 4TH INFANTRY

*Mustered in: May 2, 1861.*
*Mustered out: May 25, 1863.*
*Pfisterer 1738–51.*
*Register serial no 17, 637–776.*

Cory, Eugene A
A Private's recollections of Fredericksburg, by Eugene A. Cory, late Company E, Fourth New York. . . . 1884. 28 p. *PNRISSHS* 3rd ser. no 4. **172**

## 5TH INFANTRY

*Mustered in: May 9, 1861.*
*Mustered out: May 14, 1863.*
*Pfisterer 1751–68.*
*Register serial no 17, 777–1008.*

## 5TH VETERAN INFANTRY

*Mustered in: October 27, 1863.*
*Mustered out: August 21, 1865.*
*Pfisterer 1769–79.*
*Register serial no 17, 1009–1244.*
*Though two regiments are described, they are in effect one organization.*

Dedication services at the unveiling of the bronze statue of Maj.-Gen. G. K. Warren at Little Round Top, Gettysburg, Pa., August 8, 1888. [Brooklyn, Brooklyn Daily Eagle print., 1888] 93, (1) p. front. (illus.). 21½cm.
NHi **173**
Monument erected by the committee of the Fifth New York volunteers veteran association.

Dedicatory ceremonies held on the battlefield of Manassas or Second Bull run, Virginia, October 20th, 1906, and May 30th (Memorial day), 1907, under the auspices of the Veteran association of the Fifth regiment of New York volunteer infantry "Duryee zouaves." [Brooklyn, Eagle press, 1907] 96 p. 2 plates (illus.). 21½cm. DLC NHi **174**

Davenport, Alfred
Camp and field life of the Fifth New York volunteer infantry (Duryee zouaves), by Alfred Davenport. New York, Dick and Fitzgerald, 1879. 485 p. front. (port.), plate (illus.). 19cm. DLC NN **175**
Coulter 113. Roster of officers 475–84.

Pell, John Howland, 1830–1882.
Letters of John Howland Pell. *Pelliana* I (1934) 29–51. illus. **176**

Southwick, Thomas Paine, 1837–1892.
A Duryee zouave, by Thomas P. Southwick of the Fifth New York volunteers. Journal and reminiscences of camp life and the personal experiences on the march and in the field, of an ordinary, common soldier of the Civil war. [Washington, D. C., Acme print. co., 1930] 119 p. front. (mounted port.), 2 illus. (1 mounted). 23½cm. DLC IHi **177**
"Foreword" signed: E. M. S. [Elizabeth M. Southwick]

Tilney, Robert
My life in the army, three years and a half with the Fifth army corps, Army of the Potomac, 1862–1865, by Robert Tilney, Company D, Twelfth N.Y. volunteers, and Sergeant Company F, Fifth N.Y. veteran volunteer infantry. . . . Philadelphia, Ferris & Leach, 1912. 247 p. front. (port.). 21½cm. DLC NN **178**
Coulter 447.

Williams, George Forrester, 1837–
Bullet and shell, a soldier's romance, by Geo. F. Williams of the 5th and 146th regiments New-York volunteers. Illustrated from sketches among the actual scenes, by Edwin Forbes. New York, Fords, Howard, & Hulbert [c1882] 454 p. illus. 20½cm. NHi **179**
Coulter 478.

—— Bullet and shell, war as the soldier saw it. Camp, march, and picket; battlefield and bivouac; prison and hospital, by Geo. F. Williams. Illustrated from sketches among the actual scenes, by Edwin Forbes. New York, Fords, Howard & Hulbert, 1883. 454 p. illus. 21½cm.
NN has 1884 reprint. NN **180**

—— Lights and shadows of army life. *Century magazine* xxvIII (1884) 803–19. illus.
**180A**

### 5th Infantry (National Guard)

*Mustered in: May 1, 1861.*
*Mustered out: August 7, 1861.*
*Pfisterer 531–8.*

Meyer, Anton
Geschichte des 5. Regiments der National-Garde des Staates New York (Jefferson Guard) von seiner Entstehung bis zur Auflösung, 1834–1882. . . . [New York, Henry Rottger, printer, 1883] 92, (8) p. front. (port.). 17cm.
NHi **181**
"Vorwort" signed: Anton Meyer. "Das Jahrzehnt von 1861–1871," [30]–71. "Veteranen-Lied des 5. Regiments, von Anton Meyer," (8) p.

## 6TH INFANTRY

*Mustered in: May 25, 1861.*
*Mustered out: June 25, 1863.*
*Pfisterer 1779–1788.*
*Register serial no 18, 1–116.*

Recollections of a checkered life, by a Good Templar. Napanee, Ontario, S. T. Hammond [Toronto, Printed by Robertson & Cook, 1868] 116 p. 15½cm. NN **182**

"I was . . . a member of the 6th New York, or 'Billy Wilson's zouaves.'"

Morris, Gouverneur
The history of a volunteer regiment, being a succinct account of the organization, services and adventures of the Sixth regiment, New York volunteers, infantry, known as Wilson zouaves. Where they went, what they did, and what they saw in the War of the rebellion, 1861 to 1865. Prepared from official data by Gouverneur Morris. Illustrated by James E. Taylor. New York, Veteran Volunteer pub. co., 1891. 160 p. illus., 2 maps, ports. 23½cm.

"Muster-out roll," 147–52. DLC NN **183**

### 6th Infantry (National Guard)

Left the State: April 21, 1861.
Mustered out: July 31, 1861.
Pfisterer 539–46.

### 7TH INFANTRY

Mustered in: April 23, 1861.
Mustered out: May 8, 1863.
Pfisterer 1788–1805.
Register serial no 18, 117–287.

Hartshorn, Edmund F
Experiences of a boy, by his father's son. Newark, N. J., Baker print. co., 1910. 131 p. 21cm. DLC NN **184**

Civil war 24–56. Copyright by E. F. Hartshorn.

### 7TH VETERAN INFANTRY

Mustered in by companies: March 29 to October 31, 1864.
Mustered out: August 5, 1865.
Pfisterer 1805–15.
Register serial no 18, 288–438.

### 7th Infantry (National Guard)

Left the State: April 19, 1861; mustered in: April 26, 1861.
Mustered out: June 3, 1861.
Left the State May 25, 1862; mustered in: May 29, 1862.
Mustered out: September 5, 1862.
Mustered in: June 16, 1863.
Mustered out: July 20, 1863.
Pfisterer 546–56.

General Butler and the Seventh New York militia, extract of a letter from "a Seventh regiment man" to a former member, residing "out West," in answer to an inquiry about the aspersions Butler had cast at the Regiment. *Historical magazine* s2 iii (Morrisania 1868) 66–70. **185**

Muster roll of the Seventh regiment, N.Y.S.M. In Chronicles of the rebellion of 1861, by Charles J. Ross (1861) 5–10. **186**

Reception by the Seventh regiment, National guard, S.N.Y. of its members who served in the regular and volunteer army and navy of the United States during the great rebellion, Academy of music, January 31st, 1866. [New York, Francis & Loutrel, printers, 1866] 64 p. 7 × 11½cm. DLC **187**

Half-title: Roll of honor.

Carroll, John F
A brief history of New York's famous Seventh regiment and the events surrounding its march to the defense of the National capital. Chronology and bibliography, prepared by Lt. Colonel John F. Carroll. [New York, 1960] [17] p. illus. 28cm. DLC NN **188**

Title from cover. Text continued on p 3 of cover. "Bibliography relating to New York's Seventh regiment" [3] p. at head of text: Civil war centennial committee: The veterans of the Seventh regiment.

Clark, Emmons, 1827–1905.
History of the Second company of the Seventh regiment (National guard) N.Y.S. militia, by Captain Emmons Clark. vol. I. New York, James G. Gregory, 1864. 422 p. 24cm. DLC NHi NN **189**

No further volumes published. 1861–1863, p 284–400. RP has v 1, no 1 96 p. in paper cover.

Clark, Francis Edward, 1851–1927.
Life of William Eugene Harward, by Rev. Frank E. Clark. Portland, Me., Hoyt, Fogg & Donham, 1879. front. (port.). 19cm. NN **189A**

"His war experience," 36–76. Harward served with the 7th in 1861, 1862, and 1863.

Dalton, John Call, 1825–1889.
Dalton letters, 1861–1865. *Massachusetts historical society proceedings* LVI (1922/23) 354–495. **190**

The author's brief service in the 7th regiment is reported by several letters. His later service was as a Surgeon in the volunteers.

—— John Call Dalton, MD., U.S.V. Privately printed. [Cambridge, Riverside press] 1892. 105 p. front. (mounted port.). 20cm. DLC NN **191**

"In Washington with the Seventh," 5–34. "A volume of his war reminiscences was privately printed in 1892, by his brother, Charles H. Dalton." See footnote on p 355 of Title 190.

*7th Infantry (National Guard), continued*

Dix, John Adams, 1798–1879.

Address of Maj.-Gen. John A. Dix, at the reception by the Seventh regiment, National guard, S.N.Y., of its members who have served in the army and navy of the United States during the great rebellion, Academy of music, January 31, 1866. New York, Francis & Loutrel, printers, 1866. 17 p. 23½cm.

DLC NN      **192**

Lamb, Martha Joanna Reade (Nash), 1829–1893.

March of the New York Seventh regiment, the great uprising in New York city, 1861. *Magazine of American history* xiv (New York 1885) 58–68. illus., ports.      **193**

Peet, Frederick Tomlinson

Civil war letters and documents of Frederick Tomlinson Peet. With the Seventh New York regiment, Private in Co. H, April 18th – June 3rd, 1861. . . . Newport, R.I., 1917. 284, (1) p. 29cm.      NNC      **194**

"Prefatory note" signed: R. T. "Fifty copies — privately printed." Coulter 368.

—— Personal experiences in the Civil war, by Frederick Tomlinson Peet. With the Seventh New York regiment, Private in Co. H, April 18th – June 3rd, 1861. . . . New York, 1905. v, 107 p. 3 plates (illus., 2 ports.). 29cm.

NHi NN      **194A**

"Prefatory note" signed: R. T. "Fifty copies printed."

Shaw, Robert Gould, 1837–1863.

Letters RGS [monogram] Cambridge, University press, 1864. 328 p. 23cm.

MB NN      **195**

The author was a member of the Seventh in April and May 1861.

—— Letters from camp written by Robert Gould Shaw. *Magazine of history* xviii (New York 1914) 104–10, 226–31; xix (1914) 25–31.      **196**

Swinton, William, 1833–1892.

History of the Seventh regiment, National guard, State of New York, during the War of the rebellion, with a preliminary chapter on the origin and early history of the Regiment, a summary of its history since the war, and a roll of honor, comprising brief sketches of the services rendered by members of the Regiment in the Army and Navy of the United States, by William Swinton. Illustrated by Thomas Nast. New York, Fields, Osgood, & co., 1870. iv, 501 p. illus., plates (illus., 2 ports). 22½cm.      DLC NHi NN      **197**

Muster-in-roll, 251–62; Muster-roll for 1863, 339–48.

Viele, Egbert Ludovickus, 1825–1902.

The Seventh regiment at the Capitol, 1861, "the daylight contingent." *Magazine of American history* xiv (Morrisania 1885) 69–77. facs., illus.      **198**

Weston, Sullivan Hardy, 1816–1887.

The march of the Seventh reg't, a sermon on the providence of God, delivered in St. John's chapel in the City of New York, on Sunday, June 9th, 1861, by S. H. Weston. [New York] Association of the Veterans of the National Guard [Francis & Loutrell] 1861. 24 p. 22½cm.      NN      **199**

—— Sermons by the Rev. Mr. Weston, Chaplain of the 7th regiment, National guard, and the Rev. Byron Sunderland, pastor of the First Presbyterian church, Washington, preached in the hall of Representatives, Sunday, April 28th, 1861. Published by request of the Regiment. Washington, D. C., Henry Polinhorn, printer, 1861. 23 p. 23cm.      DLC      **200**

Winthrop, Theodore, 1828–1861.

Life in the open air, and other papers, by Theodore Winthrop. . . . Boston, Ticknor and Fields, 1863. iv, 374 p. front. (port.), plate (illus.). 19cm.      NN      **201**

Partial contents: New York Seventh regiment, our march to Washington, [217]–52; Washington as a camp, [253]–90; Fortress Monroe, [291]–301. 1873 (MWiW) and 1876 (MWiW) are reprintings.

—— New York Seventh regiment, our march to Washington. *Atlantic monthly* vii (1861) 744–56.      **202**

—— Washington as a camp. *Atlantic monthly* viii (1861) 105–18.      **203**

See also Title 59B.

## 8TH INFANTRY

*Mustered in: April 23, 1861.*

*Mustered out: April 23, 1863.*

*Pfisterer 1815–31.*

*Register serial no 18, 438–614.*

Struve, Gustav, 1805–1870.

Das 8. Regiment N.Y. Freiwilliger und Prinz Felix Salm-Salm, von Gustav Struve, ehemaligen Hauptmann in dem genannten Regimente. Washington, D. C., John F. Niedfeldt [1862] 7, (1) p. 21½cm.      DLC NN      **204**

Title and imprint from cover. "Inhaltsverzeichniss," (1) p.

### 8th Infantry (National Guard)

*Left the State: April 23, 1861; mustered in April 25, 1861.*

*Mustered out: August 2, 1861.*

*Left the State: May 29, 1862.*

*Mustered out: September 10, 1862.*
*Left the State: June 17, 1863.*
*Mustered out: July 23, 1863.*
*Pfisterer 556–67.*

Kinkaid, Thomas H          C
When we were boys in Blue, 1861–1865.
[New York, 1903] 40 p. 21cm.    IHi    **205**

"These narratives of the service in 1861, of the 8th regt., N. Y. militia; the 22d N.G.N.Y. in 1863; the 102d regt. N.G.N.Y. in 1864; and of the 192d regt. N.Y. vols. in 1865." "Explanation" signed: Thos. H. C. Kinkaid. Title from cover.

Todd, Frederick Porter
8th regiment, New York state militia (Washington Grays), circa 1850–1870. *Military collector & historian* v (Washington 1953) 101. col. plate (illus.).    **206**

**9TH INFANTRY**

*Mustered in: May 4, 1861.*
*Mustered out: May 20, 1863.*
*Pfisterer 1831–43.*
*Register serial no 18, 615–780.*

Testimonial to Col. Rush C. Hawkins, Ninth regiment, N.Y.V., "Hawkins' zouaves." New York, Latimer Brothers & Seymour, 1863. 9 p. 23½cm.    DLC NN    **207**
Presentation of a sword.

Graham, Matthew John
The Ninth regiment, New York volunteers (Hawkins' zouaves), being a history of the Regiment and Veteran association, from 1860 to 1900, by Lieut. Matthew J. Graham. New York [E. P. Corby & co., printers] 1900. xi, 634 p. front. (illus.). 23cm.    DLC NN    **208**
Muster-out roll [563]–[632]

Hawkins, Rush Christopher, 1831–1920.
An account of the assassination of loyal citizens of North Carolina for having served in the Union army, which took place at Kingston in the months of February and March 1864, by Rush C. Hawkins. New York, 1897. 46, (1) p. 22cm.    NHi NN    **209**

—— Hawkins of the Hawkins zouaves, with an introduction by Margaret B. Stillwell. In Bookmen's holiday, notes and studies written and gathered in tribute to Harry Miller Lydenberg. New York, The New York Public Library, 1943. p 86–111.    **210**

—— Why Burnside did not renew the attack at Fredericksburg. *BandL* III 126–7.    **211**

Johnson, Charles F          1843–
The long roll, being a journal of the Civil war, as set down during the years, 1861–1863, by Charles F. Johnson, sometime of Hawkins zouaves. Duluth edition. East Aurora, Roycrofters, 1911. 241, (1) p. plates (illus., map, ports.). 20½cm.    NN    **212**
Coulter 259.

Langbein, John Christopher Julius, 1845–
The colors of the 9th regiment, N.Y. volunteers, Hawkins' zouaves, a retrospect of thirty-eight years, delivered by J. C. Julius Langbein, before E. A. Kimball post, no. 100, G.A.R., department of New York, Saturday evening, June 3, 1889. 16 p. 23cm.
    WHi    **213**

Severin, John Powers and Frederick Porter Todd.
9th New York volunteer infantry regiment (Hawkins' zouaves), 1861–1863. *Military collector & historian* VIII (Washington 1956) 76–7. col. plate (illus.).    **214**

—— —— [Additional comment, by Frederick P. Todd] *Military collector & historian* IX (Washington 1957) 21.    **214A**

Thompson, David L
In the ranks to the Antietam. *BandL* II 556–8.    **215**

—— With Burnside at Antietam. *BandL* II 660–2.    **216**

Whitney, John H          E
The Hawkins zouaves (Ninth N.Y.V.), their battles and marches, by J. H. E. Whitney. . . . New York, Published by the author, 1866. x, [13]–216 p. 19cm.    DLC NN    **217**
Coulter 474.

*9th Infantry (National Guard)*
*see 83rd Infantry*

**10TH INFANTRY**

*Mustered in: April 27 – May 2, 1861.*
*Mustered out: June 30, 1865.*
*Pfisterer 1843–61.*
*Register serial no 18, 781–1072.*

Twenty-fifth anniversary of the muster into the service of the United States of the Tenth regiment of New York volunteer infantry (National zouaves), Crescent club rooms, Tuesday evening, April 27, 1886. New York, Charles H. Ludwig, printer, 1886. 28 p. 28cm.
    WHi    **218**

*10th Infantry, continued*

**Cowtan, Charles W**
Services of the Tenth New York volunteers (National zouaves) in the War of the rebellion, by Charles W. Cowtan, late Adjutant of the Regiment. . . . New York, Charles H. Ludwig, 1882. 459, (1) p. front. (illus.), plates (5 maps, 3 fold.). 19cm.    DLC NN    **219**
"Errata" (1) p. Includes unit roster.

***10th Infantry (National Guard)***
**see 177th Infantry**

**11TH INFANTRY**

*Mustered in: May 7, 1861.*
*Mustered out: June 2, 1862.*
*Pfisterer 1861–72.*
*Register serial no 18, 1072–1222.*

Life of James W. Jackson, the Alexandria hero, the slayer of Ellsworth, the first martyr in the cause of Southern independence, containing a full account of the circumstances of his heroic death, and the many remarkable incidents in his eventful life, constituting a true history more like romance than reality. Published for the benefit of his family. Richmond, West & Johnston, 1862. 48 p. 21½cm.
Crandall 2590.    NHi NN    **220**

**Ellsworth Monument Association.**
Exercises connected with the unveiling of the Ellsworth monument, Mechanicville, May 27, 1874. Albany, Joel Munsell, 1875. 85 p. front. (port.). 23½cm.    NHi NN    **221**

**Hay, John, 1838–1905.**
Ellsworth. *Atlantic monthly* VIII (1861) 119–25.    **222**

**Ingraham, Charles Anson, 1852–**
Elmer E. Ellsworth and the Zouaves of '61, by Charles A. Ingraham. . . . Chicago, Published for Chicago Historical Society by University of Chicago press [1925] xii, 167 p. plates (facs., illus., ports.). 23½cm.
    NHi NN    **223**

**Randall, Ruth Painter**
Colonel Elmer Ellsworth, a biography of Lincoln's friend and first hero of the Civil war, by Ruth Painter Randall. Boston, Little, Brown and co. [1960] xviii, 295 p. plates (facs., illus., ports.). 21cm.    NN    **224**
Civil war 229–63.

**Robinson, Luther Emerson, 1867–**
Ephraim Elmer Ellsworth, first martyr of the Civil war. *Publications of the Illinois state historical library* no 30 (1923) 11–32. plate (port.).    **225**

***11th Infantry (National Guard)***

*Left the State: May 28, 1862.*
*Mustered out: September 16, 1862.*
*Left the State: June 18, 1863.*
*Mustered out: July 20, 1863.*
*Pfisterer 570–5.*

**12TH INFANTRY**

*Mustered in: May 13, 1861.*
*Mustered out: May 17, 1863.*
*Pfisterer 1873–87.*
*Register serial no 19, 1–212.*

***12th Infantry (National Guard)***

*Left the State: April 21, 1861.*
*Mustered in: May 2, 1861.*
*Mustered out: August 5, 1861.*
*Left the State: June 6, 1862.*
*Mustered out: October 8, 1862.*
*Left the State: June 20, 1863.*
*Mustered out: July 20, 1863.*
*Pfisterer 575–86.*

*At the conclusion of the regiment's service in 1861, many members volunteered for further service forming the 12th militia which was later consolidated with the 12th infantry. The publications of the two regiments have not been separated.*

A brief memoir of Lieut. Colonel Chas. B. Randall, who fell in battle before Atlanta, Ga., fighting for the maintenance of our Union. . . . New York, 1870. 66, 11 p. 20cm.    NHi    **226**
Mustered in 12th New York infantry, May 13, 1861; mustered out, May 17, 1863; mustered in 149th New York infantry, June 8, 1863; killed in action, July 20, 1864.

. . . Independence guard. Dedication of the new armory, 12th reg't infantry, N.G.S.N.Y., Thursday, April 21st, 1887, the twenty-sixth anniversary of the departure of the Regiment for the seat of war. Official programme. [New York, Pusey & co., 1887] 54 p. 25cm.
    NHi    **227**
Advertising matter included. "Its war record," 10–14. At head of title: 1847 1861 1887.

Report annual reunion and dinner of the Old guard association, Twelfth regiment, N.G.S.-N.Y., Saturday, April 21st, 1894. . . . [New York, Ronalds press, 1894] 6, vi, [11]–223 p. facs., illus., ports., 2 plates (illus., fold. map). 23cm.    DLC NHi    **228**
"Proceedings of this year are devoted more generally to the Regiment in its connection with the war in 1861."

—— Another printing with added title page: Souvenir of the annual reunion 1894 with historical sketch of the Twelfth regiment, N.G.-S.N.Y., 1847–1861 . . . Campaign of 'sixty-one with muster rolls. Illustrated Old guard association series. Limited edition, 1895. [New York, Ronalds press, 1895]  DLC  **229**

Report of the proceedings in connection with the monument erected by Maj.-Gen. Daniel Butterfield, at Fredericksburg, Va., in honor of the Fifth corps, Army of the Potomac, and presentation of a tablet by the 12th N.Y. regiment association to the Oneida historical society, Utica, New York. [n. p., 1900] 39 p. 3 plates (illus., 2 ports.). 23cm.  NN  **230**

Butterfield, Mrs. Julia Lorrilard (Safford)
A biographical memorial of General Daniel Butterfield including many addresses and military writings. Edited by Julia Lorrilard Butterfield. New York, Grafton press, 1903. xii, 379 p. plates (facs., illus., ports.). 25cm.  NN  **231**
Partial contents: Commanding officer 12th regiment infantry (three months), 14–42; Taps and other bugle calls, 47–50; Corps badges, 116–18.

Dowley, Morris Francis
History and honorary roll of the Twelfth regiment infantry, N.G.S.N.Y., containing a full and accurate account of the various changes through which the organization has passed since the date of its formation (1847) to the present. Also biographical sketches of General Butterfield, Ward, and Barlow and Rev. Stephen H. Tyng, Jr., as well as the names and rank of several hundred members of the "Twelfth" who rose to distinction during the War for the suppression of the great rebellion, by M. Francis Dowley. New York, T. Farrell & Son, 1869. xii, 216 p. illus. t. p. 19cm.  DLC NN  **232**

McBarron, Hugh Charles and Frederick Porter Todd
12th regiment, New York state militia, 1861–1869. *Military collector & historian* IV (Washington 1952) 98. col. plate (illus.).  **233**

Scrymser, James Alexander, 1839–1918.
In President Lincoln's kitchen. *Magazine of history* XV (New York 1912) 42–3.  **234**

—— Personal reminiscences of James A. Scrymser in times of peace and war. [New York, 1915] 151, (1) p. plates (illus., double map, ports.). 23½cm.  NHi NN  **235**
Mustered in 12th New York militia, May 2, 1861 (enlisted April 19, 1861); mustered out, August 5, 1861; mustered in 43rd New York infantry, October 2, 1861; discharged, February 26, 1863.

See also Title 178.

## 13TH INFANTRY

*Mustered in: May 14, 1861.*

*Mustered out: May 14, 1863.*

*Pfisterer 1887–1901.*

*Register serial no 19, 213–382.*

Jackson, David T
. . . Petition of David T. Jackson for relief . . . New York, Howard & Stover, printers, 1869. [10] p. 22½cm.  WHi  **236**
Title and imprint from cover.

Partridge, Samuel Selden
Civil war letters of Samuel S. Partridge of the "Rochester regiment." *Rochester historical society publications* XXII (1944) 77–90.  **237**

Slater, John S
An address to the soldiers of the Army of the Potomac, and especially to the surviving members of the Fifth corps, containing a brief review of the case of Gen. Fitz John Porter, by one who served under him. Washington, D. C., Thomas McGill & co., printers, 1880. 30 p. 23cm.  CtHi NN  **238**
Title and imprint from cover, p 1. Text signed: Jno. S. Slater, 13th N.Y.V.

*13th Infantry (National Guard)*

*Left the State: April 23, 1861.*

*Mustered out: August 6, 1861.*

*Left the State: May 30, 1862.*

*Mustered out: September 12, 1862.*

*Left the State: June 20, 1863.*

*Mustered out: July 21, 1863.*

*Pfisterer 587–96.*

Bingham, Luther Goodyear, 1798–1877.
. . . The little drummer boy, Clarence D. McKenzie, the child of the Thirteenth regiment, N.Y.S.M., and the child of the mission sunday school. New York, Board of Publication of the Reformed Protestant Dutch Church, 1861. 144 p. front. (port.). 15½cm.  NHi  **239**

Kennedy, Elijah Robinson, 1846–1926.
John B. Woodward, a biographical memoir, by Elijah R. Kennedy. For private distribution. New York, Printed at the De Vinne press, 1897. 222 p. front. (port.). 23½cm.
Civil war 13–125.  DLC NHi NN  **240**

Mandeville, James de
History of the 13th regiment, N.G., S.N.Y. Compiled and published under the direction of James de Mandeville. [New York, Press of Geo. W. Rodgers, 1894] 183, (1) p. illus., ports. 25cm.  NHi NN  **241**
Advertising matter included. Partial contents: The Thirteenth in the War of the rebellion, 23–43; Clar-

*13th Infantry (National Guard), continued*

ence D. McKenzie [drummer boy] 47. On cover: History of the 13th regiment N.G.S.N.Y. with description of the grand military fair given in aid of the armory fund, October 1894, at the armory.

## 14TH INFANTRY

*Mustered in: May 17, 1861.*

*Mustered out: May 24, 1863.*

*Pfisterer 1901–12.*

*Register serial no 19, 383–534.*

Reception of the Oneida volunteers at the City of New York, June, 1861. New York, Geo. F. Nesbit & co., 1861. 10 p. 18cm.     N   **242**

Haerrer, William
With drum and gun in '61, a narrative of the adventures of William Haerrer of the Fourteenth New York state volunteers (Colonel James McQuade, commanding), in the War for the Union, from 1861 to 1863. Greenville, Pa., Beaver print. co., 1908. 119 p. front. (port.).         NNC NUt   **243**
Preface signed: D. Luther Ross.

Thomas, Howard, 1898–
. . . Boys in Blue from the Adirondack foothills. Maps by John D. Mahaffy. Prospect, Prospect Books, 1960. xiv, 297 p. maps, plates (illus., ports.). 21½cm.     NN   **244**
"Chief emphasis has been placed on New York volunteer regiments containing large numbers of foothills men; the 14th, the 26th, the 34th, the 97th, the 117th, the 121st, the 146th and the 152nd." At head of title: Howard Thomas.

*14th Infantry (National Guard)*
*see 84th Infantry*

## 15TH INFANTRY

*Mustered in: June 17, 1861.*

*Designated 15th regiment of engineers: October 25, 1861.*

*15th Infantry (National Guard)*

*Mustered in: June 6, 1864.*

*Mustered out: July 7, 1864.*

*Pfisterer 597–601.*

## 16TH INFANTRY

*Mustered in: May 15, 1861.*

*Mustered out: May 22, 1863.*

*Pfisterer 1912–22.*

*Register serial no 19, 535–680.*

Curtis, Newton Martin, 1835–1910.
From Bull run to Chancellorsville, the story of the Sixteenth New York infantry, together with personal reminiscences, by Newton Martin

Curtis. New York, G. P. Putnam's Sons, 1906. xix, 384 p. plates (4 ports.). 23½cm.
                     DLC NN   **245**
Coulter 106. Unit roster [322]–61.

Thompson, William W
Historical sketch of the Sixteenth regiment N.Y.S. volunteer infantry, April, 1861 – May, 1863. First reunion, Potsdam, N. Y., August 31st and September 1st, 1866. [Albany, Printed by Brandow, Barton & co., 1886] 58, (4) p. front, (illus.). 25cm.     MnHi NHi   **246**
"Request," [1] signed: Wm. W. Thompson. "Survivors of 16th N.Y. vols.," (4) p. Unit roster 37–58. Imprint from ms note in NHi's copy.

## 17TH INFANTRY

*Mustered in: May 28, 1861.*

*Mustered out: June 2, 1863.*

*Pfisterer 1922–35.*

*Register serial no 19, 681–818.*

## 17TH VETERAN INFANTRY

*Mustered in: October 18, 1863.*

*Mustered out: June 13, 1865.*

*Pfisterer 1935–46.*

*Register serial no 19, 819–958.*

*Though two regiments are described, they are in effect one organization.*

17th New York volunteer infantry, 3rd brigade "Westchester chausseurs" 1st div., 5th corp Army Potomac. *Historical Wyoming* xiv (Arcade, N. Y. 1960) 21–3.     **246A**

Dearing, Gilbert H
Chronological history of the 17th regiment of N.Y. infantry volunteers. Gilbert H. Dearing, historian. Sing Sing, Sunnyside print. co., 1894. 8 p. 21½cm.     DNW   **247**
"Roster of officers, [7]–8. A section of this roster is a paster.

Dudley, Harwood A
History of Company "K" of the 17th regiment, N.Y.V., compiled by Major H. A. Dudley and Captain A. M. Whaley. [Warsaw?, n. d.] [6] p. 26cm.     NHi   **248**
Title from cover.

Traver, Albert D         1815–1866.
Address at the burial services of the late George Sibbald Wilson, Adjutant of the 17th regt., N.Y.S.V., in St. Paul's church, Poughkeepsie, by Rev. A. D. Traver. [Poughkeepsie?] Osborne & Otis, printers, 1863. 8 p. 21½cm.
                     DLC NN   **249**

Westervelt, William B
Lights and shadows of army life, as seen by a private soldier, by Wm. B. Westervelt of the

27th N.Y. infantry and 17th N.Y. veteran zouaves. Marlboro, C. H. Cochrane, printer, 1886. 96 p. front. (port.). 19½cm.

                                  NHi    250

See also Title 28.

### 17th Infantry (National Guard)

*Left the State: July 3, 1863; mustered in, July 8, 1863.*

*Mustered out: August 13, 1863.*

*Pfisterer 601–03.*

## 18TH INFANTRY

*Mustered in: May 17, 1861.*

*Mustered out: May 28, 1863.*

*Pfisterer 1946–56.*

*Register serial no 19, 959–1083.*

Albany, New York. Bar.
    Memoir of William A. Jackson, a member of the Albany Bar, and Colonel of the 18th regiment, N.Y. volunteers, who died at the city of Washington, November 11, 1861. Albany, Joel Munsell, 1862. 40 p. 22cm.    NN    *251*

Jackson, William Ayrault, 1832–1861.
    The following address delivered at Albany, February 22, 1858, by the late Col. William A. Jackson, of the Eighteenth regiment of New-York volunteers, is presented as a memento of him to the officers and privates of the Regiment, by their friend Professor Jackson. [Albany?, 1863] 15 p. 22cm.    NN    *252*
    Caption-title.

—— An oration delivered at Windham Centre, Greene county, N.Y., July 4, 1859, by the late Col. William A. Jackson, of the Eighteenth regiment of New-York volunteers. Albany, C. Van Benthuysen, printer, 1863. 24 p. 22cm.
                               NN    *253*
    "Presented to the friends of Colonel Jackson, as a souvenir of him," on preliminary leaf.

### 18th Infantry (National Guard)

*Mustered in: July 3, 1863.*

*Mustered out: August 15, 1863.*

*Pfisterer 604–05.*

## 19TH INFANTRY

*Mustered in: May 22, 1861.*

*Designated 3rd regiment of light artillery: December 11, 1861.*

*Pfisterer 1956–8.*

Caulkins, Charles A
    Camp sketches of life in the old Nineteenth, by Charlie Caulkins. Auburn, 1862. 78 p. 17cm.            NHi    *254*

### 19th Infantry (National Guard)

*Left the State: June 4, 1862.*

*Mustered out: September 6, 1862.*

*Pfisterer 605–08.*

    *In January 1863, the Regiment volunteered and was accepted for a service of nine months which it rendered under the designation, 168th regiment of infantry.*

## 20TH INFANTRY

*Mustered in: May 6, 1861.*

*Mustered out: June 1, 1863.*

*Pfisterer 1958–70.*

*Register serial no 20, 1–74.*

Lehigh Valley Railroad.
    Tour of 20th (Turners) regiment of the City of New York, September 9–15, 1906. [New York, 1906] 12 p. illus. 18½cm.    NN    *255*
    Caption title: Personally conducted tour arranged for the 20th (Turners) regiment, of the City of New York, to Gettysburg, Antietam, Harper's ferry and Washington, September 9–15, 1906.

### 20th Infantry (National Guard)

*Mustered in: May 11, 1861, to date, April 23, 1861.*

*Mustered out: August 2, 1861.*

*Pfisterer 608–11.*

    *Shortly after the Regiment's return, it volunteered, organized, and was accepted for three years' service which it rendered under the designation, 80th regiment of infantry.*

## 21ST INFANTRY

*Mustered in: May 20, 1861.*

*Mustered out: May 18, 1863.*

*Pfisterer 1970–82.*

*Register serial no 20, 175–310.*

. . . Annual reunion of the Buffalo 21st veteran association, . . . addresses delivered, reports and letters. . . . vi 1884; viii 1886.   NHi    *256*

Mills, John Harrison
    Chronicles of the Twenty-first regiment, New York state volunteers, embracing a full history of the Regiment, from the enrolling of the first volunteer in Buffalo, April 15, 1861, to the final mustering out, May 18, 1863. Including a copy of muster out rolls of field and staff, and each company. Illustrated with original portraits and scenes from camp and field, by J.

*21st Infantry, continued*

Harrison Mills. Buffalo, John M. Layton, 1867.
v, [9]–294, (1) p. plates (ports.). 29½cm.
NN      **257**

Unit roster, ten folded leaves printed on rectos
following p [295] "Appendix" (1) p, is blank. Issued
by subscription and in parts, NN has the cover of
Part I. None of the examined copies had the "scenes
from camp and field."

——— ——— by J. Harrison Mills, a disabled
soldier of the Regiment. Re-published by the
21st reg't veteran association of Buffalo, by
permission of the author. Buffalo [Gies & co.]
1887. x, [11]–348, (40) p. front. (port.). 23cm.

Unit roster (40) p.           DLC NN     **258**

Nagle, Theodore M
Reminiscences of the Civil war, by Theodore
M. Nagle, formerly Sergeant Company "C,"
21st regiment, N.Y.S. vol. inf. [Erie, Penn.,
Dispatch ptg. co., 1923] 84 p. 3 plates (ports.).
21cm.                              DLC      **259**

Strong, James Clark, 1826–
Biographical sketch of James Clark Strong,
Colonel and Brigadier General by brevet. Los
Gatos, Cal., 1910. 106 p. 2 front. (ports.),
ports. 19½cm.                 DLC NN     **260**

Civil war 62–92. On cover: Biographical sketch of
General James Clark Strong written by himself. Mustered in 21st New York infantry, May 7, 1861;
mustered out, January 17, 1862; mustered in 38th
New York infantry, January 18, 1862; discharged for
disability, November 29, 1862.

### 21st Infantry (National Guard)

*Mustered in: June 27, 1863.*

*Mustered out: August 6, 1863.*

*Pfisterer 612–14.*

### 22ND INFANTRY

*Mustered in: June 6, 1861.*

*Mustered out: June 19, 1863.*

*Pfisterer 1982–93.*

*Register serial no 20, 311–430.*

Watson, Winslow Cossoul, 1803–1884.
Eulogium commemorative of Gorton T.
Thomas, Lieutenant Colonel 22d regiment,
New York volunteers, delivered at Keeseville,
N.Y., September 10, 1862, by Winslow C.
Watson. Burlington, Vt., Free Press print, 1862.
26 p. 21½cm.                       DLC      **261**

### 22nd Infantry (National Guard)

*Left the State: May 28, 1862.*

*Mustered out: September 5, 1862.*

*Left the State: June 18, 1863.*

*Mustered out: July 24, 1863.*

*Pfisterer 614–20.*

History of Company A and the 22d regiment
N.G.N.Y., 1861–1901. [New York, Printed by
Styles & Cash, 1901] 132 p. illus., ports. 23cm.
NHi     **262**

"My recollections of Company A, by Gen. Geo. W.
Wingate," p [9]–39.

Souvenir. Fiftieth anniversary of the departure
for the war of the rebellion of the Twenty-
second regiment National guard, New York,
May 28, 1912. 24 p. illus., ports. 23cm.
NHi     **263**

Todd, Frederick Porter
22d regiment, New York state militia, 1862.
*Military collector & historian* I no 1 (Washington 1949) 3–4.                           **264**

Wingate, George Wood, 1840–1928.
History of the Twenty-second regiment of
the National guard of the State of New York,
from its organization to 1895, by General
George W. Wingate. New York, Edwin W.
Dayton [1896] xxxi, 762 p. front. (port.),
illus., fold. map, ports. 24cm.     NN     **265**

Civil war 28–346.

——— The last campaign of the Twenty-second
regiment, N.G.S.N.Y., June and July, 1863.
New York, C. S. Westcott & co., printers, 1864.
47 p. 23cm.                         DLC NN     **266**

"c1864 by George W. Wingate."

See also Title 205.

### 23RD INFANTRY

*Mustered in: July 2, 1861.*

*Mustered out: May 22, 1863.*

*Pfisterer 1994–2001.*

*Register serial no 20, 431–539.*

Maxson, William P
Camp fires of the Twenty-third, sketches of
the camp life, marches, and battles of the
Twenty-third regiment, N.Y.V., during the
term of two years in the service of the United
States. Added to these are statistics of enlistments, elections, promotions, sick, discharged,
killed and wounded, and all valuable information connected with the Regiment, by Pound
Sterling. New York, Davies & Kent, printers,
1863. viii, [11]–196 p. 19cm.

Unit roster [137]–81.           DLC NN     **267**

### 23rd Infantry (National Guard)

*Mustered in: June 16, 1863.*

*Mustered out: July 22, 1863.*

*Pfisterer 621–3.*

Lockwood, John
Our campaign around Gettysburg, being a
memorial of what was endured, suffered and
accomplished by the Twenty-third regiment

(N.G.S.N.Y.) and other regiments associated with them in their Pennsylvania and Maryland campaign, during the second Rebel invasion of the Loyal states in June – July, 1863. Brooklyn, A. H. Rome & Brothers, printers, 1864. 168 p. 19½cm.    DLC NHi NN RP  **268**
Copyright by John Lockwood.

## 24TH INFANTRY

*Mustered in: July 2, 1861, to date from May 17.*

*Mustered out: May 29, 1863.*

*Pfisterer 2002–12.*

*Register serial no 20, 540–674.*

Haight, Theron Wilbur, 1840–
After the first Bull run, by Theron W. Haight, First Lieutenant 24th infantry. *MOLLUS-Wis* iii 215–25.    **269**

—— Among the pontoons at Fitzhugh crossing. *MOLLUS-Wis* i 416–23.    **270**

—— Gainesville, Groveton and Bull run. *MOLLUS-Wis* ii 357–72.    **271**

—— King's division: Fredericksburg to Manassas, an episode of Pope's Virginia campaign. *MOLLUS-Wis* ii 345–56.    **272**

Snyder, Charles M
Robert Oliver, Jr., and the Oswego county regiment. *NYH* xxxviii (1957) 276–93. plate (2 illus., port.).    **273**

## 25TH INFANTRY

*Mustered in: June 26, 1861.*

*Mustered out: July 10, 1863.*

*Pfisterer 2012–27.*

*Register serial no 20, 675–811.*

Kress, John Alexander, 1839–
Memoirs of Brigadier General John Alexander Kress. [n. p., 1925] 51 p. front. (port.). 20cm.    NN WHi  **273A**
Title from cover. Civil war 1–35. 25th New York infantry, September 10, 1861; 94th New York infantry, July 9, 1862; resigned, December 11, 1863.

### 25th Infantry (National Guard)

*Left the State: April 27, 1861.*

*Mustered out: August 4, 1861.*

*Mustered in: May 31, 1862.*

*Mustered out: September 8, 1862.*

*Pfisterer 623–9.*

## 26TH INFANTRY

*Mustered in: May 21, 1861.*

*Mustered out: May 28, 1863.*

*Pfisterer 2027–39.*

*Register serial no 21, 1–142.*

Bacon, William Johnson, 1803–1889.
Memorial of William Kirkland Bacon, late Adjutant of the Twenty-sixth regiment of New York state volunteers, by his father. Utica, Roberts, printer, 1863. 83, (1) p. front. (port.). 19cm.    NN  **274**
"Erratum" (1) p.

McClenthen, Charles S
Narrative of the Fall & Winter campaign, by a private soldier of the 2nd div., 1st army corps, containing a detailed description of the "battle of Fredericksburg," at the portion of the line where the 2nd div. were engaged, with accurate statements of the loss in killed, wounded and missing, in each regiment. Syracuse, Masters & Lee, printers, 1863. 53 p. 17½cm.    CSmH NN  **275**
"Preface" signed: Charles S. McClenthen, Co. G, 26th reg't N.Y.V.

—— A sketch of the campaign in Virginia and Maryland, from Cedar mountain to Antietam, by a soldier of the 26th N.Y.V. Syracuse, Master & Lee, printers, 1862. 45 p. 15½cm.    CSmH NHi  **276**
"Preface" and text signed: Charles S. McClenthen.

Buell, Dexter E
A brief history of Company B, 27th regiment N.Y. volunteers, its organization and the part it took in the war, by D. E. Buell. Lyons, Printed at the Office of the Republican, 1874. 22 p. 21½cm.    CtY  **276A**
See also Title 244.

## 27TH INFANTRY

*Mustered in: May 21, 1861.*

*Mustered out: May 31, 1863.*

*Pfisterer 2039–52.*

*Register serial no 21, 143–284.*

See Titles 75–78 for proceedings of reunions held 1886, 1890–1891, 1894–1897.

Fairchild, Charles Bryant, 1842–
History of the 27th regiment N.Y. vols., being a record of its more than two years of service in the War for the Union, from May 21st, 1861, to May 31st, 1863. With a complete roster and short sketches of Commanding officers. Also, a record of experience and suffering of some of the comrades in Libby and other Rebel prisons. Compiled by C. B. Fairchild, of Company "D." Published under the direction of the following committee: Gen. H. W. Slocum [and] Capt. C. A. Wells. Binghamton, Carl & Matthews, printers [1888] ix, 303, (1) p. front. (port.). illus., plates (4 maps, 2 fold.), ports. 22½cm.    DLC NN  **277**
"Errata" (1) p. Unit roster [253]–92.

*27th Infantry, continued*

Hall, Henry Seymour
Experience in the Peninsular and Antietam campaigns, January 3, 1894. *MOLLUS-Kan* 160–84.                                    278

—— Fredericksburg and Chancellorsville, April 4, 1894. *MOLLUS-Kan* 185–205.    279

—— Personal experience in organizing volunteer soldiers in April, 1861, and participating with them in the first battle of Bull run, July 21, 1861. A paper prepared and read before the Kansas commandery of the M.O.L.L.U.S., May 4th, 1892. 16 p. 22cm.            DLC   280
On cover: War paper.

—— Personal experience under Generals Burnside and Hooker, in the battles of Fredericksburg and Chancellorsville, December 11, 12, 13 and 14, 1862, and May 1, 2, 3 and 4, 1863. A paper read [April 4, 1889] before the Kansas commandery of the Military order of the loyal legion of the United States. 22 p. 22cm.                            DLC NN   281
On cover: War paper.

—— Personal experience under General McClellan, after Bull run, including the Peninsular and Antietam campaigns, from July 27, 1861, to November 10, 1862. A paper prepared and read before the Kansas commandery of the M.O.L.L.U.S., January 3, 1894. 22 p. 22½cm.
On cover: War paper.            DLC   282

—— A volunteer at the first Bull run, May 4, 1892. *MOLLUS-Kan* 143–59.        283

Kilmer, George Langdon
The Army of the Potomac at Harrison's landing. *BandL* II 427–8.            284

Merrell, William Howard,           –1897.
Five months in Rebeldom; or, notes from the diary of a Bull run prisoner, at Richmond, by Corporal W. H. Merrell, Color guard, Co. E, 27th regiment, N.Y.S.V. Rochester, Adams & Dabney, 1862. iv, [5]–64 p. front. (illus.). 21cm.                                NN   284A
"Greater portion . . . originally appeared in the columns of the Rochester evening express, in a series of twelve numbers." Coulter 321.

See also Title 250.

## 28TH INFANTRY

*Mustered in: May 22, 1861.*
*Mustered out: June 2, 1863.*
*Pfisterer 2052–62.*
*Register serial no 21, 285–412.*

Report of proceedings of the thirty-fourth annual reunion of the 28th reg't New York volunteers, held at Niagara Falls, New York, Wednesday, May 22d, 1895. . . . [Buffalo, Peter Paul book co., printers, 1895] 27 p. 1 illus., 2 ports. 25cm.                        DLC   285

Boyce, Charles William, 1842–
A brief history of the Twenty-eighth regiment, New York state volunteers, First brigade, First division, Twelfth corps, Army of the Potomac, from the author's diary and official reports, with the muster-roll of the Regiment, and many pictures, articles and letters from surviving members and friends, with the report of the proceedings of the thirty-fifth annual reunion held at Albion, New York, May 22, 1896 [by] C. W. Boyce. Buffalo [Matthews-Northrup co., 1896] 190 p. front. (port.), illus., 2 maps, ports. 25cm.            DLC NN   286
Muster-out roll, 113–38, DLC has copy with insert, "Additional photographs," dated September 1897 and paged 191–4.

—— The story of our flag, how lost, found, and restored. *Maine bugle*, campaign V (Rockland 1898) 182–9.                    287

—— The story of our flag, how lost, found, and restored. The first reunion of Blue and Gray. *BandG* I (1893) 377–82. illus., ports.
                                              288

—— A story of the Shenandoah valley in 1862. The first Provost-Marshal [Erwin A. Bowen] of Harrisonburg, Va. *BandG* III (1894) 243–8. 1 illus., ports.            289

Brown, Benjamin Balmer, 1838–1926.
Civil war letters. *North Dakota historical quarterly* I no 3 (1926/27) 60–71; no 4 61–8.
                                              289A

King, Horatio Collins, 1837–1918.
Cedar mountain. [Brooklyn, 1902?] [6] p. 2 plates (illus., port.). 22cm.    NN   289A
A poem read at the dedication of the monument to the 28th New York on the battlefield of Culpeper, Va., August 8, 1902.

Rowley, William W
The Signal corps of the army during the rebellion, by Captain W. W. Rowley, 1893. *MOLLUS-Wis* II 220–9.            290

Waller, John
With Banks from Strasburg to the Potomac. *BandG* III (1894) 194–6.            291

*28th Infantry (National Guard)*

*Left the State: April 30, 1861.*
*Mustered out: August 5, 1861.*
*Mustered in: June 16, 1863.*
*Mustered out: July 22, 1863.*
*Mustered in: August 1864.*
*Mustered out: November 13, 1864.*
*Pfisterer 629–37.*

## 29TH INFANTRY

*Mustered in: June 6, 1861.*
*Mustered out: June 20, 1863.*
*Pfisterer 2062–77.*
*Register* serial no 21, 413–555.

## 30TH INFANTRY

*Mustered in: June 1, 1861.*
*Mustered out: June 18, 1863.*
*Pfisterer 2078–89.*
*Register* serial no 21, 556–720.

## 31ST INFANTRY

*Mustered in: May 24, 1861.*
*Mustered out: June 4, 1863.*
*Pfisterer 2089–2102.*
*Register* serial no 21, 721–878.

## 32ND INFANTRY

*Mustered in: May 31, 1861.*
*Mustered out: June 9, 1863.*
*Pfisterer 2103–14.*
*Register* serial no 21, 879–1024.

## 33RD INFANTRY

*Mustered in: July 3, 1861.*
*Mustered out: June 2, 1863.*
*Pfisterer 2115–25.*
*Register* serial no 22, 1–150.

See Titles 75–77 for proceedings of reunions held 1886, 1890–1891, 1894–1897.

Judd, David Wright, 1838–1888.
   The story of the Thirty-third N.Y.S. vols.; or, two years campaigning in Virginia and Maryland, by David W. Judd (correspondent of the New York times). Illustrations from drawings by Lieut. L. C. Mix. Rochester, Benton & Andrews, 1864. iv, 349, 76 p. front. (port.), illus. 19cm.          DLC NN   **292**
   Unit roster 41–76, second pagination.

## 34TH INFANTRY

*Mustered in: June 15, 1861.*
*Mustered out: June 30, 1863.*
*Pfisterer 2125–37.*
*Register* serial no 22, 151–283.

Report of proceedings of the thirty-third annual reunion 28th regiment New York volunteers, held at Lockport, New York, Tuesday, May 22d, 1894. . . . [Buffalo, Press of Peter Paul book co., 1894] 28 p. 1 illus., port. 25cm.
                                        MnHi   **293**

Thirty-sixth annual reunion Twenty-eighth regiment New York state volunteers, held at Eldorado, on Grand island, near Buffalo, N. Y., August 26th, 1897. [Buffalo, Paul's press, 1897] 19 p. 25cm.                        MnHi   **294**
Title from cover.

Chapin, Louis N
   A brief history of the Thirty-fourth regiment N.Y.S.V., embracing a complete roster of all officers and men, and a full account of the dedication of the monument on the battlefield of Antietam, September 17, 1902, by Lieutenant L. N. Chapin. . . . [New York, 1903] 188 p. illus., ports. 24cm.              NHi   **295**
   Unit roster 113–51.

See also Titles 15 and 244.

## 35TH INFANTRY

*Mustered in: June 11, 1861.*
*Mustered out: June 5, 1863.*
*Pfisterer 2137–47.*
*Register* serial no 22, 284–428.

Shaw, Albert D
   A full report of the first re-union and banquet of the Thirty-fifth N.Y. vols., held at Watertown, N.Y., on December 13th, 1887. Also, including much valuable data pertaining to the history and members of the gallant 35th, past and present. Watertown, Times print. and pub. house, 1888. 122 p. 26½cm.          NN   **296**
   Foreword signed: Albert D. Shaw. "Muster-out-roll of field and staff," 65–101.

## 36TH INFANTRY

*Mustered in: June 17, 1861.*
*Mustered out: July 15, 1863.*
*Pfisterer 2147–59.*
*Register* serial no 22, 429–562.

Dalton, John Call, 1825–1889.
   Memorial of Edward B. Dalton, M.D. . . . New York, 1872. 40 p. plate (map). 23cm.
                                        MB NN   **297**

## 37TH INFANTRY

*Mustered in: June 7, 1861.*
*Mustered out: June 22, 1863.*
*Pfisterer 2159–72.*
*Register* serial no 22, 563–776.

O'Beirne, James Rowan
   When the Rappahannock ran red. *Hearst's magazine* xxiii (1913) 764–74. illus., plans, ports.                                        **298**

*37th Infantry, continued*

Petty, A            Milburn
History of the 37th regiment, New York
volunteers. *Journal of the Irish American historical society* xxxi (New York 1937) 101–37.
3 plates (ports.).                         **299**
"War department records of the 37th regiment,"
124–37.

### 37th Infantry (National Guard)

*Mustered in: May 29, 1862.*
*Mustered out: September 2, 1862.*
*Mustered in: June 18, 1863.*
*Mustered out: July 22, 1863.*
*Mustered in: May 6, 1864.*
*Mustered out: June 6, 1864.*
*Pfisterer 637–45.*

### 38TH INFANTRY

*Mustered in: June 3, 1861.*
*Mustered out: June 22, 1863.*
*Pfisterer 2173–87.*
*Register serial no 22, 777–961.*

Murphy, Charles J
Reminiscences of the War of the rebellion
and of the Mexican war, by Charles J. Murphy.
New York, F. J. Ficker, 1882. 80 p. 22½cm.
                                        NN   **300**
Title and imprint from cover.

Owen, Frederick Wooster
A Christmas reminiscence of Fredericksburg,
by Fred Wooster Owen, First Lieutenant and
Signal officer at the battle of Fredericksburg.
[Morristown, N. J., 1895] [4] p. 21½ × 9½cm.
P [1] title; p [4] blank.       DNW   **301**
—— The Signal service. In War talks of
Morristown veterans. Morristown, N.J., 1887,
3–6.                                       **302**

Post, Marie Caroline (de Trobriand), 1845–
1926.
The life and memoirs of Comte Regis de
Trobriand, Major-General in the Army of the
United States, by his daughter, Marie Caroline
Post (Mrs. Charles Alfred Post). New York,
E. P. Dutton & co., 1910. ix, 539 p. 2 plates
(ports.). 24½cm.                NN   **303**
Trobriand mustered in as colonel of the 55th New
York infantry, July 28, 1861; transferred to the 38th
New York infantry, December 21, 1862; mustered out,
November 21, 1863. Civil war, 226–339.

Trobriand, Philippe Régis Denis de Keredern,
compte de, 1816–1897.
Four years with the Army of the Potomac,
by Régis de Trobriand. Translated by George
K. Dauchy. Boston, Ticknor and co., 1889. xix,

757 p. front. (port.), plates (maps, partly
double and fold.). 21cm.             NN   **304**
Coulter 452.

—— Quatre ans de campagnes a l'armée du
Potomac, par Régis de Trobriand. Paris, Librairie Internationale, 1867–8. 2 v. 21½cm.
See note to Title 303.               NN   **305**
See also Title 260.

### 39TH INFANTRY

*Mustered in: May 28, 1861.*
*Mustered out: July 1, 1865.*
*Pfisterer 2188–2213.*
*Register serial no 23, 1–313.*

Soldiers memorial Company I, 39th regt. New
York volunteers. Washington, D. C., C. G.
Case, R. G. Walrad [and] B. C. Baker, c1863.
illus. broadside, 56½ × 46cm.       NHi   **306**
"Lith of Sarony, Major & Knapp, New York."

Waring, George Edwin, 1833–1898.
The Garibaldi guard, by George E. Waring, Jr. In The first book of the Authors club,
liber scriptorum (1893) 568–75.         **306A**

### 40TH INFANTRY

*Mustered in: June 21, 1861.*
*Mustered out: June 27, 1865.*
*Pfisterer 2213–37.*
*Register serial no 23, 314–676.*

Roster of the members of the Mozart regiment,
40th New York volunteers. Organized at their
camp near Alexander, Va., June 14, 1865. New
York, W. H. Rowan, 1897. 16 p. 14½cm.
                                        NN   **307**
Fletcher, Daniel Cooledge
Reminiscences of California and the Civil
war, by Daniel Cooledge Fletcher, Sergt.
Co. H, 40th regt. N.Y.V. Ayer, Mass., Press of
Huntley S. Turner, 1894. 196 p. front. (port.).
22½cm.                            DLC NN   **308**
"The War of the rebellion," [101]–96.

Floyd, Frederick Clark, 1837–
History of the Fortieth (Mozart) regiment,
New York volunteers, which was composed of
four companies from New York, four companies from Massachusetts and two companies
from Pennsylvania, by Sergeant Fred C. Floyd.
. . . Boston, F. H. Gilson co., 1909. xvi, 469 p.
facs., illus., plates (illus., ports.). 23½cm.
Unit roster 277–468.              DLC NN   **309**

Hubbell, Henry Wilson
The organization and use of artillery during
the War of the rebellion, by Captain H. W.
Hubbell. *JMSIUS* xi (1890) 396–412.      **310**

## 41ST INFANTRY

*Mustered in: June 6, 1861.*
*Mustered out: December 9, 1865.*
*Pfisterer 2237–53.*
*Register* serial no 23, 677–891.

## 42ND INFANTRY

*Mustered in: June 22, 1861.*
*Mustered out: July 13, 1864.*
*Pfisterer 2253–70.*
*Register* serial no 23, 892–1101.

Kreis, Philip, 1844–
. . . Under two flags, by Philip Kreis. [New York, 1895] 13, (1) p. front. (illus.), plate (3 ports.). 23½cm.                    NNC    *310A*
At head of title: Union forever. Title from cover. Caption title: Under two flags, the adventures of Philip Kreis. Story of the Tammany regiment of New York. Experiences of one of the members, who saw service first in the Southern army [Macon German artillery] then in the 42d New York volunteers.

Tammany Society, or Columbian Order.
A record of the proceedings at the dedication of the monument erected, September 24, 1891, on the battlefield of Gettysburg by the survivors of the Tammany regiment (Forty-second New York volunteers) in memory of those officers and men of the Regiment who fell during the Civil war, 1861–1865. [New York, Tammany Society print, 1892] 47 p. front. (illus.), 24cm.                    NN    *311*
c 1892 by Tammany Society.

## 43RD INFANTRY

*Mustered in: September 21, 1861.*
*Mustered out: June 27, 1865.*
*Pfisterer 2270–89.*
*Register* serial no 23, 1102–1361.

See Title 235.

## 44TH INFANTRY

*Mustered in: August 30, 1861 to September 24, 1861.*
*Mustered out: October 11, 1864.*
*Pfisterer 2289–2305.*
*Register* serial no 24, 1–246.

Presentation of sword, &c., to Lieut.-Colonel Rice. [Albany, 1861] 11 p. 23cm. DLC *312*
"From the Albany evening journal of October 19th, 1861."

Proceedings of the 44th Ellsworth N.Y. veteran association, on the occasion of their re-union, held at Martin's hall, Albany, N.Y., Aug. 8 and 9, 1871. Albany, Van Benthuysen print. house, 1871. 62 p. 21½cm.                    NHi    *313*

Proceedings of the Forty-fourth Ellsworth New York veteran association at their reunion and fiftieth anniversary of the organization of the Regiment, held at Albany, New York, August 8 and 9, 1911. Published by the Committee of the Forty-fourth New York veteran association. [Albany, J. B. Lyon co., printers, 1911] 67 p. front. (port.). 23cm.                    DLC    *313A*

Bridgman, Charles De Witt, 1835–1899.
Sermon commemorative of Justin R. Huntley, delivered October 23, 1864, by C. D. Bridgman, together with memoir and letters. Albany, Weed, Parsons and co., printers, 1865. 60 p. front. (port.). 22½cm.                    DLC    *314*
On cover: Memorial of Justin R. Huntley, August 26, 1864.

Knox, Edward Burgin,        –1890.
The capture of Alexandria and death of Ellsworth (read March 4, 1885). *MOLLUS-Ill* II 9–10.                                     *315*

Maret, George W
A letter from the front. Edited by Paul J. Engel. *NYH* xxxiv (1953) 204–10.    *316*

Marraro, Howard Rosario, 1897–
Lincoln's Italian volunteers from New York. *NYH* xxiv (1943) 56–67. plate (3 illus.). *317*

Nash, Eugene Arus, 1837–1911.
A history of the Forty-fourth regiment, New York volunteer infantry, in the Civil war, 1861–1865, by Captain Eugene Arus Nash. Chicago, R. R. Donnelley & Sons co., 1911. xiv, 484 p. plates (illus., maps, ports.). 23cm. NN *318*
Unit roster 351–471.

—— The People's Ellsworth regiment, 44th New York volunteer infantry, by Col. E. A. Nash. In History of Cattaraugus county (New York 1879) 505–12.                    *319*

Sprague, Charles E
"In the company street." 1893. *MOLLUS-Ill* II 126–39.                              *320*

Todd, Frederick Porter and George Woodbridge
44th New York volunteer infantry regiment (People's Ellsworth regiment), 1861–1864. *Military collector & historian* xi (Washington 1959) 10. col. plate (illus.).    *321*

Wood, Bradford Ripley
Chattanooga; or, Lookout mountain and Missionary ridge from Moccasin point. [n. p., U. S. Veteran Signal Corps Association, 1907] 24 p. 1 illus., map. 23½cm.    *322*
Author was on duty with U. S. Signal corps from January 8, 1862, until February 1864.

## 45TH INFANTRY

*Mustered in: September 9, 1861.*
*Consolidated with 58th regiment of infantry. June 30, 1865.*
*Pfisterer 2305–19.*
*Register serial no 24, 247–437.*

## 46TH INFANTRY

*Mustered in: July 29, 1861.*
*Mustered out: July 28, 1865.*
*Pfisterer 2319–37.*
*Register serial no 24, 438–625.*

## 47TH INFANTRY

*Mustered in: September 14, 1861.*
*Mustered out: August 30, 1865.*
*Pfisterer 2337–56.*
*Register serial no 24, 626–889.*

### 47th Infantry (National Guard)

*Mustered in: May 27, 1862.*
*Mustered out: September 1, 1862.*
*Left the State: June 23, 1863.*
*Mustered out: July 23, 1863.*
*Pfisterer 645–50.*

## 48TH INFANTRY

*Mustered in: August 16, 1861.*
*Mustered out: September 1, 1865.*
*Pfisterer 2357–77.*
*Register serial no 24, 890–1183.*

Monaghan, Thomas
Only a Private, a sketch of the services of a private soldier, who took part in the battles of Fort Pulaski, Fort Wagner, and Coal harbor, by himself. Boston, Pratt Brothers [n. d.] 31 p. 16cm.                                   NHi  **323**
Title and imprint from cover.

—— Only a Private, a sketch of the services of Thomas Monaghan of the Forty-eighth N.Y. regiment who took part in the battles of Fort Pulaski, Fort Wagner, Olustee and Coal harbor, by himself. Boston, Pratt Brothers [n. d.] 31 p. 16cm.                     MB  **324**

Carlton, William J
Company D, ("The die-no-mores") of the Forty-eighth regiment, New York state volunteers, 1861–5, a paper read at the first reunion of the surviving members, at Trenton, N. J., July 24, 1891, the thirtieth anniversary of the organization of the Company, by William J.

Carlton . . . Privately printed. 1892. 19. (1) p. front. (6 ports.). 23½cm.        DLC NHi  **325**

Nichols, James Moses, 1835–1886.
Perry's saints; or, the fighting Parson's regiment in the War of the rebellion, by James M. Nichols. Boston, D. Lothrop and co. [1886] 299 p. illus., maps, 2 plates (fold. map, plan). 19½cm.                              DLC NN  **326**
Coulter 343.

Palmer, Abraham John, 1847–1922.
The history of the Forty-eighth regiment, New York state volunteers, in the War for the Union, 1861–1865, by Abraham J. Palmer (formerly Private, Company D). Published by the Veteran association of the Regiment. Brooklyn, 1885. xvi, 314, (2) p. illus., maps, plates (ports.), ports. 21½cm.       DLC NN  **327**
Unit roster [245]–314. "For sale by Charles T. Dillingham, New York." Coulter 362.

Robinson, Charles Seymour, 1829–1899.
A memorial discourse, occasioned by the death of Lieut. Col. James M. Green, Forty-eighth N.Y.S.V., by his pastor, Rev. Chas. S. Robinson. Troy, Daily Times print, 1864. 17 p. 22cm.                                DLC NHi NN  **328**

Storrs, Richard Salter, 1821–1900.
One who laid down his life for his brethren, a sermon, in memory of Robert Sedgewick Edwards, preached in the Church of the Pilgrims, Brooklyn, N.Y., by R. S. Storrs, Jr. Brooklyn, "The Union" presses, 1864. 21 p. front. (mounted port.). 23cm.
                                           DLC NN  **329**

## 49TH INFANTRY

*Mustered in: September 18, 1861.*
*Mustered out: June 27, 1865.*
*Pfisterer 2378–94.*
*Register serial no 24, 1184–1374.*

Bidwell, Frederick David
History of the Forty-ninth volunteers, compiled by Frederick David Bidwell. Albany, J. B. Lyon co., printers, 1916. 317 p. front. (port.), plates (illus.). 23½cm.
Unit roster 167–292.          DLC NN  **330**

Larned, Joseph Nelson, 1836–1913.
Daniel D. Bidwell, address at dedication of the monument raised by "D" company at General Bidwell's grave, Forest Lawn, Buffalo, October 19, 1871. *Publications of the Buffalo historical society* xix (1915) 37–47.  **331**

## 50TH INFANTRY

*Mustered in: September 18, 1861.*
*Designated 50th regiment of New York engineers: October 22, 1861.*

### 50th Infantry (National Guard)

*Mustered in: September 2, 1864.*

*Mustered out: December 2, 1864.*

*Pfisterer 650–1.*

*Only Companies A and B were mustered and served as Companies L and M of the 58th infantry (National guard).*

History of the Dewitt guard, Company A, 50th regiment, National guard, State of New York. Published by the Company. Ithaca, Andrus, McChain & co., printers, 1866. 192 p. 17½cm.
NN **332**

Contents: "The name of each member of the Dewitt guard from its organization, the date of his enlistment, his profession, with such incidents as we think will be of interest to the readers," [5]–145; History of the Company [147]–92.

### 51ST INFANTRY

*Mustered in: July 27 to October 23, 1861.*

*Mustered out: July 25, 1865.*

*Pfisterer 2394–2414.*

*Register serial no 25, 1–247.*

Memoirs of the late Adjt. Andrew L. Fowler of the 51st N.Y.V., who fell at the battle of Antietam bridge, September 17th, 1862, comprising the funeral discourse preached by the Rev. Dr. S. D. Burchard, letters of condolence by friends of the family, and abstracts of letters written by the Adjt. to his parents and friends. Compiled by a friend and dedicated to the family of deceased, Brooklyn, December 12th, 1863. New York, Ferris & Pratt, printers, 1863. 67 p. 21½cm. DLC **333**

Quarter-century banquet of the 51st regiment, N.Y. volunteers (Shepard rifles) . . . 29th October, 1886. New York [American Bank Note co., 1886] 33 p. plates (illus., music). 22½cm. DLC NHi NN **334**

The bride to her regiment, words by Elliott F. Shepard, music by Jas. Hazard Wilson, [19] Freedom, truth and right, grand march, by Carl Heinemann, 1862; Bride of the regiment march, by Wm. J. Smith, arr. for piano by Jas. Hazard Wilson — at end of volume.

### 52ND INFANTRY

*Mustered in: August 3 to November 5, 1861.*

*Mustered out: July 1, 1865.*

*Pfisterer 2415–36.*

*Register serial no 25, 248–524.*

Ehlers, Edward M          L
Address by Edward M. L. Ehlers at the dedication of the monument erected by Major-General Daniel Butterfield at Fredericksburg, Virginia, to commemorate the services of the Fifth corps, Army of the Potomac, Memorial day, 1901. [New York, Press of J. J. Little & co., 1901] 16 p. 24cm. NN **335**

Frank, Emil H
Reminiscences of the Civil war, 1861–1863, by Emil H. Frank, 1st Lieut. 52d regiment New York volunteer infantry. [n. p., n. d.] 75 p. front. (port.). 23cm. NN **336**

Hegeman, George, 1845–
The diary of a Union soldier in Confederate prisons. Edited by James J. Heslin. *New-York historical society quarterly* XLI (1957) 233–78. illus., 2 maps. **337**

### 52nd Infantry (National Guard)

*Left the State: June 21, 1863.*

*Mustered out: July 25, 1863.*

*Pfisterer 651–4.*

### 53RD INFANTRY

*Mustered in: August 27 to November 15, 1861.*

*Mustered out: March 21, 1862.*

*Pfisterer 2436–41.*

*Register serial no 25, 525–652.*

Wheeler, Gerald E
The 53rd New York: a zoo-zoo tale [by] Gerald E. Wheeler and A. Stuart Pitt. *NYH* XXXVII (1956) 414–31. **338**

Zouvata, by Commissionary Sergeant James Bryant Smith, 421–31.

### 54TH INFANTRY

*Mustered in: September 5 to October 16, 1861.*

*Mustered out: April 14, 1866.*

*Pfisterer 2445–63.*

*Register serial no 25, 653–877.*

### 54th Infantry (National Guard)

*Mustered in: July 26, 1864.*

*Mustered out: November 10, 1864.*

*Pfisterer 654–7.*

### 55TH INFANTRY

*Mustered in: August 28, 1861.*

*Transferred to the 38th regiment of infantry: December 21, 1862.*

*Pfisterer 2463–71.*

*Register serial no 25, 878–977.*

See Titles 303–305.

*55th Infantry (National Guard)*

*Left State: June 24, 1863.*
*Mustered out: July 27, 1863.*
*Pfisterer 657–9.*

## 56TH INFANTRY

*Mustered in: October 28, 1861.*
*Mustered out: October 17, 1865.*
*Pfisterer 2471–89.*
*Register serial no 25, 978–1238.*

Soldiers memorial 56th regiment, Company A, New York state vols. Baltimore, J. L. Anderson [1863] col. illus. broadside, 56 × 45½cm.
"Printed by H. A. Robinson."          NHi       **339**

Fisk, Joel C          1843–
A condensed history of the 56th regiment New York veteran volunteer infantry, which was a part of the organization known as the "Tenth legion" in the Civil war, 1861–1865, together with a register or roster of all the members of the Regiment, and the war record of each member as recorded in the Adjutant general's office at Albany, New York, by Joel C. Fisk and William H. D. Blake. [Newburgh, Newburgh Journal print. house, 1906] 424 p. front. (port.), plate (illus.). 26½cm.
Unit roster [117]–[397]      DLC NN      **340**

*56th Infantry (National Guard)*

*Mustered in: June 18, 1863.*
*Mustered out: July 24, 1863.*
*Mustered in: August 2, 1864.*
*Mustered out: November 6, 1864.*
*Pfisterer 659–64.*

## 57TH INFANTRY

*Mustered in: August 12 to November 19, 1861.*
*Mustered out: July 14 to October 15, 1864.*
*Pfisterer 2489–2502.*
*Register serial no 26, 1–145.*

Cole, Jacob Henry, 1847–
Under five commanders; or, a boy's experience with the Army of the Potomac, by Jacob H. Cole of the First New York fire zouaves and the Fifty-seventh New York volunteers. Paterson, N. J., News print. co., 1906. ix, 253 p. illus., ports. 21cm.      DLC NHi      **341**
Mustered in 57th New York infantry, September 21, 1861; transferred to 61st New York infantry, no date; mustered out, September 20, 1864. Coulter 85.

Favill, Josiah Marshall
The diary of a young officer serving with the armies of the United States during the War of the rebellion, by Josiah Marshall Favill, Adjutant, Captain, and Brevet Major 57th New York infantry, Brevet Lieutenant-Colonel and Colonel U.S. volunteers. Chicago, R. R. Donnelley & Sons co., 1909. 298 p. plates (ports.). 21cm.      NHi      **342**
Coulter 155.

Frederick, Gilbert
The story of a Regiment, being a record of the military services of the Fifty-seventh New York state volunteer infantry in the War of the rebellion, 1861–1865, by Gilbert Frederick, late Captain 57th N.Y.V.I. Published by the Fifty-seventh veteran association. [Chicago, C. H. Morgan co.] 1895. xii, 349 p. front. (illus.), illus., maps, plates (ports.). 21cm.
                              DLC NN      **343**
Unit roster [298]–326. Coulter 173.

## 58TH INFANTRY

*Mustered in: August 27 to November 5, 1861.*
*Mustered out: October 1, 1865.*
*Pfisterer 2502–18.*
*Register serial no 26, 146–367.*

*58th Infantry (National Guard)*

*Mustered in: August 27, 1864.*
*Mustered out: December 2, 1864.*
*Pfisterer 664–6.*

## 59TH INFANTRY

*Mustered in: August 2 to October 30, 1861.*
*Mustered out: June 30, 1865.*
*Pfisterer 2519–38.*
*Register serial no 26, 368–656.*

O'Mara, Daniel A
Proceedings of the associated survivors of the Fifty-ninth reg't, N.Y. vet. vols. first annual re-union and dedication of monument at Gettysburg, Pa., July 3d, 1889. Compiled by the Secretary, D. A. O'Mara. New York [Wm. Finley, printer] 1889. 40 p. 21½cm.
Advertising matter, 35–40.          NN      **344**

## 60TH INFANTRY

*Mustered in: October 30, 1861.*
*Mustered out: July 17, 1865.*
*Pfisterer 2539–54.*
*Register serial no 26, 657–831.*

Eddy, Richard, 1828–1906.

History of the Sixtieth regiment, New York state volunteers, from the commencement of its organization in July, 1861, to its public reception at Ogdensburgh as a veteran command, January 7th, 1864, by Richard Eddy, Chaplain. Philadelphia, Published by the author [Crissy & Markley, printers] 1864. xii, 360 p. 19cm.                   DLC NN     **345**
Coulter 144.

Jones, Jesse H
The breastworks at Culp's hill. *BandL* III 316–17.                                                **346**

### 61ST INFANTRY

*Mustered in: September to October 1861.*
*Mustered out: July 14, 1865.*
*Pfisterer 2554–73.*
*Register* serial no 26, 832–1110.

Fuller, Charles Augustus
Personal recollections of the war of 1861, as Private, Sergeant and Lieutenant in the Sixty-first regiment, New York volunteer infantry, by Charles A. Fuller. Prepared from data found in letters, written at the time from the field to the people at home. Sherburne, News print. house, 1906. 108 p. front. (port.). 23cm.
                             MB NHi NN     **347**

Spencer, William H
How I felt in battle and in prison, by Major William H. Spencer. *MOLLUS-Me* II 122–49.
                                                    **348**
See also Title 341.

### 62ND INFANTRY

*Mustered in: June 30, 1861.*
*Mustered out: August 30, 1865.*
*Pfisterer 2573–87.*
*Register* serial no 26, 1111–1297.

Perine, Abraham T                    –1864.
In love and friendship, by Marjorie Kerr. *Staten Island historian* XVI (1955) 28–30.
                                                    **348A**
The letters are signed: Lieut. A. T. Perine. His highest rank was First Sergeant.

### 63RD INFANTRY

*Mustered in: September to November 1861.*
*Mustered out: June 30, 1865.*
*Pfisterer 2587–2608.*
*Register* serial no 27, 1–198.

Two relics of the American Civil war. *Irish sword* I (Dublin 1949/53) 88–93. plates (2 illus., port.).                               **349**
The regimental colors of the 63rd New York and sword of General Meagher at the University of Notre Dame.

### 64TH INFANTRY

*Mustered in: December 1861.*
*Mustered out: July 14, 1865.*
*Pfisterer 2608–28.*
*Register* serial no 27, 199–425.

Report of seventh annual reunion of the 64th N.Y. regimental association at Salamanca, New York, August 21 and 22, 1895. Historical sketches, letters, roster of survivors. [Salamanca?, Randolph pub. co., 1895] 66, 12 p. front. (illus.). 21cm.                    NHi     **350**
"In memoriam Captain Robert H. Renwick. Roster survivors," 12 p.

Henry, William W
Fredericksburg, my first battle. *BandG* V (1895) 99–101.                               **351**

### 65TH INFANTRY

*Mustered in: July to August 1861.*
*Mustered out: July 17, 1865.*
*Pfisterer 2628–48.*
*Register* serial no 27, 426–748.

Cochrane, John
Speech of Colonel Cochrane, delivered to his regiment First United States chasseurs, November 13, 1861. [Washington, D. C., 1861] 4 p. 23cm.                              NN     **352**
Caption title.

Hamblin, Deborah
Brevet Major-General Joseph Eldridge Hamblin, 1861–1865. Privately printed. Boston, 1902. 60 p. illus., map., plates (1 illus., ports.). 22½cm.              NHi NN     **353**
Preface signed: Deborah Hamblin.

### 65th Infantry (National Guard)

*Mustered in: June 19, 1863.*
*Mustered out: July 30, 1863.*
*Pfisterer 666–9.*

### 66TH INFANTRY

*Mustered in: November 4, 1861.*
*Mustered out: August 30, 1865.*
*Pfisterer 2648–60.*
*Register* serial no 27, 749–915.

## 67TH INFANTRY

*Mustered in: June 24, 1861.*
*Mustered out: July 4, 1864.*
*Pfisterer 2660–73.*
*Register serial no 27, 916–1118.*

### 67th Infantry (National Guard)

*Mustered in: June 25, 1863.*
*Mustered out: August 3, 1863.*
*Pfisterer 669–71.*

## 68TH INFANTRY

*Mustered in: August 1–20, 1861.*
*Mustered out: November 30, 1865.*
*Pfisterer 2673–93.*
*Register serial no 27, 1119–1339.*

Fritsch, Friedrich Otto, freiherr von, 1834–1863.

A gallant Captain of the Civil war, being the record of the extraordinary adventures of Frederick Otto Baron von Fritsch, compiled from his war record in Washington and his private papers. Edited and compiled by Joseph Tyler Butts. New York, F. Tennyson Neely [1902] xi, 163 p. front. (port.). 24cm.  DLC  **354**

### 68th Infantry (National Gurd)

*Mustered in: June 24, 1863.*
*Mustered out: July 29, 1863.*
*Pfisterer 671–3.*

Lewis, Silas W

History of the thirty days' campaign of the Sixty-eighth regiment, New York state National guards, commencing June 25th, 1863. Col. D. S. Forbes, commanding. Taken from diaries kept by different members of the Regiment, superintended by S. W. Lewis, 1st Sergeant of Company "H." Fredonia, Censor office print, 1863. 56 p. 18½cm.  NHi  **355**
Unit roster [3]–10.

## 69TH INFANTRY

*Mustered in: September 17 to November 17, 1861.*
*Mustered out: June 30, 1865.*
*Pfisterer 2694–2709.*
*Register serial no 28, 1–364.*

### 69th Infantry (National Guard)

*Mustered in: May 9, 1861.*
*Mustered out: August 3, 1861.*
*Left the State: May 29, 1862.*

*Mustered out: September 3, 1862.*
*Left the State: June 22, 1863.*
*Mustered out: July 25, 1863.*
*Mustered in: July 6, 1864.*
*Mustered out: October 6, 1864.*
*Pfisterer 673–90.*

Great historical picture of the gallant 69th Irish regiment, on their return to New York, from the seat of war, July 27th, 1861, painted by Louis Lang. [New York, 1861]  **356**
Three pages of text in boards which probably accompanied the painting. The first leaf is hinged with title on the recto, a short sketch of the Regiment on the verso. This text in NHi's copy is signed in ms: L. Savage. The second leaf is mounted on the back cover. This leaf has an outline of the painting with details keyed for the accompanying "Description of the text."

Muster roll of the sixty-ninth, N.Y.S.M. In Chronicles of the rebellion of 1861, by Charles J. Ross (1861) 17–23.  **357**

Corcoran, Michael, 1827–1863.

The captivity of General Corcoran, the only authentic and reliable narrative of the trials and sufferings endured during twelve months imprisonment in Richmond and other Southern cities, by Brig.-General Michael Corcoran, the hero of Bull run. . . . Philadelphia, Barclay & co., 1862. 100 p. front. (port.). 23½cm.
Coulter 96.  NN  **358**

Coyle, John G
General Michael Corcoran. *Journal of the American Irish historical society* xiii (1913/14) 109–26. plate (illus.).  **359**

Fitzgerald, James
The Sixty-ninth regiment, New York city. *Journal of the American Irish historical society* ix (1910) 161–82.  **360**

Halpine, Charles Graham, 1829–1868.

Baked meats of the funeral, a collection of essays, poems, speeches, histories and banquets, by Private Miles O'Reilly, late of the 47th reg't New York volunteer infantry. Collected, revised, and edited, with the requisite corrections of punctuation, spelling, and grammar, by an ex-Colonel of the Adjutant-general's department, with whom the Private formerly served as Lance Corporal of orderlies. New York, Carleton, 1866. 378 p. 19cm.  NHi NN  **361**
Halpine mustered in 69th infantry as Lieutenant, unassigned, April 20, 1861; Aide de-Camp to Colonel Hunter; mustered out with Regiment, August 3, 1861.

—— The life and adventures, songs, services, and speeches of Private Miles O'Reilly (47th regiment, New York volunteers). "The post of honor is the Private's station." With comic illustrations by Mullen. From the authentic records of the New York herald. New York, Carleton, 1864. x, [11]–237 p. illus., plates (illus.). 18½cm.                    NHi NN   **362**

—— The life and adventures, songs, services, and speeches of Private Miles O'Reilly (47th regiment, New York volunteers. . . . New York, Carleton, 1864. [Tarrytown, Reprinted, W. Abbatt, 1926] (*The magazine of history, with notes and queries.* Tarrytown, 1926. Extra number no 117).                         **363**
A reprint of title page, p [iii] [11]–41, [52]–53 and part of the preface of the original.

—— Two songs of '61. *Magazine of history* XXIII (New York 1916) 241–5.        **364**
Contents: The army to the ironclads, by Charles G. Halpine; The second mater, by Fitz-James O'Brien.

Meagher, Thomas Francis, 1823–1867.
The last days of the 69th in Virginia, a narrative in three parts, by Thomas Francis Meagher, Captain, Company K ("Irish zouaves"). New York, "Irish American," 1861. 15 p. port. 21cm.            DLC RP   **365**

## 70TH INFANTRY

*Mustered in: June 20, 1861.*
*Mustered out: July 7, 1864.*
*Pfisterer 2709–22.*
*Register serial no 28, 365–559.*

A brief memento to Captain Henry Brooks O'Reilly of the First excelsior regiment, who fell in the battle of Williamsburg, the first battle of the Army of the Potomac on its march from Yorktown to Richmond, May 5, 1862. [Rochester, 1862] 7 p. 23cm.    NN   **366**

Coyne, John N
The battle of Williamsburg, Va., May 5, 1862, by Lt. Col. John N. Coyne. [New York, Press of T. A. Wright, 1896] 26, (1) p. 18cm.                          NHi NN   **367**
Title from cover: "Printed for the Society" [of the war veterans of the 7th regiment N.G.S.N.Y.] The author served with the 7th, April 19 – June 3, 1861.

Wiley, Bell Irvin
. . . The soldier's life, North and South, letters home tell adventures of two foes. *Life* (February 3, 1961) 64–77. illus., partly col.                               **368**
At head of title: Civil war III. Samuel W. Croft, 70th New York infantry.

## 71ST INFANTRY

*Mustered in: June 20 to July 18, 1861.*
*Mustered out: July 30, 1864.*
*Pfisterer 2722–34.*
*Register serial no 28, 560–725.*

Rafferty, Thomas,        –1888.
Gettysburg, an address delivered by the late Colonel Thomas Rafferty, 1883. *MOLLUS-NY* I 1–32.                          **369**

### 71st Infantry (National Guard)

*Mustered in May 3, 1861.*
*Mustered out: July 31, 1861.*
*Mustered in: May 28, 1862.*
*Mustered out: September 2, 1862.*
*Left the State: June 17, 1863.*
*Mustered out: July 22, 1863.*
*Pfisterer 690–9.*

Addresses delivered at the unveiling of the memorial tablet presented by Colonel Henry P. Martin to the Seventy-first regiment N.G.-S.N.Y., in memory of those members of the Seventy-first who were killed or wounded at the battle of Bull run, July 21, 1861. With introduction describing the battle of Bull run and the presentation ceremonies of March 12, 1895. New York, Privately printed, 1895. 16 p. front. (illus.). 25½cm         NN   **370**

Presentation of a flag to the 71st reg. N.Y.S.M., by Mrs. Col. Thorn, at the City of New York, on the anniversary of the birthday of Washington, A.D. 1862. [New York, 1862] [3] p. 24½cm.                          CtY   **370A**
Caption title. Presentation and remarks by Charles P. Kirkland.

Report of the Seventy-first regiment, National guard, State of New York, Reprinted from the Report of the Adjutant general of the State of New York. New York, J. J. Little & co., 1882. 23 p. 23cm.                          NN   **371**
Report is dated: February 17th, 1868; and is signed: Harry Rockafeller, Lieut. Col. Comdg.

Thirty days with the Seventy-first regiment. *Continental monthly* IV (New York 1863) 404–11.                          **372**

Cook, Frederick N
Cook's war journal. [New York, 1861?] 32 p. 17cm.                          NHi   **373**
Title from cover. A diary with entries from April 21 – July 31, 1861. An "Appendix" has entry for August 18, 1861.

Francis, Augustus Theodore
History of the 71st regiment, N.G.,N.Y. . . . Published by the Veterans association 71st regiment N.G.N.Y. [New York, Press of the Eastman pub. co., 1919] xii, (3), 900, (1) p. plates (ports.). 24cm.                          NN   **374**
Civil war 88–289, 800–848. "Compiler of the present volume, Brevet Brigadier General Augustus Theodore Francis."

71st Infantry (National Guard), continued

Smith, John Wesley, 1842–
Life story of J. Wesley Smith of Ottawa, Kansas, written in his eighty-ninth year. Decatur, Ill., Printed by Decatur print. co. [1930] 126 p. front. (port.). 20½cm.
KHi NN    374A
The author's account of service with the 71st New York militia, 1862, 20–3.

Telfer, William Duff
A reminiscence of the first battle of Manassas, a camp-fire story of the Seventy-first regiment, N.G.S.N.Y., by William Duff Telfer, a volunteer in the ranks of the Regiment. . . . Brooklyn, Published and sold by the author [New York, Pratt & Grinton, 1864] vi, 58 p. front. (fold. plan). 17½cm.      NN    375
On cover: Second edition. Battle field of the 71st reg't N.G.S.N.Y.

Whittemore, Henry, 1833–1910.
History of the Seventy-first N.G.S.N.Y., including the history of the Veteran association with biographical sketches of members, by Henry Whittemore. New York, Willis McDonald & co., 1886. viii, 302 p. plates (ports.). 26cm.      NN    376
Caption and running title: The American guard.

### 72ND INFANTRY

Mustered in: July 24, 1861.
Mustered out: June 19 to October 31, 1864.
Pfisterer 2735–51.
Register serial no 28, 726–913.

. . . Report of annual reunion. 1899, 1905–1909.      DNW    377

Brown, Henri Le Fevre
˙ History of the Third regiment, Excelsior brigade, 72d New York volunteer infantry, 1861–1865, compiled by Henri Le Fevre Brown, Sergeant Company B. [Jamestown, Journal print. co.] 1902. 151, (7) p. plates (1 illus., ports.). 23cm.      DLC NN    378
Roster of officers 149–51, (7).

Eastman, William R
The army Chaplain of 1863. MOLLUS-NY IV 338–50.      379

Parker, David B
A Chautauqua boy in '61 and afterward, reminiscences by David B. Parker, Second Lieutenant, Seventy-second New York. Edited by Torrance Parker. Introduction by Albert Bushnell Hart. Boston, Small, Maynard and

co. [1912] xxvi, 388 p. plates (facs., illus., ports.). 21½cm.      NN    380
Partial contents: The war through Gettysburg, 1–36; From Gettysburg to Richmond, 37–64; War-time friends, 65–108.

Street, Owen, 1815–1887.
The young patriot, a memorial of James Hall. . . . Boston, Massachusetts Sabbath School Society [1862] 192 p. 15½cm.      NHi NN    381

### 73RD INFANTRY

Mustered in: July to October 1861.
Mustered out: June 29, 1865.
Pfisterer 2751–67.
Register serial no 28, 914–1141.

Benedict, Henry Marvin, 1827–1875.
A memorial of Brevet Brigadier General Lewis Benedict, Colonel of 162d regiment N.Y.VI., who fell in battle at Pleasant Hill, La., April 9, 1864. Albany, J. Munsell, 1866. 155 p. front. (port.). 26cm.      NHi NN    382
Benedict mustered in 73rd New York infantry, August 28, 1861; discharged for promotion to Colonel 162nd New York infantry, September 1, 1862.

Moran, Frank E
Bastiles of the Confederacy, a reply to Jefferson Davis, being a narrative of the treatment of Union prisoners in the military prisons of the South during the War of the rebellion . . . by Frank Moran, late Captain of Company H, 73d New York. Printed for the family of the author. Baltimore [1890] 201 p. front. (port.), plates (illus.). 20cm.      NHi    383

—— A thrilling history of the famous underground tunnel of Libby prison, by Captain Frank E. Moran. . . . [New York, 1893] 23 p. illus. 24½cm.      In    384
"Reprinted from the Century magazine."

O'Hagen, Joseph B      1826–1872.
The diary of . . . of the Excelsior brigade. Edited by the Rev. William L. Lucey. Civil war history VI (Iowa City 1960) 402–09.    385

### 74TH INFANTRY

Mustered in: June 30 to October 6, 1861.
Mustered out by companies: June 19 to August 3, 1864.
Pfisterer 2767–80.
Register serial no 28, 1142–1291.

Burns, James R
Battle of Williamsburgh, with reminiscences of the campaign, hospital experiences, debates,

etc., by James R. Burns. Published by the author. New York, 1865. vi, [7]–119 p. 14½cm.
          NHi NN   **386**

Heslin, James J
From the Wilderness to Petersburg, the diary of Surgeon Frank Ridgeway, by James J. Heslin. *New-York historical society quarterly* XLV (1961) 113–40. illus., maps, ports.   **386A**

### 74th Infantry (National Guard)

*Mustered in: June 18, 1863.*

*Mustered out: August 3, 1863.*

*Mustered in: November 16, 1863.*

*Mustered out: December 16, 1863.*

*Pfisterer 699–704.*

. . . Constitution and by-laws of "B" co. Spaulding guards, 74th regiment N.G.S.N.Y. Organized August 12th, 1854, adopted September 1854 . . . With an historical sketch of the Company. Buffalo, A. L. Freeman & co. printers, 1877. 88 p. 19½cm.   NHi   **387**
At head of title: "Semper fidelis." Civil war 23–9. "Salutory" signed: Wm. m. Bloomer [and] H. S. Mulligan, Committee.

### 75TH INFANTRY

*Mustered in: November 26, 1861.*

*Mustered out: August 23, 1865.*

*Pfisterer 2780–96.*

*Register serial no 29, 1–180.*

Babcock, Willoughby, 1832–1864.
Selections from the letters and diaries of Brevet-Brigadier General Willoughby Babcock of the Seventy-fifth New York volunteers, a study of camp life in the Union armies during the Civil war, by Willoughby M. Babcock, Jr. . . . [Albany] University of the State of New York, 1922. 110 p. plan, plates (illus., ports.). 22½cm. (Division of archives and history War of the rebellion series bulletin no 2.)
         DLC NHi NN   **388**
Title and imprint from cover.

Root, William H
The experiences of a Federal soldier in Louisiana in 1863. Introduction by Walter Prichard. *Louisiana historical quarterly* XIX (1936) 635–67.   **389**

See also Title 18.

### 76TH INFANTRY

*Mustered in: January 16, 1862.*

*Mustered out by companies: July 1, 1864 to January 1, 1865.*

*Pfisterer 2796–2813.*

*Register serial no 29, 181–422.*

Proceedings of the 76th New York infantry at the dedication of their battle monument, at Gettysburg, Pa., July 1, 1888. Cortland, Daily Messenger print, 1889. 34 p. front. (illus.). 21cm.   NHi   **390**

Northrop, John Worrell
Chronicles from the diary of a war prisoner in Andersonville and other military prisons of the South in 1864 . . . by John Worrell Northrop, formerly Seventy-sixth New York . . . Published and copyrighted by the author. Wichita, Kansas [Wining printery] 1904. 228 p. 17½cm.
Coulter 347.   NN   **391**

Richardson, Charles
Story of a Private, narrative of experiences in Rebel prisons and stockades, read before E. B. Wolcott post no. 1, Milwaukee, November 27, 1896, by Chas. Richardson. Milwaukee [George Richardson, printer] 1897. 100 p. front. (port.). illus. 19cm.   NN WHi   **392**

Smith, Abram P
History of the Seventy-sixth regiment, New York volunteers, what it endured and accomplished, containing desecriptions of its twenty-five battles, its marches, its camp and bivouac scenes, with biographical sketches of fifty-three officers, and a complete record of the enlisted men, by A. P. Smith, late First Lieutenant and Q.M. Cortland, Printed for the Publisher [Syracuse, Truair, Smith & Miles, printers] 1867. 429 p. front. (port.), plate (illus.), ports. 22½cm.   DLC NN   **393**
Coulter 420. Unit roster [411]–29.

### 77TH INFANTRY

*Mustered in: November 23, 1861.*

*Mustered out: June 27, 1865.*

*Pfisterer 2813–30.*

*Register serial no 29, 423–633.*

Report of the . . . annual reunion of the Survivor's association Seventy-ninth regiment New York infantry volunteers. XXIX 1901; XXXVI-XLVI 1908–1918.   DLC   **394**

Branch, Erskine B
A brief sketch of the experience of a Union soldier in the late war. Washington, D. C., Chronicle print, 1870. 8 p. 22cm. CSmH **394A**
Half-title: Reminiscences of Erskine B. Branch.

Fuller, Edward H
Battles of the Seventy-seventh New York state volunteers, Third brigade, Sixth corps, Second division. Mustered in, November 23, 1861. Mustered out, June 27, 1865. By one of the boys. [Gloversville ?, 1901] 27, (1) p. 18½cm.   DLC   **395**

*77th Infantry, continued*

Stevens, George Thomas, 1832–1921.

Three years in the Sixth corps, a concise narrative of events in the Army of the Potomac, from 1861 to the close of the rebellion, April 1865, by George T. Stevens, Surgeon of the 77th regiment New York volunteers. Albany, S. R. Gray, 1866. xii, 436 p. plan, plates (illus., ports.). 22½cm.                    DLC NN  **396**

Coulter 431.

—— —— Second edition, revised and corrected. New York, D. Van Nostrand, 1870. xvi, 449 p. illus., 2 plans, plates (illus., ports.). 19½cm.                     DLC NN  **396A**

### 77th Infantry (National Guard)

*Mustered in: August 2, 1864.*

*Mustered out: November 19, 1864.*

*Pfisterer 704–06.*

### 78TH INFANTRY

*Mustered in: October 1, 1861 to April 12, 1862.*

*Consolidated with 102nd regiment of infantry: July 2, 1864.*

*Pfisterer 2830–41.*

*Register serial no 29, 634–792.*

Elliott, Samuel McKenzie,        –1875.

The Highland brigade. [New York ?, 1861] 29 p. 23½cm.                      RP  **397**

Preface signed: Samuel M. Elliott, Col. 78th regt. Cameron Highlanders.

Greene, Albert Rowland

From Bridgeport to Ringold by way of Lookout mountain, by Albert R. Greene, late First Lieutenant Seventy-eighth New York. 1890. 46 p. PNRISSHS 4th ser no 7.          **398**

### 79TH INFANTRY

*Mustered in: May 29, 1861.*

*Mustered out: July 14, 1865.*

*Pfisterer 706, 2841–59.*

*Register serial no 29, 793–1079.*

Constitution, by-laws, regulations and ritual of the Veteran association 79th regiment Highlanders N.Y. vols. Organized, August 16th, 1865; incorporated, February, 1867. 13, (1) p. 14cm.                        NHi  **399**

Armour, Robert

The attack upon and defense of Fort Sanders, Knoxville, Tenn., November 29, 1863, prepared by Captain Robert Armour. 1898. 18 p. MOLLUS-DC no 30.                 **400**

Lusk,, William Thompson, 1838–1897.

War letters of William Thompson Lusk. Privately printed. New York, 1911. x, 304 p. plates (1 illus., 2 maps, ports.). 25cm.

Coulter 300.                        NN  **401**

New York. Monuments Commission.

. . . Report of the New York Monuments commission on the dedication of monument to the seventy-ninth regiment Highlanders, New York volunteers, Knoxville, Tenn., September 23, 1918. Albany, J. B. Lyons, printers, 1919. 56 p. front. (illus.), plate (port.). 23cm.

DLC NN  **402**

At head of title: Legislative document no. 71, State of New York.

Todd, William

The Seventy-ninth Highlanders, New York volunteers in the War of the rebellion, 1861–1865, by William Todd (of Company B). Albany, Press of Brandow, Barton & co., 1886. xv, 513 p. illus., maps. 24cm.  DLC NN  **403**

Coulter 448. Roster of officers 492–9.

Severin, John Powers and Frederick Porter Todd

79th regiment, New York state militia, 1860–61. *Military collector & historian* viii (Washington 1956) 20. col. plate (illus.).       **404**

### 80TH INFANTRY

#### 20th Infantry National Guard

*Mustered in: May 11, 1861, to April 23, 1861.*

*Mustered out: August 2, 1861.*

*Pfisterer 608–11.*

*Mustered in: Septetmber 20 to October 20, 1861.*

*Mustered out: January 29, 1866.*

*Pfisterer 2860–77.*

*Register serial no 29, 1080–1357.*

A brief history of the movements, operations and casualties of the "Ulster guard," 20th regiment N.Y.S. militia, while in the service of the United States, from April, 1861, to January, 1866, as contained in the Fourth annual report of the Bureau of military statistics of the State of New York. Republished for private distribution by Maj. Theodore B. Gates. Albany, Weed, Parsons and co., 1868. [232]–81. 23½cm.                       NHi  **405**

Services at the dedication of the monument of the Twentieth New York state militia at Gettysburg, Pa., October 4th, 1888. Roundout, Kingston Freeman print, 1888. 48 p. front. (illus.). 21½cm. N NHi **405A**
"Errata" slip inserted.

Abbey, Henry, 1842–1911.
The Ulster guard at Gettysburg on the first three days of July, 1863, by Henry Abbey, a poem, read by the author, October 4, 1888, at the dedication of the battle-field monument of the Twentieth regiment, New York state militia, Eightieth N.Y. volunteers. Roundout, Kingston Freeman, 1888. 19 p. 22cm.
DNW **406**

. . . The Ulster guard at Gettysburg on the first three days of July, 1863, verses read by the author, Henry Abbey, October 4th, 1888, at the dedication of the battlefield monument to the Twentieth regiment of New York state militia, Eightieth New York volunteers. Second edition. Roundout, 1891. 23, (1) p. 19cm.
NHi **407**

Cook, John Darwin Shepard
Personal reminiscences of Gettysburg, a paper read before the Kansas commandery of the Military order of the loyal legion of the United States, December 12, 1903, by John D. S. Cook, Captain 20th N.Y.S.M.; 80th N.Y. 24 p. 21½cm. DLC **408**
Also published as *MOLLUS-Kan* 320–41. On cover: War paper no. 24.

De Peyster, John Watts, 1821–1907.
Address delivered Wednesday, 28th November, 1866, in Feller's hall, Madalin, Township of Red Hook, Duchess co., N.Y., by Brevet Maj.-Gen. J. Watts De Peyster (S.N.Y.), upon the occasion of the inauguration of a monument erected by "this immediate neighborhood (Tivoli-Madalin) to her defenders who lost their lives in suppressing the slaveholders' rebellion and in sustaining the government of the people, for the people, by the people." . . . New York, 1867. 130, xx, lx p. 21cm.
DLC NN **409**
Title and imprint from cover. Two hundred copies printed as manuscript for private distribution by order of the "Soldiers' monument association." Supplementary pages include Annual report of the movements, service and discipline of the "Ulster guard" . . . 1862–1865.

Gates, Theodore Burr
The "Ulster guard" [20th N.Y. state militia] and the War of the rebellion, embracing a history of the early organization of the Regiment, its three months' service, its reorganization and subsequent service . . . by Theodore

B. Gates, Col. and Bvt. Brig. Gen., U.S.V. New York, Benj. H. Tyrrel, 1879. xxiii, 619 p. 23cm.
DLC NN **410**
Text is identical with Title 411. Coulter 179.

—— The War of the rebellion, with a full and critical history of the first battle of Bull run, organization of the Army of the Potomac, march to and return from Centreville, embarkation for the Peninsula, operations of the First army, corps, campaigns and battles of the Army of Virginia . . . New and illustrated edition. By Theodore B. Gates. New York, P. F. McBreen, 1884. viii, [7]–619 p. plates (illus., 2 maps, ports.). 23½cm. DLC NN **411**
Text is identical with Title 410.

Lounsbery, William
The Ulster regiment in the "Great rebellion." *Collections of the Ulster historical society* L (1860/62) 210–28. **412**

Vail, Enos Ballard, 1843–
Reminiscences of a boy in the Civil war, by Enos B. Vail. [Brooklyn] Printed by the author for private distribution, 1915. 159 p. front. (port.). 23½cm. MiU **413**

## 81ST INFANTRY

*Mustered in: December 20, 1861 to February 20, 1862.*

*Mustered out: August 31, 1865.*

*Pfisterer 2877–97.*

*Register serial no 30, 1–246.*

De Forest, Bartholomew S
Random sketches and wandering thoughts; or, what I saw in camp, on the march, the bivouac, the battle field and hospital, while with the army in Virginia, North and South Carolina, during the late rebellion. With a historical sketch of the Second Oswego regiment. Eighty-first New York state v.i., a record of all its officers and roster of its enlisted men, also, an appendix, by B. S. De Forest, late First Lieutenant and R.Q.M. Albany, Avery Herrick, 1866. 324 p. plate (illus.). 19cm.
DLC NN **414**
Coulter 122. Unit roster 269–89.

McFarlane, Carrington
Reminiscences of an army surgeon. Oswego, Lake City print shop, 1912. 82 p. front. (2 ports.). 21½cm. CtY **414A**
Mustered in 81st New York infantry, November 1, 1861; discharged for promotion to 115th New York infantry, August 15, 1863; mustered out, June 17, 1865.

## 82ND INFANTRY

*2nd Infantry National Guard*

*Mustered in: May 20 to June 7, 1861.*
*Received its numerical designation, 82nd:*
*December 7, 1861.*
*Mustered out: June 25, 1864.*
*Pfisterer 2897–2913.*
*Register serial no 30, 247–493.*

Shepard, Charles O
In a Bowery regiment, the story of my first command, by Captain Musgrove Davis (Charles O. Shepard). In Tales from McClure's. War, being true stories of camp and battlefield (1898) 17–69. illus.                   ***414B***

## 83RD INFANTRY

*9th Infantry National Guard*

*Mustered in: June 8, 1861.*
*Mustered out: June 23, 1864.*
*Pfisterer 2913–29.*
*Register serial no 30, 494–753.*

. . . Society of war veterans, Ninth regiment, New York state militia, (83d New York volunteers.). . . . Hartford, Star print. co., 1887. 19, (1) p. 23½cm.          CSmH CtHi P   ***415***
At head of title: "Camp Cameron," June 8, 1861, to "Cold harbor," June 8, 1864.

Souvenir opening of the Armory. Ninth regiment, N.G., N.Y., New York, February 22d 1897. . . . New York, Freytag press [1897] [120] p. ports 24 × 30½cm.      NHi   ***416***
Advertising matter included. Chapter II, war services, 1861–1864.

Jaques, John Wesley
Three years' campaign of the Ninth N.Y.-S.M., during the Southern rebellion, by John W. Jaques, formerly of Company D. New York, Hilton & co., 1865. 19, 47, (1) p. 19cm.
                                         DLC NN   ***417***
"Records of the Ninth regiment, New-York state militia," 47 p.

Potter, Orlando Brunson, 1823–1894.
Oration of Orlando B. Potter on the dedication of the monument erected by the Ninth regiment, N.G.S.N.Y., Eighty-third volunteers, Sunday, July 1st, 1888, at Gettysburg, Pennsylvania. 14 p. 23cm.     DLC NHi NN   ***418***

Todd, William
History of the Ninth regiment, N.Y.S.M., N.G.S.N.Y. (Eighty-third N.Y. volunteers), 1845–1888. Historian, George A. Hussey. Editor, William Todd. Published under the aus-

pices of Veterans of the Regiment. New York [J. S. Ogilvie] 1889. xvi, 737 p. front. (illus.), plates (maps, plan, ports.). 24½cm.
Unit roster 400–501.          DLC NN   ***419***

## 84TH INFANTRY

*14th Infantry National Guard*

*Mustered in: May to August, 1861.*
*Received its numerical designation, 84th,*
*December 7, 1861.*
*Mustered out: June 6, 1864.*
*Pfisterer 2929–43.*
*Register serial no 30, 754–968.*

Souvenir of the dedication of the Brooklyn Fourteenth regiment monument on the battlefield of Gettysburg, Pa., October 19th, 1887. New York, Henry Bessey, printer, 1887. 30 p. front. (illus.). 22½cm.          DLC   ***420***

Nadal, Bernard Harrison, 1812–1870.
The Christian boy soldier. The funeral sermon of Joseph E. Darrow, preached in Sands street Methodist Episcopal church, Brooklyn, on the 27th October, 1861, by B. H. Nadal. New York, Steam print. house, 1862. 28 p. 18½cm.          CSmH NN   ***420A***

Ostrander, Peter Wilson, 1829–
A narrative of the work of the Commission appointed by an Act of the Legislature of the State of New York, passed in the session of 1906: In purchasing a site and erecting thereon a monument in memory of the men who fell in the battles of the First and Second Bull run, Gainesville and Groveton, by Peter W. Ostrander, one of the Commissioners. Read before the 14th regiment war veterans' association and published by the Association. [Brooklyn, Eagle press] 1907. 47 p. illus. 23½cm.
                                         DLC NN   ***421***

Tevis, C          V
. . . The history of the fighting Fourteenth. Published in commemoration of the fiftieth anniversary of the muster of the Regiment into the United States service, May 23, 1861. [New York, Brooklyn Eagle press, 1911] 366, (1) p. col. front. (illus.), illus., ports. 28cm.
                                         DLC NN   ***422***
"Compiled by C. V. Tevis and D. R. Marquis." Unit roster [257]–366. At head of title: 1861 14th 1911.

Grube, Harry Thomson and George Woodbridge
14th regiment New York state militia, 1861–1864. *Military collector & historian* x (Washington 1958) 80–1. col. plate (illus.).   ***423***

**Low, Seth, 1850–1916.**
Address delivered by Seth Low, at Gettysburg, October 19, 1887, at the dedication of the soldiers' monument to the Fourteenth regiment of Brooklyn. New York, Henry Bessey, printer [1887] 15 p. 23cm.    DLC    *424*
Title and imprint from cover.

**Michell, Harry W**
"The fighting Fourteenth." *Brooklyn advance* xi (1885) 253–6; xii (1885) 116–20.    *424A*
Contents: The battle of South mountain; the battle of Antietam.

**New York State.**
Dedication of monument to the Fourteenth Brooklyn, N.Y.S.M. (Eighty-fourth N.Y. vols.) Antietam, Md., September 17, 1915. . . . Albany, J. B. Lyons co., printers, 1916. 29 p. front. (illus.). 23cm.    DLC NN    *424B*

### 84th Infantry (National Guard)

*Left the State: July 3, 1863.*
*Mustered out: August 4, 1863.*
*Mustered in: July 12, 1864.*
*Mustered out: October 29, 1864.*
*Pfisterer 706–11.*

### 85TH INFANTRY

*Mustered in: August to December, 1861.*
*Mustered out: June 27, 1865.*
*Pfisterer 2943–54.*
*Register serial no 30, 969–1128.*

**Langworthy, Daniel Avery, 1832–**
Reminiscences of a prisoner of war and his escape, by Daniel Avery Langworthy, late Captain 85th N.Y. Minneapolis, Minn., Byron print. co., 1915. 74 p. plates (illus., ports.). 21½cm.    NN    *425*

**Smith, William M**
The siege and capture of Plymouth, an address by Surgeon William M. Smith. *MOLLUS-NY* i 322–43.    *426*

### 86TH INFANTRY

*Mustered in: November 20, 1861.*
*Mustered out: June 27, 1865.*
*Pfisterer 2954–69.*
*Register serial no 30, 1129–1322.*

**Rathbun, Isaac R**
A Civil war diary, the diary of Isaac R. Rathbun, Co. D, 86th N.Y. volunteers, Aug. 23, 1862 — Jan. 30, 1863. Lawrence R. Cavanaugh, ed. *NYH* xxxvi (1955) 336–45.    *427*

### 87TH INFANTRY

*Mustered in: October to December, 1861.*
*Consolidated with 40th regiment of infantry: September 6, 1862.*
*Pfisterer 2969–77.*
*Register serial no 30, 1323–1446.*

**Tanner, James, 1844–1927.**
Experiences of a wounded soldier at the second battle of Bull run, by James Tanner. 1927. 121–39. 25½cm.    IHi    *428*
"Reprinted from Military surgeon for February 1927." Title from cover.

See also Title 47.

### 88TH INFANTRY

*Mustered in: September 1861 to January 1862.*
*Mustered out: June 30, 1865.*
*Pfisterer 2977–92.*
*Register serial no 30, 1–171.*

Memorial monument erected on the battlefield of Gettysburg to Very Rev. William Corby. Philadelphia, Catholic Alumni Sodality [Press of Allen, Lane & Scott] 1911. 36 p. plates (fold. facs., illus., ports.). 23cm.    MeHi    *429*
Title and imprint from cover.

**Corby, William, 1833–1897.**
Memoirs of Chaplain life, by very Rev. W. Corby. Three years Chaplain in the famous Irish brigade, "Army of the Potomac." Chicago, La Monte, O'Donnell & co., printers, 1893 391 p. plates (illus., ports.). 20½cm.
Coulter 95.    NN    *430*

—— —— Notre Dame, Ind., "Scholastic" press, 1894. 391 p. plates (illus., ports.). 20½cm.    DLC    *431*

### 89TH INFANTRY

*Mustered in: December 4, 1861.*
*Mustered out: August 3, 1865.*
*Pfisterer 2992–3003.*
*Register serial no 30, 172–341.*

### 90TH INFANTRY

*Mustered in: September to December 1861.*
*Mustered out: February 9, 1866.*
*Pfisterer 3003–17.*
*Register serial no 30, 342–551.*

*90th Infantry, continued*

**M'Cann, Thomas H**
The campaigns of the Civil war in the United States of America, 1861–1865, by Thomas H. M'Cann, Sergeant of Company "C," Ninetieth regiment, New York. [Hoboken, N. J., Hudson Observer job print, 1915] 223, 9 p. front. (2 ports.). 24cm.　　NN　**432**
"This story appeared originally in the Hudson observer." "Index," 9 p.

## 91ST INFANTRY

*Mustered in: September to December 1861.*
*Mustered out: July 3, 1865.*
*Pfisterer 3018–32.*
*Register serial no 31, 552–908.*

Company B, 91st regiment New York vol. infantry soldiers' memorial. Cincinnati, Ehrgott, Forbriger & co., lithographers, c1863. col. illus. broadside 56 × 45cm.　　NHi　**433**
Copyright by J. W. Waterman.

. . . Reunion of the 91st regiment, N.Y. veteran volunteers at Albany, N.Y., December 20th 1882. Albany, Wentworth, 1882. 24, (1) p. 22cm.　　NN　**434**
"First annual reunion." At head of title: 1861. 1882.

## 92ND INFANTRY

*Mustered in: January 1, 1862.*
*Mustered out: January 7, 1865.*
*Pfisterer 3032–41.*
*Register serial no 31, 909–1051.*

A prison song, lines supposed to be written by Dr. Sutherland, a "live Yankee" of the 92nd N.Y. regiment, who was captured by the Rebels, during the battle of "Fair Oaks," on the 31st May, 1862, and confined (with many more) in "Dixie's sunny land," during the summer and part of the autumn of 1862, being a correct history of his capture and their confinement, treatment and suffering while prisoners, also, a hit at the habits and customs of the Southern Confederacy. Hermon, 1862. broadside, 48 × 30½cm.　　MnHi　**435**
Copyright notice on paster.

## 93RD INFANTRY

*Mustered in: October 1861 to January 1862.*
*Mustered out: June 29, 1865.*
*Pfisterer 3041–59.*
*Register serial no 31, 1052–1333.*

Corser, Elwood Spencer, 1835–1917.
"A day with the Confederates," by Lieutenant Elwood S. Corser. *MOLLUS-Minn* i 364–78.　　**43**

—— Record of the life of Elwood Spence Corser of John A. Rawlins post no. 126, written for the records of the Post. Minneapolis [W. F Black & co., printers] 1911. 23 p. 2 ports 19½cm.　　MnHi　**43**

King, David H　　　1835–
History of the Ninety-third regiment, New York volunteer infantry, 1861–1865. Compiled by David H. King, A. Judson Gibbs and Jay H. Northrup. Published by the Association o the 93d N.Y.S.V. vols. Milwaukee, Wis., Swain & Tate co., printers, 1895. xii, [13]–639 p plates (illus., 1 col; 2 maps, ports.). 23cm.
Unit roster 127–256.　　DLC NN　**43**

Robertson, Robert Stoddart, 1839–1906.
The escape of Grant and Meade [May 7 1864] a correction of history. *Magazine o American history* xix (New York 1888) 248–51.　　**43**

——From Spottsylvania onward, by Captain R. S. Robertson. *MOLLUS-Ind* 344–58.　　**44(**

—— From the Wilderness to Spottsylvania, a paper read before the Ohio commandery of the Military order of the loyal legion of the United States, by Robert Stoddart Robertson, late 1st Lieut. 93rd New York. Cincinnati, Henry C Sherick, 1884. 35 p. 23cm.　　NHi NN　**44**
Also published as *Mollus-Ohio* i 252–92.

—— Personal recollections of the war, a record of service with the Ninety-third New York vol infantry and the First brigade, First division Second corps, Army of the Potomac, by Rober Stoddart Robertson. Milwaukee, Wis., Swain & Tate co., printers, 1895. 126 p. front. (port.). 23cm.　　NHi NN　**44**
On cover: War memories.

*93rd Infantry (National Guard)*

*Mustered in: July 20, 1864.*
*Mustered out: November 1, 1864.*
*Pfisterer 712–14.*

## 94TH INFANTRY

*Mustered in: March 10, 1862.*
*Mustered out: July 18, 1865.*
*Pfisterer 3059–79.*
*Register serial no 32, 1–262.*

See Title 273A.

## 95TH INFANTRY

*Mustered in: November 1861 to March 1862.*
*Mustered out: July 16, 1865.*
*Pfisterer 3079–94.*
*Register serial no 32, 263–502.*

McCowan, Archibald
The prisoners of war, a reminiscence of the rebellion, by Archibald McCowan. . . . New York, Abbey press [1901] 187 p. front. (port.). 19cm.                    MB    *443*

## 96TH INFANTRY

*Mustered in: February 20 to March 7, 1862.*
*Mustered out: February 6, 1866.*
*Pfisterer 3094–3111.*
*Register serial no 32, 503–736.*

## 97TH INFANTRY

*Mustered in: February 18, 1862.*
*Mustered out: July 18, 1865.*
*Pfisterer 3111–27.*
*Register serial no 32, 737–1017.*

Backus, Clarence Walworth, 1846–1920.
Closing war scenes. *Magazine of history* xx (New York 1915) 251–9.          *444*

Hall, Isaac
History of the Ninety-seventh regiment, New York volunteers, ("Conkling rifles,") in the War for the Union, by Isaac Hall. Utica, L. C. Childs & Son, 1890. vii, 477 p. plates (ilus., maps, ports.). 24cm.      DLC NN   *445*
Unit roster 345–453.

Hough, Franklin Benjamin, 1822–1885.
History of Duryee's brigade, during the campaign in Virginia under Gen. Pope, and in Maryland under Gen. McClellan, and the summer and autumn of 1862, by Franklin B. Hough. Albany, J. Munsell, 1864. vi, [9]–200 p. front. (port.). 23½cm.   DLC NHi NN  *446*
The author was Surgeon of the 97th infantry, July 3, 1862 – March 10, 1863.

Snow, Archibald B
A waif of the Wilderness, a story of the war, by Capt. Arch B. Snow. Gouverneur, Grand Army Journal presses, 1896. 20 p. 22½cm.                    NN   *447*

See also Titles 15 and 244.

## 98TH INFANTRY

*Mustered in: February 1–6, 1862.*
*Mustered out: August 31, 1865.*
*Pfisterer 3127–43.*
*Register serial no 32, 1018–1203.*

Kreutzer, William
Notes and observations made during four years of service with the Ninety-eighth N.Y. volunteers, in the war of 1861, by William Kreutzer, Colonel. Philadelphia, Grant, Faires & Rodgers, printers, 1878. 368 p. illus., ports., plates (2 maps, ports.). 22cm.
DLC NN   *448*

### 98th Infantry (National Guard)

*Mustered in: August 10, 1864.*
*Mustered out: December 22, 1864.*
*Pfisterer 714–716.*

## 99TH INFANTRY

*Organized as a naval brigade: May 28, 1861.*
*Reorganized as an infantry regiment: August 21, 1861.*
*Mustered out: July 15, 1865.*
*Pfisterer 3143–56.*
*Register serial no 32, 1204–1382.*

History of the Naval brigade, 99th N.Y. volunteers, Union coast guard, 1861–1865. Historian, Philip Corell. Published under the auspices of the Regimental veteran association. New York, 1905. 1 v. illus. 26cm.
DLC NHi NN   *449*
A collection of 28 articles assembled with a title page and table of contents and bound. The letter of presentation in NHi's copy has a statement that "only 73 copies of the history were bound." On spine: 99th reg't N.Y.S. vol. infantry. War reminiscences. Unit roster included.

Lopez, Joseph H
Capture, escape and re-capture of Joseph E. Lopez, Co. F, 99th N.Y. vols., Andersonville, Ga., 1864–65. [189–] 19 p.       *450*
Included in Title 449.

Mendenhall, John B
The second Peninsula campaign and its connection with the battle of Gettysburg. [189–] 24 p.                    *451*
Included in Title 449.

### 99th Infantry (National Guard)

*Mustered in: August 2, 1864.*
*Mustered out: November 9, 1864.*
*Pfisterer 717–19.*

## 100TH INFANTRY

*Mustered in September 1861 to January 1862.*

*Mustered out: August 28, 1865.*

*Pfisterer 3156–73.*

*Register serial no 33, 1–279.*

Proceedings of the . . . reunions(s) of the 100th N.Y. veteran association. . . . ɪ–ʟᴠ 1887–1941.
NBuHi **452**

Hazard, George S
Introduction to the records of the Buffalo Board of trade regiment, 100th N.Y.S. vol's. Compiled and presented to the Buffalo historical society, by George S. Hazard. [Buffalo] 1889. 15 folios. 20½cm. mimeographed.
NHi **453**

Stoddard, George N
The 100th regiment on Folly island, from the diary of Private George N. Stoddard. *Niagara frontier* ɪ (Buffalo 1954) 77–81, 113–16. **454**

Stowits, George H          1822–
History of the One hundreth regiment of New York state volunteers, being a record of its services from its muster in to its muster out, its muster in roll, roll of commissions, recruits furnished through the Board of trade of the City of Buffalo, and short sketches of deceased and surviving officers, by Geo. H. Stowits, late Major. Buffalo, Print. house of Matthews & Warren, 1870. xxix, [25]–424 p. plates (2 illus., ports.). 18½cm.          DLC NN **455**
Commissioned officers, 407–09; Muster in roll, 410–20; List of names recruited by the Board of trade, from August 1, 1862, to October 1, 1862. 421–4.

## 101ST INFANTRY

*Mustered in: September 2, 1861 to February 28, 1862.*

*Transferred to 37th regiment of infantry: December 24, 1862.*

*Pfisterer 3174–84.*

*Register serial no 33, 280–438.*

Ford, Henry E          1839–
History of the 101st regiment, by Lieut. H. E. Ford. Syracuse [Press of Times pub. co.] 155 p. front. (port.), ports. 22½cm.
DLC NN **456**
Contents: History of the Regiment [to 1868] [7]–41; Biographical sketches 42–132; Unit roster 134–55.

Nichols, Norman K          –1915.
The reluctant warrior, the diary of N. K. Nichols [edited by] T. Harry Williams. *Civil war history* ɪɪɪ (Iowa City 1957) 17–39. **457**

## 102ND INFANTRY

*Mustered in: September 9, 1861 to April 5, 1862.*

*Mustered out: July 21, 1865.*

*Pfisterer 3184–3201.*

*Register serial no 33, 439–697.*

Howe, Thomas H
Adventures of an escaped Union soldier from Andersonville prison in 1864. San Francisco, H. S. Crocker & co., printers, 1886. 48 p. port. on cover. 22cm.          MB **458**
On cover: Dedicated to the Grand army of the Republic . . . by Thomas H. Howe.

Seeley, Napoleon Bonapart
Stories of the Civil war in prose and poem. [n. p., c1905] 51 p. front. (port.). 18½cm.
NN **459**
Mustered in 178th New York infantry, January 29, 1862; transferred to 102nd New York infantry, July 12, 1864; mustered out, July 21, 1865.

### 102nd Infantry (National Guard)

*Mustered in: August 6, 1864.*

*Mustered out: November 13, 1864.*

*Pfisterer 719–22.*

See Title 205.

## 103RD INFANTRY

*Mustered in: November 1861 to March 1862.*

*Mustered out: December 7, 1865.*

*Pfisterer 3201–19.*

*Register serial no 33, 698–878.*

Kimball, Orville Samuel, 1842–
History and personal sketches of Company I, 103 N.Y.S.V., 1862–1864. Elmira, Facts print. co., 1900. 161 p. plates (ports.). 21cm.
DLC NN **460**
Personal sketches," 66–161. "Company I veteran association, its organization and meetings" [1888–1899] 58–66.

## 104TH INFANTRY

*Mustered in: September 1861 to March 1862.*

*Mustered out: July 17, 1865.*

*Pfisterer 3219–33.*

*Register serial no 33, 879–1072.*

New York. Monuments Commission for the Battlefields of Gettysburg, Chattanooga and Antietam.
. . . Report of the New York Monuments commission on the dedication of monument to

the One hundred and fourth New York volunteer regiment (Wadsworth guards), Antietam, Md., September 27, 1917. Albany, J. B. Lyons co., printers, 1918. 26 p. front. (illus.). 23cm.
DLC  *461*

At head of title: State of New York. Senate document no. 59.

Starr, George H
In and out of Confederate prisons, a paper read by Captain Geo. H. Starr. 1892. *MOLLUS-NY* II 64–103.                    *462*

### 105TH INFANTRY

*Mustered in: November 1861 to March 1862.*
*Consolidated with 94th regiment of infantry: March 10, 1863.*
*Pfisterer 3233–42.*
*Register serial no 33, 1073–1203.*

### 106TH INFANTRY

*Mustered in: August 27, 1862.*
*Mustered out: June 27, 1865.*
*Pfisterer 3242–57.*
*Register serial no 33, 1204–1381.*

Thompson, Joseph Parrish, 1819–1879.
The Sergeant's memorial, by his father. New York, Anson D. F. Randolph, 1863. 242 p. front. (port.). 15cm.                    NN  *463*

—— New York, Anson D. F. Randolph, 1863. 80 p. front. (port.). 13cm.        DLC  *464*

"An abridgement . . . prepared expressly for circulation in the army." On back cover: Presented by the United States Christian commission. Another printing 1864 (DLC).

See also Title 92A.

### 107TH INFANTRY

*Mustered in: August 13, 1862.*
*Mustered out: June 5, 1865.*
*Pfisterer 3257–68.*
*Register serial no 34, 1–172.*

### 108TH INFANTRY

*Mustered in: August 18, 1862.*
*Mustered out: May 28, 1865.*
*Pfisterer 3269–82.*
*Register serial no 34, 173–324.*

Pierce, Francis Edwin, 1833–
Civil war letters of Francis Edwin Pierce of the 108th New York volunteer infantry. *Roch-*

*ester historical society publications* XXII (1944) 150–73.                    *465*

Washburn, George H        1843–1905.
A complete military history and record of the 108th regiment N.Y. vols., from 1862 to 1894, together with roster, letters, Rebel oaths of allegiance, Rebel passes, reminiscences, life sketches, photographs, etc. etc., by Private Geo. H. Washburn, Co. D. Rochester [Press of E. R. Andrews] 1894. 521 p. plates (illus., ports.). 28cm.                    DLC NN  *466*

### 109TH INFANTRY

*Mustered in: August 27, 1862.*
*Mustered out: June 4, 1865.*
*Pfisterer 3282–94.*
*Register serial no 34, 325–510.*

### 110TH INFANTRY

*Mustered in: August 25, 1862.*
*Mustered out: August 28, 1865.*
*Pfisterer 3294–3305.*
*Register serial no 34, 511–670.*

### 111TH INFANTRY

*Mustered in: August 20, 1862.*
*Mustered out: June 4, 1865.*
*Pfisterer 3305–20.*
*Register serial no 34, 671–920.*

Proceedings of the reunion of the veterans of the 111th and the 126th reg'ts N.Y. vols. held at Gettysburg, Pa., June 10 and 11, 1886. Reported by W. G. Lightfoote. [Canandaigua, Times print. house, 1886] 38 p. 23½cm.
DLC  *467*

New York. Assembly.
Proceedings of the Assembly of the State of New York, in relation to the death of James Haggerty, held at Capitol, January 20, 1888. [Troy] Troy press co., 1888. 25 p. front. (port.). 26cm.                    NHi  *468*

### 112TH INFANTRY

*Mustered in: September 11, 1862.*
*Mustered out: June 13, 1865.*
*Pfisterer 3320–35.*
*Register serial no 34, 931–1138.*

Hyde, William Lyman, 1819–1896.
History of the One hundred and twelfth regiment N.Y. volunteers, by Wm. L. Hyde, Chaplain of the Regiment. Fredonia, W. McKinstry & co., 1866. viii, [9]–214 p. plates (4 ports.). 21cm.                    DLC NN  *469*

Unit roster [149]–214.

## 113TH INFANTRY

*Mustered in: August 1862.*
*Designated 7th regiment of heavy artillery: December 19, 1862.*

## 114TH INFANTRY

*Mustered in: September 3, 1862.*
*Mustered out: June 8, 1865.*
*Pfisterer 3335–46.*
*Register serial no 35, 1–145.*

Beecher, Harris H
Record of the 114th regiment, N.Y.S.V. Where it went, what it saw, and what it did, by Dr. Harris H. Beecher, late Assistant-surgeon. Norwich, J. F. Hubbard, Jr., 1866. x, [11]–582 p. 2 plates (ports.). 19½cm.
Unit roster 534–82.     DLC NN    **470**

Curtis, Oscar H
Proceedings of the twenty-sixth annual reunion of the 114th N.Y. regimental association and dedicatory services at Winchester, Va., October 19, 1898, with a roster of the surviving members of the 114th regiment . . . Compiled by O. H. Curtis. Washington, Conwell print, 1899. 88 p. plates (illus.). 19cm.
                      MnHi    **471**

Fitts, James Franklin
Days with the knapsack. *Galaxy* ii (1866) 405–12.                    **472**

—— Facetiae of the war. *Galaxy* vi (1868) 320–7.                    **473**

—— In the enemy's lines [Lieut. Dennis Thompson at the battle of Cedar creek] *Galaxy* iv (1867) 700–09.          **474**

—— In the ranks at Cedar creek. *Galaxy* i (1866) 534–43.             **475**

—— A June day at Port Hudson. *Galaxy* ii (1866) 121–31.            **476**

—— The last battle of Winchester *Galaxy* ii (1866) 322–32.           **477**

—— Mosby and his men. *Galaxy* ii (1866) 643–51.               **478**

—— The story of a mutiny. *Galaxy* x (1870) 224–8.              **478A**

Pellet, Elias Porter, 1837–
History of the 114th regiment, New York state volunteers, containing a perfect record of its services, embracing all its marches, campaigns, battles, sieges and sea-voyages, with a biographical sketch of each officer, and a complete register of the Regiment, wherein appears the name of every officer and enlisted man who has ever belonged to the same, with full remarks relating thereto, by Brevet-Major Elias P. Pellet, Norwich, Telegraph & Chronicle power press print, 1866. viii, ii 406 p. 20cm.
Unit roster [381]–403.     DLC NN    **479**

## 115TH INFANTRY

*Mustered in: August 26, 1862.*
*Mustered out: June 17, 1865.*
*Pfisterer 3346–58.*
*Register serial no 35, 146–365.*

Clark, James H             1842–
The iron hearted regiment, being an account of the battles, marches and gallant deeds performed by the 115th regiment N.Y. vols. Also a list of the dead and wounded, an account of hundreds of brave men shot on a score of hard fought fields of strife, a complete statement of Harper's Ferry surrender, sketches of the officers, a history of the flags and those who bore them, together with touching incidents, thrilling adventures, amusing scenes . . . by James H. Clark, late First Lieutenant, Company H, 115th N.Y.V. Albany, J. Munsell, 1865. xii, 337 p. 18½cm.    DLC NN    **480**
Coulter 80.

See Title 414A.

## 116TH INFANTRY

*Mustered in: August 10 to September 5, 1862.*
*Mustered out: June 8, 1865.*
*Pfisterer 3359–71.*
*Register serial no 35, 366–502.*

Proceedings of the first re-union of the One hundred and sixteenth New York volunteers, May 21, 1873. Buffalo, Print. house of Matthews & Warren, 1873. 16 p. 22½cm.
Title and imprint from cover.      NHi    **481**

Souvenir, 116th reg't. New York vol. infantry, twenty-fifth anniversary of muster into the U.S. service. Buffalo, Hass & Klein, printers [1887] [4] p. 24cm.           NBuHi    **481A**
Includes list of first eight reunions.

Clark, Orton S
The One hundred and sixteenth regiment of New York state volunteers, being a complete history of its organization and of its nearly three years of active service in the great rebellion, to which is appended memorial sketches, and a muster roll of the Regiment, containing the name of every man connected with it, by Orton S. Clark, late Captain Co. H. Buffalo, Print. house of Matthews & Warren, 1868. xii, [13]–348 p. front. (port.). 19cm.
Unit roster 310–48.     DLC NN    **482**

—— Sheridan's Shenandoah valley campaign. 1903. *MOLLUS-Minn* vi 28–51.            *483*

## 117TH INFANTRY

*Mustered in: August 8, 1862.*
*Mustered out: June 8, 1865.*
*Pfisterer 3371–84.*
*Register serial no 35, 503–694.*

Complete roster of the 117th N.Y. volunteers (Fourth Oneida county regiment), revised April 1, 1914, with a brief historical sketch, giving the name of every one enlisting in the Regiment, the address of survivors, and the date of death of all deceased members so far as can be ascertained. Compiled and published by James J. Guernsey of "E" company. Rome [1914] 56 p. 16½cm.            NN   *484*
"Brief historical sketch," [3]–13.

Mowris, James A
A history of the One hundred and seventeenth regiment N.Y. volunteers (Fourth Oneida), from the date of its organization, August, 1862, till that of its muster out, June, 1865, by J. A. Mowris, Regimental Surgeon. Hartford, Conn., Case, Lockwood and co., printers, 1866. xi, [12]–315 p. 20½cm.
            DLC NN   *485*
Coulter 335. "Appendix, a detail of prison life at Andersonville," by Corporal Alexander McLean, [291]–315. Unit roster 231–84.

See also Title 244.

## 118TH INFANTRY

*Mustered in: August 18–20, 1862.*
*Mustered out: June 13, 1865.*
*Pfisterer 3384–97.*
*Register serial no 35, 695–866.*

Cunningham, John Lovell, 1840–
Three years with the Adirondack regiment, 118th New York volunteers infantry, from the diaries and other memoranda of John L. Cunningham, Major 118th New York volunteer infantry. For private circulation. [Norwood, Mass., Plimpton press] 1920. v, 286 p. plates (ports.). 21cm.            NN   *486*
Unit roster 213–86. Coulter 105.

## 119TH INFANTRY

*Mustered in: September 4, 1862.*
*Mustered out: June 7, 1865.*
*Pfisterer 3397–3419.*
*Register serial no 35, 867–991.*

Ceremonies and addresses at the dedication of a monument by the 119th regiment, N.Y. state vols., at Gettysburg, July 3, 1888. Boston, Wright & Potter print. co., 1889. 35 p. plates (illus., ports.). 24½cm.      DLC NN   *487*

Dodge, Theodore Ayrault, 1842–1909.
Address at the unveiling of the monument of the 119th regiment New York volunteers on the battle field of Gettysburg, July 4, 1888.
In Title 487C, 181–91.            *487B*

—— Addresses and reviews, by T. A. D. Privately printed. Boston, Henry S. Dunn, 1898. viii, 490 p. 23cm.            NN   *487C*

—— The battle of Chancellorsville, by Colonel Theodore A. Dodge. *Southern historical society papers* xiv (Richmond 1886) 276–92.
            *488*

—— The Gettysburg campaign. *US* xiii (1885) 1–21.            *489*

—— Left wounded on the field. *Putnam's magazine* ns iv (New York 1869) 317–26.   *490*

—— The romances of Chancellorsville. *PM-HSM* iii (1886) 192–218.            *491*

—— Saaret og fanget, en episode af den nordamerikanske borgerkrig. *Rundt paa jorden* (Copenhagen 1870) 111–33.            *492*

—— Was either the better soldier? *Century magazine* xl (1890) 144–8.            *493*

## 120TH INFANTRY

*Mustered in: August 22, 1862.*
*Mustered out: June 3, 1865.*
*Pfisterer 3410–23.*
*Register serial no 35, 992–1189.*

The colors of the One hundred and twentieth. *Olde Ulster* vii (Kingston 1911) 149–51. 1 illus.
            *494*

The departure of the One hundred and twentieth. *Olde Ulster* vii (Kingston 1911) 193–206. port.            *495*

Fiftieth anniversary of the muster into service of the One hundred and twentieth regiment, N.Y.V. in the War for the Union, celebrated at Kingston, New York, August 22nd, 1912. [Kingston, Freeman pub. co., 1912] 32 (3) p. plates (illus., ports.). 23½cm.      N   *496*
"Letters of regret . . . ; Members . . . present," (3) p.

Military register Company E, 120th regiment New York volunteers. Washington, D. C., Geo. M. Lankton [1865?] col. illus. broadside, 56 × 46cm.            MWiW   *497*
"Lithographed by A. Hoen & co., Baltimore."

*120th Infantry, continued*

Coutant, Charles T
General Sharpe and Lee's surrender. *Olde Ulster* VIII (Kingston 1912) 257–79. plates (ports.). **498**

Sharpe, George Henry, 1834–1900.
General Sharpe at the unveiling. *Olde Ulster* VIII (Kingston 1912) 321–31. plate (illus.). **499**

—— Lieut.-Colonel J. Rudolph Tappan, addresses delivered at the Music hall, Kingston, at the seventh annual meeting of the 120th regimental union, by General George H. Sharpe and General Theodore B. Gates. Kingston, Daily Freeman print. house, 1875. 26 p. 22½cm. NHi **499A**

Van Santvoord, Cornelius, 1816–1801.
The One hundred and twentieth regiment, New York state volunteers, a narrative of its services in the War for the Union, by C. Van Santvoord, Chaplain. Published by the One hundred and twentieth N.Y. regimental union. Roundout, Press of the Kingston Freeman, 1894. 327 p. 3 plates (illus., ports.). 23½cm.
Unit roster [233]–324. DLC NN **500**

Zabriskie, Francis Nicoll, 1832–1901.
The post of duty, a funeral discourse in memory of Capt. Lansing Hollister (120 regt. N.Y.S. vol.,) killed at the battle of Gettysburg, July 2d, 1863, by Rev. F. N. Zabriskie. Coxsackie, F. C. Dedrick, printer [1863] 20 p. 17½cm. DLC **501**

See also Title 96.

### 121ST INFANTRY

*Mustered in: August 13, 1862.*
*Mustered out: June 25, 1865.*
*Pfisterer 3423–39.*
*Register serial no 36, 1–214.*

Adams, John Ripley, 1802–1866.
Memorial and letters of Rev. John R. Adams, Chaplain of the Fifth Maine and the One hundred and twenty-first New York regiments during the War of the rebellion, serving from the beginning to its close . . . Privately printed. [Cambridge, Mass., University press] 1890. viii, 242 p. front. (mounted port.). 24cm. NN **502**
Prefatory note signed: John McGregor Adams [and] Albert Egerton Adams. Preface signed: Emily Adams Bancroft.

Best, Isaac O
History of the 121st New York state infantry, by Isaac O. Best. Chicago, Published by Lieut.

Jas. H. Smith [W. S. Conkey co.] 1921. x, 254 p.. plates (illus., ports.). 19½cm. DLC NN **503**

Hall, Henry Seymour
With the Sixth corps at Gettysburg, a paper prepared and read before the Kansas commandery of the Military order of the loyal legion of the United States, Thursday, November 5, 1896, by H. Seymour Hall. Lawrence, Journal press, 1896. 18 p. 22cm. DLC NN **504**
On cover: War paper. "Paper no. 6 by H. Seymour Hall." Also published as *MOLLUS-Kan* 250–66.

Michie, Peter Smith, –1901.
The life and letters of Emory Upton, Colonel of the Fourth regiment of artillery, by Peter S. Michie. With an introduction by James Harrison Wilson. New York, D. Appleton and co., 1885. xxviii, 511 p. 2 plates (ports.). 19½cm. NN **505**
Upton was Colonel of the 121st New York infantry, October 23, 1862, to July 4, 1864.

Morse, Francis W
Personal experiences in the war of the great rebellion, from December, 1862, to July, 1865, by F. W. Morse, Major. Albany [Munsell, printer] 1866. 152 p. 23cm.
Coulter 333. DLC IHi MB **506**

Rice, Adam Clarke, 1840–1863.
The letters and writings of the late Lieut. Adam Clarke Rice, of the 121st regiment, N.Y. volunteers. Compiled and prepared by his brother, C. E. Rice. Little Falls, Journal & Courier press, 1864. 166 p. front. (port.). 20½cm. NHi **507**

See also Titles 15 and 244.

### 122ND INFANTRY

*Mustered in: August 28, 1862.*
*Mustered out: June 3, 1865.*
*Pfisterer 3439–54.*
*Register serial no 36, 215–350.*

Annual reunion of the 122d New York volunteers. . . . 1904 (NN), 1905 (DNW), 1907–1919 (NN). **508**

### 123RD INFANTRY

*Mustered in: September 4, 1862.*
*Mustered out: June 8, 1865.*
*Pfisterer 3454–64.*
*Register serial no 36, 351–499.*

Report of the Monument committee of the One hundred & twenty-third regiment New York infantry volunteers, 1st brig., 1st div., 20th corps, read at a meeting of the Regimental association at Argyle, N.Y., October 14, 1890. [Salem] Salem Axiom print, 1891. 21, 4 p. front. (illus.). 25cm.   DLC NHi NN   **509**

Morhous, Henry C
Reminiscences of the 123d regiment, N.Y.-S.V., giving a complete history of its three years service in the war, by Sergeant Henry C. Morhous. To which is added an appendix, containing the name, company, date of enlistment, and discharge of each man in the Regiment. Greenwich, People's journal book and job office, 1879. 220 p. 19cm.   NN   **510**
Unit roster 195–220.

### 124TH INFANTRY

*Mustered in: September 5, 1862.*
*Mustered out: June 3, 1865.*
*Pfisterer 3464–77.*
*Register serial no 36, 500–666.*

Roster of survivors of the 124th regt. N.Y. vol. infantry, August, 1891. 21 p. plates illus.). 22cm.   NHi   **511**

Roster of survivors of the 124th regt. N.Y. vol. infantry, August, 1894. [Brooklyn, Press of T. T. Donovan, 1894] 24 p. 18cm.   NHi   **512**

Weygant, Charles H                1839–1909.
History of the One hundred and twenty-fourth regiment, N.Y.S.V., by Charles H. Weygant. Newburgh, Journal print. house, 1877. vi, [7]–460 p. front. (port.), fold. chart. 24½cm.   DLC NN   **512A**
Muster in roll 17–29. Coulter 470.

### 125TH INFANTRY

*Mustered in: August 29, 1862.*
*Mustered out: June 5, 1865.*
*Pfisterer 3477–97.*
*Register serial no 36, 667–853.*

Jackson, Edward C
The bloody angle, by Captain Edward C. Jackson. *MOLLUS-Neb* i 258–62.   **513**

Lord, George A                1820–1888.
A short narrative and military experience of Corp. G. A. 'Lord, formerly a member of Company G, 125th reg't N.Y.V. Containing a four year's history of the War, the Constitution of the United States in full, a correct list of stamp duties, and also patriotic songs of the latest selection. Mr. A'Lord being honorably discharged while in the service by reason of disability is worthy of your patronage, and he

depends entirely upon the proceeds of his books for support of himself and family. [Troy, 1864] 80 p. 14½cm.   NN   **514**
Port. on title page: illus. on p 2 of cover.
MB has two undated issues with 64 p., one "Respectfully dedicated to Lieut.-Gen. U.S. Grant, the man of the day."

Simons, Ezra de Freest
A regimental history the One hundred and twenty-fifth New York state volunteers, by Chaplain Ezra D. Simons. New York, Published by Ezra D. Simmons [Judson print. co.] 1888. xxi, 352, xxix, (3) p. illus., maps, plates (ports.), ports. 24½cm.   DLC NN   **516**
"An alphabetical list of the battles of the Civil war, with dates," xxix p. Index (3) p. Unit roster [309]–52.

### 126TH INFANTRY

*Mustered in: August 22, 1862.*
*Mustered out: June 3, 1865.*
*Pfisterer 3497–3511.*
*Register serial no 36, 854–1025.*

Dedication of the monument to the 126th regiment N.Y. infantry on the battlefield of Gettysburg, October 3, 1888. Reported by W. G. Lightfoote. Canandaigua [1888] 44 p. front. (port.). 20cm.   DLC   **517**
On cover: The 126th New York infantry at Gettysburg.

Proceedings of the re-union of the 126th regiment, N.Y.V., held at Seneca point, Canandaigua lake, New York, August 22, 1867. 20, (1) p. 20½cm.   NHi   **518**

Proceedings of the re-union of the 126th regiment, N.Y.V., held at Phelps, Ontario county, N.Y., on the 22d day of August, 1868. Canandaigua, Printed at the Ontario County Times, 1868. 26 p. 22½cm.   DLC   **519**
See Title 467 for reunion of 1886.

Lounsbury, Thomas Raynesford, 1838–1915.
In the defenses of Washington. *Yale review* ns ii (New Haven 1913) 385–411.   **520**

Scott, Winfield
Pickett's charge as seen from the front line, a paper prepared and read before California commandery of the Military order of the loyal legion of the United States, February 8, 1888, by Chaplain Winfield Scott, late Captain 126th New York. 15 p. 22½cm.   NHi   **521**
On cover: War paper no. 1.

Willson, Arabella M
Disaster, struggle, triumph; adventures of 1000 "boys in Blue," from August, 1862, to June, 1865, by Mrs. Arabella M. Willson. Dedicated to the 126th regiment of New York state

*126th Infantry, continued*

volunteers. With an appendix containing a chronological record of the principal events in the history of the Regiment, and the personal history of its officers and enlisted men. Prepared by the Historical committee of the Regiment. Albany, Argus co., printers, 1870. 593 p. maps, plates (illus., maps, ports.). 23½cm.

DLC NN    **522**

"Biographical sketches," officers, non-commissioned officers and enlisted men by companies, [337]–582.

### 127TH INFANTRY

*Mustered in: September 8, 1862.*
*Mustered out: June 30, 1865.*
*Pfisterer 3511–21.*
*Register serial no 36, 1026–1161.*

Veteran association of the survivors of the 127th regiment N.Y. vols. organized at Riverhead, L. I.,, October 3d, 1889. . . . [1890] 40 p. 13 × 17½cm.    NHi    **523**

On cover: 127th regiment New York volunteers, Sept. 8th, 1862 – June 30th, 1865. Re-union, June 30th, 1890.

Abercrombie, John J
Fragment from the Army of the Potomac (read October 12, 1893). *MOLLUS-Ill* III 141–53.    **524**

Lott, Roy E
Huntington Civil war Co. E. *Long Island forum* XXII (Amityville 1959) 153–5. illus. **525**

McGrath, Franklin
The history of the 127th New York volunteers "Monitors" in the War for the preservation of the Union, September 8th, 1862, June 30th, 1865. Material collected and arranged by Franklin McGrath, Co. A. [n. p., 1898?] 222, (3) p. 2 illus., maps, plates (ports.). 22½cm.    DLC NN    **526**

Unit roster 183–222. Killed in action (3) p. "Errata" [4] p inserted.

Willis, Samuel B
Voices from the dead, a sermon preached March 26, 1865, in the Citadell square Baptist church, Charleston, S.C., before the 127th regiment, N.Y. vols. by Samuel B. Willis, Chaplain of the Regiment. New York, Thomas Daniels & Son, 1865. 16 p. 23cm.    NN    **527**

Woodford, Stewart Lyndon, 1835–1913.
The story of Fort Sumter, an address delivered by General Stewart L. Woodford. *MOLLUS-NY* I 258–84.    **528**

### 128TH INFANTRY

*Mustered in: September 4, 1862.*
*Mustered out: July 12, 1865.*
*Pfisterer 3521–32.*
*Register serial no 37, 1–150.*

128th regiment, a complete list [roster] compiled by M. P. Williams, editor *Hudson gazette*, and revised by the War committee. In The Hudson city and Columbia county directory for the year 1862–3, 178–208 **528A**

A resume of the services of the 128th regiment New York volunteers, from Sept. 4, '62, to Jan. 1, '64, with a list of losses, &c., &c. Baton Rouge, La., Printed at the Gazette and Comet book and job office, 1864. 15 p. 20cm.    NHi    **529**

Preface dated January 1st, 1864, and signed: James Smith, Colonel commanding.

De Peyster, John Watts, 1821–1907.
Address delivered at Hudson county, N.Y., 6th Sept., 1887, by Brevet Major General J. Watts de Peyster, to the 128th regiment, N.Y. vols., on the 25th anniversary of the departure of that regiment for the war. 4 p. 22cm.    NN    **530**

Caption title.

Hanaburgh, David Henry, 1839–1907.
History of the One hundred and twenty-eighth regiment, New York volunteers (U. S. infantry) in the late Civil war, by D. H. Hanaburgh, Chairman of the Committee appointed by the Regimental association. Poughkeepsie [Press of Enterprise pub. co.] 1894. xv, 280 p. front. (fold. plan), 1 illus., ports. 23½cm.

Muster-out roll 220–70.    DLC NN    **531**

Van Alstyne, Lawrence, 1839–
Diary of an enlisted man, by Lawrence Van Alstyne. New Haven, Tuttle, Morehouse & Taylor co., 1910. x, 348 p. front. (port.). 20cm.    NN    **532**

See also Title 409.

### 129TH INFANTRY

*Mustered in: August 22, 1862.*
*Designated 8th regiment of heavy artillery: November 19, 1862.*

### 130TH INFANTRY

*Mustered in: September 2, 1862.*
*Designated 19th regiment of cavalry: August 11, 1863.*

## 131ST INFANTRY

*Mustered in: September 6, 1862.*
*Mustered out: July 26, 1865.*
*Pfisterer 3532–42.*
*Register serial no 37, 152–283.*

Stearns, Albert
Reminiscences of the late war, by Captain Albert Stearns. Brooklyn, 1881. 44 p. 18cm.
Unit roster of Co. C, [41]–4.   DLC NN   **533**

## 132ND INFANTRY

*Mustered in: October 4, 1862.*
*Mustered out: June 29, 1865.*
*Pfisterer 3542–54.*
*Register serial no 37, 284–465.*

## 133RD INFANTRY

*Mustered in: September 24, 1862.*
*Mustered out: June 6, 1865.*
*Pfisterer 3554–65.*
*Register serial no 37, 466–595.*

## 134TH INFANTRY

*Mustered in: September 22, 1862.*
*Mustered out: June 10, 1865.*
*Pfisterer 3565–81.*
*Register serial no 37, 596–748.*

History of the 134th regiment, N.Y.S. vol., also a sketch of prison life. Schenectady, J. J. Marlett [n. d.] 41 p. 22½cm.   N   **534**
"Sketch of prison life," 31–41.

Levey, William T
The Blue and the Gray, a sketch of soldier life in camp and field in the army of the Civil war, by Wm. T. Levey. Schenectady, Roy Burton Myers, 1904. 53 p. 16½cm.   IHi   **535**

## 135TH INFANTRY

*Mustered in: September 2, 1862.*
*Designated 6th regiment of heavy artillery: October 3, 1862.*

## 136TH INFANTRY

*Mustered in: September 25, 1862.*
*Mustered out: June 13, 1865.*
*Pfisterer 3581–93.*
*Register serial no 37, 750–882.*

Havens, Lewis Clayton, 1873–1935.
Historical sketch of the 136th New York infantry, 1862–1865, by L. C. Havens. [Dalton, Burts print service] 1934. 21 p. 22cm.
Unit roster 9–19.   CtY   **535A**

Smith, Lucian A
Recollections of Gettysburg, by L. A. Smith, First Lieut. 136th N.Y. infantry,(read May 3, 1894). *MOLLUS-Mich* ii 297–308.   **536**

## 137TH INFANTRY

*Mustered in: September 25, 1862.*
*Mustered out: June 9, 1865.*
*Pfisterer 3593–3604.*
*Register serial no 37, 883–1028.*

## 138TH INFANTRY

*Mustered in: September 8, 1862.*
*Designated 9th regiment of heavy artillery: December 19, 1862.*

## 139TH INFANTRY

*Mustered in: September 9, 1862.*
*Mustered out: June 19, 1865.*
*Pfisterer 3604–15.*
*Register serial no 37, 1030–1172.*

## 140TH INFANTRY

*Mustered in: September 13, 1862.*
*Mustered out: June 3, 1865.*
*Pfisterer 3615–29.*
*Register serial no 38, 1–213.*

Cribben, Henry, 1834–1911.
The military memoirs of Captain Henry Cribben of the 140th New York volunteers. Edited by J. Clayton Youker. [Chicago] Privately printed [1911] xi, 154 p. front. (port.). 20cm.   WHi   **537**

Farley, Porter
Captain Farley's "Number nine," reminiscences by Porter Farley. In The attack and defense of Little Round Top, Gettysburg, July 2, 1863, by Oliver W. Norton, 1913, p 125–40.   **538**
"Is one of a series of papers written by Captain Farley describing the history of the One hundred and fortieth New York volunteers, published at intervals in a Rochester newspaper."

—— The 140th New York volunteers, Wilderness, May 5th, 1864. [Rochester, n. d.] 38 p. 15cm.   DNW NHi   **539**
Title from cover. "By Porter Farley, late Capt. 140th N.Y.V.," ms. note in DNW's copy.

*140th Infantry, continued*

*Farley, Porter, continued*

—— The 140th New York volunteers at Gettysburg. 1863. 1889. [Rochester, 1889] 14 p. 15cm.　　　　　　　　　DNW **540**

"With regards of Porter Farley, late Capt. 140th N.[Y.]" ms. note DNW's copy. "Roster of members and friends of the 140th regiment who went to Gettysburg, September 16, 1889," p 3 of cover.

—— Reminiscences of the 140th regiment New York volunteer infantry, by Porter Farley. *Rochester historical society publications* xxii (1944) 199–252.　　　　　　　　　**541**

"Only approximately a half of Porter Farley's Reminiscences of the 140th is reproduced here." NN has a photostat of the Reminiscences as originally published in the *Rochester democrat and chronicle*.

Seiser, Augustus Friedrich, 1823–1904.

August Seiser's Civil war diary. Foreword by Charles E. Seiser. *Rochester historical society publications* xxii (1944) 174–98.　　**542**

## 141ST INFANTRY

*Mustered in: September 11, 1862.*

*Mustered out: June 8, 1865.*

*Pfisterer 3630–42.*

*Register serial no 38, 214–365.*

## 142ND INFANTRY

*Mustered in: September 29, 1862.*

*Mustered out: June 7, 1865.*

*Pfisterer 3642–56.*

*Register serial no 38, 366–556.*

Curtis, Newton Martin, 1835–1910.

The capture of Fort Fisher, by Brevet Major General N. Martin Curtis. *MOLLUS-Mass* 1 299–327.　　　　　　　　　　　**543**

## 143RD INFANTRY

*Mustered in: October 8, 1862.*

*Mustered out: July 20, 1865.*

*Pfisterer 3656–67.*

*Register serial no 38, 557–687.*

143d regiment New York vols. inft., Sullivan co. Monticello, Watchman print [189–] 32, (1) p. 2 ports. 21½cm.　　DLC NHi **544**

Title and imprint from cover. Unit roster [11]–32. "Summary of constitution and by-laws," (1) p.

Young, Moses G

A condensed history of the 143d regiment New York volunteer infantry of the Civil war, 1861–1865, together with a register or roster of all the members of the Regiment, and the war record of each member, as recorded in the Adjutant-general's office at Albany, N. Y., by a Committee of the 143d regiment association, names as follows: William B. McMillen, Chairman; Moses G. Young, Editor and secretary . . . [10 names] [Newburgh, Newburgh print. house, 1909. 239 p. plates (ports.). 26½cm.　　　　　　　　　　　NN **545**

Unit roster [63]–223. "Dedication" signed: The Editor.

## 144TH INFANTRY

*Mustered in: September 27, 1862.*

*Mustered out: June 25, 1865.*

*Pfisterer 3667–79.*

*Register serial no 38, 688–901.*

McKee, James Harvey, 1840–1918.

Back "in war times," history of the 144th regiment, New York volunteer infantry, with itinerary, showing contemporaneous dates of the important battles of the Civil war, by James Harvey McKee. [Unadilla] Lieut. Horace E. Bailey, publisher [Times office] c1903. 378 p. plates (illus., maps, ports.). 23cm.　　　　　　　　　　　DLC NN **546**

On cover: Civil war record of the 144th regt., N.Y. volunteer infantry. Unit roster [301]–78.

## 145TH INFANTRY

*Mustered in: September 11, 1862.*

*Transferred to 107th, 123rd and 150th regiments of infantry: December 9, 1863.*

*Pfisterer 3679–87.*

*Register serial no 38, 902–1016.*

## 146TH INFANTRY

*Mustered in: October 10, 1862.*

*Mustered out: July 16, 1865.*

*Pfisterer 3687–3704.*

*Register serial no 38, 1017–1220.*

. . . First reunion of the 146th regiment, N.Y. vols., August 5, 1886, Rome, N.Y. [Rome, Printed by Beers & Kessinger, 1886] 20 p. 23½cm.　　　　　　　　　　NN **547**

At head of title: 1862. "Historical," 14–15.

Brainard, Mary Genevie Green

Campaign of the One hundred and forty-sixth regiment New York state volunteers, also known as Halleck's infantry, the Fifth Oneida, and Garrard's tigers. Compiled by Mary Genevie Brainard. New York, G. P. Putnam's Sons, 1915. xiii, 542 p. plates (2 fold. maps, illus., ports.). 23½cm.　　　　　　DLC NN **548**

Unit roster 311–534.

Case, A          Peirson
Notes on the taking and holding of Little
Round Top at Gettysburg. Movements of the
146th N.Y. vols. on the field of Gettysburg,
July 2, 3, 4 and 5, 1863. [Vernon, 1886] [4] p.
                                    CSmH    548A
Caption title. "Prepared for the New York state com-
missioners of Gettysburg monument by Lt. A. P.
Case of the 146th N.Y."

Erdman, Albert
A Chaplain's experiences. In War talks of
Morristown veterans, Morristown, N. J., 1887,
38–42.                                        549

Fowler, Philemon Halstead, 1814–1879.
Memorials of William Fowler. New York,
Anson D. F. Randolph & co., 1875. 172 p.
front. (port.). 19cm.            NN    550
Coulter 169. Fowler mustered in 173rd New York
infantry, October 30, 1862; mustered in 146th New
York infantry, November 11, 1863; discharged, Feb-
ruary 22, 1865.

Grindlay, James Glass
The 146th New York at Little Round Top.
BandL III 315.                                551

North, Edward
Memorial of Henry Hastings Curran, Lieutenant-Colonel of the One hundred and forty-
sixth regiment of the New York state volunteers, by Edward North . . . For private distribution. Albany, Joel Munsell, 1867. vi, [9]–
223 p. 24cm.                        NHi    552

Williams, George Forrester
Crossing the lines. BandG I (1893) 121–6.
illus., port.                                 553

Wright, Benjamin Franklin
From the Wilderness to Richmond, by
Brevet Major B. F. Wright. MOLLUS-Minn
II 7–37.                                      554

See also Titles 179–180, 244.

### 147TH INFANTRY

*Mustered in: September 22, 1862.*
*Mustered out: June 7, 1865.*
*Pfisterer 3705–18.*
*Register serial no 39, 1–217.*

Cooke, Sidney Granger
The first day of Gettysburg, a paper prepared
and read before the Kansas commandery of the
Military order of the loyal legion of the United
States (read November 4, 1897). 13 p. 22cm.
                                    DLC    555
On cover: War paper no. 17. Also published as
MOLLUS-Kan 276–89.

### 148TH INFANTRY

*Mustered in: September 14, 1862.*
*Mustered out: June 22, 1865.*
*Pfisterer 3719–31.*
*Register serial no 39, 218–374.*

### 149TH INFANTRY

*Mustered in: September 18, 1862.*
*Mustered out: June 12, 1865.*
*Pfisterer 3731–45.*
*Register serial no 39, 375–538.*

Collins, George Knapp, 1837–1931.
An abbreviated account of certain men of
Onondaga county who did service in the war
of 1861–65 in the 149th New York volunteer
regiment infantry. Collected by Captain George
K. Collins, for the Onondaga historical association. Syracuse, 1928. 53 p. front. (port.), illus.,
ports. 23cm.                        DLC NN    556
On spine: Record 149th N.Y. volunteer regt. infantry, 1861–65.

—— Memoirs of the 149th regt. N.Y. vol.
inft., 3rd brig., 2d. div., 12th and 20th A.C.,
by Capt. Geo. K. Collins. Syracuse, Published
by the author, 1891. viii, 426 p. illus., plates
(illus., ports.). 22cm.             DLC NN    557
Unit roster [341]–426. "Errors and annotations,"
inserted slip.

See also Title 226.

### 150TH INFANTRY

*Mustered in: October 10, 1862.*
*Mustered out: June 8, 1865.*
*Pfisterer 3745–56.*
*Register serial no 39, 539–697.*

The "Dutchess county regiment" (150th regiment of New York state volunteer infantry) in
the Civil war, its story as told by its members.
Based upon the writings of Rev. Edward O.
Bartlett. Edited by S. G. Cook and Charles E.
Benton. Danbury, Conn., Danbury Medical
print. co., 1907. xv, 512, (2) p. front. (port.),
2 plates (illus.). 22½cm.           DLC NN    558
Individual chapters are signed by their authors. Unit
roster [345]–507.

Historical sketch with exercises at dedication
of monument and re-union camp fire of 150th
New York volunteer infantry, Gettysburgh,
Sept. 17, 18, 1889. [Poughkeepsie] Monument
Committee of the 150th New York Volunteer
Infantry [A. V. Haight, printer, 1889] 99 p.
illus. 23cm.                        DLC NN    559
On cover: Dedication [illus. of monument] 150th
New York volunteer infantry, Gettysburg, Sept. 17,
1889.

*150 Infantry, continued*

Benton, Charles Edward, 1841–

As seen from the ranks, a boy in the Civil war, by Charles E. Benton, of the One hundred and fiftieth New York volunteers. . . . New York, G. P. Putnam's Sons, 1902. xiii, 292 p. 19cm.  NN  **560**

Cogswell, Joseph Hubert

Roster 150th N.Y. vols. Oct. 11th, 1912, 50 years from muster-in. Compiled by J. H. Cogswell, and presented to the surviving members of the Dutchess county regiment. . . . [Titusville, Penn., 1912] [4] p. 24cm.  CSmH  **561**
Caption title.

Gildersleeve, Henry Alger, 1840–1923.

Oration by Henry A. Gildersleeve, delivered on the battlefield of Gettysburg, September 17th, 1889, on the occasion of the dedication of the monument erected to the memory of the soldiers of "The Dutchess county regiment" (150th New York volunteer infantry) who were killed in the battle of Gettysburg. 19 p. 23cm.  NN  **562**

See also Title 409.

## 151ST INFANTRY

*Mustered in: October 22, 1862.*
*Mustered out: June 26, 1865.*
*Pfisterer 3756–66.*
*Register serial no 39, 698–817.*

Howell, Helena Adelaide

Chronicles of the One hundred fifty-first regiment New York state volunteer infantry, 1862–1865, contributed by its surviving members. Compiled by Helena Adelaide Howell. [Albion, A. M. Eddy, printer, 1911] 301, (1) p. illus., ports. 22½cm.  DLC N  **563**
Unit roster 131–298.

## 152ND INFANTRY

*Mustered in: October 14, 1862.*
*Mustered out: July 13, 1865.*
*Pfisterer 3767–79.*
*Register serial no 39, 818–940.*

See Titles 15 and 244.

## 153RD INFANTRY

*Mustered in: October 17, 1862.*
*Mustered out: October 2 ,1865.*
*Pfisterer 3779–90.*
*Register serial no 39, 941–1089.*

The 18th annual re-union of the 153d N.Y. veteran association, 1899. [Gloversville, 1899] [3] p. 20½cm.  DLC  **564**
Held at Elnora, Sept. 19, 1899.

## 154TH INFANTRY

*Mustered in: September 24, 1862.*
*Mustered out: June 11, 1865.*
*Pfisterer 3790–3804.*
*Register serial no 39, 1090–1232.*

## 155TH INFANTRY

*Mustered in: November 18, 1862.*
*Mustered out: July 15, 1865.*
*Pfisterer 3805–18.*
*Register serial no 39, 1233–1376.*

## 156TH INFANTRY

*Mustered in: November 17, 1862.*
*Mustered out: October 23, 1865.*
*Pfisterer 3818–31.*
*Register serial no 40, 1–155.*

The story of the One hundred and fifty-sixth. *Olde Ulster* vii (Kingston 1911) 321–8.  **565**

Kennedy, Charles W  1833–

The Civil war letters of Capt. Charles W. Kennedy. Edited by T. Livingstone and James C. Kennedy. *Staten Island historian* v (1942) 4, and continued in successive issues to ix (1948) 32.  **565A**

## 157TH INFANTRY

*Mustered in: September 19, 1862.*
*Mustered out: July 10, 1865.*
*Pfisterer 3831–43.*
*Register serial no 40, 156–318.*

[Sketch and roster of the 157th regiment New York volunteers] [Cortland, 1895] 12 leaves. 14cm.  NN  **566**
"Sketch" signed: Geo. L. Warren, Sec. On cover: 157 N. Y. volunteers.

Applegate, John Stilwell, 1837–1916.

Reminiscences and letters of George Arrowsmith of New Jersey, late Lieutenant-Colonel of the One hundred and fifty-seventh regiment, New York state volunteers, by John S. Applegate. Red Bank, N.J., John H. Cook, 1893. xiv, (2), 254 p. front. (port.). 18½cm.  NN  **567**
Mustered in 157th New York infantry, November 8, 1862: killed in action, July 1, 1863.

Barlow, Albert R
Company G, a record of the services of one company of the 157th N.Y. vols. in the War of the rebellion, from Sept. 19, 1862, to July 10, 1865, including the roster of the Company, by A. R. Barlow. Syracuse, A. W. Hall, 1899. 244 p. 18½cm.                    MnHi NN    **568**

## 158TH INFANTRY

*Mustered in: November 10, 1862.*
*Mustered out: June 30, 1865.*
*Pfisterer* 3844–55.
*Register* serial no 40, 319–495.

## 159TH INFANTRY

*Mustered in: November 1, 1862.*
*Mustered out: October 12, 1865.*
*Pfisterer* 3855–68.
*Register* serial no 40, 496–626.

Duffy, Edward
History of the 159th regiment N.Y.SV., compiled from the diary of Lieut. Edward Duffy. New York [Francis P. Harper] 1890. 48 p. 20½cm.            DLC NHi NN WHi    **569**
"One hundred and fifty copies reprinted from Hudson gazette, 1865." WHi's copy has inserted descriptive leaf signed: Francis P. Harper, no. 17 East 16th Street [New York]

Tiemann, William Francis
The 159th regiment infantry, New-York state volunteers in the war of the rebellion, 1862–1865. Compiled and published by William F. Tiemann, Captain and commissioned Major. Brooklyn, 1891. 135, liii p. plates (2 illus., maps), 23cm.            DLC NN    **570**
"Errata" inserted leaf. Unit roster, liii p.

## 160TH INFANTRY

*Mustered in: November 21, 1862.*
*Mustered out: November 1, 1865.*
*Pfisterer* 3868–79.
*Register* serial no 40, 627–742.

## 161ST INFANTRY

*Mustered in: October 27, 1862.*
*Mustered out: November 12, 1865.*
*Pfisterer* 3879–89.
*Register* serial no 40, 743–902.

Jones, William E
The military history of the One hundred & sixty-first New-York volunteers, infantry, from August 15th, 1862, to October 17th, 1865. Bath, Hull & Barnes, printers [1865] 64 p. 22cm.            NHi    **571**
Dedication signed: William E. Jones.

Merwin, John W
Roster and monograph 161st reg't. N.Y.S. volunteer infantry, rebellion 1861–1865, by J. W. Merwin. [Elmira, Gazette print, 1902] 133 p. 23½ × 29½cm.            MnHi    **572**
Unit roster 5–103.

## 162ND INFANTRY

*Mustered in: August 22 to October 18, 1862.*
*Mustered out: October 12, 1865.*
*Pfisterer* 3889–3902.
*Register* serial no 40, 903–1096.

An historical sketch of the 162d regiment N.Y. vol. infantry (3d Metropolitan guard), 19th army corps, 1862–1865. Albany, Weed, Parsons and co., printers, 1867. 45 p. front. (port.). 22½cm.            DLC NHi NN    **573**
Roster of officers 37–44.

United States. Adjutant-General's Office.
Alphabetical index of the 162d New York volunteer infantry, being an abstract of the field and staff and company rolls . . . February 16, 1889. Referred to the Committee on military affairs. Washington, Govt. print. office [1889] 247 p. 23½cm.            DLC    **574**
"10 copies printed," Catalogue of the library of John P. Nicholson, 1914.

See also Title 382.

## 163RD INFANTRY

*Mustered in: October 10, 1862.*
*Transferred to 73rd regiment of infantry: January 20, 1863.*
*Pfisterer* 3902–09.
*Register* serial no 40, 1097–1162.

## 164TH INFANTRY

*Mustered in: November 19, 1862.*
*Mustered out: July 15, 1865.*
*Pfisterer* 3909–20.
*Register* serial no 40, 1163–1317.

McAnally, John
How the 164th New York lost its colors. *BandG* iv (1894) 18–19.            **575**

*164th Infantry, continued*

United States. Adjutant-General's Office.

Alphabetical card-index of the rolls of the 164th New York infantry. Prepared and published by Brigadier-general Richard C. Drum, Adjutant-general U.S. army under instructions from the Secretary of war. . . . Washington, Govt. print. office, 1889. 273 p. 24cm.

DLC **576**

"10 copies printed," Catalogue of the library of John P. Nicholson, 1914.

## 165TH INFANTRY

*Mustered in: August to December 1862.*

*Mustered out: September 1, 1865.*

*Pfisterer 3920–28.*

*Register serial no 40, 1318–1434.*

Album of the Second battalion, Duryee zouaves, One hundred and sixty-fifth regt., New York volunteer infantry. [New York?] 1906. 1 vol. of portraits. 23½cm.     NN **577**

"Supplement to our regimental history." With the exception of the last leaf, printed on the rectos.

History of the Second battalion, Duryee zouaves, One hundred and sixty-fifth regt., New York volunteer infantry. Mustered in the United States service at Camp Washington, Staten island, N.Y., November twenty-eighth, eighteen hundred & sixty-two. [New York, Peter de Baun & co.] 1904. 1 vol. plates (illus., ports.). 23½cm.     DLC NN **578**

P 9–41, 67–74 are numbered. Unit roster included.

Roster 165th regiment, N.Y. vols. 2d Duryee zouaves, September, 1861 – September, 1865. [1903] [8] p. plates (1 illus., ports.). 22cm.

Caption title.     NHi NN **579**

Hoey, George

The 165th New York volunteers, written by George Hoey, and read by James F. Ferguson, on Decoration day, May 30th, 1890, at Tottenville, Staten island. 5 p. 20½cm.     NN **580**

Poetry.

## 166TH INFANTRY

*Failed to complete organization.*

*Pfisterer 3929.*

## 167TH INFANTRY

*Failed to complete organization.*

*Pfisterer 3929.*

## 168TH INFANTRY

*19th Infantry National Guard*

*Mustered in: February 11, 1863.*

*Mustered out: October 31, 1863.*

*Pfisterer 3930–36.*

*Register serial no 41, 1–104.*

## 169TH INFANTRY

*Mustered in: September 25 to October 6, 1862.*

*Mustered out: July 19, 1865.*

*Pfisterer 3936–51.*

*Register serial no 41, 105–300.*

## 170TH INFANTRY

*Mustered in: October 7, 1862.*

*Mustered out: July 15, 1865.*

*Pfisterer 3951–64.*

*Register serial no 41, 301–438.*

## 171ST INFANTRY

*Failed to complete organization.*

*Pfisterer 3964.*

## 172ND INFANTRY

*Failed to complete organization.*

*Pfisterer 3965.*

## 173RD INFANTRY

*Mustered in: November 10, 1862.*

*Mustered out: October 18, 1865.*

*Pfisterer 3966–78.*

*Register serial no 41, 441–581.*

Dill, Samuel Phillips

A brief sketch of the 173rd regiment, N.Y.V. [Brooklyn?] 1868. 5 p. illus. cover. 24cm.

Title from cover.     NN **581**

—— Journal of the escape and re-capture of Samuel P. Dill, late Capt. and Brevet Major 173d regt. New York vols. Brooklyn, J. H. Broach & Bro., printers, 1867. 23 p. 24cm.

CSmH NN **581A**

Peck, Lewis M

History of the One hundred and seventy-third New York volunteers, Fourth metropolitan brigade. *Brooklyn advance* xi (1884) 4–11.

**581B**

See also Title 550.

## 174TH INFANTRY

*Mustered in: October 15 to November 13, 1862.*
*Consolidated with 162nd regiment of infantry: February 17, 1864.*
*Pfisterer 3978–86.*
*Register serial no 41, 582–716.*

## 175TH INFANTRY

*Mustered in: September to November 1862.*
*Mustered out: June 30 to November 27, 1865.*
*Pfisterer 3987–96.*
*Register serial no 41, 717–848.*

## 176TH INFANTRY

*Mustered in: December 22, 1862.*
*Mustered out: April 27, 1866.*
*Pfisterer 3996–4009.*
*Register serial no 41, 849–1079.*

Duganne, Augustine Joseph Hickey, 1823–1884.
Camps and prisons, twenty months in the Department of the Gulf, by A. J. H. Duganne. New York, 1865. 424 p. plates (illus.). 19cm.
NN **582**
"Subscribers' edition." NN's presentation copy signed dated: April 1865.

—— —— Second edition. New York, J. P. Robens, 1865. 424 p. plates (illus.). 19cm.
NN **583**
This edition and a third edition (NN) are reprintings of Title 582.

Nott, Charles Cooper, 1827–1916.
Sketches in prison camps, a continuation of Sketches of the war, by Charles C. Nott, late Colonel of the 176th New York. . . . New York, Anson D. F. Randolph, 1865. 104 p. 19½cm.
DLC **584**
A third edition (NN) is a reprint.

Putnam, George Haven, 1844–1930.
The Civil war fifty years after, a veteran's experiences as recalled by the battle field pictures. *American review of reviews* XLIII (1911) 316–26. illus. **585**

—— Memories of my youth, 1844–1865, by George Haven Putnam, late Brevet Major, 176th regt. N.Y.S. vols. New York, G. P. Putnam's Sons, 1914. vi, 447 p. 2 plates (ports.). 23½cm.
NHi NN **586**
Civil war 220–442.

—— A prisoner of war in Virginia, 1864–5, by George Haven Putnam, Adt. and Bvt.-Major 176th N.Y.S. vols. . . . New York, G. P. Putnam's Sons, 1912. v, 104 p. front. (port.), illus. 21½cm.
NHi NN **587**
"Reprinted with additions, from the report of an address presented to the N.Y. commandery of the U.S. loyal legion, December 7, 1910."

—— —— *MOLLUS-NY* IV 208–48. **587A**

## 177TH INFANTRY

### 10th Infantry National Guard

*Mustered in: November 21, 1862.*
*Mustered out: September 24, 1863.*
*Pfisterer 4009–14.*
*Register serial no 41, 1080–1199.*

Albany, New York. Bar.
Memoir of Richard Marvin Strong, a member of the Albany Bar, and Adjutant of the 177th regiment, N.Y. volunteers, who died at Bonnet Carre, La., May 12, 1863. Published in pursuance of a resolution of the Bar of the City of Albany. Albany, Charles Van Benthuysen, 1863. 48 p. port. (mounted photograph). 22cm.
NN **588**

Twombly, Alexander Stevenson, 1832–1907.
The completed Christian life, a sermon commemorative of Adjt. Richard M. Strong, 177th regt. N.Y.S.V., who died at Bonnet Carre, La., May 12, 1863, preached in the State street Presbyterian church, Albany, N.Y., by Rev. A. S. Twombly, June 7, 1863. Albany, J. Munsell, 1863. 22 p. 23½cm.
NHi NN **589**

## 178TH INFANTRY

*Mustered in: June 18, 1863.*
*Mustered out: April 20, 1866.*
*Pfisterer 4015–28.*
*Register serial no 42, 1–144.*
See Title 459.

## 179TH INFANTRY

*Mustered in: April 3 to September 15, 1864.*
*Mustered out: June 8, 1865.*
*Pfisterer 4028–38.*
*Register serial no 42, 145–289.*

History of the 179th regiment N.Y.S.V., rebellion of 1861–65. [Ithaca, E. D. Norton, printer, 1900] 39, (1) p. 14½cm. DLC N NHi **590**
Unit roster 7–37. Imprint (1) p.

*179th Infantry, continued*

Starr, Frederick, 1826–1867.

The loyal soldier, a discourse delivered in the First Presbyterian church of Penn-Yan, New York, at the funeral of Major John Barnet Sloan, of the 179th regiment, N.Y.V. infantry, Monday, 2 p. m., June 27th, 1864, by Rev. Frederick Starr, Jr. Penn-Yan, G. D. A. Bridgman, printer, 1864. 28 p. 21½cm.

                                   CSmH CtY      **590A**

## 180TH INFANTRY

*Failed to complete organization.*
*Pfisterer 4038.*

## 181ST INFANTRY

*Authority to recruit this regiment was revoked.*
*Pfisterer 4038.*

## 182ND INFANTRY

*Mustered in: November 17, 1862.*
*Mustered out: July 15, 1865.*
*Pfisterer 4038–51.*
*Register serial no 42, 293–430.*

## 183RD INFANTRY

*Failed to complete organization.*
*Pfisterer 4051.*

## 184TH INFANTRY

*Mustered in: September 12, 1864.*
*Mustered out: June 29, 1865.*
*Pfisterer 4052–58.*
*Register serial no 42, 432–554.*

Post, Jacob

Discourse on the assassination of President Lincoln, preached in camp by Rev. Jacob Post, Chaplain of the 184th regiment N.Y.V., at Harrison's landing, Virginia, April 23d 1865. Oswego, S. H. Parker & co., printer, 1865. 11 p. 21½cm.                           DLC   **591**

Robinson, Wardwell G

History of the 184th regiment New York state volunteers, an address prepared by Wardwell G. Robinson, late Colonel commanding, and delivered by him at the Regimental reunion held at Oswego Falls, Oswego county, New York, June 5, 1895. . . . [Oswego, Press of R. J. Oliphant, 1895] 57 p. 23½cm.

                                   DLC N NHi    **592**

## 185TH INFANTRY

*Mustered in: September 19, 1864.*
*Mustered out: May 30, 1865.*
*Pfisterer 4058–66.*
*Register serial no 42, 555–677.*

Roster of the 185th regiment N.Y.V., prepared and revised by Major H. W. Clarke, Secretary of the 185th volunteer association.[Syracuse] Published by the direction of the Executive committee, 1889. 20 p. 23cm.     MnHi   **593**

—— Corrections to the roster published in 1889. . . . Syracuse, Syracuse Journal co., printers, 1890. 7 p. 22½cm.     NHi   **594**

## 186TH INFANTRY

*Mustered in: September 5–29, 1864.*
*Mustered out: June 2, 1865.*
*Pfisterer 4066–74.*
*Register serial no 42, 678–800.*

## 187TH INFANTRY

*Mustered in: October 8–13, 1864.*
*Mustered out: July 1, 1865.*
*Pfisterer 4074–80.*
*Register serial no 42, 801–908.*

## 188TH INFANTRY

*Mustered in: October 4–22, 1864.*
*Mustered out: July 1, 1865.*
*Pfisterer 4080–88.*
*Register serial no 43, 1–115.*

## 189TH INFANTRY

*Mustered in: August to September 1864.*
*Mustered out: June 1, 1865.*
*Pfisterer 4088–95.*
*Register serial no 43, 116–248.*

Rogers, William H

History of the One hundred and eighty-ninth regiment of New-York volunteers, by Rev. Wm. H. Rogers, Chaplain. New York, John A. Gray & Green, printers, 1865. 113 p. front. (group port.). 19cm.                           NN   **595**

Contents: Part first, Organization of the Regiment [biographies, muster roll and recruiting areas of the companies] [7]–69; Part second, Services of the Regiment, [70]–113.

## 190TH INFANTRY

*One company organized: April 7, 1865.*
*Mustered out: May 3, 1865.*
*Pfisterer 4095.*
*Register serial no 43, 249–66.*

## 191ST INFANTRY

*Two companies organized: March 30 to April 28, 1865.*
*Mustered out: May 3, 1865.*
*Pfisterer 4097.*
*Register serial no 43, 627–88.*

## 192ND INFANTRY

*Mustered in: March 13 to April 8, 1865.*
*Mustered out: August 28, 1865.*
*Pfisterer 4097–4104.*
*Register serial no 43, 289–443.*

See Title 205.

## 193RD INFANTRY

*Mustered in: March 6–28, 1865.*
*Mustered out: January 18, 1866.*
*Pfisterer 4104–10.*
*Register serial no 43, 444–596.*

## 194TH INFANTRY

*Mustered in: March 29 – April 27, 1865.*
*Mustered out: May 3–10, 1865.*
*Pfisterer 4110–14.*
*Register serial no 43, 597–804.*

## INDEPENDENT BATTALION OF INFANTRY — ENFANS PERDU

*Mustered in: April 18, 1862.*
*Transferred to 47th and 48th regiments of infantry and 1st regiment of engineers: January 30, 1864.*
*Pfisterer 4114–22.*
*Register serial no 43, 677–805.*

## MOUNTED RIFLES

### 1ST REGIMENT OF MOUNTED RIFLES

*Mustered in by companies: July 30, 1861 to September 1862.*
*Consolidated with 3rd regiment of cavalry: July 21, 1865.*
*Pfisterer 1110–33.*
*Register serial no 7, 484–853.*

Van Vechten, Henry C
At the siege of Suffolk. In National tribune scrapbook 1 83.                    **595A**

See Titles 15 and 117.

### 2ND REGIMENT OF MOUNTED RIFLES

*Left the State: March 1864.*
*Mustered out: August 10, 1865.*
*Pfisterer 1133–47.*
*Register serial no 7, 854–1059.*

Cady, Nahum Ward, 1827–
Court-martial of Major N. Ward Cady 2d mounted rifles, N.Y. vols., including the offence, defence, sentence, correspondence. . . . [Yates, 1864] 35 p. 22½cm.     DLC     **596**

See also Title 15.

## SHARPSHOOTERS

*Four companies were raised in New York for service with the United States sharpshooters — Companies A, B, D and H, 1st regiment U.S. sharpshooters.*

# *Notes*

# Regimental Publications
# & Personal Narratives
# of the Civil War

## A Checklist

Compiled by C. E. DORNBUSCH

Volume One    Northern States

PART III    NEW ENGLAND STATES

New York

The New York Public Library

1961

THIS VOLUME HAS BEEN PUBLISHED WITH HELP
FROM THE EMILY ELLSWORTH FORD SKEEL FUND

# Preface

THIS CHECKLIST of regimental histories, publications of regimental associations, and personal narratives of participants in the Civil War is a revision of and supplement to the section on "Military Organizations" in the third edition of the *Bibliography of State Participation in the Civil War*, prepared and published by the War Department Library, Washington, D. C. in 1913 as its Subject Catalogue No 6.*

The present checklist is to be published in seven Parts. The first six will cover the batteries and regiments of seventeen Northern states: I Illinois; II New York; III New England states; IV New Jersey and Pennsylvania; V Indiana and Ohio; and VI Iowa, Kansas, Michigan, Minnesota, and Wisconsin. A final section will provide an index of authors and, where required, titles of the publications listed for these seventeen states.

No subject index to the checklist is contemplated. Besides supplying references for the history of a battery or regiment, the checklist does the same for battles and engagements. To locate references on a battle or engagement, however, the user must determine from the order of battle available in Dyer's *Compendium of the War of the Rebellion* which units were involved and then turn to their entries in the checklist. It is also useful to know the other regiments of a brigade as a means of obtaining from the checklist additional narratives of an incident or battle.

The compiler has followed the arrangement of the 1913 work. Within each state military units are arranged numerically by arm of service — Artillery, Cavalry, and Infantry. While the earlier work entered only units for which publications were known, the present compilation has recorded all units which were organized. Again, while rosters and compilations of regimental histories were reported in one section headed "State Publication" in *BSP*, the present work has indexed these publications under the individual military units.

The compiler has located and personally examined each work entered in this checklist. Some entries which were listed in *BSP* have been omitted —

* The Bibliography (hereafter referred to as *BSP*) was prepared as a catalogue and index of a major Civil War collection, now part of the National War College Library, Washington.

entries based on titles taken from bibliographies, correspondence, dealers'
catalogues, and other sources but not in the War Department Library. Such
"ghosts" as have remained have been omitted here. The present checklist
also omits the *BSP* references to the *National Tribune*, and a group of articles
by George L. Kilmer which are cited in *BSP* not by original publication but
as mounted clippings in ten volumes in the War Department Library collections.

Although a monumental work, some errors found their way into the *BSP*.
For instance, Douglas Putnam's *Recollections of the battle of Shiloh* was
entered under the 92nd Ohio Regiment, the regiment to which he belonged.
But that regiment was formed some months after the battle was fought, and
Putnam could write of it not as a member but as a civilian observer. Similarly
Eagan's *Battle of Birch Coolie* is entered under the 1st Minnesota Heavy
Artillery, although that unit did not participate in the battle.

The seventeen states covered by this checklist had a total of 2,202 batteries
and regiments which took part in the Civil War. Each of these units has been
listed with a brief statement of its service, i. e. muster in and muster out
dates. Where the same number has been assigned to two regiments, they
have been distinguished by the term of original enlistments, i. e. three
months or three years. Changes in a unit's designation or arm of service
as well as amalgamations have been reported. Although some units mustered
out before the close of the war and transferred their recruits and veterans to
other units, the checklist has not reported this movement of personnel. Reference is made to regimental rosters and narratives of a unit's service where
this information may be found.

The compiler has included any articles and publications which could be
associated with a particular battery or regiment. The bulk of these are the
regimental histories, reunion proceedings, and unit rosters. Publications of
sermons preached at soldiers' funerals have been reported. Though their
size did not lend to preservation, a surprising number of soldiers' memorials
has been located. Broadsides of company rosters, often illustrated in color,
were soldiers' souvenirs of the war. The inclusion of all these types of
material has here resulted in the broadest possible bibliographical coverage
of Civil War materials. All prison narratives have been entered under the

regiment in which the author was serving at the time of his capture. Newspapers printed in the field by army units have not been included.

The value of this checklist is primarily in the listing of the personal narratives of Civil War participants, the rank and file as well as officers, from Lieutenant to Colonel. (By reason of the honorary Brevet rank, the Colonel of a regiment could be appointed Brigadier General at the close of the war, and in this case later reference to his rank is as General.) Usually the publication identifies the battery or regiment of the author. Occasionally, however, he may have served in two or more units, and the later service (often at a higher rank) is used on the title-page. Such items are entered in the checklist under the unit in which the author served at the time the events narrated took place.

Narratives which reflect service in two or more units are entered under the unit of first service, with cross references from other units in which the author served. When an author's service crossed state lines or when it was with the United States Colored Troops, his narrative has been fully entered under each unit.

The compiler has made extensive search of American journals and periodicals published since the close of hostilities. The very magnitude of this undertaking precludes even the hope of a definitive checklist. One assumes that obscure imprints with limited distribution have tended to disappear. In many cases only single surviving copies have been located. The search is continuing while other sections of the list are in preparation, and it is hoped that publication will bring new additions to light.

Following the statement of unit service, entries are given in two groups, anonymous publications followed by author entries. At least one location of each title is reported by means of the *Symbols Used in the National Union Catalogue of The Library of Congress*, seventh edition revised, 1959. Standard works such as the papers of the Military Order of the Loyal Legion and periodicals are not located in the checklist. The user is referred for these to the *Union List of Serials* and its supplements. Title-pages have been transcribed in full, including author statements which supply rank and unit. Distinction is made between illustrations which appear in the body of the text and illustrations which appear on unpaginated plates. Plates that are

paged have been considered as text illustrations. The place of publication is not identified when within same state as checklist is describing. The collation of reunion proceedings has been limited to their numbering and date.

The very size of the compiler's undertaking has meant assistance from many sources. In his inspection of collections throughout the country, the compiler has been helped by many librarians, and their contributions have been acknowledged in the appropriate sections of the checklist. Above all the compiler is indebted to the administrators of The Emily E. F. Skeel Fund of The New York Public Library for making the compilation of this checklist possible and for freedom in developing it.

# Table of Contents

# NEW ENGLAND STATES

# Acknowledgments

In the preparation of this section of the checklist acknowledgment is made of the assistance given by the following individuals and libraries:

CONNECTICUT

Miss Frances Davenport, Connecticut State Library

MAINE

Mr Richard Harwell, Librarian, Bowdoin College

MASSACHUSETTS

The Boston Public Library
Mr Stephen T. Riley, Director, Massachusetts Historical Society

NEW HAMPSHIRE

Mrs Russell B. Tobey, Librarian, New Hampshire Historical Society

RHODE ISLAND

Mr Stuart C. Sherman, Librarian, Providence Public Library

# Abbreviations

| | |
|---|---|
| *AG's report* | Annual report of the Adjutant general of the State of Rhode Island and Providence plantations for the year 1865, (1893–95) |
| *BandL* | Battles and leaders, New York, 1887–88. 4 v. |
| *Biv* | Bivouac, Boston |
| *Coulter* | Travels in the Confederate states, a bibliography, by E. Merton Coulter, 1948 |
| *Eastern Maine* | Eastern Maine and the Rebellion, by R. H. Stanley, 1887 |
| *JMSIUS* | Journal of the Military service institution of the United States |
| *JUSCA* | Journal of the United States cavalry association, Fort Leavenworth |
| *Mass soldiers* | Massachusetts soldiers, sailors and marines in the Civil war, 1931–35 |
| *Mass in the war* | Massachusetts in the War, 1861–1865, by James L. Bowen, 1889 |
| *MOLLUS* | Military order of the loyal legion of the United States |
| *DC* | War papers District of Columbia commandery |
| *Ill* | Military essays and recollections Illinois commandery |
| *Iowa* | War sketches and incidents Iowa commandery |
| *Me* | War papers Maine commandery |
| *Mass* | Civil war papers Massachusetts commandery |
| *Mich* | War papers Michigan commandery |
| *Minn* | Glimpses of the Nation's struggle Minnesota commandery |
| *Mo* | War papers and personal reminiscences Missouri commandery |
| *Neb* | Civil war sketches and incidents Nebraska commandery |
| *NY* | Personal recollections of the War of the rebellion New York commandery |
| *Ohio* | Sketches of war history Ohio commandery |

[ 13 ]

| | |
|---|---|
| *Vt* | War papers Vermont commandery |
| *Wis* | War papers Wisconsin commandery |
| *N. H. in the great rebellion* | New Hampshire in the great rebellion, by Otis F. R. Waite, 1870. |
| *PMHSM* | Papers of the Military historical society of Massachusetts |
| *PNRISSHS* | Personal narratives Rhode Island soldiers and sailors historical society |
| *Record* | Record of service of Connecticut men in the Army and Navy of the United States during the War of the rebellion, 1889 |
| *Revised register* | Revised register of the soldiers and sailors of New Hampshire in the War of the rebellion, 1895 |
| *Revised roster* | Revised roster of Vermont volunteers, 1861–66, ( 1892 ) |
| *Vermont in the Civil war* | Vermont in the Civil war, by George G. Benedict, 1886–88 |

# CONNECTICUT

# Reference Works

Connecticut. Adjutant-General.
Record of service of Connecticut men in the Army and Navy of the United States, during the War of the rebellion. Compiled by authority of the General assembly, under direction of the Adjutant-general. . . . Hartford, Press of Case, Lockwood & Brainard co., 1889. xiii, 1071 p. 30cm.
Cited herein as *Record*.

Dyer, Frederick Henry, 1849–1917.
A compendium of the War of the rebellion. 1908 (reprinted 1959).
"Regimental index" 114–116; "Regimental histories" 1006–16. The pagination is the same in the 1959 reprint.

*The Union army.*
"Record of Connecticut regiments," i (1908) 274–310.

United States. Adjutant General's Office.
Official army register of the volunteer force of the United States army for the years 1861, '62, '63, '64, '65. Part I. (New England states). Washington, 1865.
A roster of officers by regiments with an alphabetical index for the six states.

# CONNECTICUT

## ARTILLERY

### Regiments (Heavy)

#### 1ST ARTILLERY (HEAVY)

*Mustered in as 4th regiment of infantry: May 22–23, 1861.*

*Designated 1st regiment of heavy artillery: January 2, 1862.*

*Mustered out: September 25, 1865.*

*Record 116–72. History, by Henry L. Abbot.*

The City guard register, being a complete roster of the Hartford city guard since its organization in 1861. Published as a souvenir of the removal of the Company to its new quarters in the regimental armory. Hartford, 1880. 43, (1) p. 22cm.       Ct DNW       *1*

"The war company of the Hartford city guard," 34–8; Roster Company A, 1st Conn. heavy artillery, 38–40; Roll of honor, Company A, 1st Conn. heavy artillery, (1) p.

Report of the movement and operations of the 1st Conn. heavy artillery, for the year ending March 31, 1865, as given in the Annual report of the Adjutant general of Connecticut, April 1, 1865. Hartford, Press of Case, Lockwood and co., 1865. 34 p. 22½cm.       Ct DLC NHi       *2*

Roster of the First regiment Connecticut artillery, 1869. Hartford, Press of Case, Lockwood & Brainard, 1869. 8 p. 19½cm.
       Ct NHi       *3*

Abbot, Henry Larcom, 1831–1927.
    . . . Siege artillery in the campaigns against Richmond, with notes on the 15-inch gun . . . by Bvt. Brig. Gen. Henry L. Abbot. Washington, Govt. print. office, 1867. 183 p. 2 illus., 6 fold. charts. 23cm.       NN       *3A*

"Record of the First Connecticut artillery; organization," 8–16. At head of title: Professional papers Corps of engineers. No. 14.

Andrews, Elisha Benjamin, 1844–1917.
    A Private's reminiscences of the first year of the war, by E. Benjamin Andrews, Company C, Fourth Connecticut infantry. 1886. 41 p. *PNRISSHS* s3 no 18.       *4*

Bennett, Edgar B       1842–
    First Connecticut heavy artillery, historical sketch and present addresses of members. Compiled by E. B. Bennett, formerly of Co. K. East Berlin [Hartford, Star print. co., 1889] 53 p. front. (port.). 19½cm.
       Ct DLC NHi       *5*

McNamar, James B
    Official souvenir and program of monument First Connecticut heavy artillery and dedicatory exercises held on State capitol grounds, Hartford, Conn., September 25, 1902 . . . Compiled and published under the auspices of the General committee and Regimental association, by J. B. McNamar. Hartford, R. S. Peck & co. [1902] xii, 143, cxxx p. illus., ports. 23cm.
       Ct DLC NHi       *6*

Advertising matter included. Unit roster cxxx p.

Taylor, John C
    History of the First Connecticut artillery and of the siege trains of the armies operating against Richmond, 1862–1865. Hartford, Press of the Case, Lockwood & Brainard co., 1893. 270, (2), 57 p. front. (3 ports.), plates (illus., fold. maps). 30½cm.       Ct DLC NHi       *7*

Introduction signed: John C. Taylor, Historian. "Conclusion" with "errata" slip, (2) p. Unit roster reprinted from Record of Connecticut men in the war, 57 p.

Walker, Edward Ashley
    Our first year of army life, an anniversary address, delivered to the First regiment of Connecticut volunteer heavy artillery, at their camp near Gaines' Mills, Va., June, 1862, by the Chaplain of the Regiment. . . . New Haven, Thomas H. Pease, 1862. 95 p. 23cm.
       Ct DLC NN RP       *8*

"Preface" signed: E. A. W.

#### 2ND ARTILLERY (HEAVY)

*Mustered in as 19th regiment of infantry: September 11, 1862.*

*Designated 2nd regiment of heavy artillery: November 23, 1863.*

*Mustered out: August 18, 1865.*

*Record 173–219. History, by James N. Coe.*

Reunion and dedication of monument at Arlington national cemetery, Va., Wednesday, October 21, 1896. Second Connecticut heavy artillery. D. C. Kilbourn, Secretary. Hartford, Press of the Case, Lockwood & Brainard co., 1897. 34 p. map, plates (illus.). 23cm.
       Ct DLC       *9*

Finan, William J
    The mountain county regiment. *The lure of the Litchfield hills* xiv (Winsted, 1957) 6–7, 27–8. port.       *10*

Vaill, Dudley Landon, 1873–
    The county regiment, a sketch of the Second regiment of Connecticut volunteer heavy artil-

*2nd Artillery (Heavy), continued*

lery, originally the Nineteenth volunteer infantry, in the Civil war. by Dudley Landon Vaill. [Litchfield] Litchfield County University Club, 1908. xii, 108 p. plates (illus., ports.). 20½cm.                     Ct DLC NN    **11**

Vaill, Theodore Frelinghuysen, 1832–1875.

History of the Second Connecticut volunteer heavy artillery, originally the Nineteenth Connecticut vols., by Theodore F. Vaill, First Lieutenant and Adjutant. Winsted, Winsted print. co., 1868. 366 p. plates (ports.). 20cm.

Unit roster 252–318.          Ct DLC NHi    **12**

## Batteries (Light)

### 1st Battery

*Left State: January 23, 1862.*
*Mustered out: June 11, 1865.*
*Record 98–104. History, by Theron Upson.*

. . . Program of exercises at the dedication of a soldiers monument erected by the First Connecticut light battery, the Sixth, Seventh and Tenth Connecticut volunteers monument association at the Broadway park, New Haven, June 16, 1905, upon the forty-first anniversary of the battle of Bermuda Hundred and Petersburg turnpike, Virginia. [New Haven, Press of the Price, Lee & Adkins co., 1905] 45, (3) p. 23½cm.                          Ct DLC    **13**
At head of title: 1861–1905.

Beecher, Herbert W

History of the First light battery, Connecticut volunteers, 1861–1865. Personal records and reminiscences. The story of the Battery, from its organization to the present time, compiled from official records, personal interviews, private diaries, war histories and individual experiences. Historian, Herbert W. Beecher. New York, A. T. De La Mare print. co. [1901] 2 v. illus., maps, ports., plate (double map). 23½cm.                           Ct NHi NN    **14**
Unit roster II 729–821. "The Historian called to his assistance a staff of writers and artists . . . John De Morgan, who has performed the onerous duties of Editor."

### 2nd Battery

*Mustered in: September 10, 1862.*
*Mustered out: August 9, 1865.*
*Record 105–10. History, by David B. Lockwood.*

### 3rd Battery

*Left State: November 16, 1864.*
*Mustered out: June 23, 1865.*
*Record 111–15. History, by Thomas S. Gilbert.*

## CAVALRY

### 1ST CAVALRY

*Left State as a battalion: February 20, 1862.*

*Recruited and organized as a regiment: March 1864.*

*Mustered out: August 2, 1865.*

*Record 56–97. History, by Erastus Blakeslee.*

Blakeslee, Erastus

In more than ninety battles. In National tribune scrap book I 127–31.          **15**

Holmes, Theodore J

A memorial of John S. Jameson, Sergeant in the 1st Conn. cavalry, who died at Andersonville, Ga., compiled by Theodore J. Holmes, Chaplain of the Regiment. . . . [1866?] 31 p. front. (port.). 20cm.          Ct NHi NN    **15A**

Koempel, Philip, 1840–

Phil Koempel's diary, 1861–1865. [n. p., 192–] 53 p. front. (port.). 24½cm.
                                    Ct DLC    **16**
Entries from March 19, 1864, through February 15, 1865. "In explanation" signed: W. K. [Walter Koempel]

Parmelee, Uriah Nelson, 1841–1865.

The Civil war diary of Captain Uriah Nelson Parmelee. Edited by Charles Lewis Biggs. [Guilford, 1940] 11 p. 23cm.

Title from cover, p [1]          Ct NN NNC    **16A**

Turnbull, Robert, 1809–1877.

Well done, a funeral discourse for Captain Albert H. Niles, by Robert Turner. Published by request. Hartford, Press of Case, Lockwood & co., 1863. 19 p. 20½cm.          NB    **16B**

### 1ST SQUADRON OF CAVALRY

*See 2nd New York regiment of cavalry, Companies C and D.*
*Record 51–55.*

## INFANTRY

### 1ST INFANTRY

*Mustered in: May 7, 1861.*
*Mustered out: July 31, 1861.*
*Record 1–17. History, by George S. Burnham.*

## 2ND INFANTRY

*Mustered in: May 7, 1861.*
*Mustered out: August 7, 1861.*
*Record 18–33. History, by James B. Coit.*

Lucke, James Bonaparte, 1842?–1923.
History of New Haven grays, from Sept. 13,
1816, to Sept. 13, 1876, by ex-Private Jerome
B. Lucke. New Haven, Tuttle, Morehouse &
Taylor, printers, 1876. 540 p. plates (1 illus.,
ports.). 23cm.                        Ct NN      **17**
Civil war 233–329. Unit roster 528–40.

## 3RD INFANTRY

*Mustered in: May 14, 1861.*
*Mustered out: August 12, 1861.*
*Record 34–50.*

Roster of the Third regiment, Connecticut volunteers. Hartford, Calhoun print. co., 1861.
12 p. 15½cm.                          Ct      **18**
Title from cover, p [1]

Brewster, James, 1788–1866.
James Brewster's address. Officers and sol-
diers of the "Brewster rifle company." [New
Haven, 1861] 3 p. 23cm.               Ct      **19**
Caption title. Dated: September 16, 1861.

Shaw, William H          1833–
A diary as kept by Wm. H. Shaw during the
great Civil war, from April 1861, to July 1865.
[n. p., n. d.] 76 p. front. (port.). 22½cm.
                                      NN      **20**
Tyler, Elnathan B
"Wooden nutmegs" at Bull run, a humorous
account of the exploits and experiences of the
three months Connecticut brigade and the part
they bore in the national stampede, by Frinkle
Frey [pseud.] Hartford, George L. Coburn,
printer, 1872. viii, [9]–86 p. illus. 21cm.
Copyright by E. B. Tyler.   Ct DLC NN    **21**

## 4TH INFANTRY

*Mustered in: May 22–23, 1861.*
*Designated 1st regiment of heavy artil-
lery: January 2, 1862.*

Order of divine service of the Fourth regiment
Connecticut volunteers. Washington, D. C.,
M'Gill & Witherow, printers, 1861. 5, (2) p.
10½cm.                                CtHi    **22**
Title and imprint from cover, p [1]

## 5TH INFANTRY

*Mustered in: July 22–23, 1861.*
*Mustered out: July 19, 1865.*
*Record 220–56. History, by E. E: Marvin.*
Fifth Connecticut volunteers, dedication, ex-
cursion and reunion, at Gettysburg, August 8th,

9th and 10th, 1887. Hartford, Press of Wiley,
Waterman & Eaton, 1887. 27 p. front. (illus.).
23cm.                                Ct NHi    **23**

Muster roll of the Fifth Connecticut volunteers
who participated in the battle flag parade,
Hartford, September 17, 1879. Hartford, Fowler, Miller & co., printers [1879] 20 p. 19cm.
                                     Ct WHi    **24**

Roster of survivors of the 5th regiment Connecticut volunteers, so far as known' to the
Secretary. Re-revised September 9th, 1897.
[4] p. 23cm.                         Ct      **25**
Caption title.

—— Re-revised September 1, 1899. [3] p.
23½cm.                               Ct      **26**
Caption title.

Second annual reunion of the Fifth regiment
of Connecticut volunteers, proceedings, and
address by Rev. Horace Winslow. Hartford,
Geo. L. Coburn, print., 1869. 18 p. 22cm.
                                     CT NHi    **27**
Marvin, Edwin E
The Fifth regiment, Connecticut volunteers,
a history compiled from diaries and official
reports, by Edwin E. Marvin. Published for
the Reunion association of the Regiment. Hartford, Press of Wiley, Waterman & Eaton, 1889.
ix, 394, (63) p. 24cm.   DLC NHi NN    **28**
Unit roster (63) p.

Meade, Rufus, 1836–1922.
With Sherman through Georgia and the
Carolinas: letters of a Federal soldier. Edited
by James A. Padgett. *Georgia historical quarterly* xxxii (1948) 285–322; xxxiii (1949) 49–
81.                                          **29**

## 6TH INFANTRY

*Mustered in: September 12, 1861.*
*Mustered out: August 21, 1865.*
*Record 257–89. History, by Charles K.
Caldwell.*

Caldwell, Charles K
The old Sixth regiment, its war record,
1861–5, by Charles K. Caldwell. New Haven,
Tuttle, Morehouse & Taylor, printers, 1875.
227, (1) p. 21cm.        DLC NHi NN    **30**
Unit roster 127–219. Coulter 66.

Rockwell, Alfred Perkins, 1834–1903.
The operations against Charleston, by Alfred
P. Rockwell Colonel 6th Connecticut. *PMHSM*
ix 159–93.                                   **31**

—— The Tenth army corps in Virginia, May
1864. *PMHSM* ix 265–99.                     **32**

See also Title 13.

## 7TH INFANTRY

*Mustered in: September 17, 1861.*
*Mustered out: July 20, 1865.*
*Record 290–326.* History, by William H. Pierpont.

"Southern rights" and Yankee humor, a Confederate-Federal Jacksonville newspaper. *Florida historical quarterly* xxxiv (1955/56) 30–5. facs.　　　　　　　　　　　　　32A
Captain Valentine B. Chamberlain of the 7th Conn infantry completed and printed an issue of the Jacksonville *Southern rights* that was on the press.

Chamberlain, Valentine B
A letter of. . . . [Hilton head, October 10, 1862] *Florida Historical quarterly* xv (1936/37) 85–95.　　　　　　　　　　　32B

Hawley, Joseph Roswell, 1826–1905.
Comments on General Jones's paper [The battle of Olustee, or Ocean pond, Florida] *BandL* iv 79–80.　　　　　　　　　33

Tourtellotte, Jerome, 1837–
A history of Company K of the Seventh Connecticut volunteer infantry in the Civil war, compiled by a member who was second in rank in the company when the Regiment left the State for the front and second in rank in the Regiment when it returned to the State for final discharge. [n. p.] 1910. 217, (1) p. 23cm.　　　　　　　　DLC NN　34
On cover: Windham county boys in the Seventh Connecticut. Unit roster 191–209.

Walkley, Stephen, 1832–
History of the Seventh Connecticut volunteer infantry, Hawley's brigade, Terry's division, Tenth army corps, 1861–1865, compiled by Stephen Walkley. [Southington, 1905] 226, 22, lxix, 9 p. illus., plans, port., front. (port.), 2 fold. maps. 21cm.　　DLC NHi NN　35
Unit roster lxix p.

Woodford, Milton M　　　　1834–
. . . Letters from the front. Edited by Vaughn D. Bernet. *Florida historical quarterly* xxvii (1948/49) 237–59, 385–403.　　　35A
At head of title: [1st installment] A Connecticut Yankee fights at Olustee [2nd installment] A Yankee after Olustee.

See also Title 13.

## 8TH INFANTRY

*Left State: October 17, 1861.*
*Mustered out: December 12, 1865.*
*Record 327–58.* History, by J. H. Vaill.

De Kay, Sidney
. . . A night attack of cavalry, by Sidney De Kay, late U.S. vols. . . . New York, Printed for the Commandery of the State of New York by D. Appleton and co., 1888. 14 p. 24cm.
The title piece, poetry, p 3–4.　　NN　35B

Eaton, Jacob
Memorial of Marvin Wait, (1st Lieutenant Eighth regiment C.V.), killed at the battle of Antietam, September 17th, 1862. Written by Jacob Eaton (formerly 1st Lieutenant Eighth C.V.). New Haven, Thomas J. Stafford, printer, 1863. 16 p. 23cm.　　　　　DLC　36

Smith, Moses
Past mercies: present gratitudes: future duty. A discourse delivered at the camp of the Eighth regt. Conn. vet. vol. infantry, near Ft. Harrison, Virginia [sic] on the annual Thanksgiving day, November 24, 1864, with an appendix [giving the Regiment's history and roster] by Moses Smith, Chaplain 8th C.V. Published by the men of the Regiment. . . . New Haven, J. H. Benham, printer, 1865. 24 p.　　　　　　　　　　　Ct　36A

Yates, Walter J
Souvenir of excursion to Antietam and dedication of monuments of the 8th, 11th, 14th and 16th regiments of Connecticut volunteers. [New London] 1894. 61, (5) p. plates (illus., ports.). 18cm.　　　　　　NHi　37
Introduction signed: Walter J. Yates. Advertising matter, p 61, (5) p.

## 9TH INFANTRY

*Left State: November 4, 1861.*
*Consolidated into a battalion: October 12, 1864.*
*Mustered out: August 3, 1865.*
*Record 359–93.* History, by John G. Healy.

Official souvenir program. Dedication of the Ninth regt. C.V. monument at Bay view park, New Haven, Con., Wednesday, August 5, 1903. [New Haven, John J. Kiernan, 1903] 52 p. music, ports. 26½cm.　　　　　CtY　37A
Advertising matter included. Illustration of monument on cover.

Murray, Thomas Hamilton, 1857–
History of the Ninth regiment, Connecticut volunteer infantry, "The Irish regiment," in the War of the rebellion, 1861–65. The record of a gallant command on the march, in battle and in bivouac, by Thomas Hamilton Murray. New Haven, Price, Lee & Adkins, 1903. 446 p. col. front. (illus.), plates (illus., ports.). 23½cm.　　　　DLC NHi NN　38
Unit roster [239]–320.

## 10TH INFANTRY

*Mustered in: September 30, 1861.*
*Mustered out: September 5, 1865.*
*Record 394–430.* History, by John L. Otis.

Trumbull, Henry Clay, 1830–1903.
Desirableness of active service, a sermon preached to the Tenth Connecticut regiment, at St. Augustine, Fla., on Sabbath, April 10th, 1864, by Chaplain H. Clay Trumbull. Hartford, Press of Case, Lockwood and co., 1864. 21 p. 23cm.                    DLC NHi    **39**

—— A good record, a sermon preached before Petersburg, Va., on Sabbath, September 25, 1864, to the Tenth Connecticut regiment, at the close of its first three years of service, by Chaplain H. Clay Trumbull. Hartford, Press of Case, Lockwood & co., 1864. 18 p. 22½cm.                    MBLL    **40**

—— . . . The knightly soldier, a biography of Major Henry Ward Camp, Tenth Conn. vols., by Chaplain H. Clay Trumbull. Boston, Nichols and Noyes, 1865. xii, 13–331 p. front. (port.), 4 plates (illus.). 18½cm.    DLC RP    **41**
At head of title: A record of college, field and prison. "Description of plates to accompany . . . , " inserted leaf. CtY has two issues of "Sixth edition, revised," one dated [c1865] the other 1871. These issues are reprintings with the addition of "Appendix," p 332–5.

—— New and revised edition. Philadelphia, John D. Wattles, 1892. xix, 323 p. front. (port.), plates (illus.). 21cm.    DLC NN    **42**

—— War memories of an army Chaplain, by H. Clay Trumbull, formerly Chaplain of the Tenth regiment of Connecticut. New York, Charles Scribner's Sons, 1898. x, 421 p. plates (illus.). 21cm.    DLC NN    **43**

See also Title 13.

## 11TH INFANTRY

*Mustered in: October 24, 1861.*
*Mustered out: December 21, 1865.*
*Record 431–70.* History, by Charles Warren.

## 12TH INFANTRY

*Left State: February 24, 1862.*
*Consolidated into a battalion: December 2, 1864.*
*Mustered out: August 12, 1865.*
*Record 471–509.* History, by L. A. Dickinson.

Bradford, James Henry, 1836–1913.
"The Chaplains in the volunteer army," prepared by Chaplain James H. Bradford. 1892. 15 p. *MOLLUS-DC* no 11.    **44**

—— "Crises of the Civil war." 1897. 11 p. *MOLLUS-DC* no 27.    **45**

—— A tribute to Tom; or, the "servant question" among the volunteers. 1895. 16 p. *MOLLUS-DC* no 21. front. (port.).    **46**

De Forest, John William, 1826–1906.
The first time under fire. *Harper's magazine* xxix (1864) 475–82.    **47**

—— Forced marches. *Galaxy* v (New York, 1868) 708–18.    **48**
Also published as *Bio* ii (1884) 4–10.

—— Sheridan's victory of Middletown. *Harper's monthly* xxx (1864/65) 353–60.    **48A**

—— Sheridan's battle of Winchester. *Harper's monthly* xxx (1864/65) 195–200.    **48B**

—— A volunteer's adventures, a Union Captain's record of the Civil war, by John William De Forest. Edited with notes, by James H. Croushore, with an introduction, by Stanley T. Williams. New Haven, Yale University press, 1946. xviii, 237 p. front. (port.) facs., 3 maps. 24½cm.    NN    **48C**

Grant, Charles R    1846–
Marching by the flank. *Western reserve university bulletin* xv (Cleveland 1912) 44–57.    **49**

## 13TH INFANTRY

*Left State: March 17, 1862.*
*Consolidated into a battalion: December 15, 1864.*
*Mustered out: April 25, 1865.*
*Record 510–48.* History, by John C. Kinney.

Forlorn hope storming column, Port Hudson, Louisiana, June 15, 1863. Published by the Committe 13th Connecticut veteran association. [n. p.] 1912. [15] p. 21cm.    Ct    **50**
A roster by States and regiments.

Proceedings of 42nd reunion 13th Conn. veteran association. [New Britain, 1912] [3] p. 22½cm.    Ct    **51**
Caption title. "Held at Savin rock, West Haven, Conn., August 14th, 1912." "Secretary has had the minutes of the last reunion printed."

Preston, Francis W
Port Hudson, a history of the investment, siege and capture, last days of the siege, interesting particulars of the capture, the number of prisoners, the entry of our troops, the Rebel

*13th Infantry, continued*

officers detained and the men paroled, destructive effects of the bombardment, the Rebel regiments captured . . . with the partial experience of the author during three years in the march, camp, field and hospital, 19th army corps, Department of the Gulf. [Brooklyn, N.Y., F. W. Preston, c1892] 71, (1) p. illus. 17cm.                                CSmH NN    *51A*

Sprague, Homer Baxter, 1829–1918.

History of the 13th infantry regiment of Connecticut volunteers, during the great rebellion, by Homer B. Sprague. Hartford, Case, Lockwood & co., 1867. viii, [9]–353 p. 19½cm.

Unit roster [261]–311.          DLC NN    **52**

—— . . . Lights and shadows in Confederate prisons, a personal experience, 1864–5, by Homer B. Sprague. New York, G. P. Putnam's Sons, 1915. viii, 163 p. front. (7 ports.). 19½cm.                              DLC NN    **53**

### 14TH INFANTRY

*Mustered in: August 23, 1862.*

*Mustered out: May 30, 1865.*

*Record 549–86. History, by Rev. Henry S. Stevens.*

Minutes of the . . . annual reunion of the Fourteenth Connecticut regiment. . . . 1869–1924. 56 nos. 14½cm.                              Ct    **54**
Annual. Numbered [5]–60. The minutes of 1865–1868 were published with those of 1895.

Burton, Nathaniel Judson, 1822–1887.

A discourse delivered January 29th, 1865, in memory of Robert H. Gillette, by Nathaniel J. Burton. Published by request. Hartford, Press of Wiley, Waterman & Eaton, 1865. 44 p. 18½cm.                                DLC    **55**

Fiske, Samuel Wheelock, 1828–1864.

Dr. Dunn Browne's experiences in the Army. . . . Boston, Nichols and Noyes, 1866. xii, 11–390 p. front. (port.). 19cm.    DLC NN    **56**
"Biographical notice," 11–37, "from the funeral sermon of Professor W. S. Tyler, of Amherst college." "Preface" signed: A. S. F. Coulter 162.

Goddard, Henry Perkins, 1842–1916.

14th C.V. regimental reminiscences of the War of the rebellion, by Henry P. Goddard, late Captain. . . . [Middletown, C. W. Church, printer, 1877] 15 p. 22cm.   DLC NHi    **57**

—— Memorial of deceased officers of the Fourteenth regiment Connecticut volunteers, by Henry P. Goddard . . . Published by request of the Fourteenth regimental union. Hartford, Case, Lockwood & Brainard, 1872. 40 p. 22½cm.                                DLC    **58**

Page, Charles Davis, 1839–

History of the Fourteenth regiment, Connecticut vol. infantry, by Charles D. Page. Meriden, Horton print. co., 1906. 509 p. illus., ports. 23cm.                        DLC NN    **59**
Unit roster 373–509.

Stevens, Henry S

Address delivered at the dedication of monument of the 14th Conn. vols., Gettysburg, Penn., July 3d, 1884, Comrade H. S. Stevens. A description of the monument, &c. Also, an account of the trip of the 14th C.V. to Gettysburg, July 1–3, '84, by Comrade J. W. Knowlton. Middletown, Pelton & King, printers, 1884. 35, (1) p. front. (mounted illus.). 23cm.
                                   Ct DLC    **60**
"List of engagements of the 14th C.V.," (1) p.

—— Souvenir of excursion to battlefields by the Society of the Fourteenth Connecticut regiment and reunion at Antietam, September 1891, with history and reminiscences of battles and campaigns of the Regiment on the fields revisited, by Chaplain H. S. Stevens. Washington, D. C., Gibson Brothers, printers, 1893. 119 p. front. (port.), illus. 23cm.
                           CtHi DLC NHi    **61**

Stevens, John W

A descriptive account of the life and experience of John W. Stevens in Libby prison, Richmond, Va., from October 29th 1864, to March 12th, 1865, "when I was paroled." [n. p., n. d.] [4] p. 24cm.    CtHi    **62**
Caption title.

Taylor, Jeremiah, 1817–1898.

The sacrifice consumed. Life of Edward Hamilton Brewer, lately a soldier in the Army of the Potomac, by Jeremiah Taylor. . . . Boston, Henry Hoyt, 1863. x, 11–140 p. front. (port.). 17½cm.    CtHi DLC NN    **63**
On spine: The patriot soldier.

Tyler, William Seymour, 1810–1897.

. . .A sermon preached at the funeral of Capt. Samuel Fisk in the Congregational church at Shelburne Falls, on Sunday, May 29, 1864, by W. S. Tyler. New Haven, Printed by E. Hayes, 1864. 37 p. 22½cm.   Ct CtY    *63A*
At head of title: The law of sacrifice, or death the only way to a higher life.

See also Title 37.

### 15TH INFANTRY

*Mustered in: August 25, 1862.*

*Mustered out: June 27, 1865.*

*Record 587–616. History, by George M. White.*

Thorpe, Sheldon Brainerd, 1838–1914.
The history of the Fifteenth Connecticut volunteers in the War for the defense of the Union, 1861–1865, by Sheldon B. Thorpe, Sergeant Company K. New Haven, Price, Lee & Adkins co., 1893. iv, [5]–362 p. plates (illus., plan, ports.). 24cm.          DLC NHi NN    **64**
Unit roster [265]–330.

## 16TH INFANTRY

*Mustered in: August 24, 1862.*

*Mustered out: June 24, 1865.*

*Record 617–39. History, by B. F. Blakeslee.*

Roster of the survivors of the 16th Connecticut volunteers, September 1, 1909. [12] p. 1 illus., 2 ports. 19½cm.          Ct    **65**
Title from cover.

Sixteenth regiment Connecticut volunteers excursion and reunion at Antietam battlefield, September 17, 1889. Hartford, Press of the Case, Lockwood & Brainard co., 1889. 32 p. 1 illus., map. 15½cm.          Ct    **66**
"The Sixteenth at Antietam," by Lieutenant B. F. Blakeslee, 13–23.

16th regiment Conn. volunteers report of the twenty-third annual reunion at Antietam battlefield, September 17, 1889. Hartford, Press of the Case, Lockwood & Brainard co., 1890. 35 p. 23cm.          Ct    **67**

Blakeslee, Bernard F
History of the Sixteenth Connecticut volunteers, by B. F. Blakeslee, late 2d Lieut. Co. G. Hartford, Case, Lockwood & Brainard co., 1875. 116 p. 19cm.          DLC NHi NN    **68**
Coulter 39.

Burkhardt, A          W
Forty hours on the battlefield of Antietam; or, the foeman friend, by A. W. Burkhardt. [n. p., n. d.] [10] leaves. 8½ × 12½cm.
                                        NN    **69**
On cover: From the same canteen. The Northern soldier is Bela L. Burr of the 16th Conn.

Gilbert, William H
Sermon delivered in Granby, Conn., Jan. 4, 1863, at the funeral of Roswell Morgan Allen, Private in Co. E, 16th reg't C.V., who died at the hospital near Washington, Sunday, Dec. 28, 1863, by Rev. W. H. Gilbert. Hartford, Printed by Charles Montague, 1863. 23 p. 22cm.          Ct CtY    **69A**

Kellogg, Robert H
Life and death in Rebel prisons, giving a complete history of the inhuman and barbarous treatment of our brave soldiers by Rebel au-

thorities, inflicting terrible suffering and frightful mortality, principally at Andersonville, Ga., and Florence, S.C., describing plans of escape, arrival of prisoners, with numerous and varied incidents and anecdotes of prison life, by Robert H. Kellogg, Sergeant-major 16th regiment Connecticut volunteers. Prepared from his daily journal, to which is added as full sketches of other prisons as can be given without repetition of the above, by the parties who have been confined therein. . . . Hartford, L. Stebbins, 1865. viii, [11]–400 p. plans, plates (illus.). 19cm.          DLC NHi NN    **70**
"Agents wanted" for this book, p 399. Advertisement, p 400. Coulter 272.

————— ——— Hartford, L. Stebbins, 1866. viii, [11]–423 p. plans, plates (illus.). 19cm.
                                        NN    **71**
Printed from the plates of Title 70 with the addition of 399–423, Appendix. Trial and execution of Wirz. Another printing, 1867.

Mayer, Nathan
A poem read by Surgeon Nathan Mayer, October 11, 1894, at the dedication of a monument by the Sixteenth Connecticut where they fought at Antietam, September 17, 1862. Hartford, Press of the Case, Lockwood & Brainard co., 1894. 14 folios. illus., ports. 21½cm.
                                        DLC NHi    **72**
"Published by the Executive committee of the Sixteenth Connecticut association."

O'Brien, Frank P
The story of a flag and the strange bringing together of its captors and defenders, as related by one of the former. *BandG* ɪɪ (1893) 143–5.
                                        **73**
Author was a member of a Confederate artillery company.

See also Title 37.

## 17TH INFANTRY

*Mustered in: August 28, 1862.*

*Mustered out: July 19, 1865.*

*Record 640–64. History, by William H. Noble.*

Seventeenth annual reunion of the 17th regiment C.V.I., held at Fairfield, Conn., August 28th, 1883. Bridgeport, Standard Association, printers, 1884. 37 p. 22½cm.          Ct NN    **74**

17th Connecticut volunteers at Gettysburg, June 30th, and July 1st, 2d and 3d, 1884. Bridgeport, Standard Association, printers, 1884. 46, (1) p. illus., plate (illus.). 22½cm.
                                        DLC NHi NN    **75**

## 18TH INFANTRY

*Left State: August 22, 1862.*

*Mustered out: June 27, 1865.*

*Record 665–89. History, by William G. Ely.*

Roster of the 18th regt. Conn. vols. . . . Norwich, Utley's print. office, 1890. 45 p. 13½cm.
WHi   **76**

Kinney, Charles Coddington
An August morning with Farragut. *Scribner's monthly* XXII (1881) 199–208.   **76A**

—— Farragut at Mobile bay. *BandL* IV 379–400.   **76B**

Lynch, Charles H
The Civil war diary, 1862–1865, of Charles H. Lynch, 18th Conn. vol's. [Hartford, Case, Lockwood & Brainard co., 1915] 163 p. plates (2 ports.). 23½cm.   IHi NN   **77**

Walker, William Carey
History of the Eighteenth regiment Conn. volunteers in the War for the Union, by Chaplain Wm. C. Walker. Norwich, Published by the Committee [printed by Gordon Wilcox] 1885. 444 p. plates (illus., map, ports.). 24½cm.   DLC NHi NN   **78**
Unit roster 393–428.

## 19TH INFANTRY

*Mustered in: September 11, 1862.*

*Designated 2nd regiment of heavy artillery: November 23, 1863.*

Lewis, William H
Memorials of Edgar B. Lewis, late of the Junior class, Trinity college, and of the 19th regiment, C.V., by William H. Lewis. Hartford, Press of Case, Lockwood and co., 1863. 74 p. front. (port.). 18½cm.
DLC NHi NN   **79**

## 20TH INFANTRY

*Mustered in: September 8, 1862.*

*Mustered out: June 13, 1865.*

*Record 690–716. History, by Cecil A. Burleigh.*

Chapman, Horatio Dana, 1826–1910.
Civil war diary. Diary of a Forty-niner. [By] Horatio Dana Chapman, Company C, Twentieth Connecticut volunteer infantry. . . . Hartford, Allis, 1929. 115, 16 p. front. (illus., 2 ports.). 23cm.   Ct NN   **80**
Diary of a Forty-niner, 16 p.

Fenton, Ebenezer B
From the Rapidan to Atlanta, leaves from the diary of E. B. Fenton, late Twentieth Connecticut volunteer infantry, read before the Commandery of the State of Michigan, Military order of the loyal legion of the United States. . . . Detroit, Winn & Hammond, printers, 1893. 22 p. 21½cm.   DLC NHi   **81**
Also published as *MOLLUS-Mich* I no 24.

Sherman, George Witherell
A narrative of war time, a narrative connected with the heroic struggle during the Civil war for the preservation of our glorious Republic, by Captain George W. Sherman. Lynbrook, N. Y. [New Era press, 191–] 40 p. 2 illus., plan, port. 21½cm.   DLC NN   **82**
Caption title: A narrative in remembrance of the Twentieth regiment Connecticut volunteers. Title from cover.

Storrs, John Whiting
The "Twentieth Connecticut," a regimental history, by John W. Storrs. Naugatuck, Press of the "Naugatuck Valley Sentinel," 1886. 288, xviii p. 3 plates (2 mounted illus., fold. map). 19½cm.   DLC NHi NN   **83**
"Twenty years later," an account of the dedication of a monument at Gettysburg, [175]–213. Unit roster xviii p. "Further corrections" inserted slip.

## 21ST INFANTRY

*Mustered in: September 5, 1862.*

*Mustered out: June 16, 1865.*

*Record 717–38. History, by Delos D. Brown.*

The story of the Twenty-first regiment, Connecticut volunteer infantry, during the Civil war, 1861–1865, by members of the Regiment. Middletown, Stewart print. co., 1900. xx, 448, 50 p. illus., map, ports., 2 fold. maps. 22cm.
DLC NHi NN   **84**
Unit roster, 50 p. "Committee's preface" signed: W. S. Hubbell, A. M. Crane [and] D. D. Brown. Contributions are signed by their authors.

## 22ND INFANTRY

*Mustered in: September 20, 1862.*

*Mustered out: July 7, 1863.*

*Record 739–56. History, by John K. Williams.*

An allegory on the members of Company E, 22nd regiment, C.V., by a member of the Company. Hartford, Press of Case, Lockwood & co., 1863. 24 p. 18½cm.   NHi   **85**

History of the Twenty-second regiment Connecticut volunteer infantry, 1862–3. Hartford, Press of Hartford print. co., 1896. 16 p. 16½cm.   Ct NHi   **86**

A journal of incidents connected with the travels of the Twenty-second regiment Conn. volunteers, for nine months. In verse, by an Orderly Sergeant. Hartford, Williams, Wiley and Waterman, 1863. 28 p. 22½cm.

Ct NN    **87**

"Officers of the Regiment," p 4 of cover. Title from the cover. Ascribed to E. W. Waters, Orderly Sergeant of Co. E.

Reunion and 25th anniversary of the muster in of the 22d regiment Conn. vol., at Windsor, Conn., September 20, 1887. Hartford, Press of Clark & Smith, 1888. 26 p. 22cm.

Ct NHi    **88**

### 23RD INFANTRY

*Left State: November 17, 1862.*

*Mustered out: September 1, 1863.*

*Record 757–73. History, by David H. Miller.*

Quien, George
Reminiscences of the service and experience of Lieut. George Quien of Company K, Twenty-third regiment Conn. vols. Waterbury, 1906. 111, (2) p. front. (port.). 21cm.

NN    **89**

Roster of officers (2) p. On spine: Co. K in the Civil war.

Sherman, Andrew Magoun, 1844–1921.
Civil war reminiscences. *American historical magazine* iv (New York, 1909) 871–83, 997–1005.    **90**

—— In the lowlands of Louisiana in 1863, an address delivered by Rev. Andrew M. Sherman, at the forty-second annual reunion of the Twenty-third Conn. regimental association, held at Steeplechase island, Bridgeport, Connecticut, on Thursday, August 20, 1908. (Published by request) [Morristown, N.J., Howard pub. co., 1908] 40 p. front. (port.). 23cm.

DLC NN    **91**

### 24TH INFANTRY

*Mustered in: November 18, 1862.*

*Mustered out: September 30, 1863.*

*Record 774–89. History, by Augustus H. Conklin.*

### 25TH INFANTRY

*Mustered in: November 11, 1862.*

*Mustered out: August 26, 1863.*

*Record 790–806. History, by George P. Bissell.*

A memorial of Lt. Daniel Perkins Dewey of the Twenty-fifth regiment Connecticut volun-

teers. Hartford, Press of Case, Lockwood & co., 1864. 126 p. front. (port.). 18½cm.

NN    **92**

McManus, Thomas
Battle of Irish Bend, interesting reminiscences of that terrible combat . . . an address given before the people of St. Patrick's church, Collinsville, April 23, 1891, by Major Thomas McManus, of the 25th reg't., Conn. vols. [n. p., 1891] 16 p.    Ct    **93**

Title from cover.

—— Battle fields of Louisiana revisited a second time, by Thomas McManus, late Major. Hartford, Fowler & Miller co., printers, 1898. 34 p. 16cm.    Ct DLC    **94**

On cover: Battlefields of Louisiana revisited again.

—— Through the campaigning grounds of Louisiana, by a veteran of the Twenty-fifth Connecticut, forty-four years after. [n. p., 1907] [37] p. 14½cm.    Ct    **95**

Text signed: Thomas M'Manus. Title from cover.

—— Twenty-fifth regiment battle fields revisited, by Thomas McManus, Major 25th regiment, February 1896. Hartford, Clark & Smith, printers, 1896. 42 p. 19cm.    NHi    **96**

Oviatt, George Alexander, 1811–1887.
A memorial address delivered at the funeral of Captain Samuel S. Hayden, at Windsor Locks, Friday, June 19, 1863, by Rev. George A. Oviatt, lately Chaplain of the 25th reg't Conn. vols. Published by request. Hartford, Press of Case, Lockwood and co., 1863. 22 p. 23cm.    DLC    **97**

### 26TH INFANTRY

*Mustered in: November 10–12, 1862.*

*Mustered out: August 19, 1863.*

*Record 807–24. History, by Loren A. Gallup.*

Memoranda Twenty-sixth regiment, Conn. vols. [n. p., 1877?] 12 p. 22cm.    Ct    **98**

A record of the Regiment in diary form. Caption title.

Roster, muster roll and chronological record of the Twenty-sixth regiment, Connecticut volunteers, and memoranda of the Association of the Twenty-sixth regiment, Connecticut volunteers. Intended for the use of the members. . . . Norwich, Frank Utley print, 1888. 56 p. 22½cm.    Ct    **99**

Alexander, Walter Scott, 1835–1900.
Sermon occasioned by the death of Edwin Ruthven Keyes, Sergeant in the 26th Conn. regiment, who was wounded at Port Hudson, May 27th, 1863, and who died at Baton Rouge,

*26th Infantry, continued*

La., June 12th, 1863. Delivered in the First Congregational church, Pomfret, Conn., Sabbath morning, August 2nd, 1863, by Walter S. Alexander. Danielsonville, Transcript print, 1863. 15 p. 23½cm.                    DLC    *100*

### 27TH INFANTRY

*Mustered in: October 22, 1862.*

*Mustered out: August 17, 1863.*

*Record 825–44. History, by Frank D. Sloat.*

Dedication of the monument of 27th Conn. vols. at Gettysburg, October 22d, 1885, including an account of the excursion from New Haven to Gettysburg and return. New Haven, Price, Lee & co., printers, 1886. 43, (1) p. front. (illus.). 21½cm.          Ct NHi    *101*

Brand, James, 1834–1899.

James Brand, twenty-six years pastor of the First Congregational church, Oberlin, some chapters from his life . . . written by himself for his family, shortly before his death. Oberlin, Luther Day Harkness, 1899. 48 p. front. (port.). 14½cm.                         *102*
Civil war 42–8.

Sheldon, Winthrop Dudley, 1839–

The "Twenty-seventh," a regimental history, by Winthrop D. Sheldon, late Lieutenant Company H. New Haven, Morris & Benham, 1866. 144 p. 2 ports. 19cm.    DLC NHi NN    *103*
Unit roster 115–44. Coulter 412.

### 28TH INFANTRY

*Mustered in: November 15, 1862.*

*Mustered out: August 28, 1863.*

*Record 845–58. History, by W. T. Batcheller.*

Roster of the Twenty-eighth regiment, Connecticut volunteers. 1862–1897. Winsted, Press of the Dowd print. co., 1897. 31 p. 14cm.
Ct    *104*

A tribute of Company C, 27th regiment Conn. volunteers, to the memory of Captain Addison C. Taylor, died March 13th, 1863, from a wound received at the battle of Fredericks-

burg, Dec. 13, 1862. [n. p., 1863] folder, p. [2] and [4] blank. 20½cm.            CtY    *104A*

Hoag, David D

Life and letters of Capt. David D. Hoag, who fell in the siege of Port Hudson, compiled by his brother, J. C. Hoag. New York, Cutler, Tower & co., 1866. 116 p. 19½cm.
NNC    *104B*

Scofield, Loomis

History of the Twenty-eighth regiment Connecticut volunteers, by Loomis Scofield. New Canaan Advertiser, 1915. 24 p. front. (port.). 22cm.                            CtHi    *105*

### 29TH INFANTRY

*Mustered in: March 8, 1864.*

*Mustered out: October 14, 1865.*

*Record 859–81. History, by Rev. Henry G. Marshall.*

Hill, Isaac J            1826–

A sketch of the 29th regiment of Connecticut colored troops, giving a full account of its formation, of all the battles through which it passed, and its final disbandment, by J. [sic] J. Hill. Baltimore, Printed by Daugherty, Maguire & co., 1867. 42 p. 22½cm.DLC    *106*
Coulter 232.

—— New York, Baker, Goodwin, printers, 1881. 40 p. 22½cm.        DLC NHi    *106A*

Newton, Alexander Heritage, 1837–

Out of the briars, an autobiography and sketch of the Twenty-ninth regiment, Connecticut volunteers, by A. H. Newton. With an introduction by Rev. J. P. Sampson. [Philadelphia, A. M. E. Book Concern, printers, 1910] xv, 19–269 p. plates (2 illus., ports.). 21cm.                         DLC NN    *107*
"My war record and sketch of the Twenty-ninth regiment," [29]–89.

### 30TH INFANTRY

*Authorized: January 12, 1864. Four companies were organized and sent to Virginia, June 4, 1864, where they were consolidated with other companies to form the 31st United States colored troops.*

*Record 882–91.*

# MAINE

# Reference Works

Dyer, Frederick Henry, 1849–1917.

A compendium of the War of the rebellion, 1908 (reprinted 1959).

"Regimental index" 150–153; "Regimental histories" 1215–28. The pagination is the same in the 1959 reprint.

Maine. Adjutant General.

Alphabetical index of Maine volunteers, etc., mustered into the service of the United States during the war of 1861. Augusta, Stevens & Sayward, printers to the State, 1867. 1210, (1) p. 23cm.

Title cited is from cover; title page reads: Supplement to the Annual reports of the Adjutant general of the State of Maine, for the years 1861, '62, '63, '64, '65 and 1866. "Index," (1) p. In two alphabets, the second has subtitle: of persons drafted in the summer of 1863.

Stanley, Ruel H

Eastern Maine and the rebellion, being an account of the principal local events in Eastern Maine during the war, and brief histories of Eastern Maine regiments, contains accounts of mobs, riots, destruction of newspapers, war meetings, drafts, Confederate raids, peace meetings, celebrations, soldiers' letters, and scenes and incidents at the front, never before in print, by R. H. Stanley and Geo. O. Hall. Bangor, R. H. Stanley & co., 1887. 392 p. plates (illus., ports.). 22cm.

*The Union army.*

"Record of Maine regiments," I (1908) 39–67.

United States. Adjutant General's Office.

Official army register of the volunteer force of the United States army for the years 1861, '62, '63, '64, '65. Part I. (New England states). Washington, 1865.

A roster of officers by regiments with an alphabetical index for the six States.

Whitman, William Edward Seaver, 1832–

Maine in the War for the Union, a history of the part borne by Maine troops in the suppression of the American rebellion, by William E. S. Whitman and Charles H. True. Lewiston, Nelson Dingley Jr. & co., 1865. viii, 592 p. 2 plates (ports.). 22½cm.

—— —— Lewiston, Nelson Dingley Jr. & co., 1865. viii, 637 p. 2 plates (ports.). 22½cm.

"Supplement," 593–637.

# MAINE

## ARTILLERY

### 1ST ARTILLERY (HEAVY)

*Mustered in as 18th regiment of infantry: August 21, 1862.*
*Designated 1st regiment of heavy artillery: January 6, 1863.*
*Mustered out: September 11, 1865.*
*Eastern Maine 137–54.*
*Maine in the war 458–74, 602–04.*

Brown, Joel F
The charge of the heavy artillery. *Maine bugle* campaign I (1894) 3–19. **1**

—— —— Corrections and additions. *Maine bugle* campaign I (1894) 143–6.

Dole, James A
War record First Maine heavy artillery . . . presented by Lieut. James A. Dole. [n. p., n. d.] broadside, 32 × 25cm. MeBa **2**

House, Charles J
First Maine artillery in Fall of 1864, by Major Charles J. House. *Maine bugle* campaign IV (1897) 133–40. **3**

—— How the First Maine heavy artillery lost 1,179 men in 30 days. *Maine bugle* campaign II (1895) 87–95. **4**

Shaw, Horace H 1842?–
The First Maine heavy artillery, 1862–1865, a history of its part and place in the War for the Union, with an outline of causes of war and its results to our Country, by Horace H. Shaw. With organization, company, and individual records, by Charles J. House. Portland, 1903. xiii, 516, ii, a–x, (1) p. front. (port.), illus., ports., 4 double plates (illus.) 22cm.
Unit roster 222–407. DLC NN **5**

## Mounted Batteries of Artillery

### 1st Battery

*Mustered in: December 18, 1861.*
*Mustered out: July 15, 1865.*
*Maine in the war 385–91, 604–05.*

### 2nd Battery

*Mustered in: November 30, 1861.*
*Mustered out: June 16, 1865.*
*Maine in the war 392–8, 605.*

### 3rd Battery

*Mustered in: December 11, 1861.*
*Mustered out: June 17, 1865.*
*Maine in the war 399–402, 605–06.*
*Eastern Maine 281–2.*

### 4th Battery

*Mustered in: December 21, 1861.*
*Mustered out: June 17, 1865.*
*Maine in the war 403–09, 606.*

History of the Fourth Maine battery light artillery in the Civil war, 1861–65, containing a brief account of its services compiled from diaries of its members and other sources. Also, personal sketches of many of its members and an account of its reunions from 1882 to 1905. Augusta, Burleigh & Flynt, printers, 1905. vi, [7]–183 p. 2 plates (ports.). 23½cm.
Unit roster [107]–16. DLC NHi **6**

### 5th Battery

*Mustered in: December 4, 1861.*
*Mustered out: July 6, 1865.*
*Maine in the war 410–16, 606.*

Butler, Plummer H
My first experience in battle, and also the first engagement of the Fifth Maine battery. *Maine bugle* campaign III (1896) 223–6. **7**

Hunt, Charles O
Our escape from Camp Sorghum, by Lieutenant Charles O. Hunt. *MOLLUS-Me* I 85–128. **8**

Stevens, Greenlief T
Letter to the members of the 5th Maine battery association, by G. T. Stevens. Augusta, Press of Charles E. Nash, 1890. 25 p. 23½cm.
DLC NHi **9**

Whittier, Edward N
The left attack (Ewell's), Gettysburg, by Brevet Captain Edward N. Whittier. *PMHSM* III 315–50. **10**
Also published in *MOLLUS-Mass* I 75–106.

### 6th Battery

*Mustered in: June 1, 1862.*
*Mustered out: June 7, 1865.*
*Maine in the war 417–27, 606–10.*

Rhodes, James E
The Sixth Maine battery before Petersburg. *Maine bugle* campaign I (1894) 249–55. **12**

## 7th Battery

Mustered in: December 30, 1863.

Mustered out: June 12, 1865.

Maine in the war 570–2, 610.

Lapham, William Berry, 1828–1894.
My recollections of the War of the rebellion, by William B. Lapham. Privately printed. Augusta, Burleigh & Flynt, printers, 1892. 240 p. plate (port.). 19½cm.　　DLC NHi　　**13**

Partial contents: The Twenty-third Maine regiment, 41–87; Seventh Maine battery, 89–192. Unit rosters: Co. F, 23d Maine, 43–7; 7th battery, 92–103. Coulter 283.

—— With the Seventh Maine battery, by Brevet Major William B. Lapham. *MOLLUS-Me* I 145–60.　　**14**

Twitchell, Albert Sobieski, 1840–
History of the Seventh Maine light battery, volunteers in the great rebellion, containing a brief daily account of its services, without comments or attempt to criticise or praise the brave boys in this command. Also, personal sketches of a large number of members, portraits, illustrations and poems. Written and compiled by Quartermaster-Sergeant A. S. Twitchell, historian. Boston, E. B. Stillings & co., 1892. vi, [9]–248 p. front. (port.), ports. 24cm.　　DLC NN　　**15**

Unit roster 9–17. "Personal sketches, compiled from brief histories furnished by comrades on blanks furnished for that purpose," [61]–227.

—— Re-union poems as written and delivered by A. S. Twitchell. Gorham, N.H., V. V. Twitchell [Mountaineer print] 1883. front. (port.), plate (port.). 19½cm.　　NHi　　**16**

## CAVALRY

### 1ST CAVALRY

Mustered in: November 5, 1861.

Mustered out: August 1, 1865.

Maine in the war 350–82, 597–9.

Eastern Maine 246–66.

First Maine bugle, campaign I [–II] July 1890–October 1893. . . . Rockland, First Maine Cavalry Association [1890–93] 2 v. ports., plates (illus., ports.). 23½cm.　　DLC NHi　　**17**

Quarterly. Contains the Proceedings of the yearly reunions of the First Maine cavalry. Organ of the Cavalry society of the armies of the United States, July 1892 – October 1893. E. P. Tobie, editor. Preceded by Title 18. Superseded by the Maine bugle.

First Maine cavalry association record of proceedings at the . . . annual reunion. . . . Augusta, 1872–82. 7 v. 23cm.
　　DLC NN (1, 3–11)　　**18**

Eleven meetings were held. The record of the meetings, 3/4, 5/7, 8/9, were published in three volumes as indicated. Continued by Title 17.

Unveiling of monument to the First Maine cavalry at Gettysburg, Oct. 3d, 1889. [Boston, C. A. F. Emery, printer, 1889] [12] leaves. front. (port.), plate (illus.). 18cm.
　　MeHi NHi　　**19**

On cover: Gettysburg First Maine cavalry monument. Contents: Address, by Charles H. Smith; Poem, by Edward P. Tobie.

Benson, Andrew M
My capture, prison life and escape, by Brevet-Major Andrew M. Benson. *MOLLUS-Mass* I 109–38.　　**20**

Bowman, Martin T　　V
My experience on Pope's retreat. *MOLLUS-Iowa* II 48–56.　　**21**

Cilley, Jonathan Prince, 1835–1920.
A plea for regimental histories. *Maine bugle* campaign II (1895) 144–57.　　**21A**
"The debate in the Maine Senate," 151–7.

—— Regimental histories, by Gen. J. P. Cilley. *Maine bugle* campaign I (1894) 175–8.　　**21B**
Includes "List of regimental histories and publications pertaining to Maine regiments."

Coburn, Jefferson L
Adventures at Farmville, Virginia, by Lieutenant Jeff. L. Coburn. *Maine bugle* campaign IV (1897) 22–8.　　**22**

—— An episode of the Wilson raid, City point to Roanoke, Va., June 21–30, 1864. *Maine bugle* campaign II (1895) 187–203. 3 ports., map.　　**23**

—— A visit to the battlefield of Dinwiddie court house, incidents and anecdotes relating to that battle. *Maine bugle* campaign II (1895) 52–75. plan, 3 ports.　　**24**

Darling, Joseph T　　1833–
Nine months in a Rebel prison. *Maine bugle* campaign V (1898) 1–13, 115–26.　　**25**

Ford, Charles W
Charge of the First Maine cavalry at Brandy station, by Captain Charles W. Ford. *MOLLUS-Me* II 268–89.　　**26**

Hall, Henry C
Some recollections of Appomattox, by Major H. C. Hall. *Maine bugle* campaign I (1894) 133–40.　　**27**

Merrill, Samuel Hill, 1805–1873.

The campaigns of the First Maine and First District of Columbia cavalry, by Samuel H. Merrill, Chaplain. Portland, Bailey & Noyes, 1866. xv, [17]–436 p. plates (ports.). 19½cm.

DLC NN **28**

Unit roster [389]–431. Coulter 323.

Smith, Charles Henry,        –1902.

A reconnaissance with the First Maine cavalry. [Fort Clark, Texas, 1885] 9 p. 21cm.

MeBa **29**

Caption title. Text dated and signed: C. H. Smith, formerly Colonel 1st Maine cavalry, Fort Clark, Texas, May, 1885. Also published as *JUSCA* III (1890) 253–62.

Thaxter, Sidney Warren, 1839–1908.

A remarkable reconnaissance, by Major Sidney W. Thaxter. *MOLLUS-Me* I 20–8.    **30**

—— Stonewall Jackson. *Maine bugle* campaign II (1895) 315–34.    **31**

Tobie, Edward Parsons, 1838–

The boys in Blue and the boys in Gray. *BandG* II (1893) 51–4.    **32**

—— First Maine cavalry historical sketch and recollections, by Lieut. Edward P. Tobie. [n. p., n. d.] 48 p. plates (2 illus., 4 maps). 24cm.    MeHi **33**

Title from cover.

—— History of the First Maine cavalry, 1861–1865, by Edward P. Tobie. Published by the First Maine cavalry association. Boston, Press of Emery & Hughes, 1887. xix, 735, (1) p. plates (illus., ports.).    23½cm.    NN **34**

Unit roster [449]–658. "Card of Committee on publishing history," (1) p.

—— Personal recollections of General Sheridan. 1889. 40 p. *PNRISSHS* s4 no 5.    **35**

—— Service of the cavalry in the Army of the Potomac. 1882. 56 p. *PNRISSHS* s2 no 14.    **36**

—— Supporting a battery. *BandG* II (1893) 257–60.    **37**

—— A trip to Richmond as a prisoner of war. 1879. 48 p. *PNRISSHS* s1 no 6.    **38**

—— A "Yank" in the hands of the enemy. *BandG* I (1893) 173–8.    **39**

## 2ND CAVALRY

*Left State: April 1864.*
*Mustered out: December 6, 1865.*
*Maine in the war 563–9, 599–602.*
*Eastern Maine 306–10.*

Roberts, C        C

A story of General Andrew B. Spurling and Second Maine cavalry, compiled from official, individual and newspaper reports, historical notes, incidents, etc., for distribution at reunion in Boston, Mass., Aug. 17, 1904, by C. C. Roberts. 91 p. front. (port.). 21½cm.

MeBa **40**

## INFANTRY

### 1ST INFANTRY

*Mustered in: April 28, 1861.*
*Mustered out: August 5, 1861.*
*Maine in the war 26–36.*

Bosworth, George W

The soldier's commission against rebellion, a sermon preached before a portion of the First regiment of the volunteer militia of Maine, Portland, April 28, 1861, by Rev. G. W. Bosworth. Portland, James S. Staples, printer, 1861. 20 p. 21cm.    Me **41**

Gould, John Mead, 1839–1930.

Directory of the First-Tenth-Twenty-ninth Maine regiment association, compiled for the use of the association, by Major John M. Gould, Sec'y, 1889. Portland, Stephen Berry, printer, 1889. 40 p. 23cm.    NN **42**

Title and imprint from cover.

—— History of the First-Tenth-Twenty-ninth Maine regiment, in service of the United States, from May 3, 1861, to June 21, 1866, by Maj. John M. Gould. With the history of the Tenth Me, battalion, by Rev. Leonard G. Jordan. Portland, Stephen Berry, 1871. 709 p. illus., map, plates (2 maps, ports.). 22½cm.

DLC NN **43**

Unit roster: 1st regiment, 66–79; 10th regiment, 313–32; 10th battalion, 377–82; 29th regiment, 615–36. Coulter 198.

—— —— Additions and corrections to 1-10-29 Maine regiment. Correcting all errors that have been noticed up to February, 1893. 8 p. 22½cm.    NN **43A**

Title from cover.

## 2ND INFANTRY

*Mustered in: May 28, 1861.*
*Mustered out: June 9, 1863.*
*Maine in the war 37–57.*
*Eastern Maine 41–61, 118–23, 161–8.*

## 3RD INFANTRY

*Mustered in: June 4, 1861.*
*Mustered out: June 28, 1864.*
*Maine in the war 58–61.*

Eaton, James R                    1841–
Sixteen years on the dark blue sea, four
years with the Army of the Potomac: or, footprints in many lands, being the life, suffering,
and hair-breadth escapes on land and sea of
James R. Eaton, served in the War for the
Union in the 3d and 17th Maine. Written by,
and published for, the author. [Indianapolis,
Press of Frank H. Smith] 1894. 152 p. front.
(port.). 18cm.                     DLC    44
Civil war 24–8.

Howard, Oliver Otis, 1830–1909.
Autobiography of Oliver Otis Howard,
Major-General. New York, Baker & Taylor co.,
1907. 2 v. plates (facs., 2 illus., ports.). 22cm.
                                NN WHi    45
"Colonel of the Third Maine regiment," June 4 –
September 3, 1861, I 111–222.

Johnson, Hannibal Augustus, 1841–
The sword of honor, from captivity to freedom. 1903. 72 p. *PNRISSHS* s6 no 6.    46

—— The sword of honor, a story of the Civil
war, by Lieut. H. A. Johnson, Third Maine
regt. . . . Worcester, Mass., Blanchard press
[1906] 103 p. plates (1 illus., ports.). 18cm.
                                     NHi    47

—— —— Hallowell, Register print. house,
1906. 96, (1) p. plates (ports.). 18cm.
Coulter 260.                         DLC    48

Wing, Samuel B                     1832–
The soldier's story, a personal narrative of
the life, army experiences and marvelous sufferings since the war of Samuel B. Wing. Phillips,
Phonograph print, 1898. 118, (2) p. illus.,
ports. 20½cm.                        WHi    49

## 4TH INFANTRY

*Mustered in: June 15, 1861.*
*Mustered out: July 19, 1864.*
*Maine in the war 82–110.*
*Eastern Maine 98–102, 209–12, 224–5.*

Fernald, Charles O
Life in Libby. *Maine bugle* campaign I
(1894) 232–7.                         50

Gould, Edward Kalloch, 1865–
Major-General Hiram G. Berry, his career
as a contractor, bank president, politician and
Major-General of volunteers in the Civil war,
together with his war correspondence, embrac-

ing the period from Bull run to Chancellorsville, by Edward K. Gould. Rockland, Press of
the Courier-Gazette, 1899. 312 p. plates (illus.,
ports.). 23cm.                       DLC    51
As Colonel of the 4th Maine, 81–105.

Robbins, Nathaniel A
Life in Rebel prisons, by First Lieutenant
Nathaniel A. Robbins. 1906. 12 p. *MOLLUS-
DC* no 65.                            52

## 5TH INFANTRY

*Mustered in: June 24, 1861.*
*Mustered out: July 27, 1864.*
*Maine in the war 111–35.*

Adams, John Ripley, 1802–1866.
Memorial and letters of Rev. John R. Adams,
Chaplain of the Fifth Maine and the One hundred and twenty-first New York regiments during the War of the rebellion, serving from the
beginning to its close. [Cambridge, Mass., University press] 1890. viii, 242 p. front. (mounted
port.). 24cm.                         NN    53
Prefatory note signed: John McGregor Adams [and]
Albert Egerton Adams. Preface signed: Emily Adams
Bancroft.

Bicknell, George W
History of the Fifth regiment Maine volunteers, comprising brief descriptions of its
marches, engagements, and general services
from the date of its muster in, June 24, 1861,
to the time of its muster out, July 27, 1864, by
Rev. Geo. W. Bicknell, First Lieutenant and
Adjutant. Portland, Hall L. Davis, 1871. xii,
[13]–404 p. front. (port.), 2 plates (ports.).
19cm.                             DLC NN    54
Coulter 32. Unit roster [377]–404.

Daggett, Aaron Simon, 1837–
The battle of Rappahannock station, Va., by
Brigadier-General A. S. Daggett. *MOLLUS-
Me* IV 190–9.                         55

McIntyre, Philip Willis, 1847–
Alonzo Palmer Stinson, the first Portland
soldier who fell in battle during the Civil war.
Exercises at the dedication of the memorial to
his memory erected by his comrades of Company H, Fifth Maine volunteer infantry. Edited by Philip Willis McIntyre. . . . Portland,
Lefavor-Tower co., 1909. 62 p. plates (illus.,
ports.). 25cm.                    DLC NN    56
On cover: Stinson memorial. Unit roster Co. H, Fifth
Maine, 57–60.

Mason, Edwin Cooley
Recollections of the Mine run campaign, by
Lieutenant-Colonel Edwin C. Mason. *MOL-
LUS-Minn* I 308–36.                   57

—— Through the Wilderness to the Bloody angle at Spottsylvania court house. *MOLLUS-Minn* iv 281–312.                  58

Morse, William H
The "rebellion record" of an enlisted man. In National tribune scrap book iii 33–101.
58A

Shannon, James H
A few incidents and reminiscences of the Civil war, by Captain James H. Shannon. *MOLLUS-Me* iv 320–39.                  59

Stevens, William E
In battle and in prison, a reminiscence of the War of the rebellion. *Granite monthly* ii (Concord 1879) 210–17.                  60

Weston, Edward Payson, 1819–1879.
The Christian soldier-boy, an address to the young people of Gorham on the death of Joseph D. Harmon, of Company A, 5th regiment Maine volunteers, by Edward P. Weston, on Sabbath evening, July 20th. Portland, Office of the Maine Teacher, 1862. 16 p. 22½cm.
CtY NN    60A

Williams, Isaiah Thornton
Address of Isaiah Thornton Williams on the presentation of colors to the Fifth regiment of Maine volunteers, in City hall park, in the City of New York, on the 27th day of June, 1861. New York, S. Bradford, printer, 1862. 8 p. 22cm.                  DLC  61

## 6TH INFANTRY

*Mustered in: July 15, 1861.*
*Mustered out: August 15, 1864.*
*Maine in the war 136–62.*
*Eastern Maine 124–37.*

Fiftieth anniversary Sixth Maine association, Hancock hall, Ellsworth, Maine, Friday, July 14, 1911. 38 p. 22½cm.        MeHi  62

Ambler, Isaac
'Truth is stranger than fiction,' the life of Sergeant I. W. Ambler, embracing his nativity, poverty, and toil. . . . Boston, Lee and Shepard [c1873] xii, [13]–319 p. front. (port.), plates (illus.).      23cm.                  NN  63

—— —— Boston, Lee and Shepard, 1883. 311 p. front. (port.), plates (illus.). 22cm.
PPLL  64

A reprinting. Pages 313–19, a list of the author's friends, in the first printing, has been omitted. Though not mustered, the author was with the Sixth Maine as drillmaster.

Clark, Charles Amory, 1841–1913.
Campaigning with the Sixth Maine, a paper read before the Iowa commandery, Military order of the loyal legion of the United States, by Brevet-Lieut.-Colonel Charles A. Clark. Des Moines, Iowa, Kenyon press, 1897. 53 p. front. (port.). 23cm.                  DLC NHi  65
Also published as *MOLLUS-Iowa* ii 389–439.

—— General McClellan, a paper read before the Iowa commandery Military order of the loyal legion of the United States, Des Moines, Kenyon press, 1897. 41 p. front. (port.). 23cm.
NHi  66
Also published as *MOLLUS-Iowa* ii 9–47.

Forsyth, William
A sprig of myrtle for the "old Sixth Maine." Address of welcome by Rev. Wm. Forsyth, at 21st reunion of 6th Maine veteran association at Emery hall, Bucksport, Me., Oct. 1, 1901. [7] p. 20½cm.                  DNW  66A
Title from cover.

## 7TH INFANTRY

*Mustered in: August 21, 1861.*
*Mustered out: August 21, 1864.*
*Maine in the war 163–91.*

## 8TH INFANTRY

*Mustered in: September 7, 1861.*
*Mustered out: January 18, 1866.*
*Maine in the war 192–208, 610–11.*
*Eastern Maine 284–92.*

Doble, Erastus
Reminiscences of prison life and escape. *Maine bugle* campaign i (1894) 105–15, 214–28, 317–32.                  67

Pollard, Kendall
Early services of the Eighth Maine. *Maine bugle* campaign i (1894) 23–6.                  68

Ulmer, George T
Adventures and reminiscences of a volunteer; or, a drummer boy from Maine, by Geo. T. Ulmer, Company H, 8th Maine. . . . [Chicago, 1892] 77 p. front. (port.), illus., plates (illus.). 22cm.                  NN  69

Wright, J    E    M
From Petersburg to Appomattox court house. *Maine bugle* campaign i (1894) 115–23.  70

## 9TH INFANTRY

*Mustered in: September 22, 1861.*
*Mustered out: July 13, 1865.*
*Maine in the war 209–24, 611–12.*

## 10TH INFANTRY

*Mustered in: October 4–5, 1861.*
*Mustered out: May 7–8, 1863. Recruits
and veterans formed 10th battalion until
their transfer to 29th infantry, November
1, 1863.*
*Maine in the war 225–60.*

Gould, John Mead, 1839–1930.
Joseph K. F. Mansfield, a narrative of events
connected with his mortal wounding at Antietam, Sharpsburg, Maryland, September 17,
1862, by John Mead Gould, late Acting Adjutant 10th Maine and Major 29th Maine.
Portland, Stephen Berry, printer, 1895. 32 p.
map with port. 22½cm.             NHi NN    *71*

Russell, Benjamin
The marching and fighting of the Tenth
Maine regiment. Also, departed heroes and
the soldier's dream. By Benj. Russell, Jr., of
Company G. Boston, Morrill & Son, printers,
1863. 20 p. 17½cm.                    DLC    *72*
Poetry.

See also Titles 42–43.

## 11TH INFANTRY

*Mustered in: November 12, 1861.*
*Mustered out: February 2, 1866.*
*Maine in the war 261–87.*
*Eastern Maine 293–9.*

Brady, Robert
The story of one regiment, the Eleventh
Maine infantry volunteers in the War of the
rebellion. Compiled by a Committee of the
Regimental association. New York [Press of
J. J. Little & co.] 1896. xv, 435, lxx p. front.
(port.). 23cm.                      DLC NN    *73*
Unit roster, lxx p. c1896 by Albert Maxfield, a
member of the Historical committee. "Preface" signed:
J. A. Hill, Chairman of the Historical committee.
"Lieutenant Brady compiled the historical sketch."

Daggett, Monroe
A cavalryman in the Eleventh Maine infantry [by] Capt. Monroe Daggett. *Maine bugle*
campaign I (1894) 71–6.                     *74*

Holmes, Thomas J
Eleventh Maine at Appomattox court house.
*Maine bugle* campaign I (1894) 76–9.     *76*

Maxfield, Albert
Roster and statistical record of Company D,
of the Eleventh Maine infantry volunteers, with
a sketch of its services in the War of the
rebellion, prepared by Albert Maxfield and

Robert Brady, Jr. [New York, Press of Thos.
Humphrey] 1890. 83 p. 25cm.
Unit roster Co. D, 66–72.  DLC NHi NN    *77*

Wharff, William H
From Chapin's farm to Appomattox. *Maine
bugle* campaign III (1896) 231–5.          *78*

## 12TH INFANTRY

*Mustered in: November 16, 1861.*
*Mustered out: April 18, 1866.*
*Maine in the war 288–99, 613–14.*

Chase, Freeman H
A story of adventures and incidents in a
Rebel prison in Texas. *Maine bugle* campaign
IV (1897] 28–38.                            *79*

Cousens, Oliver M
Discourse on the death of Sergeant Enoch
L. Snow, of Company C, 12th regiment Maine
volunteers, who received fatal injuries at the
battle of Ponchatoula, September 15, 1862,
by Oliver M. Cousens. Portland, Printed by
Brown Thurston, 1863. 22 p. 22½cm.
                                     MeHi    *80*
"Discourse on the death of Sergeant Edwin A.
Harmon, of Company C, 12th regiment Maine volunteers, who received fatal injuries at the battle of Ponchatoula, September 15, 1862, and died February 25,
1863, by Oliver M. Cousens," [13]–22.

Curtis, A          H
Short history of the Twelfth Maine infantry.
*Maine bugle* campaign I (1894) 169–74.   *81*

## 13TH INFANTRY

*Mustered in: December 13, 1861.*
*Mustered out: January 5, 1865.*
*Maine in the war 300–17.*

Gordon, Seth C
Reminiscences of the Civil war from a Surgeon's point of view. *MOLLUS-Me* I 129–44.
                                             *82*

Hawes, Levi Lindley
Personal experiences of a Union veteran.
*Historical leaves* (Somerville historical society)
IV (1905) 25–37, 49–62.                     *83*

Hesseltine, Francis S
Amusing the enemy, by Lieut.-Colonel Francis S. Hesseltine. *MOLLUS-Mass* I 27–44.  *84*

Lufkin, Edwin B          1841–
Extracts from an unpublished history of the
Thirteenth Maine. *Maine bugle* campaign III
(1896) 193–204. ports.                      *85*

——— History of the Thirteenth Maine regiment, from its organization in 1861 to its

muster-out in 1865, by Edwin B. Lufkin, a Private of Co. E. With a sketch of the Thirteenth Maine battalion attached to the Thirtieth Maine. And an appendix containing a complete roster of the Regiment. Brighton, H. A. Shorey & Son, 1898. xiii, 140, 67, (1) p. plates (ports.). 21½cm.　　DLC NN　86

Unit roster, 67 p. "Errata," (1) p. Page of text accompanying each portrait is not included in the pagination.

## 14TH INFANTRY

*Mustered in: December 31, 1861.*

*Mustered out: August 28, 1865.*

*Maine in the war 318–33, 614–15.*

Carver, Willard
Fourteenth regt. Maine infantry roster of survivors, revised by Willard Carver, Secretary of the Regimental association, with abstract of Regimental history. 1890. 20 p. 14½cm.
　　　　　　　　　　　　　　　DLC　87

Title and imprint date from cover. "Brief summary of history of the 14th regiment, Maine infantry," [1]–7.

Gardner, Ira Bernard, 1843–
Personal experiences with the Fourteenth Maine volunteers from 1861–1865, by Brevet Lieutenant-Colonel Ira B. Gardner. *MOLLUS-Me* IV 90–113.　　　　　　　　　89

—— Recollections of a boy member of Co. I, Fourteenth Maine regiment 1861 to 1865. Lewiston, Journal printshop [190–] [20] p. 23cm.　　　　　　　　　　MeBa　90

—— Personal recollections of a boy member of Co. I, 14th Maine vols., from 1862 to 1865. Privately printed. 1901. 71 p. 18½cm.
"Preface" signed: Ira B. Gardner.　MeBa　91

—— Recollections of a boy member of Co. I, Fourteenth Maine volunteers, 1861 to 1865, by Ira B. Gardner. Lewiston, Printed by Lewiston Journal co., 1902. 55 p. front. (port.). 23cm.　　　　　　　　　DLC NN　92

## 15TH INFANTRY

*Mustered in: January 23, 1862.*

*Mustered out: July 5, 1866.*

*Maine in the war 334–42, 615–17.*

The Maine Fifteenth's reunion annual. . . . IV 1888 (MeHi); 1893 (MeBa); XI 1895 (Me); 1901 (NHi); 1903–1904 (MeBa); 1906 (Me); 1909 (MeBa); 1909–1912 (MeBa); 1913 (MeHi); 1915–1917 (MeHi); 1918 (MeBa). 1916–1917 issued in one volume.　　　　　93

Shorey, Henry Augustus
The story of the Maine Fifteenth; being a brief narrative of the more important events in the history of the Fifteenth Maine regiment, together with a complete roster of the Regiment, embracing the name of every officer and enlisted man serving with it at any time during its term of service, and illustrations and brief biographical sketches of nearly all the commissioned officers of the Regiment, by Henry A. Shorey. Bridgton, Press of the Bridgton News, 1890. 178, 26 p. plates (ports.). 26cm.　　　　　　　　　DLC NN　94

Unit roster, 26 p.

## 16TH INFANTRY

*Mustered in: August 14, 1862.*

*Mustered out: June 4, 1865.*

*Maine in the war 428–45, 618–19.*

Memorial of Lieut. Frederick Henry Beecher. Portland, Stephen Berry, printer, 1870. 47 p. 26cm.　　　　　　　　　　CSmH NB　95

"This edition is limited to 200 copies." Beecher later served in the 3rd U.S. infantry and was killed September 17, 1868, in action with Indians in Kansas.

Report of the thirteenth annual reunion of the 16th Maine regimental association. Portland, B. Thurston & co., 1888. 12 p. 15½cm.
　　　　　　　　　　　　　　　NHi　96

Andrews, Henry Franklin, 1844–
Company D, 16 Maine vols., a brief history of the individual services of its members, 1862–1865, by H. F. Andrews. Exira, Iowa, Exira print. co., 1906. [12] leaves. 2 plates (ports.). 26½cm.　　　　　　DLC MeHi NHi　97

Bisbee, George D
Three years a volunteer soldier in the Civil war, Antietam to Appomattox, by Second Lieutenant George D. Bisbee. *MOLLUS-Me* IV 114–49.　　　　　　　　　　98

Bolton, Horace Wilbert, 1839–
Personal reminiscences of the late war, by H. W. Bolton. Introduced by F. A. Hardin. Edited by H. G. Jackson. Chicago, H. W. Bolton, 1892. viii, [9]–219 p. illus., ports. 20cm.
　　　　　　　　　　　　　　DLC NN　99

Gilmore, Pascal Pearl, 1845–
Civil war memories, personal experiences and observations of the author with quotations from the highest authorities, by Pascal Pearl Gilmore. [Bangor, 1928] xi, 7–170 p. plates (illus., ports.). 19½cm.　　DLC NN　99A

O'Dea, Thomas,　　　　　–1926.
History of O'Dea's famous picture of Andersnoville [sic] prison as it appeared August 1, 1864, when it contained 35,000 prisoners of war . . . by Thomas O'Dea, late Private Co. E, 16th regt. Maine infantry. Cohoes, N.Y., Clark & Foster, printers, 1887. 20 p. 22cm.
　　　　　　　　　　　　　　DLC NB　99B

*16th Infantry, continued*

Small, Abner Ralph, 1836–1910.
Personal observations and experiences in Rebel prisons, 1864–1865. *MOLLUS-Me* i 295–317. **100**
Also published as *Maine bugle*, campaign iii (1896) 37–53.

—— The Sixteenth Maine regiment in the War of the rebellion, 1861–1865, by Major A. R. Small. With an introduction by Gen. James A. Hall . . . Published for the Regimental association. Portland, B. Thurston & co., 1886. iv, 323 p. plates (illus., ports.). 22cm. DLC NN **101**
Unit roster [225]–52. "Errata" slip inserted.

—— The road to Richmond, the Civil war memoirs of Major Abner R. Small of the Sixteenth Maine volunteers, together with the diary which he kept when he was a prisoner of war. Edited by Harry Adams Small. Berkeley, University of California press, 1939. xiii, 314 p. front. (port.), plates (illus., map). 22½cm. NN **102**
Coulter 419.

Stratton, Albion W
What became of the flag, how the Sixteenth Maine saved their flag from the disgrace of capture. *Maine bugle* campaign iii (1896) 95–7. **102A**

Wiggin, Francis
Sixteenth Maine at Gettysburg, by Lieutenant Francis Wiggin. *MOLLUS-Me* iv 150–70. **103**

## 17TH INFANTRY

*Mustered in: August 18, 1862.*
*Mustered out: June 4, 1865.*
*Maine in the war 446–57, 620–1.*

Seventeenth Maine regiment at Gettysburg. [188–] 72 p. plates (illus., maps). 27½cm.
Title from cover. In **104**

Green, William H
From the Wilderness to Spotsylvania, by Brevet Major William H. Green. *MOLLUS-Me* ii 91–104. **105**

Houghton, Edwin B
The campaigns of the Seventeenth Maine, by Edwin B. Houghton, a member of the Regiment. Portland, Short & Loring, 1866. x, 333 p. 18½cm. DLC NN **106**
Unit roster, muster in, [312]–33.

Mattocks, Charles Porter, 1840–1910.
In six prisons. *MOLLUS-Me* i 161–80. **107**

—— Oration, by General Charles P. Mattocks. In The equestrian statue of Major General

Joseph Hooker, published by the State of Massachusetts (1903) [123]–66. **108**

Roberts, Charles W
At Gettysburg in 1863 and 1888, by Lieutenant Charles W. Roberts. *MOLLUS-Me* i 49–57. **109**

Verrill, George W
The Seventeenth Maine at Gettysburg and in the Wilderness, by Captain George W. Verrill. *MOLLUS-Me* i 260–82. plate (map). **110**
See also Title 44.

## 18TH INFANTRY

*Mustered in: August 21, 1862.*
*Designated 1st regiment of heavy artillery: January 6, 1863.*

## 19TH INFANTRY

*Mustered in: August 25, 1862.*
*Mustered out: May 31, 1865.*
*Maine in the war 475–89, 621–3.*

Reunions of the Nineteenth Maine regiment association at. . . . Augusta, Press of Sprague, Owen & Nash, 1878. 140, (2) p. 23cm.
DLC MeHi NHi **111**
Proceedings of the 1st – 6th reunions 1873–1878. Unit roster 95–126. "Notes. Index to contents," (2) p.

Adams, Silas
The Nineteenth Maine at Gettysburg, by Captain Silas Adams. *MOLLUS-Me* iv 250–63. **112**

Connor, Selden, 1839–
In the Wilderness, by Brigadier-General Selden Connor. *MOLLUS-Me* iv 200–29. **113**

Smith, John Day, 1845–
The history of the Nineteenth regiment of Maine volunteer infantry, 1862–1865, by John Day Smith, late a Corporal in Company F. Prepared at the request of the Nineteenth Maine regimental association. With an introduction written by Brevet Major-General Alexander S. Webb. Minneapolis, Minn., Great Western print. co., 1909. xv, 356 p. plates (illus., maps, ports.). 23cm. DLC NN **114**
Unit roster 317–49.

—— What war meant to a Maine soldier, 1861–1865. Minneapolis, 1927. [8] p. 15½cm.
Title from cover. MnHi **115**

Spaulding, Joseph W
Nineteenth Maine at High bridge, by Lieutenant-Colonel Joseph W. Spaulding. *MOLLUS-Me* iv 294–306. **116**

## 20TH INFANTRY

*Mustered in: August 29, 1862.*

*Mustered out: June 4, 1865.*

*Maine in the war 490–9, 623–7.*

Dedication of the Twentieth Maine monument at Gettysburg, Oct. 3, 1889, with report of annual reunion, Oct. 2d, 1889. Waldoboro, News print, 1891. 35 p. 2 plates (illus.). 22cm.

IHi NHi **117**

Reunions of the Twentieth Maine regiment association, at Portland. . . . Waldoboro, Samuel L. Miller, 1881. 30, (1) p. 22½cm.

DLC NHi **118**

Proceedings of the 1st (1876) and 2nd (1881) reunions.

Roster of the 20th Maine regiment association, organized Aug. 10th, 1876. Waldoboro, Samuel L. Miller, printer, 1893. [14] leaves. 14cm.

NHi **119**

Chamberlain, Joshua Lawrence, 1828–1914.

Five Forks. *MOLLUS-Me* II 220–67. fold. map. **120**

—— The military operations on the White Oak road, Virginia, March 31, 1865. *MOLLUS-Me* I 207–52. **121**

—— My story of Fredericksburg. *Cosmopolitan* LIV (1912) 148–59. illus., ports. **122**

—— The passing of the armies, an account of the final campaign of the Army of the Potomac, based upon personal reminiscences of the Fifth army corps, by Joshua Lawrence Chamberlain. New York, G. P. Putnam's Sons, 1915. xxi, 392 p. 5 plates (3 maps, 2 fold.; 2 ports.). 22cm. DLC NHi NN **123**

—— Through blood and fire at Gettysburg. *Hearst's magazine* XXIII (1913) 894–909. illus., ports. **124**

Gerrish, Theodore, 1846–

Army life, a Private's reminiscences of the Civil war, by Rev. Theodore Gerrish, late a member of the 20th Maine vols. With an introduction by Josiah H. Drummond. Portland, Hoyt, Fogg & Donham [1882] 372 p. 18½cm.

Coulter 182. DLC NN **125**

—— The Blue and the Gray, a graphic history of the Army of the Potomac and that of Northern Virginia, including the brilliant engagements of these forces from 1861 to 1865. The campaigns of the Shenandoah valley and the Army of the James, together with reminiscences of tent and field, acts of personal daring, deeds of heroic suffering and thrilling adventure, coupled with which, will be found many tales of individual achievements, army

yarns, and pen pictures of officers and privates . . . by Rev. Theodore Gerrish, Private in the Army of the Potomac, and Rev. John S. Hutchinson. . . . Bangor, Brady, Mace, & co., 1884. 816 p. maps. 22cm. DLC NN **126**

Melcher, Holman S

An experience in the battle of the Wilderness, by Brevet-Major Holman S. Melcher. *MOLLUS-Me* I 73–84. **127**

—— The 20th Maine at Little Round Top. *BandL* III 314–15. **128**

Pullen, John J

The Twentieth Maine, a volunteer regiment in the Civil war, by John J. Pullen. Philadelphia, J. B. Lippincott co. [1957] 338 p. illus., maps, plates (illus., ports.). 22cm.

"Bibliography," 295–302. DLC NN **129**

Simonton, Edward

Recollections of the battle of Fredericksburg, by Brevet Lieutenant-Colonel Edward Simonton. *MOLLUS-Minn* II 245–66. **129A**

Spear, Ellis, 1834–

The hoe cake of Appomattox, by Ellis Spear, Brevet Brigadier-General. 1913. 12 p. *MOLLUS-DC* no 92. **130**

—— The story of the raising and organization of a regiment of volunteers in 1862. 1903. 15 p. *MOLLUS-DC* no 46. **131**

Wallace, Willard M

Soul of the lion, a biography of General Joshua L. Chamberlain, by Willard M. Wallace. New York, Thomas Nelson & Sons [1960] 357 p. maps, plans, plates (illus., ports.). 22cm.

Civil war 36–202. DLC NN **131A**

## 21ST INFANTRY

*Mustered in: October 14, 1862.*

*Mustered out: August 25, 1863.*

*Maine in the war 500–05.*

Woodward, Joseph T 1838–

Historic record and complete biographic roster 21st Me. vols. with reunion records of the 21st Maine regimental association, by Adj't Jos. T. Woodward. Augusta, Press of Charles E. Nash & Son, 1907. 251, (5) p. front. (map), plates (ports.). 23½cm. DLC NN **132**

"Reunions," 47–104. "Biographical sketches," 115–248. "Index," (5) p.

## 22ND INFANTRY

*Mustered in: October 10, 1862.*

*Mustered out: August 14, 1863.*

*Maine in the war 506–14.*

*Eastern Maine 278–81.*

## 23RD INFANTRY

*Mustered in: September 29, 1862.*
*Mustered out: July 15, 1863.*
*Maine in the war 515–19.*

Nichols, George Ward, 1837–1885.
Major Soule, a memorial of Alfred B. Soule, late Major of the Twenty-third regiment, Maine volunteers, by Chislon. Salem, Geo. W. Pease & co., 1866. 199 p. front. (mounted port.). 19½cm.  MB NHi  *133*

See also Title 13.

## 24TH INFANTRY

*Mustered in: October 16, 1862.*
*Mustered out: August 25, 1863.*
*Maine in the war 520–2.*

## 25TH INFANTRY

*Mustered in: September 29, 1862.*
*Mustered out: July 10, 1863.*
*Maine in the war 523–6.*

Soldiers' memorial Company A, 25th regiment Maine volunteers. Washington, D. C. Gibson Brothers, prs., c1863. broadside, 55 × 45cm.  NHi  *134*

## 26TH INFANTRY

*Mustered in: October 11, 1862.*
*Mustered out: August 17, 1863.*
*Maine in the war 527–33.*
*Eastern Maine 281.*

Brown, William F
History of Company F, Twenty-sixth Maine regiment, by Lieutenant William F. Brown. *Maine bugle* campaign IV (1897) 297–313.  *135*

Maddocks, Elden B  1843–
History of the Twenty-sixth Maine regiment. Published under vote of the Twenty-sixth Maine association passed August 26, 1898. Compiled by comrade Elden B. Maddocks. Bangor, Chas. H. Glass & co., printers, 1899. viii, [3]–374 p. 1 illus., ports. 23½cm.  DLC NN  *136*

Unit roster [46]–69. Biographical sketches [126]–316. Report of reunions 1–13 (1886–1898), [70]–125.

## 27TH INFANTRY

*Mustered in: September 30, 1862.*
*Mustered out: July 17, 1863.*
*Maine in the war 534–9.*

Stone, James M
The history of the Twenty-seventh regiment Maine volunteer infantry, by Lieut.-Colonel James M. Stone. [Portland, Thurston print] 1895. 44 p. 23½cm.  DLC NN  *137*

"Roll of officers and men in the Twenty-seventh Maine regiment who volunteered, in June, 1863, to remain after their term of service had expired, and assist in the defense of Washington," [21]–30.

## 28TH INFANTRY

*Mustered in: October 18, 1862.*
*Mustered out: August 31, 1863.*
*Maine in the war 540–7.*
*Eastern Maine 283–4.*

## 29TH INFANTRY

*Mustered in: November 13 to December 29, 1863.*
*Mustered out: June 21, 1865.*
*Maine in the war 548–53, 627–8.*

See Titles 42–43.

## 30TH INFANTRY

*Mustered in: January 8, 1864.*
*Mustered out: August 20, 1865.*
*Maine in the war 554–62, 628–30.*

Burrage, Henry Sweetser, 1837–1926.
Thomas Hamlin Hubbard, Bvt. Brigadier General U.S. vols., by Henry S. Burrage. Portland, 1923. 66 p. front. (port.). 23½cm.  DLC NHi  *138*

Fairbanks, Henry N
The Red river expedition of 1864, by Lieutenant Henry N. Fairbanks. *MOLLUS-Me* I 181–90.  *139*

Hall, Charles Badger
Notes on the Red river campaign of 1864, by Major-General Chas. B. Hall. *MOLLUS-Me* IV 264–81.  *140*

Hubbard, Thomas Hamlin, 1838–1915.
The lost cause, address delivered to the Commandery of the State of New York, Military order of the loyal legion of the United States, by Thomas H. Hubbard. . . . [1912] 13 p. 24cm.  WHi  *141*

## 31ST INFANTRY

*Left State: April 18, 1864.*
*Mustered out: July 15, 1865.*
*Maine in the war 577–81, 630–1.*

Report of the eleventh annual meeting of the Thirty-first Maine regimental association at

Bangor, August 28th, 1907, with roster of surviving members and brief history of the Regiment. 24 p. 15½cm. NHi **142**

Beals, Thomas P
In a charge near Fort Hell, Petersburg, April 2, 1865, by Captain Thomas P. Beals. *MOLLUS-Me* II 105–15. **142A**

Burbank, Horace Harmon, 1837–1905.
The battle of "the Crater," by Captain Horace H. Burbank. *MOLLUS-Me* I 283–94. **143**

—— My prison life. *MOLLUS-Me* II 11–27. **144**

### 32ND INFANTRY

*Left State: April 20, 1864, six companies; May 11, 1864, four companies.*
*Consolidated with 31st Infantry: December 12, 1864.*
*Maine in the war 582–6.*

Chase, James Judson, 1847–
The charge at day-break, scenes and incidents at the battle of the mine explosion, near Petersburg, Va., July 30th, 1864, written by Lieut. J. J. Chase. . . . Lewiston, Printed at the Journal office, 1875. 32 p. 18cm.
DLC NHi **145**

Houston, Henry Clarence, 1847–
The Thirty-second Maine regiment of infantry volunteers, an historical sketch, by Henry C. Houston of Co. C. Portland, Press of Southworth Brothers, 1903. xii, 537 p. plates (ports.). 24cm. NN **146**
Unit roster [459]–534.

### SHARPSHOOTERS

One company was raised in Maine for service with the United States sharpshooters: Company D, 2d regiment U.S. sharpshooters.

# MASSACHUSETTS

# Reference Works

Bowen, James Lorenzo

Massachusetts in the war, 1861–1865, by James L. Bowen, with an introduction by Henry L. Dawes. Springfield, Clark W. Bryan & co., 1889. xv, 1029 p. ports. 23cm.

"Sketches of general officers," [875]–1010. Cited herein as *Mass in the war.*

Dyer, Frederick Henry, 1849–1917.

A compendium of the War of the rebellion, 1908 (reprinted 1959).

"Regimental index" 155–64; "Regimental histories" 1237–68. The same pagination is used in the 1959 reprint.

Massachusetts. Adjutant General.

Massachusetts soldiers, sailors and marines in the Civil war. Compiled and published by the Adjutant general. . . . Brookline, Printed at the Riverdale press [v. 1–7, Norwood, Printed at the Norwood press] 1931–35. 8 v. 26½cm.

Cited herein as *Mass soldiers.*

—— Index to army records. Boston, Wright & Potter print. co., 1937. 634 p. 26½cm.

Does not index names of officers and men who served in the Navy and Marine corps.

*The Union army.*

"Record of Massachusetts regiments," i (1908) 168–227.

United States. Adjutant General's Office.

Official army register of the volunteer force of the United States army for the years 1861, '62, '63, '64, '65. Part i. (New England states). Washington, 1865.

A roster of officers by regiments with an alphabetical index for the six states.

# MASSACHUSETTS

## ARTILLERY

### Regiments (Heavy)

#### 1ST ARTILLERY (HEAVY)

*Mustered in as 14th regiment of infantry:
July 5, 1861.
Designated 1st regiment of heavy artillery: January 2, 1862.
Mustered out: August 16, 1865.
Mass soldiers v 545–656.
Mass in the war 723–9.*

. . . A directory of the commissioned and noncommissioned officers and privates, of each company, attached to the Fourteenth regiment heavy artillery, Massachusetts volunteers, Col. Wm. B. Greene, Commanding, stationed at the forts near Washington. Compiled and published by "Typo." Lawrence, American office, printer, 1862. 32 p. 21½cm.

      DLC MHi NHi *1*

At head of title: Essex county regiment.

Soldier's memorial 14th regiment, Company C, Mass. heavy artillery. New York, Currier & Ives, 1862. col. illus. broadside, 50½ × 40cm.

      MB *2*

Souvenir. First regiment of heavy artillery Massachusetts volunteers. Excursion to battle fields. Dedication of monument, May 19, 1901. Historical sketch of Regiment. 60 p. plates (illus., ports.). 23cm. DLC MHi NN *3*

Title from cover.

Bradley, Leverett, 1846–
 Leverett Bradley, a soldier-boy's letters, 1862–1865, a man's work in the ministry. Edited by Susan Hinckley Bradley . . . Privately printed. Boston [Everett press] 1905. 91 p. front. (port.), 2 plates (ports.). 24½cm.

      NN *4*

Carter, Robert Goldthwaite, 1845–1936.
 Four brothers in Blue; or, sunshine and shadow of the War of the rebellion, a story of the great Civil war, from Bull run to Appomattox, by Captain Robert Goldthwaite Carter. Washington, D. C., Press of Gibson Bros., 1913. xii, 509 p. front. (group of ports.). 28cm. NN *5*

Based on the letters and diaries of the author and his three brothers. John H. Carter served in the 1st Mass heavy artillery; Robert G. Carter and Walter Carter in the 22nd Mass infantry. A part of the work was published serially in the *Maine bugle* (July 1896 to October 1898).

Dearborn, Stanley B
 From Washington, D. C., to Spottsylvania court house, original poem, by Stanley B. Dearborn. . . . [Boston, Press of S. B. Dearborn, n. d.] 9 folios. col. front. (illus.), 3 plates (illus.). 14½cm. MHi *6*

On cover Spottsylvania poem. Enclosed in folder with cover title: Souvenir of Spottsylvania.

Kimball, George –1916.
 P. H. O'Connell's experience as a prisoner. *Biv* II (1884) 164–8, 196–9, 230–3. *7*

Littlefield, Roger S
 Address of welcome to Southwestern Oregon veteran association at Marshfield, Oregon, August 30, 1895, by R. S. Littlefield. [3] leaves. 22½cm. DNW *7A*

Mustered in 2nd Mass battery, July 31, 1861; discharged for disability, September 10, 1861; mustered in 1st Mass heavy artillery, September 28, 1861; mustered out, August 18, 1865.

Morgan, William Henry, 1843–
 A narrative of the service of Company D, First Massachusetts heavy artillery, in the War of the rebellion, 1861 to 1865, from the organization of the Company to its final discharge, with a list of members, and individual history of each, as far as obtainable. Compiled by Sergeant Wm. H. Morgan. Adopted as the Company history, at the annual reunion, February 22, 1905. Boston, Press of S. Woodberry & co., 1907. 79 p. 19cm. DLC *8*

Unit roster [57]–69.

Putnam, Arthur Alwyn, 1829–1910.
 The Putnam guards of Danvers, Mass., story of the Company in the early war time of 1861, by Arthur A. Putnam. . . . Danvers, Danvers Mirror office, 1887. 22 p. 23cm.

      DLC MHi *9*

"Republished from the *Danvers mirror* of July 2, 9, 16, & 23, 1887."

Roe, Alfred Seelye, 1844–1917.
 History of the First regiment of heavy artillery Massachusetts volunteers, formerly the Fourteenth regiment of infantry, 1861–1865, by Alfred Seelye Roe and Charles Nutt. Published by the Regimental association. [Worcester, Commonwealth press] 1917. xi, 507 p. plates (illus., ports.). 23½cm.

 Unit roster [330]–498. DLC NN *10*

——— The Melvin memorial, Sleepy hollow cemetery, Concord, Massachusetts, a brother's tribute. Exercises at dedication, June 16, 1909. Cambridge, Riverside press, 1910. xii, 148 p.

*1st Artillery (Heavy), continued*

plates, 2 double, 1 fold. (facs., illus., ports.).
24½cm.                                         NN    *11*
"Preface" signed: Alfred S. Roe, editor. Diary of
Samuel Melvin, [77]–133.

Washburn, Andrew
Documents in the case of Major Andrew
Washburn, late of the Fourteenth regiment
Massachusetts volunteers, (heavy artillery).
[1862] 27 p. 22½cm.          CSmH NN    *12*

## 2ND ARTILLERY (HEAVY)

*As the companies were mustered in, July
28 to December 24, 1863, they left the
State.*

*Mustered out: September 3, 1865.*

*Mass soldiers v 657–69.*

*Mass in the war 730–3.*

Fiske, Joseph Emery, 1839–1909.
An involuntary journey through the Confed-
eracy, by Captain Joseph E. Fiske. *MOLLUS-
Mass* ii 513–29.                                *13*

—— War letters of Capt. Joseph E. Fiske
<Harvard '61>, written to his parents during
the War of the rebellion from Andover theo-
logical seminary and encampments in North
Carolina and from Southern prisons. Wellesley,
Maugus press [190–] 60 p. 21cm.
                                         DLC    *13A*
Mustered in 43rd Mass infantry, September 24,
1862; discharged for promotion to 2nd Mass heavy
artillery, May 29, 1863; mustered out, May 15, 1865.

Goss, Warren Lee, 1838–1925.
Jack Alden: a story of adventures in the
Virginia campaigns, 1861–65, by Warren Lee
Goss. New York, Thomas Y. Crowell & co.
[1895] xii, 402 p. plates (illus.). 18cm.
                                    CSmH NN    *13B*
"Is the third, perhaps the last, of a series of his-
torical stories of the War for the Union."

—— Recollections of a Private, a story of the
Army of the Potomac, by Warren Lee Goss.
New York, Thomas Y. Crowell & co. [1890]
xi, 354 p. illus., plates (illus.). 22½cm.
                                     DLC NN    *14*
"The writer has availed himself of the reminiscences of many comrades known by him to be
trustworthy."

—— Recollections of a Private. *BandL* i 149–
59; ii 153–9, 189–99.                           *15*
Contents: I Going to the front; II Campaigning to
no purpose; III Yorktown to Williamsburg.

—— The soldier's story of his captivity at
Andersonville, Belle isle and other Rebel prisons, by Warren Lee Goss of the Second Massachusetts regiment of heavy artillery, with an

appendix, containing the names of Union soldiers who died at Andersonville . . . Sold only
by subscription. Boston, Lee & Shepard [1866]
357 p. front. (port.), plates (illus., map, 2
plans). 22cm.                                  NN    *16*
"Names of Union soldiers buried at Andersonville,"
275–356. "Graves of unknown U.S. soldiers," 357.
Reprinted 1869 (NB) and 1870 (NB NN). Coulter
197.

—— —— Boston, I. N. Richardson & co.,
1871. 357 p. front. (port.), plates (illus., maps,
2 plans). 22cm.                                NB    *16A*

—— The soldier's story of his captivity at
Andersonville, Belle isle and other Rebel pris-
ons, by Warren Lee Goss. Boston, Lee Shepard,
1868. 274 p. plates (illus.). 19½cm.
                                              NN    *17*
Printed from the plates of Title 16 omitting the
"Names of Union soldiers buried in Andersonville."

## 3RD ARTILLERY (HEAVY)

*Eight companies were recruited during
1863, for garrisoning the forts of Massachusetts. These companies were consolidated and designated 3rd regiment of
heavy artillery: September 8, 1864.*

*Mustered out: Company M, June 17,
1865; ten companies, September 18, 1865;
Company I, September 26, 1865.*

*Mass soldier v 770–847.*

*Mass in the war 734–6.*

Blanding, Stephen F
In the defences of Washington; or, the sunshine in a soldier's life, by Stephen F. Blanding.
Providence, E. L. Freeman & Son, printers,
1889. 54 p. 2 plates (illus.). 20cm.
                                         DLC NN    *19*

## 4TH ARTILLERY (HEAVY)

*Twelve companies of heavy artillery were
raised in the late summer of 1864, for
coast defense. These companies were consolidated and designated 4th regiment of
heavy artillery: November 12, 1864.*

*Mustered out: June 17, 1865.*

*Mass soldiers vi 1–66.*

## Battalions (Heavy)

### 1st Battalion of Heavy Artillery

*Organized from separate companies: May
15, 1863.*

*Mustered out: Companies E and F, June
28, 1865; B, June 29, 1865; D. September
12, 1865; A and C, October 20, 1865.*

*Mass soldiers vi 80–128.*

Cabot, Stephen, 1826–1906.

Report of the "draft riot" in Boston, July 14th, 1863, from the diary of Major Stephen Cabot, 1st batt. Mass. vol. heavy artillery, who had command of Cooper street armory the night of the riot. Printed by vote of the Veteran association of Co. A, 1st battalion of Massachusetts volunteer heavy artillery. [Boston, n. d.] 6 leaves. 19½cm. MB **20**

## Companies (Heavy)

*Companies 1 to 28 were organized principally for garrison duty in Boston harbor. When the companies were transferred to Washington, they were assigned to existing regiments of heavy artillery.*

### 29th Company

*Organized: September 20, 1864.*
*Mustered out: June 16, 1865.*
*Mass soldiers* vi 67–73.

### 30th Company

*Organized: September 1, 1864.*
*Mustered out: June 16, 1865.*
*Mass soldiers* vi 67, 74–9.

## Batteries (Light)

### 1st Battery

*Left State: April 21, 1861; mustered in: May 18, 1861. Cook's. (3 months)*
*Mustered out: August 2, 1861.*
*Mass soldiers* v 337–42.
*Mass in the war* 785–6.
*Mustered in: August 28, 1861. (3 years)*
*Mustered out: October 19, 1864.*
*Mass soldiers* v 343–54.
*Mass in the war* 786–9.

Bell, John W

Address at the fifth annual re-union of the First Massachusetts light battery association, held at Young's hotel, Boston, Mass., October 3, 1882, by comrade John W. Bell. Boston, Franklin press, 1882. 24 p. 22cm. MB **21**

Bennett, Andrew J

The story of the First Massachusetts light battery, attached to the Sixth army corps, a glance at events in the Armies of the Potomac and Shenandoah, from the summer of 1861, to the Autumn of 1864, by A. J. Bennett, Private. Boston, Press of Deland and Barta,

1886. 200 p. plates (facs., illus., ports.). 23½cm. DLC NN **22**
<small>Unit roster, October 3, 1861, [13]–15. Coulter 26.</small>

### 2nd Battery

*Mustered in: July 31, 1861.*
*Mustered out: August 11, 1865.*
*Mass soldiers* v 335–70.
*Mass in the war* 790–6.

Whitcomb, Caroline Elizabeth, 1862–

History of the Second Massachusetts battery (Nims' battery) of light artillery, 1861–1865, compiled from records of the rebellion, official reports, diaries and rosters, by Caroline E. Whitcomb. Concord, N.H., Rumford press [1912] 111 p. plates (illus., ports.). 22½cm. DLC NN **23**
<small>On cover: Nims' Second Massachusetts battery.</small>

### 3rd Battery

*Mustered in: September 5, 1861.*
*Mustered out: September 16, 1864.*
*Mass soldiers* v 373–82.
*Mass in the war* 797–801.

See Title 248.

### 4th Battery

*Organized: November 17, 1861.*
*Mustered out: November 10, 1865.*
*Mass soldiers* v 383–96.
*Mass in the war* 802–08.

### 5th Battery

*Mustered in: December 3, 1861.*
*Mustered out: June 12, 1865.*
*Mass soldiers* v 397–411.
*Mass in the war* 809–16.

History of the Fifth Massachusetts battery. Organized October 3, 1861; mustered out, June 12, 1865. Boston, Luther E. Cowles, 1902. xiv, 991 p. col. front. (illus.), illus., plans, plates (illus., maps, ports.). 25cm. DLC NN **24**
<small>"Roster and index," 979–91. c1902, by Luther E. Cowles. "Preface" signed: Nathan Appleton, Henry D. Scott, John F. Murray, Thomas E. Chase [and] George L. Newton, Committee.</small>

### 6th Battery

*Mustered in: January 20, 1862.*
*Mustered out: August 7, 1865.*
*Mass soldiers* v 412–27.
*Mass in the war* 817–21.

## 7th Battery

*Mustered in as Richardson's light guard:*
*May 21, 1861.*
*Designated 7th battery of light artillery:*
*March 17, 1862.*
*Mustered out: November 10, 1865.*
*Mass soldiers* v 428–43.
*Mass in the war* 822–6.

## 8th Battery

*Left State: June 25, 1862.*
*Mustered out: November 29, 1862.*
*Mass soldiers* v 444–51.
*Mass in the war* 827–8.

## 9th Battery

*Mustered in: August 10, 1862.*
*Mustered out: June 6, 1865.*
*Mass soldiers* v 452–66.
*Mass in the war* 829–33.

Baker, Levi Wood
History of the Ninth Mass. battery. Recruited, July, 1862; mustered in Aug. 10, 1862; mustered out June 9, 1865, at the close of the rebellion, by Levi W. Baker. South Framingham, Lakeview press, 1888. vi, [7]–261, (1) p. front. (illus.), illus., ports. 22½cm.
Unit roster 244–52.          DLC NN    **25**

Bigelow, John, 1841–
The battle of Marye's heights and Salem church, by Captain John Bigelow. *PMHSM* iii 240–314.                                **26**

—— The Peach orchard, Gettysburg, July 2, 1863, explained by official reports and maps, by Major John Bigelow, Captain 9th Mass. battery. An appeal to have Trostle lane (a battle avenue) now named "United States avenue" renamed Hunt avenue, for the credit of the artillery arm of the service, which exclusively fought all along it, and in honor General Henry J. Hunt, Chief of the artillery (1862–1865), Army of the Potomac. Minneapolis, Kimball-Storer co., 1910. plans, fold. map. 22½cm.                          NHi NN    **27**

—— —— Supplement to Peach orchard, Gettysburg, an appeal for the information of veterans. . . . Minneapolis, Kimball-Storer co., 1911. 57, (9) p. maps, fold. map. 22½cm.
                                    NHi NN    **28**
Maps and accompanying text, (9) p. Titles 27–28 also found under one cover.

## 10th Battery

*Mustered in: September 9, 1862.*
*Mustered out: June 9, 1865.*
*Mass soldiers* v 467–78.
*Mass in the war* 834–43.

Billings, John Davis, 1842–1933.
Hardtack and coffee; or, the unwritten story of army life, including chapters on enlisting, life in tents and log huts, Jonahs and beats, offences and punishments, the army mule, the Engineer corps, the Signal corps, etc., by John D. Billings. Illustrated by Charles W. Reed. Boston, George M. Smith & co., 1887. vi, 408 p. illus., col. plates (illus.). 22½cm.    NN    **29**
NHi has a reprint, Minneapolis, G. S. Richards & co., 1889. NN has reprint published by Smith, 1888.

—— . . . Hardtack and coffee, the unwritten story of army life, by John D. Billings. Edited by Richard Harwell. Chicago, Lakeside press, 1960. xxxii, 483 p. front. (port.), illus., music. 17½cm.                          NN    **29A**
At head of title: The Lakeside classics [no. 58]

—— The history of the Tenth Massachusetts battery of light artillery in the War of the rebellion, formerly of the Third corps, and afterwards of Hancock's Second corps, Army of the Potomac, 1862–1865, by John D. Billings, a member of the Company. Boston, Hall & Whiting, 1881. xii, 400 p. plates (illus., 1 col.; 2 plans; ports.). 24cm.    DLC NN    **30**
On cover: Sleeper's Tenth Massachusetts battery. Unit roster 374–83. Coulter 33.

—— The history of the Tenth Massachusetts battery of light artillery in the War of the rebellion, formerly of the Third corps, and afterwards of Hancock's Second corps, Army of the Potomac, 1862–1865, by John D. Billings. Authorized and sanctioned by the Tenth Massachusetts battery association. Boston, Arakelvan press, 1909. 496 p. illus. (1 col.), 2 plans, 2 ports. 24cm.            DLC    **31**
Unit roster 470–7. Page 470A was distributed as an insert after publication of the volume.

## 11th Battery

*Mustered in: August 25, 1862.* (9 months)
*Mustered out: May 29, 1863.*
*Mass soldiers* v 479–85.
*Mass in the war* 844–5.
*Mustered in: January 2, 1864.* (3 years)
*Mustered out: June 16, 1865.*
*Mass soldiers* v 486–94.
*Mass in the war* 845–6.

### 12th Battery

*Organized: October 3 to December 29, 1863.*

*Mustered out: July 25, 1865.*

*Mass soldiers v 495–506.*

*Mass in the war 847–8.*

### 13th Battery

*Organized: November to December 1862. Transferred to 6th Mass battery, February 17, 1864; to Battery L, 1st U.S. artillery, March 6, 1864; again an independent command, July 1, 1865.*

*Mustered out: July 28, 1865.*

*Mass soldiers v 507–21.*

*Mass in the war 849–51.*

### 14th Battery

*Mustered in: February 27, 1864.*

*Mustered out: June 15, 1865.*

*Mass soldiers v 522–31.*

*Mass in the war 852–5.*

### 15th Battery

*Mustered in: February 17, 1863.*

*Mustered out: August 4, 1865.*

*Mass soldiers v 532–45.*

*Mass in the war 867–7.*

### 16th Battery

*Left State: April 17, 1864.*

*Mustered out: June 27, 1865.*

*Mass soldiers v 546–53.*

*Mass in the war 858–9.*

### CAVALRY

### 1ST CAVALRY

*Mustered in: September 12 to October 31, 1861.*

*Mustered out: June 26, 1865.*

*Mass soldiers vi 129–227.*

*Mass in the war 742–54.*

Twenty-ninth annual reunion, held at Holyoke, Mass., October twenty-fourth, 1894. [8] p. 23cm.          DNW  **32**

"Mortuary list First regiment Massachusetts cavalry, 1894," wrapper.

Adams, Charles Francis, 1835–1915.
A cycle of Adams letters, 1861–1865. Edited by Worthington Chauncey Ford. Boston,

Houghton Mifflin co., 1920. 2 v. plates (illus., ports.). 22½cm.          NHi NN  **33**

Allen, Stanton P
Down in Dixie, life in a cavalry regiment in the war days, from the Wilderness to Appomattox, by Stanton P. Allen of the First Massachusetts cavalry. Illustrated by H. G. Laskey. Boston, D. Lothrop co., 1893. xiii, [13]–494, (2) p. illus., plates (illus.). 22½cm.
DLC NN  **34**

Babbitt, Benjamin B
A sermon on the death of Walter L. Raymond, a Union soldier, delivered on Sunday, April 3, 1865, by Benjamin B. Babbitt. Andover, Printed by Warren F. Draper, 1865. 32 p. 17½cm.          DLC  **35**

Bowditch, Henry Ingersoll, 1808–1892.
Memorial [of Nathaniel Bowditch, Lieutenant First Massachusetts cavalry, 1839–1863] Boston, Privately printed by John Wilson & Son, 1865. vi, (1), 134 p. plate (mounted port.). 24cm.          DLC NN  **36**

Dedication signed: Henry I. Bowditch. On spine: N.B.

Crowninshield, Benjamin William, 1837–1892.
The battle of Cedar creek, October 19, 1864, a paper read before the Massachusetts military historical society, December 8, 1879, by Col. B. W. Crowninshield. Cambridge, Printed at the Riverside press, 1879. 36 p. front. (double map). 24cm.          InHi  **37**

—— Cavalry in Virginia during the War of the rebellion. *PMHSM* xiii 1–31.          **38**

Also published in *JMSIUS* xii (1891) 527–51.

—— Cedar creek. *PMHSM* vi 153–81.          **39**

—— —— Extract from letter to Colonel Benjamin W. Crowninshield from General W. H. Emory. *PMHSM* xiv 117.          **40**

—— A history of the First regiment of Massachusetts cavalry volunteers, by Benjamin W. Crowninshield, Major. With roster and statistics, by D. H. L. Gleason. For the First Massachusetts cavalry association. Boston, Houghton, Mifflin and co., 1891. x, [3]–490 p. plates (illus., maps [fold. map in pocket], plans, ports.). 24½cm.          DLC NN  **41**

Unit roster [316]–457.

—— Sheridan at Winchester. *Atlantic monthly* xlii (1878) 683–91.          **42**

Curtis, Greely Stevenson,          –1897.
The cause of the Confederate failure at Gettysburg, by Brevet-Brigadier-General Greeley S. Curtis. *PMHSM* iii 367–75.          **43**

*1st Cavalry, continued*

—— Gettysburg (report of Committee). *PM-HSM* iii 357–65.　　　　　　　**44**

The other members of the Committee were John C. Ropes and Brevet Major Herbert C. Mason whose task was to ascertain the numbers of the two armies that fought at Gettysburg.

Davis, George Breckenridge, 1847–1914.
The Antietam campaign, by Bvt. Lieutenant-Colonel George B. Davis. *PMHSM* iii 27–72.　　　　　　　　　　　**45**

—— The Bristoe and Mine run campaigns. *PMHSM* iii 470–502.　　　　　　**46**

—— The cavalry combat at Kelly's ford in 1863. *JUSCA* xxv (1914) 390–402.　　**47**

—— The cavalry operations in Middle Tennessee in October, 1862. *JUSCA* xxiv (1914) 879–91.　　　　　　　　　　　**48**

—— A comparison between certain aspects of the War of the rebellion and the Russo-Japanese war in Manchuria. *PMHSM* xiii 155–74.　　　　　　　　　　　　　　**49**

—— From Gettysburg to Williamsport. *PM-HSM* iii 449–69.　　　　　　　**50**

—— The operations of the cavalry in the Gettysburg campaign. *JUSCA* i (1888) 325–48.　　　　　　　　　　　　**51**

—— The Richmond raid of 1864. *JUSCA* xxiv (1914) 707–22.　　　　　　**52**

—— "Some reminiscences of the early days of the Army of the Potomac." 1914. 18 p. *MOLLUS-DC* no 96.　　　　　**53**

—— The Stoneman raid. *JUSCA* xxiv (1914) 533–52.　　　　　　　　　**54**

—— The strategy of the Gettysburg campaign. *PMHSM* iii 376–414.　　　　**55**

Higginson, Henry Lee, 1834–1919.
Life and letters of Henry Lee Higginson, by Bliss Perry. Boston, Atlantic Monthly press [1921] 2 v. plates (facs., illus., ports.). 24½cm.
　　　　　　　　　　　　　**55A**
Mustered in 2nd Mass infantry, May 25, 1861; discharged for promotion to 1st Mass cavalry, October 25, 1861; resigned August 9, 1864. Civil war i 140–238.

—— —— Boston, Atlantic Monthly press [1921] viii, (2), 557 p. plates (facs., illus., ports.). 23cm.　　　　　　NN　**55B**
Printed from the plates of Title 55A.

Smith, Charles M
From Andersonville to freedom. 1894. 74 p. *PNRISSHS* s5 no 3.　　　　　**56**

## 2ND CAVALRY

*Companies A, E, F, L and M were raised in California. Companies A, B, C, D and K left State, February 12, 1863; the rest of the Regiment, May 11, 1863.*

*Mustered out: July 20, 1865.*

*Mass soldiers* vi 228–328.

*Mass in the war* 755–66.

*Records of California men in the War of the rebellion, 1861 to 1867, compiled by the Adjutant-general of California, 1890,* 848–70.

Alvord, Henry Elijah, 1844–1904.
"Early's attack upon Washington, July, 1864," by Major Henry E. Alvord. 1897. 32 p. *MOLLUS-DC* no 26.　　　　　**57**

—— A New England boy in the Civil war. Edited by Caroline B. Sherman. *New England quarterly* v (1932) 310–44.　　**58**

Backus, Samuel W
Californians in the field, historical sketch of the organization and services of the California "Hundred" and "Battalion," 2d Massachusetts cavalry. A paper prepared and read before California commandery of the Military order of the loyal legion of the United States, December 17, 1889, by Samuel W. Backus, late Co. "L," 2d Massachusetts cavalry. 21 p. 23½cm.　　　　　　　NHi　**59**
On cover: War paper no. 4. . . .

Bartol, Cyrus Augustus, 1813–1900.
The purchase by blood, a tribute to Brig.-Gen. Charles Russell Lowell, Jr., spoken in the West church, Oct. 30, 1864, by C. A. Bartol. Boston, Printed by John Wilson and Son, 1864. 21 p. 23½cm.　　　　NN WHi　**60**

California. Adjutant General.
Report of the organization and services of the California cavalry battalion, with the name and rank of its officers and enlisted men, from the Adjutant-General's report of the State of California for 1866 and 1867. Sacramento, Dan Gelwicks, State printer, 1867. p 131–53. 22cm.
　　　　　　　　　　CtY NHi　**60A**

Drew, Samuel S
The California battalion claim, argument before the Committee of the Legislature of Massachusetts, on military claims, in the case of Henry H. Wyatt and others, members of the California battalion, for State bounty, March 19, 1866, by S. S. Drew. 14 p. 23½cm.
Caption title.　　　　　　　MHi　**61**

Emerson, Edward Waldo, 1844–1930.
Life and letters of Charles Russell Lowell, Captain Sixth United States cavalry, Colonel

Second Massachusetts cavalry, Brigadier-General United States volunteers, by Edward W. Emerson. Boston, Houghton, Mifflin and co., 1907. viii, 499 p. plates (1 illus., fold. map, ports.). 20cm.                    NN    62

Humphreys, Charles Alfred, 1838–1921.
Field, camp, hospital and prison in the Civil war, 1863–1865 [by] Charles A. Humphreys, Chaplain Second Massachusetts cavalry. Boston, Press of Geo. H. Ellis co., 1918. xi, 428 p. front. (port.). 20½cm.          NN    63
Coulter 249.

Hunt, Aurora
The California five hundred. In her The Army of the Pacific (1951) 281–300.    63A

Lawrence, William H
Prison-pen and swamp, Massachusetts cavalryman's escape and sufferings attending his attempt to reach the Union lines, by Wm. H. Lawrence, Sergt. Co. M, 2d Mass. cav. [Boston, 189–] 42 p. front. (port.). 16cm.
                                            MB    64

Morison, John Hopkins, 1808–1896.
Dying for our country, a sermon on the death of Capt. J. Sewall Reed and Rev. Thomas Starr King, preached in the First Congregational church in Milton, March 13, 1864, by John H. Morison. Boston, Printed by John Wilson & Son, 1864. 28 p. 23½cm.
                                       CSmH NN    64A
Captain Reed was a member of the California hundred

Rogers, Henry Munroe, 1839–1837.
The Second Massachusetts cavalry, by Henry M. Rogers. [Cambridge, 1919] 6 p. 24½cm.
                                          PPLL    65
"Reprinted from the Harvard graduates' magazine for March, 1919." A tribute to Charles A. Humphreys.

Rogers, J            Henry
The California hundred, a poem, by J. Henry Rogers. San Francisco, H. H. Bancroft and co., 1865. 100 p. 18cm.           MB NNC    66

### 3RD CAVALRY

*Formed from four cavalry companies organized during the Fall of 1861, and the 41st regiment of infantry recruited in the late Summer and Autumn of 1862, later to become the 41st mounted infantry.*

*These units were consolidated and designated the 3rd regiment of cavalry: June 17, 1863.*

*Mustered out: September 28, 1865.*

*Mass soldiers vi 329–420.*

*Mass in the war 767–75.*

Allen, John Fisk
Memorial of Pickering Dodge Allen, by his father. Boston, Printed by Henry W. Dutton and Son, 1867. 174 p. front. (port.). 19½cm.
                                            DLC    67

Ewer, James Kendall, 1846–
The Third Massachusetts cavalry in the War for the Union, by Rev. James K. Ewer, Company C. Published by direction of the Historical committee of the Regimental association. [Maplewood, Wm. G. J. Perry press] 1903. 452, cxiv, (ii) p. illus., maps, ports., plates (fold. map, ports.). 23cm.    DLC NN    68
Unit roster, cxiv p. "Reunions of Third Mass. cavalry," "Errors and corrections," (ii) p.

### 4TH CAVALRY

*Organized from separate companies: November 12, 1864.*

*Mustered out: November 14, 1865.*

*Mass soldiers vi 421–91.*

*Mass in the war 776–80.*

Arnold, William B
The Fourth Massachusetts cavalry in the closing scenes of the War for the maintenance of the Union, from Richmond to Appomattox. [Boston?, 191–] 32, (4) p. ports. 24cm.
                                       CSmH DLC    69
"Presented by William B. Arnold." Title from cover. Contents: The battle at High bridge, by Major Edward T. Bouvé; The first United States flag raised in Richmond after the war, by Mrs. Lasalle Corbell Pickett; The Fourth Massachusetts cavalry in the closing scenes of the War for the maintenance of the Union, from Richmond to Appomattox, by Wm. B. Arnold.

Bouvé, Edward Tracy
The battle at High bridge, by Major Edward T. Bouvé. MOLLUS-Mass ii 403–12.    70

Dorr, Henry Gustavus
Mohawk Peter, legends of. the Adirondacks and Civil war memories, by Henry G. Dorr. Illustrations by Nellie L. Thompson. Boston, Cornhill pub. co. [1921] 275 p. plates (illus.). 19cm.                    NN    71
The author served in the 14th Illinois cavalry, September 25, 1862, to December 9, 1863; 8th Tennessee cavalry, December 9, 1863 to February 12, 1864; 4th Massachusetts cavalry, April 21, 1864 to May 15, 1865. "Civil war memories," 161–275.

Scott, Henry Bruce, 1839–
The surrender of General Lee and the Army of Northern Virginia at Appomattox, Virginia, April 9, 1895, paper read at a meeting of surviving officers of the Second Massachusetts infantry, at Boston, August 9, 1916, by H. B. Scott, late Lieut. Colonel 4th Massachusetts cavalry. [4] folios. 28½cm.    Ct M    72
Caption title.

## 5TH CAVALRY

*Mustered in: January 9 to May 5, 1864.*
*Mustered out: October 31, 1865.*
*Mass soldiers VI 492–544.*
*Mass in the war 781–3.*

Bowditch, Charles Pickering
War letters of Charles P. Bowditch. *Massachusetts historical society proceedings* LVII (1923/24) 414–95. facs., plate (port.).    **73**

### 1st Battalion of Cavalry

*Mustered in and attached to 26th regiment of New York cavalry: December 30, 1864 to January 2, 1865.*
*Mustered out: June 30, 1865.*
*Mass soldiers VI 545–65.*
*Mass in the war 784.*

## INFANTRY

### 1ST INFANTRY

*Mustered in: May 23–27, 1861.*
*Mustered out: May 25, 1864.*
*Mass soldiers I 1–68.*
*Mass in the war 99–112.*

Constitution, by laws, and rules of order of the First regiment relief association, organized, June 15, 1863. Boston, J. E. Farwell & co., printers, 1863. 9, (1) p. 14cm.    MHi    **74**

First regiment Massachusetts volunteer infantry veteran association. Boston, Mass., February, 1911. Fiftieth anniversary roster [Boston, 1911] [32] p. port. 23½cm.    DLC    **75**
Caption title.

First regiment of infantry Massachusetts volunteer militia, Colonel Robert Cowdin, commanding. In service of the United States, in answer to the President's first call for troops to suppress the rebellion, April 5, 1861. Compiled from original papers in the Adjutant general and Auditor's offices of the Commonwealth. Boston, Wright and Potter print co., 1903. 50 p. 2 plates (facs., port.). 24cm.
    DLC NN    **76**
Unit roster [15]–50. On cover: 1st regiment infantry M.V.M., 1861. "Introduction" signed: Luke Edward Jenkins, Private Company B.

Memorial service in memory of the dead of the First regt. Massachusetts volunteer infantry, 1861–64, Faneuil hall, Boston, Mass., May 21, 1911. [16] p. 23cm.    DLC NN    **77**
Title from cover which includes the program. A roster of those killed in action and those who have died since the war.

Bardeen, Charles William, 1847–1924.
A little fifer's war diary, by C. W. Bardeen, formerly of Co. D., 1st Mass. vol. inf. With an introduction by Nicholas Murray Butler. Syracuse, N. Y., C. W. Bardeen, 1910. 329 p. illus., maps, ports. 24cm.    NN    **78**
Facsimile of the author's discharge printed on inside of back cover.

Cowdin, Robert, 1806?–1874.
Gen. Cowdin and the First Massachusetts regiment of volunteers. Boston, J. E. Farwell and co., printers, 1864. 19 p. 23cm.
    DLC M MHi    **79**

Cudworth, Warren Handel, 1825–1883.
History of the First regiment (Massachusetts infantry), from the 25th of May, 1861, to the 25th of May, 1864, including brief references to the operations of the Army of the Potomac, by Warren H. Cudworth, Chaplain of the Regiment. . . . Boston, Walker, Fuller and co., 1866. 528 p. plates (illus.). 20cm.    DLC NN    **80**
Unit roster [498]–528. Coulter 103.

Cutler, Frederick Morse, 1874–
The old First Massachusetts coast artillery in war and peace, by Frederick Morse Cutler. Boston, Pilgrim press [1917] 180 p. plates (illus., ports.). 19½cm.    NN    **81**
Civil war 46–79.

Darling, Charles B
Historical sketch of the First regiment infantry, Massachusetts volunteer militia, compiled by Chas. B. Darling. Boston. [Alfred Mudge & Sons, printers] 1890. [40] p. illus., ports. 27½ × 35½cm.    DLC    **82**
Advertising matter included. On cover: Souvenir of the dedication of the new armory, June, 1890.

Frye, James A          1863–1933.
The First regiment of heavy artillery, 1844–1899. In Regiments and armories of Massachusetts, edited by Charles W. Hall, 1899 I 338–60.    **83**
Civil war, 344–52.

Holden, Leverett Dana, 1843–1932.
My first and last fights, delivered before the Malden club, Feb. 5, 1914. Fredericksburg to Gettysburg. Memories of the Civil war, by Leverett D. Holden. Malden, Samuel Tilden, printer [1914] 85 p. front. (port.). 16½cm.
    NN    **84**

Kingsbury, Allen Alonzo, 1840–1862.
The hero of Medfield, containing the journals and letters of Allen Alonzo Kingsbury, of Medfield, member of Co. H, Chelsea volunteers, Mass. 1st reg., who was killed by the Rebels near Yorktown, April 26, 1862. Also, notice of the other three soldiers belonging to the same company and killed at the same time,

funeral services at Chelsea and Medfield. Historic and poetic account of Medfield. . . . Boston, John M. Hewes, printer, 1862. 144 p. front. (port.). 18½cm.　　MHi NN　85

"Introduction" signed: E. A. J[ohnson] the editor.

Ryan, J　　　　　　W
The Massachusetts First at Gettysburg, July 2, 1863, read at the dedication of their monument, July 1, 1886, by Mrs. T. R. Mathews, by J. W. Ryan. [4] p. 21½cm.　　MHi　86

Caption title. Poetry.

Thompson, Augustus Charles, 1812–1901.
Soldier and Christian, address at the funeral of Robert M. Carson, Private in the First regiment Mass. volunteers, by A. C. Thompson, Roxbury, Mass., Dec. 18, 1862. 11 p. 19cm.

Caption title.　　　　　　MHi　87

## 2ND INFANTRY

*Mustered in: May 25, 1861.*

*Mustered out: July 14, 1865.*

*Mass soldiers* i 69–147.

*Mass in the war* 113–35.

In memoriam Charles Redington Mudge Lieut.-Col. Second Mass. infantry. Born in New York city, October 22d, 1839. Killed at Gettysburg, July 3d, 1863 . . . Privately printed. Cambridge [Riverside press] 1863. 32 p. 22½cm.　　　　　　MHi　88

Second Massachusetts infantry association . . . annual meeting. . . . xxix 1900 (MHi); xxxiv 1905 (MB); xli 1911 (MHi); xliv 1914 (MHi).　　　　　　89

Dwight, Wilder, 1833–1862.
Life and letters of Wilder Dwight. Lieut-Col. Second Mass. inf. vols. . . . Boston, Ticknor and Fields, 1868. 349, (2) p. front. (port.). 23½cm.　　MHi NHi NN　90

Edited by his mother, Elizabeth A. Dwight.

Gordon, George Henry, 1825?–1886.
Brook farm to Cedar mountain in the War of the great rebellion, 1861–62. A revision and enlargement (from the latest and most authentic sources) of Papers numbered I, II and III, entitled, "A history of the Second Massachusetts regiment," and the "Second Massachusetts regiment and Stonewall Jackson." By George H. Gordon. Boston, James R. Osgood and co., 1883. x, 376 p. plates (illus., 3 maps, 2 fold.). 21cm.　　DLC NN　91

—— History of the campaign of the Army of Northern Virginia, under John Pope,

from Cedar mountain to Alexandria, 1862, by George H. Gordon. Boston, Houghton, Osgood and co., 1880. xiv, 498 p. fold. maps. 24cm.
　　　　　　DLC NHi NN　92

—— History of the Second Mass. regiment of infantry, second paper, delivered by George H. Gordon, at the annual meeting of the Second Mass. infantry association, on May 11, 1874. Boston, Alfred Mudge & Son, 1874. 68 p. 24cm.　　　　M NHi　93

—— History of the Second Mass. regiment of infantry, third paper, delivered by George H. Gordon, Colonel Second Mass. regiment of infantry, at the annual meeting of the Second Mass. infantry association, on May 11, 1875. Boston, Alfred Mudge & Son, printers, 1875. viii, [3]–231 p. 23½cm.　　DLC NN　94

On cover: The Second Massachusetts and "Stonewall" Jackson.

—— Major Anderson at Fort Sumter. *PMHSM* ix 1–52.　　　　　　95

—— The organization and early history of the Second Mass. regiment of infantry, an address delivered by George H. Gordon, at the annual meeting of the Second Massachusetts infantry association, on the 11th May, 1873. Boston, Press of Rockwell & Churchill, 1873. 35 p. 24cm.　　　　　　NHi　96

The first paper in the series, History of the Second Mass. regiment. See Titles 93–94.

—— The twenty-seventh day of August, 1862, (being Chapter VII of the history of the campaign of the Army of Virginia, from Cedar mountain to Alexandria). *PMHSM* ii 99–132.
　　　　　　97

Morse, Charles Fessenden, 1839–1936.
From second Bull run to Antietam, by Col. Charles F. Morse. *MOLLUS-Mo* i 268–77.　98

—— History of the Second Massachusetts regiment of infantry. Gettysburg, a paper read at the officers' reunion in Boston, May 10, 1878, by Charles F. Morse, Colonel Second Massachusetts regiment. Boston, George H. Ellis, printer, 1882. 20 p. 24cm.
　　　　　　DLC NHI NN　99

—— Letters written during the Civil war, 1861–1865. Privately printed. [Boston, T. R. Marvin & Son, printers] 1898. 222 p. front. (port.). 23½cm.　　DLC　100

"Note" signed: Charles F. Morse. Coulter 332.

—— The relief of Chatanooga, October, 1863, and guerrilla operations in Tennessee. *PMHSM* xiv 65–81.　　　　　101

—— The Twelfth corps at Gettysburg. *PMHSM* xiv 19–42.　　　　　102

*2nd Infantry, continued*

Oakey, Daniel
History of the Second Massachusetts regiment of infantry. Beverly ford, a paper read at the officers' reunion in Boston, May 12, 1884, by Daniel Oakey, Captain Second Massachusetts regiment. Boston, Geo. H. Ellis, printer, 1884. 15 p. 23cm. NHi **103**

—— Marching through Georgia and the Carolinas. *BandL* IV 671–9. **104**

Pattison, Everett Wilson, 1839–
Some reminiscences of army life, by Captain Everett W. Pattison. St. Louis, Smith & Owens print. co., 1887. 20 p. 23cm.
DLC **105**
Title and imprint from cover. Also published as *MOLLUS-Mo* I 243–6.

Quincy, Samuel Miller, 1833–1887.
The character of General Halleck's military administration in the summer of 1862, with special reference to the removal by his orders of the Army of the Potomac from the Peninsula, and to the share which belongs to him in the campaign of General Pope. *PMHSM* II 1–30. **106**

—— History of the Second Massachusetts regiment of infantry. A prisoner's diary, a paper read at the officers' reunion in Boston, May 11, 1877, by Samuel M. Quincy, Captain Second Massachusetts regiment. Boston, George H. Ellis, printer, 1882. 24 p. 24cm.
Coulter 384. NHi NN **107**

Quint, Alonzo Hall, 1828–1896.
The Potomac and the Rapidan, army notes from the failure at Winchester to the reenforcement of Rosecrans, 1861–3, by Alonzo H. Quint, Chaplain of the Second Massachusetts infantry. Boston, Crosby and Nichols, 1864. 407 p. fold. map. 18½cm. NN **108**
Coulter 385.

—— The record of the Second Massachusetts infantry, 1861–65, by Alonzo H. Quint, its Chaplain. Boston, James P. Walker, 1867. viii, 528 p. plates (ports.). 21cm. NN **109**
Unit roster [295]–514. Coulter 386.

Shaw, Robert Gould, 1837–1863.
Letters RGS [monogram] Cambridge, University press, 1864. 328 p. 23cm.
MB NN **110**
Mustered in 2nd Mass infantry, May 25, 1861; discharged for promotion in 54th Mass infantry, April 17, 1863; killed in action, July 18, 1863. Shaw had prior service in the 7th regiment New York militia.

—— Letters from camp written by Robert Gould Shaw. *Magazine of history* XVIII (New York 1914) 104–10, 226–31; XIX (1914) 25–31. **111**

Thayer, George Augustine, 1839–
The draft riots of 1863, a historical study, read at the meeting of the Ohio commandery, Military order of the loyal legion of the United States, April 5, 1916, by George A. Thayer, late Captain of the Second Massachusetts infantry. 13 p. 22cm. NHi **112**
Title from cover.

—— "Gettysburg," "as we men on the right saw it," a paper read before the Ohio commandery of the Military order of the loyal legion of the United States. Cincinnati, H. C. Sherick & co., 1886. 22 p. 23½cm.
NHi **113**
Also published as *MOLLUS-Ohio* II 24–43.

—— "The heroic period of the Union," a sermon delivered before the Ohio commandery of the Military order of the loyal legion of the United States. . . . Cincinnati, H. C. Sherick & co., 1886. 22 p. 22cm. NHi **114**

—— History of the Second Massachusetts regiment of infantry, Chancellorsville, a paper read at the officers' reunion in Boston, May 11, 1880, by George A. Thayer. Boston, George H. Ellis, printer, 1882. 33 p. 24cm.
MHi NN RP **115**

—— A railroad feat of war. *MOLLUS-Ohio* IV 214–34. **116**

Thompson, James William, 1805–1881.
Funeral tribute, words spoken at the obsequies of William Blackstone Williams, late Captain in the Second regiment of Massachusetts infantry, Sunday, Aug. 17, 1862, by James W. Thompson. Boston, John Wilson and Son, 1862. 15 p. 23½cm. DLC M **117**

See also Title 55A.

### 3RD INFANTRY

*Left State: April 18, 1861.* (3 months)
*Mustered out: July 23, 1861.*
*Mass soldiers* I 148–65.
*Mass in the war* 136–8.
*Mustered in: September 23–26, 1862.* (9 months)
*Mustered out: June 26, 1863.*
*Mass soldiers* I 166–203.
*Mass in the war* 138–41.

Historical souvenir of fiftieth anniversary of First volunteer company (Co. C., 3rd reg't, M.V.M.). Issued April 17, 1912, by direction of First volunteers citizens' association. Cambridge [L. F. Weston] 1912. 36 p. illus., ports. 23cm. M **118**
"The soldier's story, as told by Captain John Kinnear," 10–13.

Gammons, John Gray
The Third Massachusetts regiment volunteer militia in the War of the rebellion, 1861–1863, by Rev. John G. Gammons. Providence, Snow & Farnham co., printers, 1906. x, 326 p. plates (double map, ports.). 19½cm.
Unit roster included.                DLC NN    *119*

### 4TH INFANTRY

*Left State: April 17, 1861.* (3 months)
*Mustered out: July 22, 1861.*

*Mass soldiers* 1 204–27.

*Mass in the war* 142–4.

*Mustered in: September 1–26, 1862; field and staff, December 16, 1862.* (9 months)

*Mustered out: August 28, 1863.*

*Mass soldiers* 1 228–68.

*Mass in the war* 144–7.

Dollard, Robert, 1842–
Recollections of the Civil war, and going West to grow up with the country, by Robert Dollard. Scotland, S.D., Published by the author, 1906. 296 p. plates (ports.). 23cm.
                                        DLC NN    *120*
Mustered in 4th Mass infantry, April 22, 1861; mustered out, July 22, 1861; mustered in 23rd Mass infantry, September 28, 1861; discharged for promotion in 2nd U.S. colored cavalry, June 1, 1864.

Maglathlin, Henry Bartlett, 1819–1910.
Company I, Fourth Massachusetts regiment, nine months volunteers, in service, 1862–3. Boston, Press of Geo. C. Rand & Avery, 1863. 40, (1) p. 23½cm.    M MHi NHi    *121*
Foreword signed: Henry B. Maglathlin. "Additions and corrections," (1) p.

Stephenson, Luther, 1830-
Three months service in 1861, with the Fourth regiment, M.V.M. *MOLLUS-Mass* II 533–50.    *122*

### 5TH INFANTRY

*Mustered in: May 1, 1861.*

*Mustered out: July 31, 1861.*

*Mass soldiers* 1 269–99.

*Mass in the war* 148–50.

*Mustered in: September 16–29, 1862.* (9 months)

*Mustered out: July 2, 1863.*

*Mass soldiers* 1 300–35.

*Mass in the war* 151–5.

*Mustered in: Later part of July 1864.* (100 days)

*Mustered out: November 16, 1864.*

*Mass soldiers* 1 336–70.

*Mass in the war* 155–6.

Company I, Fifth regiment, Mass. volunteer militia. April 20, 1861. Somerville light infantry. Broadside, 46 × 50cm.    M    *123*
A roster.

History of the Richardson light guard of Wakefield, Mass., 1851–1901. Published under the direction and authority of the General committee on the occasion of the semi-centennial celebration of the Company, October 11, 1901. Wakefield, Printed at the Citizen and Banner office, 1901. 216, (33) p. illus., ports. 23½cm.
                                        NN    *123A*
Unit roster, (33) p. Members of the Richardson light guard served as Company E in the following Mass regiments: 5th (3 months), 7th, 8th (100 days) and 50th. Civil war 38–97.

A souvenir history of the Charlestown city guard, Company "H," 5th regiment infantry, M.V.M., 1897. Boston, Hanover print. co., 1897. 46 p. ports. 20 × 28cm.    M    *124*
Civil war 38–44. Advertising matter included.

Barrett, Edwin Shepard, 1833–1898.
What I saw at Bull run. An address by Edwin S. Barrett, delivered in the Town hall, Concord, Mass., July 21st, 1886, on the 25th anniversary of the battle of Bull run, at the re-union of the veterans of Co. G (Concord artillery), Fifth regiment, M.V.M. Capt. George L. Prescott. Boston, Beacon press, 1886. 48 p. front. (port.). 23cm.    NN    *125*
"Staff [Company] officers Fifth regiment M.V.M. (three months)," 35–48. The author was present at the battle as a non-combatant.

Bennett, Edwin Clark
Musket and sword; or, camp, march, and firing line in the Army of the Potomac, by Edwin C. Bennett. Boston, Coburn pub. co., 1900. viii, 344 p. front. (port.). 18cm.
                                        DLC NN    *126*
Mustered in 5th Mass infantry, May 1, 1861; mustered out, July 31, 1861; mustered in 22nd Mass infantry, September 17, 1861; mustered out, October 17, 1864.

Robinson, Frank Torry, 1845–1898.
History of the Fifth regiment, M.V.M., by Frank T. Robinson, ex-member of Co. H, and A, and Regimental historian. . . . Boston, W. F. Brown & co., printers, 1879. vi, 237, (1) p. front. (illus.), plates (ports.). 22½cm.
                                        DLC NN    *127*
Unit roster: First three months troops, 18–28; Nine months' campaign, 57–69. "Errata" (1) p.

Roe, Alfred Seelye, 1844–1917.
The Fifth regiment Massachusetts volunteer infantry in its three tours of duty, 1861, 1862–'63, 1864, by Alfred S. Roe. Regimental committee on history . . . [5 names] Published by the Fifth regiment veteran association. Boston

*5th Infantry, continued*

[Worcester, Blanchard press] 1911. 510 p. illus., maps and plans, ports. 23cm.
DLC NN **128**

Unit roster: Three months' service, 317–71; Nine months' service, 373–435; One hundred days' service, 437–88.

Wild, Silas F

Expedition to Goldsboro, N.C. Edited by Emma Wild Goodwin. *Medford historical register* VII (1904) 88–95. **129**

## 6TH INFANTRY

*Left State: April 17, 1861. (3 months)*

*Mustered out: August 2, 1861.*

*Mass soldiers* I 371–97.

*Mass in the war* 157–61.

*Mustered in: August 31 to September 8, 1862. (9 months)*

*Mustered out: June 3, 1863.*

*Mass soldiers* I 398–432.

*Mass in the war* 161–5.

*Mustered in: July 14–19, 1864. (100 days)*

*Mustered out: October 27, 1864.*

*Mass soldiers* I 433–68.

*Mass in the war* 166–7.

April 19, 1861. "Old Sixth" Mass. regt., April 19, 1870. Lowell, Marsden & Rowell, printers, 1871. 22 p. 22cm. DLC NHi **130**

Caption title: Ninth anniversary of "Old Sixth" Massachusetts regiment at Worcester, April 19, 1870.

Adams, Herbert Lincoln

Worcester light infantry, 1803–1922, a history. Worcester, Worcester Light Infantry Association, 1924. 608 p. front. (port.), facs., illus., ports., fold. plate (port.). 27½cm.
DLC NN **131**

"History, period of the Civil war, 1861–1865, Company G, "Old 6th," 47–70.

Andrew, John Albion, 1818–1867.

An address on the occasion of dedicating the monument to Ladd and Whitney, members of the Sixth regiment, M.V.M., killed at Baltimore, Maryland, April 19, 1861, delivered at Lowell, Massachusetts, June 17, 1865, by John Andrew, Governor of the Commonwealth. Boston, Wright & Potter, State printers, 1865. 31 p. 23cm. NN **132**

Andrews, Matthew Page, 1879–1947.

Passage of the Sixth Massachusetts regiment through Baltimore, April 19, 1861. *Maryland historical magazine* XIV (1919) 60–76. **133**

Brown, George William, 1812–1891.

The Sixth Massachusetts regiment in Baltimore. . . . In his Baltimore and the nineteenth of April, 1861 (1887) 42–55. **134**

Clark, Charles Branch, 1913–

Baltimore and the attack on the Sixth Massachusetts regiment, April 19, 1861. *Maryland historical magazine* LVI (1961) 39–71. **134A**

Darling, Charles Kimball

Sixth regiment of infantry, M.V.M., by Colonel Charles K. Darling. In Regiments and armories of Massachusetts, edited by Charles W. Hall (1899) I 412–54. **135**

Civil war 414–31.

Dennis, John Benjamin, –1894.

March of the old 6th Massachusetts through Baltimore, April 19, 1861, a paper read before the Nebraska commandery of the Military order of the loyal legion of the United States, by Bvt. Brig. Gen'l John B. Dennis, late a Private of Company G, 6th Mass. [Omaha, Neb., Ackermann Bros. & Heintze, printers, 1888] 23cm. NHi **136**

Originally published in *MOLLUS-Neb* I 122–40.

Dickinson, Kendrick

Life of Luther C. Ladd, the first martyr that fell a sacrifice to his country, in the city of Baltimore, on the 19th of April, 1861, while bravely defending the flag of the nation, exclaiming with his dying breath, "all hail to the Stars and stripes!" Accompanied with a likeness taken from life, together with an account of his parentage, and a description of his home in Alexandria, N.H. Also, an account of the brilliant naval engagement at Port Royal, by a citizen of Alexandria. Belfast, Me., J. W. Dickinson, 1862. viii, [9]–40 p. front. (port.). 22cm. DLC NhHi **137**

Hanson, John Wesley, 1823–1901.

Historical sketch of the old Sixth regiment of Massachusetts volunteers during its three campaigns, in 1861, 1862, 1863, and 1864, containing the history of the several companies previous to 1861, and the names and military record of each man connected with the Regiment during the war, by John W. Hanson, Chaplain. Boston, Lee and Shepard, 1866. 352 p. 3 plates (2 illus., 26 ports.). 20cm.
NN **138**

Unit roster: The three months' campaign, 85–138, 339; The nine months' campaign, 256–94; The hundred days' campaign, 306–338. Coulter 212.

Massachusetts. General Court.

. . . Proceedings in the Legislature of Massachusetts, upon the Act of the State of Maryland appropriating seven thousand dollars for the families of those belonging to the Sixth

regiment of Massachusetts volunteers, who were killed or disabled by wounds received in the riot at Baltimore, April 19th, 1861. Boston, Wright & Potter, printers, 1862. 15 p. 23½cm.
NN  *139*

At head of title: Maryland and Massachusetts.

Sampson, Walter S
. . . Capt. Sampson's statement [of the passage of his command through the City of Baltimore on April 19, 1861] [Boston, 1886] 4 p. 23cm.                                    MB  *140*

Caption title. At head of title: From Boston herald of April 19th, 1886.

Smith, Charles S
The slain at Baltimore! Boston, E. L. Mitchell, printer [1861] Broadside, 20 × 13cm.
Text signed: C. S. S. Poetry.       MB  *141*

Watson, Benjamin Frank, 1826–1905.
Addresses, review and episodes chiefly concerning the "Old Sixth" Massachusetts regiment, by B. F. Watson, Brevet-Colonel. New York, 1901. 142 p. 23½cm.       NN  *142*

——— An oration delivered at Huntington hall, Lowell, Massachusetts, by Col. B. F. Watson, April 19, 1886 . . . in commemoration of the 25th anniversary of the passage through Baltimore of the 6th regiment of Massachusetts volunteers, April 19th, 1861. Oration printed by order of the Association. [New York, Livingston Middleditch, 1886] 54, (4) p. 23½cm.
NHi NN  *143*

"From Boston herald of April 19th, 1866. Capt. Sampson's statement," (4) p.

## 7TH INFANTRY

*Mustered in: June 15, 1861.*
*Mustered out: June 27, 1864.*
*Mass soldiers* I 469–515.
*Mass in the war* 168–80.

Bowen, James Lorenzo
Dedication of the monuments of the 7th, 10th and 37th Mass. vols., at Gettysburg, Pa., October 6, 1886, with the dedicatory address, by James L. Bowen. Springfield, 1886. 56 p. 14cm.                                    NB  *143A*

Hutchinson, Nelson V
History of the Seventh Massachusetts volunteer infantry in the War of the rebellion of the Southern states against constitutional authority, 1861–1865, with description of battles, army movements, hospital life, and incidents of the camp, by officers and privates . . . by the author, Nelson V. Hutchinson. Taunton, Published by authority of the Regimental Association [Ezra Davol, printer] 1890. vii, 320 p. plates (1 illus., ports.). 23cm.
Unit roster [252]–72.       DLC NN  *144*

See also Title 123A

## 8TH INFANTRY

*Left State: April 18, 1861.* (3 months)
*Mustered out. August 1, 1861.*
*Mass soldiers* I 516–43.
*Mass in the war* 181–3.
*Mustered in: September 15 to October 30, 1862.* (9 months)
*Mustered out: August 7, 1863.*
*Mass soldiers* I 544–81.
*Mass in the war* 184–7.
*Mustered in: July 13–21, 1864.* (100 days)
*Mustered out: November 10, 1864.*
*Mass soldiers* I 582–615.
*Mass in the war* 187–8.

Hincks, Edward Winslow, 1830–1904.
The Forty-fifth regiment Massachusetts volunteer militia, nine months' men, and the Eighth regiment at Annapolis in 1861. Extracts from speech by General Edward W. Hincks, at Peabody, November 5th, 1883. Cambridge, Printed by William H. Wheeler, 1883. 23 p. 21½cm.                                    MHi NN  *145*
"The Forty-fifth regiment," [3]–10, "The Eighth regiment at Annapolis," 10–23.

Peach, Benjamin Franklin
Eighth regiment, M.V.M. In Regiments and armories of Massachusetts, edited by Charles W. Hall (1901) II 37–64.       *146*
Civil war 38–58.

Sewall, John S
Echoes from life in camp, by Chaplain Rev. John S. Sewall. MOLLUS-Me IV 73–89.  *147*

Whipple, George M
History of the Salem light infantry, from 1805 to 1890. Salem, Essex Institute, 1890. 148 p. plate (facs.). 23½cm.       NN  *147A*
The Company served in the 8th Mass (90 days). Civil war 65–70.

See also Title 123A

## 9TH INFANTRY

*Mustered in: June 11, 1861.*
*Mustered out: June 21, 1864.*
*Mass soldiers* I 616–81.
*Mass in the war* 189–95.

*9th Infantry, continued*

Flynn, Frank J
"The Fighting Ninth" for fifty years and the semi-centennial celebration, by Frank J. Flynn. [1911] 109 p. ports. 26½cm.                     **148**
Civil war 4–49.

McNamara, Daniel George
The history of the Ninth regiment Massachusetts volunteer infantry, Second brigade, First division, Fifth army corps, Army of the Potomac, June, 1861 — June, 1864, by Daniel George McNamara. Boston, E. B. Stillings & co., printers, 1899. xii, 543 p. 24cm.
Unit roster [427]–542.                   NN   **149**

MacNamara, Michael H
The Irish Ninth in bivouac and battle; or, Virginia and Maryland campaigns, by M. H. MacNamara, late Captain. . . . Boston, Lee & Shepard, 1867. 306 p. plates (illus.). 19½cm.
                                      NN RP   **150**
Unit roster 249–306. Coulter 313.

**10TH INFANTRY**

*Mustered in: June 21, 1861.*

*Mustered out: July 1 and 6, 1864.*

*Mass soldiers* I 682–734.

*Mass in the war* 196–206.

Newell, Joseph Keith
"Ours," annals of 10th regiment Massachusetts volunteers, in the rebellion. Edited by Captain Joseph Keith Newell, Historian of the Regiment, from personal observation, private journals of officers and men, selections from the press of the day, and from letters from soldiers of the Regiment published in the local newspapers. Springfield, C. A. Nichols & co., 1875. 609 p. plates (ports.). 23½cm.
Unit roster [295]–609.                   NN   **151**

Parsons, Joseph Bailey
The 10th regiment, salient points in its history, a paper prepared by its commander, Col. Joseph B. Parsons, delivered before the Loyal legion on Wednesday, April 3, 1901, also read at the 34th annual reunion of the 10th regiment association at Orange, Mass., June 21, 1901. 19 p. port. 22cm.            M   **152**
Title from cover.

Rockwell, Francis Williams, 1844–1929.
Address at the unveiling of the memorial tablet of Colonel Henry S. Briggs, and the Tenth Massachusetts volunteer infantry, at Pittsfield, Massachusetts, June 21, 1907, by Francis W. Rockwell. [Pittsfield, Eagle print. co., 1907] 18 p. fold. plate (illus.). 23½cm.
                                          M   **153**

Roe, Alfred Seelye, 1844–1917.
The Tenth regiment Massachusetts volunteer infantry, 1861–1864, a Western Massachusetts regiment, by Alfred S. Roe. Regimental committee on history . . . [seven names] Published by the Tenth regiment veteran association. Springfield [F. A. Bassette co.] 1909. 535 p. front. (illus.), illus., ports. 24cm.   NN   **154**
Unit roster 332–517.

Williams, Sidney S
From Spottsylvania to Wilmington, N.C., by way of Andersonville and Florence, by Sidney S. Williams, late First Sergeant, Company C, Tenth Massachusetts. 1899. 47 p. *PNRISSHS* s5 no 10.                                    **155**
See also Title 143A.

**11TH INFANTRY**

*Mustered in: June 13, 1861.*

*Mustered out: July 14, 1865.*

*Mass soldiers* I 735–816.

*Mass in the war* 207–18.

Blake, Henry Nicholls, 1838–1933.
Three years in the Army of the Potomac, by Henry N. Blake, late Captain in the Eleventh Massachusetts volunteers. . . . Boston, Lee and Shepard, 1865. vi, [7]–319 p. 19cm.
Coulter 38.                         DLC NN   **156**

Hutchinson, Gustavus B
A narrative of the formation and services of the Eleventh Massachusetts volunteers, from April 15, 1861, to July 14, 1865, being a brief account of their experiences in the camp and in the field, to which is added a roster, containing the names of all surviving members known to the Veteran association, compiled from such authentic sources of information as were available, and from the personal recollections of the participants. Published by Gustavus B. Hutchinson, late Sergeant, Co. D, 11th Mass. Boston, Alfred Mudge & Sons, printers, 1893. 96 p. 18cm.         NHi   **157**

Means, James Howard, 1823–1894.
A sermon preached in the Second church, Dorchester, after the death of Lieutenant William R. Porter, Eleventh regiment Massachusetts volunteers, by Rev. James H. Means, September 7, 1862. . . . Boston, Press of T. R. Marvin & Son, 1862. 21 p. 23cm.
                                    DLC MHi   **158**

**12TH INFANTRY**

*Mustered in: June 26, 1861.*

*Mustered out: July 8, 1864.*

*Mass soldiers* II 1–68.

*Mass in the war* 219–34.

Secretary's annual circular number . . . Twelfth Massachusetts (Webster) regiment association. . . . no [1]–22, 1896–1916. 23½cm.

DLC  *159*

Until his death, February 10, 1916, George Kimball was the Secretary.

Appleton, Samuel
The battle of Malvern hill (read June 7, 1882). *MOLLUS-Ill* III 37–43.    *160*

Beale, James
The battle flags of the Army of the Potomac at Gettysburg, Penna., July 1st, 2d, & 3d, 1863. Philadelphia, Compiled and published by James Beale, 1885. 1 v. 32 col. plates (illus.). 30cm.    DLC NHi  *161*

Descriptive text on rectos of leaves facing plates. Versos are blank. "Edition limited to 125 copies."

—— "Chancellorsville," a paper read before the United service club, Philadelphia, Penna., on Wednesday, February 8, 1888, by James Beale, late Private Company I, 12th regiment Massachusetts volunteer infantry. [Philadelphia, 1888?] 32 p. 18½ × 21cm.
25 copies printed.    CSmH  *162*

—— —— Second edition. [Philadelphia, James Beale, printer] 1892. 11 folios. plans. 18½ × 21cm.    NHi  *163*

Text on rectos, plans and notes on versos.

—— Echoes from the wagon wheels, heard at a regimental reunion. [Philadelphia, 189–] 30 folios. 21½ × 27½cm.
CSmH NHi NN  *164*

Title from cover. Colophon on p 3 of cover. "Sixty copies printed."

—— A famous war song, a paper read before the United service club, Phila., by James Beale. [Philadelphia, 1888] 18 folios. 20cm.
"One hundred copies printed."    CSmH  *165*

—— —— [Philadelphia, James Beale, printer, 1894] 22, (1) folios. 17½ × 22cm.    PP  *166*
"One hundred copies privately printed September, 1894."

—— A famous war song. *Magazine of history* XII (New York 1910) 70–2.    *167*

—— The following letter and memoranda from Mr. James Beale, of Philadelphia, is published in answer to the attack made upon me at Gettysburg, on the 1st ult., by Col. A. Wilson Morris, in an address. . . . [Philadelphia, 1886] 4 folios.    CSmH  *168*

Caption title. Dated in caption: 23 Fifth avenue, New York, August 5th, 1886. Note of transmittal is signed: D. E. Sickles.

—— From Marsh run to Seminary ridge [a paper read before the United service club, Philadelphia . . . March 6, 1889, by James Beale . . . ] [Philadelphia, J. Beale, printer, 1889] 38 folios. 20½ × 24½cm.
"Fifty copies privately printed." CSmH  *168A*

—— —— Revised edition. [Philadelphia] 1891. 20 folios. plate (illus.). 18 × 20½cm.
NHi  *169*

—— Gettysburg, a paper read before the United service club, Philadelphia, Pennsylvania, January 5, 1887, by James Beale. [Philadelphia, James Beale, printer, 1887] 36, (1) p. 17½ × 17½cm.    MnHi  *170*
"Ten copies privately printed." Distribution of copies, (1) p.

—— Percentages of loss by death in Massachusetts regiments, by James Beale. [Boston, 1878] broadside, 20 × 22cm.    CSmH  *171*
Caption title.

—— The statements of time on July 1st at Gettysburg, Pa., 1863. An examination of the official reports, by James Beale. . . . Philadelphia, James Beale, printer, 1897. 29 p. plates (maps). 24½cm.    CSmH DLC  *172*
"One hundred copies privately printed."

—— Tabulated roster of the Army of the Potomac at Gettysburg, Penna., July 1, 2, 3, 1863. Arranged by States, showing the brigade, division, and corps with which each organization served during the battle. Philadelphia, Compiled and published by James Beale [Philadelphia, 1888] 32 p. 15½cm.
DLC NHi  *173*

Cook, Benjamin F
History of the Twelfth Massachusetts volunteers (Webster regiment), by Lieutenant-Colonel Benjamin F. Cook. Boston, Published by the Twelfth (Webster) Regiment Association, 1882. 167 p. plates (1 illus., fold. map in pocket, 2 ports.). 23½cm.    NN  *174*

On cover: Twelfth Webster regiment. "Though the History bears the name of Col. Cook, it was written by Private James Beale, Co. I," Catalogue of library of John P. Nicholson, 1914. Coulter 90.

Haviland, Thomas P
A brief diary of imprisonment. Contributed by Thomas P. Haviland. *Virginia magazine of history and biography* L (1952) 230–7. *174A*

Jenkins, James Howard
The author of the John Brown song. *Magazine of history* XI (New York 1910) 337–41.    *175*

Kimball, George          –1916.
A day in camp. *Biv* II (1885) 256–9.  *176*

—— The John Brown song. *Biv* III (1885) 1–6.    *177*

—— Origin of the John Brown song. *New England magazine* ns I (1889) 371–6. facs., music.    *178*

*12th Infantry, continued*

—— Ornamented stationery. *Biv* III (1885) 94–8.　　　　　　　　　　　　　　　**179**

Stutler, Boyd Blynn, 1889–
Glory, glory, hallelujah!, the story of "John Brown's body" and "Battle hymn of the Republic" [by] Boyd B. Stutler. [Cincinnati, C. J. Krehbiel co., 1960] 47 p. front. (port.). 16½cm.　　　　　　　　　NN　**179A**
"Our Christmas greeting."

### 13TH INFANTRY

*Mustered in: July 16, 1861.*
*Mustered out: August 1, 1864.*
*Mass soldiers* II 69–130.
*Mass in the war* 235–48.

Thirteenth Massachusetts regiment. Testimonial to Charles E. Davis, Jr. From the "Boston journal," April 28, 1895. [4] p. 2 plates (illus.). 25cm.　　　　　　　　　　　M　**180**
Caption title.

Circular no . . . Thirteenth Massachusetts regiment. [Boston, 1888–1922] 35 v. 25½cm.
　　　　　　　　DLC NN [3–26]　**181**
Title from cover. Nos. 1–8 are not numbered. Annual. "Circular no. 35, final."

Thirteenth Massachusetts regiment association [report of annual reunion] [Dorchester?, 1923–25] 3 nos. 22½cm.　　　　　MB　**182**
Report of the proceedings of the year previous to the date on the cover. Title from cover.

Bell, Clarence H
[Contributions to *Bivouac*]
Being a Private. II (1885) 353–6.　　**183**

The Confederate soldier. III (1885) 201–5. **184**

"Frills," II (1885) 225–30.　　　　　**185**

Guns. III (1885) 41–6.　　　　　　**186**

How we opened the railroad. II (1884) 75–8.
　　　　　　　　　　　　　　　　**187**

Some camp amusements. II (1884) 175–9. **188**

Victuals and drink. II (1884) 110–14.　**189**

When you were mad. II (1885) 302–8.　**190**

Bingham, Charles H
Recruits. *Biv* III (1885) 57–60.　　**191**

Davis, Charles E　　　　　　　–1915.
Three years in the army, the story of the Thirteenth Massachusetts volunteers, from July 16, 1861, to August 1, 1864, by Charles E. Davis, Jr. Boston, Estes and Lauriat, 1894. xxxv, 476 p. plates (maps). 23cm.　NN　**192**
Unit roster 392–470. Coulter 115.

## 12th – 15th Massachusetts Infantry

Freeman, Warren Hapgood
Letters from two brothers serving in the War for the Union to their family at home in West Cambridge, Mass. Printed for private circulation. Cambridge [Printed by H. O. Houghton] 1871. 164, (2) p. front. (mounted port.). 18cm.　　　　　　　　DLC NN　**193**
Mustered in 13th Mass infantry, December 1, 1861; transferred to 39th Mass infantry, July 14, 1864; mustered out, September 13, 1864. Eugene H. Freeman was an engineer in the transport service.

Grand Army of the Republic. Massachusetts Department. John A. Rawlins Post, No. 43, Marlboro.
The story of the John Brown bell, by direction of John A. Rawlins post 43, G.A.R. [Marlboro] Rawlins Building Association, c1910. 19 p. illus., ports. 20½cm.　　M　**194**

Hill, Nathaniel
An address given in the First church, Dorchester, June 19th, 1864, commemorative of Walter Humphreys, by Nathaniel Hill. Printed for private circulation. Boston, Printed by Alfred Mudge & Son, 1864. 19 p. 19cm.
　　　　　　　　　　　　NB　**194A**

### 14TH INFANTRY

*Mustered in: July 5, 1861.*
*Designated 1st regiment of heavy artillery: January 2, 1862.*
*Mass in the war* 249–50.

### 15TH INFANTRY

*Mustered in: July 12, 1861.*
*Mustered out: July 26, 1864.*
*Mass soldiers* II 131–204.
*Mass in the war* 251–63.

Cutler, Ebenezer, 1822–1897.
A memorial of Lieut. John W. Grout of the 15th Massachusetts volunteers, killed at Ball's Bluff, October 21, 1861, by the Rev. E. Cutler. Printed for the family. [Worcester, 1861] 199–204, (1) p. front. (port.). 27cm.
　　　　　　　　　　　　NB　**194B**
"The vacant chair — Thanksgiving, 1861, by Henry S Washburn," (1) p.

Devens, Charles, 1820–1891.
Address commemorative of Fifteenth regiment Massachusetts volunteers, delivered at dedication of monument to the Regiment at Gettysburg, June 2, 1886, by Br. Maj.-Gen. Devens and remarks at dedication of monument to Col. Geo. H. Ward. . . . Worcester, Press of Charles Hamilton, 1886. 18 p. front. (port.). 28½cm.　　　　MHi NN　**195**
On cover: Addresses commemorative of the Fifteenth regiment Massachusetts volunteers.

Earle, David M

History of the excursion of the Fifteenth Massachusetts regiments and its friends to the battle-fields of Gettysburg, Pa., Antietam, Md., Ball's bluff, Virginia, and Washington, D.C., May 31 – June 12, 1886, by Capt. David M. Earle. Worcester, Press of Charles Hamilton, 1886. 58 p. plates (illus., fold. map, port.). 27½cm.      DLC M NN   **196**

Fay, Eli

Discourse at the funeral of Hans P. Jorgensen, Capt. of Co. A, 15th regiment, Mass. volunteers, who was killed in the battle of Gettysburg, July 2, 1863, by Eli Fay. . . . Fitchburg, Printed by Caleb C. Curtis, 1863. 17 p. 22½cm.            DNW   **197**

Ford, Andrew Elmer

The story of the Fifteenth regiment Massachusetts volunteer infantry in the Civil war, 1861–1864, by Andrew E. Ford. Clinton, Press of W. J. Coulter, 1898. 422 p. maps, plates (2 fold. maps, 2 ports.). 23cm.   DLC NN   **198**
Unit roster [7]–8, [344]–411.

Hanaford, Phoebe Ann (Coffin), 1829–1921.

The young Captain, a memorial of Capt. Richard C. Derby, Fifteenth reg. Mass. volunteers, who fell at Antietam, by Mrs. P. A. Hanaford. Boston, Degen, Estes, & co., 1865. 226 p. front. (illus.). 17cm.     MHi NHi   **199**

Hill, Alonzo, 1800–1871.

In memoriam, a discourse preached in Worcester, Oct. 5, 1862, on Lieut. Thomas Jefferson Spurr, Fifteenth Massachusetts volunteers, who, mortally wounded at the battle of Antietam, died in Hagerstown, Sept. 27th following, by Alonzo Hill. . . . Boston, Printed by John Wilson and Son, 1862. 32 p. 23cm.
                      MHi NN   **200**

Hooper, J        Harris

Twelve days "absence without leave." *Overland monthly* v (1870) 201–13.    **201**

Ward, George W

History of the excursion of the Fifteenth Massachusetts regiment and its friends to the battlefields of Gettysburg, Antietam, Ball's Bluff, and the City of Washington, D.C., September 14–20, 1900. Published under the direction of the Excursion committee. Worcester, Press of O. B. Wood, 1901. 61 p. plates (illus., ports.). 27½cm.      NB   **201A**
"Introductory" signed: George W. Ward.

## 16TH INFANTRY

*Mustered in: June 29 to July 12, 1861.*

*Mustered out: July 27, 1864.*

*Mass soldiers* II 214–69.

*Mass in the war* 264–73.

Order of services at the dedication of the chapel tent of the Sixteenth regiment of Massachusetts volunteers, at Fortress Monroe, Va., December 22d, 1861. [Baltimore, Murphy & co., printers, 1861] [2] p. 24cm.   MHi   **202**
Caption title.

Fuller, Richard Frederick, 1821–1869.

Chaplain Fuller, being a life sketch of a New England clergyman and army Chaplain, by Richard F. Fuller. . . . Boston, Walker, Wise and co., 1863. vi, 342 p. front. (port.). 19½cm.      DLC NN RP   **203**
Civil war 167–342. Another printing, 1864, NN.

Warren, William G

Richmond and way stations, '61 and '64, by Didama (Mrs. B. A. White). Massachusetts, 1889. 54, (1) p. 18cm.    NB   **203A**
Letters of William G. Warren of the 16th Massachusetts infantry to his wife.

## 17TH INFANTRY

*Mustered in: July 22, 1861.*

*Mustered out: July 11, 1865.*

*Mass soldiers* II 270–348.

*Mass in the war* 274–80.

Galloupe, Isaac Francis, 1823–

Reminiscences of a prisoner of war, by Brevet Colonel Isaac Francis Galloupe. *MOLLUS-Mass* II 499–510.              **204**

Kirwan, Thomas, 1829–1911.

Memorial history of the Seventeenth regiment Massachusetts infantry (old and new organizations) in the Civil war from 1861–1865. Issued by the authority of the Supervisors, authorized to write and publish the history. Written and compiled in part by Thomas Kirwan. Edited and completed by Henry Splaine . . . Published for the Committee on history. Salem, Salem press co., 1911. 402, (1) p. plates (maps, ports.). 23½cm.
                      MHi NN   **205**
Unit roster: 1861, [7]–65; 1864, 263–94. "The bivouac of the dead, by Theodore O'Hare," (1) p.

—— Soldering in North Carolina, being the experience of a 'typo' in the pines, swamps, fields, sandy roads, towns, cities, and among the fleas, wood-ticks, "gray-backs," mosquitoes, blue-tail flies, moccasin snakes, lizards, scorpions, Rebels, and other reptiles, pests and vermin of the "old North state," embracing an account of the three-years and nine months Massachusetts regiments in the Department, the freedmen, etc., etc., by "one of the Seventeenth." Boston, Printed and published by Thomas Kirwan, 1864. 126 p. 3 illus. 16½cm.
                DLC NHi   **206**

## 18TH INFANTRY

*Mustered in: August 24, 1861.*
*Mustered out: September 2, 1864.*
*Mass soldiers* II 349–408.
*Mass in the war* 281–92.

De Costa, Benjamin Franklin, 1831–1904.
The Eighteenth Massachusetts regiment, a discourse in commemoration of Washington's birthday, delivered in Falls church, Fairfax co., Va., on Sunday, February 23, 1862, by Rev. B. F. De Costa, Chaplain. . . . Charlestown, 1862. 15 p. 23cm.　　M MHi NN　**207**

Guild, Amasa, 1843–
The mule and the army wagon in the Civil war. *Dedham historical register* XIII (1902) 77–80.　　**208**

—— The Eighteenth Massachusetts regiment volunteer infantry in the rebellion, together with some personal reminiscences. *Dedham historical register* XIII (1902) 98–105; XIV (1903) 2–11, 48–55, 75–83, 108–17.　**209**
"To be continued."

Mann, Thomas H
A Yankee in Andersonville. *Century magazine* XL (1890) 447–61, 606–22.　**210**

—— —— Comment by E. A. Craighill, 2d Va. *Century magazine* XLI (1890) 154–5.　**211**

Weld, Stephen Minot, 1842–1920.
War diary and letters of Stephen Minot Weld, 1861–1876. Privately printed. [Cambridge] Riverside press, 1911. xiii, 428 p. plates, partly double and fold. (facs., illus., map, ports.). 24½cm.　　DLC NN　**212**
"This edition consists of fifty numbered copies."
Mustered in 18th Mass infantry, January 24, 1862; discharged for promotion in 56th Mass infantry, December 23, 1863; mustered out, July 12, 1865.

## 19TH INFANTRY

*Mustered in: August 28, 1861.*
*Mustered out: June 30, 1865.*
*Mass soldiers* II 409–91.
*Mass in the war* 293–310.

Brigadier General Edmund Rice, a brief record of his military career and tribute to his memory. [1907] 14 p. front. (port.). 18cm.　　NN　**213**
On cover: From "The reveille," January, 1907. Caption title.

Adams, John Gregory Bishop, 1841–1900.
. . . Reminiscences of the Nineteenth Massachusetts regiment, by Capt. John G. B. Adams.

Boston, Wright & Potter print. co., 1899. viii, 186 p. plates (ports.). 21½cm.　　DLC NN　**214**
At head of title: "Follow the colors of the Nineteenth" — General Webb. Coulter 3.

—— Sunshine and shadows of army life. *MOLLUS-Mass* II 447–63.　**215**

Devereaux, Arthur Forrester
Some account of Pickett's charge at Gettysburg. *Magazine of American history* XVIII (New York 1887) 13–19. 1 illus.　**216**

Rice, Edmund, 1842–1906.
Repelling Lee's last blow at Gettysburg. *BandL* III 387–90.　**217**

Waitt, Ernest Linden, 1872–
History of the Nineteenth regiment Massachusetts volunteer infantry, 1861–1865. Issued by the History committee. Salem, Salem press co., 1906. vi, 446 p. plates (facs., illus., ports.). 22cm.　　DLC NN　**218**
"Compiled by Ernest Linden Waitt." Unit roster 369–419.

—— —— Appendix. p [447]–56. front. (illus.). 22cm.　**218A**
Contents: Return of the captured flag; Reunion . . . by Captain Thomas F. Winthrop.

Weston, Henry Grant
Random shots, by Henry Grant Weston, given before the Massachusetts commandery of the Military order of the loyal legion, at Boston, Massachusetts, November 5, 1913. 13 p. 25½cm.　　M　**219**

Weymouth, Albert Blodgett, 1839–1913.
A memorial sketch of Lieut. Edgar M. Newcomb of the Nineteenth Mass. vols. Edited by Dr. A. B. Weymouth. Printed for private distribution. Malden, Alvin G. Brown, printer, 1883. 134 p. front. (port.), 2 plates (illus.). 19½cm.　　NHi NN　**220**

Weymouth, Harrison G　　　O
The crossing of the Rappahannock by the 19th Massachusetts. *BandL* III 121.　**221**

## 20TH INFANTRY

*Mustered in: August 28, 1861.*
*Mustered out: July 15, 1865.*
*Mass soldiers* II 492–593.
*Mass in the war* 311–26.

A memorial of Paul Joseph Revere and Edward H. R. Revere. Privately printed. Boston, Wm. Parsons Lunt, 1874. 218 p. 19½cm.　M　**222**

—— Reprinted. [Clinton, W. J. Coulter press] 1913. 209 p. plates (illus., ports.). 21½cm.　　IHi　**223**

The return of the sword. . . . [n. p.] Privately printed, 1897. 24 p. 18cm. NN **224**

An account of the sword belonging to William Lowell Putnam who was killed October 21, 1862.

Bartol, Cyril Augustus, 1813–1900.

Our sacrifices, a sermon preached in the West church, November 3, 1861, being the Sunday after the funeral of Lieut. William Lowell Putnam, by C. A. Bartol. . . . Boston, Ticknor and Fields, 1861. 23 p. 22½cm.

DLC **225**

Bruce, George Anson, 1839–1929.

The Twentieth regiment of Massachusetts volunteer infantry, 1861–1865, by Brevet Lt.-Colonel George A. Bruce, at the request of the Officers' association of the Regiment. Boston, Houghton, Mifflin and co., 1906. viii, 519 p. plates (illus., plans, 2 ports.). 22½cm.

Unit roster [443]–519.         DLC NN **226**

Holmes, Oliver Wendell, 1809–1894.

My hunt after "the Captain." In his Pages from an old volume of life (1883) 16–77. **227**

First published in the *Atlantic monthly* x (1862) 738–64.

Holmes, Oliver Wendell, 1841–1935.

Touched with fire, Civil war letters and diary of Oliver Wendell Holmes, Jr., 1861–1864. Edited by Mark de Wolfe Howe. Cambridge, Harvard University press, 1946. ix, 158 p. facs., plans, plates (ports.). 21½cm.

NN **228**

Palfrey, Francis Winthrop, 1831–1889.

The battle of Antietam, by Bvt. Brigadier-General Francis W. Palfrey. *PMHSM* iii 1–26.

**229**

—— The battle of Malvern hill. *PMHSM* i 253–75. **230**

—— In memoriam H. L. A. [Henry Livermore Abbott] ob. May VI., A.D. MDCCLXIV . . . Printed for private distribution. Boston, 1864. 31 p. 23cm. NN **231**

—— —— Memoir of William Francis Bartlett, by Francis Winthrop Palfrey. Boston, Houghton, Osgood & co., 1878. front. (port.) fold. plan. 17½cm. NN **232**

Coulter 361. Mustered in 20th Mass infantry, August 8, 1861; Colonel 49th Mass infantry, November 12, 1862; mustered out, September 1, 1863; Colonel 57th Mass infantry, April 9, 1864; Brigadier General, June 20, 1864; Major General, March 13, 1865; mustered out, July 18, 1866.

—— The period which elapsed between the fall of Yorktown and the beginning of the seven days' battle. *PMHSM* i 153–215. **233**

—— The seven days' battle to Malvern hill. *PMHSM* i 217–51. **234**

Peirson, Charles Lawrence, 1834–1920.

A monograph. Ball's bluff, an episode and its consequences to some of us, a paper written for the Military historical society of Massachusetts, by Charles Lawrence Peirson. Privately printed . . . for the information later on of Charles Lawrence Peirson . . . and Charles Peirson Lyman. . . . Salem, Salem press co., 1913. 54 p. front. (port.). 22½cm. DLC NN **235**

"Extracts from a diary written in Libby prison," Nov. 5, 1861 – Jan. 31, 1862, 43–54.

Perry, John Gardner,          –1926.

Letters from a surgeon of the Civil war, compiled by Martha Derby Perry. Boston, Little, Brown, and co., 1906. xii, 225 p. (illus., 2 ports.). 21cm. DLC NN **236**

Coulter 370.

## 21ST INFANTRY

*Mustered in: July 19 to August 23, 1861.*

*Reduced to a battalion of three companies, August 18, 1864.*

*Consolidated with the 36th infantry: October 21, 1864.*

*Mass soldiers* ii 594–648.

*Mass in the war* 327–45.

. . . Observance of the fiftieth anniversary of the departure of Co. G, 21st Mass. vols. from Ashburnham to the Civil war, Wednesday, July 19, 1911, Ashburnham, Mass. Issued under the auspices of Company G veteran association of the Town of Ashburnham. 25 p. plates (illus., ports.). 22cm. NB **236A**

At head of title: 1861   1911.

Deane, Nathaniel Carter

. . . Roster 21st Massachusetts volunteer infantry, August 23d, 1861, to September 30, 1864. Battles fought, men engaged and losses. [Carnegie, Pa., J. B. Knepper] c1914. [4] p. illus., ports. 28cm. DLC **237**

At head of title: Why comrades are comrades. Caption title.

Stearns, William Augustus, 1805–1876.

Adjutant Stearns. . . . Boston, Massachusetts Sabbath School Society [1862] 160 p. front. (port.). 15½cm. NN **238**

Dedication signed: By His father.

Stone, James Madison

Personal recollections of the Civil war, by one who took part in it as a private soldier in the 21st volunteer regiment of infantry from Massachusetts, by James Madison Stone. Boston, Published by the author, 1918. 193 p. front. (port.). 19cm. DLC MB **239**

*21st Infantry, continued*

Tyler, William Seymour, 1810–1897.

A memorial of Adj. Frazar A. Stearns, of the 21st Massachusetts volunteers, killed at Newbern, March 14, 1862, by the Rev. W. S. Tyler. Printed for the Junior class of Amherst college. p 227–38. front. (port.). 26cm.

NHi **240**

Walcott, Charles Folsom,            –1887.

The battle of Chantilly, by Bvt. Brig.-Gen. Charles F. Walcott. *PMHSM* ii 133–72. **241**

—— History of the Twenty-first regiment Massachusetts volunteers in the War for the preservation of the Union, 1861–1865, with statistics of the war and of Rebel prisons, by Charles F. Walcott. Boston, Houghton, Mifflin and co., 1882. xiii, 502 p. plans, 2 plates (ports.). 22cm.            DLC NN **242**

Unit roster 429–89. "George A. Hitchcock's diary of his life in Southern prisons," 401–26. Coulter 461.

—— A revisit to the fields of Manassas and Chantilly. *PMHSM* ii 133–72.            **243**

Willard, Wells

Narrative of the personal services of Wells Willard in the War of the rebellion, 1861–1865. New York, Baker & Godwin, printers, 1874. 61 p. 22cm.            NN **244**

NN's copy has manuscript note, Only 52 copies printed.

Mustered in 21st Mass infantry, August 5, 1861; discharged for promotion in 34th Mass infantry, October 1, 1862; mustered out, June 16, 1865.

## 22ND INFANTRY

*Mustered in: September to October 5, 1861.*

*Mustered out: August 17, 1864.*

*Mass soldiers* ii 649–710.

*Mass in the war* 346–58.

Barnard, Walter F

The "Everett guard," Co. D, 22d Massachusetts volunteers in the War of the rebellion, compiled by Walter F. Barnard, Company historian. 1880. 40 p. 17cm.            NB **244A**

Carter, Robert Goldthwaite, 1845–1936.

Record of the military service of First Lieutenant and Brevet Captain Robert Goldthwaite Carter, U.S. army, 1862 to 1876. Washington, D.C. Gibson Bros., printers, 1904. 48 p. 22½cm.            DLC **245**

—— Reminiscences of the campaign and battle of Gettysburg. *MOLLUS-Me* ii 150–83. **246**

Cutler, Cyrus Morton, 1841–1870?

Letters from the front, from October, 1861, to September, 1864, by Cyrus Morton Cutler, while a member of Co. F 22nd Massachusetts volunteer infantry regiment and Battery C 1st New York (light) artillery regiment. [San Francisco, 1892] 39 p. front. (port.). 26cm.

MHi **247**

Preface signed: A. D. Cutler. Letter of Fitz John Porter, dated Oct. 15, 1892, on services of 22d Mass., p [6]

Parker, John Lord, 1837–1917.

. . . History of the Twenty-second Massachusetts infantry, the Second company sharpshooters, and the Third light battery, in the War of the rebellion, by John L. Parker, assisted by Robert G. Parker and the Historical committee. Published by the Regimental association. Boston, Press of Rand Avery co., 1887. xxii, 591 p. plates (illus., ports.). 23½cm.

DLC NN **248**

Unit roster [550]–80. At head of title: Henry Wilson's regiment.

Winthrop, Robert Charles, 1802–1894.

"The flag of the Union, a speech on the presentation of a flag to the Twenty-second regiment of Massachusetts volunteers, on Boston common, October 8, 1861." In his Addresses and speeches on various occasions from 1852 to 1867, p 505–10.            **249**

See also Titles 5 and 126.

## 23RD INFANTRY

*Mustered in: September 28, 1861.*

*Mustered out: June 25, 1865.*

*Mass soldiers* ii 719–73.

*Mass in the war* 359–70.

Emilio, Luis Fenallosa, 1844–

Roanoke island, its occupation, defense and fall, by Luis F. Emilio (23d Mass. infantry), a paper read before the Roanoke associates, New York city, Feb. 9th, 1891. Printed for the Associates. 18 p. front. (map). 21cm.

CSmH NN **249A**

Emmerton, James Arthur, 1834–1888.

A record of the Twenty-third regiment Mass. vol. infantry in the War of the rebellion, 1861–1865, with an alphabetical roster, company rolls, portraits, maps, etc., by James A. Emmerton, Corporal of Co. F and Assis't Surg. Boston, William Ware & co., 1886. xx, 352 p. plates (illus.; maps, partly fold.; ports.). 23cm.

DLC NN **250**

Unit roster 253–334. Coulter 151.

Stevens, Munroe        –1917.
A tribute to the Twenty-third reg't Mass. volunteers, at their reunion at Gloucester, 1876. Broadside, 29½ × 23½cm.        **M    251**
Author's name printed on paster.

Valentine, Herbert Eugene, 1841–1917.
Dedication of the boulder commemorating the service of the Twenty-third regiment Massachusetts volunteer infantry, in the Civil war, 1861–1865, at Salem, Massachusetts, September 28, 1905. Salem, Newcomb & Gauss, printers, 1905. 35, (1) p. front. (illus.), plates (ports.). 23cm.        DLC NHi NN    **252**
"Prepared and printed by the 'Boulder committee' . . . compiled and edited by comrade Herbert E. Valentine."

—— Story of Company F, 23d Massachusetts volunteers in the War for the Union, 1861–1865, by Herbert E. Valentine. Boston, W. B. Clarke & co., 1896. xii, [9]–166 p. plates (illus., ports.). 23cm.        DLC NN    **253**
Unit roster [145]–62.

Welch, William W
The Burnside expedition and the engagement at Roanoke island. 1890. 48 p. *PNRISSHS* s4 no 9.        **254**

See also Title 120.

### 24TH INFANTRY

*Left State: December 9, 1861.*
*Mustered out: January 10, 1866.*
*Mass soldiers* II 774–833.
*Mass in the war* 371–81.

By-laws of the Twenty-fourth club, organized May 23, 1865. [Boston] Watson's press, 1865. 8 p. 17cm.        MHi    **255**

Roster of Company I, 24th regiment Massachusetts volunteers. Boston, E. B. Stillings & co., 1902. 15 p. 21cm.        DLC NHi    **256**

Rules and regulations of the Association of members of the 24th regiment Mass. volunteer infantry. Boston, Lewis & co., stationers [1866?] 8 p. 12cm.        MHi    **257**

Amory, Charles Bean, 1841–
A brief record of the army life of Charles B. Amory, written for his children. Privately published. [Boston?] 1902. 43 p. front. (port.). 22cm.        M NN    **258**
Officers of the 24th Mass. infantry, December, 1861, 41–3. Coulter 6.

Edmands, Thomas Franklin
Operations in North Carolina, 1861–62. *PMHSM* IX 53–83.        **259**

Osborn, Francis Augustus
Bermuda Hundred, June 16–17, 1864. *PMHSM* v 187–204.        **260**

Roe, Alfred Seelye, 1844–1917.
The Twenty-fourth regiment Massachusetts volunteers, 1861–1866, "New England guard regiment," by Alfred S. Roe . . . Regimental committee on history, Charles B. Amory, John C. Cook [and] George Hill. Published by the Twenty-fourth veteran association. Worcester [Blanchard press] 1907. 573 p. front. (port.), illus., maps, ports. 23½cm.        DLC NN    **261**
Unit roster 448–562.

Stevenson, Joshua Thomas,        –1876.
[Memorial of Thomas Greely Stevenson, 1836–1864] [Cambridge, Printed by Welch, Bigelow & co., 1864] 129 p. front. (mounted port.). 20½cm.        DLC MB NHi NN    **262**
No title page. On cover: Gen. Stevenson.

Trumbull, Henry Clay, 1830–1903.
The captured scout of the Army of the James, a sketch of the life of Sergeant Henry H. Manning of the Twenty-fourth Mass. regt., by Chaplain H. Clay Trumbull. Boston, Nichols and Noyes, 1869. 60 p. 17½cm.        NN    **263**

### 25TH INFANTRY

*Mustered in: September 26 – October 12, 1861.*
*Mustered out: July 21, 1865.*
*Mass soldiers* III 1–60.
*Mass in the war* 382–92.

Clark, Harvey
My experience with Burnside's expedition and 18th army corps [by] Harvey Clark, Private Company F, 25th Massachusetts. [Gardner, 1914] 119 p. front. (port.), illus., ports. 22cm.        NN    **264**
On cover: Three years in the Civil war. Contents: My experience . . . , 7–95: Record of the men from Ashburnham in Company F, 96; My three visits to Southern battlefields, 97–119.

Day, David L
My diary of rambles with the 25th Mass. volunteer infantry, with Burnside's coast division, 18th army corps, and Army of the James, by D. L. Day. [Milford, King & Billings, printers, 1884] 153 p. 23cm.        DLC NHi    **265**

Denny, Joseph Waldo
Address delivered at second re-union K association, 25th Massachusetts volunteers, at Worcester, Mass., Sept. 26, 1870, by J. Waldo Denny, late Captain Co. K. (Published by request of the Association.) Comprising also, proceedings of Association, etc., together with

*25th Infantry, continued*

roster of Company K. . . . Boston, Alfred
Mudge and Son, printers, 1871. 32 p. 21½cm.
DLC NHi **266**

—— Wearing the Blue in the Twenty-fifth
Mass. volunteer infantry, with Burnside's coast
division, 18th army corps, and Army of the
James, by J. Waldo Denny. Worcester, Putnam
& Davis, 1879. xi, 523 p. plates (ports.).
23cm. DLC NHi **267**
Unit roster [443]–509.

Draper, William Franklin, 1842–1910.
Recollections of a varied career, by William
F. Draper. Boston, Little, Brown, and co., 1908.
411 p. plates (illus., ports.). 23cm.
NN **267A**
Civil war 34–176. Mustered in 25th Mass infantry,
October 12, 1861; discharged to accept promotion in
the 36th Mass infantry, August 26, 1862; mustered
out, October 12, 1864. NN has a 1909 reprint.
"Preface" paged vii.

Hill, Alonzo, 1800–1871.
Revelation by fire, a sermon preached in
Worcester, Aug. 17, 1862, the Sunday after
the burial of Mr. William Hudson, a Private
in the Twenty-fifth regiment of Massachusetts
volunteers, by Alonzo Hill. . . . Boston, Press
of John Wilson & Son, 1862. 23 p. 23½cm.
MHi NN **268**

James, Horace, 1818–1875.
The two great wars of America, an oration
delivered in Newbern, North Carolina, before
the Twenty-fifth regiment Massachusetts volunteers, July 4, 1862, by Rev. Horace James,
Chaplain. Boston, Printed by W. F. Brown &
~o., 1862. 30 p. 23½cm. MHi NN **269**

McCarter, John Gray
How Rogers and I made our first and second
excursion to the old "Tar heel" state, 1862–
1903. [Boston, Frank Wood, printer, 1903]
38 p. 3 plates (ports.). 19½cm.
CSmH NB **270**

Parkhurst, Veranus P
Proceedings of a court of inquiry, in regard
to reports made by Maj. M. J. McCafferty and
others, of misconduct at the battle of Roanoke
island February 8, 1862, by Capt. V. P. Parkhurst, Co. I, 25th regiment, Mass. vols. Ordered
on the demand of Captain Parkhurst. Fitchburg, Curtis and Bushnell, printers, 1864. 55 p.
21½cm. DLC NN **271**
"Introduction" signed and dated: V. P. Parkhurst,
Portsmouth, Va., April, 1864. Title and imprint from
cover.

Putnam, Samuel Henry
The story of Company A, Twenty-fifth regiment, Mass. vols. in the War of the rebellion,
by Samuel H. Putnam. Worcester, Putnam,

Davis and co., 1886. 324 p. front. (port.),
plates (maps). 24½cm. DLC NN **272**
Muster in roll 14–19. Coulter 383.

Sprague, Augustus Brown Reed, 1827–1910.
The Burnside expedition, by Brevet Brig-
adier-General A. B. R. Sprague. *MOLLUS-
Mass* II 427–44. **273**

Stearns, Amos Edward
Narrative of Amos E. Stearns, member Co.
A., 25th regt. Mass. vols., a prisoner at Ander-
sonville. With an introduction by Samuel H.
Putnam. Worcester, Franklin P. Rice, 1887.
57 p. front. (port.). 23cm. NHi NN **274**

## 26TH INFANTRY

*Mustered in: September to October 1861.*

*Mustered out: August 26, 1865.*

*Mass soldiers* III 61–119.

*Mass in the war* 393–400.

Estabrooks, Henry L
Adrift in Dixie; or, a Yankee officer among
the Rebels, with an introduction by Edmund
Kirke [pseud] New York, Carleton, 1866.
224 p. 19cm. DLC NN **275**
Coulter 153.

Farnsworth, Ezra K            1843–1923.
At the rear in war times, by Captain Ezra
K. Farnsworth. *MOLLUS-Minn* VI 405–24.
**276**

—— The battle of Cedar creek. *MOLLUS-
Minn* VI 169–97. **277**

—— Brown's experiences as a wounded soldier. *MOLLUS-Minn* VI 309–30. **278**

—— The capture of New Orleans. *MOLLUS-
Minn* VI 108–39. **279**

—— Reminiscences of the Shenandoah valley
in 1864. *MOLLUS-Minn* V 314–31. **280**

## 27TH INFANTRY

*Left State: November 2, 1861.*

*The Regiment was surrounded and
largely captured, March 8, 1865. The
few remaining were mustered out, June
26, 1865.*

*Mass soldiers* III 120–87.

*Mass in the war* 401–18.

Derby, William P
Bearing arms in the Twenty-seventh Massa-
chusetts regiment of volunteer infantry during
the Civil war, 1861–1865, by W. P. Derby.
Boston, Wright & Potter print. co., 1883. xvi,
607 p. plates (maps, 2 double; ports.). 23½cm.
DLC NN **281**
Unit roster [551]–601. Coulter 124.

## 28TH INFANTRY

*Mustered in: December 13, 1861.*
*Mustered out: June 30, 1865.*
*Mass soldiers* III 188–274.
*Mass in the war* 419–34.

## 29TH INFANTRY

*In July 1861 with the mustering out of the 3d and 4th regiments, seven companies re-enlisted forming a battalion. Near the close of 1861 three companies were added completing the organization of the 29th regiment.*
*Mustered out: July 29, 1865.*
*Mass soldiers* III 275–332.
*Mass in the war* 435–51.

Osborne, William H
The history of the Twenty-ninth regiment of Massachusetts volunteer infantry, in the late War of the rebellion, by William H. Osborne. Boston, Albert J. Wright, printer, 1877. 393 p. 24cm.         NN   *282*
Unit roster [343]–68. "Reunions of the Regiment," 1870–1877, 384–90. Coulter 355.

## 30TH INFANTRY

*Mustered in: September 15 to December 1861.*
*Mustered out: July 5, 1866.*
*Mass soldiers* III 333–94.
*Mass in the war* 452–65.

Howe, Henry Warren, 1841–1900.
Passages from the life of Henry Warren, consisting of diary and letters written during the Civil war, 1861–1865, a condensed history of the Thirtieth Massachusetts regiment and its flags, together with the genealogies of the different branches of the family. Privately printed. Lowell, Courier-Citizen co., printers, 1899. 211 p. plates (ports.). 21½cm.
"Errata" slip inserted.     DLC NN   *283*

## 31ST INFANTRY

*Mustered in: November to December 1861.*
*Mustered out: September 9, 1865.*
*Mass soldiers* III 395–447.
*Mass in the war* 466–78.

The color-bearer, Francis A. Clary. New York, American Tract Society [1864] 106 p. 16cm.
    DLC MHi NN   *284*

Tupper, James B     T
Civil war memories, occupation of New Orleans by the 31st Massachusetts regiment and the forces under command of Gen. Butler, May 1, 1862, personal reminiscences, paper read before the Burnside post, G.A.R., Washington, D. C., May 9, 1917, by J. B. T. Tupper, 31st Mass. 10 p. 22cm.     MB   *285*

## 32ND INFANTRY

*Mustered in: Companies A-E, November–December 1861; Company F, February 1862; other companies during the summer of 1862.*
*Mustered out: June 28, 1865.*
*Mass soldiers* III 448–535.
*Mass in the war* 479–95.

Ewing, Thomas, 1829–1896.
Address in defence of J. Cushing Edmands, late Colonel 32d Massachusetts infantry volunteers, to the General court martial, of which Major-General J. B. Ricketts is President, sitting at Annapolis, Maryland, September, 1865. Tried on charges of violation of orders and of neglect of duty to the prejudice of good order and military discipline. Washington, D. C., Printed by R. A. Waters, 1865. 13 p. 21½cm.
    CSmH NN   *285A*
Thomas Ewing, Jr., Counsel.

James, Henry B     1841–1920.
Memories of the Civil war, by Henry B. James, Co. B, 32nd Mass. volunteers. . . . New Bedford, Franklin E. James, 1898. 133, (2) p. 2 plates (ports.). 18cm.     DLC M   *286*
"Contents," (2) p.

Meacham, Henry H
The empty sleeve; or, the life and hardships of Henry H. Meacham in the Union army, by himself. Springfield [Boston, Pratt Brothers, printers, 1869] 32 p. 19cm.     NN   *287*
—— —— Springfield [1869?] 24 p. 19½cm.
A reprint.     MHi   *288*

Parker, Francis Jewett, 1825–1909.
The story of the Thirty-second regiment Massachusetts infantry, whence it came, where it went, what it saw, and what it did, by Francis J. Parker, Colonel. Boston, C. W. Calkins & co., 1880. xi, 260 p. 20cm.     DLC NN   *289*
Coulter 365.

Stephenson, Luther, 1830–
Addresses and papers, by Luther Stephenson, Jr. (late 32d regiment Mass. vols.), Brevet Brigadier General. Printed for private use. Togus, Maine, 1885. 71 p. 23cm.     NHi   *290*
—— A sketch giving some incidents during the service of the Thirty-second Massachusetts volunteer infantry, presented by General Luther Stephenson, at the annual re-union,

*32nd Infantry, continued*

August 4, 1900. Published by the Thirty-second regiment association. [Boston, Wheelman press, 1900] 22 p. plates (2 illus., ports.). 22½cm.
DLC NHi   *291*

### 33RD INFANTRY

*Mustered in: Early August 1862.*

*Mustered out: June 10, 1865.*

*Mass soldiers* III 536–87.

*Mass in the war* 496–506.

Boies, Andrew J
Record of the Thirty-third Massachusetts volunteer infantry, from Aug. 1862 to Aug. 1865, by Andrew J. Boies. Fitchburg, Sentinel print. co., 1880. 168 p. front. (port.). 23½cm.
DLC NN   *292*
Unit roster [137]–67. Coulter 44.

Cady, Daniel Reed, 1813–1879.
Memorial of Lieut. Joseph P. Burrage, a funeral sermon, preached December 25, 1863, by Rev. Daniel R. Cady. Boston, Gould and Lincoln, 1864. 48 p. 19cm.   DLC MHi   *293*

Ryder, John J                 1833–
Reminiscences of three years' service in the Civil war, by a Cape Cod boy, John J. Ryder. New Bedford, Reynolds print., 1928. 85 p. plates (illus., facs., ports.). 24½cm.
IHi NN   *294*

Underwood, Adin Ballou, 1828–1888.
The three years' service of the Thirty-third Mass. infantry regiment, 1862–1865, and the campaigns and battles of Chancellorsville, Beverley's ford, Gettysburg, Wauhatchie, Chattanooga, Atlanta, the march to the sea and through the Carolinas in which it took part, by Adin B. Underwood, formerly Colonel of the Regiment. Boston, A. Williams & co., 1881. xiv, 299, (35) p. 23½cm.   DLC NN   *295*
Unit roster (35) p.

### 34TH INFANTRY

*Left State: August 15, 1862.*

*Mustered out: June 15, 1865.*

*Mass soldiers* III 588–644.

*Mass in the war* 507–24.

Soldiers' memorial. Company F, 34th regt. Massachusetts infty. vols. New York, Major & Knapp [186–] Broadside, 55 × 44cm.
NHi   *296*

Buell, P          L
The poet soldier, a memoir of the worth, talent and patriotism of Joseph Kent Gibbons, who fell in the service of his country during the great rebellion, by P. L. Buell. With an introduction by Nelson Sizer. New York, Samuel R. Wells, 1868. 48 p. front. (port.). 19½cm.   DLC NN   *297*

Clark, William H
Poems and sketches, with reminiscences of the "Old 34th," by William H. Clark. South Framington, Lakeview press, 1890. 55 p. 17½cm.   DLC NHi NN   *298*
On cover: Souvenir.

—— Reminiscences of the Thirty-fourth regiment, Mass. vol. infantry, by William H. Clark, Private Co. E. Published for the author. Holliston, J. C. Clark & co., 1871. 31 p. 18½cm.
DLC NN   *299*
"Up to May 15th, 1864, when he received the wound which disabled him."

—— The soldier's offering, by William H. Clark. Boston [South Framingham, J. C. Clark print. co.] 1875. 76 p. 19cm.   DLC NN   *300*
Contents: Part I, Reminiscences of the Thirty-fourth regiment Mass. vol. inf.; Part II, Original poems; Part III, Pencillings.

Lincoln, Levi
A memorial of William Sever Lincoln, Colonel 34th Mass. infantry and Brevet Brig.-Gen. U.S. volunteers, 1811–1889. [Worcester, 1889] 55 p. front. (port.). 22cm.   DLC   *301*
"Imprisonment and escape" [by Colonel W. S. Lincoln] p 33–55. Dedication signed: L. L.·

Lincoln, William Sever, 1811–1889.
Life with the Thirty-fourth Mass. infantry in the War of the rebellion, by William S. Lincoln, late Colonel of the Regiment. Worcester, Press of Noyes, Snow & co., 1879. 459, 18 p. front. (mounted photograph with 39 ports.). 24cm.   DLC NN   *302*
Unit roster 422–59. "Imprisonment and escape of Lieut. Colonel Lincoln," 18 p. On cover: Army of West Virginia.

Roe, Alfred Seelye, 1844–1917.
An angel of the Shenandoah, a life sketch of Mrs. Jessie Haining Rupert, New Market, Virginia, "daughter of the Regiment" (Thirty-fourth Massachusetts infantry) by Alfred S. Roe. Privately printed by Thirty-fourth regiment veteran association. Worcester, Commonwealth press, 1913. 30 p. illus., ports. 20½cm.
MWiW   *303*

See also Title 244.

### 35TH INFANTRY

*Mustered in: August 9–19, 1862.*

*Mustered out: June 9, 1865.*

*Mass soldiers* III 645–708.

*Mass in the war* 525–41.

Annual souvenir . . . annual reunion of the Thirty-fifth regiment Mass. vol. infantry at. . . . viii 1873 (MHi), xi–xii 1876–1877 (MHi), xxix 1894 (DNW), xxx–xliv 1895–1909 (DLC).                                            304

History of the Thirty-fifth regiment Massachusetts volunteers, 1862–1865, with roster, by a Committee of the Regimental association. Boston, Mills, Knight & co., 1884. viii, 409, 66 p. 19½cm.                              DLC NN    305

Prisoner of war narratives: by Sergeant Henry W. Tisdale, 330–63; by Lieutenant Alfred Blanchard, Jr., 363–87. Unit roster, 66 p.

Bartol, Cyrus Augustus, 1813–1900.
The Nation's hour, a tribute to Major Sidney Willard, delivered in the West church, December 21, Forefather's day, by C. A. Bartol. Boston, Walker, Wise, and co., 1862. 58 p. 24cm.                                DLC NN    306

"Extracts from Major Willard's letters, Aug. 25 – Dec. 12" [1862], 30–49.

Hodges, Thorndike D            1836–1900.
Scattering fire, a paper read by Thorndike D. Hodges, late Brevet Major. MOLLUS-NY i 71–7.                                               307

Lee, Amos William
'61 to '65, recollections of the Civil war, by Amos William Lee, Private, Company B, Thirty-fifth Massachusetts infantry. . . . Put into print for private circulation by Edward B. Lee and Christine G. Lee. 1913. 100 p. front. (port.). 23cm.                   In    308

Portrait mounted on front cover.

Munsell, George N            –1905.
An address delivered Sept. 17, 1872, at the seventh reunion of the Thirty-fifth regiment Mass. volunteers' association, held at Parker house, Boston, by Ass't surgeon George N. Munsell. Harwich, Goss and Richards print. office, 1872. 10 p. 22½cm.        MHi    309

Park, John Cochran, 1804–1889.
A memorial of Major Edward Granville Park of the 35th Massachusetts volunteers . . . Printed for private circulation. Boston, Press of John Wilson and Son, 1865. 41 p. 19½cm.
                                       DLC NHi    310

Dedication signed: By his father.

### 36TH INFANTRY

Left State: September 2, 1862.
Mustered out: June 8, 1865.
Mass soldiers iii 709–68.
Mass in the war 542–62.

Hollis correspondence. Indiana magazine of history xxxvi (1940) 275–94.          311

Frank W. Knowles 36th Mass.

Burrage, Henry Sweetser, 1837–1926.
Burnside's East Tennesee campaign. PMH-SM viii 559–603.                              312

—— History of the Thirty-sixth regiment Massachusetts volunteers, 1862–1865, by a Committee of the Regiment. Boston, Press of Rockwell and Churchill, 1884. xiii, 405 p. 23½cm.                                 DLC NN    313

"Preface" signed: H. S. B. Burrage "was assigned the editorial supervision of the work." Individual chapters are signed by their authors, Alonzo A. White, S. Alonzo Ranlett, Henry S. Burrage, William H. Hodgkins, Edmund W. Noyes and William M. Olin. Unit roster 316–84.

—— How I recovered my sword. MOLLUS-Me ii 61–76.                                    314

—— My capture and what came of it. MOLLUS-Me i 1–19.                            315

—— Reminiscences of prison life at Danville (read Sept. 3, 1884). MOLLUS-Me iii 43–60.
                                              316

—— The retreat from Lenoir's and the siege of Knoxville. Atlantic monthly xviii (1866) 21–32.                                       317

—— Some added facts concerning my capture. MOLLUS-Me iv 171–89.             318

—— 'Tis fifty years since, extract from a student diary at Brown, April, 1861. Brown Alumni monthly xi (Providence 1911) 221–6.
                                              320

Hodgkins, William Henry, 1840–1905.
Address deliverd before Theodore Winthrop encampment, Post 35, G.A.R., at Academy of music, Chelsea, Mass., Memorial day, May 30, 1873, by Major William H. Hodgkins. Boston, Rockwell and Churchill, printers, 1873. 22 p. 22½cm.                                WHi    321

—— The battle of Fort Stedman (Petersburg, Virginia), March 25, 1865, by William H. Hodgkins, Thirty-sixth regiment Massachusetts. Privately printed. [Boston, Press of Rockwell & Churchill, 188–] 49 p. front. (fold. map). 25cm.                          NHi NN    322

Ranlett, Seth Alonzo
The capture of Jackson, by Lieutenant Seth A. Ranlett. MOLLUS-Mass i 249–68.    323

Swords, Henry L
My campaigning with the Army of the Tennessee, by Major H. L. Swords. MOLLUS-Iowa i 74–88.                               324

Woodward, Philip Grenville, 1837–1921.
The siege of Knoxville, by Captain Philip Grenville Woodward. MOLLUS-Minn v 382–95.                                           325

See also Title 267A.

## 37TH INFANTRY

*Mustered in: August 30 to September 4, 1862.*

*Mustered out: June 21, 1865.*

*Mass soldiers* III 769–824.

*Mass in the war* 563–75.

Bowen, James Lorenzo
General Edward's brigade at the Bloody angle. *BandL* IV 177.            **326**

—— History of the Thirty-seventh regiment Mass. volunteers, in the Civil war of 1861–1865, with a comprehensive sketch of the doings of Massachusetts as a State, and of the principal campaigns of the war, by James L. Bowen. Holyoke, Clark W. Bryan & co., 1884. 431, li p. front. (illus.), plate (illus.). 20½cm.

Unit roster xiv–xliii.            NN     **327**

Nichols, Samuel Edmund, 1842–1898.
"Your soldier boy Samuel," Civil war letters of Lieut. Samuel Edmund Nichols of the 37th regiment Massachusetts volunteers. Arranged by Charles Sterling Underhill. Privately printed. [Buffalo, N.Y.] 1929. 133 p. plates (illus., ports.). 20cm.            NN     **328**

"Map covering the region of activity of the Army of the Potomac from the Fall of 1862 to 1865," end paper. A slip has been inserted correcting the scale as printed.

Shaw, William H            1833–
A diary as kept by Wm. H. Shaw during the great Civil war, from April, 1861 to July, 1865. [n. p., n. d.] 76 p. front. (port.). 22½cm.
            NN     **329**

The author also served in the 3rd Conn infantry.

Tyler, Mason Whiting, 1840–1907.
Recollections of the Civil war with many original diary entries and letters, written from the seat of the war, and with annotated references, by Mason Whiting Tyler, late Lieut.-Colonel and Brevet-Colonel 37th reg't. Mass. vols. Edited by William S. Tyler. New York, G. P. Putnam's Sons, 1912. xix, 379 p. plates (3 fold. maps, ports.). 22½cm.

Coulter 456.            DLC NN     **330**

See also Title 143A.

## 38TH INFANTRY

*Mustered in: July to August 1862.*

*Mustered out: July 13, 1865.*

*Mass soldiers* IV 1–45.

*Mass in the war* 578–88.

Flinn, Frank M
Campaigning with Banks in Louisiana, '63, and '64, and with Sheridan in the Shenandoah valley, by Frank M. Flinn. Lynn, Press of Thos. P. Nichols, 1887. viii, 239 p. 19½cm.
            NN     **331**

—— —— Second edition. Boston, W. B. Clarke & co., 1889. viii, 239 p. 20cm.

A reprinting.            NN     **332**

Powers, George Whitefield, 1834–1903.
Bitter and sweet. *Biv* III (1885) 342–5.  **333**

—— The story of the Thirty eighth regiment of Massachusetts volunteers, by George W. Powers. Cambridge, Cambridge press, Dakin and Metcalf, 1866. x, 308 p. 20cm.
            DLC NHi NN     **334**

Unit roster [241]–308. Coulter 378.

—— Types of recruits. *Biv* III 305–9.     **335**

Taylor, Charles H            1846–1921.
The North in wartime . . . an address by Charles H. Taylor of Company F to his comrades of the Thirty-eighth Massachusetts regiment of Massachusetts volunteers at a dinner given by him in commemoration of the fiftieth anniversary of their leaving for the war. . . . Boston, 1912. 23½cm.            MB     **336**

Wood, William
Shameful treatment of the Union dead! False imprisonment and barbarous treatment of a disabled Union soldier by the Federal government, at Winchester, Va., during the Fall of 1864, and Spring of 1865. [n. p., 187–] 12 p. 22½cm.            MHi     **337**

Caption title.

## 39TH INFANTRY

*Left State: September 6, 1862.*

*Mustered out: May 23, 1865.*

*Mass soldiers* IV 46–106.

*Mass in the war* 589–602.

The soldier's record, Thirty-ninth regiment, Company F, Mass. volunteers. New York, Currier & Ives [1862] col. illus. broadside, 51 × 38cm.            NN     **337A**

Dusseault, John H
Company E, Thirty-ninth infantry in the Civil war, by John H. Dusseault. Somerville, Journal print, 1908. 49 p. front. (port.). 24½cm.            MBLL     **338**

First published in *Historical leaves* Somerville historical society VI (1907) 17–23, 43–7, 56–72; VII (1908) 1–20. Unit roster in last installment.

Peirson, Charles Lawrence, 1834–1920.
The mine run affair. *PMHSM* XIV 55–64.  **339**

—— The operations of the Army of the Potomac, May 7–11, 1864. *PMHSM* IV 205–41.
            **340**

Porter, Charles Hunt
The battle of Cold harbor, by Captain Charles H. Porter. *PMHSM* IV 319–40. **341**

—— The Fifth corps at the battle of Five Forks. *PMHSM* VI 235–55. **342**

—— Opening of the campaign of 1864. *PMHSM* IV 1–24. **343**

—— Operations against the Weldon railroad, August 18, 19, 21, 1864. *PMHSM* V 241–66. **344**

—— Operations of the Fifth corps on the left, March 29, to nightfall, March 31, 1865; Gravelly run. *PMHSM* VI 209–34. **345**

—— Operations of Generals Sigel and Hunter in the Shenandoah valley, May and June, 1864. *PMHSM* VI 59–82. **346**

—— The Petersburg mine. *PMHSM* V 221–39. **347**

Roe, Alfred Seelye, 1844–1917.
The Thirty-ninth regiment Massachusetts volunteers, 1862–1865, by Alfred S. Roe. Regimental committee on history . . . [seven names] Published by the Regimental veteran association. Worcester [Commonwealth press] 1914. 493 p. plates (facs., 1 illus., ports.). 22cm.
Unit roster 330–465.        DLC NN    **348**

See also Title 193.

### 40TH INFANTRY

*Mustered in: August 22 to September 5, 1862.*
*Mustered out: June 17, 1865.*
*Mass soldiers IV 106–50.*
*Mass in the war 603–12.*

Roster of the living members of the Fortieth regiment Mass. infantry. Boston, Press of C. W. Calkins & co., 1891. 40 p. 23cm.
                                MBLL    **349**

Buck, George H
A brief sketch of the service of Co. G, 40th Mass. vol. infantry, 1862–1865, by comrade Geo. H. Buck. Chelsea, Chas. H. Pike & co., printers, 1910. 24 p. 15cm.        MB    **350**

### 41ST INFANTRY

*Recruited in the late summer and autumn of 1862.*
*Designated 3d regiment of cavalry: June 17, 1863.*
*Mass in the war 613–16.*

Diary of Forty-first regiment infantry, Massachusetts volunteers. Colonel, Thomas E. Chick-

ering. Boston, J. E. Farwell & co., printers, 1863. 11, (1) p. 14½cm.        NHi    **351**

### 42ND INFANTRY

*Mustered in: September 13 to October 14, 1862. (9 months)*
*Mustered out: August 20, 1863.*
*Mass soldiers IV 151–93.*
*Mass in the war 617–22.*
*Mustered in: July 14–22, 1864. (100 days)*
*Mustered out: November 11, 1864.*
*Mass soldiers IV 194–228.*
*Mass in the war 622–3.*

Bosson, Charles Palfray
History of the Forty-second regiment infantry, Massachusetts volunteers, 1862, 1863, 1864, by Sergeant-Major Charles P. Bosson. Boston, Mills, Knight & co., printers, 1886. vi, 465 p. 3 plates (2 illus., port.). 19½cm.
                                DLC NN    **352**

### 43RD INFANTRY

*Mustered in: September 12 to October 11, 1862.*
*Mustered out: July 30, 1863.*
*Mass soldiers IV 229–69.*
*Mass in the war 624–8.*

Manning, Jacob Merrill, 1824–1882.
The soldier of freedom, a sermon preached before the officers of the Forty-third regiment, M.V., in the Old South church, Boston, Sunday morning, Oct. 5, 1862, by Jacob M. Manning. Printed for the use of the Regiment. Boston, J. E. Farwell and co., printers, 1862. 20 p. 24½cm.        M NN    **353**

Rogers, Edward H
Reminiscences of military service in the Forty-third regiment Massachusetts infantry, during the great Civil war, 1862–63, by Edward H. Rogers, Company H. Boston, Franklin press, 1883. 210 p. 4 plates (illus.). 24cm.
                                DLC NN    **354**
Unit roster [199]–210. Coulter 397.

Winthrop, Robert Charles, 1802–1894.
"A flag to the Forty-third, a speech on the presentation of a flag to the Forty-third regiment, on Boston common, November 5, 1862." In his Addresses and speeches on various occasions from 1852 to 1867, 546–52.        **355**

See also Title 13A.

## 44TH INFANTRY

*Mustered in: September 12, 1862.*
*Mustered out: June 18, 1863.*
*Mass soldiers* IV 270–308.
*Mass in the war* 629–33.

Record of the service of the Forty-fifth Massachusetts volunteer militia in North Carolina, August 1862 to May 1863. Privately printed. Boston [Cambridge, University press] 1887. xvi, 364 p. illus., plates (illus., plans, ports.). 26½cm.                    DLC NN    **356**

Unit roster [301]–35. "Signatures of members of the 44th regiment Massachusetts vols., reproduced from photographic copy of pay rolls," [341–55] paged 1–15. James B. "Gardner has done by far the greater part of getting this book together."

Roll of Association of Company "F," 44th regiment Mass. volunteers, prepared by the Secretary. . . . Dedham, Press of Hugh H. McQuillen, 1876. 24 p. 23½cm.          MHi NHi    **357**

Roster of the 44th Mass. regiment, Jan. 1, 1908. [24] p. 15½cm.                  MHi    **358**

Title from cover.

—— [Supplement, changes from January 1, 1909, to January 1, 1910] [2] p. 14cm.
MHi    **359**

Baldwin, Frank
A Virginia raid in 1906, by Frank Baldwin, hereafter known as the "Dough boy." [n. p., 1906] 49 p. 23cm.          NN    **359A**

Title from cover. "Francis" in the roster.

Bartol, Cyrus Augustus, 1813–1900.
Conditions of peace, a discourse delivered in the West church, in memory of David Kimball Hobart, June 14, 1863, by C. A. Bartol. Boston, Walker, Wise, and co., 1863. 28 p. 23½cm.                DLC M    **360**

Haines, Zenas T
Letters from the Forty-fourth regiment M.V.M., a record of the experience of a nine month's regiment in the Department of North Carolina in 1862–3, by "Corporal." Boston, Printed at the Herald job office, 1863. 121 p. 23½cm.                DLC NN    **361**

Coulter 207.

James, Garth W          –1883.
The assault on Fort Wagner, by Capt. Garth W. James. *MOLLUS-Wis* I 9–30.    **362**

Safford, De Forest
. . . The Bay state Forty-fourth, a regimental record, edited by De Forest Safford, of the 44th regiment. Boston, M. O. Hall & co. [1863] 32 p. 23cm.                  DLC    **363**

At head of title: Price, 15 cents. Title from cover. Unit roster 29–32.

Wyeth, John Jasper
Leaves from a diary written while serving in Co. E, 44 Mass. Dep't of No. Carolina, from September, 1862, to June, 1863. Boston, L. F. Lawrence & co., 1878. 76 p. plates (fold. facs.; plans, 1 fold.; ports.). 23cm.
DLC M NN    **364**

"Preface" signed: John J. Wyeth. "Descriptive roll of Company E," fold. facs. facing p 6.

## 45TH INFANTRY

*Mustered in: September 26 to October 7, 1862.*
*Mustered out: July 8, 1863.*
*Mass soldiers* IV 309–47.
*Mass in the war* 634–6.

Hubbard, Charles Eustis, 1842–
The campaign of the Forty-fifth regiment Massachusetts volunteer militia, "the cadet regiment." Boston, Printed by James S. Adams, 1882. xiv, 126 p. plates (illus.). 25½cm.
DLC NN    **365**

"Published by the "Company A associates" of the Forty-fifth regiment, M.V.M." "Co. A 45 Mass., Dep't of No. Carolina," from device on title page. Unit roster [xiii]–xiv. "In 1882, under the auspices of this association, a diary of one of the members, Corporal Charles Eustis Hubbard, was published, bearing the title, "The campaign of the Forty-fifth," which was illustrated by . . . Frank H. Shapleigh," from History of the Forty-fifth regiment, 1908. Coulter 246.

Mann, Albert William, 1841–
History of the Forty-fifth regiment Massachusetts volunteer militia, "the cadet regiment," compiled by Albert W. Mann, historian of the Regiment. [Boston, Printed by Wallace Spooner, 1908] vi, 562, (3) p. plates (illus., ports.). 23cm.          DLC NN    **366**

"Cadet waltz," music (3) p. Unit roster 470–552.

—— Poem read at the fifty-second annual reunion of the Company A associates 45th regiment M.V.M., at the Parker house, January 19, 1915, by Albert W. Mann. [3] p. illus. on cover. 20cm.                  MHi    **367**

Title from cover.

See also Title 145.

## 46TH INFANTRY

*Mustered in: September 24 to October 22, 1862.*
*Mustered out: July 29, 1863.*
*Mass soldiers* IV 348–86.
*Mass in the war* 637–41.

Roster Forty-sixth regiment M.V.M. Compiled and verified from the Adjutant-general's report by vote of the Association. 1886. 20 p. 25cm.
DLC    **368**

Greene, Aella, 1838–
Reminiscent sketches, by Aella Greene.
[Florence, Press of Bryant print] 1902. 208 p.
16½cm.                                        M   *369*
"Concerning the Forty-sixth," 131–54.

Higgins, William C
Scaling the eagle's nest, the life of Russell
H. Conwell, by an old army comrade. Spring-
field, James D. Gill [1889] iv, [7]–212 p. front.
(port.), plates (illus.). 17cm.
                                        MeB NN   *370*
"The soldier," 54–72. "The editor . . . has en-
larged and arranged the writings of Mr. Wm. C.
Higgins."

Parker, Addison
A year of service in North Carolina. In War
talks of Morristown veterans, Morristown, N.J.
(1887) 22–9.                                  *371*

### 47TH INFANTRY

*Mustered in: September 19 to October 31,*
*1862.*
*Mustered out: September 1, 1863.*
*Mass soldiers* iv 387–429.
*Mass in the war* 642–4.

Barker, Frederick I
Captured by the grand rounds! In National
tribune scrap book i 157–9.            *371A*

Miles, James Browning, 1822–1875.
The soldier's trust, a discourse addressed
to the Putnam blues, in the First church,
Charlestown, on Sunday morning, Sept. 21,
1862, by Rev. James B. Miles. Published by
request of the Company. Boston, Mass. Sabbath School Society [1862] 64 p. 11½cm.
Unit roster [2]                          M   *372*

### 48TH INFANTRY

*Left State: December 27, 1862.*
*Mustered out: September 3, 1863.*
*Mass soldiers* iv 430–69.
*Mass in the war* 645–9.

Cross, Henry Martyn, 1843–1931.
A Yankee soldier looks at the negro. Edited
by William Cullen Bryant, II. *Civil war his-*
*tory* vii (1961) 133–48. plate (illus., group
port.).                                   *372A*

Plummer, Albert
History of the Forty-eighth regiment M.V.M.
during the Civil war. [Boston, New England
Druggist pub. co.] 1907. 133 p. plates (illus.,
ports.). 23½cm.            DLC NN   *373*
Unit roster [69]–133. "Preface" signed: Albert
Plummer, historian.

### 49TH INFANTRY

*Mustered in: September 18 to October 28,*
*1862.*
*Mustered out: September 1, 1863.*
*Mass soldiers* iv 470–507.
*Mass in the war* 650–3.

Dewey, Orville, 1794–1882.
A talk with the camp. New York, Anson
D. F. Randolph, 1863. 16 p. 11½cm.
                                        NN RP   *374*
Title and imprint from cover. Signed: Orville
Dewey, Sheffield, February 16, 1863. "We have nearly
a hundred from Sheffield in the Forty-ninth Massa-
chusetts."

Johns, Henry T
Life with the Forty-ninth Massachusetts
volunteers, by Henry T. Johns, late Quartermaster's clerk. Published for the author. Pittsfield [C. A. Alvord, printer] 1864. 391 p.
plates (1 illus., ports.). 19cm.
                                        DLC NN   *375*
Unit roster [381]–91. Coulter 256.

—— —— Washington, D. C. [Ramsey & Bisbee, printers] 1890. 435 p. front. (port.).
19½cm.                                    NN   *376*
c1864. "I could not improve on it; so, except the
correction of a few errors, it is just the book your
fathers read and prized" (the edition of 1864). Unit
roster [425]–35.

Summer, Samuel Barstow, 1830–1891.
A poem delivered at the reunion of the
Forty-ninth regiment Massachusetts volunteers,
at Pittsfield, Mass., May 21, 1867, by Samuel
B. Summer, Lieutenant Colonel of the Regiment. With notes and an appendix. Springfield, Samuel Bowles & co., printers, 1867. 36 p.
22½cm.                              MB NHi   *377*

Torrey, Rodney Webster, 1836–
War diary of Rodney W. Torrey, 1862–
1863. [n. p., 1904?] 93 p. front. (port.). 20cm.
Coulter 450.                              NN   *378*

Winsor, Frederick, 1829–1889.
The surgeon at the field hospital. *Atlantic*
*monthly* xlvi (1880) 183–8.            *379*

See also Title 232.

### 50TH INFANTRY

*Mustered in: September 15–30, 1862.*
*Mustered out: August 24, 1863.*
*Mass soldiers* iv 508–45.
*Mass in the war* 654–7.

Barrows, William, 1815–1891.
Honor to the brave, a discourse delivered
in the old South church, Reading, Mass., Au-

*50th Infantry, continued*

gust 23, 1863, on the return of Company D. Fiftieth reg., Mass. vols., by the Rev. William Barrows. . . . Boston, John M. Whittemore & co., 1863. 19 p. 21½cm.          IHi MB      *380*
Killed, deceased and wounded, 18–19.

Stevens, William Burnham, 1843–
History of the Fiftieth regiment of infantry Massachusetts volunteer militia in the late War of the rebellion, by William B. Stevens, a member of Co. C. Boston, Griffiths-Stillings press, 1907. xii, 399 p. plates (1 illus., map, ports.). 23½cm.          DLC NN      *381*
Unit roster [289]–394.

See also Title 123A.

### 51ST INFANTRY

*Mustered in September 25 to October 14, 1862.*

*Mustered out: July 27, 1863.*

*Mass soldiers* iv 546–82.

*Mass in the war* 658–62.

Baldwin, John S          1834–
The old Fifty-first Massachusetts volunteers, verses written for and read at some of the reunions, by John S. Baldwin, Captain of Company F. [n. p., 1909] 20 p. front. (illus.). 19½cm.          NN      *382*

Pierce, Charles F
History and camp life of Company C, Fifty-first regiment, Massachusetts volunteer militia, 1862–1863, by C. F. Pierce. Worcester, Printed by Charles Hamilton, 1886. ix, [9]–130, (1) p. plates (illus.; maps, 1 fold.; ports.). 23cm.
          DLC NN      *383*
Unit roster 23–32. "The deserted camp of the Massachusetts Fifty-first, by Henry S. Washburn," (1) p.

—— Souvenir army life Co. C 51 Mass., Dep't of No. Carolina, 1862. 1863. Gardner, Autoglyph prints by W. P. Allen [1885] 29 leaves. plates (illus., ports.). 29cm. DLC NN      *384*
Preface signed: Charles F. Pierce. Unit roster included.

Robbins, Gilbert
The Christian patriot, a biography of James E. McClellan, by Gilbert Robbins. Worcester, Grout & Bigelow, 1865. vi, [9]–127 p. front. (port.). 17½cm.          NN      *385*

### 52ND INFANTRY

*Mustered in: October 2–11, 1862.*

*Mustered out: August 14, 1863.*

*Mass soldiers* iv 583–618.

*Mass in the war* 663–6.

Hosmer, James Kendall, 1834–1927.
The color-guard, being a Corporal's notes of military service in the Nineteenth army corps, by James K. Hosmer, of the Fifty-second regiment Mass. volunteers. Boston, Walker, Wise, and co., 1864. xii, [9]–244 p. 17½cm.
Coulter 242.          DLC NN      *386*

—— The thinking bayonet, by James K. Hosmer. . . . Boston, Walker, Fuller, and co., 1865. vii, 9–326 p. 18cm.          NN WHi      *387*
Continuing the author's The color-guard in publishing his "diary of a military life."

Moors, John Farwell, 1819–
History of the Fifty-second regiment Massachusetts volunteers by the Chaplain, J. F. Moors. Boston, Press of George H. Ellis, 1893. 220, lxiii p. plates (map, 2 ports.). 24cm.
Unit roster [i]–xlix.          DLC NN      *388*

Spear, Asa Adams, 1841–
The Civil war in history, an address delivered at the reunion of the 52d regiment Massachusetts volunteers, Wednesday, August 14, 1912, at Greenfield, Mass., the 50th anniversary of the enlistment of the Regiment in the U.S. army for service in the Civil war, by Lieutenant Asa A. Spear of Company G. Northampton, Gazette print. co., 1912. 15, (1) p. 23cm.          DLC NN      *389*

### 53RD INFANTRY

*Mustered in: October 17–18; November 6, 1862.*

*Mustered out: September 2, 1863.*

*Mass soldiers* iv 619–55.

*Mass in the war* 667–71.

Simes, William
John Green Mudge, the valiant soldier and public spirited citizen, a memorial address, delivered in Petersham, by William Simes, August 2, 1899. [10] p. port. 24cm.
Caption title.          DLC      *390*

Stratton, Joel A          1837–
Recollections of a soldier in the Civil war, by Joel A. Stratton, Captain Company C, Fifty-third Massachusetts volunteers, 1862–1863. Fitchburg, Published by vote of the Fifty-third regiment association, 1919. 24 p. 21cm.          NN      *391*

Willis, Henry Augustus, 1830–1918.
The Fifty-third regiment Massachusetts volunteers, comprising also a history of the siege of Port Hudson, by Henry A. Willis. Fitchburg, Press of Blanchard & Brown, 1889. 247 p. front. (port.). 24cm.          DLC NN      *392*
Unit roster [217]–47.

## 54TH INFANTRY

*Mustered in: March 30 to May 13, 1863.*
*Mustered out: August 20, 1865.*
*Mass soldiers* iv 656–714.
*Mass in the war* 672–81.

Justice to the negro soldiers . . . the Fifty-fourth regiment. [1864?] 2 p. 25cm.
MHi **393**
Caption title. "The letter was published in the Boston *Liberator*, and is thus endorsed by its Editor, Lloyd Garrison."

Memorial RGS [monogram, Robert Gould Shaw] Cambridge, University press, 1864. 195 p. front. (port.). 23½cm. NN **394**

Souvenir of the Massachusetts Fifty-fourth (colored) regiment. [Boston, 1863] 10 p. 22cm. DLC MHi **395**
Caption title. Purchase and presentation of a flag to the Regiment, its departure to the front, etc.

Appleton, John W M
That night at Fort Wagner, by one who was there. *Putnam's magazine* ns iv (1869) 9–16.
**396**

Bartlett, Samuel Ripley, 1837–
The charge of the Fifty-fourth [by] S. R. Bartlett . . . Fifty copies for private circulation. Chicago [Church, Goodman & Donnelley, printers] 1869. [7] leaves. 19½cm.
A Christmas publication. NHi **397**

Boston, City Council.
Exercises at the dedication of the monument to Colonel Robert Gould Shaw and the Fifty-fourth regiment of Massachusetts infantry, May 31, 1897. Published by order of the City council of Boston. Boston, Municipal print. office, 1897. 71 p. front. (illus.). 26cm.
M NN **398**
Partial contents: Oration by Professor William James, 37–53; Address of Booker T. Washington, 55–61.

Coulter, Ellis Merton, 1890–
Robert Gould Shaw and the burning of Darien, Georgia. *Civil war history* v (1959) 363–73. **398A**

Duren, Charles M          –1869.
The occupation of Jacksonville, February 1864, and the battle of Olustee. Letters of Lt. C. M. Duren, 54th Massachusetts regiment. *Florida historical quarterly* xxxii (1953/54) 262–87. illus. **398B**

Emilio, Luis Fenallosa, 1844–
The assault on Fort Wagner, July 18, 1863, the memorable charge of the Fifty-fourth regiment of Massachusetts volunteers, written for "The Springfield republican," by Captain Luis

F. Emilio. Boston, Rand Avery co., 1887. 16 p. 22½cm. DLC NN **399**

—— History of the Fifty-fourth regiment of Massachusetts volunteer infantry, 1863–1865, by Luis F. Emilio. Boston, Boston Book co., 1891. xvi, 410 p. plates (maps and plans, partly fold.; ports.). 22cm. DLC NN **400**
On cover: A brave black regiment. Unit roster [327]–90.

—— —— Second edition, revised and corrected, with appendix upon treatment of colored prisoners of war. Boston, Boston Book co., 1894. xvi, 452 p. plates (maps and plans, partly fold.; ports.). 22cm. NHi **401**
Unit roster [327]–90.

Hagood, Johnson, 1829–1898.
[Letter to Thomas W. Higginson, dated Columbia, S.C., Sept. 21, 1881, on the burial of Colonel Robert G. Shaw, at Battery Wagner, July 19, 1863] *Mass historical society proceedings* xlvii (1914) 341–3. **401A**

Higginson, Henry Lee, 1834–1919.
Robert Gould Shaw, an address delivered in Sanders theatre, Cambridge, May 30, 1897. In his Four addresses (1902) 71–107. **402**

McKay, Martha Nicholson, 1847–
When the tide turned in the Civil war, by Martha Nicholson McKay. Indianapolis, Hollenbeck press, 1929. 66 p. front. (illus.). 21½cm. NN **403**
"To the memory of Colonel Robert Gould Shaw and his regiment, the 54th Massachusetts." "The following pages were written about the time of the unveiling of the Shaw monument in 1897."

Massachusetts. Shaw Monument Committee.
The monument to Robert Gould Shaw, its inception, completion and unveiling, 1865–1897. Boston, Houghton, Mifflin and co., 1897. 97, (1) p. front. (illus.). 26cm. M **404**
Much of the text uses the plates of Title 398.

See also Titles 110–111.

## 55TH INFANTRY

*Mustered in: May 31 to June 22, 1863.*
*Mustered out: August 29, 1865.*
*Mass soldiers* iv 715–61.
*Mass in the war* 682–91.

Fox, Charles Barnard
Record of the service of the Fifty-fifth regiment of Massachusetts volunteer infantry. Printed for the Regimental association. Cambridge, Press of John Wilson and Son, 1868. 144 p. 25cm. NN **405**
Unit roster [90]–144. "Voted to print in pamphlet form the diary kept by Colonel Fox during the Regi-

*55th Infantry, continued*

mental service . . . very little change, however, has been made from the original draft."

Hallowell, Norwood Penrose, 1839–1914.
The negro as a soldier in the War of the rebellion, by Norwood P. Hallowell, read before the Military historical society of Massachusetts, January 5, 1892. Boston, Little Brown, and co., 1897. 29 p. plates (1 illus., ports.). 22cm.                       WHi    **406**
Also published in *PMHSM* xiii 287–313.

Wilder, Burt Green, 1841–1925.
. . . Professor Wilder talks of his regiment.
. . . [Brookline, 1914] [2] p. 23cm.
                                             MHi    **407**
At head of title: Reprinted, revised, from the Brookline (Mass.) chronicle of May 30, 1914. Caption title.

—— . . . The Fifty-fifth Massachusetts volunteer infantry colored, June, 1863 – September, 1865, address before the Brookline historical society, May 28, 1914, by Burt G. Wilder. [1917] [4] p. 25½cm.                       M    **408**
Caption title. Additional text, inserted leaf. At head of title: To replace the print of August 17. The only change is the addition of the Appendix on page four.

—— The Fifty-fifth regiment of the Massachusetts volunteer infantry colored, June 1863 — September 1865, by Burt G. Wilder. Third edition. Brookline, Riverdale press, 1919. 8 p. 24cm.                                   DLC NN    **409**
"Revised, with additions and in simplified spelling."

—— Two examples of the negro's courage, physical and moral, by Burt G. Wilder, an address at the Garrison centenary, December 10, 1905. [Boston, 1906] p [21]–8. 2 ports. 24cm.                                     CtY    **409A**
Title from cover. "Reprinted from Alexander's magazine for January 1906."

## 56TH INFANTRY

*Left State: March 20, 1864.*
*Mustered out: July 12, 1865.*
*Mass soldiers* iv 762–814.
*Mass in the war* 692–6.

Adams, Zabdield Boylston, 1829–1902.
In the Wilderness, by Brevet Major Z. Boylston Adams. *MOLLUS-Mass* ii 373–99.    **410**

Griswold, Anna
Colonel Griswold. [Brookline, 1866] 67 p. 19½cm.                                      NHi    **411**

Weld, Stephen Minot, 1842–1920.
The case of Fitz-John Porter, by Bvt. Brig.-Gen. Stephen M. Weld. *PMHSM* ii 221–62.
                                                   **412**

—— The conduct of General McClellan during his stay at Alexandria in August, 1862; the

nature and extent of his command, and his alleged neglect to support the army of General Pope. *PMHSM* ii 287–302.            **413**

—— The Petersburg mine. *PMHSM* v 205–19.                                           **414**

See also Title 212.

## 57TH INFANTRY

*Left State: April 18, 1864.*
*Mustered out: July 30, 1865.*
*Mass soldiers* iv 815–74.
*Mass in the war* 697–704.

Lt.-Col. Charles Lyon Chandler [a memorial] [Cambridge, Printed by Welch, Bigelow, and co., 1864?] 40 p. front. (port.). 19cm.
                                             NHi    **415**

Anderson, John, 1841–
The Fifty-seventh regiment of Massachusetts volunteers in the War of the rebellion, Army of the Potomac, by Captain John Anderson. Boston, E. B. Stillings & co., printers, 1896. xiv, 512 p. plates (ports.). 23½cm.
Unit roster [419]–504.               DLC NN    **416**

Stewart, William Henry, 1838–1912.
The "no name" battle.... *BandG* v (1895)    **417**
Contents: I. From the Confederate side, by Colonel William H. Stewart, 29–32; From the Union side, by Whitman V. White, 32–5.

Sturgis, Thomas, 1846–
Prisoners of war, 1861–65, a record of personal experiences, and a study of the condition and treatment of prisoners on both sides during the War of the rebellion, by Thomas Sturgis, late 1st Lieut. 57th regt., Mass. vet. vols.... New York, G. P. Putnam's Sons, 1912. iv, 266–328 p. plates (facs., illus.). 24½cm.
                                           NHi NN    **418**
"Reprinted from the report of an address delivered before the N.Y. commandery of the Military order of the loyal legion, Feb. 1, 1911."

—— Shall Congress erect statues at national expense to Confederate officers in Washington? Resolutions adopted by the New York commandery of the Military order of the loyal legion, October 6th, 1909. Confederate officers and the right of secession. By Thomas Sturgis. New York, 1910. 15 p. 23cm.    NN    **419**
Title and imprint from cover.

Tarbox, Increase N
Missionary patriots, memoirs of James H. Schneider and Edward M. Schneider, by Increase N. Tarbox. Boston, Massachusetts Sabbath School Society, 1867. 357 p. 2 plates (ports.). 17½cm.                       NHi    **420**
Civil war 118–82, 288–357. Edward M. Schneider served in the 57th Mass infantry.

See also Title 232.

## 58TH INFANTRY

*Mustered in: January 14 to April 18, 1864.*
*Mustered out: July 14, 1865.*
*Mass soldiers v 1–47.*
*Mass in the war 705–9.*

Cushman, Frederick E
  History of the 58th regt. Massachusetts vols., from the 15th day of September, 1863, to the close of the rebellion, by F. E. C. Washington, D. C., Gibson Brothers, printers, 1865. 38 p. 17½cm.                    DLC NHi    **421**
  Unit roster [24]–38.

Wilson, John
  Seven months in a Rebel prison, by John Wilson, Co. A, 58th Mass. vol. [n. p., n. d.] 28 p. front. (port.). 21cm.          NHi    **422**

## 59TH INFANTRY

*Mustered in: December 5, 1863 to April 21, 1864.*
*Consolidated with 57th infantry, June 20, 1865, to be effective as of June 1, 1865.*
*Mass soldiers 48–92.*
*Mass in the war 710–15.*

Moody, Joseph E
  Life in Confederate prisons, by Lieutenant Joseph E. Moody. MOLLUS-Mass II 351–69.
                                            **423**

Sweet, John D          1838–1916.
  The speaking dead, a discourse occasioned by the death of Serg't Edward Amos Adams, 59th regiment, M.V.M., delivered at Billerica, Mass., July 31st, 1864, by Rev. John D. Sweet. . . . Boston, Commercial print. house, 1864. 28 p. front. (mounted port.). 23cm.
                                      MHi    **424**

## 60TH INFANTRY

*Organized: August 1, 1864.*
*Mustered out: November 30, 1864.*
*Mass soldiers 93–126.*
*Mass in the war 716–17.*

## 61ST INFANTRY

*Organized: August to September 1864.*
*Mustered out: June 4, July 16, 1865.*
*Mass soldiers 127–64.*
*Mass in the war 718–21.*

## 62ND INFANTRY

*Organization was not completed. Recruits for the regiment were mustered out, May 5, 1865.*
*Mass soldiers v 165–80.*
*Mass in the war 722.*

## NATIONAL GUARD

### BOSTON CADETS

*Mustered in for duty at Fort Warren: May 26, 1862.*
*Mustered out: July 2, 1862.*
*Mass soldiers v 317–20.*

Gore, Henry Watson, 1842–
  The Independent corps of cadets of Boston, Mass. at Fort Warren, Boston harbor in 1862. Compiled by H. W. Gore. Boston, Press of Rockwell and Churchill, 1888. 447 p. ports. 25cm.                        DLC NN    **425**
  "Portraits and personal records," [31]–443. Edition limited to one hundred copies.

Todd, Frederick Porter
  Independent corps of cadets, Massachusetts volunteer militia, 1858–1864. *Military collector & historian* II (Washington 1950) 29. col. plate (illus.).                              **426**

### SALEM CADETS

*Mustered for duty at Fort Warren: May 26, 1862.*
*Mustered out: October 11, 1862.*
*Mass soldiers v 316, 321–5.*

## SHARPSHOOTERS

### 1ST COMPANY

*Mustered in: September 2, 1861.*
*Mustered out: June 30, 1865.*
*Mass soldiers v 205–13.*
*Mass in the war 862–6.*

### 2ND COMPANY

*Mustered in: September 1861.*
*Mustered out: October 17, 1864.*
*Mass soldiers v 711–18.*
*Mass in the war 867.*

See Title 248.

  *Three companies were raised in Massachusetts for service with the United States sharpshooters: Company E. 1st regiment U.S. sharpshooters. Companies F and G, 2nd regiment U.S. sharpshooters.*

# NEW HAMPSHIRE

# Reference Works

Dyer, Frederick Henry, 1849–1917.

A compendium of the War of the rebellion, 1908 (reprinted 1959).

"Regimental index" 176–8; "Regimental histories" 1345–53. The pagination is the same in the 1959 reprint.


New Hampshire. Adjutant General.

Revised register of the soldiers and sailors of New Hampshire in the War of the rebellion, 1861–1866. Prepared and published by authority of the Legislature, by Augustus D. Ayling, Adjutant general. Concord, Ira C. Evans, Public printer, 1895. xii, 1347 p. 31cm.

Cited herein as *Revised register*.


*The Union army.*

"Record of New Hampshire regiments," I (1908) 81–92.

United States. Adjutant General's Office.

Official army register of the volunteer force of the United States army for the years 1861, '62, '63, '64, '65. Part I. (New England states). Washington, 1865.

A roster of officers by regiments with an alphabetical index for the six states.


Waite, Otis Frederick Reed, 1818–1895.

New Hampshire in the great rebellion containing histories of the several New Hampshire regiments, and biographical notices of many of the prominent actors in the Civil war of 1861–65, by Major Otis F. R. Waite. Claremont, Tracy, Chase & co., 1870. vi, [9]–608 p. plates (illus., ports.). 21½cm.

Cited by title.

# NEW HAMPSHIRE

## ARTILLERY

### 1ST ARTILLERY (HEAVY)

Mustered in: September 2 to October 17, 1864.

Mustered out: June 9, 15; September 15, 1865.

Revised register 920–63. Historical sketch by Charles H. Long.

N.H. in the great rebellion 560–6.

#### 1st Company of Heavy Artillery

Mustered in: May 26 to July 22, 1863.

Became Company A 1st regiment of heavy artillery: September 15, 1864.

Revised register 906–11. Historical sketch by Charles H. Long.

#### 2nd Company of Heavy Artillery

Mustered in: August 18 to September 17, 1863.

Became B company 1st regiment of heavy artillery: October 1, 1864.

Revised register 912–19. Historical sketch by Charles H. Long.

#### 1st Battery of Light Artillery

Mustered in: September 26, 1861.

Became Company M 1st regiment of heavy artillery: November 5, 1864.

Revised register 892–905.

N.H. in the great rebellion 555–9.

Articles of war, printed for the use of the First New-Hampshire battery of light artillery. Manchester, Printed by Charles F. Livingston, 1861. 23 p. 18cm.    **NhHi   1**

History of the First N.H. battery, during the War of the rebellion, together with the by-laws of Platoon A, First N.H. light artillery, S.M. Manchester, Thomas H. Tuson, printer, 1878. 20 p. 13½cm.    **NHi   2**

Names and record of all the members who served in the First N.H. battery of light artillery, during the late rebellion, from September 26, 1861, to June 15, 1865, when the Battery was mustered out of the service of the United States. Manchester, 1884. 15 p. 22½cm.    **IHi NHi   3**

—— Manchester, Budget job print, 1891. 40, (1) p. 23½cm.    **NHi NN   4**

"Monument at Gettysburg," (1) p.

## Lafayette Artillery

Mustered in: June 30, 1864.

Mustered out: September 23, 1864.

Revised register 998–1001.

## CAVALRY

### 1ST CAVALRY

New Hampshire raised four companies of cavalry, October 24 to December 24, 1861, which became Companies I, K, L and M of the First New England cavalry.

First New England cavalry designated 1st regiment of Rhode Island cavalry: March 31, 1862.

Four New Hampshire companies were returned to the State, January 7, 1864, to become the nucleus of the 1st regiment of New Hampshire cavalry. Companies A to H were mustered in: April 19 to July 24, 1864.

Mustered out: July 15, 1865.

Revised register 829–91. Historical sketch: New Hampshire battalion of 1st New England cavalry, by Ezra B. Parker; 1st New Hampshire cavalry, by Ervin H. Smith.

N.H. in the great rebellion 545–54.

### 2ND CAVALRY

Mustered in as 8th regiment of infantry: October 25 to December 29, 1861.

Designated 2nd regiment of cavalry: December 1863.

Mustered out: January 18, 1865; Veteran battalion, October 28, 1865.

Revised register 404–56. Historical sketch by John M. Stanyan.

N.H. in the great rebellion 365–95.

Complete roster of the Eighth regiment New Hampshire volunteers. [Concord?, 189–] 106 p. 23½cm.    **NHi NN   5**

"Supp. vol. Stanyan's History of the 8th," ms. note in NHi's copy. The bindings of the two volumes are identical. Reprinted from the Revised register, 1895.

Stanyan, John Minot, 1828–1905.

A history of the Eighth regiment of New Hampshire volunteers, including its service as infantry, Second N.H. cavalry, and veteran battalion in the Civil war of 1861–1865, covering a period of three years, ten months, and nineteen days, by J. M. Stanyan, late Captain

*2nd Cavalry, continued*

of Company B. Concord, Ira C. Evans, printer, 1892. 583 p. plates (ports.). 23½cm.
On cover: "The old Eighth."　DLC NN　**6**

## INFANTRY

### 1ST INFANTRY

*Mustered in: May 1–7, 1861.*

*Mustered out: August 9, 1861.*

*Revised register 1–24. Historical sketch by Stephen G. Abbott.*

*N.H. in the great rebellion 57–86.*

Abbott, Stephen G
The First regiment New Hampshire volunteers in the great rebellion, containing the story of the campaign, and account of the "great uprising of the people of the State," and other articles upon subjects associated with the early war period, map of the route of the Regiment, tables, biographies, portraits and illustrations, by Rev. Stephen G. Abbott, Chaplain of the Regiment. Keene, Sentinel print. co., 1890. 511 p. illus., map, ports., plates (ports.). 24cm.　DLC NN　**7**
Original roster 375–418.

### 2ND INFANTRY

*Mustered in: May 31 to June 10, 1861.*

*Mustered out: December 19, 1865.*

*Revised register 25–98. Historical sketch by Martin A. Haynes.*

*N.H. in the great rebellion 103–68.*

Ten months in Confederate prisons, by a member of Company B, 2nd New Hampshire regiment volunteers. In Richmond prisons, 1861–1862, by William H. Jeffrey (1893) 123–59.
**7A**

Fitts, J　　　Lane
My experience as a prisoner of war. In Richmond prisons, 1861–1862, by William H. Jeffrey (1893) 110–15.　**7B**

Gorman, Thomas
Sermon on the death of Lieut. Sylvester Rogers, son of Freeman S. Rogers, of Nashua, who was killed in the battle of August 29th, 1862, near Bull run, by Rev. Thomas Gorman. Preached on Sunday, September 28, at the Universalist church, Nashua. Nashua, Printed at the N.H. Telegraph office, 1862. 18 p. 21½cm.　DLC　**8**

Gunnison, Elisha Norman, 1836?–1880.
Our stars. For the Army of the Potomac, by Norman Gunnison, Second New Hampshire

volunteers. Philadelphia, Ringwalt & Brown, printers, 1863. 120 p. plates (ports.). 17½cm.
Title and imprint from cover.　NHi　**9**

Haynes, Martin A　　　1845–
History of the Second regiment, New Hampshire volunteers, its camps, marches and battles, by Martin A. Haynes, Private of Company I. . . . Manchester, Charles F. Livingston, printer, 1865. viii, [9]–223, (1) p. 20cm.
　　　　DLC NN　**10**
"List of battles. . . ," (1) p. Unit roster [179]–218.
Coulter 223.

―― A history of the Second regiment, New Hampshire volunteer infantry in the War of the rebellion, by Martin A. Haynes. Lakeport, 1896. xv, 350, (2), 125, (1) p. illus., plans, ports., 3 plates (ports.). 22½cm.
　　　　DLC NN　**11**
"Errata and addenda," (1) p. Unit roster, 125 p.

―― A minor war history, compiled from a soldier boy's letters to "the girl I left behind me," 1861–1864. Dramatis personae: the soldier boy, Martin A. Haynes; "the girl I left behind me," Cornelia T. Lane. Lakeport, Private print of Martin A. Haynes, 1916. 171 p. plates (2 illus., ports.). 23½cm.
"Edition sixty copies."　IHi NhHi　**12**

―― Muster out roll of the Second New Hampshire regiment in the War of the rebellion, a partial record of members who have died since the printing of the Regimental history and roster in 1896, with various contemporary obituary notices and biographical sketches, compiled by Martin A. Haynes. Lakeport, Private print of Martin A. Haynes, 1917. 55 p. front. (illus.). 23½cm.　Nh　**13**
"Edition eighty copies."

―― A poem read at the second reunion of New Hampshire veterans held at Weirs landing, N.H., (Camp Phin P. Bixby,) August 13, 14 & 15, 1878, by Martin A. Haynes. Printed and sold for the N.H. veteran association. 1878. 12 p. 20½cm.　NHi　**14**

Severin, John Powers and Frederick Porter Todd
2d regiment New Hampshire volunteer militia, 1861. *Military collector & historian* v (Washington 1953) 17–18. col. plate (illus.).
　　　　**15**

### 3RD INFANTRY

*Mustered in August 22–26, 1861.*

*Mustered out: July 20, 1865.*

*Revised register 99–152. Historical sketch by Daniel Eldredge.*

*N.H. in the great rebellion 169–214.*

Dedication of the monument erected in memory of Gen. John Bedel, by his surviving comrades of the Third regiment, New Hampshire volunteers, at Bath, N.H., October 10th, 1888. [Concord, Press of Ira C. Evans, 1888] 32, (1) p. ports. 22cm. DNW **16**

Extract history of officers & enlisted men, Cp. F, 3d N.H. vols. [n. p., n. d.] 15 p. 18½cm.
A roster. Title from cover. NhHi **17**

Bedel, John, 1822–1875.
Historical sketch of the Third regiment, New Hampshire volunteers. *Granite monthly* III (Concord 1880) 516–34. **18**
General John Bedel, by Walter Harriman, 513–15.

Copp, Elbridge J 1844–
Reminiscences of the War of the rebellion, 1861–1865, by Col. Elbridge J. Copp. the youngest commissioned officer in the Union army who rose from the ranks. Published by the author. Nashua, Printed by the Telegraph pub. co., 1911. 536, iv p. illus., ports. 23cm.
Coulter 94. DLC NN **19**

Eldredge, Daniel
... The Third New Hampshire and all about it, by D. Eldredge, Captain Third New Hampshire vol. inf. Boston, Mass., E. B. Stillings and co., 1893. xxxi, 1054 p. illus., maps, plans, plates (fold. maps, ports.). 24cm.
DLC NN **20**
At head of title: 1861    1865. Unit roster 797–967. Two blank leaves with printed border at end of volume for "Memoranda."

Hamilton, Henry S 1836?–
Reminiscences of a veteran, by Henry S. Hamilton. Concord, Republican Press Association, 1897. 180 p. front. (port.). 18½cm.
DLC NHi NN WHi **21**

Linehan, John Cornelius, 1840–1905.
War pictures. *Granite monthly* XVIII (Concord 1895) 343–50; XIX (1895) 83–8, 143–51, 208–15, 307–14, 356–60, 456–7. illus., ports. **22**

**4TH INFANTRY**

*Mustered in: September 18–20, 1861.*

*Mustered out: August 23, 1865.*

*Revised register 153–208. Historical sketch by Francis W. Parker.*

*N.H. in the great rebellion 215–51.*

Bouton, John Bell, 1830–1902.
A memoir of General Louis Bell, late Col. of the Fourth N.H. regiment, who fell at the assault on Fort Fisher, N.C., January 15th, 1865, by John Bell Bouton. Read before the N.H. historical society, Sept. 14th, 1865. . . . New York, 1865. 53 p. 23cm. DLC NhHi **23**

Bryant, Elias A
The diary of Elias A. Bryant, as written by him while in his more than three years' service in the U.S. army in the Civil war. [Concord, Rumford press, n. d.] 197 p. front. (3 ports.). 23½cm. Nh **24**

Hutchinson, John G
Roster Fourth regiment New Hampshire volunteers, compiled and published by authority of the Fourth regiment veteran association, by John G. Hutchinson, First Sergt. Co. E, historian. Manchester, Printed by John B. Clarke co., 1896. 188 p. ports. 16½cm.
Nh NHi **25**

Jewett, Albert Henry Clay, 1841–1898.
A boy goes to war, by Albert Henry Clay Jewett, war memories of 1860 to 1864, written by Dr. Jewett in the last year of his life . . . Poem-preface by his daughter, Grace Jewett Austin. Bloomington, Ill., 1944. x, 73 p. front. (illus.). 20cm. DLC **26**

Towle, George Francis, –1900.
Terry's Fort Fisher expedition, by G. F. Towle, Inspector of the expedition. *Our living and our dead* III (Raleigh, N.C. 1875) 464–72, 592–604. **26A**

**5TH INFANTRY**

*Mustered in: October 12–26, 1861.*

*Mustered out: June 28, 1865.*

*Revised register 209–82. Historical sketch by William Child.*

*N.H. in the great rebellion 252–96.*

Child, William, 1834–
A history of the Fifth regiment, New Hampshire volunteers, in the American Civil war, 1861–1865. In two parts. By William Child, Major and Surgeon, Historian of the Veterans' association of the Regiment. Bristol, R. W. Musgrove, printer, 1893. xv, 336, 228 p. plates (illus., ports.). 22½cm. DLC NN **27**
Unit roster [1]–202, second pagination.

Livermore, Thomas Leonard, 1844–1918.
Patterson's Shenandoah campaign. *PMHSM* I 1–58. **28**

**6TH INFANTRY**

*Mustered in: November 27–30, 1861.*

*Mustered out: July 17, 1865.*

*Revised register 283–349. Historical sketch by Lyman Jackson.*

*N.H. in the great rebellion 297–337.*

Crawford, A         B
General S. G. Griffin. *Granite monthly* V (Concord 1882) 101–08. plate (port.). **29**

*6th Infantry, continued*

Jackman, Lyman
History of the Sixth New Hampshire regiment in the War for the Union. Captain Lyman Jackman, historian. Amos Hadley, editor. Concord, Republican Press Association, 1891. vi, 630 p. plates (ports.). 23½cm.
Unit roster [408]–[602]          DLC NN    **30**

## 7TH INFANTRY

*Mustered in: October 29 to December 15, 1861.*

*Mustered out: July 20, 1865.*

*Revised register 350–403. Historical sketch by Henry F. W. Little.*

*N.H. in the great rebellion 338–64.*

Day, Pliny Butts, 1806–1869.
A tribute to the memory of Lieut. John Howard Worcester, in a discourse delivered at Hollis, N.H., on Sabbath, January 24, 1864, by P. B. Day. . . . Nashua, Printed at the N.H. Telegraph office, 1864. 16 p. 22cm.
DLC    **31**

Douglass, Malcolm, 1825–1877.
A sermon commemorative of Haldimand Sumner Putnam (Capt. Engineers, U.S.A.), Colonel of the 7th regiment, New-Hampshire volunteers and acting Brigadier general, commanding the column of assault on Fort Wagner, upon whose ramparts he fell, July 18, 1863 . . . Preached on the 30th August, 1863, in Trinity church, Cornish N.H., by the Rev. Malcolm Douglass. Claremont, Press of the Claremont Manufacturing co., 1863. 16 p. 21½cm.          DLC    **32**

Little, Henry F          W          1842–
. . . The Seventh regiment, New Hampshire volunteers in the War of the rebellion, by Henry F. W. Little, Lieutenant Seventh N.H. volunteers, Regimental historian. Published by the Seventh New Hampshire veteran association. Concord, Ira C. Evans, printer, 1896. xviii, 567, 110, xxi p. illus., maps (1 fold.), plans, ports. 23cm.          DLC NN    **33**
At head of title: 1861      1865. Unit roster, 110 p.
"Index to contents," xxi p.

Spalding, Winslow J
A Yankee boy's experience in the war.
*BandG* II (1893) 63–4.          **33A**

## 8TH INFANTRY

*Mustered in: October 25 to December 29, 1861.*

*Designated 2nd regiment of cavalry; December 1863.*

## 9TH INFANTRY

*Mustered in: July 3 to August 23, 1862.*

*Mustered out: June 10, 1865.*

*Revised register 457–512. Historical sketch by George L. Wakefield.*

*N.H. in the great rebellion 396–420.*

Major William I. Brown, a sketch prepared for W. I. Brown post, no. 31, Grand army of the Republic, Fisherville, N.H. Published by request, January, 1876. Concord, Republican Press Association, 1876. 13 p. 21½cm.
DLC    **34**
On cover: Major William I. Brown, 18th N. H. vols.
Brown mustered in 9th New Hampshire infantry, August 15, 1862; discharged for promotion in 18th New Hampshire infantry, October 20, 1864; killed in action, March 29, 1865.

Canfield, William A
A history of William A. Canfield's experience in the army . . . by himself. . . . Manchester, Printed by Charles F. Livingston, 1869. 34 p. 17½cm.          MB WHi    **35**

Case, Ervin T
Battle of the mine, by Ervin T. Case, late Captain Ninth New Hampshire. 1879. 37 p. *PNRISSHS* s1 no 10.          **35A**

Lord, Edward Oliver, 1856–
History of the Ninth regiment, New Hampshire volunteers in the War of the rebellion. Edited by Edward O. Lord. Concord, Republican Press Association, 1895. xii, 761, (1), 171 p. plates (ports.). 23½cm.  DLC NN    **36**
Unit roster 1–111, second pagination

## 10TH INFANTRY

*Mustered in: August to September 18, 1862.*

*Mustered out: June 21, 1865.*

*Revised register 513–34. Historical sketch by James A. Sanborn.*

*N.H. in the great rebellion 421–43.*

Memorial services. Address of welcome, poem, responses, ceremonies, and oration, at the dedication of the Soldiers' monument in Amherst, N.H., on the reunion of the Tenth regiment of N.H. veterans, June 19, 1890, with an appendix. Manchester, Printed by John B. Clarke, 1890. 47 p. front. (illus.). 22cm.   Nh    **36A**
Prefatory material signed: J. G. D. [Josiah G. Davis]
W. B. R. [William B. Roth]

## 11TH INFANTRY

*Mustered in: August 21 to September 10, 1862.*

*Mustered out: June 4, 1865.*

*Revised register 555–606. Historical sketch by Leander W. Cogswell.*

*N.H. in the great rebellion 446–61.*

Cogswell, Leander Winslow, 1825–
A history of the Eleventh New Hampshire regiment, volunteer infantry in the rebellion war, 1861–1865, covering its entire service, with interesting scenes of army life, and graphic details of battles, skirmishes, sieges, marches, and hardships, in which its officers and men participated, by Leander W. Cogswell, Company D. Concord, Republican Press Association, 1891. xi, 784, (1) p. plates (illus., fold. map, plan, ports.). 23cm.    DLC NN  **37**
"Addenda, errata," (1) p. Unit roster, unpaged, following p [672]

Currier, John Charles
From Concord to Fredericksburg, a paper prepared and read before California commandery of the Military order of the loyal legion of the United States, Feburary 12, 1896, by John Charles Currier, Capt. 11th New Hamp. 17 p. 22½cm.    DLC  **38**
On cover: War paper no. 15. . . .

Hadley, Amos
Life of Walter Harriman with selections from his speeches and writings, by Amos Hadley. Boston, Houghton, Mifflin and co., 1888. vii, 385 p. plates (1 illus., ports.). 23cm.
Civil war 107–216.    DLC MB  **39**

Morrill, James        –1892.
[Items copied from the diary of James Morrill, February 1, 1864 – July 3, 1865] In The early history of Wilmot, New Hampshire, by Casper L. LeVarn (1957) 125–31.    **40**

Nason, William A
With the Ninth army corps in East Tennessee, by First Sergeant W. A. Nason. 1891. 70 p. PNRISSHS s4 no 15.    **41**

Paige, Charles C
Story of the experiences of Lieut. Charles C. Paige in the Civil war of 1861–5, as told by himself. Franklin, Journal-Transcript press, 1911. 146 p. plates (illus., ports.). 22cm.
Portrait on front cover.    Nh  **42**

## 12TH INFANTRY

*Mustered in: August 28 to September 25, 1862.*

*Mustered out: June 21, 1865.*

*Revised register 607–49. Historical sketch by Asa W. Bartlett.*

*N.H. in the great rebellion 462–77.*

By-laws of the 12th regt. association adopted at Alton, Sept. 26, 1884. Bristol, Printed by

R. W. Musgrove, 1885. 5 p. leaf 14½ x 32cm. folded to 14½ x 11cm.    NhHi  **43**
Title from cover.

Bacheler, Albert William
Libby and how we got out of it, by Albert William Bacheler . . . Discovered in the Regimental history and reprinted for his classmates at Dartmouth college. Boston, Melvin O. Adams, 1916. 19 p. 23cm.    MnHi  **44**
Title from cover p [1]

Bartlett, Asa W        1839–
History of the Twelfth regiment New Hampshire volunteers in the War of the rebellion, by Capt. A. W. Bartlett, Historian Twelfth regiment association. Concord, Ira C. Evans, printer, 1897. x, 752, 87 p. front. (port.), plates (illus.), ports. 27cm.    DLC NN  **45**
Unit roster and "Summary," 87 p.

Haynes, Martin Alonzo, 1842–1919.
New Hampshire independence, an address delivered at the twentieth reunion, 12th N.H. vols., at Gilmanton I.W., Friday, September 25, 1885, by Martin A. Haynes. Printed for private circulation. 1885. 20 p. 21½cm.
        NhHi  **46**

Musgrove, Richard Watson, 1840–1914.
Autobiography of Captain Richard W. Musgrove. Published by Mary D. Musgrove. [Bristol] 1921. front. (port.), illus., port. 24cm.
        NN  **47**
Mustered in September 5, 1862; discharged, April 23, 1864, for promotion in 1st U. S. volunteers.

## 13TH INFANTRY

*Mustered in: September 12 to October 9, 1862.*

*Mustered out: June 21, 1865.*

*Revised register 650–92. Historical sketch by S. Millett Thompson.*

*N.H. in the great rebellion 478–96.*

Aaron Fletcher Stevens, August 9, 1819, May 10, 1887. [Nashua, 190–] 133 p. front. (port.). 24cm.    NhHi  **48**
"As a soldier," by R. B. Prescott, 11–73.

Bruce, George Anson, 1839–1929.
The battle of Fredericksburg, December 13, 1862, by Brevet Lieutenant-Colonel George A. Bruce. PMHSM ix 497–537.    **49**

—— The capture and occupation of Richmond. PMHSM xiv 119–45.    **50**

—— The Donelson campaign. PMHSM vii 1–29.    **51**

—— General Buell's campaign against Chattanooga. PMHSM viii 99–148.    **52**

*13th Infantry, continued*

—— General Butler's Bermuda campaign. *PMHSM* IX 301–46. **53**

—— Memorial address of Geo. A. Bruce, May 30, 1878. Somerville, Mass., Somerville Journal print, 1878. 12 p. CSmH **53A**
Caption title: Oration. "Contains as an incident of the war of 1861–65, one of the best descriptions of the burning of Richmond," Catalogue of the John P. Nicholson library, 1914.

—— Petersburg, June 15 – Fort Harrison, September 29: a comparison. *PMHSM* XIV 83–115. **54**

—— The strategy of the Civil war. *PMHSM* XIII 391–483. **54A**

Prescott, Royal B
The capture of Richmond, by Lieutenant R. B. Prescott. *MOLLUS-Mass* I 47–72. **55**

Thompson, S     Millett, 1838–
Thirteenth regiment of New Hampshire volunteer infantry in the War of the rebellion, 1861–1865, a diary covering three years and a day, by S. Millett Thompson, Lieutenant Thirteenth N.H. volunteers. Boston, Houghton, Mifflin and co., 1888. xi, 717 p. col. front. (illus.), 2 illus., maps, plans. 24cm.
DLC NN **56**
Unit roster 638–85. "Reunion of 1887," [686]–707.

## 14TH INFANTRY

*Mustered in: September 16 to October 16, 1862.*

*Mustered out: July 8, 1865.*

*Revised register 693–733. Historical sketch by Francis H. Buffum.*

*N.H. in the great rebellion 497–515.*

Buffum, Francis Henry, 1844–1927.
A memorial of the great rebellion, being a history of the Fourteenth regiment, New Hampshire volunteers, covering its three years of service, with original sketches of army life, 1862–1865. Issued by the Committee of publication. Boston, Franklin press, 1882. xii, 423 p. plates (illus., plans, ports.). 23½cm.
Original roster 379–402. DLC NN **57**
"The author kept a diary throughout the service of the Regiment. This diary was the nucleus of the Regimental history which Buffum wrote while Military editor of the Boston herald," information supplied to the compilor by Francis A. Lord, grandson of Buffum.

—— Sheridan's veterans, a souvenir of their two campaigns in the Shenandoah valley, the one, of war, in 1864, the other, of peace, in 1883. Being the record of the excursion to the battle-fields of the valley of Virginia, September 15–24, 1883. By one of the veterans. Bos-

ton [W. F. Brown & co., printers] 1883. vi, [9]–128 p. plates (illus., ports.). 21½cm.
"Prefatory note" signed: F. H. B. NHi **58**

—— Sheridan's veterans, no. II, a souvenir of their third campaign in the Shenandoah valley, 1864–1883–1885, September 15–24, 1885, by F. H. Buffum. Boston [W. F. Brown & co., printers] 1886. iv, [5]–128 p. 2 plates (illus.). 22½cm. NB NHi **59**

Gerould, Samuel Lankton, 1834–1906.
Roll call Company G, Fourteenth New Hampshire volunteers, June 1, 1894. [Hollis, 1894] 8 p. 22½cm. Nh **60**
Caption title. Text signed: Samuel L. Gerould, Company Secretary.

—— Roll-call number 2 Company G, Fourteenth N.H. volunteers, compiled by Samuel L. Gerould, Secretary, June 1, 1901. [Lebanon, Press of H. E. Waite & co., 1901] 18 p. 22½cm.
Nh **61**

Hadley, Elbridge Drew, 1842–1923.
The battle of Cedar creek, popular history refuted, by Captain E. D. Hadley. *MOLLUS-Iowa* II 441–77. **62**

—— Vindication of the Army of West Virginia (or Eighth corps), at the battle of Cedar creek, Oct. 19, 1864. *Granite monthly* XXVII (Concord 1899) 280–6. **63**
"This compilation of authorities and argument thereon is furnished by E. D. Hadley."

—— A young soldier's career. *Annals of Iowa* s3 XIII (Des Moines 1922) 323–61. 2 ports. **64**

## 15TH INFANTRY

*Mustered in: October 4 to November 12, 1862.*

*Mustered out: August 13, 1863.*

*Revised register 734–61. Historical sketch by Charles McGregor.*

*N.H. in the great rebellion 516–27.*

McGregor, Charles
History of the Fifteenth regiment New Hampshire volunteers, 1862–1863, by Charles McGregor. Published by order of the Fifteenth regiment association. [Concord, Printed by Ira C. Evans] 1900. xiv, 624 p. illus., ports., plates (illus., ports.). 24cm. DLC NN **65**
"Roll and preliminary sketch of Company A [-K] 40–109; "The field and staff," 114–33.

## 16TH INFANTRY

*Mustered in: October 10 to December 2, 1862.*

*Mustered out: August 20, 1863.*

*Revised register 762–90. Historical sketch by Daniel E. Howard.*

*N.H. in the great rebellion 528–34.*

Johnson, Henry L

Souvenir roster, 1895, of the 371 living members of the Sixteenth regiment New Hampshire volunteers, thirty-three years after enlistment. [Washington, D. C., John F. Sheiry, printer, 1895] 39 p. 1 illus., ports. 15 × 23½cm.

"Preface" signed: Henry L. Johnson.  NN  **66**

Townsend, Luther Tracy, 1838–1922.

History of the Sixteenth regiment, New Hampshire volunteers, by Adjutant Luther Tracy Townsend. Published by Henry L. Johnson and Luther T. Townsend. Washington, D. C., Norman T. Elliott, 1897. 574 p. illus., plans, ports. 23½cm.          DLC NN  **67**

Unit roster [331]–561. First published in the *Granite monthly* xxii–xxiii (Concord 1897).

## 17TH INFANTRY

*Mustered in: November 13, 1862 to January 10, 1863. Organization was not completed and the men were transferred to the 2nd infantry April 16, 1863.*

*Revised register 791–800. Historical sketch by Henry O. Kent.*

*N.H. in the great rebellion 535–7.*

Kent, Charles Nelson, 1843–1906.

History of the Seventeenth regiment, New Hampshire volunteer infantry, 1862–1863, by Lieut. Charles N. Kent . . . Published by order of the Seventeenth New Hampshire veteran association. Concord [Rumford press] 1898. 325 p. ports., plates (illus., ports.). 23½cm.          DLC NN  **68**

Partial contents: The music and songs of the war, by John C. Linehan, 184–212; Regimental histories and their relation to the annals of the state [with bibliography] 213–60; Roster of the Seventeenth New Hampshire infantry including only men in camp during winter of 1862–'63, and not including the nearly seven hundred from the Third district transferred to the Fifteenth and Sixteenth infantry, 267–93.

## 18TH INFANTRY

*Mustered in: September 18, 1864 to April 6, 1865.*

*Mustered out: June 10, July 29, 1865.*

*Revised register 801–28. Historical sketch by Thomas L. Livermore.*

*N.H. in the great rebellion 538–44.*

Chadwick, Hale, 1841–

Sketch of "ours" and reminiscences, by comrade Hale Chadwick, Co. B, 18th regiment, N.H. volunteers. Penacook [1910] 23 p. 2 ports. 20½cm.          NhHi  **69**

Mustered in 17th New Hampshire infantry, December 29, 1862; mustered out, April 16, 1863; mustered in 18th New Hampshire infantry, September 13, 1864; mustered out, June 10, 1865.

Livermore, Thomas Leonard, 1844–1918.*

The Appomattox campaign, an examination of the question whether a captured letter of General Lee's disclosed his plan of retreat to General Grant. *Proceedings of the Massachusetts historical society* s2 xx (1907) 87–112.          **70**

—— Days and events, 1860–1866, by Thomas L. Livermore, late Colonel of the 18th New Hampshire volunteers. Boston, Houghton Mifflin co., 1920. x, 485 p. front. (port.). 23cm.          NN  **71**

Coulter 294. "Introduction" signed: Henry M. Rogers. "Author's note" dated: March 31, 1867.

—— The failure to take Petersburg, June 15, 1864. *PMHSM* v 33–73.          **72**

—— The generalship of the Appomattox campaign. *PMHSM* vi 449–506.          **73**

—— The Gettysburg campaign. *PMHSM* xiii 485–542.          **74**

—— Grant's campaign against Lee. *PMHSM* iv 407–59.          **75**

—— History of the Eighteenth New Hampshire volunteers, 1864–5, by Thomas L. Livermore. Boston, Fort Hill press, 1904. 124 p. plates (illus., ports.). 24cm.          DLC NN  **76**

Unit roster 80–120.

—— The Mine run campaign, November, 1863. *PMHSM* xiv 43–54.          **77**

—— The Northern volunteers. *Granite monthly* x (Concord 1887) 239–47, 257–66.

Also published in *JMSIUS* xii (1891) 905–37.  **78**

—— The numbers in the Confederate army, 1861–1865. *PMHSM* xiii 315–43.          **79**

—— The siege and relief of Chattanooga. *PMHSM* viii 273–339.          **80**

See also Title 34.

### Martin Guards

*Mustered in: July 25, 1864.*

*Mustered out: September 16, 1864.*

*Revised register 995–7.*

### Strafford Guards

*Mustered in: April 24, 1864.*

*Mustered out: July 28, 1864.*

*Revised register 989–91.*

---

* As Livermore was appointed Colonel of the 18th New Hampshire on January 17, 1865, most of his service was with the 5th New Hampshire.

# RHODE ISLAND

# Reference Works

Dyer, Frederick Henry, 1849–1917.

A compendium of the War of the rebellion, 1908 (reprinted 1959).

"Regimental index" 228–30; "Regimental histories" 1627–36. The pagination is the same in the 1959 reprint.


Rhode Island. Adjutant General.

Annual report of the Adjutant general of the State of Rhode Island and Providence plantations for the year 1865. Corrected, revised, and republished in accordance with provisions of Chapters 705 and 767 of the Public laws, by Brigadier-General Elisha Dyer, Adjutant general. Providence, E. L. Freeman & Sons, printers to the State, 1893–95. 2 v. 25½ cm.

Added title: Official register of Rhode Island officers and men who served in the United States army and navy, from 1861 to 1866. Contents: v. I, Infantry regiments; v. II, Cavalry and artillery regiments. The routine Report is omitted from this revised edition.

Herein cited as *AG's report.*


*The Union army.*

"Record of Rhode Island regiments," I (1908) 244–257.


United States. Adjutant General's Office.

Official army register of the volunteer force of the United States army for the years 1861, '62, '63, '64, '65. Part I. (New England states). Washington, 1865.

A roster of officer's by regiments with an alphabetical index for the six states.

# RHODE ISLAND

## ARTILLERY

### 3RD ARTILLERY (HEAVY)

*Organized as an infantry regiment: August 1861.*

*Designated 3rd regiment of heavy artillery: December 19, 1861.*

*Mustered out: August 27, 1865.*

*AG's report II 319–485. The historical sketch by Edwin M. Stone, 1865, revised by George M. Turner.*

Roster of commissioned officers Third regiment Rhode Island heavy artillery, from date of organization to August 31, 1864. Port Royal, S.C., New South office, 1864. [6] p. 20cm.
RHi RP **1**

Third regiment Rhode Island heavy artillery veteran association, organized, August 28, 1872. [Providence, Snow & Farnham, printers, 189–] 41, (7) p. 14½cm.          NHi **2**

Denison, Frederic, 1819–1901.
Army hymns, written for the Third regiment R.I. heavy artillery, by their Chaplain, Rev. F. Denison. . . . Providence, A. Crawford Greene, 1863. 16 p. 9½cm.          RHi **3**
Dated: Jan., 1863. Title and imprint from cover.

—— Shot and shell, the Third Rhode Island heavy artillery regiment in the rebellion, 1861–1865; camps, forts, batteries, garrisons, marches, skirmishes, sieges, battles, and victories. Also, the roll of honor and roll of the Regiment. By Rev. Frederic Denison, Chaplain. Published for the Third R.I.H. art. vet. association. Providence, J. A. & R. A. Reid, 1879. front. (port.), illus., maps, plates (3 illus., 2 col.; map). 23cm.          DLC NN **4**
Unit roster [336]–62.

Egan, Patrick, 1846–1912.
The Florida campaign with Light battery C. 1905. 25 p. *PNRISSHS* s6 no 10. 2 front. (ports.).          **5**

Irwin, David
Chief [Patrick] Egan's war record, written for the archives. *Journal of the American Irish historical society* VIII (Providence 1909) 177–82.          **6**

James, Martin S
War reminiscences, by Martin S. James, late Captain Light battery C. 1911. 38 p. *PNRISSHS* s7 no 4. front. (port.).          **7**

Metcalf, Edwin, 1848–1915.
Personal incidents in the early campaigns of the Third regiment Rhode Island volunteers and the Tenth army corps, by Edwin Metcalf, late Colonel Third regiment. 1879. 31 p. *PNRISSHS* s1 no 9          **8**

Stone, Edward Martin, 1805–1883.
Extract from the history of the Third regiment R.I. heavy artillery, published in the Adjutant general's report of the State of Rhode Island, (reprint of 1865), 1893. Printed by the Third Rhode Island veteran association for its members. Providence, E. L. Freeman & Son, printers, 1894. 23 p. 23½cm.          DHL RHi **9**

Williams, Alonzo, 1842–1901.
The investment of Fort Pulaski, by Alonzo Williams, late Second Lieutenant. 1887. 59 p. *PNRISSHS* s3 no 20.          **10**

Williams, Charles H
The last tour of duty at the siege of Charleston, by Charles H. Williams, formerly Second Lieutenant. 1882. 29 p. *PNRISSHS* s2 no 16.          **11**

### 5TH ARTILLERY (HEAVY)

*Mustered in as a regiment of infantry: December 16, 1861.*

*Designated 5th regiment of heavy artillery: May 27, 1863.*

*Mustered out: June 26, 1885.*

*AG's report II 487–586. The historical sketch by Edwin M. Stone, 1865, revised by William H. Chenery.*

Barney, Caleb Henry
A country boy's first three months in the army, by C. Henry Barney, formerly Corporal. 1880. 47 p. *PNRISSHS* s2 no 2.          **12**

Burlingame, John K
History of the Fifth regiment of Rhode Island heavy artillery during three years and a half of service in North Carolina, January 1862 – June 1865, compiled under the supervision of John K. Burlingame. Providence, Snow & Farnham, printers. xv, 382 p. illus., ports, plates (4 maps, 2 fold.; 3 ports.). 23½cm.          DLC NN **13**
Unit roster [261]–338.

Chenery, William H
Reminiscences of the Burnside expedition, by William H. Chenery, late Sergeant Company D. 1905. 48 p. *PNRISSHS* s7 no 1. front. (port.).          **14**

5th Artillery (Heavy), continued

Douglas, William Wilberforce, 1841–1929.
Relief of Washington, North Carolina, by
the Fifth Rhode Island volunteers, by William
W. Douglas, late Captain. 1886. 28 p. *PNRIS-
SHS* s3 no 17.                                    **15**

Hopkins, George C
Battle of Newbern as I saw it, a paper read
by Brevet Major George G. Hopkins. *MOL-
LUS-NY* iii 138–47.                               **16**

## 14TH HEAVY ARTILLERY (COLORED)

*Organized: August 1863 to January 1864.*

*Designated 8th regiment U.S. colored
heavy artillery: April 4, 1864.*

*Designated 11th regiment U.S. colored
heavy artillery: May 21, 1864.*

*Mustered out: October 2, 1865.*

*AG's report ii 587–705. The historical
sketch by Edwin M. Stone, 1865, revised
by William H. Chenery.*

Addeman, Joshua Melancthon, 1840–
Reminiscences of two years with the colored
troops, by J. M. Addeman, late Captain. 1880.
38 p. *PNRISSHS* s2 no 7.                        **17**

Chenery, William H
The Fourteenth regiment Rhode Island
heavy artillery (colored) in the War to pre-
serve the Union, 1861–1865, by William H.
Chenery, late First Lieutenant, Company F.
Providence, Snow & Farnham, printers, 1898.
viii, 343 p. plates (ports.). 23½cm.
Unit roster [151]–266.            DLC NN     **18**

## 1ST ARTILLERY (LIGHT)

### Battery A

*Mustered in: June 6, 1861.*

*Transferred to Battery B, 1st regiment of
light artillery: September 23, 1864.*

*AG's report ii 741–60. The historical
sketch by Edwin M. Stone, 1865, revised
by Theodore Reichardt.*

Aldrich, Thomas M
The history of Battery A, First regiment
Rhode Island light artillery in the War to pre-
serve the Union, 1861–1865, by Thomas M.
Aldrich. Providence, Snow & Farnham, printers,
1904. vii, 408 p. plates (2 illus., ports.). 24cm.
Unit roster [389]–403.            DLC NN     **19**

Child, Benjamin H
From Fredericksburg to Gettysburg, by Ben-
jamin H. Child, late Sergeant. 1895. 36 p.
*PNRISSHS* s5 no 4                                **20**

## Rhode Island Artillery Batteries

Peck, George Bacheler, 1843–1934.
Historical address delivered at the dedica-
tion of the memorial tablet on the arsenal,
Benefit street, corner of Meeting, Providence,
R.I., Thursday, July 19, 1917 [by] George B.
Peck. [Providence, Rhode Island print. co.,
1917] 17, (1) p. plate (illus.). 20cm.
                                  DLC RHi     **21**
On cover: Historical address Rhode Island light
artillery, 1801–1874, in the Civil and Spanish wars.

Reichardt, Theodore
Diary of Battery A. First regiment, Rhode
Island light artillery, by Theodore Reichardt.
Written in the field. Providence, N. Bangs
Williams, 1865. v, [6]–153 p. 19½cm.
Unit roster [145]–53.             DLC RP     **22**

### Battery B

*Mustered in: August 13, 1861.*

*Mustered out: June 13, 1865.*

*AG's report ii 761–90. The historical
sketch by Edwin M. Stone, 1865, revised
by John H. Rhodes.*

Battery B, First R.I. light artillery, August 13,
1861 — June 12, 1865 [roster of surviving
members] [Central Falls, E. L. Freeman co.,
1907] 32 p. illus., ports. 25cm.      RHi     **23**
Preface signed: Charles Tillinghast Straight. Title
from cover.

Soldiers' home bazaar. History of the Gettysburg gun. Battery "B," Rhode Island light artillery. [187–] [4] p. 22cm.             NHi     **24**
Caption title.

Rhodes, John H
The Gettysburg gun, by John H. Rhodes,
late Sergeant. 1892. 57 p. *PNRISSHS* s4 no 19.
front. (illus.).                                 **25**

—— The history of Battery B. First regiment
Rhode Island light artillery in the War to preserve the Union, 1861–1865, by John H.
Rhodes. Providence, Snow & Farnham, printers,
1894. xi, 406, (1) p. 2 illus., map, ports.,
plates (maps, 1. fold.; ports.). 23½cm.
                                  DLC NN     **26**
Unit roster 351–75. "Errata," (1) p.

### Battery C

*Mustered in: August 25, 1861.*

*Transferred to Battery G, 1st regiment of
light artillery: December 23, 1864.*

*AG's report ii 791–814. The historical
sketch by Edwin M. Stone, 1865, revised
by John B. Peck.*

## Battery D

Mustered in: September 4, 1861.
Mustered out: July 17, 1865.
AG's report II 815–41. The historical
sketch by Edwin M. Stone, 1865, revised
by George C. Sumner.

John Albert Monroe, a memorial. Recollections
of him as Commander of Battery D, by G. C.
Sumner. A biographical sketch, by George B.
Peck. A eulogy, by Edward P. Tobie. 1892.
50 p. PNRISSHS s4 no 18. front. (port.).    27

Monroe, John Albert, 1836–1891.
Battery D, First Rhode Island light artillery
at the battle of Antietam, September 17, 1862.
1886. 45 p. PNRISSHS s3 no 16. 1 illus.    28

—— Battery D, First Rhode Island light artillery at the second battle of Bull run. 1890.
33 p. PNRISSHS s4 no 10.                    29

—— Reminiscences of the War of the rebellion of 1861–5, by J. Albert Monroe, late Lieutenant-Colonel. 1881. 78 p. PNRISSHS s2 no
11.                                         30

—— The Rhode Island artillery at the first
battle of Bull run. 1878. 31 p. PNRISSHS s1
no 2.                                       31

Parker, Ezra Knight, 1832–
Campaign of Battery D, First Rhode Island
light artillery in Kentucky and East Tennessee,
by Ezra K. Parker, late First Lieutenant. 1913.
48, (1) p. PNRISSHS s7 no 6.                32

Sumner, George C
Battery D, First Rhode Island light artillery,
in the Civil war, 1861–1865, by Dr. George C.
Sumner, a member of the Battery. Providence,
Rhode Island print. co., 1897. 192 p. 2 plates
(illus., port.). 21½cm.         DLC NN    33
Unit roster [157]–92.

—— Recollections of service in Battery D,
First Rhode Island light artillery. 1891. 52 p.
PNRISSHS s4 no 11.                          34

## Battery E

Left for Washington: October 5, 1861.
Mustered out: June 11, 1865.
AG's report II 842–71. The historical
sketch by Edwin M. Stone, 1865, revised
by George Lewis.

Bucklyn, John Knight, 1834–
Battle of Cedar creek, October 19, 1864, by
John K. Bucklyn, late Captain. 1883. 24 p.
PNRISSHS s2 no 19.                          35

Butts, Francis Banister
The organization and first campaign of Battery E, First Rhode Island light artillery, by

Francis B. Banister, late Corporal. 1896. 85 p.
PNRISSHS s5 no 6. front (port.).            36

Lewis, George, 1831–
The history of Battery E, First regiment
Rhode Island light artillery, in the War of 1861
and 1865 to preserve the Union, by George
Lewis. Providence, Snow & Farnham, printers,
1892. xi, 540 p. plates (1 illus., fold. map,
ports.). 23½cm.                DLC NN      37
Unit roster [483]–529.

Parker, Ezra Knight, 1832–
From the Rapidan to the James under Grant,
by Ezra K. Parker, late First Lieutenant. 1909.
38 p. PNRISSHS s7 no 2. front. (port.).    38

## Battery F

Left for Washington: October 28–29, 1861.

Mustered out: June 27, 1865.

AG's report II 872–99. The historical
sketch by Edwin M. Stone, 1865, revised
by Philip S. Chase.

Chase, Philip Stephen, 1843–1918.
Battery F, First regiment Rhode Island light
artillery, in the Civil war, 1861–1865, by Philip
S. Chase, late Second Lieutenant. Providence,
Snow & Farnham, printers, 1892. viii, 332 p.
2 illus., 6 maps (5 fold.), ports. 20cm.
                                DLC RP     39
Unit roster [249]–86. "Appendix. My four months'
experience as a prisoner of war, by Captain Thomas
Simpson," [287]–312; "A summer in Southern prisons,
an account of the experiences of Private Charles C.
Vars," [313]–19.

—— Organization and service of Battery F,
First Rhode Island light artillery, to January
1st, 1863. 1880. 48 p. PNRISSHS s2 no 3.   40

—— Service with Battery F, First Rhode Island light artillery. 1884. 31 p. PNRISSHS s3
no 7.                                       41

—— —— 1889. 41 p. PNRISSHS s4 no 3.    42

Simpson, Thomas
My four month's experience as a prisoner of
war, by Thomas Simpson, late Captain. 1883.
40 p. PNRISSHS s3 no 2.                     43

## Battery G

Left for Washington: December 2, 1861.

Mustered out: June 24, 1865.

AG's report II 900–27. The historical
sketch by Edwin M. Stone, 1865, revised
by Edward P. Adams.

*Battery H*

Left for Washington: October 23, 1862.
Mustered out: June 28, 1865.
AG's report II 928–52. The historical
sketch by Edwin M. Stone, 1865, revised
by Earl Fenner.

Fenner, Earl, 1841–
The history of Battery H, First regiment
Rhode Island light artillery in the War to pre-
serve the Union, by Earl Fenner. Providence,
Snow & Farnham, printers, 1894. vii, 216 p.
map, plates (ports.). 23½cm.   DLC NN   **44**
Unit roster [157]–92. Errata slip inserted.

Noyes, Isaac Pitman, 1840–
Battery H and the Light brigade compared.
Published by the author because of his inability
to otherwise reach the public. [1906] 5 p.
22cm.                                 DLC   **45**
Text signed: Isaac P. Noyes, No. 3 on 3d piece.

## INDEPENDENT BATTERIES
## LIGHT ARTILLERY

*1st Battery*

Organized: April 1861.
Mustered out: August 6, 1861.
AG's report II 707–18. The historical
sketch by Edwin M. Stone, 1865, revised
by Augustus Woodbury.

*10th Battery*

Organized: May 1862.
Mustered out: August 30, 1862.
AG's report II 719–29. The historical
sketch by Edwin M. Stone, 1865, revised
by Samuel A. Pearce.

Spicer, William Arnold, 1845–1913.
History of the Ninth and Tenth regiments
Rhode Island volunteers, and the Tenth Rhode
Island battery, in the Union army in 1862.
Providence, Snow & Farnham, printers, 1892.
415 p. illus., maps, music, ports. 22½cm.
                                      DLC NN   **46**
Unit rosters: 9th R. I., [361]–84; 10th R. I., [385]–
409; Tenth light battery (Company L), [410]–13.
"The end — at last," the author's statement on the
writing of the volume signed William Arnold Spicer,
Company B., Tenth R. I. vols. Author's name on
cover and in half-title.

—— —— A letter from Chaplain Clapp . . .
printed in this separate form to accompany the
book. [Providence, 1893?] [4] p. 22½cm.
                                              **46A**
Caption title. Dated: New York, December 15,
1893.

## CAVALRY

### 1ST CAVALRY

Organized as 1st New England cavalry:
December 14, 1861 to March 3, 1862.
Designated 1st Rhode Island cavalry:
March 31, 1862.
New Hampshire companies, I, K, L and M,
returned to their State, January 7, 1864.
Mustered out: August 3, 1865.
AG's report II 1–58. The historical sketch
by Edwin M. Stone, 1865, revised by
George N. Bliss.

Constitution of the First Rhode Island cavalry
veteran association, with roll and post office
address of regimental comrades; also, roll of
membership, both active and honorary. Providence, E. L. Freeman & Son, 1886. 29, (1) p.
14½cm.                                RHi   **47**

—— —— Providence, E. L. Freeman & Son,
1894. 48 p. 14½cm.                    RHi   **48**

Bliss, George Newman, 1837–1928.
The cavalry affairs at Waynesboro, letter
from Captain George Bliss. Southern historical
society papers XIII (Richmond 1885) 427–30.
                                              **49**

—— Cavalry service with General Sheridan,
and life in Libby prison. 1884. 103 p. PNRIS-
SHS s3 no 6. front. (port.).            **50**

—— Duffié and the monument to his memory, by George N. Bliss, late Captain, Company K, First Rhode Island cavalry. Providence
[Snow & Farnham, printers] 1890. 64 p. 2
plates (illus., port.). 20½cm.        RHi   **51**
Originally published as PNRISSHS s4 no 8.

—— The First Rhode Island cavalry at Middleburg, Va., June 17 and 18, 1863. 1889. 56 p.
PNRISSHS s4 no 4.                       **52**

—— How I lost my sabre in war and found it
in peace. 1903. 71 p. PNRISSHS s6 no 2. plates
(1 illus., ports.).                     **53**

—— Prison life of Lieut. James M. Fales.
1882. 70 p. PNRISSHS s2 no 15.          **54**

—— Reminiscences of service in the First
Rhode Island cavalry. 1878. 32 p. PNRISSHS
s1 no 3.                                **55**

—— A review of Aldie. Maine bugle campaign
I (Rockland 1894) 123–32.               **56**

—— —— A rebuttal to Captain Bliss' review
of Aldie, by Major Henry C. Hall. Maine bugle
campaign I (Rockland 1894) 256–62.      **57**

Cooke, Jacob B
The battle of Kelly's ford, March 17, 1863, by Jacob B. Cooke, late First Lieutenant. 1887. 38 p. *PNRISSHS* s3 no 19.             **58**

Denison, Frederic, 1819–1901.
The battle of Cedar mountain, a personal view, August 9, 1862. 1881. 45 p. *PNRISSHS* s2 no 10.             **59**

—— The battle of Groveton, August 28, 1862. 1885. 35 p. *PNRISSHS* s3 no 9.             **60**

—— A Chaplain's experience in the Union army. 1893. 45 p. *PNRISSHS* s4 no 20.     **61**

—— Sabres and spurs, the First regiment Rhode Island cavalry in the Civil war, 1861–1865, its origin, marches, scouts, skirmishes, raids, battles, sufferings, victories, and appropriate official papers, with the roll of honor and roll of the Regiment, by Rev. Frederic Denison, Chaplain. Published by the First Rhode Island cavalry veteran association. [Central Falls, Press of E. L. Freeman & co.] 1876. 600 p. 4 plates (1 col. illus., fold. map, 6 ports.). 20cm.             NN  **62**
Unit roster 478–597.

Gardiner, William
Incidents of cavalry experiences during General Pope's campaign, by William Gardiner, late Sergeant. 1883. 36 p. *PNRISSHS* s2 no 20.             **63**

—— Operations of the cavalry corps, Middle military division, Armies of the United States, from February 27 to March 8, 1865, participated in by the First Rhode Island cavalry. 1896. 31 p. *PNRISSHS* s5 no 5.     **64**

Green, Charles O
An incident in the battle of Middleburg, Va., June 17, 1863, by Charles O. Green. 1911. 38 p. *PNRISSHS* s7 no 3. 3 plates (map, 2 ports.).             **65**

Leeds, Samuel Penniman, 1824–1910.
Address at the funeral of Capt. Lorenzo D. Gove, slain by Rebels in Virginia, delivered in the Congregational church at Dartmouth college, by S. P. Leeds. Hannover, Printed at the Dartmouth press, 1863. 12 p. 22cm.
                    WHi  **66**

Meyer, William E          1843–
The sailor on horseback, by William E. Meyer, late Corporal. 1912. 71 p. *PNRISSHS* s7 no 5. 2 plates (ports.).             **67**

Stevens, Leverett C
A forlorn hope, by Leverett C. Stevens, late Corporal. 1903. 44 p. *PNRISSHS* s6 no 1.  **68**

## 2ND CAVALRY

*Organized: November 21, 1862.*

*Transferred to 1st Louisiana cavalry: August 24, 1863.*

*Transferred to 3rd Rhode Island cavalry: January 14, 1864.*

*AG's report* ii 159–220. *The historical sketch by Edwin M. Stone, 1865, revised by Augustus W. Corliss.*

Sabre, Gilbert E
Nineteen months a prisoner of war, narrative of Lieutenant G. E. Sabre, Second Rhode Island cavalry, of his experience in the war prisons and stockades of Morton, Mobile, Atlanta, Libby, Belle Island, Andersonville, Macon, Charleston, and Columbia, and his escape to the Union lines. To which is appended, a list of officers confined at Columbia, during the winter of 1864 and 1865. New York, American News co., 1865. 207 p. 2 plates (illus.). 18½cm.             DLC NHi  **69**
Coulter 404.

## 3RD CAVALRY

*Organized: September 12, 1863.*

*Mustered out: November 29, 1865.*

*AG's report* ii 221–305. *The historical sketch by Edwin M. Stone, 1865, was not revised.*

Parkhurst, Charles H
Incidents of cavalry service in Louisiana, by Charles H. Parkhurst, late Lieutenant-Colonel. 1879. 25 p. *PNRISSHS* s1 no 7.             **70**

Scott, Livingston, 1839–1909.
A soldier writes to his Congressman, by Frank F. White, Jr. *Rhode Island history* xviii (1959) 97–114; xix (1960) 13–25.     **71**
Mustered in 10th Rhode Island infantry, May 26, 1862; mustered out, September 1, 1862, mustered in 3rd Rhode Island cavalry, August 24, 1863; mustered out, November 29, 1864.

## 7TH SQUADRON OF CAVALRY

*Mustered in: June 24, 1862.*

*Mustered out: September 26, 1862.*

*AG's report* ii 305–17. *The historical sketch by Edwin M. Stone, 1865, revised by Augustus W. Corliss.*

Alvord, Henry Elijah, 1844–1904.
A New England boy in the Civil war. Edited by Caroline B. Sherman. *New England quarterly* v (1932) 310–44.     **72**

Corliss, Augustus Whittemore, 1837–1908.
History of the Seventh squadron, Rhode Island cavalry, by a member. 1862. Yarmouth,

*7th Squadron of Cavalry, continued*

Me., "Old Times" office, 1879. 11 p. port.
24cm.                              DLC NHi NN    73
"From Adjutant-general's report, 1865." Unit
roster 3–8. "Notes from the diary of First-Sergeant
Henry E. Alvord...," 8–11. Title from cover.

Heysinger, Isaac Winter, 1842–1917.
   Antietam and the Maryland and Virginia
campaigns of 1862, from the government records, Union and Confederate, mostly unknown
and which now first disclosed the truth. Approved by the War department. By Captain
Isaac W. Heysinger. New York, Neale pub. co.,
1912. 322 p. 19cm.                   NN    73A
—— The cavalry column from Harper's ferry
in the Antietam campaign. *JUSCA* xxiv (1914)
587–638. 1 illus., 2 maps.                        74

Nichols, William H
   The siege and capture of Harper's ferry, by
the Confederates, September 1862, by William H. Nichols, 3d, late Corporal. 1889. 48 p.
*PNRISSHS* s4 no 2                                 75

Pettengill, Samuel B
   The college cavaliers, a sketch of the service
of a company of college students in the Union
army in 1862, by S. B. Pettengill. Chicago,
H. McAllaster & co., printers, 1883. 94, (1) p.
front. (port.). 19cm.              DLC NN    76
"Appendix. Roster Troop B, Seventh Squadron
R. I. cavalry," (1) p.

Scales, John
   The Dartmouth cavalry. *Granite monthly* iv
(Concord 1881) 463–6.                             77

## INFANTRY

## 1ST INFANTRY

*Organized: April 1861.*

*Mustered out: August 2, 1861.*

*AG's report i 1–63. The historical sketch
by Edwin M. Stone, 1865, revised by Augustus Woodbury.*

Clarke, Charles H
   History of Company F, 1st regiment, R.I.
volunteers, during the spring and summer of
1861, by Charles H. Clarke. Newport, B. W.
Pearce, printer, 1891. 76 p. 15cm.   NN    78
Unit roster 8–10.

Poore, Benjamin Perley, 1820–1887.
   The life and public services of Ambrose E.
Burnside, soldier, citizen, statesman, by Ben.
Perley Poore, with an introduction by Henry
B. Anthony. Providence, J. A. & R. A. Reid,
1882. illus., maps, ports., plates (ports.). 23cm.
                                   DLC NN    79

Partial contents: Organization of the First Rhode
Island regiment; Presentation of a flag; Journey to
Washington; Barrack and camp life..., 92–102.

Severin, John and Frederick Porter Todd
   1st regiment of Rhode Island detached militia, 1861. *Military collector & historian* vii
(Washington 1955) 49–50. col. plate (illus.).
                                                   80

Sholes, Albert E
   Personal reminiscences of Bull run, read at
the thirty-eighth annual reunion of the First
R.I. regiment and First battery association, at
Lakewood, R.I., Thursday, July 21, 1910, by
Albert E. Sholes. [Flushing, N.Y.?, 1910] 8 p.
28cm.                              RP    81

Smith, George B
   Formation and service of the First regiment
Rhode Island detached militia, April 17th –
Aug. 2nd, 1861. *Bulletin of the Newport his-
torical society* no 58 (1926) 14–29.            82

Stone, Edwin Martin, 1805–1883.
   First regiment Rhode Island detached militia. [Providence, Providence press co., 1866]
96 p. 27cm.                        RP    83
Caption title. Reprinted from the Annual report of
the Adjutant general...1865.

Woodbury, Augustus, 1825–1895.
   Ambrose Everett Burnside. 1882. 97 p. *PN-
RISSHS* s2 no 17.                                 84

—— The memory of the first battle, a discourse preached in Westminster church, Providence, R.I., on the 28th anniversary of Bull run,
July 21, 1889, before the Veteran association
of the First and Second Rhode Island regiments and their batteries, by Augustus Woodbury, Chaplain of the First Rhode Island regiment of detached militia. Providence, E. L.
Freeman & Son, 1889. 34 p. front. (port.).
22½cm.                             RHi RP    85
On cover: Chaplain Woodbury's anniversary sermon, July 21, 1889, with Appendix. The following
extracts from the Reports of the Secretary of the Veteran association of the First regiment and First battery
R.I. detached militia, Geo. Edward Allen, for the
years 1884 and 1889, show the number and position
of those members of the First regiment and First battery who re-enlisted, and of those who received commissions in other regiments, batteries and staff appoint-
ments ... ," p 27–34.

—— A narrative of the campaign of the First
Rhode Island regiment in the Spring and Summer of 1861, by Augustus Woodbury, Chaplain
of the Regiment. Providence, Sidney S. Rider,
1862. 260 p. front. (port.), plate (map).
19½cm.                             DLC NN    86
Unit roster [169]–223. "Occupations of the members of the Regiment" by companies, 225–30. Coulter
484.

Wyman, Mrs. Lillie Buffum (Chace), 1847–1929.
A Grand army man [Augustine A. Mann] of Rhode Island, by Lillie Buffum Chace Wyman. Newton, Graphic press, 1925. xiii, [15]–33 p. plates (ports.). 21cm.　　　DLC NN　87

## 2ND INFANTRY

*Left for Washington: June 19, 1861.*

*Mustered out: July 13, 1865.*

*AG's report* i 65–229. *The historical sketch by Edwin M. Stone, 1865, revised by Horatio Rogers and Elisha H. Rhodes.*

The campaign life of Lt.-Col. Henry Harrison Young, Aide-de-camp to General Sheridan and Chief of his scouts. Providence, Sidney S. Rider, 1882. 66 p. front. (port.). 18½cm.
　　　　　　　　　　　　　　MB NB　88

Colonel Henry H. Young in the Civil war. Sheridan's chief of scouts, a noted Rhode Island fighter. Providence, E. A. Johnson & co., 1910. 55 p. front. (port.), 2 illus. 23½cm.
　　　　　　　　　　　　　　R NN　89
Contents: Foreword, by William A. Spicer, 5–10; A brave Rhode Island fighter, Col. Henry Young, by Col. Joseph P. Manton, 11–16; War memories, by Gen. Oliver Edwards, 17–26; Young, by William Gilmore, 27–54.

Ames, William, 1842–1914.
Civil war letters of William Ames, from Brown university to Bull run. Edited by William Greene Roelker. *Rhode Island historical society collections* xxxiii (1940) 73–92; xxxiv (1941) 5–24. 2 plans.　　　90

Caldwell, Samuel Lunt, 1820–1887.
A sermon preached in the First Baptist meeting-house, Providence, Sunday morning, June 9, 1861, before the Second regiment of Rhode Island volunteers, by Samuel L. Caldwell. Providence, Knowles, Anthony & co., printers, 1861. 12 p. 23½cm.　　　DLC　91

Crossley, William J
Extracts from my diary, and from my experiences, while boarding with Jefferson Davis, in three of his notorious hotels, in Richmond, Va., Tuscaloosa, Ala., and Salisbury, N.C., from July, 1861, to June, 1862, by William J. Crossley, late Sergeant, 1903. 49 p. *PNRISSHS* s6 no 4.　　　92

Grand Army of the Republic. Department of Rhode Island. Slocum Post, No. 10.
Memorial of Colonel John Stanton Slocum, First Colonel of the Second Rhode Island volunteers, who fell in the battle of Bull run, Virginia, July 21, 1861. Prepared and published by Slocum post, no. 10, Department of Rhode

Island, G.A.R. Providence, J. A. & R. A. Reid, printers, 1886. 92 p. front. (port.), map, plan, plate (illus.). 22½cm.　　　NN　93

Peck, George Bacheler, 1843–1934.
Camp and hospital, by George B. Peck, Jr., late Second Lieutenant. 1884. 50 p. *PNRISSHS* s3 no 5. front. (port.).　　　94

—— A recruit before Petersburg. 1880. 74 p. *PNRISSHS* s2 no 8. front. (port.).　　　95

—— Reminiscences of the War of the rebellion, by George B. Peck, Jr. (late Second Lieutenant, Second Rhode Island volunteers). Providence, Printed by Providence press co., 1884. 48 p. front. (port.). 20½cm.
　　　　　　　　　　　　　　CtY　95A

Rhodes, Elisha Hunt, 1842–1917.
The first campaign of the Second Rhode Island infantry, by Elisha H. Rhodes, late Lieutenant-Colonel. 1878. 26 p. *PNRISSHS* s1 no 1.　　　96

—— The Second Rhode Island volunteers at the siege of Petersburg. 1915. 37 p. *PNRISSHS* s7 no 10. 2 plates (ports.).　　　97

Rogers, Horatio, 1836–1904.
Personal experiences of the Chancellorsville campaign, by Horatio Rogers, late Colonel. 1881. 33 p. *PNRISSHS* s2 no 9.　　　98

Woodbury, Augustus, 1825–1895.
The Second Rhode Island regiment, a narrative of military operations in which the Regiment was engaged from the beginning to the end of the War for the Union, by Augustus Woodbury. Providence, Valpey, Angell and co., 1875. 633 p. front. (port.), fold. map. 25cm.
Unit roster [427]–618.　　　DLC NN　99

## 3RD INFANTRY

*Organized: August 1861.*

*Designated 3rd regiment of heavy artillery: December 19, 1861.*

## 4TH INFANTRY

*Left for Washington: October 5, 1861.*

*Mustered out: October 15, 1864.*

*AG's report* i 231–323. *The historical sketch by Edwin M. Stone, 1865 revised by Henry J. Spooner and Thomas J. Griffin.*

Allen, George H
Forty-six months with the Fourth R.I. volunteers, in the War of 1861 to 1865, comprising a history of its marches, battles, and camp life, compiled from journals kept while on duty in the field and camp, by Corp. Geo. H. Allen

*4th Infantry, continued*

of Company B. Sold by subscription only.
Providence, J. A. & R. A. Reid, printers, 1887.
389 p. front. (port.). 22½cm.
                           DLC NN    **100**
Unit roster, Company B, [369]–87.

Rhode Island.   Fourth Regiment Rhode Island
Volunteers Commissioner.
. . . Report of the . . . to Royal C. Taft, Gov-
ernor of Rhode Island. Providence, E. L. Free-
man & Son, 1889. 8 p. 23½cm.    RP    **101**
At head of title: State of Rhode Island and Provi-
dence plantation. George Carmichael, Commissioner.
Reimbursement of money deducted by the United
States from their pay for clothing given them by the
State of Rhode Island.

Rhode Island.   Governor.
. . . Fourth regiment Rhode Island volunteers. Communication from the U.S. Treasury
department relative to clothing account, etc.
Providence, E. L. Freeman & co., 1885. 33 p.
23½cm.                             RHi    **102**
At head of title: State of Rhode Island and Providence plantation.

Sherman, Sumner Upham, 1839–
Battle of the crater, and experiences of
prison life, Sumner U. Sherman, late Captain.
1898. 38 p. *PNRISSHS* s5 no 8.         **103**

Sholes, Albert E
. . . "A dream of the past," written by A. E.
Sholes, read at the annual reunion of the
Fourth Rhode Island, July 29, 1889. Savannah,
Ga., Press of M. S. & D. A. Byck [1889] [8] p.
19½cm.                             RHi    **104**
Title and imprint from cover. Poetry.

Spooner, Henry Joshua, 1839–1918.
The Maryland campaign with the Fourth
Rhode Island, by Henry J. Spooner, late First
Lieutenant. 1903. 27 p. *PNRISSHS* s6 no 5.
                                          **105**

## 5TH INFANTRY

*Mustered in: December 16, 1861.*
*Designated 5th regiment of heavy artil-*
*lery: May 27, 1863.*

## 6TH INFANTRY

*Failed to complete organization.*

## 7TH INFANTRY

*Left for Washington: September 10, 1862.*
*Mustered out: June 9, 1865.*
*AG's report* ɪ *325–427. The historical*
*sketch by Edwin M. Stone, 1865, revised*
*by Percy Daniels and W. P. Hopkins.*

Seventh regiment Rhode Island volunteers. Ex-
hibition of the Vicksburg statue. Exercises on
the grounds of the Gorham manufacturing
company, Saturday, March 28, 1908. . . .
[Providence, Standard print. co., 1908] [4] p.
2 illus. (1 col.). 23cm.            DLC    **106**

Hopkins, William Palmer, 1845–1920.
The seventh regiment Rhode Island volunteers in the Civil war, 1862–1865, by William
P. Hopkins. Providence, Providence press,
Snow & Farnham, printers, 1903. xxiv, 543,
(1) p. plates (illus., 2 fold. maps, plan, ports.).
23½cm.                             DLC NN   **107**
Unit roster [431]–525. "Errata," (1) p. Edited
by George B. Peck from material assembled by William P. Hopkins.

## 8TH INFANTRY

*Failed to complete organization.*

## 9TH INFANTRY

*Organized: May 26, 1862.*
*Mustered out: September 2, 1862.*
*AG's report* ɪ *429–73. The historical*
*sketch by Edwin M. Stone, 1865, revised*
*by William A. Spicer.*

See Title 46.

## 10TH INFANTRY

*Organized: May 26, 1862.*
*Mustered out: September 1, 1862.*
*AG's report* ɪ *475–517. The historical*
*sketch by Edwin M. Stone, 1865, revised*
*by William A. Spicer.*

Bailey, William Whitman, 1843–1914.
My boyhood at West Point. 1891. 38 p.
*PNRISSHS* s4 no 12.                     **108**

Spicer, William Arnold, 1845–1913.
The high school boys of the Tenth R.I. regiment, with a roll of teachers and students of
the Providence high school who served in the
Army or Navy of the United States during the
rebellion. 1882. 83 p. *PNRISSHS* s2 no 13.
                                          **109**

——— A souvenir of the fortieth anniversary of
the Tenth Rhode Island veteran association,
May 26, 1902, and of battle flag day, October
17, 1903. A supplement to the History of the
Regiment, prepared by the author for the 42d
anniversary, May 26, 1904. William Arnold
Spicer, Company B. [Providence, 1904] 6
leaves. illus. 23cm.               IHi NN   **110**

See also Titles 46 and 71.

## 11TH INFANTRY

*Mustered in: October 1, 1862.*
*Mustered out: July 13, 1863.*
*AG's report I 519–78. The historical sketch by Edwin M. Stone, 1865, revised by J. C. Thompson.*

Eleventh Rhode Island regiment veteran association eighth winter reunion, 1888–9. . . . [Providence, McCausland & co., 1889] 5, (19) folios. illus. 13½ × 21cm.  RHi  *111*

"Series of sketches illustrating camp scenes and incidents . . . during 1862 and 1863." On cover: Souvenir. 1862. 11th regt., R.I.V. Mid-winter reunion.

Secretary's report of the second 5 year reunion, of the Company I veterans, 11th regiment, R.I.V., July 13, 1888. [Providence, 1888] [8] p. 17½cm.  RHi  *112*

Title from cover

Mowry, William Augustus, 1829–1917.
Camp life in the Civil war, Eleventh R.I. infantry, by Captain William A. Mowry. Privately published. Boston, 1914. 80 p. 4 plates (2 illus., 2 ports.). 18½cm.  NN RP  *113*

Nickerson, Ansel D  –1896.
A raw recruit's war experiences, by Ansel D. Nickerson, late Private Co. B, Eleventh Rhode Island volunteers. Providence, Printed by the Press co., 1888. viii, 64 p. front. (port.). 17½cm.  NHi RP  *114*

—— Souvenir. 1862. 11th regt. R.I.V. 1890. By the "Raw recruit." Mid-winter reunion. [Providence, Snow & Farnham, 1890] [50] folios. 13½ × 20½cm.  RHi  *115*

Title from cover. Poetry.

Parkhurst, Charles H
Incidents of service with the Eleventh regiment Rhode Island volunteers. 1883. 32 p. *PNRISSHS* s2 no 18.  *116*

Remington, George H
A statistical history of Co. I, 11th R.I. volunteers, together with an account of the 20th reunion, holden on the grounds of the Warwick club, Friday, July 13, 1883. Providence, E. A. Johnson & co., 1884. 35 p. 15cm.  RHi  *117*

"Arranged and written by George H. Remington." On cover: 1863. Company I, 11th regt., R.I.V. 1883. The first reunion.

Thompson, John C
History of the Eleventh regiment, Rhode Island volunteers in the War of the rebellion,

by R. W. Rock. Published by a Committee of the Eleventh regiment veteran association. Providence, Providence press co., printers, 1881. vii, 217 p. 20cm.  DLC NN  *118*

"Preface" signed: J. C. Thompson. Unit roster 201–16. "The writer has drawn freely from the following sources. . .the letters of R. W. Rock to the Providence evening press."

## 12TH INFANTRY

*Mustered in: October 18, 1862.*
*Mustered out: July 29, 1863.*
*AG's report I 579–654. The historical sketch by Edwin M. Stone, 1865, revised by Pardon E. Tillinghast.*

Ballou, Daniel Ross, 1837–1923.
The military services of Maj.-Gen. Ambrose Everett Burnside in the Civil war, and their value as an asset of his country and its history, by Daniel R. Ballou, late Second Lieutenant. 1914. 38, 59 p. *PNRISSHS* s7 no 8–9. 3 plates (ports.).  *119*

Part I–II appears on covers.

Grant, Joseph W
My first campaign. Boston, Wright & Potter, 1863. 152 p. 16cm.  DLC NN  *120*

The author identifies himself on p [5] and served in Company F, 12th Rhode Island. On spine: The flying regiment.

—— The flying regiment, journal of the campaign of the 12th regt. Rhode Island volunteers, by Capt. J. W. Grant. Providence, Sidney S. Rider & Bro., 1865. 152 p. 16cm.  DLC RHi  *121*

Printed from the plates of Title 120.

Lapham, Oscar, 1837–1926.
Recollections of service in the Twelfth regiment, R.I. volunteers, by Oscar Lapham, late First Lieutenant. 1885. 39 p. *PNRISSHS* s3 no 11.  *122*

Tillinghast, Pardon Elisha, 1836–1905.
History of the Twelfth regiment Rhode Island volunteers in the Civil war, 1862–1863. Prepared by a Committee of the survivors in 1901–4. [Providence, Snow & Farnham, printers, 1904] xiv, 394 p. plates (illus., map, ports.). 24cm.  NN  *123*

Unit roster [311]–87. Chapters are signed by their authors. "Compiler's preface" signed: P.E.T.

—— Reminiscences of services with the Twelfth Rhode Island volunteers and a memorial of Col. George H. Browne. 1885. 53 p. *PNRISSHS* s3 no 15.  *124*

# VERMONT

# Reference Works

Benedict, George Grenville, 1826–1907.

Vermont in the Civil war, a history of the part taken by the Vermont soldiers and sailors in the War for the Union, 1861–5, by G. G. Benedict. Burlington, Free Press Association, 1886–88. 2 v. maps, plates (maps, ports.). 23cm.

Cited as *Vermont in the Civil War.*

Dyer, Frederick Henry, 1849–1917.

A compendium of the War of the rebellion. 1908 (reprinted 1959).

"Regimental index" 233–4; "Regimental histories" 1647–55. The pagination is the same in the 1959 reprint.

*The Union army.*

"Record of Vermont regiments," I (1908) 108–30.

United States. Adjutant General's Office.

Official army register of the volunteer force of the United States army for the years 1861, '62, '63, '64, '65. Part I. (New England states). Washington, 1865.

A roster of officers by regiments with an alphabetical index for the six states.

Vermont. Adjutant General.

Revised roster of Vermont volunteers and lists of Vermonters who served in the army and navy of the United States during the War of the rebellion, 1861–66. Compiled by authority of the General assembly under direction of Theodore S. Peck, Adjutant-General. Montpelier, Press of the Watchman pub. co., 1892. vii, 1,863 p. 29cm.

Herein cited as *Revised roster.*

# VERMONT

## ARTILLERY

### 1ST ARTILLERY (HEAVY)

*Mustered in as 11th regiment of infantry: September 1, 1862.*
*Designated 1st regiment of heavy artillery: December 10, 1862.*
*Mustered out: August 25, 1865.*
*Revised roster 408–55. Narrative by James M. Warner and Aldace F. Walker.*
*Vermont in the Civil war* II 343–96.

Anson, Charles H
Assault on the lines of Petersburg, April 2, 1865, by Bvt. Major Charles H. Anson. *MOLLUS-Wis* I 85–98.     **1**

—— Battle of Cedar creek, October 19th, 1864. *MOLLUS-Wis* IV 355–67. fold. map.  **2**

—— General Robert E. Lee. *MOLLUS-Wis* I 241–50.     **3**

—— The last week's campaign of the Army of the Potomac. *MOLLUS-Wis* III 188–97.  **4**

—— Reminiscences of an enlisted man. *MOLLUS-Wis* IV 279–90.     **5**

Ayer, Don C
Battle of Cedar creek, by Lieut. Don C. Ayer. *MOLLUS-Neb* I 262–8.     **6**

Benton, Reuben Clark
From Yorktown to Williamsburg, by Lieutenant-Colonel Reuben C. Benton. *MOLLUS-Minn* II 204–22.     **7**

Chamberlin, George Ephraim, 1838–1864.
Letters of George E. Chamberlin, who fell in the service of his country near Charlestown, Va., August 21st, 1864. (Lieutenant-Colonel 1st artillery, 11th Vermont volunteers.) . . . Springfield, H. W. Rokker's pub. house, 1883. vii, 393 p. 21cm.     DLC IHi   **8**
Edited by Mrs Caroline Chamberlin Lutz.

Chittenden, Lucius Eugene, 1824–1900.
An unknown heroine, an historical episode of the War between the States, by L. E. Chittenden. New York, George H. Richmond, 1894. 314 p. front. (port.). 19cm.   DLC MiU   **9**
The "unknown heroine" is Mrs Van Metre of Clarke co., Va., who befriended Lieutenant Henry E. Bedell, 1st Vermont heavy artillery, wounded at the battle of Opequan, September 13, 1864, and deserted by his comrades. On Bedell's return North, Mrs. Van Metre accompanied him, and through the assistance of Secretary Stanton and others found her husband, a Confederate soldier confined in a Northern prison under an assumed name, and secured his release.

Lewis, Henry C     H
Roster Society 1st artillery 11th regiment Vermont volunteers, 1890, by H. C. H. Lewis, Secretary. Burlington, Free Press Association, 1890. 82 p. 23½cm.   DNW Vt   **10**
Slip inserted addressed: Comrades.

Ross, Charles
An Andersonville prison diary. Edited by C. M. Destler. *Georgia historical quarterly* (1940) 56–76.     **10A**

—— A Vermonter in Andersonville, diary of Charles Ross, 1864. *Vermont history* ns XXV (1957) 229–45.     **11**

—— A Vermonter returns from Andersonville. Edited by Chester McArthur Destler. *Vermont history* ns XXV (1957) 344–51.   **12**

Thomas, Cyrus
The frontier schoolmaster, the autobiography of a teacher . . . by C. Thomas. Montreal, Printed by John Lovell & Son, 1880. xii, [5]–465 p. 22cm.   TxU VtU   **13**
Civil war 366–95.

Walker, Aldace Freeman, 1842–1901.
The old Vermont brigade (read December 11, 1890). *MOLLUS-Ill* II 189–209.   **14**
Also published as *MOLLUS-NY* II 316–35.

—— A Rebel heroine (read January 11, 1894). *MOLLUS-Ill* IV 416–29.   **15**

—— The Vermont brigade in the Shenandoah valley, 1864, by Aldace F. Walker. Burlington, Free Press Association, 1869. xi, [13]–191 p. 3 plates (maps). 19cm.   DLC NN   **16**
Coulter 462.

### *1st Company of Heavy Artillery*

*Organized: March 1, 1865.*
*Mustered out: July 28, 1865.*
*Revised roster 652–4.*

## Batteries of Light Artillery

### *1st Battery*

*Mustered in: February 18, 1862.*
*Mustered out: August 10, 1864.*
*Revised roster 625–32. Narrative by Edward E. Greenleaf.*
*Vermont in the Civil war* II 696–710.

[ 101 ]

## 2nd Battery

*Mustered in: December 24, 1861.*
*Mustered out: July 31, 1865.*
*Revised roster 633–42. Narrative by John W. Chase.*
*Vermont in the Civil war II 710–19.*

## 3rd Battery

*Mustered in: January 1, 1864.*
*Mustered out: June 15, 1865.*
*Revised roster 643–51.*
*Vermont in the Civil war II 720–30.*

## CAVALRY

### 1ST CAVALRY

*Mustered in: November 19, 1861.*
*Mustered out: August 9, 1865.*
*Revised roster 214–66. Narrative by William L. Greenleaf.*
*Vermont in the Civil war II 533–694.*

In memoriam. Gen. William Wells, died April 29, 1892. [Burlington, 1892] 29 p. front. (port.). 18½cm.                CSmH NN     **16A**

Clark, Stephen A
Brandy station, October, 1863. *Maine bugle* campaign III (Rockland 1896) 226–9.     **17**

—— Buckland Mills. *Maine bugle* campaign IV (Rockland 1897) 108–10.     **18**

Clarke, Almon
In the immediate rear, experience and observations of a field surgeon. *MOLLUS-Wis* II 87–101.     **19**

Cummings, William G
Six months in the Third cavalry division under Custer. *MOLLUS-Iowa* I 296–315.     **20**

Dufur, Simon Miltimore, 1843–
Over the dead line; or, tracked by bloodhounds, giving the author's personal experience during eleven months that he was confined in Pemberton, Libby, Belle island, Andersonville, Ga., and Florence, S.C., as a prisoner of war. Describing plans of escape, arrival of prisoners, his escape and recapture, with numerous and varied incidents and anecdotes of his prison life, by S. M. Dufur, Company B, 1st Vermont cavalry. Burlington, Printed by Free Press Association, 1902. viii, 283 p. front. (ports.). 21cm.          DLC NN     **21**
"Kilpatrick's famous cavalry raid round Richmond," 9–23. Coulter 134.

Goodrich, John Ellsworth, 1831–1915.
Captain Hiram Henry Hall of the First Vermont cavalry, read at the twenty-first anniversary of the Vermont commandery of the Military order of the loyal legion of the United States, by Chaplain J. E. Goodrich, November 19, 1912. Burlington, Free Press print. co., 1913. 7, (1) p. 24cm.          VtHi     **22**

Jackson, Horatio Nelson, 1872–
Dedication of the statue to Brevet Major-General William Wells and the officers and men of the First regiment Vermont cavalry on the battlefield of Gettysburg, July 3, 1913. Privately printed. [Burlington?] 1914. 225, (1) p. facs., illus. (1 col.) ports. 23cm.
                      DLC NHi NN     **23**
"Preface" signed: H. Nelson Jackson. On cover: In affectionate memory of Major-General William Wells. "First regiment cavalry, by Lieutenant William L. Greenleaf and Sergeant Seymour H. Wood," 151–69.

Parsons, Henry C
Farnsworth's charge and death. *BandL* III 393–6.     **24**

Shatzel, Albert Harry          –1908.
Imprisoned at Andersonville, the diary of Albert Harry Shatzel, May 5, 1864 – September 12, 1864. Edited by Donald F. Danker. *Nebraska history* XXXVIII (1957) 81–125. plates (illus., port.).     **25**

Tompkins, Charles H
With the Vermont cavalry, 1861–2, some reminiscences. *The Vermonter* XVII (White river junction 1912) 505–7.     **26**

### FRONTIER CAVALRY

*Two Vermont companies were organized early in January 1865, and formed part of the 26th New York cavalry.*
*Mustered out: June 27, 1865.*
*Revised roster 656–61. Narrative by Josiah Grout.*
*Vermont in the Civil war II 694–5.*

### 1st Vermont Brigade

*2d, 3rd, 4th, 5th, and 6th infantry regiments.*
*Vermont in the Civil war I 235–620.*

Grant, Lewis Addison, 1829–1918.
The old Vermont brigade at Petersburg, by Brigadier-General Lewis A. Grant. *MOLLUS-Minn* I 381–403.     **27**

For other references on the Vermont brigade, see the entries under the regiments that formed the Brigade.

INFANTRY

**1ST INFANTRY**

*Mustered in: May 9, 1861.*

*Mustered out: August 15, 1861.*

*Revised roster 5–26. Narrative by Roswell Farnham.*

*Vermont in the Civil war* I 28–61.

Connor, Selden, 1839–
The boys of 1861. *MOLLUS-Me* I 323–43.
28

Also published in *Magazine of history* XIV (New York 1911) 73–92, and *Maine bugle* campaign II (Rockland 1895) 242–57.

McKeen, Silas, 1791–1877.
. . . A sermon delivered at Bradford, Vt., Sabbath afternoon, April 28, 1861, in the presence of the Bradford guards, when under call to join the First regiment of Vermont volunteers, and go forth in their country's service. By Rev. Silas McKeen. Published by request of the Company. Windsor, Printed at the Chronicle press, 1861. 16 p. 22½cm.
NN VtU    29
At head of title: Heroic patriotism. Unit roster, 14–16.

Washburn, Peter Thacher, 1814–1870.
An oration before the Re-union society of Vermont officers, in the Representatives' hall, Montpelier, Vt., October 22d, 1868, by Gen. P. T. Washburn. Montpelier, J. & J. M. Poland, printers, 1869. 29 p. 22½cm.    DLC    31
Also published in the *Proceedings of the Reunion society of Vermont officers* I 82–100.

**2ND INFANTRY**

*Mustered in: June 20, 1861.*

*Mustered out: July 15, 1865.*

*Revised roster 27–66. Narrative by Amasa S. Tracy.*

*Vermont in the Civil war* I 61–125.

Aubery, Cullen Bullard
Recollections of a newsboy in the Army of the Potomac, 1861–1865. His capture and confinement in Libby prison. After being paroled sharing the fortunes of the famous Iron brigade. By Doc Aubery. [Milwaukee, 1904] 166, (1) p. facs., 1 illus., ports. 19½cm.    NN    32
The author was not a soldier but ran away with his three brothers who were enrolled in the 2nd Vermont. "Echoes from the marches of famous Iron brigade (unwritten stories of that famous organization)," commences on p 19.

Chase, Peter S
Reunion greeting, together with an historical sketch and a complete descriptive list of the members of Co. I, 2d regt., Vt. vols., in the War for the Union, 1861 to 1865, with final statement of the Regiment. Also, the by-laws of Co. I, 2d regiment, Vt. vols., infantry association, with each member's name, and post-office address so far as known. By Peter S. Chase. Brattleboro, Phoenix print. office, 1891. 61, (3) p. 15 x 23½cm.    VtHi    33

Dayton, Durell W
Chaplain Dayton's address. In *Proceedings of the Reunion society of Vermont officers* II 77–86.    34

Edwards, John Harrington, 1834–
. . . A sermon in memory of Capt. Charles C. Morey, of the Second Vermont regiment, preached in the Congregational church, West-Lebanon, N.H., May 14, 1865, by the pastor Rev John H. Edwards. Hanover, N.H., Printed at the Dartmouth press, 1865. 12 p. 23½cm.
DLC    35
At head of title: Life given, not lost.

Folsom, William R           1873–
Vermont at Bull run. *Vermont quarterly* ns XIX (1951) 5–21.    36

**3RD INFANTRY**

*Mustered in: July 16, 1861.*

*Mustered out: July 11, 1865.*

*Revised roster 67–105. Narrative by Samuel E. Pingree.*

*Vermont in the Civil war* I 126–55.

Cook, John F
The bloody seven days' battle. Edited by George A. McDonald. *Vermont quarterly* ns XV (1947) 230–5. map.    37

Glover, Waldo F
. . . Abraham Lincoln and the sleeping sentinel of Vermont. Montpelier, Vermont Historical Society, 1936. 114 p. front. (port.), 2 facs., illus. 19cm.    NN    38
At head of title: By Waldo F. Glover.

—— The sleeping sentinel, a postscript. *Vermont quarterly* ns XVI (1948) 83–95.    39

Janvier, Francis De Haes, 1817–1885.
The sleeping sentinel, by Francis De Haes Janvier. Philadelphia, T. B. Peterson & Brothers, 1863. 19 p. 18cm.    DLC NN WHi    40

**4TH INFANTRY**

*Mustered in: September 21, 1861.*

*Mustered out: July 13, 1865.*

*Revised roster 106–41. Narative by Stephen M. Pingree.*

*Vermont in the Civil war* I 156–79.

*4th Infantry, continued*

Roster and roll of the survivors of the 4th regiment, Vermont volunteers, 1861–1865, first reunion, held at Montpelier, October 19, 1888. [Montpelier, Watchman pub. co., 1889] 12 p. 22cm.                                              NhHi  *41*

<small>Excusing errors and promising a nearly perfect roll for the next reunion, inserted slip signed: Secretary and committee. Title from cover.</small>

Clark, Charles A
To an unsung hero. *The Vermonter* XLII (White river junction 1937) 109–10.      *42*

Conline, John
Recollections of the battle of Antietam and the Maryland campaign (read January 7, 1897). 12 p. 23cm.                          NN  *43*
<small>Also published as *MOLLUS-Mich* II 110–16.</small>

Hosmer, Francis J
A glimpse of Andersonville and other writings, by Francis J. Hosmer. Springfield, Mass., Press of Loring & Axtell, 1896. 90 p. plates (illus., ports.). 21cm.               Ct NN  *44*
<small>"Published by F. J. Hosmer, Greenfield, Mass.," inserted slip. Contents: Andersonville, 1–65; Letters from the old battle-fields, 67–80; Memorial address, 1887, 82–90.</small>

Pringle, Cyrus Guernsey, 1838–1911.
The record of a Quaker conscience, Cyrus Pringle's diary, with an introduction by Rufus M. Jones. New York, Macmillan co., 1918. 93 p. 17cm.                                           NN  *45*

—— The United States versus Pringle. *Atlantic monthly* CXI (1913) 145–62.      *46*

## 5TH INFANTRY

*Mustered in: September 16, 1861.*
*Mustered out: June 29, 1865.*
*Revised roster 142–76. Narrative by Lewis A. Grant, John R. Lewis and Charles G. Gould.*
*Vermont in the Civil war* I 180–207.

Keyes, Charles
Major-General Lewis Addison Grant. *Annals of Iowa* s3 XII (1921) 511–32. 1 illus., ports, plate (port.).                                      *47*

## 6TH INFANTRY

*Mustered in: October 15, 1861.*
*Mustered out: June 26, 1865.*
*Revised roster 177–213. Narrative by Frank G. Butterfield.*
*Vermont in the Civil war* I 208–34.

## 7TH INFANTRY

*Mustered in: February 12, 1862, to date from June 1, 1861.*
*Mustered out: March 14, 1866.*
*Revised roster 267–98. Narrative by William C. Holbrook.*
*Vermont in the Civil war* II 1–79.

Proceedings of the first and second reunions. Roster and roll of surviving members, also, list of actions and skirmishes participated in by officers or detached portions of 7th regiment Vermont volunteers (veterans). New York, American Bank Note co., 1883. 91 p. front. (port.). 21½cm.                          DLC NN  *48*
<small>Unit roster 25–86. On cover: 1862. 1866. 1882. 1883.</small>

Holbrook, William C
Colonel Holbrook's oration. In *Proceedings of the Reunion society of Vermont officers* I 413–29.                                            *49*

—— A narrative of the officers and enlisted men of the 7th regiment of Vermont volunteers (veterans), from 1862 to 1866, by Wm. C. Holbrook, late Colonel. New York, American Bank Note co., 1882. viii, 219 p. front. (port.). 21½cm.                                 DLC NN  *50*

## 8TH INFANTRY

*Mustered in: February 18, 1862.*
*Mustered out: June 28, 1865.*
*Revised roster 299–337. Narrative by S. E. Howard.*
*Vermont in the Civil war* II 80–181.

Eighth Vermont association constitution and by-laws, and names and p.o. address of surviving members. Burlington, Published by authority, 1888. (2), (10) folios. 17½cm.
                                                     DNW  *51*
<small>"Errata," "Additions," p 3 of cover. Title and imprint from cover.</small>

Eighth Vermont regimental association twenty-second reunion, Montpelier, Oct. 1st, 1895. In memoriam Colonel George Nathaniel Carpenter, by Capt. S. E. Howard. (6) p. front. (port.). 20½cm.                               DNW  *52*
<small>Title from cover.</small>

Second re-union of Eighth regiment Vermont volunteers, at White river junction, September 2, 1873. Report of the meetings. Poem, by George N. Carpenter. [n. p.] Kenosha print, 1874. 16 p. 21½cm.                     DNW Vt  *53*

Carpenter, George Nathaniel
History of the Eighth regiment, Vermont volunteers, 1861–1865, by Geo. N. Carpenter.

Issued by the Committee of publication. Boston, Press of Deland & Barta, 1886. x, 335 p. plates (illus., maps, ports.). 23½cm.
Original roster 286–318.   DLC NN   **54**

Childe, Charles B
General Butler at New Orleans, 1862, by Charles Butler, late Captain. *MOLLUS-Ohio* v 175–98.   **55**

Hill, Herbert E     1845–1895.
Campaign in the Shenandoah valley, 1864, a paper read before the Eighth Vermont volunteers and First Vermont cavalry, at the annual reunion, in Montpelier, Vermont, November 2, 1886, by Colonel Herbert E. Hill. . . . Boston, 1886. 13, (3) p. 2 plates (illus.).   NHi   **56**

Howard, S     Edward
The morning surprise at Cedar creek, by Captain S. E. Howard. *MOLLUS-Mass* ii 415–24.   **57**

McFarland, Moses
Some incidents touching the battle of the "Cotton," as related by Moses McFarland, late Captain of Company A, 8th Vt. Morrisville, News and Citizen, 1896. 18 p. port. 18cm.
  VtHi   **58**

Pollard, Henry M
Recollections of Cedar creek, by Major H. M. Pollard. *MOLLUS-Mo* i 278–86.   **59**

## 9TH INFANTRY

*Mustered in: July 9, 1862.*
*Mustered out: December 1, 1865.*
*Revised roster 338–78. Narrative by Joel C. Baker.*
*Vermont in the Civil war* ii 182–275.

Baker, Joel C
The fall of Richmond, by Joel C. Baker, First Lieut. 1892. 16 p. *MOLLUS-Vt* no 2.   **60**

—— Lieut. J. C. Baker's address. In *Proceedings of the Reunion society of Vermont officers* ii 280–91.   **61**

Bisbee, Lewis H
Captain Bisbee's address, life and service of Gen. Sheridan. In *Proceedings of the Reunion society of Vermont officers* ii 89–108.   **62**

Kimball, Moses, 1799–1868.
A discourse commemorative of Major Charles Jarvis of the Ninth Vermont volunteers, who was mortally wounded, Dec. 1, 1863, in an encounter with the enemy, near Cedar point, N.C., delivered at his funeral in the Congregational church, at Weathersfield Bow, Vt., December 13, 1863, by Rev. M. Kimball. New

York, Edward O. Jenkins, printer, 1864. 24 p. 21½cm.   DLC NN WHi   **63**

Leavenworth, Abel E
Vermont at Richmond. *Proceedings of the Rutland historical society* ii 24–9.   **64**

Ripley, Edward Hastings, 1839–1915.
The capture and occupation of Richmond, April 3rd, 1865, by Edward H. Ripley, Col. 9th Vt. inf. [New York] G. P. Putnam's Sons, 1907. front. (port.), plates (facs., illus.). 31 p. 24½cm.   NHi NN   **65**
Also published as *MOLLUS-NY* iii 472–502.

—— General Edward H. Ripley's address. In *Proceedings of the Reunion society of Vermont officers* ii 334–58.   **66**

—— Memories of the Ninth Vermont at the tragedy of Harper's ferry, Sept. 15, 1862. *MOLLUS-NY* iv 133–61.   **67**

—— Vermont General, the unusual war experiences of Edward Hastings Ripley, 1862–1865, edited by Otto Eisenschiml. New York, Devin-Adair co., 1960. viii, 340 p. maps, plates (illus., ports.). 21cm.   DLC NN   **67A**

Sherman, Elijah B
. . . A letter from Camp Douglas, read before the Illinois commandery of the Loyal legion, April 7, 1927 . . . by Lieutenant E. B. Sherman. [4] p. 21cm.   MnHi   **68**
Letter dated, October 4, 1862.

## 10TH INFANTRY

*Mustered in: September 1, 1862.*
*Mustered out: June 22, 1865.*
*Revised roster 379–408. Narrative by Rev. Edwin M. Haynes.*
*Vermont in the Civil war* ii 276–341.

Abbott, Lemuel Abijah, 1842–1911.
Personal recollections and Civil war diary, 1864, by Major Lemuel Abijah Abbott, late Captain 10th regt. Vt. vol. infantry. Burlington, Free Press print. co., 1908. x, 296 p. front. (port.), plates (illus.). 21cm.   NN   **69**

Burnell, George W
The development of our armies, 1861–5, by Captain W. G. Burnell. *MOLLUS-Wis* ii 70–80.   **70**

Haynes, Edwin Mortimer, 1836–
A history of the Tenth regiment, Vermont volunteers, with biographical sketches of the officers who fell in battle and a complete roster of all the officers and men connected with it showing all changes by promotion, death or resignation, during the military existence of the

*10th Infantry, continued*

Regiment, by Chaplain E. M. Haynes. Published by the Tenth Vermont regimental association. [Lewiston, Me., Journal steam press, 1870] viii, [9]–249 p. 22½cm.     DLC NN    **71**
Unit roster [205]–42. Coulter 222.

—— A history of the Tenth regiment, Vt. vols., with biographical sketches of nearly every officer who ever belonged to the Regiment, and many of the non-commissioned officers and men, and a complete roster of all the officers and men connected with it, showing all changes by promotion, death or resignation, during the military existence of the Regiment. Second edition. Revised, enlarged and embellished by over sixty engravings and fully illustrated by maps and charts of battlefields, by the Chaplain, E. M. Haynes. Rutland, Tuttle co., printers, 1894. v, 504 p. plates (illus.; maps, partly fold.; ports.). 24cm.     DLC NN    **72**
Unit roster 447–500.

## 11TH INFANTRY

*Mustered in: September 1, 1862.*
*Designated 1st regiment of heavy artillery: December 10, 1862.*

## 12TH INFANTRY

*Mustered in: October 4, 1862.*
*Mustered out: July 14, 1863.*
*Revised roster 456–77. Narrative by George G. Benedict.*
*Vermont in the Civil war* II 402–5.

Benedict, George Grenville, 1826–1907.
Army life in Virginia. Letters from the Twelfth Vermont regiment and personal experiences of volunteer service in the War for the Union, 1862–63, by George Grenville Benedict, Private and Lieutenant Twelfth regiment, Vermont volunteers and Aide-de-camp upon the staff of the Second Vermont brigade. Burlington, Free Press Association, 1895. 194 p. plates (illus., ports.). 21½cm.     DLC NN    **73**
First published in the Burlington free press.

—— The battle of Gettysburg and the part taken therein by Vermont troops, by G. G. Benedict. Burlington, Free Press print, 1867. 24 p. plates (illus.). 22cm.     NHi    **74**

—— Lieutenant Benedict's oration. In *Proceedings of the Reunion society of Vermont officers* I 385–406.     **75**

—— The element of romance in military history. 1893. 19 p. *MOLLUS-Vt* no 4.     **76**

—— The service of the Vermont troops, an oration before the Re-union society of Vermont officers, in the Representative's hall, Montpelier, Vt., November 2, 1882, by Lieut. Geo. Grenville Benedict. Montpelier, Watchman and Journal press, 1882. 31 p. 22½cm.     NN    **76A**

Jackson, William Henry, 1843–
Time exposure, the autobiography of William Henry Jackson. New York, G. P. Putnam's Sons [1940] x, 341 p. plates (illus., ports.). 22cm.     NN Vt    **77**
Civil war 30–77.

## 13TH INFANTRY

*Mustered in: October 10, 1862.*
*Mustered out: July 21, 1863.*
*Revised roster 478–501. Narrative by Albert Clarke.*
*Vermont in the Civil war* II 405–8.

Report of the Sixth annual re-union of the Thirteenth Vermont volunteer association, held at Northfield, June 22d and 23d, 1893, with addresses and poems attending the exercises of the dedication of the monument erected to the memory of the late Colonel Francis V. Randall. Also a roster of the Thirteenth regiment, prepared and published by the Secretary, under the authority of the Thirteenth regiment association. Burlington, Free Press Association, 1893. 64 p. front. (illus.). 20cm.     NN    **78**
Unit roster 38–64.

Bancroft, Charles De Forest, 1853–1926.
Roster Company I, 13th Vermont regiment. Was enlisted Aug. 25, 1862, mustered into the service of the United States, Oct. 10, 1862; mustered out of service, July 21, 1863. [Montpelier, 1907] [3] p. 34½cm.     VtHi    **79**
Caption title. "Compiled. . .by C. DeF. Bancroft."

Bliss, Joshua Isham, 1830–
Sermon preached at the funeral of Capt. Lucius H. Bostwick, in Calvary church, Jericho, Vt., June 10, 1863, by Rev. J. Isham Bliss. Montpelier, Printed by E. P. Walton, 1863. 16 p. 22cm.     DLC    **80**

Clarke, Albert
Hancock and the Vermont brigade. *JMSIUS* XLVIII (1911) 224–9.     **81**

—— Lieutenant Clarke's oration. In *Proceedings of the Reunion society of Vermont officers* I 362–76.     **82**

Palmer, Edwin Franklin, 1836–1914.
The Second brigade; or, camp life, by a volunteer. . . . Montpelier, Printed for the author by E. P. Walton, 1864. 224 p. 19½cm.     NN    **83**
c1864 by E. F. Palmer.

Sturtevant, Ralph Orson
Pictorial history Thirteenth regiment Vermont volunteers War of 1861–1865. Ralph Orson Sturtevant, historian. [n. p., 1910] 896 p. illus., ports., fold. plates (ports.). 27cm.

DLC NHi NN   **84**

On cover: History of the 13th regiment Vermont volunteers, 1910. Ralph Orson Sturtevant. Carmi Lathrop Marsh.

—— —— Supplement to the History of the Thirteenth regiment Vermont volunteers, 1911. Compiled by Eli Nelson Peck. Published and presented by "the self-appointed committee of three." p 865–96. illus., ports. 26½cm.

NHi   **85**

Also found bound with Title 84 where the phrase "the self-appointed committee . . . " is dropped from the title page of this section.

Scott, George Hale, 1839–1907.
Vermont at Gettysburg, an address delivered before the Society, July 6th, 1870. *Proceedings of the Vermont historical society* ns i (1930) 51–74.   **86**

## 14TH INFANTRY

*Mustered in: October 21, 1862.*

*Mustered out: July 30, 1863.*

*Revised roster 502–23. Narrative by Rev William S. Smart.*

*Vermont in the Civil war* ii 408–11.

Benedict, George Grenville, 1826–1907.
A short history of the 14th Vermont reg't, by Colonel G. G. Benedict . . . An account of the reunion held July 4th, 1887. Also, a roster of the Regiment, with present addresses of members. Published by Co. F, 14th Vermont regiment. Bennington, Press of C. A. Pierce, 1887. 97, (1) p. front. (port.), plan, ports. 22cm.

"Errata," (1) p. Unit roster 87–97.   NN   **87**

Williams, John C          1843–
Life in camp, a history of the nine months' service of the Fourteenth Vermont regiment, from October 21, 1862, when it was mustered into the U.S. service, to July 21, 1863, including the battle of Gettysburg, by J. C. Williams, Corp. Co. B, 14th Vt. reg't . . . Published for the author. Claremont, N.H., Claremont Manufacturing co., 1864. viii, [9]–167, (1) p. 17½cm.

DLC NN   **88**

## 15TH INFANTRY

*Mustered in: October 22, 1862.*

*Mustered out: August 5, 1863.*

*Revised roster 524–44. Narrative by Redfield Procter and William W. Grout.*

*Vermont in the Civil war* ii 411–13.

United States military record Co. K, 15th reg. Vermont state volunteer militia. Baltimore, Schroeder & Sanders, chromo lithogr., 1862. col. illus. broadside, 58 × 46cm.   VtHi   **89**

Copyright by N. B. Adams.

Grout, William W
Address. In *Proceedings of the Reunion society of Vermont officers* i 114–32.   **90**

## 16TH INFANTRY

*Mustered in: October 23, 1862.*

*Mustered out: August 10, 1863.*

*Revised roster 545–67. Narrative by Chandler M. Russell and Lyman S. Emery.*

*Vermont in the Civil war* ii 413–16.

Sixteenth regiment Vermont volunteers. Reunions and roster, 1878 and 1888. Montpelier, Argus and Patriot print. house, 1889. 27 p. front. (port.). 21½cm.   VtHi   **91**

Goulding, Joseph H
Memorial day address, Wheelock G. Veazey, as a soldier and comrade, by Col. J. H. Goulding. Brattleboro, Vermont, May 30, 1898. 19 p. 22cm.   VtHi   **92**

Stevens, Alfred, 1810–1893.
The duty of Christians in times of national calamity. A sermon, preached on the day of national thanksgiving, Aug. 6th, 1863, at the funeral of Sergt. Walter W. Ranney, who died of wounds received in the battle of Gettysburg, by Rev. A. Stevens. Bellows Falls, Printed at the Phenix office, 1863. 15 p. 22½cm.

DLC   **93**

Veazey, Wheelock Graves, 1835–1898.
An oration before the Re-union society of Vermont officers, in the Representative's hall, Montpelier, Vt., October 25th, 1886. Rutland, Tuttle, Gay & co., 1866. 26 p.   DLC   **94**

Also published in the *Proceedings of the reunion society of Vermont officers* i 34–48.

## 17TH INFANTRY

*Mustered in: January 5 to April 12, 1864.*

*Mustered out: July 14, 1865.*

*Revised roster 568–97. Narrative by Joel H. Lucia.*

*Vermont in the Civil war* ii 496–532.

## SHARPSHOOTERS

Three companies were raised in Vermont for service with the United States sharpshooters: Company F, 1st regiment U.S. sharpshooters; Companies E and H, 2d regiment U.S. sharpshooters.

# Regimental Publications
# & Personal Narratives
# of the Civil War

## *A Checklist*

*Compiled by* C. E. DORNBUSCH

Volume One    Northern States

PART IV   NEW JERSEY AND PENNSYLVANIA

New York

The New York Public Library

1962

THIS VOLUME HAS BEEN PUBLISHED WITH HELP
FROM THE EMILY ELLSWORTH FORD SKEEL FUND

# Preface

THIS CHECKLIST of regimental histories, publications of regimental associations, and personal narratives of participants in the Civil War is a revision of and supplement to the section on "Military Organizations" in the third edition of the *Bibliography of State Participation in the Civil War*, prepared and published by the War Department Library, Washington, D. C. in 1913 as its Subject Catalogue No 6.*

The present checklist is to be published in seven Parts. The first six will cover the batteries and regiments of seventeen Northern states: i Illinois; ii New York; iii New England states; iv New Jersey and Pennsylvania; v Indiana and Ohio; and vi Iowa, Kansas, Michigan, Minnesota, and Wisconsin. A final section will provide an index of authors and, where required, titles of the publications listed for these seventeen states.

No subject index to the checklist is contemplated. Besides supplying references for the history of a battery or regiment, the checklist does the same for battles and engagements. To locate references on a battle or engagement, however, the user must determine from the order of battle available in Dyer's *Compendium of the War of the Rebellion* which units were involved and then turn to their entries in the checklist. It is also useful to know the other regiments of a brigade as a means of obtaining from the checklist additional narratives of an incident or battle.

The compiler has followed the arrangement of the 1913 work. Within each state military units are arranged numerically by arm of service — Artillery, Cavalry, and Infantry. While the earlier work entered only units for which publications were known, the present compilation has recorded all units which were organized. Again, while rosters and compilations of regimental histories were reported in one section headed "State Publication" in *BSP*, the present work has indexed these publications under the individual military units.

The compiler has located and personally examined each work entered in this checklist. Some entries which were listed in *BSP* have been omitted —

* The Bibliography (hereafter referred to as *BSP*) was prepared as a catalogue and index of a major Civil War collection, now part of the National War College Library, Washington.

[ 5 ]

entries based on titles taken from bibliographies, correspondence, dealers' catalogues, and other sources but not in the War Department Library. Such "ghosts" as have remained have been omitted here. The present checklist also omits the *BSP* references to the *National Tribune*, and a group of articles by George L. Kilmer which are cited in *BSP* not by original publication but as mounted clippings in ten volumes in the War Department Library collections.

Although a monumental work, some errors found their way into the *BSP*. For instance, Douglas Putnam's *Recollections of the battle of Shiloh* was entered under the 92nd Ohio Regiment, the regiment to which he belonged. But that regiment was formed some months after the battle was fought, and Putnam could write of it not as a member but as a civilian observer. Similarly Eagan's *Battle of Birch Coolie* is entered under the 1st Minnesota Heavy Artillery, although that unit did not participate in the battle.

The seventeen states covered by this checklist had a total of 2,202 batteries and regiments which took part in the Civil War. Each of these units has been listed with a brief statement of its service, i. e. muster in and muster out dates. Where the same number has been assigned to two regiments, they have been distinguished by the term of original enlistments, i. e. three months or three years. Changes in a unit's designation or arm of service as well as amalgamations have been reported. Although some units mustered out before the close of the war and transferred their recruits and veterans to other units, the checklist has not reported this movement of personnel. Reference is made to regimental rosters and narratives of a unit's service where this information may be found.

The compiler has included any articles and publications which could be associated with a particular battery or regiment. The bulk of these are the regimental histories, reunion proceedings, and unit rosters. Publications of sermons preached at soldiers' funerals have been reported. Though their size did not lend to preservation, a surprising number of soldiers' memorials has been located. Broadsides of company rosters, often illustrated in color, were soldiers' souvenirs of the war. The inclusion of all these types of material has here resulted in the broadest possible bibliographical coverage of Civil War materials. All prison narratives have been entered under the

regiment in which the author was serving at the time of his capture. Newspapers printed in the field by army units have not been included.

The value of this checklist is primarily in the listing of the personal narratives of Civil War participants, the rank and file as well as officers, from Lieutenant to Colonel. (By reason of the honorary Brevet rank, the Colonel of a regiment could be appointed Brigadier General at the close of the war, and in this case later reference to his rank is as General.) Usually the publication identifies the battery or regiment of the author. Occasionally, however, he may have served in two or more units, and the later service (often at a higher rank) is used on the title-page. Such items are entered in the checklist under the unit in which the author served at the time the events narrated took place.

Narratives which reflect service in two or more units are entered under the unit of first service, with cross references from other units in which the author served. When an author's service crossed state lines or when it was with the United States Colored Troops, his narrative has been fully entered under each unit.

The compiler has made extensive search of American journals and periodicals published since the close of hostilities. The very magnitude of this undertaking precludes even the hope of a definitive checklist. One assumes that obscure imprints with limited distribution have tended to disappear. In many cases only single surviving copies have been located. The search is continuing while other sections of the list are in preparation, and it is hoped that publication will bring new additions to light.

Following the statement of unit service, entries are given in two groups, anonymous publications followed by author entries. At least one location of each title is reported by means of the *Symbols Used in the National Union Catalogue of The Library of Congress*, seventh edition revised, 1959. Standard works such as the papers of the Military Order of the Loyal Legion and periodicals are not located in the checklist. The user is referred for these to the *Union List of Serials* and its supplements. Title-pages have been transcribed in full, including author statements which supply rank and unit. Distinction is made between illustrations which appear in the body of the text and illustrations which appear on unpaginated plates. Plates that are

paged have been considered as text illustrations. The place of publication
is not identified when within same state as checklist is describing. The collation of reunion proceedings has been limited to their numbering and date.

The very size of the compiler's undertaking has meant assistance from
many sources. In his inspection of collections throughout the country, the
compiler has been helped by many librarians, and their contributions have
been acknowledged in the appropriate sections of the checklist. Above all
the compiler is indebted to the administrators of The Emily E. F. Skeel Fund
of The New York Public Library for making the compilation of this checklist
possible and for freedom in developing it.

# Table of Contents

NEW JERSEY AND PENNSYLVANIA

# Acknowledgments

In the preparation of this section of the Checklist acknowledgment is made of the assistance given by the following individuals:

NEW JERSEY

Mr Donald Sinclair, Curator of Special Collections, Rutgers University Library

PENNSYLVANIA

Mr Robert E. Scudder, Head, Social Science and History Department, The Free Library of Philadelphia

Mr Charles W. Mann, Jr, Curator, Rare Books & Manuscripts, The Pennsylvania State University Library

# Abbreviations

| | |
|---|---|
| *Bates* | History of Pennsylvania volunteers, 1861–5 (1869–71) 5 v. |
| *BandL* | Battles and leaders, New York, 1887–88   4 v. |
| *BandG* | Blue and Gray, Philadelphia |
| *Biv* | Bivouac, Boston |
| *Coulter* | Travels in the Confederate states, a bibliography. By E. Merle Coulter. 1948 |
| *JMSIUS* | Journal of the Military service institution of the United States |
| *JUSCA* | Journal of the United States cavalry association, Fort Leavenworth |
| *MOLLUS* | Military order of the loyal legion of the United States |
| *DC* | War papers District of Columbia commandery |
| *Ill* | Military essays and recollections Illinois commandery |
| *Iowa* | War sketches and incidents Iowa commandery |
| *Minn* | Glimpses of the Nation's struggle Minnesota commandery |
| *Mo* | War papers and personal reminiscences Missouri commandery |
| *NY* | Personal recollections of the War of the rebellion New York commandery |
| *Ohio* | Sketches of war history Ohio commandery |
| *Wis* | War papers Wisconsin commandery |
| *New Jersey and the rebellion* | New Jersey and the rebellion . . . by John Y. Foster, 1868 |
| *PMHSM* | Papers of the Military historical society of Massachusetts |
| *PNRISSHS* | Personal narratives Rhode Island soldiers and sailors historical society |
| *Philadelphia in the Civil war* | Philadelphia in the Civil war, 1861–1865. By Frank H. Taylor. 1913 |
| *PNJHS* | Proceedings New Jersey historical society |
| *Record* | Record of officers and men of New Jersey in the Civil war. 1876 |
| *US* | The united service, Philadelphia |

*Location symbols are those of National Union Catalog.*

# NEW JERSEY

# Reference Works

Dyer, Frederick Henry, 1849–1917.

A compendium of the War of the rebellion, 1908 (reprinted 1959).

"Regimental index" 177–9; "Regimental histories" 1352–66. The pagination is the same in the 1959 reprint.


Foster, John Young

New Jersey and the rebellion, a history of the services of the troops and people of New Jersey in aid of the Union cause, by John Y. Foster. Published by authority of the State. Newark, Martin R. Dennis & co., 1868. viii, 872 p. front. (port.), maps. 23cm.


New Jersey. Adjutant General.

Record of officers and men of New Jersey in the Civil war, 1861–1865. Compiled in the office of the Adjutant general. Published by authority of the Legislature. William S. Stryker, Adjutant general. Trenton, John L. Murphy, printer, 1876. 2 v., 1758, 176 p. 29½cm.

"Index" of names, 176 p.


*The Union army.*

"Record of New Jersey regiments," III (1908) 32–71.


United States. Adjutant General's Office.

Official army register of the volunteer force of the United States army for the years 1861, '62, '63, '64, '65. Part II. New York and New Jersey. Washington, 1865.

A roster of officers by regiments with an alphabetical index for the two states.

# NEW JERSEY

## ARTILLERY

### Batteries (Light)

#### Battery A

Mustered in: August 12, 1861.
Mustered out: June 22, 1865.
New Jersey and the rebellion 680–91.
Record 1369–79.

#### Battery B

Mustered in: September 3, 1861.
Mustered out: June 16, 1865.
New Jersey and the rebellion 692–6.
Record 1380–90.

Hanifen, Michael, 1841–
History of Battery B, First New Jersey artillery, by Michael Hanifen. . . . [Ottawa, Ill., Republican-Times, printers, 1905] 174 p. plates (1 illus., ports.). 23½cm.
Unit roster 151–73.      DLC NjN NN      *1*

#### Battery C

Mustered in: September 11, 1863.
Mustered out: June 19, 1865.
New Jersey and the rebellion 697–703.
Record 1391–7.

#### Battery D

Mustered in: September 16, 1863.
Mustered out: June 17, 1865.
New Jersey and the rebellion 704–25.
Record 1398–1407.

#### Battery E

Mustered in: September 8, 1863.
Mustered out: June 12, 1865.
New Jersey and the rebellion 726.
Record 1408–20.

## CAVALRY

### 1ST CAVALRY

Organized as Halsted's cavalry and left State: September 1, 1861.
Transferred to State authority and designated 1st regiment of cavalry: February 19, 1862.

Mustered out: May 8 to July 24, 1865.
New Jersey and the rebellion 408–85.
Record 1180–1254.

Report of the operations of the First New Jersey cavalry, from the 28th of March to the 25th of May, 1865, with a portion of the number of engagements in which the Regiment has participated, and a complete roster of the commissioned officers. Published for the officers and men. Trenton, Printed at the True American office, 1865. 19 p. 20½cm.      NHi      *2*

Bray, John
My escape from Richmond. Harper's magazine xxviii (1863/64) 662–5.      *2A*

Godfrey, Carlos Emmor,      –1941.
Sketch of Major Henry Washington Sawyer, First regiment cavalry, New Jersey volunteers, a Union soldier and a prisoner of war in Libby prison under sentence of death, by Dr. C. E. Godfrey. . . . Trenton, MacCrellish & Quigley, printers, 1907. 11 p. front. (port.). 23cm.
      DLC NjR NHi NN      *3*

Pyne, Henry Rogers, 1834–1892.
The history of the First New Jersey cavalry, (Sixteenth regiment, New Jersey volunteers), by Henry R. Pyne, Chaplain. Trenton, J. A. Beecher, 1871. 350 p. 2 fronts. (col. illus., port.). 18½cm.      DLC NjR NN      *4*
Unit roster [321]–50.

—— Ride to war, the history of the First New Jersey cavalry, by Henry R. Pyne. Edited, with an introduction and notes, by Earl Schenck Miers. New Brunswick, Rutgers University press [1961] xxxiii, 340 p. maps. 21½cm.
      DLC NjR NN      *4A*
Unit roster 296–340. Map of Eastern theater, end paper.

Robbins, Walter Raleigh, 1843–1923.
War record and personal experiences of Walter Raleigh Robbins, from April 22, 1861, to August 4, 1865. Edited by Lilian Rea. Privately printed. [Chicago?] 1923. vii, 220 p. 3 plates (ports.). 19cm.      DLC NjR NN      *5*

Schuyler, Colfax, 1835–
A day with Mosby's men. BandG iii (1894) 334–9. illus.      *6*

Stradling, James M
The lottery of death, two death prizes drawn by Major Henry Sawyer, of New Jersey, and Captain John M. Flinn, of Indiana, by Lieutenant James M. Stradling. McClure's magazine xxvi (1905) 94–101. ports.      *7*
Author and Henry W. Sawyer were members of the 1st New Jersey cavalry.

## 2ND CAVALRY

*Mustered in: August 11 to September 25, 1863.*
*Mustered out: November 1, 1865.*
*New Jersey and the rebellion 589–608.*
*Record 1255–1320.*

Andrews, Edwin N
  The Chaplain's address to the soldiers of the First brigade, Second division, Cavalry corps . . . Memphis, Tenn., July, 1864, written by Edwin N. Andrews, Chaplain, 2nd N. J. cavalry. broadside, 28½ x 21cm.    NjR   **8**
Poetry.

Packard, William Alfred, 1830–1909.
  Joseph Karge, a memorial sketch, by William A. Packard. New York, Anson D. F. Randolph and co. [1893] 32 p. 24½cm.
                     DLC NN   **9**
"Reprinted from the Princeton college bulletin of April, 1893, for private circulation."

## 3RD CAVALRY

*Mustered in: December 2, 1863 to March 24, 1864.*
*Mustered out: May 8 to August 1, 1865.*
*New Jersey and the rebellion 661–9.*
*Record 1321–68.*

Risley, Clyde Alan and Frederick Porter Todd
  3rd New Jersey cavalry regiment, 1864–1865 (1st regiment, U. S. hussars). *Military collector & historian* ix (Washington, 1957) 44–5. col. plate (illus.).    **10**

Schmitt, Frederick Emil, 1837–1923.
  Prisoner of war, experiences in Southern prisons. *Wisconsin magazine of history* xlii (1958/59) 83–93. illus., plan.    **10A**

### INFANTRY

## New Jersey Brigades

### 1st Brigade

1st, 2nd, 3rd, 4th, 10th, 15th, 23rd, and 40th infantry regiments.

Baquet, Camille
  History of the First brigade, New Jersey volunteers, from 1861 to 1865. Compiled under the authorization of Kearny's First New Jersey brigade society, by Camille Baquet, Second Lieutenant, Company A, First regiment, New Jersey volunteers. Published by the State of New Jersey. Trenton, MacCrellish &

Quigley, printers, 1910. iii, 515 p. plates (illus., partly col.; ports.). 23½cm.
            DLC NjR NN   **11**
On cover and spine: History of Kearny's First New Jersey brigade.

Society of Kearney's First New Jersey Brigade.
  . . . Annual reunion. . . . v 1886 (DLC, NjR, NHi); vi 1887 (Nj); xii 1893 (NjR); xvii 1898 (NHi).    **12**

For other references on the 1st New Jersey brigade, see the entries under the regiments forming the Brigade.

### 2nd Brigade

5th, 6th, 7th, 8th, and 11th infantry regiments.

Report of the . . . annual reunion . . . 1888–97. 9 nos. 18cm.    **12A**
  DLC (ii, ix); Nj (iv–viii); NjR (iv); NHi (i–iii).

For other references on the 2nd New Jersey brigade, see the entries under the regiments forming the Brigade.

## Regiments

### 1ST INFANTRY

*Mustered in: April 30, 1861. (3 months)*
*Mustered out: July 31, 1861.*
*New Jersey and the rebellion 24–62.*
*Record 15–27.*

*Mustered in: May 21, 1861. (3 years)*
*Mustered out: June 29, 1865.*
*New Jersey and the rebellion, the First brigade 63–128.*
*Record 68–101.*

Ferguson, Joseph
  Life-struggles in Rebel prisons, a record of the sufferings, escapes, adventures and starvation of the Union prisoners, by Joseph Ferguson, late Captain First New Jersey. Containing an appendix with the names, regiments, and date of death of Pennsylvania soldiers who died at Andersonville. With an introduction by Rev. Joseph T. Cooper. . . . Philadelphia, James M. Ferguson, 1865. 206, xxiv p. front. (port.), plates (illus.). 18cm.
            DLC NN   **13**
NjR has an 1865 reprint with "Third edition" at head of title. "Appendix, roll of honor. Names of the Pennsylvania soldiers who died at Andersonville," xxiv p.

Stockton, Robert Field, –1891.
Memorial address delivered by Gen. R. F. Stockton at the service held in memory of Brevet Maj. Gen. A. T. A. Torbet, at Milford, Delaware, September 30th. 1880. Trenton, William S. Sharp, printer, publisher, 1880. 19 p. 23½cm. NjR **14**

Townsend, George Alfred, 1841–1914.
. . . General Alfred T. A. Torbet memorial, by George Alfred Townsend, taken from the Army and navy journal, November 13th, 1880. [Wilmington] Historical Society of Delaware, 1922. 122 p. 23cm. NjR NN **15**

## 2ND INFANTRY

*Mustered in: May 1, 1861.* (3 months)
*Mustered out: July 31, 1861.*
*New Jersey and the rebellion 24–62.*
*Record 28–39.*
*Mustered in: May 26, 1861.* (3 years)
*Mustered out: July 11, 1865.*
*New Jersey and the rebellion, the First brigade 63–128.*
*Record 102–49.*

Craven, Elijah Richardson, 1824–1908.
In memoriam, sermon and oration. Sermon preached by E. R. Craven in the Third Presbyterian church, Newark, N. J., July 20, 1862, on occasion of the death of Col. I. M. Tucker, 2d reg't N. J. vols., who fell at the battle of Gaines' Mills, before Richmond, June 27, 1862. Oration delivered by Bro. John D. Foster on invitation of Protection lodge no. 28, I.O.O.F., in 3d Pres. church Newark, N. J., July 29, 1862, in commemoration of the death of P. G. representative, Isaac M. Tucker, Col. 2d reg't N. J. vols., and a member of said Lodge. Newark, Published by Protection Lodge No. 28 I.O.O.F., 1862. 42 p. 22½cm.
DLC NHi **16**
Goddu, Louis
The new recruit. *BandG* II (1893) 153–9. **17**

The author associates himself with Company K of the 14th New Jersey. The roster has a Louis Goddee in the 2nd New Jersey as a transfer from the 14th New Jersey. He mustered in, March 25, 1865; deserted, July 7, 1865.

## 3RD INFANTRY

*Mustered in: April 27, 1861.* (3 months)
*Mustered out: July 31, 1861.*
*New Jersey and the rebellion 24–62.*
*Record 40–52.*
*Mustered in: June 4, 1861.* (3 years)

*Mustered out: June 29, 1865.*
*New Jersey and the rebellion, the First brigade 63–128.*
*Record 150–81.*

Grubb, Edward Burd, 1841–1913.
An account of the battle of Crampton's pass [Maryland, Sept. 14, 1862] being an address delivered by Edward Burd Grubb at the reunion of Kearny's First New Jersey brigade, at Edgewater Park, September 20, 1888. 21 p. 23cm. Nj NjR **18**
Caption title.

—— Notes of a staff officer of our First New Jersey brigade on the seven day's battle on the Peninsula in 1862. Morristown, Moorestown print. co., 1910. 32 p. 22cm.
DLC NjR NHi **19**
Also published in Title 11.

Wamsley, James A 1851–
Co. A, Third regiment New Jersey volunteers, by Dr. J. A. Wamsley. [n. p., 19—] broadside, 30½ x 15½cm. NjR **20**
Poetry.

## 4TH INFANTRY

*Mustered in: April 27, 1861.* (3 months)
*Mustered out: July 31, 1861.*
*New Jersey and the rebellion 24–62.*
*Record 53–65.*
*Mustered in: August 19, 1861.* (3 years)
*Mustered out: July 9, 1865.*
*New Jersey and the rebellion, the First brigade 63–128.*
*Record 182–227.*

Forbes, Eugene, –1865.
Diary of a soldier and prisoner of war in the Rebel prisons, written by Eugene Forbes, Sergeant Company B, 4th regiment New Jersey. Trenton, Murphy & Bechtel, printers, 1865. iv, 5–68 p. 22cm. CSmH WHi **21**

Jackson, Huntington Wolcott, 1841–1901.
The battle of Chancellorsville (read May 1, 1883). *MOLLUS-Ill* II 49–78. **22**

—— The battle of Gettysburg (read April 5, 1882). *MOLLUS-Ill* I 147–84 **23**

—— Sedgwick at Fredericks and Salem heights. *BandL* III 224–32. **24**

## 5TH INFANTRY

*Mustered in: August 22, 1861.*
*Consolidated with 7th regiment of infantry: November 6, 1864.*
*New Jersey and the rebellion, the Second brigade 129–202.*
*Record 228–66.*

## 6TH INFANTRY

*Mustered in: August 19, 1861.*
*Mustered out: September 7, 1864.*
*New Jersey and the rebellion, the Second brigade 129–202.*
*Record 267–99.*

Crawford, Joseph U
Hooker's division at Seven Pines. *US* ns I
(1889) 290–302.         **25**

## 7TH INFANTRY

*Mustered in: September 3, 1861.*
*Mustered out: October 7, 1864 (non-veterans); July 17, 1865.*
*New Jersey and the rebellion, the Second brigade 129–202.*
*Record 300–65.*

By-laws of the Seventh regiment veteran asso'n of New Jersey. Newark, Wm. H. Holloway, printer, 1896. 16 p. 14½cm    NHi   **26**

Martin's soldiers record. Morris county pioneers. Company "K," Seventh regiment, New Jersey vols. Milwaukee, Lith. by L. Kurz & co. [1863] col. illus. broadside, 52 x 42cm.
          DLC   **26A**

Francine, Albert Philip, 1873–
Louis Raymond Francine, 1837–1863.
[1910] 29 p. front. (port.). 23cm.
          DLC   **27**
Caption title: Brigadier-General Louis Raymond Francine by Albert Phillip [sic] Francine. Carte de visite in DLC copy "Philip."

Hamilton, Edward John, 1834–1918.
A Union Chaplain's diary. Edited by Chase C. Mooney. *PNJHS* LXXV (1957) 1–17. 2 plates (illus., fold. map).   **28**

Hillyer, William R
Chancellorsville, May 2 and 3, 1863, by Captain William R. Hillyer. 1904. 40 p. *MOLLUS-DC* no 55. 2 plans.   **29**

Lloyd, George William,   –1906.
The patriot's death, its bloody lessons, a funeral discourse on the death of Corp'l James S. Gustin, who fell in the advanced guard before Williamsburg, Va., preached in the Presbyterian church of Branchville, N. J., by Rev. G. W. Lloyd. New York, John F. Trow, printer, 1862. 24 p. 23½cm.    DLC NjR   **30**

Revere, Joseph Warren, 1812–1880.
Keel and saddle, a retrospect of forty years of military and naval service, by Joseph W. Revere. Boston, James R. Osgood and co., 1872. xiii, 360 p. 20cm.    NjR NHi NN   **31**
Civil war as Colonel of the 7th New Jersey 269–78.

## 8TH INFANTRY

*Mustered in: September 14, 1861.*
*Mustered out: July 17, 1865.*
*New Jersey and the rebellion; the Second brigade 129–202.*
*Record 366–429.*

Todd, Henry Hugh
The narrative of a prisoner of war. California commandery of the Military order of the loyal legion of the United States, March 25, 1893, by Henry Hugh Todd, late Captain 8th New Jersey. 20 p. 22½cm.
On cover: War paper no. 11.    DLC NN   **32**

## 9TH INFANTRY

*Organized: September 13 to October 15, 1861.*
*Mustered out: July 12, 1865.*
*New Jersey and the rebellion 203–66.*
*Record 430–87.*

Memorial of Colonel Abram Zabriskie, by the Bar of Hudson county, New Jersey. Jersey City, Printed by John H. Lyon, 1864. 34 p. 22cm.    CSmH NjR   **32A**

Minutes of meeting, held at the . . . annual reunion of the 9th New Jersey veteran volunteers. . . .   **33**

1 Elizabeth, February 8, 1887. 27 p.
          DLC NHi NjR

2 Trenton, September 13, 1887. 20 p.
          DLC NHi

8 Camden, September 20, 1893. 9, (2) p.
          DNW

Cleveland, Edmund Janes, 1842–1902.
[Diary] Edited by Edmund J. Cleveland, Jr. *PNJHS* LXVI-LXXI (1948–1953).   **34**
Contents: The second battle of Cold harbor LXVI 25–37. The siege of Petersburg LXVI 76–95, 176–96. The campaign of promise and disappointment LXVII 218–40, 308–28. The early campaigns in North Carolina LXVIII 119–61, 216–66; LXIX 143–67, 248–73, 362–86; LXX 61–5, 137–40, 278–83; LXXI 62–4, 136–41, 204–09.

Drake, James Madison, 1837–1913.
Adventurous escape from prison life, an incident of the late Civil war. *Magazine of American history* XIV (New York 1885) 404–06.   **35**

—— Fast and loose in Dixie, an unprejudiced narrative of personal experience as a prisoner of war at Libby, Macon, Savannah, and Charleston. With an account of a desperate leap from a moving train of cars, a weary tramp of forty-five days through swamps and mountains, places and peoples visited, etc., by

J. Madison Drake. New York, Authors' pub. co., 1880. x, [11]–310 p. front. (port.), illus., ports. 20cm. NjR NN 36
Coulter 132.

—— Historical sketches of the Revolutionary and Civil wars, with an account of author's desperate leap from a swiftly moving train of cars, and a fatiguing tramp of 1,000 miles through three Confederate states, in making his escape, by J. Madison Drake. Printed for the author. New York, Webster press, 1908. 272 p. front. (port.), illus. 24cm.
NjR NN 37

—— The history of the Ninth New Jersey veteran vols., a record of its service, from Sept. 13th, 1861, to July 12th, 1865, with a complete official roster, and sketches of prominent members, with anecdotes, incidents and thrilling reminiscences, by Captain J. Madison Drake. Elizabeth, Journal print. house, 1889. 501 p. illus., map, plates (illus., ports.). 23½cm. DLC NjR NN 38
Unit roster 422–501.

—— Narrative of the capture, imprisonment and escape of J. Madison Drake, Captain Ninth New Jersey veteran volunteers. . . . 1868. 93 p. illus. cover. 21cm. DLC NjR NHi 39
Title and print date from cover. Text in double columns. NjJ has variant printing without date and illustration on cover and with the text extended to 94 pages by three "congratulatory letters."

Everts, Hermann
A complete and comprehensive history of the Ninth regiment New Jersey vols. infantry, from its first organization to its final muster out, by Hermann Everts. Newark, A. Stephen Holbrook, printer, 1865. 197 p. 21½cm.
Unit roster [5]–71. DLC NjR NN 40

Hightstown Gazette, Hightstown, N. J.
The Gazette souvenir, fifth reunion of the Ninth regt. New Jersey veteran vols., held at Hightstown, N. J., September 16th, 1890. . . . [Hightstown] Hightstown Gazette [1890] [20] p. NjR 40A
Proceedings of the reunion events and texts of addresses by local persons and by Surgeon F. B. Gillette.

New Jersey. Monument to Ninth New Jersey Volunteers at New Berne, North Carolina, Commission for Erection of.
. . . Report . . . Dedication National cemetery, New Berne, N. C., May 18, 1905. Published by authority of the Commission. [Philadelphia, John C. Winston co.] 1905. 112 p. front. (illus.), 2 facs., ports. 26cm. NjR NN 41
On cover: New Jersey's Ninth regiment, 1861–1905. At head of title: 1861–1865. Mustered in October, 1861; mustered out, July 1865; total enlistments 2,720 men; three years and nine months of continued active service in the field.

Runyan, Morris C
Eight days with the Confederates and capture of their archives, flags, &c. by Company "G" Ninth New Jersey vol., written by Captain Morris C. Runyan. Princeton, Wm. C. C. Zapf, printer, 1896. 44 p. front. (port.). 22cm.
DLC NjJ NN 42
Coulter 400. Unit roster [43]–4.

## 10TH INFANTRY

*Organized as Olden legion and left State: December 26, 1861.*

*Accepted as State organization and designated 10th regiment of infantry: January 29, 1862.*

*Mustered out: June 22, 1865.*

*New Jersey and the rebellion 267–75.*

*Record 488–51.*

Weiser, George
Nine months in Rebel prisons, by George Weiser, Company A, 10th regiment, New Jersey volunteers. Philadelphia, John N. Reeve & co., 1890. 53, (1) p. 3 plates (ports.). 20cm.
DLC In 43

## 11TH INFANTRY

*Mustered in: August 18, 1862.*

*Mustered out: June 6, 1865.*

*New Jersey and the rebellion 276–98.*

*Record 542–84.*

Kearny, Philip J 1841–1863.
Letters from the field written to his relatives, by Major Philip J. Kearney, Eleventh New Jersey. *Historical magazine* s2 vii (Morrisania 1870) 184–95. 44
For comment on the letters by "John Schoonover, late Lt. Col., 11th N. J. vols." with editorial statement, see *Historical magazine* s3 i (1872/73) 122–3.

McAllister, Robert, 1813–1891.
McAllister's brigade at the Bloody angle [May 12, 1864] *BandL* iv 176. 45

Marbaker, Thomas D 1846–
History of the Eleventh New Jersey volunteers, from its organization to Appomattox, to which is added experiences of prison life and sketches of individual members, by Thos. D. Marbaker, Serg't Co. E. Trenton, MacCrellish & Quigley, printers, 1898. viii, 364 p. front. (port.), illus., ports. 22½cm.
DLC NjR NN 46

Union Soldiers' Alliance, Washington, D. C.
Octavius Longworth Pruden. In memoriam. Union soldiers' alliance, Washington, D. C. The following brief sketch of the military serv-

*11th Infantry, continued*

ice of comrade Pruden was prepared by the Committee appointed for that purpose. . . . [Washington, D. C. 1902] [8] p. front. (port.). 24cm.                                        DLC    47

Welling, Edward Livingston
An address delivered before the Temperance association of the Eleventh regiment N. J. vols. . . . April 25, 1864. . . . Trenton, Murphy & Bechtel, printers, 1864. 29 p.    NjR    47A
"History of the Association," [27]–9.

## 12TH INFANTRY

*Mustered in: September 4, 1862.*
*Mustered out: July 15, 1865.*
*New Jersey and the rebellion 299–315.*
*Record 585–627.*

Proceedings of the First [-sixth] annual reunion of the Society of the Twelfth regiment New Jersey volunteers held at . . . 1875 [-1880] 56 p. 23½cm.                         NHi    48
Caption title.

[Roster of the Twelfth New Jersey volunteers. Oration of Colonel William E. Potter delivered before the surviving members of the Twelfth regiment New Jersey volunteers in the War of the rebellion at their first reunion, held at Woodbury, New Jersey, February 22, 1875.] [Woodbury ? 1875] 32 p. 23½cm.
                                        DLC NHi    49
Souvenir pamphlet of dedication of a marker in memory of the 12 N. J. vols. at the battle of Wilderness, located at the Old Orange plank and Brock road, near Fredericksburg, Va., Memorial day, May 30th, 1942. . . . [18] p. illus., ports. 23cm.                 NjR    49A

Haines, William P        1840–
Historique, a sketch of the Twelfth regiment New Jersey volunteers. Dedicated to Ellwood Griscom "he was my pard," by Wm. P. Haines, Private Co. F. Mickleton, 1896. sheet 18 x 33cm. folded to [8] p., 18 x 9cm.
Dated: Sept. 4, 1896.               NjR    50

—— History of the men of Co. F, with description of the marches and battles of the 12th New Jersey vols . . . by Wm. P. Haines. Mickleton, [Camden, C. S. Magrath, printer] 1897. vii, 293 p. 22½cm.
                                    DLC NjR NN    51
"Life sketches, men of Co. F" [97]–169.

Riley, Frank M        1842–1923.
Libby prison experience of Frank M. Riley, Captain Co. F, Twelfth New Jersey volunteers. In Almanac and year book First national

11th – 13th New Jersey Infantry

bank, Woodston, N. J., 1917, p [32]–40. plate (port.).                                    52
Originally published in Title 51.

Slater, Thomas Ogden, 1842–
Incidents of personal experiences, given by Capt. T. O. Slater, at the forty-third reunion of the Twelfth regiment New Jersey volunteers, held at Elmer, Salem county, N. J., Sept. 4, 1916. [New York, Knickerbocker press, 1916] 24 p. 20½cm.              NjR    53

Thompson, Richard S        1837–
A scrap of Gettysburg (read February 11, 1897). *MOLLUS-Ill* iii 97–109.        54

## 13TH INFANTRY

*Mustered in: August 25, 1862.*
*Mustered out: June 8, 1865.*
*New Jersey and the rebellion 316–55.*
*Record 628–61.*

Historical sketch of Co. "D," 13th regiment, N. J. vols., part of the 3d brigade, 1st division, 12th army corps, U. S. A., with the muster roll of the Company. Compiled and printed for the use of its members by the authority of "D" society. New York, D. H. Gildersleeve & co., 1875. 87, (1) p. 19½cm.
                                    DLC NjR NN    55
"A brief record of the members of Company D" [47]–80.

Report of the Monument committee of the Veteran association of the 13th regiment, New Jersey volunteers, 1862–1865, the dedicatory exercises at Gettysburg, on Friday, July 1st, 1887, and the campfire on Friday evening, June 30th, with a list of the contributors to the monument fund. New Brunswick, Fredonian pub. co.'s print, 1887. 63 p. 22cm
                                        DLC NjR    56

Some rhymes read at the annual re-union of "D" society, held at the Continental hotel, Newark, N. J., on the evening of Tuesday, January 15, 1907. [4] p. 17½ x 9cm.
Caption title.                        NjR    57

Veteran association of the Thirteenth New Jersey volunteers. Proceedings of the . . . reunion at. . . . i–xx 1886–1905; xxviii–xxix 1913–1914. DLC (i–vii, xiii), DNW (vi, viii–xii, xiv–xx), Nj (i–xviii), NjR (i–xix, xxviii–xxix).                                    58

Allen, Edward Livingston, 1846–
Descriptive lecture, both sides of army life, the grave and the gay, by Rev. E. Livingston Allen, late Sergeant Co. K, 13th N. J. vols. [Poughkeepsie, N. Y., 1885] 16 p. 25½cm.
Title from cover.                    DLC    59

Carman, Ezra Ayers, 1834–1909.
"General Hardee's escape from Savannah,"
prepared by Brevet Brigadier General E. A.
Carman. 1893. 30 p. *MOLLUS-DC* no 13.
plan.                                            **60**

Crowell, Joseph Edgar, 1844–
The young volunteer, a record of the expe-
riences of a private soldier, by Joseph E.
Crowell, late Private Company K, 13th N. J.
New York, F. Tennyson Neely [1899] 490 p.
19½cm.                               Nj     **61**

—— The young volunteer, the everyday experiences of a soldier boy in the Civil war, by
Joseph E. Crowell. Second edition, revised
and illustrated. New York, G. W. Dillingham
co. [c1906] vi, [7]–492 p. plates (illus.,
ports.). 18½cm.              DLC NN     **62**

—— —— Paterson, Published by Joseph E.
Crowell, The Call [1906] vi, [7]–492 p. plates
(illus., ports.). 18½cm.           NjR     **63**

Hopkins, Charles A
The march to the sea, by Charles A. Hopkins, late Captain 13th regiment, New Jersey.
1885. 32 p. *PNRISSHS* s3 no 12.        **64**

Smith, James O          1844–
My first campaign and battles, a Jersey boy
at Antietam, seventeen days from home.
*BandG* i (1893) 280–90. illus., plan, ports. **65**

Toombs, Samuel, 1884–1889.
Reminiscences of the war, comprising a detailed account of the experiences of the Thirteenth regiment New Jersey volunteers in
camp, on the march, and in battle, by Samuel
Toombs. With the personal recollections of
the author. Orange, Printed at the Journal
office, 1878. 232, 47 p. 17½cm.
                            DLC NjR NN     **66**
Unit roster, 47 p. Coulter 449.

## 14TH INFANTRY

*Mustered in: August 26, 1862.*

*Mustered out: June 18, 1865.*

*New Jersey and the rebellion 356–81.*

*Record 662–96.*

Report of the Commissioners appointed by
Edward C. Stokes, Governor of New Jersey,
to erect a monument to commemorate the services of the 14th reg't N. J. volunteers in the
Civil war of 1861 to 1865. Services of dedication at Monocacy, Frederick county, Maryland, July 9, 1907. [Asbury Park, Pennypacker
press, 1907] 34 p. plates (illus., ports.). 20cm.
                                    DLC NHi     **67**

... Report of the fiftieth anniversary of the
muster in of the Fourteenth regiment N. J.

volunteers and the thirty-fourth reunion at
the home of James B. Vredenburgh, Freehold,
N. J., August 26, 1912. 40 p. 1 illus., ports.
20½cm.                               Nj     **68**
At head of title: 1862 1912.

Terrill, John Newton,          –1916.
Campaign of the Fourteenth regiment New
Jersey volunteers, by Sergeant J. Newton Terrill, Co. K, Fourteenth regiment. New Brunswick, Terhune & Van Anglen's press, 1866.
132 p. 22½cm.                  NjR NHi     **69**

—— —— Second edition. New Brunswick,
Daily Home News press, 1884. 132 p. 18½cm.
                            DLC NjR NN     **70**
"Commenced Sept. 1st, 1865; finished July 15th,
1866."

Vredenburgh, Peter, 1837–1864.
... Letters of Major Peter Vredenburgh ...
of the battles and marches of the old Fourteenth regiment N. J. vols ... Printed for private circulation. [n. p. 187–?] 37, (1) p.
23½cm.                             DLC NN     **70A**
Title from cover, p [1]. At head of title: For the
satisfaction of his family, and to preserve the evidence
furnished by the. "In memoriam. Major P- V- Sept.
19, 1864," (1) p. signed: H.

## 15TH INFANTRY

*Mustered in: August 25, 1862.*

*Mustered out: June 22, 1865.*

*New Jersey and the rebellion 382–407.*

*Record 697–740.*

Report of Monument commissioners appointed
to erect a monument on battlefield of Salem
church, and to place a tablet on the battlefield
of Spottsylvania, Va. Transmitted by the Governor to the Legislature, session of 1910. Trenton, MacCrellish & Quigley, printers, 1910.
7 p. 23½cm.                        DLC NN     **71**
"To commemorate the service of the Fifteenth regiment, New Jersey volunteer infantry, in the battles of
Salem church and Spottsylvania, and other engagements of the Civil war."

... Re-union Fifteenth N. J. volunteers at ...
                                        NHi     **72**
[1st] Hackettstown, October 19, 1880. Dover, "Iron
Era" print, 1880. 24 p. 23cm.
2nd, Flemington, August 25th, 1881. Trenton,
Wm. S. Sharp, printer, 1881. 20 p. 23cm.
3rd. Morristown, August 17th, 1882. Morristown,
"Chronicle" print, 1883. 8 p. 22cm.

Roster of the officers and men of the 15th
regiment association, New Jersey volunteers.
Somerville, Somerville pub. co., 1896. 37 p.
14½cm.                             DLC NHi     **73**

*15th Infantry, continued*

Andrews, Frank G

Fourth annual pilgrimage of the Fifteenth regiment New Jersey volunteers' veteran association, May 11th to 15th, 1909, Fredericksburg, Washington and Gettysburg. Washington, Washington Star printery [1909] 81 p. illus., ports. 23½cm.                     Nj    **74**
Frank G. Andrews, pilgrimage historian.

Campbell, Edward Livingston

Historical sketch of the Fifteenth regiment New Jersey volunteers, First brigade, First division, Sixth corps. Trenton, Wm. S. Sharp, printer, 1880. 25 p. 23cm.          NHi    **75**

Haines, Alanson Austin, 1830–1891.

History of the Fifteenth regiment New Jersey volunteers, by Alanson A. Haines, Chaplain of the Regiment. New York, Jenkins & Thomas, printers, 1883. 388 p. front. (port.). illus., maps. 22½cm.    DLC NjR NN    **76**
Unit roster [321]–88.

Lindsley, J        Frank

Pilgrimage of the Fifteenth regiment New Jersey volunteers veteran association to the White Oak church camp ground and battlefields of Fredericksburg, Va. and vicinity, May 22 to 26, 1906. Newark, Madison & co., printers [1906] 62, (1) p. illus., map, ports. 23cm.
                                NjR NHi    **77**
"J. Frank Lindsley, historian," (1) p.

**16th Regiment see 1st Cavalry**

**17TH, 18TH, 19TH, and 20TH REGIMENTS**

The four militia regiments numbered 1–4 raised in response to the Presidential proclamation of April 15, 1861, were subsequently counted as the 17th, 18th, 19th, and 20th regiments and are so carried on the rolls of the Adjutant general of New Jersey, *Record* 741.

**21ST INFANTRY**

*Mustered in: September 15, 1862.*
*Mustered out: June 19, 1863.*
*New Jersey and the rebellion 486–96.*
*Record 742–60.*

**22ND INFANTRY**

*Mustered in: September 22, 1862.*
*Mustered out: June 25, 1863.*
*New Jersey and the rebellion 497–9.*
*Record 761–78.*

**23RD INFANTRY**

*Mustered in: September 13, 1862.*
*Mustered out: June 27, 1863.*
*New Jersey and the rebellion 500–14.*
*Record 779–98.*

History of the Re-union society of the 23d regiment N. J. volunteers, organized December 13, 1888. Philadelphia, Keystone print. co., 1890. 111 p. facs., 3 plates (ports.). 25cm.
Unit roster 47–90.    DLC NjR NHi    **78**

Dobbins, Edward L        1838–

Fragments from the history of a Quaker regiment. In War talks of Morristown veterans (Morristown, N. J. 1887) 30–4.          **79**

**24TH INFANTRY**

*Mustered in: September 16, 1862.*
*Mustered out: June 29, 1863.*
*New Jersey and the rebellion 515–27.*
*Record 799–818.*

Borton, Benjamin

Awhile with the Blue; or, memories of war days, the true story of a Private, by Benjamin Borton. Published by the author. Passaic, Wm. Taylor, printer, 1898. 168 p. plates (illus., ports.). 19½cm.    DLC NN PU    **80**
Unit roster [153]–68.

—— On the parallels; or, chapters of inner history, a story of the Rappahannock, by Benjamin Borton. . . . Woodstown, Monitor-Register print, 1903. 333, (1) p. front. (port.), illus. 19½cm.          NjR NN    **81**

Reeves, James Johnson, 1839–

History of the Twenty-fourth regiment, New Jersey volunteers, by James J. Reeves. Printed by direction of the Society at their reunion in Woodbury, N. J., December 13, 1888. Camden, S. Chew, printer, 1889. 45 p. 22cm.
                                DLC NjR NN    **82**
"Constitution and by-laws of 'The reunion society of the Twenty-fourth regiment, New Jersey volunteers' " . . . [39]–45.

**25TH INFANTRY**

*Mustered in: September 18–26, 1862.*
*Mustered out: June 20, 1863.*
*New Jersey and the rebellion 528–38.*
*Record 819–38.*

**26TH INFANTRY**

*Mustered in: September 18, 1862.*
*Mustered out: June 27, 1863.*
*New Jersey and the rebellion 529–52.*
*Record 839–58.*

Dodd, Ira Seymour, 1842–1922.
The household of the hundred thousand, social life in the Army of the Union. *McClure's magazine* xi (1898) 154–61.                    **82A**

——— The making of a regiment. What a service of seven months did for a troop of raw recruits. By Ira Seymour. *McClure's magazine* ix (1897) 1031–44.                    **,83**

——— The song of the Rappahannock, the real experience in battle of a young soldier of the Army of the Potomac. *McClure's magazine* viii (1896/97) 314–20.                    **83A**

——— The song of the Rappahannock, sketches of the Civil war, by Ira Seymour Dodd. New York, Dodd, Mead and co., 1898. viii, 254 p. 17½cm.                    DLC NN    **83B**

——— One young soldier, formerly published as The song of the Rappahannock, by Ira Seymour Dodd. New York, Dodd, Mead and co., 1918. 253 p. 18½cm.         DLC NN    **84**
Printed from the plates of Title 83B, the Preface and last paragraph are omitted.

## 27TH INFANTRY

*Mustered in: September 19, 1862.*
*Mustered out: July 2, 1863.*
*New Jersey and the rebellion 553–68.*
*Record 859–80.*

. . . In memoriam William Harrison Lambert, May, 1842–June, 1912, first President of the Lincoln fellowship . . . Edited by the First vice-president. New York, 1912. 36, (3) p. front. (port.). 24cm.         CSmH NN    **85**
Mustered in 15th Pennsylvania cavalry, August 22, 1862; discharged for promotion in the 27th New Jersey infantry, November 24, 1862; mustered out, July 2, 1863; 33rd New Jersey infantry, July 25, 1863; mustered out, July 17, 1865. At head of title: No. 4 of the publications of the Lincoln fellowship of New York.

[In memoriam William H. Lambert] Memorial service in the Second Presbyterian church, Germantown, Philadelphia, Sunday, June the sixteenth, at four-fifteen, nineteen hundred and twelve. 30 p. front. (port.). 25cm.
Supplied portion of title from cover. NHi    **85A**

Condict, Alfred H
The Army of the Potomac, its heroic dead and living. In War talks of Morristown veterans (Morristown, N. J. 1887) 10–16.    **86**

Richmond, John Brown, 1829–1911.
Our deceased comrades, read at the reunion of the Twenty-seventh regiment New Jersey volunteers at Morristown, N. J., October 7, 1896, by John B. Richmond, Major and Surgeon. 8 p. 22cm.         NHi    **87**

## 28TH INFANTRY

*Mustered in: September 22, 1862.*
*Mustered out: July 6, 1863.*
*New Jersey and the rebellion 569–74.*
*Record 881–900.*

## 29TH INFANTRY

*Mustered in: September 20, 1862.*
*Mustered out: July 6, 1863.*
*New Jersey and the rebellion 574–8.*
*Record 901–19.*

Souvenir program, unveiling of the monument in commemoration of the services of the Twenty-ninth regiment New Jersey volunteer infantry in the War between the States, 1861–1865. Fairview cemetery, Monmouth county, New Jersey, Memorial day, Saturday, May 30, 1925, at three o'clock. [8] p. mounted col. illus. on cover, port. inserted. 27½cm.
                    NHi    **88**

## 30TH INFANTRY

*Mustered in: September 17, 1862.*
*Mustered out: June 27, 1863.*
*New Jersey and the rebellion 579–81.*
*Record 920–39.*

Bowman, James, 1833–1913.
A record of the services of the Thirtieth regiment, New Jersey volunteers in the War of the rebellion. . . . Somerville, printed by Unionist-Gazette Association, 1912. 20 p. 23cm.
                    NjR (P)    **89**

## 31ST INFANTRY

*Mustered in: September 17, 1862.*
*Mustered out: June 24, 1863.*
*New Jersey and the rebellion 582–8.*
*Record 940–58.*

Honeyman, Robert R        1836–1873.
Col. Honeyman and his war journal. *Our home* i (Somerville 1873) 347–53, 396–99, 463–7, 499–503, 544–50.         NjR    **90**
Text signed: "V. D." [Abraham Van Doren Honeyman, 1849–1936]

*32nd Regiment see 2nd Cavalry*

## 33RD INFANTRY

*Mustered in: September 3, 1863.*
*Mustered out: July 17, 1865.*
*New Jersey and the rebellion 609–41.*
*Record 959–1003.*

*33rd Infantry, continued*

Pierson, Stephen, 1830–1900.
From Chattanooga to Atlanta in 1864, a personal reminiscence. *PNJHS* xvi (1931) 324–56.      **91**
Foreword, 324–7, by Major-General Henry G. Sharpe.

Taylor, Benjamin Cook, 1801–1881.
A sermon delivered in the Reformed Dutch church at Bergen, N. J., July 10, 1864, on the death of Capt. Wm. H. Cochran, who was killed in battle, June 16, 1864, at Pine Knoll, near Marietta, Ga., by Benjamin C. Taylor. . . . New York, C. S. Westcott & co., 1864. 21 p. 18½cm.      DLC NjR   **92**

See also Title 85–85A.

### 34TH INFANTRY

*Mustered in: September 3 to November 9, 1863.*
*Mustered out: April 30, 1866.*
*New Jersey and the rebellion 642–7.*
*Record 1004–53.*

### 35TH INFANTRY

*Mustered in: August 28 to October 14, 1863.*
*Mustered out: July 20, 1865.*
*New Jersey and the rebellion 648–60.*
*Record 1054–94.*

*36th Regiment see 3rd Cavalry*

### 37TH INFANTRY

*Mustered in: June 23, 1864.*
*Mustered out: October 1, 1864.*
*New Jersey and the rebellion 670–3.*
*Record 1095–1109.*

. . . Souvenir of the first annual reunion, 37th regiment New Jersey volunteers at the home of Gen. E. Burd Grubb, Edgewater park, New Jersey, September 12th, 1889. [New York, J. Henry Probst, printer, 1889] 26 p. 12 x 17cm.      DLC NHi   **93**

Rodgers, Richard N
Epitome of the 37th reg't, New Jersey volunteers, by R. N. Rodgers, Co. E. [New York, J. Craft, printer, 1864] broadside, 48½ x 36cm., fold and mounted in boards, 26½ x 16cm.      DLC NN   **94**
"Epitome 37th regiment, N.J. vols., by R. N. Rodgers, Co. E. Privately printed, October 25th, 1864," label mounted on p 2 of cover. On cover: Epitome 37th regt. N.J. vols.

### 38TH INFANTRY

*Mustered in: September 9 to October 3, 1864.*
*Mustered out: June 30, 1865.*
*New Jersey and the rebellion 674–5.*
*Record 1110–28.*

### 39TH INFANTRY

*Organized: October 3, 1864.*
*Mustered out: June 17, 1865.*
*New Jersey and the rebellion 676–8.*
*Record 1129–51.*

### 40TH INFANTRY

*Mustered in: October 24, 1864 to March 10, 1865.*
*Mustered out: July 13, 1865.*
*New Jersey and the rebellion 679.*
*Record 1152–79.*

PENNSYLVANIA

# Reference Works

Bates, Samuel Penniman, 1827–1902.

History of Pennsylvania volunteers, 1861–5, prepared in compliance with Acts of the Legislature, by Samuel P. Bates. . . . Harrisburg, B. Singerly, State printer, 1869–71. 5 v. plates (col. illus.; maps, partly fold.). 27½cm.


Dyer, Frederick Henry, 1849–1917.

A compendium of the War of the rebellion, 1908 (reprinted 1959).

"Regimental index" 214–28; "Regimental histories," p 1557–1627. The pagination is the same in the 1959 reprint.


Taylor, Frank Hamilton, 1846–

Philadelphia in the Civil war, 1861–1865 [by] Frank H. Taylor. Illustrated from contemporary prints and photographs and from drawings by the author. Published by the City. [Philadelphia, Dunlap print. co.] 1913. 360 p. illus., 2 maps, 1 fold., plates (illus.). 23cm.


*The Union army.*

"Record of Pennsylvania regiments," I (1908) 359–506.


United States. Adjutant General's Office.

Official army register of the volunteer force of the United States army for the years 1861, '62, '63, '64, '65. Part III. Pennsylvania, Delaware, Maryland, District of Columbia. Washington, 1865.

A roster of officers by regiments with an alphabetical index to the three states and the District of Columbia.

# PENNSYLVANIA

## First Defenders

Ringgold Light Artillery of Reading
Logan Guard of Lewiston
Washington Artillery of Pottsville
National Light Infantry of Pottsville
Allen Rifles of Allentown

*Tendered services: April 13, 1861.*
*Mustered in: April 18, 1861.*
*Assigned to 25th regiment of infantry as*
*Companies A, D, E, G and H.*

Heister, William Muhlenberg
The place of the Ringgold light artillery of
Reading, among the first five companies from
Pennsylvania which marched to the defense
of Washington, April, 1861, a paper read be-
fore the Historical society of Berks county,
June 14, 1870. . . . Reading, 1870. 16 p. front.
(facs.). 22cm.                                 NHi    *1*

—— —— [n. p., 1904] 13 p. 22cm.
"Reprinted 1904."                              DNW    *2*

Thompson, Heber Samuel, 1840–1911.
The first defenders, by Heber S. Thompson,
President of the First defenders' association.
1910. xiii, (1), 179 p. plates (facs.; ports, 1
double). 22½cm.                    DLC NHi    *3*
Muster in and out rolls, 26–93.

### ARTILLERY

### 1ST ARTILLERY (LIGHT)
### (43RD VOLUNTEERS)

*For muster in and out dates, see the in-*
*dividual batteries.*
Bates I 944–1013.
*Philadelphia in the Civil war 147–9.*

### Battery A

*Organized: August 5, 1861.*
*Mustered out: July 25, 1865.*

### Battery B

*Organized: August 5, 1861.*
*Mustered out: June 9, 1865.*

Cooper's "Battery B" before Petersburg, by
one of its members *BandG* IV (1894) 41–4.  *4*

Stewart, John Q
An address delivered by John Q. Stewart at
the twenty-second annual reunion of the Association of Battery B, First artillery, Pennsyl-

vania reserve corps, at Mount Jackson, Law-
rence county, Penn'a., Monday, June 8, 1891.
[New Castle, New Castle News, 1891] 20 p.
23cm.                                         DLC NHi    *5*
Also printed in the *New Castle News*, Wednesday,
June 10, 1891.

—— Address of John Q. Stewart at the thirty-
first annual reunion of Battery B, First Pennsylvania light artillery, P.R.V.C., Mount Jackson, Lawrence county, Penna., Friday, June
8, 1900. 16 p. 23½cm.                         DNW    *6*

### Battery C

*Organized: August 5, 1861.*
*Consolidated with Battery D, 1st regi-*
*ment of light artillery: October 23, 1863.*
*Second battery organized: December 1864.*
*Mustered out: June 30, 1865.*

### Battery D

*Organized: August 5, 1861.*
*Mustered out: June 30, 1865.*

### Battery E

*Organized: August 5, 1861.*
*Mustered out: July 20, 1865.*

### Battery F

*Organized: August 5, 1861.*
*Mustered out: July 9, 1865.*

### Battery G

*Organized: August 5, 1861.*
*Mustered out: June 29, 1865.*

Rudisill, James Jefferson, 1900–
The days of our Abraham, 1811–1899 [by]
James Jefferson Rudisill. York, York print. co.,
1936. 530 p. plates (facs., illus., maps, ports.).
23cm.                                         DLC NjN    *7*
Book three, the soldier, 61–490. "There have been
200 copies . . . printed — after which the type was
destroyed."

### Battery H

*Organized: August 5, 1861.*
*Mustered out: June 27, 1865.*

### Battery I

*Organized: March 2, 1865.*
*Mustered out: July 1, 1865.*

**2ND ARTILLERY (HEAVY)**
**(112TH VOLUNTEERS)**

*Organized: January 8, 1862.*
*Mustered out: January 29, 1866.*
*Bates* III 1059–1142.
*Philadelphia in the Civil war* 150–1.

Memorial of Edward S. Colwell. [Philadelphia, 1864] [29] p. 23½cm.    DLC   **8**
"40 copies only printed," ms note in DLC s copy.

Humphreys, Henry Hollingsworth, 1840–
Major General Andrew Atkinson Humphreys United States volunteers at Fredericksburg, Va., December 13th, 1862, and Farmville, Va., April 7th, 1865, by Henry H. Humphreys. Chicago, Press of R. R. McCabe & co. [1896] 60 p. 21½cm.          DLC NN   **9**

—— Reply to General Porter's articles which have appeared in the Century magazine during the years 1896 and 1897. *JMSIUS* XXIII (1898) 1–34.                  **10**

Ward, George Washington, 1845–
History of the Second Pennsylvania veteran heavy artillery, (112th regiment Pennsylvania volunteers), from 1861 to 1866, including the Provisional second Penn'a heavy artillery, by George W. Ward. Revised. Philadelphia, Geo. W. Ward, printer, 1904. xii, 311 p. maps, ports, plates (ports.). 24cm.
Unit roster [227]–311.   DLC NN PSt   **11**

Wells, Stephen F
Forts Harrison and Gilmer. In National tribune scrap book III 32.            **12**

**3RD ARTILLERY (HEAVY)**
**(152ND VOLUNTEERS)**

*Organized from existing units: February 17, 1863.*
*Mustered out: Companies A and B, July 11, 1865; Company H, July 25, 1865; Regiment, November 9, 1865.*
*Bates* IV 698–771.
*Philadelphia in the Civil war* 152–3.

Sanderson, Joseph Warren, 1839–
"Chaplains and Chaplains," by Rev. Jos. W. Sanderson. *MOLLUS-Wis* III 372–6.   **13**

—— The James river during the war. *MOLLUS-Wis* III 33–40.        **14**

—— Memoirs and memoranda of forty and fifty years ago, by Joseph W. Sanderson (former Capt. Battery "G," 3rd Pa. arty.). Milwaukee, Burdick & Allen, printers, 1907. 18 p. 23cm.            DLC   **15**

—— —— Cincinnati, Lotz print. co., 1910. 21 p. 23½cm.             MB   **16**
Text dated: Beaver dam, Wis., April, 1907.

**5TH ARTILLERY (HEAVY)**
**(204TH VOLUNTEERS)**

*Organized: August – September 1864.*
*Mustered out: June 30, 1865.*
*Bates* V 603–35.

**6TH ARTILLERY (HEAVY)**
**(212TH VOLUNTEERS)**

*Organized: September 15, 1864.*
*Mustered out: June 13, 1865.*
*Bates* V 771–801.

## Independent Batteries of Light Artillery

### Battery A

*Organized: September 19, 1861.*
*Mustered out: June 30, 1865.*
*Bates* V 854–8.
*Entire service was garrison duty at Fort Delaware.*

### Battery B

*Organized: August 1861.*
*Mustered out: October 12, 1865.*
*Bates* V 859–64.

### Battery C

*Organized: November 6, 1861.*
*Mustered out: June 30, 1865.*
*Bates* V 865–74.

### Battery D

*Mustered in: September 24, 1861.*
*Mustered out: June 13, 1865.*
*Bates* V 875–82.

Roster of Durell's battery. [n. p., n. d.] 6 p. 23cm.              DNW   **18**
Caption title. Contents: Roster [survivors] Wanted, either the present address, or that at the time of enlistment; In memoriam; Deserted.

Cuffel, Charles A
Durell's battery in the Civil war (Independent battery D, Pennsylvania volunteer artillery), a narrative of the campaigns and battles of Berks and Bucks counties' artillerists in the War of the rebellion, from the Battery's organization, September 24, 1861, to its mus-

ter out of service, June 13, 1865, by Lieutenant Charles A. Cuffel. [Philadelphia, Craig, Finley & co., 1900] 265 p. plates (illus., maps, ports.). 24cm.                                    DLC NN    **19**
Unit roster 258–65.

—— History of Durell's battery in the Civil war (Independent battery D, Pennsylvania volunteer artillery.) A narrative of the campaigns and battles of Berks and Bucks counties' artillerists in the War of the rebellion, from the Battery's organization, September 24, 1861, to its muster out of service, June 13, 1865. [Philadelphia, Craig, Finley & co., printers, 1903] 265 p. plates (illus., maps, ports.). 24cm.                                    DLC    **20**
Published with the "Approval of Durell's battery association." "Preface" signed: Charles A. Cuffel, Battery historian.

Rhoads, Samuel H
Oration delivered by Samuel H. Rhoads, late Captain commanding Battery "D" Pennsylvania volunteer artillery, from October 4, 1864, to June 13, 1865, at the dedication of the monument erected by the State of Pennsylvania on the battle field of Antietam, to commemorate the battle record and services of Durell's battery "D" Pennsylvania volunteer artillery, from September 24th, 1861, to June 13th, 1865. [Philadelphia, 1904] 47 p. plates (ports.). 23cm.            NHi NN    **21**
On cover: 1862 September seventh 1904.

### Battery E

*Organized: September 1861.*
*Mustered out: June 14, 1865.*
*Bates v 883–92.*
*Philadelphia in the Civil war 154.*

Brown, Henry E
The 28th and 147th regiments Penna. vols. at Gettysburg [by] H. E. Brown. [n. p. 189–] 7 p. 22½cm.                        DNW    **22**
Caption title. On cover: The 28th regt. P.V.V.I. The 147th regt. P.V.V.I., and Knap's ind. battery "E" at Gettysburg, July 1, 2, 3, 1863.

Nicholson, John Page, 1842–1922.
Association of the 28th and 147th regiments infantry and Independent battery "E," light artillery. Philadelphia, Allen, Lane & Scott [1882] 8 p. 23½cm.    CSmH DLC NHi    **23**
A transcript of the organization and services. 250 copies printed. "Compiled by the Secretary of the Association, John P. Nicholson."

### Battery F

*Organized: December 7, 1861.*
*Mustered out: June 26, 1865.*
*Bates v 893–9.*

Clark, William
History of Hampton Battery F independent Pennsylvania light artillery, organized at Pittsburgh, Pa., October 8, 1861, mustered out in Pittsburgh, June 26, 1865, compiled by William Clark. [Akron, Ohio, Werner co., 1909] 179 p. illus., ports, plate (double map). 24½cm.                        DLC NN    **24**
"Errata" slip inserted. Unit roster 73–101.

### Battery G

*Organized: August 22, 1862.*
*Mustered out: June 15, 1865.*
*Bates v 900–04.*

### Battery H

*Organized October 21, 1862.*
*Mustered out: June 1865.*
*Bates v 905–11.*

### Battery I

*Organized: December 31, 1863 to January 7, 1864.*
*Mustered out: June 23, 1865.*
*Bates v 912–17.*

## Named Artillery Organizations

### Commonwealth Company of Heavy Artillery

*Organized: April 24, 1861.*
*Mustered out: August 5, 1861.*

Copy of the muster-out roll of the Commonwealth artillery company of Pennsylvania volunteers, Philadelphia, 1861, together with the individual "records of service" of the members of the Company subsequent to the expiration of its term of service, as furnished by the Adjutant-general of the United States . . . with further particulars of service, compiled by Flor. W. Grugan, April 24th, 1885. Philadelphia, Royal print. house, 1885. 27 p. 22½cm.                                    NHi    **25**

### Keystone Battery of Light Artillery

*Organized: August 13, 1862.*
*Mustered out: August 24, 1863.*

### Keystone Militia Battery No. 2

*Organized: July 6, 1863.*
*Mustered out: August 24, 1863.*

Howard-Smith, Logan
The history of Battery A (formerly known as the Keystone battery) and Troop A, N.G.P.

*Keystone Militia Battery No. 2, continued*

Compiled and edited by Logan Howard-Smith and J. F. Reynolds Scott. Philadelphia, John C. Winston co., 1912. xii, 13–272 p. plates (illus., ports.). 21½cm.　　NN PSt　**26**
Civil war including roster, 13–69.

In memoriam William Houston Patterson, 1832–1904. [Philadelphia?, 1904] 17, (1) p. front. (port.). 25cm.　CSmH DLC　**26A**

### Ringgold Light Artillery

*Bates* i 3–8, 12.
See First defenders, p 29.

### Washington Artillery

*Bates* i 3-8, 10–11.
See First defenders, p 29.

## CAVALRY

### 1ST CAVALRY (44TH VOLUNTEERS)

*Organized: July – August, 1861.*
*Mustered out: September 9, 1864. Veterans and recruits consolidated to a battalion. Battalion consolidated with 6th and 17th regiments of cavalry, June 17, 1865, with designation, 2nd provisional regiment of cavalry.*
*Bates* i 1014–56.

Bayard, Samuel John
The life of George Dashiell Bayard . . . by Samuel J. Bayard. New York, G. P. Putnam's Sons, 1874. ix, [11]–337 p. front. (port.), 2 plates (illus., fold. map). 19½cm.
　　　　　　　　　　　　　NN　**26B**
As Colonel 1st Penn cavalry, 187–209.

Lloyd, William Penn, 1837–1911.
History of the First reg't Pennsylvania reserve cavalry, from its organization, August, 1861, to September, 1864, with list of names of all officers and enlisted men who have ever belonged to the Regiment, and remarks attached to each name, noting change. . . . Philadelphia, King & Baird, printers, 1864. 216 p. 19½cm.　　　　　　　DLC NN　**27**
"Preface' signed: Wm. P. Lloyd, Adjutant. Unit roster [138]–216. Coulter 295.

Scott, James Knox Polk, 1845–
The story of the battles at Gettysburg, by James K. P. Scott, H. 1st Penna. cavalry. . . . Harrisburg, Telegraph press, 1927. 301 p. plates (illus., ports.). 22½cm.　　NN　**28**
On spine: Book 1. "The story of the battles at Gettysburg, a trilogy, three books, [one to each day of the battle] each with its story complete." "Officers killed and mortally wounded at Gettysburg," 253–70, includes regiment and where the officer was killed.

Thomas, Hampton Sidney, 1837–
Some personal reminiscences of service in the cavalry of the Army of the Potomac, by Colonel Hampton S. Thomas. . . . Philadelphia, L. R. Hammersly & co., 1889. 26 p. 25cm.
　　　　　　　　　　　DLC NHi　**29**
Title and imprint from cover. "Reprinted from "The United service," January 1889.

### 1ST PROVISIONAL REGIMENT

*Formed by consolidation of 2nd and 3rd regiments of cavalry: June 17, 1865.*
*Mustered out: July 13, 1865.*

### 2ND CAVALRY (59TH VOLUNTEERS)

*Organized: September 1861 to April 1862.*
*Consolidated with 20th regiment of cavalry with designation, 1st provisional regiment of cavalry: June 17, 1865.*
*Bates* ii 320–59.
*Philadelphia in the Civil war 155–6.*

### 2ND PROVISIONAL REGIMENT

*Formed by consolidation of 1st, 6th and 17th regiments of cavalry: June 17, 1865.*
*Mustered out: August 7, 1865.*

### 3RD CAVALRY (60TH VOLUNTEERS)

*Organized: July – August 1861.*
*Consolidated with 5th regiment of cavalry: May 8, 1865.*
*Bates* ii 360–406.
*Philadelphia in the Civil war 157–9.*

Constitution and by-laws of Company H, Third Pennsylvania cavalry, with a brief history and muster roll. Shippensburg, D. K. and J. C. Wagner, printers, 1878. 58 p. 15cm.
　　　　　　　　　DLC NHi PSt　**30**

History of the Third Pennsylvania cavalry, Sixtieth regiment Pennsylvania volunteers in the American Civil war, 1861–1865. Compiled by the Regimental history committee in accordance with a resolution of the Third Pennsylvania cavalry association. Philadelphia, Franklin print. co., 1905. xxxvi, 614 p. plates (illus., 2 fold. maps, ports.). 25½cm.
　　　　　　　　　　　　DLC NN　**31**
Unit roster 561–614. Signed chapters: VI, With the cavalry on the Peninsula, by General William W. Averell; XIV, The first cavalry battle of the Civil war, Kelly's ford, Va., by Lt.-Col. Frank W. Hess; XVII, The Second cavalry division in the Gettysburg cam-

paign, by Brevet Lt.-Col. William Brooke Rawle; XVIII, The Third Penn. cavalry at Gettysburg, by Capt. William E. Miller.

Averell, William Woods, –1900.
With the cavalry of the Peninsula. *BandL* II 429–33. **32**

Edmonds, Howard Owen, 1867–
Owen-Edmonds, incidents of the American Civil war, 1861–1865, prepared from family records, by Howard Owen Edmonds. Printed for private circulation. Chicago, Lakeside press, 1928. 93 p. illus., plates (illus., ports.). 24½cm. NN **33**
"Samuel Wilson Owen was Lieutenant Colonel of the Third Pennsylvania cavalry from the outbreak of the American Civil war in 1861, until shortly after the battle of Antietam, September 17, 1862. Howard Edmonds was First Lieutenant and subsequently Captain of Company L of the same regiment during the entire period of the war." Edmonds served also in the 6th Penn. infantry.

Gilmore, David McKinney
Cavalry, its use and value as illustrated by reference to the engagements of Kelly's ford and Gettysburg, by Captain D. M. Gilmore. *MOLLUS-Minn* II 38–51. **34**

—— With General Gregg at Gettysburg. *MOLLUS-Minn* IV 92–111. **35**

Hess, Frank W
The first cavalry battle at Kelly's ford, Va., by Maj. Frank W. Hess. *First Maine bugle* campaign III (Rockland, 1893), call 3, p 3–16; call 4, p 8–22. **36**

Miller, William E
The cavalry battle near Gettysburg. *BandL* III 397–406. **37**

—— War history. Operations of the Union cavalry on the Peninsula, in which some Cumberland county soldiers took part. By Capt. Wm. E. Miller. Read before the Hamilton library association, Carlisle, Pa., October 23, 1908, and reprinted for the Historical department. 12 p. 22cm. NN **37A**
Caption title. Printed from type used for newspaper publication of the text.

Rawle, William Brooke, 1843–1915.
Further remarks on the cavalry fight on the right flank at Gettysburg. *JUSCA* IV (1891) p 157–60. **38**

—— Gregg's cavalry fight at Gettysburg, July 3, 1863. *JUSCA* IV (1891) 257–75. fold. map. **39**
The right flank at Gettysburg "revised with the aid of additional information and official records."

—— Gregg's cavalry fight at Gettysburg, historical address delivered Oct. 15th, 1884, upon the dedication of monumental shaft erected

upon the site of the cavalry engagement on the right flank of the Army of the Potomac, July 3d, 1863, during the battle of Gettysburg, by William Brooke-Rawle. Philadelphia [Allen, Lane & Scott, printers] 1884. 29 p. front. (fold. map). 26cm. NN PPLL **40**

—— The right flank at Gettysburg, an account of the operations of General David McM. Gregg's cavalry command and their important bearing on the results of the battle. Reprinted from Chapters of unwritten history in the annals of the war, Philadelphia weekly times, September 14, 1878. Philadelphia, McLaughlin Brothers' job print, 1878. 24 p. 15cm. PPLL **41**
Author's name a part of caption title. "Published in season for the reunion . . . Sept. 17th, 1878," ms note in PPLL's copy.

—— —— Philadelphia, McLaughlin Brothers' print. estab., 1878. 24 p. 23cm. DLC **42**

—— The right flank at Gettysburg, an account of the operations of General Gregg's cavalry command, showing their important bearing upon the results of the battle, by William Brooke-Rawle, formerly Captain Third Pennsylvania cavalry. Philadelphia, Allen, Lane & Scott's print. house, 1878. 24 p. fold. map. 24½cm. NHi **43**
"Preface" dated: November, 1878.

—— —— 27 p. fold. map. 26½cm. "Preface" dated: November, 1878. DLC **44**

—— With Gregg in the Gettysburg campaign. Reprinted from chapters of Unwritten history in the annals of the war, Philadelphia weekly times, February 2, 1884, by William Brooke-Rawle. Philadelphia, McLaughlin Bros. co. job print. estab., 1884. 30 p. 23cm. DLC NN **45**

Speese, Andrew Jackson
Story of Companies H, A and C, Third Pennsylvania cavalry at Gettysburg, July 3, 1863. [Germantown, 1906] 22, (1) p. front. (port.), 2 fold. plates (facs.). 15cm. DLC NHi NN **46**
Text signed: A. J. Speese, late Corporal Company H.

Treichel, Charles
Major Zagonyi's horse-guard, a paper by Brevet Lieutenant-Colonel Charles Treichel. *MOLLUS-NY* III 240–6. **47**

Wister, Sarah (Butler) "Mrs. O. J. Wister," 1835–1908.
Walter S. Newhall, a memoir . . . Published for the benefit of the Sanitary commission. [Philadelphia, Press of C. Sherman, Son & co.] 1864. iv, [9]–140 p. front. (port.). 20½cm. DLC NHi NN **48**

## 3RD PROVISIONAL REGIMENT

*Formed by consolidation of 18th and 22nd regiments of cavalry: June 24, 1865.*
*Mustered out: October 31, 1865.*

## 4TH CAVALRY (64TH VOLUNTEERS)

*Organized: August to October 1861.*
*Mustered out: July 1, 1865.*
*Bates* II 522–67.

A brief history of the Fourth Pennsylvania veteran cavalry, embracing organization, reunions, dedication of monument at Gettysburg and address of General W. E. Doster, Venango county battalion, reminiscences, etc. Pittsburgh, Ewens & Eberle, printers, 1891. 113 p. 23cm.                                    DLC NN     **49**

Doster, William Emile, 1837–
   Lincoln and episodes of the Civil war, by William E. Doster, late Brevet Brigadier General U.S.V., Provost Marshal of Washington. New York, G. P. Putnam's Sons, 1915. v, 282 p. 20½cm.                                        NN     **49A**
   Partial contents: Incidents of provost duty; The campaign ending with Chancellorsville; The campaign ending with Gettysburg.

Hyndman, William, 1842, or 1843–
   History of a cavalry company, a complete record of Company "A," 4th Penn'a cavalry, as identified with that Regiment, and with the Second brigade, Second division, Cavalry corps, in all the campaigns of the Army of the Potomac, during the late Civil war, by Capt. William Hyndman. Philadelphia, Jas. B. Rodgers co., printers, 1872. xxiv, [25]–343 p. 19cm.
   Unit roster 331–43.          DLC NN     **50**

## 5TH CAVALRY (65TH VOLUNTEERS)

*Organized: July to September 1861.*
*Mustered out: August 7, 1865.*
*Bates* II 568–631.
*Philadelphia in the Civil war* 160–2.

Grubbs, John Cloud          –1878.
   War record of Dr. J. C. Grubbs. Only enough of the incidents connected with the journey from Oregon to the East, and subsequent events and adventures of Dr. Grubbs, to make a connected narrative, are published in this transcript. Compiled by F. H. Grubbs. Portland, Ore., 1908. 32 p. 24cm.
                                              DLC     **51**

## 6TH CAVALRY (70TH VOLUNTEERS)

*Organized: August to October 1861.*
*Consolidated with 1st and 17th regiments of cavalry and designated, 2nd provisional regiment of cavalry: June 17, 1865.*
*Bates* II 741–87.

. . . Dedication of the monument of the Sixth Penna. cavalry "lancers" on the battlefield of Gettysburg, October 14, 1888. Philadelphia [James Beale, printer] 1889. 37, (1) p. front. (illus.). 22½cm.                     DLC NHi     **52**
   At head of title: 1861. 1865. Partial contents: Address of Colonel Frederick C. Newhall, 8–25; Killed in action, [29]–37.

James Starr. In Report of the Class of 1857 in Harvard college, 1882, 123–138.     **52A**

Gracey, Samuel Levis, 1835–1911.
   Annals of the Sixth Pennsylvania cavalry, by Rev. S. L. Gracey, Chaplain of the Regiment. Published for the officers of the Regiment. [Philadelphia] E. H. Butler & co., 1868. 371, (1) p. fold. map. 23cm.     DLC NN     **53**
   "Errata," (1) p.

Newhall, Frederic Cushman
   With General Sheridan in Lee's last campaign, by a staff officer. Philadelphia, J. B. Lippincott & co., 1866. vii, 9–235 p. front. (port.), fold. map. 20½cm. DLC NN     **54**
   Also published in *Maine bugle* campaign I (1894) 201–13, 297–317; campaign II (1895) 1–7, 96–112, 236–56, 289–308; campaign III (1896) 1–14.

Strang, Edgar B
   General Stoneman's raid; or, the amusing side of army life. Philadelphia, E. B. Strang, 1911. 30 p. front. (port.), 2 plates (illus.). 18½cm.                     CSmH MB     **56**

—— Sunshine and shadows of the late Civil war, by E. B. Strang, Company M, 6th Pennsylvania cavalry. Philadelphia, 1898. vi, [7]–80 p. 2 illus., 2 ports. 22½cm.     MB     **57**

Todd, Frederick Porter and Harry G. Larter
   6th Pennsylvania cavalry (Rush's lancers), 1862. *Military collector & historian* VI (Washington, 1954) 102. col. plate (illus.).     **58**

## 7TH CAVALRY (80TH VOLUNTEERS)

*Organized: September to December 1861.*
*Mustered out: August 13, 1865.*
*Bates* II 1114–66.
*Philadelphia in the Civil war* 162–4.

History and roster of the Seventh Pa. cavalry veteran volunteers, 1861–1865. Prepared by

the officers of the organization. Pottsville, Miners' journal, 1904. 141 p. 22½cm.
Unit roster [13]–141.  NN  **59**

Dornblaser, Thomas Franklin, 1841–1941.
My life-story for young and old, by Thomas Franklin Dornblaser. Published for the author. [Chicago] 1930. 222 p. illus., ports. 23cm.
Civil war 44–76.  NN  **60**

—— Sabre strokes of the Pennsylvania dragoons in the War of 1861–1865, interspersed with personal reminiscences, by T. F. Dornblaser. Published for the author. Philadelphia, Lutheran Publication Society, 1884. viii, [9]–264 p. fold. map. 19½cm.  DLC NN  **61**
Coulter 128. On cover: The independent dragoons.

Sipes, William B  –1905.
The Seventh Pennsylvania veteran volunteer cavalry, its record, reminiscences and roster, by William B. Sipes. Pottsville, Miners' Journal print [1906] 169, 60, 143, (3) p. plates (1 illus., ports.). 24cm.  DLC NN PSt  **62**
Unit roster, 143 p. "Contents," "Appendix," "Index to roster," (3) p. Coulter 418.

Straub, Edward Adlum, 1845–
Life and Civil war services of Edward A. Straub of Co. B, 7th Pennsylvania cavalry, written by himself. Milwaukee, Press of J. H. Yewdale & Sons co., 1909. front. (port.). 22cm.  DLC  **62A**

Thompson, Heber Samuel, 1840–1911.
Diary of Capt. Heber S. Thompson, Seventh Pennsylvania cavalry, Pottsville, May to December, 1864. [Pottsville? 191–] 32 p. 23cm.
Title from cover.  CtY  **63**

Vale, Joseph G
Minty and the cavalry, a history of cavalry campaigns in the Western armies, by Joseph G. Vale, late Captain Seventh Pennsylvania cavalry. Harrisburg, Edwin K. Meyers, printer, 1886. xxxi, 550 p. plates (maps, ports.). 24cm.
DLC NN  **64**
Includes rosters of officers of the 4th Michigan cavalry, 7th and 9th Penn cavalry and 4th United States cavalry.

## 8TH CAVALRY (89TH VOLUNTEERS)

*Organized: August to October 1861.*
*Mustered out: July 24, 1865.*
*Bates* III 111–50.
*Philadelphia in the Civil war 165–7.*

Ceremonies at dedication of monument of the Eighth Penna. cavalry regiment at Gettysburg, September 1, 1890, with historical sketch of the Regiment. 35 p. front. (illus.). 23½cm.
Address of Capt. J. E. Giles, 10–25. NHi  **65**

The charge of the Eighth Pennsylvania cavalry. *BandL* III 186–8.  **68**
Accounts by Pennock Huey, J. Edward Carpenter and Andrew B. Wells.

Carpenter, James Edward, 1841–1901.
A list of the battles, engagements, actions and important skirmishes in which the Eighth Pennsylvania cavalry participated during the war of 1861–1865, compiled by J. Edward Carpenter. Philadelphia, Allen, Lane & Scott's print. house. 1886. 8 p. 23cm.  DLC  **69**

Collins, John L
A prisoner's march from Gettysburg to Staunton. *BandL* III 429–33.  **70**

—— When Stonewall Jackson turned our right. *BandL* III 183–6.  **70A**

Dykins, Daniel B
A case of hunger cure, and the tragedy that followed. *The now and then* III (Muncy 1890/92) 139–40.  **71**

Huey, Pennock
A true history of the charge of the Eighth Pennsylvania cavalry at Chancellorsville, by Pennock Huey, formerly Colonel of the Eighth. Philadelphia, Porter & Coates [1883] 76 p. 3 plates (maps). 19½cm.  DLC NN  **72**

Wickersham, Charles I
Personal recollections of the cavalry at Chancellorsville, by Major Charles I. Wickersham. *MOLLUS-Wis* III 453–62.  **73**

## 9TH CAVALRY (92ND VOLUNTEERS)

*Organized: October to November 1861.*
*Mustered out: July 18, 1865.*
*Bates* III 234–83.
*Philadelphia in the Civil war 167–8.*

Jordan, Thomas Jefferson,  –1895.
Battle of Thompson's station and the trial of the spies at Franklin, Tennessee. *US* ns III (1890) 300–14.  **74**

—— Some military reminiscences of the rebellion. *US* ns II (1889) 508–21.  **75**

Moore, James
Kilpatrick and our cavalry, comprising a sketch of the life of General Kilpatrick, with an account of the cavalry raids, engagements, and operations under his command, from the beginning of the rebellion to the surrender of Johnston, by James Moore, Surgeon Ninth Pennsylvania cavalry. New York, W. J. Widdleton, 1865. 245 p. front. (port.), plates (illus.). 18cm.  DLC NN  **76**

36

10th – 15th Penn Cavalry

## 10TH CAVALRY

*Organization not completed.*

## 11TH CAVALRY (108TH VOLUNTEERS)

*Organized as Harlan's light cavalry: August to October 1861.*
*Designated 11th regiment of cavalry: Noverber 13, 1861.*
*Mustered out: August 13, 1865.*
*Bates III 902–51.*
*Philadelphia in the Civil war 169–70.*

For historical sketch and roster of Company A, see *Roster and record of Iowa soldiers . . . ,* Adjutant general IV 1781–95. Company M, see *Official roster of the soldiers of the State of Ohio* XI 745–50, 811.

History of the Eleventh Pennsylvania volunteer cavalry, together with a complete roster of the Regiment and Regimental officers. Philadelphia, Franklin print. co., 1902. 289 p. 24cm.　　　　DLC NN　　77
Unit roster [189]–285. "Preface" signed: John L. Roper, Henry C. Archibald [and] G. W. Coles, History committee.

Military register Company "B," 11th regiment Penna. vol. cavalry, 2d brigade, Kautz's cavalry, Army of the James. Baltimore, Printed by Bross & co. [1864] illus. broadside, 56½ x 45cm.　　　　　　NN　　78
"Lith. by H. Schroeder."

Register of the commissioned officers of the Eleventh regiment of Pennsylvania cavalry volunteers, from the organization of the Regiment on the fifth day of October, 1861, to the time of its muster-out on the thirteenth day of August, 1865. With an Appendix containing historical memoranda of the Regiment during the same period. Philadelphia, J. B. Lippincott & co., 1866. 55 p. 24½cm.　　NHi NN　79

Cruikshank, George L
　Fort Dodge soldiers in the East. *Annals of Iowa* s3 VI (1905) 571–80. 2 plates (ports.).
　　　　　　　　　　　　80

Tripp, Stephen
　The cavalry at Appomattox, April 9, 1865, by Captain Stephen Tripp. *Maine bugle* campaign V (Rockland, 1898) 212–16.　81

## 12TH CAVALRY (113TH VOLUNTEERS)

*Organized: December 1861 to April 1862.*
*Mustered out: July 20, 1865.*
*Bates III 1143–82.*
*Philadelphia in the Civil war 170–1.*

## 13TH CAVALRY (117TH VOLUNTEERS)

*Organized: December 1861 to April 1862.*
*Mustered out: July 14, 1865.*
*Bates III 1267–1309.*
*Philadelphia in the Civil war 172–3.*

Dougherty, Michael
　Prison diary of Michael Dougherty, late Co. B, 13th Pa. cavalry, while confined in Pemberton, Barrett's, Libby, Andersonville, and other Southern prisons. Sole survivor of 127 of his regiment captured the same time, 122 dying in Andersonville. Bristol, C. A. Dougherty, printer, 1908. 75, (1) p. front. (port.). 19½cm.　　　　　　　DLC　82

—— Diary of a Civil war hero, Michael Dougherty. With a pictorial history of the war, by James Boylan. New York, Pyramid books [1960] 128 p. illus. 18cm.　　DLC　82A
"War: a commentary in text and pictures, by James Boylan," 48–80.

## 14TH CAVALRY (159TH VOLUNTEERS)

*Organized: October to November 1862.*
*Mustered out: August 24, 1865.*
*Bates IV 851–97.*
*Philadelphia in the Civil war 174.*

Mowrer, George H
　History of the organization and service, during the War of the rebellion, of Co. A, 14th Pennsylvania cavalry, compiled by G. H. Mowrer, appointed Historian by action of the Survivors' association. [n. p., 189–] 91 p. 19½cm.　　　　　　　　NN　83
Unit roster 41–55.

Slease, William Davis
　The Fourteenth Pennsylvania cavalry in the Civil war, a history of the Fourteenth Pennsylvania volunteer cavalry from its organization until the close of the Civil war, 1861–1865, by Rev. William Davis Slease. [Pittsburgh, Art Engraving & print. co., 1915] 299 p. plates (illus., double map, ports.). 22½cm.
Unit roster [19]–81.　　　　　　NN　84

## 15TH CAVALRY (160TH VOLUNTEERS)

*Organized: July to October 1862.*
*Mustered out: June 21, 1865.*
*Bates IV 902–49.*
*Philadelphia in the Civil war 175–8.*

Annual report of the Society of the 15th Pennsylvania cavalry. 23cm. 56, 1928 DLC　85
Continues Title 88.

In memory of Lieut.-Col. Chas. Malone Betts, 15th Penn. vol. cav., died November 10, 1905. [8] p. front. (2 ports.). 28cm.　MeHi　*86*

... In memoriam William Harrison Lambert, May, 1842 – June, 1912, first President of the Lincoln fellowship... Edited by the First vice-president. New York, 1912. 36, (3) p. front. (port.). 24cm.　CSmH NN　*87*

At head of title: No. 4 of the publications of the Lincoln fellowship of New York. Lambert mustered in 15th Penn cavalry, August 22, 1862; discharged for promotion in 27th New Jersey infantry, November 24, 1862.

To the members of the Society of the 15th Pennsylvania volunteer cavalry a short account of the annual banquet, held at Philadelphia ... With fraternal greetings of John F. Conway. Philadelphia, 1884–1927. 44 v. illus., ports. 23cm. (1884–1885, 17cm.; 1886–1895, 20cm.).　DLC　*88*

Numbered, 12–55. An account of the first eleven banquets was not published. The annual banquets were discontinued by Resolution adopted Sept. 25, 1928. Continued by Title 85.

Carraway, William E
The mutiny of the 15th Pennsylvania volunteer cavalry. *Denver Westerners monthly roundup* XVII 11 (November 1961) 5–15. 2 ports.　*88A*

Colton, Matthias Baldwin, 1839–1915.
The Civil war journal and correspondence of Matthias Baldwin Colton. Edited by Jessie Sellers Colton. Philadelphia, Macrae-Smith co., 1931. xii, 412 p. plates (ports.). 21½cm.　DLC　*89*

Kirk, Charles H
History of the Fifteenth Pennsylvania volunteer cavalry, which was recruited and known as the Anderson cavalry in the rebellion of 1861–1865. Edited and compiled by Charles H. Kirk, First Lieutenant Company E, assisted by the Historical committee of the Society of the Fifteenth Pennsylvania cavalry. Philadelphia, 1906. 784 p. plates (illus., fold. map in pocket, ports.). 25½cm.　DLC NN　*90*

Unit roster 739–84. Chapters are signed by their authors.

Palmer, William Jackson, 1836–1909.
Letters, 1853–1868, Gen'l Wm. J. Palmer. Compiled by Isaac H. Clothier. Philadelphia [Ketterlinus] 1906. v, 9–128 p. plates (illus., ports.). 24cm.　NN　*91*

Plates have guard sheets with titles of plates. "Addendum" inserted slip.

Williams, John A　　Bedford　　–1893.
In commemoration of the eleventh annual reunion of the Anderson cavalry, December 5, 1883. [3] p. 17½cm.　DLC　*92*

Text signed: J. A. B. Williams.

—— Leaves from a trooper's diary. Published by the author. Philadelphia [Bell, printer] 1869. 103 p. 17½cm.　DLC NHi NN　*93*

"An account of the mutiny in the Anderson cavalry, at Nashville, Tenn., December, 1862," by Geo. S. Fobes, late Quartermaster of the Anderson cavalry, [78]–103.

Wilson, Selden L
Recollections and experiences during the Civil war, 1861–1865, in the 15th Penna. vol. cavalry, better known as the Anderson cavalry, by Second Lieut. Selden L. Wilson. Washington 1913. 168 p. plates (1 illus., plan, ports.). 23cm.　PHi　*94*

Wilson, Suzanne (Colton), 1895–
Column south, with the Fifteenth Pennsylvania cavalry from Antietam to the capture of Jefferson Davis. Compiled by Suzanne Colton Wilson. Edited by J. Ferrell Colton and Antoinette G. Smith. Drawings by Barton A. Wright. Flagstaff, Arizona, J. F. Colton & co., 1960. xxi, 389, 35 p. illus., maps, plates (illus., fold. maps, ports.). 27cm.　DLC NN　*95*

Cover illustrated in color. Includes selections from the diaries and letters of Mathias Baldwin Colton, 1839–1915, and William Francis Colton, 1841–1921. Index, 35 p. "Battle lines at Chattanooga," plan, end paper.

## 16TH CAVALRY (161ST VOLUNTEERS)

*Organized: September to November 1862.*

*Mustered out: August 11, 1865.*

*Bates* IV 950–1000.

*Philadelphia in the Civil war* 179.

History of the 16th regiment, Pennsylvania cavalry, for the year ending October 31st, 1863. Commanded by Colonel John Irvin Gregg. Philadelphia, King & Baird, printers, 1864. 44 p. 22cm.　DLC　*96*

Prepared as an official report by the Adjutant, Charles H. Miller.

## 17TH CAVALRY (162ND VOLUNTEERS)

*Organized: September to November 1862.*

*Consolidated with the 1st and 6th regiments of cavalry with designation 2nd provisional regiment of cavalry: June 17, 1865.*

*Bates* IV 1001–41.

Bean, Theodore Weber, 1833–1891.
The roll of honor of the Seventeenth Pennsylvania cavalry; or, one hundred and sixty-second of the line, Pennsylvania volunteers. Philadelphia, James S. Claxton, 1865. 88 p. 18½cm.　PPLL　*97*

Preface signed: Theo W. Bean, Captain Co. L.

*17th Cavalry (22nd Volunteers), continued*

Clark, James Albert, 1841–1908.
The making of a volunteer cavalryman, by
First Lieutenant James Albert Clark. 1907.
28 p. *MOLLUS-DC* no 70.                        **98**

Moore, James B
Two years in the service. [n. p., 186–] 16 p.
21cm.                               NHi      **99**
Caption title.

Moyer, Henry P
History of the Seventeenth regiment Pennsylvania volunteer cavalry; or, One hundred
and sixty-second in the line of Pennsylvania
volunteer regiments, war to suppress the rebellion, 1861–1865. Compiled from records of
the rebellion, official reports, recollections,
reminiscences, incidents, diaries and company
rosters. With an appendix. By H. P. Moyer,
formerly Bugler, Co. E. [Lebanon, Sowers
print. co., 1911] 472 p. plates (illus., ports.).
24cm.                           DLC NN     **100**
Unit roster 411–48.

**18TH CAVALRY (163RD VOLUNTEERS)**

*Organized: October to December 1862.*
*Mustered out: May 14, 1866.*
*Bates* iv 1042–83.
*Philadelphia in the Civil war 180.*

History of the Eighteenth regiment of cavalry
Pennsylvania volunteers (163rd regiment of
the line). Compiled and edited by the Publication committee of the Regimental association. New York [Wynkoop Hallenbeck Crawford co.] 1909. 299 p. col. front. (illus.),
plates (illus., maps, ports.). 23cm.
                                DLC NN     **101**
"Historical sketch," by Brigadier-General T. F.
Rodenbough, [13]–30. Other chapters are signed by
their authors. Unit roster [179]–288.

Phillips, John Wilson, 1837–1896.
The Civil war diary of . . . Edited by Robert
G. Athearn. *Virginia magazine of history and
biography* LXII (1954) 95–123.           **102**

—— Experiences in Libby prison, by Lieut.-
Colonel J. W. Phillips. *MOLLUS-Mo* i 54–73.
                                           **103**

**19TH CAVALRY (180TH VOLUNTEERS)**

*Organized: June to October 1863.*
*Mustered out: May 14, 1866.*
*Bates* v 1–31.
*Philadelphia in the Civil war 181–2.*

**20TH CAVALRY (181ST VOLUNTEERS)**

*Organized: June to August 1863.*
*(6 months)*
*Mustered out: January 7, 1864.*
*Bates* v 32–52.
*Philadelphia in the Civil war 183.*
*Organized: February 1864.* (3 years)
*Consolidated with 2nd regiment of cav-
alry with designation 1st provisional regi-
ment of cavalry: June 17, 1865.*
*Bates* v 32–5, 52–76.
*Philadelphia in the Civil war 183–4.*

Savior, Livingstone
My experience while a prisoner of war. *Publications of the Historical society of Schuykill
county* ii (Pottsville, 1910) 385–403.     **104**

Smith, Joshua, 1841–
Map and description of the main battlefields,
routes, camps and Headquarters in the Gettysburg, Wilderness, and Appomattox campaigns
of the Civil war in the United States, by Joshua
Smith 1st Lieut. Co. K, 20th Pa. vol. cav. Chicago, Joshua Smith, 1900. 24 p. fold. map.
23cm.                           DLC NHi    **105**
On cover: From Gettysburg to Appomattox.

**21ST CAVALRY (182ND VOLUNTEERS)**

*Organized: June 28 to August 1, 1863.*
*(6 months)*
*Mustered out: February 20, 1864.*
*Bates* v 77, 81–97.
*Organized: February 1864.* (3 years)
*Mustered out: July 8, 1865.*
*Bates* v 76–81, 97–127.

Annual report survivors of the 21st Penn'a vol.
cavalry asso'n . . . reunions. . . . 1891–1908.
16 v. (420 p.). plates (illus., ports.). 23cm.
                                        P    **106**

Title varies: Organization and first and second reunions; Third [-thirteenth] annual reunion; Tri-annual
report . . . fifteenth, sixteenth and seventeenth reunions. Proceedings of the 14th and 18th reunions
were not seen. There is a gap in the pagination.

**22ND CAVALRY (185TH VOLUNTEERS)**

*Organized: June to July 1863.* (6 months)
*Mustered out: February 5, 1864.*
*Bates* v 170–204.
*Organized by consolidation of Ringgold
battalion, an unnamed battalion, Wash-
ington county cavalry company and
Lafayette cavalry company: February
1864.* (3 years)

*Consolidated with 18th regiment of cavalry and designated 3rd provisional regiment of cavalry: June 24, 1865.*

*Bates v 170–204.*

Elwood, John William, 1842–
Elwood's stories of the old Ringgold cavalry, 1847–1865, the first three year cavalry of the Civil war, with introduction by the Rev. H. H. Ryland. Coal Center, Published by the author, 1914. xvi, [17]–326 p. front. (port.), illus., ports. 23cm.                    DLC      *107*

Farrar, Samuel Clarke
The Twenty-second Pennsylvania cavalry and the Ringgold battalion, 1861–1865. Written and compiled by Samuel Clarke Farrar, Company C. Published under the auspices of the Twenty-second Pennsylvania Ringgold cavalry association. [Pittsburgh, New Werner co.] 1911. xi, 538 p. illus., maps, ports, plates (1 illus., fold. map, ports.). 23½cm.
Unit roster 468–531.      DLC NN      *108*

Hasson, Benjamin F
Escape from the Confederacy, overpowering the guards, midnight leap from a moving train, through swamps and forest, blood hounds, thrilling events, by B. F. Hasson, late Lieut. Ringgold battalion. [Bryant, Ohio 1900] 59, (1) p. 1 illus. 20cm.      DLC      *109*
"List of members of the Regiment captured," (1) p.

## Named Cavalry Organizations

### Anderson Troop of Cavalry

*Organized: November 30, 1861.*

*Mustered out: March 24, 1863.*

*Bates IV 898–907.*

### Comley's Independent Company

### Militia Cavalry

*Organized: July 19, 1863.*

*Mustered out: July 30, 1863.*

Atkinson, Wilmer, 1840–1920.
Wilmer Atkinson, an autobiography, founder of the Farm journal. Philadelphia, Wilmer Atkinson co., 1920. xviii, 375 p. plates (illus., ports.). 20½cm.      NN      *109A*
Mustered in 11th Penn militia infantry, September 12, 1862; mustered out September 25, 1862; mustered in Comley's independent company militia cavalry, July 2, 1863; mustered out, July 30, 1863; mustered in 197th Penn infantry, July 22, 1864; mustered out, November 11, 1864.

### Ringgold Battalion of Cavalry

*Organized by consolidation of existing companies: September 1862.*

*Consolidated with existing battalions and companies to form 22nd regiment of cavalry: February 22, 1864.*

See Title 108.

## ENGINEERS

### Independent Company C (Acting Engineers)

*Mustered in: August 9, 1862.*

*Mustered out: June 20, 1865.*

*Bates v 918–24.*

*Philadelphia in the Civil war 146.*

## INFANTRY

### PENNSYLVANIA RESERVE CORPS

Pennsylvania. Governor.
Messages of Gov. Andrew G. Curtin, relative to the Reserve corps, Pennsylvania volunteers. [Harrisburg, Singerly & Myers, State printers, 1863?] 15 p. 24cm.
CSmH DLC      *109B*

Pennsylvania Reserve Association.
The report of the Committee on the services of the Pennsylvania reserves at Gettysburg. Philadelphia, Printed by J. B. Lippincott co., 1889. 29 p. map. 22cm.      DNW      *109C*

Rauch, William Harrison
Pennsylvania reserve volunteer corps "round-up," Wednesday and Thursday, June 24, 25, Harrisburg, Pa., together with a roster of comrades present. [Philadelphia, Electric print. co., 1903] 89 p. 3 plates (2 illus., 6 ports.). 23cm.
DLC NN      *109D*
"Compiled by William H. Rauch."

Sypher, Josiah Rinehart, 1832–
History of the Pennsylvania Reserve corps, a complete record of the organization, and of the different companies, regiments and brigades, containing descriptions of expeditions, marches, skirmishes and battles, together with biographical sketches of officers and personal records of each man during his term of service. Compiled from official reports and other documents, by J. R. Sypher. Lancaster, Elias Barr & co., 1865. 723 p. plates (maps, ports.). 23cm.      DLC NN      *109E*
Unit roster, 1st–13th regiments 562–723.

### Philadelphia Brigade

Comprised of 69th, 71st, 72nd, and 106th Pennsylvania infantries.

Banes, Charles H
History of the Philadelphia brigade, Sixty-ninth, Seventy-first, Seventy-second, and One hundred and sixth Pennsylvania volunteers, by Charles H. Banes. Philadelphia, J. B. Lippincott & co., 1876. 315 p. 19½cm.
DLC NN    *110*

Cunnington, W    H
The Philadelphia brigade and their monument at Antietam. *BandG* IV (1894) 269–73. illus., ports.    *111*
For other references on the Philadelphia brigade, see the entries under the regiments that formed the brigade.

## Regiments

### 1ST INFANTRY

*Mustered in: April 18–21, 1861.*
*Mustered out: July 27, 1861.*
*Bates* I 13–22.

Schaadt, James L
Company I, First regiment Pennsylvania volunteers, a memoir of its service for the Union in 1861. *Penn germania* XIII (1912) 538–50.    *112*

*1st Reserve Infantry see 30th Infantry*

### 2ND INFANTRY

*Mustered in: April 20, 1861.*
*Mustered out: July 26, 1861.*
*Bates* I 23–31.

*2nd Reserve Infantry see 31st Infantry*

### 3RD INFANTRY

*Mustered in: April 20, 1861.*
*Mustered out: July 29, 1861.*
*Bates* I 32–9.

*3rd Reserve Infantry see 32nd Infantry*

### 4TH INFANTRY

*Mustered in: April 20, 1861.*
*Mustered out: July 27, 1861.*
*Bates* I 40–9.

*4th Reserve Infantry see 33rd Infantry*

### 5TH INFANTRY

*Mustered in: April 20–21, 1861.*
*Mustered out: July 25, 1861.*
*Bates* I 50–7.

*5th Reserve Infantry see 34th Infantry*

### 6TH INFANTRY

*Mustered in: April 21–23, 1861.*
*Mustered out: July 27, 1861.*
*Bates* I 58–67.

See Title 33.

*6th Reserve Infantry see 35th Infantry*

### 7TH INFANTRY

*Mustered in: April 22–23, 1861.*
*Mustered out: July 29, 1861.*
*Bates* I 68–76.

Holmes, James Rush, 1827–1882.
The Civil war letters of . . . Edited by Ida Bright Adams. *Western Pennsylvania historical magazine* XLIV (1961) 105–27.    *112A*
After service in the three month 7th Penn infantry, Rush re-enlisted in the 61st Penn infantry.

*7th Reserve Infantry see 36th Infantry*

### 8TH INFANTRY

*Mustered in: April 21–24, 1861.*
*Mustered out: July 29, 1861.*
*Bates* I 77–85.

See Title 338.

*8th Reserve Infantry see 37th Infantry*

### 9TH INFANTRY

*Mustered in: April 22–24, 1861.*
*Mustered out: July 29, 1861.*
*Bates* I 86–95.

*9th Reserve Infantry see 38th Infantry*

### 10TH INFANTRY

*Mustered in: April 24–29, 1861.*
*Mustered out: July 31, 1861.*
*Bates* I 96–105.

*10th Reserve Infantry see 39th Infantry*

### 11TH INFANTRY

*Mustered in: April 24–26, 1861. (three months)*
*Mustered out: August 1, 1861.*

*Bates* I 106–16.
*Organized: August 1861.* (three years)
*Mustered out: July 1, 1865.*
*Bates* I 247–306.

Coulter, Richard
[Sallie] a war dog. *Biv* III (1885) 17–20.
*113*

Locke, William Henry
The story of the Regiment, by William
Henry Locke, Chaplain. Philadelphia, J. B.
Lippincott & co., 1868. xii, [13]–401 p.
19½cm.                    DLC NN    *114*

—— —— New York, James Miller, 1872. xii,
[13]–401 p. 19cm.              DLC    *115*

*11th Reserve Infantry see 40th Infantry*

## 11TH INFANTRY (MILITIA)

*Called September 4, 1862, to repel Lee's
invasion of Maryland.*
*Disbanded: September 24, 1862.*

See Title 109A

## 12TH INFANTRY

*Mustered in: April 25, 1861.*
*Mustered out: August 5, 1861.*
*Bates* I 117–24.

Fleming, George Thornton, 1855–1928.
Life and letters of Alexander Hays ... Edited
and arranged with notes and contemporary
history, by George Thornton Fleming, from
data compiled by Gilbert Adams Hays. . . .
Pittsburgh, 1919. viii, 708, (16) p. plates
(illus., ports.). 24cm.   DLC NN P    *116*
Major 12th Penn infantry, April 25, 1861; mustered
out, August 5, 1861; Colonel 63rd Penn infantry,
October 9, 1861; Brigadier General, September 29,
1862. "Index," (16) p.

Niebaum, John Henry, 1852–
History of the Pittsburgh Washington infantry, 102nd (old 13th) regiment, Pennsylvania
veteran volunteers and its forebears ... by
John H. Niebaum. [Pittsburgh, Burgum print.
co., 1931] 325 p. illus., ports. 27cm.
                         DLC NN    *117*
Civil war 64–189. Rosters: 12th infantry, 66–72;
102nd infantry 118–86.

*12th Reserve Infantry see 41st Infantry*

## 13TH INFANTRY

*Mustered in: April 25, 1861.*
*Mustered out: August 6, 1861.*
*Bates* I 125–33.

History of the Washington infantry of Pittsburgh, Pennsylvania. Thirty-sixth anniversary,
1855–1891. [Pittsburgh, 1891] 60 p. ports.
19 x 27½cm.                    PSt    *118*
Advertising matter on versos. Services in the 13th
and 102nd infantry regiments with rosters, 25–39.

Stewart, Alexander Morrison, 1814–1875.
Camp, march and battle-field; or, three years
and a half with the Army of the Potomac, by
Rev. A. M. Stewart, Chaplain of 102nd regiment P.V. Philadelphia, Jas. B. Rodgers,
printer, 1865. x, 413 p. front. (port.). 20cm.
                         DLC NN    *119*
Served in the 13th Pennsylvania infantry; mustered
in 102nd Pennsylvania infantry, August 6, 1861; discharged, September 14, 1862. Coulter 435.

See also Title 117.

*13th Reserve Infantry see 42nd Infantry*

## 14H INFANTRY

*Mustered in: April 24 to May 2, 1861.*
*Mustered out: August 7, 1861.*
*Bates* I 134–41.

*14th Reserve Infantry see 1st Cavalry*

## 15TH INFANTRY

*Mustered in: April 23 to May 1, 1861.*
*Mustered out: August 8, 1861.*
*Bates* I 142–50.

## 15TH INFANTRY (MILITIA)

*Called, September 4, 1862, to repel Lee's
invasion of Maryland.*
*Disbanded: September 24, 1862.*

Biggert, Florence C       –1900.
Some leaves from a Civil war diary. Edited
by Harry R. Beck. *Western Pennsylvania historical magazine* XLII (1959) 363–82.    *120*

## 16TH INFANTRY

*Mustered in: April 23–30, 1861.*
*Mustered out: July 30, 1861.*
*Bates* I 151–8.

## 17TH INFANTRY

*Mustered in: April 25, 1861.*
*Mustered out: August 2, 1861.*
*Bates* I 159–67.

# 42

## 18TH INFANTRY

*Mustered in: April 24, 1861.*
*Mustered out: August 6, 1861.*
*Bates* I 168–75.

## 19TH INFANTRY

*Mustered in: May 18, 1861.*
*Mustered out: August 29, 1861.*
*Bates* I 176–84.

## 20TH INFANTRY

*Mustered in: April 30, 1861.*
*Mustered out: August 6, 1861.*
*Bates* I 185–92.

## 21ST INFANTRY

*Mustered in: April 29, 1861.*
*Mustered out: August 9, 1861.*
*Bates* I 193–200.

## 22ND INFANTRY

*Mustered in: April 23, 1861.*
*Mustered out: August 7, 1861.*
*Bates* I 201–08.

## 23RD INFANTRY

*Mustered in: April 21, 1861.*
*Mustered out: July 31, 1861.*
*Bates* I 209–17.
*Organized: August 1861.* (3 years)
*Mustered out: September 8, 1864.*
*Bates* I 307–43.
*Philadelphia in the Civil war 49–51.*

Birney, David Bell, 1825–1864.
A brief statement of the part which Brig.-General David B. Birney of Philadelphia has taken in the present rebellion <prepared and printed (not published) at the request of a few of his personal friends, for private circulation> 11 p. 23cm.    CSmH OCl WHi    *121*
Dated: Philadelphia, February 17th, 1863. Title from cover.
Served in both 23rd Penn regiments; Brigadier-General, February 17; 1862; Major-General, May 20, 1863.

Cutler, Elbridge Jefferson, 1831–1870.
Fitzhugh Birney, a memoir. Cambridge [University press] 1866. 40 p. 19cm.
    DLC    *122*

[Davis, Oliver Wilson]
Life of David Bell Birney, Major-General United States volunteers. Philadelphia, King & Baird, 1867. xii, 418 p. front. (port.). 26cm.
    DLC DNW    *122A*

Wray, William James
History of the Twenty-third Pennsylvania volunteer infantry, Birney's zouaves, three months and three years service, Civil war, 1861–1865. Compiled by the Secretary, by order of the Survivors association Twenty-third regiment Pennsylvania volunteers, 1903–1904. [Philadelphia, 1904] 432 p. illus., ports. 25cm.
    DLC NN    *123*
Unit rosters: Three months' service, 14–27; Three years' service, 189–247. "Having authorized its Secretary, William J. Wray, to prepare a history. . . ."

——— . . . Report of the first annual reunion of the Survivors' association, 23d Penna. vols., held at Maennerchor hall, Philadelphia, Penna., May 31, 1882 . . . compiled by W. J. W. Philadelphia, William P. Kildare, printer, 1883. 52, (2) p. 23cm.    DNW    *124*
At head of title: "Fair Oaks." Fair Oaks and the 23d Penna. vols. at Fair Oaks, by James K. Shinn, [8]–34.

## 24TH INFANTRY

*Mustered in: May 1, 1861.*
*Mustered out: August 10, 1861.*
*Bates* I 218–25.

## 25TH INFANTRY

*Organized by consolidation of the First defenders and five new companies.*
*Mustered out: August 1, 1861.*
*Bates* I 226–31.

Davis, William Watts Hart, 1820–1910.
The campaign of 1861 in the Shenandoah valley, a paper read before the Commandery of the State of Pennsylvania of the Military order of the loyal legion of the United States, May 3, 1893, by W. W. H. Davis, Captain of the 25th Pa. Doylestown, Doylestown pub. co., printers, 1893. 18 p. 22cm.    NHi NN    *125*
The author also served in the 104th Penn infantry.

Schaadt, James L
The Allen infantry in 1861. *Pennsylvania-German* XII (1911) 149–62. ports.    *125A*

## 26TH INFANTRY

*Mustered in: May 25, 1861.*
*Mustered out: June 18, 1864.*
*Bates* I 344–81.
*Philadelphia in the Civil war 52–3.*

Cooper, Thomas Valentine, 1835–1909.
Pennsylvania's memorial days, September
11 and 12, 1889. The 26th Pennsylvania volunteers, address of Thomas C. Cooper, Private
of Co. C. [4] p. 22cm.  DLC NHi  *126*
Caption title.

## 26TH INFANTRY (MILITIA)

*Organized: June 22, 1863.*
*Mustered out: July 31, 1863.*

Pennypacker, Samuel Whitaker, 1843–1916.
26th Pennsylvania emergency infantry. Ad-
dress of Samuel W. Pennypacker, Private Co.
"F" at the dedication, Sept. 1, 1892, of the
monument to commemorate the services of the
Regiment on the battlefield of Gettysburg.
Philadelphia, 1892. 26 p. 23½cm.
 DNW  *127*
On cover: 26th Pennsylvania emergency infantry at
Gettysburg.

Richards, Henry Melcher Muhlenberg, 1848–
Citizens of Gettysburg in the Union army.
BandL III 289.  *128*

—— Pennsylvania's emergency men at Gettys-
burg, a touch of bushwhacking, by H. M. M.
Richards. Reading 1895. 35 p. 22cm.
Title and imprint from cover.  DNW  *129*

## 27TH INFANTRY

*Mustered in: May 31, 1861, to date from
May 5, 1861.*
*Mustered out: June 11, 1864.*
*Bates* I 381–417.
*Philadelphia in the Civil war 54–6.*

## 28TH INFANTRY

*Mustered in: June 28, 1861.*
*Mustered out: July 18, 1865.*
*Bates* I 418–83.
*Philadelphia in the Civil war 57–60.*

McLaughlin, John
A memoir of Hector Tyndale ... born March
24, 1821, died March 19, 1880. Philadelphia
[Collins, printer] 1882. 118 p. front. (port.).
fold. map. 25cm.  DLC NHi NN  *130*
"Preface" signed: J. McL. "Selections from the
military reports, public addresses, letters, etc. of ...
General Hector Tyndale," [27]–115.

Tyndale, Hector, 1821–1880.
Re-union of the 28th & 147th regiments,
Pennsylvania volunteers, Philadelphia, Nov.

24th, 1871. Philadelphia, Pawson & Nicholson,
1872. 21 p. 23cm.  DLC  *131*
Remarks of Brevet Major General Hector Tyndale,
[1]–21.
See also Titles 22–23.

## 29TH INFANTRY

*Mustered in: July 1–29, 1861.*
*Mustered out: July 11, 1865.*
*Bates* I 484–536.
*Philadelphia in the Civil war 61–4.*

## 30TH INFANTRY (1ST RESERVE)

*Organized: June 9, 1861.*
*Mustered out: June 10, 1864.*
*Bates* I 545–74.

Gilbert, Charles E
A sketch of the seven days' fight in front of
Richmond, by Charles E. Gilbert, late of Co.
K, First reg"t Penn'a reserve. Gettysburg, J. E.
Wible, printer, 1880. 22 p. 21½cm.
 NHi  *132*

Minnigh, Henry N
History of Company K, 1st (inft), Penn'a
reserves, "the boys who fought at home," by
H. N. Minigh, Captain. Introductory edition.
Duncansville, "Home Print" [1891] 41, 39,
44 p. 17½cm.  DLC NN  *133*
Contents: Transcript of the muster out roll of Co.
K, preliminary leaves; A history of Company K, 41 p;
Historical record of the members of Co. K, 39 p;
Papers and reminiscences, 44 p.

Urban, John W
Battle field and prison pen; or, through the
war, and thrice a prisoner in Rebel dungeons
... by John W. Urban, Company "D," First
regiment Pennsylvania reserve infantry. Philadelphia, Hubbard Brothers [1882] xi, [13]–
486 p. plates (illus., plans, ports.). 20cm.
 NN  *134*
Author mustered in 30th infantry, June 8, 1861;
transferred to 190th infantry, May 31, 1864; mustered out, June 28, 1865. Coulter 458.

—— My experience mid shot and shell and in
Rebel den, a graphic recital of personal experiences throughout the entire Civil war, in
which the author was actually engaged in 25
battles and skirmishes, was three times captured ... by John W. Urban. Lancaster, Published for the author, 1882. xi, (1), xiii–633 p.
plates (illus., plans, ports.). 20cm.
 DLC  *135*

—— Through the war and thrice a prisoner
in Rebel dungeons, a graphic recital of personal experiences throughout the whole period

*30th Infantry (1st Reserve), continued*
of the late war for the Union, during which the author was actively engaged in 25 battles and skirmishes, was three times taken prisoner of war ... by John W. Urban. Philadelphia, J. H. Moore & co., 1892. xii, 13–486 p. plates (illus., plans, ports.). 20cm.  DLC **136**

**31ST INFANTRY (2ND RESERVE)**

*Organized: May 1861.*
*Mustered out: June 16, 1864.*
*Bates* I 575–608.
*Philadelphia in the Civil war 67–8.*

Woodward, Evan Morrison
Our campaigns; or, the marches, bivouacs, battles, incidents of camp life and history of our Regiment during its three years term of service, together with a sketch of the Army of the Potomac, under Generals McClellan, Burnside, Hooker, Meade and Grant, by E. M. Woodward, Adjutant. Philadelphia, John E. Potter and co. [1865] 363 p. 19cm.
                                        DLC NN  **137**
Unit roster 334–58. Coulter 486.

**32ND INFANTRY (3RD RESERVE)**

*Organized: May 1861.*
*Mustered out: June 17, 1864.*
*Bates* I 609–35.
*Philadelphia in the Civil war 69–70.*

Woodward, Evan Morrison
History of the Third Pennsylvania reserve, being a complete record of the Regiment, with incidents of the camp, marches, bivouacs, skirmishes and battles, together with the personal record of every officer and man during his term of service, by Major E. M. Woodward. Trenton, N. J., MacCrellish & Quigley, printers, 1883. 256, 60, 11 p. 4 plates (illus., 3 ports.). 24cm.        DLC NN  **138**
Unit roster 9–60 of 60 p. "Index," 11 p.

**33RD INFANTRY**

*Organized: August 31, 1861.*
*Designated 62nd regiment of infantry: November 18, 1861.*

**33RD INFANTRY (4TH RESERVE)**

*Organized: July 1861.*
*Mustered out: June 8, 1864.*
*Bates* I 636–64.
*Philadelphia in the Civil war 71–2.*

Vanscoten, M      H
The conception, organization and campaigns of "Company H," 4th Penn. reserve, volunteer corps, 33 regiment in line, 1861–5. Historian: Sergeant M. H. Vanscoten. Compiled by Mrs. M. H. France. Tunkhannock, Baldwin & Chapman, 1885. 130 p. 21½cm.        NN  **139**

**34TH INFANTRY (5TH RESERVE)**

*Organized: June 1861.*
*Mustered out: June 13, 1864.*
*Bates* I 664–91.

Moyer, Henry C
A remarkable gunshot wound, the case of Daniel V. Moyer, Company H, Fifth Pennsylvania reserves. *The now and then* II (Muncy 1888–90) 177–82.

**35TH INFANTRY**

*Mustered in: July 27, 1861.*
*Mustered out: June 11, 1864.*
*Bates* I 692–719.

Hull, Charles T
Monumental day at Gettysburg, of the Sixth reserves, Pennsylvania volunteers, Tuesday, September 2, 1890, biographical sketches, speeches, etc. Athens, Gazette print., 1892. 44 p. plates (ports.). 21cm.   MnHi  **140**
"Preface" signed: Chas. T. Hull.

**36TH INFANTRY (7TH RESERVE)**

*Mustered in: July 27, 1861.*
*Mustered out: June 16, 1864.*
*Bates* I 720–55.
*Philadelphia in the Civil war 72–3.*

Wilson, William
Yankee letters from Andersonville prison. Edited by Spencer B. King, Jr. *Georgia historical quarterly* XXXVIII (1954) 394–8.   **140A**

**37TH INFANTRY (8TH RESERVE)**

*Organized: June 28, 1861.*
*Mustered out: May 24, 1864.*
*Bates* I 756–83.

Darby, George W
Incidents and adventures in rebeldom, Libby, Belle-isle, Salisbury, by Geo. W. Darby. Drawings by J. W. Rawsthorne. Pittsburg, Press of Rawsthorne engrav. & print. co., 1899. 228 p. front. (port.). illus. 23½cm.
                                        DLC NHi  **141**
Author mustered in 37th Penn infantry, April 24, 1861; transferred to 191st Penn infantry, May 15, 1864. Coulter 112.

Hill, Archibald F
Our boys, the personal experiences of a soldier in the Army of the Potomac, by A. F. Hill of the Eighth Pennsylvania reserves. Philadelphia, John E. Potter, 1864. xii, 13–412 p. front. (illus.). 18cm.　　DLC NN　　**142**
Coulter 231.

#### 38TH INFANTRY (9TH RESERVE)

*Mustered in: July 27, 1861.*

*Mustered out: May 12, 1864.*

*Bates i 784–812.*

Torrance, Eliakim
The Pennsylvania reserves, by Lieutenant Eli Torrance. *MOLLUS-Minn* iii 57–76.　**143**

#### 39TH INFANTRY (10TH RESERVE)

*Mustered in: July 21, 1861.*

*Mustered out: June 11, 1864.*

*Bates i 813–44.*

Roy, Andrew
Recollections of a prisoner of war, by Andrew Roy. Columbus, Ohio, J. L. Trauger print. co., 1905. 170 p. front. (port.). 19½cm.
On cover: Roy.　　WvU　　**144**

—— —— Second edition, revised. Columbus, Ohio, J. L. Trauger print. co., 1909. 216 p. 3 plates (ports.). 20cm.　　NN　　**145**
On cover: Roy.

#### 39TH INFANTRY (MILITIA)

*Organized: July 4, 1863.*

*Mustered out: August 2, 1863.*

Paxson, Isaac
Reminiscences of Schuykill Haven in the Civil war. *Publications of the Historical society of Schuykill county* ii (Pottsville, 1910) 418–44.　　**146**

#### 40TH INFANTRY (11TH RESERVE)

*Mustered in: June 29, 1861.*

*Mustered out: June 13, 1864.*

*Bates i 845–75.*

Jackson, Frank W
Colonel Samuel M. Jackson and the Eleventh Pennsylvania reserves. *Western Pennsylvania historical magazine* xviii (1935) 45–7.　**147**

Jackson, Samuel McCartney, 1833–1907.
Diary of General S. M. Jackson for the year 1862. [Apollo, 1925] 64 p. front. (port.). 19½cm.　　DLC　　**148**
Preface signed: John H. Jackson.

McBride, Robert Ekin, 1846–
In the ranks, from the wilderness to Appomattox court-house, the war as seen and experienced by a private soldier in the Army of the Potomac, by Rev. R. E. M'Bride. Cincinnati, Printed by Walden & Stowe, 1881. 246 p. front. (port.). 18cm.　　DLC NN　　**149**
Enlisted 40th Penn infantry, December 15, 1863; transferred to 190th Penn infantry, June 1, 1864; mustered out, June 28, 1865. "Muster rolls," 231–46. Coulter 304.

#### 41ST INFANTRY (12TH RESERVE)

*Organized: August 1861.*

*Mustered out: June 11, 1864.*

*Bates i 876–906.*

*Philadelphia in the Civil war 74.*

Hardin, Martin D　　　1837–
The defence of Washington against Early's attack in July, 1864, read January 7, 1885. *MOLLUS-Ill* ii 121–44.　　**150**

—— Gettysburg not a surprise to the Union commander, by General Martin D. Hardin, read March 10, 1892. *MOLLUS-Ill* iv 265–75.　　**151**

—— History of the Twelfth regiment Pennsylvania reserve volunteer corps (41st regiment of the line), from its muster into the United States service, August 10th, 1861, to its muster out, June 11th, 1864, together with biographical sketches of officers and men and a complete muster-out roll. Compiled from official reports, letters, and other documents, by M. D. Hardin, late Col. 12th reserves. Published by the author. New York, 1890. 224, (24) p. plates (map and plans, ports.). 23½cm.　　DLC NN　　**152**
Muster-out roll and Duty roster of officers by the month, (24) p.

#### 42ND INFANTRY (13TH RESERVE)

*Organized: June 21, 1861.*

*Mustered out: June 11, 1864.*

*Bates i 907–43.*

...Annual reunion of the Regimental association of the Bucktails; or, First rifle regiment, P.R.V.C. i 1887 (P); ii 1888 (NN); iii–iv 1889–1890 (NHi); x 1896 (WHi); xii 1898 (NHi); xv 1901 (NN); xvi 1902 (NHi).　**153**

Dedication of monument and 20th and 21st annual reunions of the Regimental association of the "Old bucktails" or First rifle regiment P.R.V.C., Driftwood, Penna., September 14th and 15th, 1906; and April 27th and 28th, 1908. ...[61] p. plates (ports.). 21½cm.　　NN　　**154**

42nd Infantry (13th Reserve), continued

Glover, Edwin A
Bucktailed wildcats, a regiment of Civil war
volunteers, by Edwin A. Glover. New York,
Thomas Yoseloff [1960] 328 p. plans, plates
(illus., ports.). 22cm.    DLC NN    155
"Bibliography," 275–9.

Goldsborough, William Worthington, 1831–
1901.
How Ashby was killed, a correspondent re-
views the fighting before the battle of Cross
Keys. Southern historical society papers XXI
(1893) 224–6.    156
Text signed: W. W. Goldsborough, late Major
Maryland infantry.

Shoemaker, Henry Wharton, 1880–    , supposed author.
Two famous Pennsylvania Civil war regiments. [n. p., 1951?] 10 folios. 28cm. Mimeographed.    PSt    157
Caption title. The 42nd and 100th Pennsylvania
infantry.

Thomson, Osmund Rhodes Howard, 1873–
History of the "Bucktails," Kane rifle regiment of the Pennsylvania reserve corps (13th
Pennsylvania reserves, 42nd of the line). Published by William H. Rausch, Historian for the
Regimental association. By O. R. Howard
Thomson and William H. Rausch, with a dedicatory note by Edward A. Irvin, late Lieutenant-Colonel. Philadelphia, Electric print.
co., 1906. x, 466, (1) p. plates (illus., ports.).
24cm.    DLC NN    158
On cover: Bucktails. Unit roster 335–437. "Corri-
genda et addenda," (1) p. "Printed sources most fre-
quently consulted," 455–6.

43rd Regiment of the Line
see 1st Light Artillery

43RD INFANTRY (MILITIA)

Organized: July 6, 1863.
Mustered out: August 13, 1863.

Landreth, Burnet
Ninety-day men of '63. US ns XII (1894)
111–16.    159
"Captain in the Forty-third ninety-day regiment."

44th Regiment of the Line see 1st Cavalry

45TH INFANTRY

Organized: October 21, 1861.
Mustered out: July 17, 1865.
Bates I 1057–1110.

Albert, Allen Diehl, 1844–1913.
A grandfather's oft told tales of the Civil
war, 1861–1865, by Allen D. Albert, Private,
Company D, Forty-fifth Pennsylvania. [Wil-
liamsport, Grit pub. co., 1913] 30 p. front.
(2 ports.), 3 plates (1 illus., 3 ports.). 25½cm.
DLC NN    160

——— History of the Forty-fifth regiment Pennsylvania veteran volunteer infantry, 1861–
1865. Written by the comrades, edited and
arranged by Allen D. Albert, Private of Company D. Williamsport, Grit pub. co., 1912.
530 p. plates (illus., ports.). 23½cm.
DLC NN    161
Chapters are signed by their authors. Unit roster
[421]–524.

Myers, Ephraim E
A true story of a Civil war veteran, by
Ephraim E. Myers, Lieutenant Company K,
45th regiment Penna. vet. vol. inf. Including
an escape from a Rebel prison, by Capt. R. G.
Richards. [York, 1910] 81 p. front. (port.),
ports. 22½cm.    NN    162
Unit roster of Co. K, 72–81. Contents: by Ephraim
E. Myers: Three years' and five months' experience
of an orange recruit, 7–41; by Rees G. Richards: In
the Wilderness, 43–5; The Forty-fifth in the battle of
the Crater, 45–56; From Columbia, S.C., to Knoxville, Tenn., 57–71.

46TH INFANTRY

Organized: September 1, 1861.
Mustered out: July 16, 1885.
Bates I 1111–49.

Harmon, George D
The military experiences of James A. Pfeifer,
1861–1865. North Carolina historical review
XXXII (1955) 385–409, 544–72.    162A
Pfeifer served also in the 1st Penn infantry.

47TH INFANTRY

Mustered in: August 19 to September 20,
1861.
Mustered out: December 25, 1865.
Bates I 1150–90.

48TH INFANTRY

Organized: September 1861.
Mustered out: July 17, 1865.
Bates I 1191–1235.

Bausum, Daniel F
Personal reminiscences of Sergeant Daniel
F. Bausum, Co. K, 48th regt., Penna. vol. inf.,
1861–1865. Publications of the Historical society of Schuykill county IV (Pottsville 1914)
240–9.    163

Bosbyshell, Oliver Christian, 1839–
The 48th in the war, being a narrative of
the campaigns of the 48th regiment, infantry,
Pennsylvania veteran volunteers, during the
War of the rebellion, by Oliver Christian Bosbyshell, late Major. Philadelphia, Avil print
co., 1895. 205 p. plates (illus., ports.). 23½cm.
    Coulter 48.       DLC NN   **164**

——— The Petersburg mine. *Maine bugle* campaign III (Rockland 1896) 211–23. plates
(plan, 3 ports.).            **165**

Featherston, John C
... The work of the 48th regiment, Pennsylvania V.V.I., at Petersburg mine, and which
resulted in the great battle of the Crater, as
detailed by John C. Featherston, late a Captain in the Alabama brigade of General
Mahone's division, which recaptured this important point in the Confederate lines. A lecture delivered at Pottsville, Schuykill county,
the home of the 48th regiment, by Capt. John
C. Featherston. [1906] 30 p. 2 plates (illus.).
23cm.              DLC P   **166**

Gould, Joseph, 1840–
The story of the Forty-eighth, a record of
the campaigns of the Forty-eighth regiment
Pennsylvania veteran volunteer infantry dur-
ing the four eventful years of its service in the
War for the preservation of the Union, by
Joseph Gould, late Quartermaster Sergeant.
Published by authority of the Regimental asso-
ciation. [Philadelphia, Printed by Alfred M.
Slocum co.] 1908. 471 p. illus., maps, ports.,
fold. map. 23½cm.      DLC NN   **167**
Unit roster [399]–462.

Pleasants, Henry, 1884–
The tragedy of the Crater, by Henry Pleasants, Jr. Boston, Christopher pub. house [1938]
110 p. front. (port.). 20½cm.
               DLC NN   **168**
"The spirit of my cousin is really telling his version
of the exploit, for it was from the notes, documents,
letters, and current newspaper accounts left by General Pleasants on his death that the tale has been
pieced together by the author.'"

## 49TH INFANTRY

*Organized: September 14, 1861.*
*Mustered out: July 15, 1865.*
*Bates* I 1236–76.

Westbrook, Robert S
History of the 49th Pennsylvania volunteers,
by Robert S. Westbrook, late Sergeant of Company "B." A correctly compiled roll of the
members of the Regiment and its marches
from 1861 to 1865. Altoona [Altoona Times

print] 1898. 272, (2) p. plans, plates (ports.).
28½cm.               DLC   **169**
"Contents," (2) p. Unit roster 7–85.

## 50TH INFANTRY

*Organized: September 25, 1861.*
*Mustered out: July 30, 1865.*
*Bates* I 1277–1315.

Crater, Lewis, 1843–
History of the Fiftieth regiment, Penna. vet.
vols., 1861–65, by Lewis Crater, Adjutant.
Reading, Coleman print. house, 1884. 88, L,
(1) p. 3 plates (7 ports.). 23½cm.
              DLC NN   **170**
Unit roster, L p. A resolution of thanks by the Committee on Regimental history to the author, (1) p.
Circular dated, June 12, 1889, apportioning remaining copies of the History on the basis of contributed
dues. The bindings are described: best cloth-bound,
common cloth-bound and paper-bound.

## 51ST INFANTRY

*Organized: November 16, 1861.*
*Mustered out: July 27, 1865.*
*Bates* II 1–46.

Public services of Brevet Major-General John
F. Hartranft, Union candidate for Auditor gen-
eral.... Norristown, Wills & Iredell, printers,
1868. 15 p. port. on cover. 22½cm.
                  DLC   **171**
Caption title: A biographical sketch of Bvt. Maj.
Gen. John F. Hartranft.

Sixth annual meeting of the Association of the
51st regiment P.V. Dedication of monument
at Antietam bridge, October 8th, 1887. 28 p.
2 plates (illus.). 24cm.     P PHi   **172**
Caption title.

Society of the Fifty-first regiment Pennsylvania veteran volunteers record of proceedings
of the ... annual reunion held at.... Harrisburg, Lane S. Hart, printer, 1880–81. 22cm.
                    NHi   **173**
1st, Norristown, Sept. 17, 1880. 47 p.
2nd, Lewisburg, Sept. 14, 1881. 56 p.

Chain, B     Percy
Report of presentation of battle flag of the
51st regiment, Penna. volunteers. *Historical
sketches Historical society of Montgomery
county* VI (Norristown 1929) 71–5. plate
(port.).                     **174**

Parker, Thomas H
History of the 51st regiment of P.V. and
V.V., from its organization at Camp Curtin,
Harrisburg, Pa., in 1861, to its being mustered
out of the United States service at Alexandria,

51st Infantry, continued

Va., July 27th, 1865, by Thomas H. Parker, late Captain Co. I. Philadelphia, King & Baird, printers, 1869. xx, [9]–703 p. plates (ports.). 21cm.          DLC NN   *175*

Unit roster 622–89. "Price list of United States clothing, camp and garrison equipage as charged the 51st regt. for the year, 1865," p 703. Coulter 366.

## 52ND INFANTRY

*Organized: October 7, 1861.*
*Mustered out: July 12, 1865.*
*Bates* ii 47–91.

The third annual meeting of the 52d regimental association, held at Tunkhannock, Wyoming county, Penn'a, Thursday, Sept. 25, 1890. [24] p. 14½cm.        NHi   *176*

Fourth reunion of the survivors of the 52d regt. Pa. vols., (known as the Luzerne regiment), held in G.A.R. memorial hall, Wilkes Barre, Sept. 25, 1891. 32 p. 14½cm.        NHi   *177*

Fuller, Frederick
Frederick Fuller, late Lieutenant in the Civil war, 52d reg't P.V. and Signal officer U.S.A., 1861–1865. [Philadelphia, 191–] 15 p. 23½cm.
Title from cover.        PPLL   *178*

Mott, Smith B
The campaigns of the Fifty-second Pennsylvania volunteer infantry, first known as "The Luzerne regiment," being the record of nearly four years' continuous service, from October 7, 1861, to July 12, 1865, in the War for the suppression of the rebellion. Compiled under authority of the Regimental association, by Smith B. Mott, late Quartermaster. Philadelphia, Press of J. B. Lippincott co., 1911. 266 p. plates (1 illus., 2 maps, ports.). 21½cm.
Unit roster [203]–56.    DLC NN   *179*

Powell, W    George
Sumter regained. Dedicated to the Fifty-second regiment, Pennsylvania volunteers, and read at their second annual re-union, held at Scranton, Pa., September 25, 1889. 9 p. 16½cm.        NHi   *180*
Title from cover. Poem signed: W. George Powell.

## 53RD INFANTRY

*Organized: October 1861.*
*Mustered out: June 30, 1865.*
*Bates* ii 92–134.

Ludwig, Mahlon S
My escape from a Rebel prison. In National tribune scrap book i 104–12.

## 54TH INFANTRY

*Organized: August to September 1861.*
*Mustered out: July 15, 1865.*
*Bates* ii 135–75.

Biographical sketch of Col. Jacob Miller Campbell, Union candidate for Surveyor general. [1868] 8 p. 23½cm.    DLC   *181A*

Caption title. On cover: Our leader risen from the ranks! A working man, first in the field, and ever ready with sword and purse to defend his country.

Leonard, Albert Charles, 1845–
The boys in Blue of 1861–1865, a condensed history worth preserving. Lancaster, A. C. Leonard [Press of New Era print. co., 1904] 79 p. front. (port.), illus., port. 22½cm.
Coulter 290.        NN   *181*

## 55TH INFANTRY

*Organized: November 1861.*
*Mustered out: August 30, 1865.*
*Bates* ii 176–215.

## 56TH INFANTRY

*Organized: March 7, 1862.*
*Mustered out: July 1, 1865.*
*Bates* ii 216–45.
*Philadelphia in the Civil war* 75–6.

[Documents in the transfer of the 56th Penn flag to the Union league club, Philadelphia] [Kelly's Ford, Va.?, 1863] 4 folios. 1 col. illus. 26 x 21cm.    DLC NB   *181A*

Contents of each sheet: [1] Letter of Col. J. Wm. Hofmann dated December 5, 1863, to the President of the Union league club offering the flag; [2] illus in color of the flag; [3] Letter of Brigadier General Cutler dated September 5, 1863, to the Governor of Penn commending the 56th Penn for its part in the battle of Gettysburg; [4] Letter of Geo. W. Boker, Secretary Union league club dated December 28, 1863, to Col. Hofmann acknowledging receipt of the flag. Until June 1863 when the Regiment's engagements were sewn on, the flag was a camp flag.

Hofmann, John William, 1824–1902.
Address delivered by Brevet Brigadier General J. William Hofmann, U. S. vols. (late Colonel 56th regiment Pennsylvania veteran volunteer infantry), at the dedication of the Regimental memorial erected upon the field of Gettysburg, by the liberality of the Commonwealth of Pennsylvania, September 11th, 1889. Philadelphia, A. W. Auner, printer, 1890. 14 p. 24cm.        DLC   *182*

—— Military record of Brevet Brigadier General John William Hofmann, United States volunteers (late Colonel of the Fifty-sixth regiment Pennsylvania). Philadelphia, A. W.

Auner, printer, 1884. 23, (1) p. front. (port.).
22cm.                                        NHi      *183*

—— Remarks on the battle of Gettysburg.
Operations on the right of the First corps,
Army of the Potomac. First day of the fight.
By Bvt. Brig. Gen'l J. Wm. Hofmann . . . read
before the Historical society of Pennsylvania,
March 8th, 1880. Philadelphia, A. W. Auner,
printer, 1880. 8 p. 23½cm.        DLC      *184*

### 57TH INFANTRY

*Organized: December 14, 1861.*
*Mustered out: June 29, 1865.*
*Bates* ii 246–84.

History of the Fifty-seventh regiment, Pennsylvania veteran volunteer infantry, First brigade, First division, Third corps, and Second
brigade, Third division, Second corps, Army
of the Potomac. Compiled by James M. Martin, E. C. Strouss, R. G. Madge, R. I. Campbell
[and] M. C. Zahniser. [Meadville, printers,
Calvin, printers, 1904] 196 p. plates (ports.).
20cm.                               DLC NHi      *185*

Ferguson, Leonard C           1839–1873.
The Civil war diaries of Leonard C. Ferguson. Notes by William Hunter. *Pennsylvania
history* xiv (1947) 196–224, 289–313.    *186*

Nelson, Alanson Henery, 1828–
The battles of Chancellorsville and Gettysburg, by Captain A. H. Nelson, 57th Penna.
vols. Minneapolis, 1899. 183 p. 1 illus., maps.
18½cm.                      DLC NHi NN      *187*
"Errata" slip inserted.

Sallada, William Henry, 1846–
Silver sheaves gathered through clouds and
sunshine. In two parts. Part first, Civil and
military life of the author; Part second, Miscellaneous collection of prose and poetry. By
William H. Sallada. Second edition. Published
by the author. Des Moines [Mills & co., print-
ers] 1879. 360 p. front. (port.)., 2 illus.
19½cm.                          DLC NHi      *188*
Civil war 51–160.

### 58TH INFANTRY

*Organized: February 13, 1862.*
*Mustered out: January 24, 1866.*
*Bates* ii 285–319.
*Philadelphia in the Civil war 77–8.*

Clay, Cecil, 1842–1907.
"A personal narrative of the capture of Fort
Harrison," prepared by Brevet Brigadier General Cecil Clay. 1891. 12 p. *MOLLUS-DC*
no 7.                                            *189*

*59th Regiment of the Line* see *2nd Cavalry*

*60th Regiment of the Line* see *3rd Cavalry*

### 61ST INFANTRY

*Organized: September 7, 1861.*
*Mustered out: June 28, 1865.*
*Bates* ii 407–50.
*Philadelphia in the Civil war 79–80.*

Brewer, Abraham Titus, 1841–
History Sixty-first regiment Pennsylvania
volunteers, 1861–1865, under authority the
Regimental association . . . [by] A. T. Brewer,
historian. [Pittsburgh, Art engrav. and print.
co., 1911] 234 p. plates (ports.). 26cm.
Unit roster [159]–225.               DLC NN      *190*

—— . . . Oration delivered July 24th, 1886,
on Wolf's hill, Gettysburg, by A. T. Brewer,
at dedication of battle monument in memory
of the Sixty-first Pennsylvania volunteers. . . .
Cleveland, Cleveland print. and pub. co.
[1888] p [21]–41. map. 22½cm.
                                                 DNW      *191*
At head of title: Second division, Sixth corps. Title
and imprint from cover. "Fragments of battle flags
under which the 61st Pennsylvania volunteers marched
and fought from 1861 to 1865," col. plate with text.

Mindil, George Washington,              –1907.
The battle of Fair Oaks, a reply to General
Joseph E. Johnston, by George W. Mindil, late
Brevet Major-General. Philadelphia [New
York, American Church and press co.] 1874.
16 p. map. 24½cm.                   DLC      *192*
250 copies printed for private distribution.

See item 112A.

### 62ND INFANTRY

*Organized as 33rd regiment of infantry:
August 31, 1861.*
*Designated 62nd regiment of infantry:
November 18, 1861.*
*Mustered out: July 13, 1864.*
*Bates* ii 451–88.

The Sixty-second Pennsylvania volunteers in
the War for the Union dedicatory exercises at
Gettysburg, September 11, 1889. . . . [Pitts-
burgh ?, Barker, 1889] plates (1 illus., ports.).
20cm.                                    MnHi      *193*
Title and imprint from cover.

### 63RD INFANTRY

*Organized: August to September 1861.*
*Mustered out: September 9, 1864.*
*Bates* ii 489–521.

*63rd Infantry, continued*

Hays, Gilbert Adams
Under the Red patch, story of the Sixty-third regiment Pennsylvania volunteers, 1861–1864 ... Compiled by Gilbert Adams Hays, with personal narrative, by William H. Morrow, Company A. Published by Sixty-third Pennsylvania volunteers Regimental association. Pittsburgh [Press of Market Review pub. co.] 1908. 476, (3) p. plates (illus., ports.). 23cm.         DLC NN    *194*
"Company history and roster," [281]–407. "Bully for you," "The bully old Sixty-third," words and music, (3) p.

Marks, James Junius, 1809–1899.
The Peninsula campaign in Virginia; or, incidents and scenes on the battle-fields and in Richmond, by Rev. J. J. Marks. Philadelphia, J. B. Lippincott & co., 1864. xx, 21–444 p. plates (illus.). 18½cm.       NN   *195*
Coulter 315. "Introduction" signed: John Swinburne. The author mustered in, August 26, 1861; resigned, December 20, 1862.

See also Title 116.

*64th Regiment of the Line see 4th Cavalry*

*65th Regiment of the Line see 5th Cavalry*

#### 66TH INFANTRY

*Organized as 30th Regiment of Infantry: July to August 1861.*

*Designated 66th regiment of infantry: October 10, 1861.*

*Consolidated with 73rd and 99th regiments of infantry: March 1, 1862.*

*Bates II 632–3.*

*Philadelphia in the Civil war 81.*

#### 67TH INFANTRY

*Organized: March 31, 1862.*

*Mustered out: July 17, 1865.*

*Bates II 634–72.*

*Philadelphia in the Civil war 82–3.*

#### 68TH INFANTRY

*Organized: August 1862.*

*Mustered out: June 9, 1865.*

*Bates II 673–96.*

*Philadelphia in the Civil war 83–4.*

#### 69TH INFANTRY

*Mustered in: August 19, 1861.*

*Mustered out: July 1, 1865.*

*Bates II 696–740.*

*Philadelphia in the Civil war 87–8.*

McDermott, Anthony Wayne
A brief history of the 69th regiment Pennsylvania veteran volunteers, from its formation until final muster out of the United States service, by Adjutant Anthony W. McDermott. Also an account of the reunion of the survivors of the Philadelphia brigade and Pickett's division of Confederate soldiers and the dedication of the monument of the 69th regiment Pennsylvania infantry at Gettysburg, July 2d and 3d, 1887, and of the rededication, September 11th, 1889, by Captain John E. Reilly. [Philadelphia, D. J. Gallagher & co., printers, 1889] 106 p. plates (illus., ports.). 21cm.       DLC NN   *196*

*70th Regiment of the Line see 6th Cavalry*

#### 71ST INFANTRY

*Organized: April to May 1861.*

*Mustered out: July 2, 1864.*

*Bates II 788–828.*

*Philadelphia in the Civil war 85–6, 89–90.*

Fifth anniversary banquet of the Survivors' association, 71st P.V. (California regiment), Monday evening, April 13, 1891, at Colonnade hotel, Philadelphia, and the report of the Committee on the monument at Gettysburg. [Philadelphia, 1891] 83 p. 2 plates (illus., port.). 21cm.       NN   *197*

Baltz, John D
Battle of Ball's bluff. Death of Senator E. D. Baker. *US* s3 iv (1903) 46–66.   *198*

—— Hon. Edward D. Baker, U. S. Senator from Oregon, one of America's heroes ... Colonel E. D. Baker's defense in the battle of Ball's bluff, fought October 21st, 1861, in Virginia, and slight biographical sketches of Colonel Baker and Generals Wistar and Stone, by John D. Baltz, late Lieutenant, formerly a Private, Co. H, 71st Penna. vols. Published for the author. Lancaster, Inquirer print. co., 1888. 248 p. 5 plates (2 illus., fold. map, 2 ports.). 19½cm.     DLC NHi NN   *199*

Harris, William Charles, 1830–1905.
Prison-life in the tobacco warehouse at Richmond, by a Ball's bluff prisoner, Lieut. Wm. C. Harris of Col. Baker's California regiment. Philadelphia, George W. Childs, 1862. 175 p. front. (illus.). 17½cm.     NN PP   *200*

Moore, John Hampton, 1864–1950.
Baker at Ball's bluff, address of J. Hampton Moore at reunion of survivors of the Seventy-

first Pennsylvania (California) regiment, G.A.R., and the Confederate veterans, at Ball's bluff, Potomac river, Virginia, on the fiftieth anniversary of the battle, October 21, 1911. 7 p. 23cm.       DLC    *201*
Caption title.

United States. Congress.
Addresses on the death of Edward D. Baker, delivered in the Senate and House of representatives on Wednesday, December 11, 1861. Washington, Govt. print. office, 1862. 87 p. front. (port.). 23cm.      WHi    *202*

Wistar, Isaac Jones, 1827–1905.
Autobiography of Isaac Jones Wistar, 1827– 1905, half a century in war and peace. Philadelphia, Wistar Institute of Anatomy and Biology, 1937. vii, 528 p. plates (illus., fold. map, ports.). 26½cm.      NN    *203*
Civil war 355–456. A note mentions "the first confidential printing."

## 72ND INFANTRY

*Organized: August 10, 1861.*

*Mustered out: August 24, 1864.*

*Bates* II 829–61.

*Philadelphia in the Civil war* 91–2.

Fiftieth anniversary of Baxter's Philadelphia fire zouaves, 72nd regt. Penna. vols., August 10th, 1861, to August 10th, 1911, Association of the survivors of the 72nd regt. Penna vols., organized Sept. 30, 1882. [Philadelphia, Bowers print. co., 1911] 16 p. plates (illus.). 23cm.      CSmH P    *204*

The Seventy-second regiment, Pennsylvania volunteers, at Bloody angle, Gettysburg. [Order of exercises, and addresses by John Reed and Capt. W. W. Ker, on the occasion of the temporary erection of the Regiment's monument on the battlefield of Gettysburg, September 2, 1889. Philadelphia ?, 1889] 15 p. plan. 23½cm.      DLC    *205*

Furness, William Henry, 1802–1896.
A word of consolation for the kindred of those who have fallen in battle, a discourse delivered September 28, 1862, by W. H. Furness ... with the funeral service at the burial of Lieut. A. W. Peabody, September 26, 1862. 23 p. 23cm.      DLC    *206*

Pennsylvania. Courts. Court of Common Pleas, Adams County.
Between survivors of the 72d regiment of Pennsylvania volunteers, plaintiffs and Gettysburg battle-field memorial association and Commissioners appointed by the Governor of the State of Pennsylvania, defendants. Bill of complaint by the plaintiffs. [1889] 20 p. plan. 23cm.      NHi    *207*

Pennsylvania. Courts. Supreme Court, Middle district.
Appeal of the Gettysburg battlefield memorial association and Commissioners appointed by the Governor of the State of Pennsylvania, from the decree of the Court of common pleas of Adams county. Paper book of appellants. [1889] cxiv, 400 p. plates (plans). 22½cm.      NHi    *208*

—— Paper-book of appellants. [1889] 35 p. 22½cm.      NHi    *209*

—— Paper-book of appellees. [1889] 24 p. plan. 22½cm.      NHi    *210*

Webb, Alexander Stewart, 1835–1911.
An address delivered at Gettysburg, August 27, 1883, by Gen. Alexander S. Webb, at the dedication of the 72d Pa. vols. monument. Also, an historical sketch of the 72d regiment, by Charles H. Banes, Assistant Adjutant-General. Philadelphia, Porter & Coates, 1883. 25 p. front. (mounted illus.). 22½cm.
     DLC NN    *211*
"Historical sketch of the 72d Pennsylvania volunteers (Philadelphia fire zouaves)," [19]–25.

## 73RD INFANTRY

*Left State: September 24, 1861.*

*Mustered out: July 14, 1865.*

*Bates* II 862–92.

*Philadelphia in the Civil war* 96–7.

The Seventy-third regiment Pennsylvania volunteers at Gettysburg. [1889] 28 p. 23½cm.      NHi    *212*

## 74TH INFANTRY

*Mustered in: September 14, 1861.*

*Mustered out: August 29, 1865.*

*Bates* II 893–914.

*Philadelphia in the Civil war* 98–9.

## 75TH INFANTRY

*Organized as 40th regiment of infantry: August to September 1861.*

*Designated 75th regiment of infantry.**

*Mustered out: September 1, 1865.*

*Bates* II 915–44.

*Philadelphia in the Civil war* 99–102.

* "The 75th regiment infantry was organized at Philadelphia in August – September, 1861, under the mistaken identity of the 40th regiment infantry. The regiment never formally bore this designation, the designation 40th regiment infantry having already been assigned to the 11th reserves." (Pennsylvania Department of military affairs to the compiler.)

75th Infantry, continued

Nachtigall, Hermann
    Geschichte des 75sten Regiments, Pa. vols., von Hermann Nachtigall, als Festgabe zum Andenken an die Errichtung und Einweihung des Denkmals zu Ehren ihrer um Bürgerkriege gefallenen Kameraden, herausgegeben von der Vereinigung der überlebenden Veteranen des 75sten Regiments, Pa. vols. Philadelphia, Druck von C. B. Kretchman, 1886. 10 p. 23½cm.                                         DLC   *213*
    Title and imprint from cover.

## 76TH INFANTRY

*Organized: October 18, 1861.*
*Mustered out: July 18, 1865.*
*Bates* II 945–84.

## 77TH INFANTRY

*Organized: October 15, 1861.*
*Mustered out: December 6, 1865.*
*Bates* II 985–1028.

Andersonville, diary of a prisoner, from the original manuscript, now first printed. *Historical magazine* s2 IX (Morrisania 1871) 1–7.
                                                      *214*
    "The writer was probably Alfred W. Letteer, Sergeant-Major of a regiment of Pennsylvania volunteers commanded by Colonel Thomas E. Rose."

Obreiter, John
    The Seventy-seventh Pennsylvania at Shiloh. History of the Regiment. The battle of Shiloh. [Harrisburg, Harrisburg pub. co., State printer] 1905. 406 p. plates (illus., 2 fold. maps, ports.). 24cm.                        DLC NN   *215*
    Added title page, p [67] History of the Seventy-seventh Pennsylvania volunteers, by John Obreiter. Report of the Shiloh battlefield commission and dedication of the monument, 11–65. Unit roster 165–251. "Shiloh, by Major David W. Reed," 253–352.

—— The Seventy-seventh Pennsylvania at Shiloh. History of the Regiment. [Harrisburg, Harrisburg pub. co., State printer] 1908. 341 p. plates (illus., 4 double maps, ports.). 24cm.
                                                  NN   *216*
    Added title page, p [63] History of the Seventy-seventh Pennsylvania volunteers, by John Obreiter. Revised edition. Report of the Shiloh battlefield commission and dedication of the monument, 11–61. Unit roster 239–317.

Rose, Thomas Ellwood, 1830–1907.
    Col. Rose's story of the famous tunnel escape from Libby prison, a thrilling account of the daring escape of 109 Union officers from Libby prison through the famous Yankee tunnel. [188–] [12] p. illus., 2 ports., plan. 23½cm.
    Title from cover.                          DLC In   *217*

## 78TH INFANTRY

*Organized: October 15, 1861.*
*Mustered out: September 11, 1865.*
*Bates* II 1029–74.

Blakeley, Archibald, 1827–1915.
    Address by comrade Archibald Blakeley, delivered at Leechburg, Pa., September, 1880, at the re-union of the 78th regiment of Pennsylvania volunteers. [Pittsburgh] W. V. Dermitt, print [1880] 12 p. 25cm.            IHi   *218*
    Title and imprint from cover.

—— Address of General Archibald Blakeley at the reunion of the Society of the Army of the Cumberland, Louisville, Ky., October, 1901. Cincinnati, Robert Clarke co., 1902. 23 p. 23½cm.                                WHi   *219*

Gibson, Joseph Thompson, 1844–1922.
    History of the Seventy-eighth Pennsylvania volunteer infantry, edited by T. J. Gibson, under the direction of the Historical committee of the Regimental association. [Pittsburgh, Pittsburgh print. co.] 1905. 267 p. illus., maps, ports. 23½cm.                        DLC NN   *220*
    Unit roster 195–267.

## 79TH INFANTRY

*Organized: October 1861.*
*Mustered out: July 12, 1865.*
*Bates* II 1075–1113.

Muster roll of the 79th Pa. vol. Philadelphia, H. Blickenderfer, 1865. broadside, 50 x 66cm.
                                                  PPLL   *221*
    "Printed in oil colors by P. S. Duval & Son, Philadelphia."

Johnston, Adams S
    The soldier boy's diary book; or, memorandums of the alphabetical first lessons of military tactics, kept by Adams S. Johnston, from September 14, 1861, to October 2, 1864. Pittsburgh, 1866. v, [7]–139 p. 18cm.
                                                  DLC NN   *222*

Johnston, John M
    A night with bushwackers. *BandG* II (1893) 328–31.                                              *223*

Martin, Edwin K
    Oration, by E. K. Martin, delivered in Fulton hall, Lancaster, Pa., October 8th, 1877. Lancaster, New Era print, 1877. 34 p. 19cm.
                                                  DNW   *224*
    Title and imprint from cover, p [1] Delivered before the first re-union of the 79th Penn.

*80th Regiment of the Line see 7th Cavalry*

## 81ST INFANTRY

*Organized: October 1861.*

*Mustered out: June 29, 1865.*

*Bates* II 1167–1201.

*Philadelphia in the Civil war* 102–4.

Wilson, Harry
Oration at the unveiling of the monument erected by the State of Pennsylvania on the battle-field of Gettysburg in honor of, and upon the spot where fought the Eighty-first regiment of Pennsylvania veteran volunteers, delivered by Harry Wilson, Captain Company F, at the request of the Survivors' association. ... [Philadelphia, Sprangler Davis, prs.] 1889. 16 p. 23cm.                           NB     224A

## 82ND INFANTRY

*Organized as 31st Regiment of infantry: August 1861.*

*Designated 82nd regiment of infantry.\**

*Mustered out: July 13, 1865.*

*Bates* II 1202–47.

*Philadelphia in the Civil war* 104–5.

Davis, Charles Lukens, 1839–1919.
A signal officer with Grant: the letters of Captain Charles L. Davis. Edited by Wayne C. Temple. *Civil war history* VII (1961) 428–37.                                    224B

## 83RD INFANTRY

*Mustered in: September 8, 1861.*

*Mustered out: June 28, 1865.*

*Bates* II 1248–1306.

Judson, Amos M
History of the Eighty-third regiment Pennsylvania volunteers, by A. M. Judson, of Company "E." Erie, B. F. H. Lynn [1865] xv, 17–139, (1) p. 24½cm.
DLC NN     225
Unit roster 111–139. Coulter 268.

Norton, Oliver Willcox
Army letters, 1861–1865, being extracts from private letters to relatives and friends from a soldier in the field during the late Civil war, with an appendix containing copies of some official documents, papers and addresses of a later date, by Oliver Willcox Norton, Private Eighty-third regiment Pennsylvania volunteers, First Lieutenant Eighth United States

*     "This was a case of mistaken assignment of a number that had already been awarded to another organization. The mistake was not corrected until some time after the battle of Fair Oaks, 31 May 1862." (Pennsylvania Department of military affairs to the compiler.)

colored troops. Printed for private circulation only. [Chicago, Printed by O. L. Deming, 1903] 355 p. 22½cm.         DLC NN     226
Coulter 348.

—— The attack and defense of Little Round Top, Gettysburg, July 2, 1863, by Oliver Willcox Norton. New York, Neale pub. co., 1913. 350 p. plates (1 illus., ports.). 21cm.
NHi NN     227

—— Strong Vincent and his brigade at Gettysburg, July 2, 1863 [by] Oliver W. Norton. Chicago, 1909. 57 p. 2 plates (illus., port.). 23½cm.         DLC NN     228

—— Two bugle calls. [190–] 7, (1) p. 21½cm.         DLC NHi     229
Title from cover. Also published in Title 226, p 323–9.

Stafford, David W
In defense of the flag, a true war story, a pen picture of scenes and incidents during the great rebellion, thrilling experiences during escape from Southern prisons, etc., by David W. Stafford. [Erie] Warren Mirror print, 1917. 95 p. illus., ports. 17cm.     DLC WHi     230

## 84TH INFANTRY

*Organized: August to October 1861.*

*Consolidated with 57th regiment of infantry: January 13, 1865.*

*Bates* II 1307–56.

United States. Works Progress Administration. Illinois.
Calendar of the Robert Weidensall correspondence, 1861–1865, at George Williams College, Chicago, Illinois. Prepared by the Illinois historical records survey project, Division of professional and service projects, Works project administration. Chicago, 1940. xiii, 34 folios. front. (port.). 27½cm. Mimeographed.
DLC NN     231
Letters of Jacob Weidensall, 84th Pennsylvania.

Merchant, Thomas Edward
Eighty-fourth regiment, Pennsylvania volunteers (infantry.) Address by Captain Thomas E. Merchant, at the dedication of monument on battlefield of Gettysburg, 1889. [Philadelphia, Press of Sherman & co., 1890] 109 p. 22cm.         DLC     232

Young, Jesse Bowman, 1844–1914.
The battle of Gettysburg, a comprehensive narrative, by Jesse Bowman Young. New York, Harper & Brothers, 1913. ix, (1), 462, (1) p. plans, plates (illus.; maps, 1 double and partly fold.; ports.). 21½cm.     NHi NN     233

*84th Infantry, continued*

—— What a boy saw in the army, a story of sight-seeing and adventure in the War for the Union, by Jesse Bowman Young. 100 original drawings by Frank Beard. New York, Hunt & Eaton [1894] 398 p. illus., ports. 25cm.

NN   234

## 85TH INFANTRY

*Organized: November 12, 1861.*

*Mustered out: November 22, 1864.*

*Bates* III 1–27.

Dickey, Luther Samuel, 1846–
History of the Eighty-fifth regiment Pennsylvania volunteer infantry, 1861–1865, comprising an authentic narrative of Casey's division at the battle of Seven Pines, by Luther S. Dickey. New York [J. C. & W. E. Powers] 1915. xii, 467 p. plates (illus., maps, ports.). 26cm.     DLC NN   235

Unit roster 434–62. "Battle of Seven Pines," 65–172.

Gordon, Marquis Lafayette, 1843–1900.
M. L. Gordon's experiences in the Civil war, from his narrative, letters and diary. Edited by Donald Gordon. Privately printed. Boston [Merrymount press] 1922. 72 p. 2 facs., plates (facs., 2 fold.; 1 illus.; ports.). 28cm.

Coulter 196.     MnHi   236

Hadden, James, 1845–1923.
History of the old flag of the 85th reg't Uniontown, News Standard. 1902. 21 p. front. (illus.), plates (ports.). 22cm.

MnHi   237

Includes roster of survivors. "By James Hadden."

## 86TH INFANTRY

*Organization not completed.*

## 87TH INFANTRY

*Organized: September 25, 1861.*

*Mustered out: June 29, 1865.*

*Bates* III 28–66.

Prowell, George Reeser, 1849–1928.
History of the Eighty-seventh regiment, Pennsylvania volunteers, prepared from official records, diaries, and other authentic sources of information, by George R. Prowell. Published under the auspices of the Regimental association. York, Press of the York Daily, 1901. vii, 306, xxv p. illus., ports., plates (ports.). 23cm.

Unit roster xxv p.     DLC NN   238

## 88TH INFANTRY

*Organized: September 1861.*

*Mustered out: June 30, 1865.*

*Bates* III 67–110.

*Philadelphia in the Civil war* 106–08.

Grant, George W
The First army corps on the first day at Gettysburg. *MOLLUS-Minn* v 45–58.   239

—— Under fire at Charleston while a prisoner of war, by Lieutenant George W. Grant. *MOLLUS-Minn* IV 351–63.   240

Vautier, John D
History of the 88th Pennsylvania volunteers in the War for the Union, 1861–1865, by John D. Vautier, Co. I. . . . Philadelphia, Printed by J. B. Lippincott co., 1894. 280 p. plates (illus., 2 maps, ports.). 23½cm.     DLC NN   241

Unit roster 229–77.

Wagner, George Emil
88th regiment, infantry, Pennsylvania volunteers. Address delivered at the dedication of its monument at Gettysburg, September 11, 1889, by Geo. E. Wagner, formerly First Lieutenant Co. D, Eighty-eighth regiment. 16 p. 22½cm.     NNC NHi   242

Title from cover.

*89th Regiment of the Line see 8th Cavalry*

## 90TH INFANTRY

*Organized: October 1, 1861.*

*Mustered out: November 26, 1864.*

*Bates* III 151–85.

*Philadelphia in the Civil war* 108–10.

Sellers, Alfred Jacob
Souvenir Survivors' association Gettysburg, 1888–9. [Philadelphia, John W. Clark's Sons, 1889] 111 p. plates (illus., ports.). 22cm.

DLC NHi   243

"Compiled by comrade A. J. Sellers."

Smedley, Charles, 1836–1864.
Life in Southern prisons, from the diary of Corporal Charles Smedley, of Company G, 90th regiment Penn'a volunteers, commencing a few days before the "battle of the Wilderness," in which he was taken prisoner, in the evening of fifth month fifth, 1864. Also, a short description of the march to and battle of Gettysburg, together with a biographical sketch of the author. . . . [Lancaster?] Ladies' and Gentlemen's Fulton Aid Society, 1865. 60 p. front. (port.). 19cm.     DLC   244

## 91ST INFANTRY

*Mustered in: December 4, 1861.*
*Mustered out: July 10, 1865.*
Bates III 186–233.
*Philadelphia in the Civil war* 111–12.

*92nd Regiment of the Line see 9th Cavalry*

## 93RD INFANTRY

*Organized: September to October 1861.*
*Mustered out: June 27, 1865.*
Bates III 284–334.

Mark, Penrose G
Red: white: and blue badge, Pennsylvania veteran volunteers, a history of the 93rd regiment, known as the "Lebanon infantry" and "One of the 300 fighting regiments," from September 12th, 1861, to June 27th, 1865, by Penrose G. Mark. Authorized by the executive committee of the 93rd Pennsylvania veteran volunteers association [Harrisburg, Aughinbaugh press, 1911] 578 p. plates (ports.). 22½cm.                          DLC    245

## 94TH INFANTRY

*Organization not completed.*

## 95TH INFANTRY

*Organized: August to October 1861.*
*Mustered out: July 17, 1865.*
Bates III 335–81.
*Philadelphia in the Civil war* 113–15.

Galloway, George Norton
Hand-to-hand fighting at Spotsylvania.
BandL IV 170–4.                            246

—— The Ninety-fifth Pennsylvania volunteers ("Gosline's Pennsylvania zouaves") in the Sixth corps, an historical paper, by G. Norton Galloway (late Co. "A," 95th P.V.), read by Charles Snyder, at a re-union of the surviving members of the 95th Pennsylvania volunteers, held at Germantown, Pa., on the 12th October, 1883, to which is added a narrative of the Chancellorsville campaign, the Sixth corps' part in that campaign, which includes an official list of casualties in each regiment in the Corps, and also the name of every commissioned officer killed or wounded. Prepared from the manuscript of the forthcoming history of the Sixth corps, by G. Norton Galloway. . . . Philadelphia [Collins, printer] 1884. 87 p. 24½cm.                          DLC NN    247

Reed, George E
Campaign of the Sixth army corps, Summer of 1863, by George E. Reed. Philadelphia

[McLaughlin Brothers, printers] 1864. 35 p. 15cm.                          DLC NN    247A
The poem was republished by Charles L. Cummings. See the 28th Michigan infantry.

## 96TH INFANTRY

*Mustered in: September 23, 1861.*
*Mustered out: October 21, 1864.*
Bates III 382–410.

## 97TH INFANTRY

*Organized: August 22 to October 28, 1861.*
*Mustered out: August 28, 1865.*
Bates III 411–62.

Price Isaiah, 1822–
History of the Ninety-seventh regiment Pennsylvania volunteer infantry during the War of the rebellion, 1861–65, with biographical sketches of its field and staff officers, and a complete record of each officer and enlisted man. Prepared at the request of the Regiment, by Isaiah Price, Major. Published by the author for the subscribers. Philadelphia [B. & P., printers] 1875. 608, (1) p. illus., maps, plates (ports.). 27cm.          DLC NN    248
Unit roster 457–564. "Biographical sketches of field officers who commanded, and some of the staff officers," 391–456. Coulter 379.

—— Reunion of the Ninety-seventh regiment Pennsylvania volunteers, October 29th, 1884, "on the old camp ground," at Camp Wayne, West Chester, Pa. An account of the proceedings with a roster of the comrades present, prepared by Brevet-Colonel Isaiah Price. Philadelphia [Press of Donaldson & Magrath] 1884. 64 p. front. (port.). 22½cm.
                                          DLC NN    249

Torrence, Eliakim
General George H. Thomas. *MOLLUS-Minn* IV 494–516.                      250

## 98TH INFANTRY

*Organized: August 23 to November 6, 1861.*
*Mustered out: June 29, 1865.*
Bates III 463–505.
*Philadelphia in the Civil war* 116–17.

## 99TH INFANTRY

*Organized as 32nd regiment of Infantry: July 26, 1861 to January 18, 1862.*
*Designated 99th regiment of infantry: January 1862.*
*Mustered out: July 1, 1865.*

*99th Infantry, continued*

Bates III 506–52.
Philadelphia in the Civil war 118–19.

Fasnacht, Charles H
Historical sketch, by C. H. Fasnacht, and oration, by E. L. Martin, delivered at dedication of 99th Pennsylvania monument, Gettysburg, Pa., July 2, 1886. Lancaster, Examiner print, 1886. 37 p. 19cm.
"Errata" slip inserted.    DLC NHi NN    **251**

Magnin, Albert
Address by Captain Albert Magnin, dedication of monument 99th reg't Penna. vols., Gettysburg, Pa. [1889] 8 p. 18cm.
NHi    **252**
Title from cover. Caption title: The 99th at Gettysburg.

## 100TH INFANTRY

*Organized: August 31, 1861.*
*Mustered out: July 24, 1864.*
*Bates III 553–600.*

Bates, Samuel Penniman, 1827–1902.
A brief history of the One hurdredth [sic] regiment, (Roundheads,) by Samuel P. Bates, to which is added short sketches of Colonel Leasure, and Chaplain Browne, with a few poems by H. B. Durant, of Company A, composed while in the service. New Castle, W. B. Thomas, printer, 1884. 32 p. plates (2 ports.). 20cm.    DLC NN    **253**
On cover: Published by Jas. C. Stevenson. "Preface" signed: Jas. C. Stevenson, Secretary Society of the 100th P.V.V.

Leasure, Daniel
Personal observations and experiences in the Pope campaign in Virginia, by Colonel Daniel Leasure. MOLLUS-Minn I 135–66.    **254**

See also Title 157.

## 101ST INFANTRY

*Organized: November 21, 1861 to February 24, 1862.*
*Mustered out: June 25, 1865.*
*Bates III 601–46.*

Re-union of the 101st reg't Pa. vet. vols., at Leechburg, Armstrong county, Pa., September 10th, 1879. Minutes of proceedings, address of welcome, by H. H. Wray and oration by Col. A. W. Taylor. Bedford, Jordan & Mullin, printers [1879] 18 p. 22½cm.    NHi    **255**
Title and imprint from cover.

Boots, Edward Nicholas, 1842–1864.
Civil war letters of E. N. Boots from New Bern and Plymouth. Edited by Wilfred W. Black. *North Carolina historical review* XXXVI (1959) 205–23.    **255A**

Creelman, Samuel
... Collections of a coffee cooler, consisting of daily prison scenes in Andersonville, Ga., and Florence, S. C., with poetic effusions on foraging, army beans, army corns, soldier's oration, soldier's widow, soldier's death, and the soldier's funeral, silent sentinels, etc., by S. Creelman, late Co. A. 101st Reg't Penn'a vols. Wilkinsburg [Pittsburgh, Press of Pittsburgh photo-engraving co.] c1889. 74 p. illus. 19½cm.    DLC NHi    **256**

Reed, John A    1845–
History of the 101st regiment Pennsylvania veteran volunteer infantry, 1861–1865, by John A. Reed, Private of Company H (appointed 2d Lieut., N. C. Union vols., Dec. 1863), with Luther S. Dickey as collaborator. Chicago, L. S. Dickey & co., 1910. 285 p. plates (illus.; maps and plans, 1 double, 1 fold.; ports.). 26½cm.    DLC NN    **257**
Unit roster 87–122.

## 102ND INFANTRY

*Organized: August 1861.*
*Mustered out: June 28, 1865.*
*Bates III 647–94.*

See Titles 117–119.

## 103RD INFANTRY

*Organized: September 7, 1861 to February 22, 1862.*
*Mustered out: June 25, 1865.*
*Bates III 695–732.*

Dickey, Luther Samuel, 1846–
History of the 103d regiment Pennsylvania volunteer infantry, 1861–1865, by Luther S. Dickey, Corporal of Company C, with Sergeant Samuel M. Evans as collaborator. Chicago, L. S. Dickey, 1910. xiv, 400 p. plates (illus.; maps and plans, 1 double, 1 fold.; ports.). 26½cm.    DLC NN    **258**
Unit roster 361–400. "Diary of Maj. James F. Mackey, a daily record of events covering the entire period he was a prisoner of war...," 314–40.

Donaghy, John, 1837–
Army experience of Capt. John Donaghy, 103d Penn'a vols., 1861–1864. Deland, Fla., E. O. Painter print co. [1926] 244 p. front. (port.). 24cm.    DLC NN    **259**
"Written in 1886, printed in 1926," paster on title page.

McCluskey, William C
Yankee letters from Andersonville prison.
Edited by Spencer B. King, Jr. *Georgia histori-
cal quarterly* xxxviii (1954) 394–8.        **259A**

McNary, Oliver R
What I saw and did inside and outside of
Rebel prisons, a paper prepared and read be-
fore the Kansas commandery of M.O.L.L.U.S.,
by O. R. McNary, 1st Lieutenant 103d Penna.
vols. 22 p. 19½cm.                 DLC    **260**
On cover: War paper. Also published as *MOLLUS-
Kan* War papers (1906) 24–44.

## 104TH INFANTRY

*Organized: September to October 1861.*

*Mustered out: August 25, 1865.*

*Bates* iii 733–78.

"Rescue of the colors," painting presented to
Bucks county. Exercises and addresses, October 20, 1899. *A collection of papers, Bucks
county historical society* ii (Riegelsville 1909)
576–88. plate (illus.).                **261**

Davis, William Watts Hart, 1820–1910.
Address in memory of William Richard
Cries, late Chaplain of 104th regt. Penna. vols.,
by W. W. H. Davis, late Col. of said regt., at
the unveiling of the window of St. Paul's P. E.
church, Doylestown, Sunday, Sept. 27th, 1884.
9 p. 18cm.                        NN    **261A**
The author also served in the 25th Penn infantry.

—— The battle of Fair Oaks. *A Collection of
papers, Bucks county historical society* ii
(Riegelsville 1909) 337–47.            **262**

—— History of the 104th Pennsylvania regiment, from August 22nd, 1861, to September
30th, 1864, by W. W. H. Davis, late Colonel.
Philadelphia, Jas. B. Rodgers, printer, 1866.
vii, [9]–364 p. plates (illus., ports.). 23½cm.
Unit roster [339]–64.          DLC NN    **263**

## 105TH INFANTRY

*Organized: September 9, 1861.*

*Mustered out: July 11, 1865.*

*Bates* iii 779–827.

Roster of the surviving members of the One
hundred and fifth Pennsylvania infantry, service from 1861–1865. . . . Brookville, Republican office [1901] 17 p. 19cm. MnHi    **263A**

Craig, Samuel Alfred, 1839–1920.
Captain Samuel A. Craig's memoirs of Civil
war and reconstruction. *Western Pennsylvania
historical magazine* xiii (1930) 215–36; xiv

(1931) 43–60, 115–37, 191–206, 258–79. plate
(port.).                             **264**

Scott, Kate M
History of the One hundred and fifth regiment of Pennsylvania volunteers, a complete
history of the organization, marches, battles,
toils, and dangers participated in by the Regiment, from the beginning to the close of the
war, 1861–1865, by Kate M. Scott. Philadelphia, New-World pub. co., 1877. xiii, [17]–
329 p. plates (ports.). 23½cm.
                          DLC NN    **265**
Unit roster 257–327. The author was one of the
Regimental nurses.

Thompson, Albert C
Major-General Philip Kearney, as known in
history and as known to me as one who served
under him while he commanded the First division of the Third corps of the Army of the
Potomac. *MOLLUS-Ohio* vi 78–88.        **266**

## 106TH INFANTRY

*Organized: August 14 to October 31, 1861.*

*Mustered out: June 30, 1865.*

*Bates* iii 828–53.

*Philadelphia in the Civil war* 93–5.

Sanders, Richard A        1834–1862.
Civil war diary. *Now and then* iv (Muncy
1929/32) 232–4, 276–7, 302–03. port.
"To be continued." Republished in *Now and then*
xii (1961).

Ward, Joseph Ripley Chandler, 1845–
History of the One hundred and sixth regiment Pennsylvania volunteers, 2d brigade, 2d
division, 2d corps, 1861–1865, by Joseph R. C.
Ward. Philadelphia, Grant, Faires & Rodgers,
1883. viii, 351 p. plates (ports.). 23cm.
                          DLC NN    **267**
Unit roster 249–311. Coulter 463.

—— —— Philadelphia, F. McManus, Jr. &
co., 1906. xii, 457 p. plates (illus., ports.).
23cm.                            DLC    **268**
Unit roster 298–375.

## 107TH INFANTRY

*Organized: March 5, 1862.*

*Mustered out: July 13, 1865.*

*Bates* iii 854–901.

Byrnes, William
An artillery fight at short range. *BandG* ii
(1893) 160–2.                         **269**

Hernbaker, Henry
True history. Jefferson Davis answered. The
horrors of Andersonville prison pen. The per-

*107th Infantry, continued*

sonal experience of Henry Hernbaker, Jr. and John Lynch, Philadelphia, Merihew & Son, printers, 1876. 14 p. 22cm.　　DLC　270

Contents: Statement of Henry Hernbaker, Jr., late of the 107th regiment, Penn'a vols., [3]–6; Statement of John Lynch, late Company F, 13th New York cavalry, [7]–14.

Linn, George Wilds, 1844–

An echo of the Civil war. From Richmond to Appomattox, some account of the evacuation of Richmond and Petersburg and the surrender of General Robert E. Lee, by an eyewitness in the advance column, George Wilds Linn. [Lebanon, Press of Sowers print. co., 1911] 25 p. front. (illus.). 20cm.

DLC　271

On cover: By George Wilds Linn of the 107th regt. Penna. infantry volunteers.

*108th Regiment of the Line see 11th Cavalry*

### 109TH INFANTRY

*Organized: March to May 1862.*

*Consolidated with the 11th regiment of infantry: March 31, 1865.*

*Bates III 953–77.*

*Philadelphia in the Civil war 120–1.*

Veale, Moses, 1832–1917.

The 109th regiment Penn. veteran volunteers, an address delivered at the unveiling of their monument on Culps hill, Gettysburg, Pa., September 11, 1889, by Moses Veale. Philadelphia [James Beale, printer] 1890. 40 p. front. (mounted illus.). 23cm.

"Errata" slip inserted. DLC NHi NN　272

### 110TH INFANTRY

*Organized: August 19, 1861. Left State: January 2, 1862.*

*Mustered out: June 28, 1865.*

*Bates III 978–1012.*

*Philadelphia in the Civil war 122–3.*

Headquarters. Commander of the Post. Winchester, Va., April 17th, 1862. Citizens of Winchester: Upon me has devolved the duty of commanding this Post . . . Wm. D. Lewis, Jr., Col. 110th reg't P.V. commanding Post. broadside, 31 x 26cm.　　DLC　272A

Shaw, Edmund

Dedication services and historical address of Edmund Shaw at the dedication of the monument erected to mark the position held by

110th regiment, Pennsylvania volunteers, in the battle of July 2, 1863. 4 p. 22½cm.

NHi　273

Caption title. On cover: The 110th regiment, Pennsylvania volunteers at Gettysburg, September 11th and 12th, 1889.

### 111TH INFANTRY

*Organized: January 24, 1862.*

*Mustered out: July 19, 1865.*

*Bates III 1013–58.*

Boyle, John Richards

Soldiers true, the story of the One hundred and eleventh regiment Pennsylvania veteran volunteers, and of its campaigns in the War for the Union, 1861–1865, by John Richards Boyle, late Adjutant. Published by authority of the Regimental association. New York, Eaton & Mains, 1903. 368 p. illus., 2 fold. maps, ports. 23½cm.　　DLC NN　274

Unit roster 323–62.

*112th Regiment of the Line*

*see 2nd Regiment of Heavy Artillery*

*113th Regiment of the Line see 12th Cavalry*

### 114TH INFANTRY

*Organized: August 1862.*

*Mustered out: May 29, 1865.*

*Bates III 1183–1207.*

*Philadelphia in the Civil war 124–6.*

Cavada, Frederick Fernandez, 1832–1871.

Libby life, experiences of a prisoner of war in Richmond, Va., 1863–64, by Lieut.-Colonel F. F. Cavada, U.S.V. Philadelphia, J. B. Lippincott & co., 1865. 221 p. illus., plates (illus.). 19cm.　　DLC NN PP　274A

Collis, Charles Henry Tucky, 1838–1902.

The affair at Guiney's station. *Century magazine* LIV (1897) 318.　　275

—— Case of F. F. Cavada. [Philadelphia] King & Baird, printers [1866] 14 p.

CSmH　275A

Cavada was cashiered for misbehavior before the enemy at Fredericksburg, re-instated, and similar charges were made at Chancellorsville and Gettysburg but Cavada resigned before trial. The publication which prints the documents is prefaced by a letter signed by Collis and dated December 4, 1865, protesting Cavada's appointment as a Consul general. At the end of the publication is a list of officers of the 114th Pennsylvania infantry who endorse their Commanding officer's action.

—— [Letters and testimony presented by Mr. Collis defending himself against accusations made to the Military order of the loyal legion

as to his military record. New York, 1891]
38 p. 23cm.                    DLC    **276**
"Printed only for private circulation." On cover:
1st brigade, 1st div., 3rd corps. (57th, 63rd, 68th,
105th, 114th, 141st Pennsylvania volunteers.)

Collis, Septima Maria (Levy), 1842–1917.
A woman's war record, 1861–1865, by Septima M. Collis (Mrs. Genl. Charles H. T. Collis). New York, G. P. Putnam's Sons, 1889.
78 p. plates (illus., ports.). 18½cm.
                              NN    **277**

Rauscher, Frank
Music on the march, 1862–'65, with the Army of the Potomac, 114th regt., P.V. Collis' zouaves, by Frank Rauscher. Philadelphia, Press of Wm. F. Fell & co., 1892. vii, [9]–270 p. plates (ports.). 18½cm.
Coulter 389.              DLC NN    **278**

Todd, Frederick Porter
114th Pennsylvania volunteer infantry (Collis zouaves), 1862–1865. *Military collector & historian* iv (Washington, 1952) 42–4. col. plate (illus.).                    **279**

## 115TH INFANTRY

*Organized: January 28, 1862.*
*Consolidated with 110th Regiment of Infantry: June 22, 1864.*
*Bates* iii 1208–27.
*Philadelphia in the Civil war 128–30.*

## 116TH INFANTRY

*Organized: June 11 to September 4, 1862.*
*Mustered out: June 1, 1865.*
*Bates* iii 1228–66.
*Philadelphia in the Civil war 128–30.*

Mulholland, St Clair Augustin, 1839–1910.
The American volunteer, the most heroic soldier the world has ever known. Letters written to the "Public ledger," by St. Clair A. Mulholland, formerly Colonel 116th Pa. infantry. Philadelphia, Town print. co., 1909. 75 p. 23cm.                          NN    **280**

—— Annals of the war. Chapters of unwritten history. The Gettysburg campaign. The story of the Second corps on the march and in battle. Philadelphia, McLaughlin Brothers, printers, 1880. 16 p. 23cm.
                          CSmH NN    **280A**
Caption title: Hancock's heroism under fire, a graphic recital of the stirring deeds of an eventful day [by] Maj. Gen. St. Clair A. Mulholland. "In the Philadelphia weekly times, February 14, 1880."

—— Heroism of the American volunteer. [Philadelphia, 1904] 40 p. plates (1 illus., ports.). 24cm.                    WHi    **281**

—— Percentage of losses at Gettysburg greatest in history. Gettysburg, W. H. Tipton, 1903.
8 p. front. (port.). 24½cm.    In    **282**

—— The story of the 116th regiment, Pennsylvania infantry, War of secession, 1862–1865, by Brevet Major General St. Clair A. Mulholland. [Philadelphia, F. McManus, Jr. & co., printers, 1899] 422 p. plates (illus., fold. map, ports.). 23cm.    DLC NN    **283**
Unit roster [385]–422.

—— The story of the 116th regiment Pennsylvania volunteers in the War of the rebellion, the record of a gallant campaign, by St. Clair A. Mulholland, Jr. [Philadelphia, F. McManus, Jr. & co., printers] 1903. xxii, 462 p. plates (illus., fold. map, ports.). 23cm.
Unit roster [419]–62.          DLC    **284**

*117th Regiment of the Line see 13th Cavalry*

## 118TH INFANTRY

*Mustered in: August 30, 1862.*
*Mustered out: June 1, 1865.*
*Bates* iii 1310–42.
*Philadelphia in the Civil war 130–2.*

Cattell, Alexander Gilmore, 1816–1894.
An address at the unveiling of the monument erected by the Commercial exchange association of Philadelphia (late Corn exchange association) to commemorate the heroic services of the Corn exchange regiment, 118th Penn'a volunteers, delivered at "Round Top," on the Gettysburg battlefield, September 8, 1884, by Alexander G. Cattell. Philadelphia, Commercial List print. house, 1884. 30 p. front. (illus.). 23½cm.                    DNW    **285**

Corn Exchange Association, Philadelphia.
Eleventh annual report of the Corn exchange association of Philadelphia, January 31, 1865. Philadelphia, E. C. Markley & Son, printers, 1865. 72 p. 22cm.            IHi NN    **286**
"Roster of officers of the 118th regiment," [39]–43.
"Journal of the 118th regiment," [45]–72.

—— Twelfth annual report . . . January 30, 1866. Philadelphia, E. C. Markley & Son, printers, 1866. 39 p. 22cm.        IHi NN    **287**
"Journal of the Corn exchange regiment (concluded)," [35]–9.

Peck, Henry Thomas
Historical sketch of the 118th regiment Pennsylvania volunteers "Corn exchange regt.," by H. T. Peck, formerly Adjutant of the Regiment. Read at the ceremonies of dedicating the monument on Round Top, Gettysburg, September 8th, 1884. p 193–209. 23½cm.
                              NHi    **288**

*118th Infantry, continued*

Smith, John L     1846–

History of the Corn exchange regiment 118th Pennsylvania volunteers, from their first engagement at Antietam to Appomattox, to which is added a record of its organization and a complete roster . . . by the Survivors' association 118th (Corn exchange) regt., P.V. Philadelphia, J. L. Smith, 1888. xvi, 746 p. illus., maps, ports., plates (illus., maps, ports.). 22½cm.     NN     **289**

c1888, by J. L. Smith. Smith's name is signed to the appeal for assistance reproduced on p 680. "Comrades! Touch the elbow," words by Gen. J. H. Martindale and music, 27–8. "The army mule, by Tom of Co. K,' poem, two plates following p 208. Unit roster 681–743.

——— Antietam to Appomattox with the 118th Penna. vols. Corn exchange regiment, with descriptions of marches, battles, and skirmishes, together with roster and sketches of officers and men, compiled from official reports, letters and diaries, with addenda. Philadelphia, J. L. Smith, 1892. xvi, 746 p. illus., maps, ports., plates (illus., maps, ports.). 23cm.     DLC     **290**

Printed from the plates of Title 289. On cover: " 'Charge!!' " 118th P.V.

——— History of the 118th Pennsylvania volunteers, Corn exchange regiment, from. . . . Philadelphia, J. L. Smith, 1905. xvi, 743 p. illus., maps, ports., plates (illus., maps, ports.). 23cm.     DLC     **291**

Printed from the plates of Title 289. Pages 744–6 have been dropped in this printing.

## 119TH INFANTRY

*Organized: August 1862.*

*Mustered out: June 19, 1865.*

*Bates* iv 1–29.

*Philadelphia in the Civil war* 133–4.

Gordon, Harmon Yerkes

History of the First regiment infantry of Pennsylvania and antecedent and successor echelons to the 103d engineer battalion (infantry division) Pennsylvania army National guard (the Dandy first), 1777–1961, by Harmon Yerkes Gordon. Philadelphia [Printed by the Legal Intelligencer] 1961. xvii, 336 p. plates (facs., illus., ports.). 23½cm.     NN     **291A**

"The War of the rebellion, Fredericksburg to Appomattox," 35–86.

## 120TH INFANTRY

*Failed to complete organization.*

## 121ST INFANTRY

*Organized: September 1862.*

*Mustered out: June 2, 1865.*

*Bates* iv 30–53.

*Philadelphia in the Civil war* 135–6.

Addenda to history of the 121st regiment Pennsylvania volunteers, by the Survivors' association. "An account from the ranks." Philadelphia, Press of Burk & McFetridge co., 1893. 16 p. 24½cm.     DLC     **292**

Preface signed: Wm. W. Strong.

History of the 121st regiment Pennsylvania volunteers, by the Survivors' association. "An account from the ranks." Philadelphia, Press of Burk & McFetridge co., 1893. 292 p. plates (illus., 2 fold. maps, ports.). 24½cm.

Unit roster [239]–97.     DLC NN     **293**

——— Revised edition. Philadelphia, Press of Catholic Standard and Times, 1906. 299, (3) p. plates (illus., 2 fold. maps, ports.). 24½cm.     DLC NN     **294**

Unit roster 247–99. "Illustrations" and "Contents," (3) p.

Memorial of Thomas M. Hall. Privately printed. Philadelphia, King & Baird, printers, 1865. 26 p. 23cm.     DLC NHi     **295**

Thomas Mifflin Hall, born in Philadelphia, June 2, 1835, died in Philadelphia, November 6, 1864. broadside, 30 x 48cm.     PPLL     **296**

Proceedings of a meeting of the Bar of Philadelphia at which tributes to Colonel Hall were read by Colonel Chapman Biddle, J. S. Rosengarten, W. Rotch Wister, etc. Also, Preamble and resolutions adopted at Petersburg, Virginia, November 15, 1864, by the 121st Penn. on the death of Colonel Hall.

Baird, Henry Carey, 1825–1912.

Memoir of Col. Alexander Biddle (read before the American philosophical society, October 20, 1899). In *Proceedings* . . . Memorial volume i (1900) 196–205.     **297**

Biddle, Chapman, 1822–1880.

The first day of the battle of Gettysburg, an address delivered before the Historical society of Pennsylvania, on the 8th of March, 1880, by Chapman Biddle, formerly Colonel of the One hundred and twenty-first Pennsylvania volunteers. Philadelphia, Printed by J. B. Lippincott & co., 1880. 50 p. 2 fold. maps. 25cm.     DLC NHi     **298**

Biddle, Walter Livingston Cochrane

Address P.V. 121st regiment, by Walter L. C. Biddle, July 2d, 1886, at Gettysburg. 10 p. front. (illus.). 23½cm.     NHi     **299**

Leland, Charles Godfrey
A memoir of Chapman Biddle, read before the Historical society of Pennsylvania, by Charles Godfrey Leland. Philadelphia, Collins, printer, 1882. 24 p. front. (port.). 25cm.
NNC 299A

### 122ND INFANTRY

Organized: August 12, 1862.
Mustered out: May 16, 1863.
Bates IV 54–70.

Transactions of the first annual reunion of the 122d regiment Pennsylvania volunteers, held at Lancaster, Pa., Thursday, May 17, 1883. Lancaster, New Era print. house, 1884. 49 p. 22cm. DLC NHi 300
Partial contents: Oration, by K. Allen Lovell, 6–23; History, by John Smith, 24–49.

Sprenger, George F
Concise history of the camp and field life of the 122d regiment, Penn'a volunteers, compiled from notes, sketches, facts and incidents, as recorded in the diary of George F. Sprenger, First Sergeant, Company K. Lancaster, New Era print, 1885. vii, [9]–372 p. illus., maps, plates (ports.). 20cm. DLC NN 301
Unit roster [331]–41.

### 123RD INFANTRY

Organized: August 1862.
Mustered out: May 13, 1863.
Bates IV 71–89.

### 124TH INFANTRY

Organized: August 1862.
Mustered out: May 16, 1863.
Bates IV 90–107.

Secretary's report of annual re-union of the Survivors' association 124th regiment, P.V., from 1885 to 1890 (inclusive.) Wilmington, Del., Delaware print. co., 1890. 79 p. 22½cm.
DNW 302

Green, Robert McCay, 1842–
History of the One hundred and twenty-fourth regiment Pennsylvania volunteers in the War of the rebellion, 1862–1863. Regimental re-unions, 1885–1906. History of monument. Compiled by Robert M. Green. Approved by the Regimental committee. Philadelphia, Ware Bros. co., printers, 1907. 396, (1) p. illus., ports. 24½cm. DLC NN 303
Unit roster 61–81. "Reminiscences of Thos. V. Cooper," (1) p.

### 125TH INFANTRY

Organized: August 1862.
Mustered out: May 18, 1863.
Bates IV 108–26.

History of the One hundred and twenty-fifth regiment Pennsylvania volunteers, 1862–1863, by the Regimental committee. Philadelphia, Printed by J. B. Lippincott co., 1906. 324 p. illus., maps, ports. 24cm. DLC 304
Chapters are signed by their authors. Unit roster 293–325.

—— Second edition. Philadelphia, Printed by J. B. Lippincott co., 1907. 342 p. illus., maps, ports. 24cm. DLC NN 305
A reprint of Title 304.

Huyette, Miles Clayton, 1844–
The Maryland campaign and the battle of Antietam, by Miles Clayton Huyette. Buffalo, N. Y., 1915. 59 p. plates, 1 fold. (illus., maps, ports.). 22½cm. NB PPL 306

—— Reminiscences of a private. In National tribune scrap book I 83–103. 306A

—— Reminiscences of a soldier in the American Civil war ... by M. C. Huyette. Buffalo, N. Y. [Vosburgh & Whiting co.] 1908. illus., 2 maps, ports. 23cm. MiDB NB 307

McCamant, Thomas, 1840–
Dedication of monument of 125th regiment Pennsylvania volunteer infantry, on Antietam battlefield, Sept. 17th, 1904. Address of Lieutenant Thomas McCamant. [n. p., 1904] 26 p. 23cm. NN PSt 308

### 126TH INFANTRY

Organized: August 1862.
Mustered out: May 20, 1865.
Bates IV 127–46.

MacCauley, Clay, 1843–1925.
From Chancellorsville to Libby prison, by Rev Clay MacCauley. MOLLUS-Minn I 179–201. 309

—— Through Chancellorsville, into and out of Libby prison. I, From Chancellorsville into Libby prison. II, In Libby prison, and out of it, home again. By Clay MacCauley, late Lieutenant. 1904. 70 p. PNRISSHS s6, no 7. 2 plates (ports.). 310

—— Memories and memorials: gatherings from an eventful life, by Clay MacCauley. Tokyo [Printed by the Fukuin print. co.] 1914. xiv, 781, (1) p. plates (illus., ports.). 19½cm. NN 311
"Memorials of the Civil war, 1859–1865," 574–675. Colophon in Japanese, (1) p.

*126th Infantry, continued*

Rowe, David Watson
A sketch of the 126th regiment Pennsylvania volunteers, prepared by an officer, and sold for the benefit of the Franklin county Soldiers' monumental association. Chambersburg, Printed at the office of the "Franklin Repository"-Cook & Hays, publishers, 1869. 89 p. 22cm.                           DLC NN PSt    *312*
Unit roster [53]–89. "Note to the reader" inserted slip.

Welsh, George Wilson and Philip Rudisil Welsh.
Civil war letters from two brothers. *Yale review* xviii (1928) 148–61.          *312A*

### 127TH INFANTRY

*Organized: August 16, 1862.*
*Mustered out: May 29, 1863.*
*Bates* iv 147–65.

History of the 127th regiment Pennsylvania volunteers, familiarly known as the "Dauphin county regiment." Authorized by the Regimental association and prepared by its Committee. [Lebanon, Press of Report pub. co., 1902] 335 p. plates (1 illus., 1 double; ports.). 20cm.
                                          DLC NN    *313*
Unit roster included. Chapter authors are identified in the "Preface."

Gregg, John Chandler
Life in the army, in the Departments of Virginia, and the Gulf, including observations in New Orleans, with an account of the author's life and experience in the ministry, by Rev. J. Chandler Gregg. Philadelphia, Perkinpine & Higgins, 1866. 271 p. plates (illus.). 19cm.
                                          DLC    *314*
—— —— Second edition, revised and corrected. Philadelphia, Perkinpine & Higgins, 1868. 271 p. plates (illus.). 19cm.
Reprint of Title 314.            NN    *315*

### 128TH INFANTRY

*Mustered in: August 13–15, 1862.*
*Mustered out: May 19, 1863.*
*Bates* iv 166–83.

### 129TH INFANTRY

*Organized: August 15, 1862.*
*Mustered out: May 18, 1863.*
*Bates* iv 184–203.

[Armstrong, William H          ]
Red-tape and pigeon hole generals, as seen from the ranks during a campaign in the Army

of the Potomac, by a citizen-soldier. New York, Carleton, 1864. viii, [9]–318 p. 19cm.
                          CSmH DLC NN    *316*
Coulter 328. CSmH's copy has autograph letter signed William H. Armstrong in which he states that he wrote the story and that it was instigated by the action of a superior in regard to a trifling clothing order.

### 130TH INFANTRY

*Mustered in: August 10–15, 1862.*
*Mustered out: May 21, 1863.*
*Bates* iv 204–23.

Hays, John
The 130th regiment, Pennsylvania volunteers in the Maryland campaign and the battle of Antietam, an address delivered June 7, 1894, before Capt. Colwell post 201 G.A.R., by John Hays, late 1st Lieut. and Adjt. Carlisle, Herald print. co., 1894. 21 p. 23cm.
                                      CSmH NN    *317*

Spangler, Edward Webster, 1846–
My little war experiences with historical sketches and memorabilia, by Edward W. Spangler, Private Company K, 130th regiment Pennsylvania. [York, York Daily pub. co., 1904] xv, 202, (4) p. plates (facs., illus., ports.). 23½cm.              DLC NHi    *318*
"Index," (4) p. Coulter 426.

### 131ST INFANTRY

*Organized: August 1862.*
*Mustered out: May 23, 1863.*
*Bates* iv 224–42.

Hutchison, Joseph G
Fredericksburg, by Captain J. G. Hutchison. *MOLLUS-Iowa* ii 255–73.          *319*

Orwig, Joseph Ray, 1838–
History of the 131st Penna. volunteers, War of 1861–5, by Capt. Joseph R. Orwig. Published by direction of the 131st regimental association. Compiled and edited by the Historical committee: William Sweeley, M. L. Wagenseller [and] J. R. Orwig. Williamsport, Sun Book and job print. house, 1902. 269, (1) p. plates (ports.). 23cm.
                                          DLC NN    *320*
Unit roster [248]–69. "Reunions held," (1) p.

### 132ND INFANTRY

*Mustered in: August 11–18, 1862.*
*Mustered out: May 24, 1863.*
*Bates* iv 243–62.

Fourth re-union of the Regimental association of the 132d Pennsylvania volunteers, Antietam,

Md., September 17th, 1891. 27 p. front. (port.).
19½cm.                                   NHi    *321*
"Dedicated and presented to the surviving members of the 132d regiment Pennsylvania volunteers by V. M. Wilcox."

Hitchcock, Frederick Lyman, 1837–
War from the inside, the story of the 132nd regiment Pennsylvania volunteer infantry in the War for the suppression of the rebellion, 1862–1863, by Frederick L. Hitchcock, late Adjutant and Major 132nd Pennsylvania volunteers. Published by authority of the 132nd regiment Pennsylvania volunteer infantry association. Philadelphia, Press of J. B. Lippincott co., 1904. 308 p. plates (illus., ports.). 20½cm.                              PSt    *322*
Unit roster 251–308.

—— War from the inside; or, personal experiences, impressions, and reminiscences of one of the "boys" in the War of the rebellion, by Col. Frederick L. Hitchcock. Philadelphia, Press of J. B. Lippincott, 1904. 308 p. plates (illus., ports.). 20½cm.    DLC NN    *323*
On cover: 132nd Pennsylvania.

Wilcox, Vincent M
An address by Vincent M. Wilcox, Colonel, 132d regiment Pennsylvania volunteers, delivered at the first re-union of the Regiment on the 26th anniversary of the battle of Antietam, at Danville, Pennsylvania, September 17th 1888. [New York, Printed by Albert B. King, 1888] 19 p. front. (port.), plates (illus.). 22cm.                                   NHi    *324*

Wright, Orestes B
The record of a nine months regiment. In National tribune scrap book I 125–6.    *324A*

### 133RD INFANTRY

*Organized: August 1862.*
*Mustered out: May 26, 1863.*
*Bates* IV 263–81.

### 134TH INFANTRY

*Organized: August 1862.*
*Mustered out: May 26, 1863.*
*Bates* IV 282–301.

### 135TH INFANTRY

*Organized: August 19, 1862.*
*Mustered out: May 24, 1863.*
*Bates* IV 302–17.

McClune, Hugh H
Miscellanea, by H. H. McClune. [York, Gazette co.] 1907. 214 p. front. (port.). 19cm.
                                          NN    *325*

Court-martialled and dismissed, November 16, 1862.

### 136TH INFANTRY

*Organized: August 20, 1862.*
*Mustered out: May 29, 1863.*
*Bates* IV 318–34.

### 137TH INFANTRY

*Organized: August 25, 1862.*
*Mustered out: June 1, 1863.*
*Bates* IV 335–50.

### 138TH INFANTRY

*Organized: August 26, 1862.*
*Mustered out: June 23, 1865.*
*Bates* IV 351–77.

Harrold, John
Libby, Andersonville, Florence, the capture, imprisonment, escape and rescue of John Harrold.... Philadelphia, Wm. B. Selheimer, printer, 1870. 132 p. 17cm. DLC NN    *326*

Lewis, Osceola
History of the One hundred and thirty-eighth regiment, Pennsylvania volunteer infantry, by Osceola Lewis. Norristown, Wills, Iredell & Jenkins, 1866. 198 p. front. (3 ports.). 18cm.                              DLC NN    *327*
Unit roster, muster out 163–86.

Mauk, John W
The man who killed General A. P. Hill, statement of Mr. Mauk, who says he fired the fatal shot. *Southern historical society papers* XX (1892) 349–51.    *328*

### 139TH INFANTRY

*Organized: September 1, 1862.*
*Mustered out: June 21, 1865.*
*Bates* IV 378–406.

### 140TH INFANTRY

*Mustered in: September 8, 1862.*
*Mustered out: May 31, 1865.*
*Bates* IV 406–36.

Paxton, John Randolph, 1843–1923.
Sword and gown, by John R. Paxton, soldier and preacher, a memorial volume, a gift to his friends, issued by his daughter, Mary Paxton Hamlin. Edited, with a biography, by Calvin Dill Wilson. New York, Knickerbocker press, 1926. ix, 517 p. plates (illus., ports.). 23½cm.
                                          NN    *329*
"The sword: War lecture: on to Richmond: War stories; War letters home"; 297–401.

*140th Infantry, continued*

Stewart, Robert Laird, 1840–
History of the One hundred and fortieth regiment, Pennsylvania volunteers, by Professor Robert Laird Stewart, Historian. Published by authority of the Regimental association. [Philadelphia, Printed by the Franklin bindery] 1912. 504 p. 2 plans, plates (illus., fold. map, ports.). 22½cm.　　DLC NN　*330*
Imprint supplied from Library of Congress entry. Unit roster [457]–96.

### 141ST INFANTRY

*Organized: August 29, 1862.*

*Mustered out: May 28, 1865.*

*Bates* IV 437–63.

Bloodgood, John D　　–1915.
Personal reminiscences of the war, by Rev. J. D. Bloodgood, late Sergeant Company I, 141st Pennsylvania. New York, Hunt & Eaton, 1893. 324 p. 18cm.　　DLC NHi　*331*

Craft, David, 1832–1908.
History of the One hundred forty-first regiment, Pennsylvania volunteers, 1862–1865, by David Craft, Chaplain of the Regiment. Published by the author. Towanda, Reporter-Journal print. co., 1885. ix, 270, (4) p. 4 plates (1 illus., ports.). 23cm.　　DLC NN　*332*
"Notes," "Errata" and "Index," (4) p. Unit roster [250]–69. "Appeared in the Bradford reporter, 1884–85. Contains material not in printed volume," Catalogue of the John P. Nicholson library, 1914. Nicholson's copy of mounted clips of the newspaper text is in CSmH. Coulter 98.

Powelson, Benjamin F
History of Company K of the 140th regiment Pennsylvania volunteers (1862–'65), by B. F. Powelson, under the direction of Brevet Capt. Aleck Sweeney, and with the co-operation of others of the Company. Steubenville, Ohio, Carnahan print. co., 1906. 78 p. plates (ports.). 23½cm.　　DLC　*333*

Ward, Lester Frank, 1841–1913.
Young Ward's diary, a human and eager record of the years between 1860 and 1870 ... by Lester Ward ... Edited by Bernhard J. Stern. New York, G. P. Putnam's Sons [1935] x, 321 p.　　NN　*333A*
"A rank and file soldier in the Union army," 115–54.

### 142ND INFANTRY

*Organized: September 1, 1862.*

*Mustered out: May 29, 1865.*

*Bates* IV 464–86.

Gearhart, Edwin R
Reminiscences of the Civil war [by] E. R. Gearhart. Stroudsberg, Daily Record press [1901?] 86 p. front. (port.). 21cm.
　　NB　*333B*

McCalmont, Alfred Brunson
Extract from letters written by Alfred B. McCalmont late Lt.–Col. 142d regt., Col. 208th regt., from the front during the War of the rebellion ... Printed for private circulation by his son, Robert McCalmont. [Franklin, 1908] 134 p. plates (2 illus., ports.). 23cm.
　　DLC　*334*

Warren, Horatio N　　1838–1916.
The Declaration of independence and war history, Bull run to Appomattox, by Col. Horatio N. Warren. War songs, recitations, poems, familiar songs, Decoration day poems and speeches, concluding with a war drama in four acts, entitled "Tilmon Joy, the emancipator," composed and copyrighted by Col. H. N. Warren. Buffalo, Courier co., printers, 1894. vi, [7]–189, (1) p. front. (port.), plate (illus.). 23½cm.　　DLC NN　*335*
On cover: Rally round the Flag, boys. Edited and compiled by Col. H. N. Warren. Unit roster [71]—91. "This third revised edition." Much of the text is printed from the plates of Title 336.

—— Two reunions of the 142d regiment, Pa. vols., including a history of the Regiment, dedication of the monument, a description of the battle of Gettysburg, also a complete roster of the Regiment, by Col. Horatio N. Warren. Buffalo, Courier co., printers, 1890. vi, [7]–152 p. front. (port.), plate (illus.). 23½cm.
　　NN　*336*
On cover: War history, by Col. H. N. Warren, 1861–1865. Unit roster [63]–83.

### 143RD INFANTRY

*Organized: October 18, 1862.*

*Mustered out: June 12, 1865.*

*Bates* IV 487–517.

Association of the 143d Pennsylvania volunteers dedication of monument and re-union at Gettysburg, September 11 and 12, 1889. Scranton, Sunday News [1889] 67, (1) p. 22cm.
Title and imprint from cover.　　NHi　*337*

Zierdt, William Henry, 1881–
Narrative history of the 109th field artillery, Pennsylvania National guard, 1775–1930, by William H. Zierdt. Special publication Wyoming historical and genealogical society. Wilkes-Barre, Printed by E. B. Yordy co., 1932. xxii, 298 p. col. front. (illus.), plates (ports.). 24½cm.　　NN　*338*
"143rd Pennsylvania volunteers (1862–1865)," 70–87. Unit rosters: 8th Penn., 162–7; 143rd Penn., 168–95.

## 144TH INFANTRY

*Failed to complete organization.*

## 145TH INFANTRY

*Organized: September 5, 1862.*
*Mustered out: May 31, 1865.*
*Bates* iv 518–50.

Black, John D
Reminiscences of the Bloody angle, by
Brevet-Major John D. Black. *MOLLUS-Minn*
iv 420–36.                                         339

## 146TH INFANTRY

*Failed to complete organization.*

## 147TH INFANTRY

*Organized: October 10, 1862.*
*Mustered out: June 6, 1865.*
*Bates* iv 551–76.
*Philadelphia in the Civil war* 137.

Moore, Joseph Addison
Address on the three days' operations of the
One hundred and forty-seventh P.V.V.I., at
Gettysburg, July 1, 2 and 3, 1863, by Joseph
Addison Moore, late Captain Company B
147th P.V.I. Delivered September 12, 1889,
on the occasion of the dedication of the 147th
regiment P.V.V.I. monument on Gettysburg
battle-field on Culp's hill. Harrisburg, Meyers
print. and pub. house, 1889. 23 p. 22½cm.
                                   NHi      340

Russ, William Adam, editor.
Civil war letters concerning members of Co.
G, 174th [sic! 147th] reg. P.V.I. Edited by
William A. Russ, Jr. *Susquehana university
studies* v (1953/56) 179–220.

See also Titles 22–23 and 131.

## 148TH INFANTRY

*Organized: September 8, 1862.*
*Mustered out: June 1, 1865.*
*Bates* iv 577–610.

Burr, Frank A          1843–1894.
Life and achievements of James Addams
Beaver, early life, military services and public
career, by Frank A. Burr. Philadelphia, Ferguson Bros. & co., printers, 1882. 224 p. 2 facs.,
plates (1 illus., 3 plans, 2 pórts.). 19½cm.
                                   DLC      341
"Respectfully dedicated to the One hundred and
forty-eighth Pennsylvania volunteers."

Forster, Robert H
Pennsylvania days. Historical address of
Major R. H. Forster, at the dedication of the
monument of the 148th Penna. volunteers,
Gettysburg, Sept. 11–12, 1889. Harrisburg,
Meyers print. house, 1889. 16 p. 22cm.
                                   P       342

Muffly, Joseph Wendel, 1840–
The story of our regiment, a history of the
148th Pennsylvania vols., written by the comrades, Adjt. J. W. Muffly, editor. Des Moines,
Iowa, Kenyon print. & mfg. co., 1904. 1096 p.
plates (2 illus., ports.). 23½cm.
                                   DLC NN   343
Unit roster 921–1037. Chapters are signed by their
authors.

## 149TH INFANTRY

*Organized: August 1862.*
*Mustered out: June 24, 1865.*
*Bates* iv 611–48.

Proceedings of reunion and dedication of State
monument held by the survivors of the 149th
P.V. regiment at Gettysburg, Pennsylvania day,
Sept. 11th and 12th, 1889. Pittsburgh, Ferguson & co., printers, 1889. 16 p. 20cm.
                                   IHi In    344

Bassler, John H
The color episode of the One hundred and
forty-ninth regiment Pennsylvania volunteers
in the first day's fight at Gettysburg, July 1,
1863 ... by J. H. Bassler, late Captain of the
Color company. *Papers and addresses of the
Lebanon county historical society* iv (Lebanon
1907) 77–110.                             345

——— Reminiscences of the first day's fight at
Gettysburg, an address delivered by J. H. Bassler before the faculty and students of Albright
collegiate institute, June, '95. . . . [Myerstown,
Press of Myerstown Enterprise, 1895] 12,
(2) p. 22cm.                           In     346
Title from cover.

——— ——— [another printing] 16, (2) p. port.
21cm.                                  CSmH   347

Nesbit, John Woods
. . . General history of Company D, 149th
Pennsylvania volunteers and personal sketches
of the members, compiled by John W. Nesbit,
with the assistance of the Committee and other
members and friends of the Company. Oakdale, Cal., Oakdale print. and pub. co., 1908.
104 p. plates (illus., ports.). 23½cm.
                                   NN       348
Unit roster 93–6. Biographical sketches [50]–92.
At head of title: 1862 1865 Revised edition. Originally published 1899.

**150TH INFANTRY**

*Organized: September 4, 1862.*

*Mustered out: June 23, 1865.*

*Bates* IV 649–76.

*Philadelphia in the Civil war* 138–9.

Association of the 150th regiment Pennsylvania volunteers, Bucktail brigade. Account of the proceedings at the dedication of the Regimental monument and annual meeting of the Association, at Gettysburg, September 11, 1889.... 47 p. 2 plates (illus.). 24½cm.

                         In   **349**

Ashhurst, Richard Lewis, 1838–1911.

    Address to the Survivors' association of the 150th regiment, Pennsylvania volunteers, read at Gettysburg, September 25th, 1896, by Brevet-Major R. L. Ashhurst.... Philadelphia, Printing house of Allen, Lane & Scott, 1896. 19 p. 25½cm.         DLC   **350**

—— Remarks on certain questions relating to the first day's fight at Gettysburg, a paper read February 10th, 1896, before the Pennsylvania commandery of the Loyal legion, by R. L. Ashhurst. Philadelphia, Press of Allen, Lane & Scott, 1897. 29 p. 23½cm.    In   **351**

Chamberlin, Thomas

    History of the One hundred and fiftieth regiment Pennsylvania volunteers, second regiment, Bucktail brigade, by Lieutenant-Colonel Thomas Chamberlin, historian of the Survivors' association. Philadelphia, Printed by J. B. Lippincott co., 1895. 277 p. plates (ports.). 23½cm.      NN   **352**

—— Revised and enlarged edition, with complete roster. Philadelphia, F. McManus, Jr. & co., printers, 1905. 362, (6) p. plates (2 illus., ports.). 24½cm.      NN   **353**

Unit roster [323]–62. "Index of persons and places," (6) p.

Huidekoper, Henry Shippen, 1839–1918.

    Gettysburg. *Book of the royal blue* v 11 (August 1902) 1–7. illus.      **353A**

—— ...A short story of the first day's fight at Gettysburg, by H. S. Huidekoper, one-time Colonel 150th P.V. Philadelphia, Bicking print, 1906. 12 p. plates (2 illus., map, port.). 23½cm.      NN   **354**

At head of title: Reprinted after revision, from "The military order of Congress, Medal of honor, Legion of the United States," by Gen. Mulholland.

—— A short story of Gettysburg forty years after the battle. *Book of the royal blue* VI 10 (July 1903) 1–13. illus., map, ports.   **354A**

Kieffer, Henry Martyn, 1845–

    An address delivered at the second reunion of the survivors of the One hundred and fiftieth

regiment Pennsylvania volunteers, "Bucktails," held at Meadville, Pa., September 10th, 1890, by the Rev. H. M. Kieffer. Published by order of the Regimental association. Philadelphia, Allen, Lane & Scott, printers, 1890. 18 p. 23½cm.      NN   **355**

—— The recollections of a drummer-boy, by Harry M. Kieffer, late of the One hundred and fiftieth regiment Pennsylvania volunteers.... Boston, James R. Osgood and co., 1883. 332 p. plates (illus.). 17½cm.     DLC   **356**

—— —— Sixth edition, revised and enlarged. ... Boston, Ticknor and co., 1889. 250 p. illus. 22cm.      NHi   **357**

—— —— Boston, Houghton Mifflin co. [1911] 250 p. illus. 21cm.   NN   **358**

"Illustrations signed A. C. R. were drawn by Allen C. Redwood, who served in the Confederate army."

**151ST INFANTRY**

*Organized: October 18 to November 24, 1862.*

*Mustered out: July 27, 1863.*

*Bates* IV 677–97.

Record of a nine months' regiment at the battle of Gettysburg. The 151st regiment, Penna. volunteers. Hamburg, Item print. house [188–] illus. broadside, 35 x 27½cm.    PSt   **359**

Includes "List of losses at Gettysburg, by companies."

Potts, Charles P

    A first defender in Rebel prison pens. *Publications of the Historical society of Schuylkill county* IV (Pottsville 1914) 341–52.   **360**

*152nd Regiment of the Line*
*see 3rd Regiment of Heavy Artillery*

**153RD INFANTRY**

*Organized: September 1862.*

*Mustered out: July 24, 1863.*

*Bates* IV 772–94.

Kiefer, William R

    History of the One hundred and fifty-third regiment Pennsylvania volunteers infantry, which was recruited in Northampton county, Pa., 1862–1863, written by Rev. W. R. Kiefer, historian (one of the musicians), assisted by Newton H. Mack. Easton, Press of the Chemical pub. co., 1909. 352 p. illus., ports., plates (illus., ports.). 23½cm.  DLC NN   **361**

Unit roster 276–351.

Rice, Owen, 1836–1892.

    Afield with the Eleventh army corps at Chancellorsville, a paper read before the Ohio commandery of the Loyal legion of the United States, October 7, 1885, by Owen Rice, late Captain Co. A, 153d Penn. Cincinnati, H. C. Sherick & co., 1885. 38 p. 21½cm.

DLC NHi      362

Also published in *MOLLUS-Ohio* I 358–91.

Simmers, William
The volunteers manual; or, ten months with the 153d Penn'a volunteers, being a concise narrative of the most important events of the history of the said regiment, by William Simmers and Paul Bachschmid, late Lieutenants, 153d P.V. Easton, D. H. Neiman, printer, 1863. 52 p. 22cm.      DLC NHi      363
Unit roster 39–52.

—— —— Easton, Reprinted by Free Press pub. co., 1907. 69 p. 23cm.      NN      364
Unit roster [51]–65.

Weaver, Ethan Allen, 1853–
Owen Rice, Christian, scholar and patriot, a genealogical and historical memoir, by Ethan Allen Weaver. Inscribed to the boys of Company A, 153d Pennsylvania. [Germantown, 1911] 24 p. front. (2 ports.). 23½cm.
DLC      365

## 154TH INFANTRY

*Organized: October 29, 1862.*

*Mustered out: September 29 to October 21, 1863.*

*Bates IV 795–99.*

Seven companies were detailed for special duty.

## 155TH INFANTRY

*Organized: September 2–19, 1862.*

*Mustered out: June 2, 1865.*

*Bates IV 800–32.*

... Fifth reunion of the One hundred and fifty-fifth regiment Penna. volunteers, held at Normal hall, Clarion, Penna., July 20th and 30th, 1896. Pittsburgh, Rawsthorne engrav. and print. co. [1896] 47 p. ports. 23cm.
At head of title: 1862. 1896.      DNW      366

Under the Maltese cross, Antietam to Appomattox, the loyal uprising in Western Pennsylvania, 1861–1865, campaigns 155th Pennsylvania regiment narrated by the rank and file. Published by the 155th regimental association. Pittsburgh [Akron, Ohio, Werner co.] 1910. xiii, 817 p. illus., partly double; map; ports; plates, partly col. (illus., fold. map, ports.). 26cm.      DLC NN      367
Unit roster [743]–91. Company histories, contributed articles and memoirs and sketches are signed by their authors.

Kerr, John
... Oration delivered at the first reunion of the One hundred and fifty-fifth regiment, Penn'a veteran volunteers, at Lafayette hall, Pittsburgh, Friday evening, September 17, 1875, by John Kerr. Pittsburgh, Sam'l F. Kerr, printer, 1875. 20 p. 22cm.      DNW      368
At head of title: 13th anniversary of the battle of Antietam.

Laughlin, George McCully
Memories of Appomattox, by George McCully Laughlin. Edited by Charles A. McClintock. *Western Pennsylvania historical magazine* XLII (1949) 259–63.      369

McBarron, Hugh Charles and Frederick Porter Todd
155th Pennsylvania volunteer infantry regiment, 1864–1865. *Military collector & historian* I no 3 (Washington 1949) 3–4. col. plate (illus.).      370

Marshall, D      Porter
Company "K," 155th Pa, volunteer zouaves, a detailed history of its organization and service to the country during the Civil war, from 1862 until the collapse of the rebellion, together with many incidents and reminiscences of the camp, the march and the battle field, also much of the history of the grand old 155th, by B'v't. Maj. D. P. Marshall, assisted by Maj. J. A. Cline and Serg't W. D. Porter. [n. p., 1888?] xiv, [17]–288 p. 19½cm. NN      371
Unit roster 271–84.

## 156TH INFANTRY

*Failed to complete organization.*

## 157TH INFANTRY

*Organized: October 1862 to February 1863.*

*Consolidated with 191st regiment of infantry: March 21, 1865.*

*Bates IV 833.*

*Philadelphia in the Civil war 140.*

Only a battalion of four companies was organized.

## 158TH INFANTRY

*Organized: November 1, 1862.*

*Mustered out: August 12, 1863.*

*Bates IV 834–50.*

*159th Regiment of the Line see 14th Cavalry*

*160th Regiment of the Line see 15th Cavalry*

*161st Regiment of the Line see 16th Cavalry*

*162nd Regiment of the Line see 17th Cavalry*

*163rd Regiment of the Line see 18th Cavalry*

### 164TH INFANTRY
*Failed to complete organization.*

### 165TH INFANTRY
*Organized: November 25 to December 5, 1862.*
*Mustered out: July 28, 1863.*
*Bates* iv 1084–99.

### 166TH INFANTRY
*Organized: November 10 to December 6, 1862.*
*Mustered out: August 12, 1863.*
*Bates* iv 1100–15.

### 167TH INFANTRY
*Organized: November 10 to December 6, 1862.*
*Mustered out: August 12, 1863.*
*Bates* iv 1116–33.

### 168TH INFANTRY
*Organized: October 16 to December 1, 1862.*
*Mustered out: July 25, 1863.*
*Bates* iv 1134–49.

### 169TH INFANTRY
*Organized: October 16, 1862.*
*Mustered out: July 27, 1863.*
*Bates* iv 1150–64.

### 170TH INFANTRY
*Failed to complete organization.*

### 171ST INFANTRY
*Organized: October to November 1862.*
*Mustered out: August 8, 1863.*
*Bates* iv 1165–81.

Cox, Robert Courton
Memories of the war, by General Robert C. Cox. Wellsboro, Agitator book print, 1893. 47, (1) p. 2 fronts (illus., port.), fold. plate (illus.). 22½cm.          NHi     372
Major 171st Penn infantry, November 19, 1862; mustered out, August 8, 1863; Colonel 207th Penn infantry, September 9, 1864; mustered out, May 31, 1865.

### 172ND INFANTRY
*Organized: October 27 to November 29, 1862.*
*Mustered out: August 1, 1863.*
*Bates* iv 1182–96.

### 173RD INFANTRY
*Organized: October to November 1862.*
*Mustered out: August 18, 1863.*
*Bates* iv 1197–1212.

### 174TH INFANTRY
*Organized: November 19, 1862.*
*Mustered out: August 7, 1863.*
*Bates* iv 1213–25.

### 175TH INFANTRY
*Organized: November 6, 1872.*
*Mustered out: August 7, 1863.*
*Bates* iv 1226–37.

### 176TH INFANTRY
*Organized: November 3–11, 1862.*
*Mustered out: August 19, 1863.*
*Bates* iv 1238–52.

### 176TH INFANTRY
*Organized: November 3–11, 1862.*
*Mustered out: August 19, 1863.*
*Bates* iv 1238–52.

### 177TH INFANTRY
*Organized: November 20, 1862.*
*Mustered out: August 4 and 7, 1863.*
*Bates* iv 1253–68.

### 178TH INFANTRY
*Organized: October 22 to November 27, 1862.*
*Mustered out: July 27, 1863.*
*Bates* iv 1269–84.

### 179TH INFANTRY
*Organized: October 23 to December 6, 1862.*
*Mustered out: July 27, 1863.*
*Bates* iv 1285–98.

*180th Regiment of the Line see 19th Cavalry*

*181st Regiment of the Line see 20th Cavalry*

*182nd Regiment of the Line see 21st Cavalry*

## 183RD INFANTRY

*Organized: December 24, 1863.*
*Mustered out: July 13, 1865.*
*Bates v 128–50.*
*Philadelphia in the Civil war 141–2.*

## 184TH INFANTRY

*Organized: May 1864.*
*Mustered out: July 14, 1865.*
*Bates v 151–69.*

*185th Regiment of the Line see 22nd Cavalry*

## 186TH INFANTRY

*Organized: January 29 to May 31, 1864.*
*Mustered out: August 15, 1865.*
*Bates v 205–21.*

## 187TH INFANTRY

*Organized: March 3 to May 4, 1864.*
*The First battalion upon expiration of its term re-organized and recruited as a part of the 187th infantry.*
*Mustered out: August 3, 1865.*
*Bates v 222–4, 232–51.*
*Philadelphia in the Civil war 143–4.*

Report of the . . . annual meeting of the Survivors' association of the 187th regiment, P.V.I.
P     374
1. Philadelphia, Sept. 6, 1899. 23 p. Text refers to meeting as the second.
2. Gettysburg, June 5, 1900. 37 p.
3. Gettysburg, June 4, 1901. 49 p.
5. Danville, October 8, 1903. 48 p.

Gibbs, James M
History of the First battalion Pennsylvania six months volunteers and 187th regiment Pennsylvania volunteer infantry, six months and three years service, Civil war, 1863–1865, compiled by James M. Gibbs. [Harrisburg, Central print. and pub. house] 1905. 320 p. illus., 2 maps, ports. 24cm. DLC NN    375
Unit rosters: six months' volunteers, 21–72; 187th regiment, 235–320.

## 188TH INFANTRY

*Organized: April 1, 1864.*
*Mustered out: December 14, 1865.*
*Bates v 252–78.*
*Philadelphia in the Civil war 145–6.*

## 189TH INFANTRY

*Failed to complete organization.*
*Bates v 279.*

## 190TH INFANTRY

*Organized: May 31, 1864.*
*Mustered out: June 28, 1865.*
*Bates v 279–304.*

The greater portion of the rank and file was captured before they had been three months with the Regiment.

See Titles 134–136 and 149.

## 191ST INFANTRY

*Organized: May 31, 1864.*
*Mustered out: June 28, 1865.*
*Bates v 279–87, 304–40.*

The greater portion of the rank and file was captured before they had been three months with the Regiment.

See Title 141.

## 192ND INFANTRY

*Organized: July 1864.*
*Mustered out: November 11, 1864. (100 days' service)*
*Bates v 341–60.*
*Mustered out: August 24, 1865. (1 years' service)*
*Bates v 341–2, 361–75.*

Myers, John C
A daily journal of the 192d reg't Penn'a volunteers, commanded by Col. William B. Thomas, in the service of the United States for one hundred days, by John C. Myers. Philadelphia, Crissy & Markley, printers, 1864. 203 p. front. (port.). 19½cm.
DLC NN    376
Unit roster officers and non-commissioned officers [183]–98.

## 193RD INFANTRY

*Organized: July 19, 1864.*
*Mustered out: November 19, 1864.*
*Bates v 376–90.*

## 194TH INFANTRY

*Organized: July 22, 1864.*
*Mustered out: November 6, 1864.*
*Bates v 391–404.*

70

## 195TH INFANTRY

*Organized: July 24, 1864.*
*Mustered out: November 4, 1864.*
*Bates v 405–18.*
*Reorganized: February 1865.*
*Mustered out: January 31, 1866.*
*Bates v 405, 419–35.*

## 196TH INFANTRY

*Organized: July 20, 1864.*
*Mustered out:. November 17, 1864.*
*Bates v 436–49.*

## 197TH INFANTRY

*Organized: July 22, 1864.*
*Mustered out: November 11, 1864.*
*Bates v 450–63.*

See Title 109A.

## 198TH INFANTRY

*Organized: September 9, 1864.*
*Mustered out: June 4, 1865.*
*Bates v 464–94.*

Mitchell, Thomas
The kindred organizations, the Society of the Cincinnati and the Military order of the loyal legion of the United States, a paper prepared and read before California commandery of the Military order of the loyal legion of the United States, January 18, 1889, by Thomas Mitchell, late Captain 198th Penn. vol. infantry. 8 p. 22½cm.        DLC NHi    **377**
On cover: War paper no. 2. . . .

Woodward, Evan Morrison
History of the One hundred and ninety-eighth Pennsylvania volunteers, being a complete record of the Regiment, with its camps, marches and battles, together with the personal record of every officer and man during his term of service, by Major E. M. Woodward. Trenton, N. J., MacCrellish & Quigley, printers, 1884. xiv, 136 p. plates (ports.). 24cm.
Unit roster 70–132.      DLC NN    **378**

## 199TH INFANTRY

*Organized: September to October 1864.*
*Mustered out: June 28, 1865.*
*Bates v 494–518.*

## 200TH INFANTRY

*Organized: September 3, 1864.*
*Mustered out: May 30, 1865.*
*Bates v 519–41.*

## 201ST INFANTRY

*Organized: August 29, 1864.*
*Mustered out: June 21, 1865.*
*Bates v 542–58.*

## 202ND INFANTRY

*Organized: September 3, 1864.*
*Mustered out: August 3, 1865.*
*Bates v 559–77.*

## 203RD INFANTRY

*Organized: September 10, 1864.*
*Mustered out: June 22, 1865.*
*Bates v 578–602.*

Recollections in the Army of Virginia and North Carolina, by "Hermit" of the 203rd Pennsylvania volunteers, a full and graphic account of Gen. Butler's expedition to Fort Fisher; also, of the second expedition under Gen. Alfred H. Terry; details of the capture of Forts Fisher, Caswell, Anderson and Sugarloaf. . . . Wilkes-Barre, Printed on the Record of the Times press, 1865. 53 p. 21cm.
Unit roster Company F [52]–3.    NHi    **379**

*204th Regiment of the Line*
*see 5th Regiment of Heavy Artillery*

## 205TH INFANTRY

*Organized: September 2, 1864.*
*Mustered out: June 2, 1865.*
*Bates v 636–54.*

## 206TH INFANTRY

*Organized: September 1864.*
*Mustered out: June 26, 1865.*
*Bates v 655–70.*

## 207TH INFANTRY

*Organized: September 8, 1864.*
*Mustered out: May 11, 1865.*
*Bates v 671–90.*

See Title 372.

## 208TH INFANTRY

*Organized: August 16 to September 12, 1864.*
*Mustered out: June 1, 1865.*
*Bates v 691–709.*

See Title 334.

## 209TH INFANTRY

*Organized: September 16, 1864.*
*Mustered out: May 31, 1865.*
Bates v 710–28.

## 210TH INFANTRY

*Organized: September 12–24, 1864.*
*Mustered out: May 30, 1865.*
Bates v 729–50.

## 211TH INFANTRY

*Organized: September 16, 1864.*
*Mustered out: June 2, 1865.*
Bates v 751–70.

Soldier's memorial Company H, 211th regt.
Pa. vol. infantry, 2d brigade, 3d division, 9th
army corps. Baltimore, J. C. Fuller & co., 1865.
col. illus. broadside, 52 x 45cm.    PSt    *380*
"Lith. of Major & Knapp . . . New York."

*212th Regiment of the Line*
*see 6th Regiment of Heavy Artillery*

## 213TH INFANTRY

*Organized: February 4 to March 2, 1865.*
*Mustered out: November 18, 1865.*
Bates v 802–18.

## 214TH INFANTRY

*Organized: March 1865.*
*Mustered out: March 21, 1866.*
Bates v 819–37.

## 215TH INFANTRY

*Organized: April 1865.*
*Mustered out: July 31, 1865.*
Bates v 838–53.

# Miscellaneous Infantry
# Organizations

## 1ST BATTALION OF INFANTRY

*Organized: June to July 1863.*
*Mustered out: January 9, 1864. Reorganized and recruited as a part of the 187th regiment of infantry.*
Bates v 222–32.

See Title 375.

## INDEPENDENT COMPANY C

*Mustered in: September 4, 1862.*
*Mustered out: July 20, 1865.*
Bates v 922–24.

## ALLEN GUARD

Bates i 3–10.

See First defenders, page 29.

## COLLIS INDEPENDENT COMPANY ZOUAVES DE AFRIQUE

*Mustered in: August 17, 1861.*
*Transferred to 114th regiment of infantry as Company A: August 1862.*
*Philadelphia in the war 124.*

## LOGAN GUARDS

Bates i 3–9.

See First defenders, page 29.

## NATIONAL LIGHT INFANTRY

Bates i 3–8, 11.

See First defenders, page 29.

# Regimental Publications
# & Personal Narratives
# of the Civil War

## A Checklist

*Compiled by* C. E. DORNBUSCH

Volume One    Northern States
PART V  INDIANA AND OHIO

New York
The New York Public Library
1962

THIS VOLUME HAS BEEN PUBLISHED WITH HELP
FROM THE EMILY ELLSWORTH FORD SKEEL FUND

# Preface

THIS CHECKLIST of regimental histories, publications of regimental associations, and personal narratives of participants in the Civil War is a revision of and supplement to the section on "Military Organizations" in the third edition of the *Bibliography of State Participation in the Civil War*, prepared and published by the War Department Library, Washington, D. C. in 1913 as its Subject Catalogue No 6.*

The present checklist is to be published in seven Parts. The first six will cover the batteries and regiments of seventeen Northern states: I Illinois; II New York; III New England states; IV New Jersey and Pennsylvania; V Indiana and Ohio; and VI Iowa, Kansas, Michigan, Minnesota, and Wisconsin. A final section will provide an index of authors and, where required, titles of the publications listed for these seventeen states.

No subject index to the checklist is contemplated. Besides supplying references for the history of a battery or regiment, the checklist does the same for battles and engagements. To locate references on a battle or engagement, however, the user must determine from the order of battle available in Dyer's *Compendium of the War of the Rebellion* which units were involved and then turn to their entries in the checklist. It is also useful to know the other regiments of a brigade as a means of obtaining from the checklist additional narratives of an incident or battle.

The compiler has followed the arrangement of the 1913 work. Within each state military units are arranged numerically by arm of service — Artillery, Cavalry, and Infantry. While the earlier work entered only units for which publications were known, the present compilation has recorded all units which were organized. Again, while rosters and compilations of regimental histories were reported in one section headed "State Publication" in *BSP*, the present work has indexed these publications under the individual military units.

The compiler has located and personally examined each work entered in this checklist. Some entries which were listed in *BSP* have been omitted —

---

* The Bibliography (hereafter referred to as *BSP*) was prepared as a catalogue and index of a major Civil War collection, now part of the National War College Library, Washington.

entries based on titles taken from bibliographies, correspondence, dealers' catalogues, and other sources but not in the War Department Library. Such "ghosts" as have remained have been omitted here. The present checklist also omits the *BSP* references to the *National Tribune*, and a group of articles by George L. Kilmer which are cited in *BSP* not by original publication but as mounted clippings in ten volumes in the War Department Library collections.

Although a monumental work, some errors found their way into the *BSP*. For instance, Douglas Putnam's *Recollections of the battle of Shiloh* was entered under the 92nd Ohio Regiment, the regiment to which he belonged. But that regiment was formed some months after the battle was fought, and Putnam could write of it not as a member but as a civilian observer. Similarly Eagan's *Battle of Birch Coolie* is entered under the 1st Minnesota Heavy Artillery, although that unit did not participate in the battle.

The seventeen states covered by this checklist had a total of 2,202 batteries and regiments which took part in the Civil War. Each of these units has been listed with a brief statement of its service, i. e. muster in and muster out dates. Where the same number has been assigned to two regiments, they have been distinguished by the term of original enlistments, i. e. three months or three years. Changes in a unit's designation or arm of service as well as amalgamations have been reported. Although some units mustered out before the close of the war and transferred their recruits and veterans to other units, the checklist has not reported this movement of personnel. Reference is made to regimental rosters and narratives of a unit's service where this information may be found.

The compiler has included any articles and publications which could be associated with a particular battery or regiment. The bulk of these are the regimental histories, reunion proceedings, and unit rosters. Publications of sermons preached at soldiers' funerals have been reported. Though their size did not lend to preservation, a surprising number of soldiers' memorials has been located. Broadsides of company rosters, often illustrated in color, were soldiers' souvenirs of the war. The inclusion of all these types of material has here resulted in the broadest possible bibliographical coverage of Civil War materials. All prison narratives have been entered under the

regiment in which the author was serving at the time of his capture. Newspapers printed in the field by army units have not been included.

The value of this checklist is primarily in the listing of the personal narratives of Civil War participants, the rank and file as well as officers, from
Lieutenant to Colonel. (By reason of the honorary Brevet rank, the Colonel
of a regiment could be appointed Brigadier General at the close of the war,
and in this case later reference to his rank is as General.) Usually the publication identifies the battery or regiment of the author. Occasionally, however, he may have served in two or more units, and the later service (often
at a higher rank) is used on the title-page. Such items are entered in the
checklist under the unit in which the author served at the time the events
narrated took place.

Narratives which reflect service in two or more units are entered under
the unit of first service, with cross references from other units in which the
author served. When an author's service crossed state lines or when it was
with the United States Colored Troops, his narrative has been fully entered
under each unit.

The compiler has made extensive search of American journals and periodicals published since the close of hostilities. The very magnitude of this
undertaking precludes even the hope of a definitive checklist. One assumes
that obscure imprints with limited distribution have tended to disappear. In
many cases only single surviving copies have been located. The search is
continuing while other sections of the list are in preparation, and it is hoped
that publication will bring new additions to light.

Following the statement of unit service, entries are given in two groups,
anonymous publications followed by author entries. At least one location of
each title is reported by means of the *Symbols Used in the National Union
Catalogue of The Library of Congress*, seventh edition revised, 1959. Standard works such as the papers of the Military Order of the Loyal Legion and
periodicals are not located in the checklist. The user is referred for these to
the *Union List of Serials* and its supplements. Title-pages have been transcribed in full, including author statements which supply rank and unit.
Distinction is made between illustrations which appear in the body of the
text and illustrations which appear on unpaginated plates. Plates that are

paged have been considered as text illustrations. The place of publication is not identified when within same state as checklist is describing. The collation of reunion proceedings has been limited to their numbering and date.

The very size of the compiler's undertaking has meant assistance from many sources. In his inspection of collections throughout the country, the compiler has been helped by many librarians, and their contributions have been acknowledged in the appropriate sections of the checklist. Above all the compiler is indebted to the administrators of The Emily E. F. Skeel Fund of The New York Public Library for making the compilation of this checklist possible and for freedom in developing it.

# Table of Contents

# INDIANA AND OHIO

# Acknowledgments

In the preparation of this section of the Checklist acknowledgment is made of the assistance given by the following individuals:

INDIANA

Miss Caroline Dunn, Librarian, The William Henry Smith Memorial Library, The Indiana Historical Society
Mrs Hazel W. Hopper, Indiana State Library

OHIO

Mrs Elizabeth R. Martin, Librarian, The Ohio Historical Society

# Abbreviations

| | |
|---|---|
| *AGR* | Report of the Adjutant general of the State of Indiana, 1865–69. 8 v. |
| *AI* | Annals of Iowa |
| *Coulter* | Travels in the Southern states, a bibliography, by E. Merle Coulter, 1948 |
| *InMH* | Indiana magazine of history |
| *Indiana battle flags* | Indiana battle flags, compiled by David I. McCormick. 1929 |
| *MOLLUS* | Military order of the loyal legion of the United States |
| *DC* | War papers District of Columbia commandery |
| *Ill* | Military essays and recollections Illinois commandery |
| *Ind* | War papers Indiana commandery |
| *Iowa* | War sketches and incidents Iowa commandery |
| *Mich* | War papers Michigan commandery |
| *Minn* | Glimpses of the Nation's struggle Minnesota commandery |
| *NY* | Personal recollections of the War of the rebellion New York commandery |
| *Ohio* | Sketches of war history Ohio commandery |
| *Wis* | War papers Wisconsin commandery |
| *Official roster* | Official roster of the soldiers of the State of Ohio in the War of the rebellion, 1886–95. 12 v. |
| *OHQ* | Ohio historical quarterly |
| *Ohio in the war* | Ohio in the war: her statesmen, her Generals, and soldiers, by Whitelaw Reid, 1868. 2 v. |
| *PMHSM* | Papers of the Military historical society of Massachusetts |
| *Ryan* | The Civil war literature of Ohio, a bibliography, by Daniel J. Ryan, 1911. |
| *US* | The united service, Philadelphia. |

# INDIANA

# Reference Works

Dyer, Frederick Henry, 1849–1917.

A compendium of the War of the rebellion. 1908 (reprinted 1959).
"Regimental index" 131–40; "Regimental histories" 1103–58. The pagination is the same in the 1959 reprint.


Indiana.   Adjutant General.

Report of the Adjutant general of the State of Indiana . . . Indianapolis, Alexander H. Conner, State printer, 1865–69. 8 v. 23cm.

Contents: I Indiana in the War of the rebellion, and statistics and documents; II–III Containing rosters of officers and historical memoranda of Indiana regiments; IV–VII Containing rosters of Indiana regiments; VIII Containing additional information, corrections of previous volumes, a list of officers and men who lost their lives in the service, and a list of deserters.


McCormick, David Isaac, 1849–1937.

Indiana battle flags and record of Indiana organizations in the Mexican, Civil and Spanish-American wars, including the movements of troops in the Civil war, as follows: actions, affairs, attacks, battles, campaigns, defenses, expeditions, marches, movements, raids and reconnaissances, by the Indiana Battle flag commission. Compiled by David I. McCormick. Edited by Mrs. Mindwell Crampton Wilson. Indianapolis, 1929. 682 p. col. front. (illus.), 3 plates (illus.). 23½cm.


*The Union army.*

"Record of Indiana regiments," III (1908) 110–207.


United States.   Adjutant General's Office.

Official army register of the volunteer forces of the United States army for the years 1861, '62, '63, '64, '65. Part VI. Indiana, Illinois. Washington, 1865.

A roster of officers by regiments with an alphabetical index for the two states.

# INDIANA

## ARTILLERY

### Regiments

#### 1ST ARTILLERY (HEAVY)

*Organized as 21st Regiment of Infantry: July 24, 1861.*
*Designated 1st Regiment of Heavy Artillery: February 1863.*
*Mustered out: January 10, 1866.*
*Indiana battle flags 569–72.*
*AGR* II 194–209; IV 447–91.

Annual reunion of the Twenty-first regiment, First Indiana heavy artillery.... 1887–1896.
Annual. InHi **1**

Proceedings of the ... annual reunion Company A, 21st regiment Indiana vols., First regt. heavy art.... [III–IV] 1892–1893 (NNC); VII 1896 (NNC); IX–XIII 1898–1902 (NHi); XXII–XXVI 1911–1915 (NNC). **2**

Harding, George Canaday, 1829–1881.
The miscellaneous writings of George C. Harding. Indianapolis, Carlon & Hollenbeck, printers, 1882. 358 p. front. (port.). 20½cm.
DLC NN **3**
"Shifting scenes from the drama of the late war," 190–337.

—— Some Civil war letters from Geo. C. Harding, 2d Lieutenant, Co. F, Twenty-first Indiana volunteers to his wife. [Indianapolis?] 1904. 48 p. 14cm. MnHi **4**
Title from cover.

### Batteries of Light Artillery

#### 1st Battery

*Mustered in: August 16, 1861.*
*Mustered out: August 22, 1865.*
*Indiana battle flags 508–11.*
*AGR* III 384–6; VII 693–6.

#### 2nd Battery

*Mustered in: August 9, 1861.*
*Mustered out: July 3, 1865.*
*Indiana battle flags 511–13.*
*AGR* III 387–9; VII 696–701.

#### 3rd Battery

*Mustered in: August 24, 1861.*
*Mustered out: August 21, 1865.*
*Indiana battle flags 513–16.*
*AGR* III 390–2; VII 701–04.

#### 4th Battery

*Mustered in: September 30, 1861.*
*Mustered out: August 1, 1865.*
*Indiana battle flags 516–19.*
*AGR* III 393–6; VII 705–09.

#### 5th Battery

*Mustered in: November 22, 1861.*
*Mustered out: November 26, 1864.*
*Indiana battle flags 519–22.*
*AGR* III 397–400; VII 709–12.

Holm, David D
History of the Fifth Indiana battery, compiled and written from the "Field diary" of Lieutenant Daniel H. Chandler, and from official reports of officers of the Army of the Cumberland, by Private D. D. Holm. [n. p., n. d.] 62 p. 20cm. In **5**
"Errata" slip inserted. Unit roster 54–62.

Hupp, Ormund
My diary [by] Ormund Hupp. [Odessa, Mo., Ewing printers, 1923] 107, (1) p. 21cm.
InHi NN (M) **5A**

Kendall, Henry Myron
The battle of Perryville, prepared by Major Henry M. Kendall. 1902. 13 p. MOLLUS-DC no 43. **6**

—— The battle of Stone river. 1903. 14 p. MOLLUS-DC no 49. **7**

#### 6th Battery

*Mustered in: September 7, 1861.*
*Mustered out: July 22, 1865.*
*Indiana battle flags 522–4.*
*AGR* III 401–02; VII 712–15.

#### 7th Battery

*Mustered in: December 2, 1861.*
*Mustered out: July 20, 1865.*
*Indiana battle flags 524–7.*
*AGR* II 403–05; VII 715–20.

Morgan, Otho H
History of the 7th independent battery of Indiana light artillery, by O. H. Morgan and E. R. Murphy. War of the rebellion, 1861 to 1865. [Bedford, Press of the Democrat, 1898] 45 p. 21cm. InHi NN (M) **7A**

## 8th Battery

*Mustered in: December 13, 1861.*
*Mustered out: January 25, 1865.*
*Indiana battle flags 527–9.*
AGR III 406–08; VII 720–3.

Fislar, John C
John C. Fislar's valedictory. Ocean Park,
Cal., 1926. 20 p. port. on cover. 27½cm.
              MB    8
Title and imprint from cover, p [1]. "Transcription
by Clara Wheeler [and] M. Harriet Wheeler."

## 9th Battery

*Mustered in: December 20, 1861.*
*Mustered out: June 25, 1865.*
*Indiana battle flags 529–32.*
AGR III 409–12; VII 723–5.

## 10th Battery

*Mustered in: January 25, 1862.*
*Mustered out: July 10, 1865.*
*Indiana battle flags 532–4.*
AGR III 413–15; VII 726–9.

## 11th Battery

*Mustered in: December 17, 1861.*
*Consolidated with 18th battery of light
artillery: November 21, 1864.*
*Indiana battle flags 534–7.*
AGR III 416–17; VII 729–32.

Otto, John, 1826–
History of the 11th Indiana battery, connected with an outline history of the Army of
the Cumberland during the War of the rebellion, 1861–1865, by John Otto, late Senior 1st
Lieutenant. Auburn [Fort Wayne, W. D. Page,
printer] 1891. 109, (2) p. 22½cm.
              DLC NHi    9
Unit roster 101–09. "Contents," (2) p. Coulter 356.

## 12th Battery

*Mustered in: January 25, 1862.*
*Mustered out: July 7, 1865.*
*Indiana battle flags 537.*
AGR III 418–19; VII 732–7.

## 13th Battery

*Mustered in: February 22, 1862.*
*Mustered out: July 10, 1865.*
*Indiana battle flags 538–9.*
AGR III 420–1; VII 737–40.

## 14th Battery

*Mustered in: March 24, 1862.*
*Mustered out: September 1, 1865.*
*Indiana battle flags 539–41.*
AGR III 422–3; VII 740–3.

## 15th Battery

*Mustered in: July 5, 1862.*
*Mustered out: June 30, 1865.*
*Indiana battle flags 541–4.*
AGR III 424–6; VII 743–6.

Fout, Frederick W
The dark days of the Civil war, 1861 to
1865, the West Virginia campaign of 1861, the
Antietam and Harper's ferry campaign of
1862, the East Tennessee campaign of 1863,
the Atlanta campaign of 1864, by Frederick
W. Fout, late First Lieutenant Fifteenth Indiana battery. [St. Louis] Printed by F. A. Wag-
enfuehr, 1904. 422 p. plates (2 illus., maps,
ports.). 24cm.
              NN    10
—— Die schwersten Tage des Bürgerkrieges
von 1864 und 1865. Der Feldzug unter Schofield und Thomas gegen Hood in Tennessee.
Die Schlachten von Franklin und Nashville.
Erinnerungen von Fred'k W. Fout, herausgegeben von Albert E. Fout. [St. Louis, 1902]
317 p. plates (illus., 2 maps, plan, ports.).
24cm.              DLC NN    11

## 16th Battery

*Mustered in: March 24, 1862.*
*Mustered out: July 5, 1865.*
*Indiana battle flags 545–6.*
AGR III 427–8; VII 746–50.

## 17th Battery

*Mustered in: May 20, 1862.*
*Mustered out: July 8, 1865.*
*Indiana battle flags 546–8.*
AGR III 429–30; VII 750–4.

## 18th Battery

*Mustered in: August 20, 1862.*
*Mustered out: June 23, 1865.*
*Indiana battle flags 548–52.*
AGR III 431–2; VII 754–7.

## 19th Battery

*Mustered in: August 5, 1862.*
*Mustered out: June 10, 1865.*
*Indiana battle flags 552–5.*
AGR III 433–5; VII 758–60.

### 20th Battery

Mustered in: Sepember 19, 1862.
Mustered out: June 28, 1865.
Indiana battle flags 555–6.
AGR III 436–7; VII 760–3.

### 21st Battery

Mustered in: September 9, 1862.
Mustered out: June 26, 1865.
Indiana battle flags 556–8.
AGR III 438–9; VII 764–6.

Andrew, Abram Piatt, 1843–
Some Civil war letters of A. Piatt Andrew, III. Privately printed. Gloucester, Mass. [Boston, McGrath-Sherrill press] 1925. x, 146 p. plates (illus., ports.). 21cm.  DLC NN     **12**
"Foreword" signed: A. P. A., IV. Coulter 9.

### 22nd Battery

Mustered in: December 15, 1862.
Mustered out: July 7, 1865.
Indiana battle flags 558–9.
AGR III 440–1; VII 767–9.

Van Arsdel, John S
Hood's invasion of Tennessee. In National tribune scrap book I 132–4.     **12A**

### 23rd Battery

Mustered in: November 8, 1862.
Mustered out: July 2, 1865.
Indiana battle flags 560–2.
AGR III 442–3; VII 770–2.

### 24th Battery

Mustered in: November 29, 1862.
Mustered out: August 3, 1865.
Indiana battle flags 562–4.
AGR III 444–5; VII 772–5.

### 25th Battery

Mustered in: November 28, 1864.
Mustered out: July 20, 1865.
Indiana battle flags 564–5.
AGR III 446; VII 775–8.

### 26th Battery

Mustered in as Company A, 17th Regiment of Infantry: June 12, 1861.
Designated 26th battery of light artillery: October 1861.

Mustered out: July 19, 1865.
Indiana battle flags 565–7.
AGR III 447–9; VII 778–81.

Graham, H          Clay
Hialmer's poetical pencilings by the way; or, sketches of three years' service in Uncle Sam's army. Indianapolis, H. C. Chandler & co., printers, 1864. 47 p. 14½cm. DLC     **13**
Text signed: H. Clay Graham.

## CAVALRY

### 1ST CAVALRY (28TH REGIMENT)

Mustered in: August 20, 1861.
Mustered out: May 31, 1865.
Indiana battle flags 572–8.
AGR II 270–9; IV 630–54.

### 2ND CAVALRY (41ST REGIMENT)

Organized: September 20, 1861.
Mustered out: July 12, 1865.
Indiana battle flags 581–8.
AGR II 400–12; V 273–302.

### 3RD CAVALRY (45TH REGIMENT)

Organized: August 22, 1861. Right Wing, Companies A-F.
Mustered out: August 7, 1865.
Indiana battle flags 589–96.
AGR II 440–52; V 387–95, 409–11.
Organized: October 1, 1861. Left Wing, Companies G-M, transferred to 8th regiment of cavalry: December 1864.
Indiana battle flags 597–601.
AGR II 440–52; V 395–408.

Beck, Elias W          H
Letters of a Civil war surgeon. InMH XXVII (1931) 132–63.     **14**

McCain, Warren
A soldier's diary; or, the history of Co. "L," Third Indiana cavalry, by General Warren McCain, late Sergeant of the Company. Indianapolis, William A. Patton, 1885. 60 p. 20cm.
Unit roster [59]–60.     IHi NHi     **15**

Pickerill, William N
History of the Third Indiana cavalry, by W. N. Pickerill. Indianapolis [Aetna print. co.] 1906. 201 p. plates (ports.). 24cm.
DLC NN     **16**

*3rd Cavalry (45th Regiment), continued*

Weaver, Augustus C
Third Indiana cavalry, a brief account of the actions in which they took part as seen by comrade A. C. Weaver . . . 1861–1865. [Greenwood, 1919] [12] p. 16cm.                In    **17**
Title from cover.

**4TH CAVALRY (77TH REGIMENT)**

*Mustered in: August 22, 1862.*
*Mustered out: June 29, 1865.*
*Indiana battle flags 601–08.*
*AGR III 12–20; VI 245–67.*

**5TH CAVALRY (90TH REGIMENT)**

*Organized: August 22 to October 30, 1862.*
*Mustered out: June 16, 1865.*
*Indiana battle flags 608–13.*
*AGR III 102–11; VI 455–80.*

. . . Annual reunion of the Fifth Indiana cavalry association. . . . [I] 1883 (DNW); II/III 1884/1885; IV 1886 (DNW); V–VI 1887–1888; IX–XVI 1891–1898; XVIII–XXII 1900–1904; XXIV–XXVIII 1906–1910.                **18**
All at InHi, unless indicated.

Finney, Russell P
Maj. R. P. Finney's address, a digest history of the Fifth Indiana cavalry during the War of the rebellion. In Title 18, 1895. 36–47.
                **18A**

Sammons, John H
Personal recollections of the Civil war, by John H. Sammons, a Private in the 5th Ind. cav. vol. Greensburg, Montgomery and Son, printers [188–] 79 p. 23cm.          NN    **19**

Whitenack, David S          1837?–1931.
Reminiscences of the Civil war, Andersonville. InMH XI (1915) 128–43.          **20**

**6TH CAVALRY (71ST REGIMENT)**

*Organized from the 71st Regiment of Infantry: February 23, 1863.*
*Mustered out: September 15, 1865.*
*Indiana battle flags 613–17.*
*AGR II 647–65; VI 138–62.*

The first execution of a deserter in the West. [Indianapolis, 1863] [4] p. 22½cm.
                In    **20A**
Caption title. Robert Gay, Company D.

**7TH CAVALRY (119TH REGIMENT)**

*Mustered in: October 1, 1863.*
*Mustered out: February 18, 1866.*
*Indiana battle flags 617–20.*
*AGR III 209–18; VII 100–30.*

Cogley, Thomas Sydenham, 1840–
History of the Seventh Indiana cavalry volunteers, and the expeditions, campaigns, raids, marches, and battles of the armies with which it was connected, with biographical sketches of Brevet Major General John P. C. Shanks, and of Brevet Brig. Gen. Thomas M. Browne, and other officers of the Regiment. With an account of the burning of the steamer Sultana on the Mississippi river, and of the capture, trial, conviction and execution of Dick Davis, the guerrilla, by Thomas S. Cogley, late First Lieutenant Company "F." Laporte, Herald co., printers, 1876. v, [5]–267 p. 1 illus., 3 plates (ports.). 18½cm.          DLC NHi NN    **21**
Unit roster 68–84. Coulter 84. On cover: Seventh Indiana cavalry and sketches of its officers.

Lowes, James Harvey S          –1920.
Unwritten history of the 7th Indiana cavalry in the War of the rebellion, by James H. S. Lowes. Baltimore, Md., Press of John Cox's Sons, 1899. 11 p. 20½cm.          In    **22**
Poetry.

**8TH CAVALRY (39TH REGIMENT)**

*Mustered in: October 15, 1863.*
*Mustered out: July 20, 1865.*
*Indiana battle flags 620–5.*
*AGR II 381–91; V 222–50.*

Report of the proceedings of the . . . annual reunion of the Eighth Indiana veteran cavalry. . . . I–II 1884–1885; V–VIII 1888–1891; X–XXIX 1893–1912.          In    **23**

Bartmess, Jacob W          1836–1907.
Jacob W. Bartmess Civil war letters . . . Edited by Donald F. Carmony. InMH LII (1956) 49–74, 157–86.          **24**

Clifton, William Baldwin
Libby and Andersonville, a true sketch, by William Baldwin Clifton. Indianapolis, 1910. [24] p. port. 15cm.          In    **25**

**9TH CAVALRY (121ST REGIMENT)**

*Organized: December 7, 1863 to March 29, 1864.*
*Mustered out: August 23, 1865.*
*Indiana battle flags 625–6.*
*AGR III 226–32; VII 148–66.*

Comstock, Daniel Webster, 1840–1917.
Ninth cavalry, One hundred and twenty-first regiment Indiana volunteers. Richmond, J. M. Coe, 1890. 56 p. fold. map. 22½cm.
                DLC NHi    **26**
"Preface" signed: D. W. Comstock. "Papers here collected were read by the Regimental historian . . . at annual re-unions."

**10TH CAVALRY (125TH REGIMENT)**

*Organized: December 30, 1863 to April 30, 1864.*

*Mustered out: August 31, 1865.*

*Indiana battle flags 627–8.*

*AGR* iii 249–54; vii 198–215.

**11TH CAVALRY (126TH REGIMENT)**

*Organized: November 10, 1863 to April 2, 1864.*

*Mustered out: September 19, 1865.*

*Indiana battle flags 629–31.*

*AGR* iii 255–62; vii 216–34.

Eighth reunion of the Eleventh Indiana cavalry association held at Portland, Ind., September 23 and 24, 1894, and regimental roster. Indianapolis, Baker & Randolph, printers [1890] 24 p. 14½cm.    DLC In    **27**
Title and imprint from cover. "A brief history of the Eleventh Indiana cavalry," [1]–5.

Report of the Eleventh Indiana cavalry association for 1898. [Anderson, Benham printery, 1898] 12 p. port. 15cm.    DLC NHi    **28**
Includes Report of proceedings of the 14th annual reunion, 1898.

Doster, Frank, 1847–
    Eleventh Indiana cavalry in Kansas in 1865. *Transactions of the Kansas state historical society* xv (1923) 524–9. port.    **29**

Zornow, William Frank
    Lincoln and Private [John Doyle] Lennan. *InMH* xlix (1953) 267–72.    **30**

**12TH CAVALRY (127TH REGIMENT)**

*Organized: December 10, 1863 to April 28, 1864.*

*Mustered out: November 10, 1865.*

*Indiana battle flags 631–3.*

*AGR* iii 262–8; vii 235–53.

Anderson, Edward, 1833–
    Camp fire stories, a series of sketches of the Union army in the Southwest, by Edward Anderson, Colonel 12th Indiana volunteer cavalry. Chicago, Star pub. co., 1896. vi, 222 p. illus., plates (illus.). 20cm.  DLC MB   **31**
—— Missouri in 1861–1862. *PMHSM* viii 1–19.    **32**

**13TH CAVALRY (131ST REGIMENT)**

*Organized: December 23, 1863 to April 29, 1864.*

*Mustered out: November 18, 1865.*

*Indiana battle flags 633–5.*

*AGR* iii 290–6; vii 303–24.

## Independent Cavalry Companies

### Bracken's Company

*Mustered in: July 9, 1861.*

*Assigned to 1st regiment of cavalry as Company K: August 20, 1861.*

*Mustered out: May 31, 1865.*

*Indiana battle flags 579–81.*

*Detached from the 1st regiment during its entire service.*

### Stewart's Company

*Mustered in: July 4, 1861.*

*Assigned to 1st regiment of cavalry as Company I: August 20, 1861.*

*Mustered out: May 31, 1865.*

*Indiana battle flags 578–9.*

*Detached from the 1st regiment during its entire service.*

### INFANTRY *

### 6TH INFANTRY

*Mustered in: April 27, 1861. (3 months)*

*Mustered out: August 2, 1861.*

*Indiana battle flags 31.*

*AGR* ii 2–6; iv 2–13.

*Mustered in: September 20, 1861. (3 years)*

*Mustered out: September 22, 1864.*

*Indiana battle flags 31–7.*

*AGR* ii 32–9; iv 74–90.

Reunion of the Sixth regimental association on the anniversary of the battle of Shiloh, Columbus, Indiana, April 6, 1895. 17 p. ports. 22½cm.      In    **33**
Caption title. Includes a roster of survivors.

Briant, Charles C
    History of the Sixth regiment Indiana volunteer infantry, of both the three months' and three years' services . . . Written from personal knowledge and the records by the chosen Historian of the Regiment, C. C. Briant, Captain Company K. Indianapolis, Wm. B. Burford, printer, 1891. iv, 423 p. plates (ports.). 19½cm.    DLC NHi NN    **34**
Unit roster 344–423. Coulter 50.

Doll, William Henry Harrison
    History of the Sixth regiment Indiana volunteer infantry in the Civil war, April 25, 1861, to September 22, 1864 [by] William H.

* Indiana Civil War regiments commenced numbering with the sixth infantry. Regiments one to five served in the Mexican War.

*6th Infantry, continued*

Doll. Columbus, Republican print, 1903. 130 p. plates (illus., ports.). 23cm.   DNW   **35**
Unit roster 102–30.

Fletcher, William B        1837–1907.
The Civil war journal of William B. Fletcher. Contributed and edited by Loriman S. Brigham. *InMH* LVII (1961) 41–76. facs., 2 maps, ports.                                     **35A**

Grayson, Andrew J        1838–
. . . History of the Sixth Indiana regiment in the three months' campaign in Western Virginia. Full of humor and originality, depicting battles, skirmishes, forced marches, incidents in camp life, etc., with the names of every officer and private in the Sixth regiment, by A. J. Grayson. [Madison, Courier print, 1875?] 52 p. 21½cm.                       DLC NHi   **36**
At head of title "The spirit of 1861." Unit roster 10–15. Coulter 200.

Smith, William Henry, 1846–
The Sixth Indiana regiment, its historical record, by William Henry Smith. *The Indianian* IV (Indianapolis 1899) 276–85. 1 illus., port.                                        **37**

## 7TH INFANTRY

*Mustered in: April 27, 1861. (3 months)*
*Mustered out: August 2, 1861.*
*Indiana battle flags 37–8.*
*AGR* II 7–12; IV 14–25.
*Mustered in: September 13, 1861.*
*(3 years)*
*Mustered out: September 20, 1864. Veterans and recruits transferred to the 19th regiment of infantry.*
*Indiana battle flags 38–45.*
*AGR* II 40–7; IV 91–109.

A partial list of survivors of Seventh regiment of Indiana volunteers, May 2, 1887. Franklin, Republican print, 1887. 14 p. 15cm.
Title and imprint from cover.   In   **38**

Roster of the survivors of the Seventh regiment, Indiana volunteers, according to company reports, in July, 1897. . . . Indianapolis, Engle print [1897] 32 p. 18cm.   In   **39**
Title and imprint from cover.

Hadley, John Vestal, 1840–
A day with escaping prisoners, by Judge John V. Hadley. *MOLLUS-Ind* 278–94.   **40**

——— Seven months a prisoner; or, thirty-six days in the woods, giving the personal experience of prison life in Gordonsville. . . . Indi-

anapolis, J. M. & F. J. Meikel & co., printers, 1868. 180 p. 20½cm.   In   **41**

——— Seven months a prisoner, by J. V. Hadley. New York, Charles Scribner's Sons, 1898. 258 p. 17 x 10cm.   DLC NN   **42**
"The ivory series."

Howe, Daniel Wait, 1839–1920.
Civil war times, by Daniel Wait Howe. . . . Indianapolis, Bowen-Merrill co. [1892] x, 421 p. 20½cm.                       DLC   **43**

Kemper, General William Harrison, 1839–1927.
The Seventh regiment Indiana volunteers, three months enlistment, by G. W. H. Kemper. Muncie, Press of R. H. Cowan print. co., 1903. 16 p. 1 illus. 24cm.             DLC   **44**
Also published in *MOLLUS-Ind* 117–31. Coulter 273.

——— The surgeons of the Civil war. Muncie [1918] 12 p. port. 20cm.             WHi   **45**
Title from cover. "Reprinted from the Journal of the Indiana state medical association, October, 1918, vol. XI, p. 367."

Thomson, Orville
From Philippi to Appomattox, narrative of the service of the Seventh Indiana infantry in the War for the Union. Published by the author [190–] 200, xliii p. 19½cm.   IHi   **46**
Unit roster, xliii p. On cover: 7th Indiana infantry in the War for the Union, much of which I saw, some of which I was, by O. Thompson, Co. G.

## 8TH INFANTRY

*Mustered in: April 27, 1861. (3 months)*
*Mustered out: August 6, 1861.*
*Indiana battle flags 45.*
*AGR* II 12–16; IV 26–37.
*Mustered in: September 5, 1861. (3 years)*
*Mustered out: August 28, 1865.*
*Indiana battle flags 45–57.*
*AGR* II 48–56; IV 110–28.

Bigelow, James K        1833–1886.
Abridged history of the Eighth Indiana volunteer infantry, from its organization, April 21st, 1861, to the date of re-enlistment as veterans, January 1, 1864, by James K. Bigelow, Surgeon Eighth Indiana. Indianapolis, Ellis Barnes, printer, 1864. 40 p. 22½cm.
                                            DLC   **47**

## 9TH INFANTRY

*Mustered in: April 27, 1861. (3 months)*
*Mustered out: August 2, 1861.*
*Indiana battle flags 57.*
*AGR* II 17–21; IV 38–49.

*Mustered in: September 5, 1861.* (3 years)
*Mustered out: September 28, 1865.*
*Indiana battle flags 58–65.*
AGR ii 57–66; iv 129–54.

Partial roster of the survivors of the 9th regiment Ind. vet. vol. infantry, compiled by Alex L. Whitehall. [Watseka, Ill., n. d.] [8] p. 21½cm.                                   In   48
Caption-title.

Proceedings of the ... annual reunion of the Ninth regiment Indiana veteran volunteer infantry association. ... i–xiii 1884–1899 (NHi); xiv–xviii 1900–1904 (In); xxv 1911 (In); xxvii–xxix 1913–1915 (In); xxxi 1917 (In).                                                      49

Bierce, Ambrose, 1842–1914?
... Ambrose Bierce's Civil war. Edited and with an introduction by William McCann. Chicago, Henry Regnery co. [1956] xi, (1), 257 p. 18cm.                  DLC   50
At head of title: Ambrose Bierce. "A gateway edition."

—— Battle sketches, by Ambrose Bierce with eight engravings on wood, by Thomas Derrick. Oxford, Printed at Shakespeare Head press for the First Editions Club, 1930. 88, (1) p. front. (illus.), illus. chapter headings. 29cm.
DLC IaU NN   51

—— Battlefields and ghosts, by Ambrose Bierce. After forty-odd years there are neither enemies nor victories, but only gracious mountains & sleepy valleys all aflame with autumn foliage, hazy & dim as old memories. [Stanford, Cal.] Harvest press, 1931. 16, (1) p. front. (port.). 23cm.       DLC In NN   52
Prepared for the 24th [sic! 18th] annual reunion of the Ninth Indiana (1904) and first published in the Proceedings. "One hundred and fifteen copies of this book have been printed."

—— In the midst of life, tales of soldiers and civilians, by Ambrose Bierce. New York, G. P. Putnam's Sons, 1898. vi, 362 p. 17½cm.
NN   53

—— Tales of soldiers and civilians, by Ambrose Bierce. San Francisco, E. L. G. Steele, 1891. 300 p. 18cm.          NN   54
"Soldiers," 9–163.

Dunn, Byron Archibald, 1842–1928.
... Battling for Atlanta. Chicago, A. C. McClurg & co., 1900. 380 p. plates (illus., map). 19cm.                     NB   54A
At head of title: The young Kentuckians series. NN has "Seventh edition," 1917, a reprint.

—— ... The boy scouts of the Shenandoah. With five illustrations by J. Allen St. John.

Chicago, A. C. McClurg & co., 1916. vi, (3), 355 p. plates (illus.). 18½cm.   DLC   54B
At head of title: The young Virginians series.

—— ... The courier of the Ozarks. With eight illustrations by H. S. DeLay. Chicago, A. C. McClurg & co., 1912. ix, (1), 363 p. plates (illus.). 19cm.              DLC   54C
At head of title: The young Missourians series.

—— ... From Atlanta to the sea. Chicago, A. C. McClurg & co., 1901. 408 p. plates (illus.). 19cm.                  NB   54D
At head of title: The young Kentuckians. NN has "Fifth edition," 1910, a reprinting.

—— General Nelson's scout. Seventh edition. Chicago, A. C. McClurg and co., 1909. 320 p. plates (illus.). 19½cm.        NN   54E
On cover: The young Kentuckians series.

—— ... On General Thomas's staff. Chicago, A. C. McClurg & co., 1899. 379 p. plates (illus.). 19cm.                  NB   54F
At head of title: The young Kentuckians.

—— The scout of Pea ridge. With eight illustrations by H. S. DeLay. Chicago, A. C. McClurg & co., 1911. ix, (1), 344 p. plates (illus.). 19½cm.                      DLC   54G
On cover: The young Missourians series.

—— ... Scouting for Sheridan. With five illustrations by J. Allen St. John. Chicago, A. C. McClurg & co., 1918. 389 p. plates (illus.). 18½cm.                       NN   54H
At head of title: The young Virginians series.

—— ... With the Army of the Potomac. With five illustrations by J. Allen St. John. Chicago, A. C. McClurg & co., 1917. vi, (2), 322 p. plates (illus.). 19½cm.               NN   54 I
At head of title: The young Virginians series.

—— ... With Lyon in Missouri. With eight illustrations by H. S. DeLay. Chicago, A. C. McClurg & co., 1910. viii, (2), 336 p. plates (illus.). 19½cm.          NN   54 J
At head of title: The young Missourians series.

**10TH INFANTRY**

*Mustered in: April 25, 1861.* (3 months)
*Mustered out: August 2, 1861.*
*Indiana battle flags 65–6.*
AGR ii 22–6; iv 50–62.

*Mustered in: September 18, 1861.*
(3 years)
*Mustered out: September 19, 1864. Veterans and recruits transferred to 58th regiment of infantry.*
*Indiana battle flags 66–74.*
AGR ii 67–74; iv 155–72.

*10th Infantry, continued*

Soldiers memorial Clinton rangers, Company K, 10th reg. Indiana volunteers. Cincinnati, Lithogr. & printed in colors by Ehrgott, Forbriger & co [1863] col. illus. broadside, 55½ x 45½cm.                                    InHi     **55**
    c1863 by J. Wesley Waterman & co.

Johnson, Lewis,         –1900.
    General Thomas's first victory, the battle of Mill Springs. *US* xiii (1885) 385–99.     **56**

Shaw, James Birney
    History of the Tenth regiment Indiana volunteer infantry, three months and three years organizations, by James Birney Shaw. Lafayette [Burt-Hayward co.] 1912. 325 p. illus., ports. 19½ x 27cm.          DLC NHi     **57**
    Unit roster 17–52.

### 11TH INFANTRY

*Mustered in: April 25, 1861.* (3 months)
*Mustered out: August 2, 1861.*
*Indiana battle flags 74.*
*AGR* ii 27–32; iv 62–73.
*Mustered in: August 31, 1861.* (3 years)
*Mustered out: July 26, 1865.*
*Indiana battle flags 74–7.*
*AGR* ii 75–88; iv 173–200.

Second annual report of the Eleventh Indiana infantry association, held at Crawfordsville, October 19, 1876. Indianapolis, Journal co., printers, 1877. 20 p. 22cm.          In     **58**

Third annual report of the Eleventh Indiana infantry association, held at Indianapolis, October 19, 1877. Indianapolis, Journal co., printers, 1878. 36 p. 21½cm.       In WHi     **59**

McBarron, Hugh Charles and Frederick Porter Todd
    11th Indiana volunteers (Wallace zouaves), 1861. *Military collector & historian* iii (1951) 84–5. col. plate (illus.).     **60**

McGinnis, George Francis, 1826–1910.
    Shiloh, by Brigadier-General George F. McGinnis. *MOLLUS-Ind* 1–41. fold. map.     **61**

Wallace, Lewis, 1827–1905.
    Lew Wallace, an autobiography. New York, Harper & Brothers, 1906. 2 v. (1028 p.). plates (illus., ports.). 21½cm.          NN     **62**
    11th Indiana, 268–347.

### 12TH INFANTRY

*Mustered in: May 11, 1861.* (1 year)
*Mustered out: May 16, 1862.*

*Indiana battle flags 86–7.*
*AGR* ii 86–91; iv 201–16.
*Mustered in: August 17, 1862.* (3 years)
*Mustered out: June 8, 1865. Veterans and recruits transferred to 48th and 59th regiments of infantry.*
*Indiana battle flags 87–93.*
*AGR* ii 92–8; iv 217–36.

Gage, Moses D         1828–1912.
    From Vicksburg to Raleigh; or, a complete history of the Twelfth regiment Indiana volunteer infantry, and the campaigns of Grant and Sherman, with an outline of the great rebellion, by M. D. Gage, Chaplain. Chicago, Clarke & co., 1865. xiv, [15]–356 p. 19½cm.
                                    DLC In NN     **63**
    Coulter 177. Unit roster [323]–56.

Matthews, James Louis, 1839–1924.
    Civil war diary of Sergeant James Louis Matthews. Edited by Roger C. Hackett. *InMH* xxiv (1928) 306–16.     **64**

Williams, Reuben, 1831–1905.
    ... Officers and soldiers; your commanding officer addresses you for the last time as an organization. broadside, 28 x 21½cm.
                                    In     **65**
    At head of title: Head-quarters 12th regiment Indiana infantry, Indianapolis, Ind., 19th June, 1865.

### 13TH INFANTRY

*Mustered in: June 19, 1861.*
*Mustered out: September 5, 1865.*
*Indiana battle flags 93–102.*
*AGR* ii 99–111; iv 237–72.

Long, Lessel
    Twelve months in Andersonville, on the march, in the battle, in the Rebel prison pens, and at last in God's country, by Lessel Long, Private Co. F, 13th Indiana infantry. Huntington, Thad and Mark Butler, 1886. 199, L p. illus. 22½cm.          DLC NHi     **66**
    List of Indiana soldiers who died in Andersonville, L p. Coulter 297.

Ross, Charles H
    Old memories, 1885. *MOLLUS-Wis* i 149–63.     **67**

—— Scouting for bushwhackers in West Virginia in 1681, by Charles H. Ross, Bvt. Major 13th Indiana. 1900. *MOLLUS-Wis* iii 399–412.     **68**

Smock, Mathias, 1818–
    Mathias Smock's sermons and a sketch of his life, written by himself. Second edition [Maryville, Mo.] 1901. 95 p. crude portrait of author. 18½cm.          MoSM     **68A**
    Civil war, 14–16; a photostat of these pages is in InHi.

## 14TH INFANTRY

*Mustered in: June 7, 1861.*
*Mustered out: June 16, 1864. Veterans and recruits transferred to 20th regiment of infantry.*
*Indiana battle flags 102–12.*
AGR II 112–22; IV 273–90.

Roster of the Fourteenth Indiana volunteers, twenty-fifth annual reunion, 1909, Bloomfield, Indiana. Bloomfield, News print [1909] [8] leaves. 14½cm.      InHi    **69**
Title and imprint from cover.

Allen, Amory K
Civil war letters of. . . . *InMH* xxxi (1935) 338–86.      **70**

Kimball, Nathan,      –1898.
Fighting Jackson at Kernstown. *BandL* II 302–13.      **70A**

Landon, William D    F    –1866?.
Fourteenth Indiana regiment, letters to the Vincennes Western sun. *InMH* xxix (1933) 350–71; xxx (1934) 275–98; xxxiii (1937) 325–48; xxxiv (1938) 71–98; xxxv (1939) 76–94.      **71**
The writer of these letters used the pen name Sprock.

Pool, J    T
Under canvass; or, recollections of the Fall and Summer campaign of the 14th regiment Indiana volunteers, Col. Nathan Kimball, in Western Virginia, in 1861, containing incidents of scouting parties, skirmishes, battles, anecdotes of the war, life around the camp-fires, &c., by J. T. Pool, and respectfully dedicated to the Union troops of Indiana. Terre Haute, O. Bartlett, 1862. 64 p. 23cm.      DLC    **72**

Van Dyke, Augustus Mortimer, 1838–
Early days; or, the school of the soldier, by Augustus M. Van Dyke, Captain, 1899. *MOLLUS-Ohio* v 18–31.      **73**

—— A fruitless victory, 1900. *MOLLUS-Ohio* v 199–203.      **74**

## 15TH INFANTRY

*Mustered in: June 14, 1861.*
*Mustered out: June 16, 1864. Veterans and recruits transferred to 17th regiment of infantry.*
*Indiana battle flags 113–24.*
AGR II 123–30; IV 291–307.

Historical sketch of the organization and service of the Fifteenth regiment Indiana volunteers, and third annual reunion of the Fifteenth regiment Ind. volunteers, Frankford, Indiana, September 20th and 21, 1888. Also, a roster of surviving members of the "Regiment." 84, (1) p. fold. map. 19cm.    MnHi    **75**
"Historical sketch . . . by E[dward] M. Burns," 9–34. Title from cover.

## 16TH INFANTRY

*Mustered in: July 23, 1861. (1 year)*
*Mustered out: May 14, 1862.*
*Indiana battle flags 124–5.*
AGR II 131–6; IV 308–22.

*Mustered in: August 19, 1862. (3 years)*
*Mustered out: June 30, 1865. Veterans and recruits transferred to 13th regiment of cavalry.*
*Indiana battle flags 125–32.*
AGR II 137–45; IV 323–43.

Jordan, William H      –1911.
The Sixteenth Indiana regiment in the last Vicksburg campaign. Edited by Willie D. Halsell. *InMH* xlvii (1947) 67–82.      **76**

## 17TH INFANTRY

*Mustered in: June 12, 1861.*
*Mustered out: August 8, 1865.*
*Indiana battle flags 132–44.*
AGR II 145–57; IV 344–71.

Seventeenth regiment Indiana veteran volunteer mounted infantry roster of surviving members and sketch of history. [Pendleton, 1912] [12] p. 2 ports. 15½cm.    In    **77**
Title from cover. "Remarks" signed: W. H. H. Benefiel, Secretary and Treasurer.

Souvenir the Seventeenth Indiana regiment. A history from its organization to the end of the war giving description of battles, etc. Also list of the survivors. . . . [Elwood, Model print. co., 1913] [118] p. illus., ports. 23cm. NHi    **78**
Unit roster included. "Closing remarks" signed: W. H. H. Benefiel, Secretary-Treasurer and Historian.

Wilder, John Thomas, 1830–1917.
The battle of Hoover's gap, by John T. Wilder, Brevet Brigadier-General. *MOLLUS-Ohio* vi 168–73.      **79**

—— Paper of John T. Wilder . . . read before the Ohio commandery of the Loyal legion, November 4, 1908. 10 p. 23cm.      DLC    **79A**
Caption title: Preliminary movements of the Army of the Cumberland before the battle of Chickamauga. Title from cover.

—— The siege of Mumfordville. *MOLLUS-Ohio* vi 296–304.      **79B**

17th Infantry, continued

Williams, Samuel C
General John T. Wilder. InMH xxxi (1935)
169–203. 2 ports.                                    80

Wilson, George Spencer,          –1897.
Wilder's brigade of mounted infantry in
Tullahoma-Chickamauga campaigns, a paper
prepared and read before the Kansas comman-
dery of the M.O.L.L.U.S., November 4th, 1891,
by George S. Wilson. 29 p. fold. map. 22cm.
                                    DLC    81
On cover: War paper. Also published as MOLLUS-
Kan 45–76.

See also Title 13.

### 18TH INFANTRY

Mustered in: August 16, 1861.
Mustered out: August 28, 1865.
Indiana battle flags 144–51.
AGR II 158–67; IV 372–89.

Black, James Buckley, 1838–1916.
General Philip Henry Sheridan, by Major
James B. Black. MOLLUS-Ind 42–72.        82

### 19TH INFANTRY

Mustered in: July 29, 1861.
Mustered out: July 28, 1864. Veterans
and recruits consolidated with 20th regi-
ment of infantry: October 18, 1864.
Indiana battle flags 151–6.
AGR I 168–77; IV 390–410.

Second annual re-union of the Nineteenth
regiment Indiana volunteers, held at Walling
hall, Muncie, December 12 and 13, 1872. 17 p.
15cm.                                    In    83

Third annual re-union of the Nineteenth regiment Indiana volunteers . . . Indianapolis, September 17th and 18th, 1873. 22 p. 14cm.
Title from cover.                        In    84

Roster of the survivors of the 19th Indiana
regiment of infantry, also a brief history of the
regiment, revised to. . . .        15cm. In    85

October 2, 1907. 20 p.
January 1, 1912. 20 p.
November 1, 1915. 17, (1) p.
Includes report of 1912 and 1915 reunions.

Dudley, William Wade, 1842–1909.
The Iron brigade at Gettysburg, official report of the part borne by the 1st brigade, 1st
division, 1st army corps, Army of the Potomac,
in action at Gettysburg, Pennsylvania, July 1st,

2d and 3d, 1863. Cincinnati [Peter G. Thomp-
son] 1879. iv, [5]–15 p. 22½cm.    In    86
Text signed: Wm. W. Dudley.

Ebersole, Jacob
Incidents of field hospital life with the Army
of the Potomac, by Jacob Ebersole, late Major
and Surgeon Nineteenth Indiana, 1894. MOL-
LUS-Ohio IV 327–33.                      87

### 20TH INFANTRY

Mustered in: July 22, 1861.
Mustered out: July 12, 1865.
Indiana battle flags 157–68.
AGR II 178–93; IV 411–46.

Fifth annual reunion of the 20th vet. vol. asso.
Ind., at Crown Point, Indiana, on September
3rd and 4th, 1890. [Valpariso] Valpariso Messenger print [1890] 48 p. 23cm.    In    88
Title and imprint from cover.

Osbourn, Francis A
One of the "Fighting three hundred," the
Twentieth Indiana infantry, by Francis A. Os-
bourn, a member of Company "L." [n. p.,
n. d.] [18] p. 26½cm.            In MB    89
Title from cover.

Stiles, Israel Newton, 1833–1895.
The Merrimac and the Monitor (read April
5, 1885). MOLLUS-Ill I 125–33.            90

### 21ST INFANTRY

Mustered in: July 23, 1861.
Designated 1st regiment of heavy artil-
lery: February 1863.
Indiana battle flags 168–70.

### 22ND INFANTRY

Mustered in: August 15, 1861.
Mustered out: July 24, 1865.
Indiana battle flags 170–7.
AGR II 210–19; IV 492–519.

Charlton, Thomas Jefferson, 1846–1904.
"The private soldier," address of T. J. Charlton, delivered at Tomlinson hall, at the G.A.R.
department campfire, Wednesday evening,
March 13, 1889. Indianapolis, Sentinel print.
co. [1889] 11 p. 22cm.            WHi    91

Davis, Jefferson Columbus,        –1879.
Campaigning in Missouri, Civil war memoir
of General Jefferson C. Davis. Missouri historical review LIV (1959/60) 39–45. illus., port.
                                       91A

Griffit, Reuben C          1845–1910.
Six months in Rebel prisons. Dedicated to the memory of the Union soldier of 1861–1865. [Martinsville, 1908?] 149 p.

            InHi (M)          *91B*

The work is the "result of the publication of a series of letters in The Republican, published at Martinsville, Ind." The author was a member of the Commission in charge of the establishment and dedication of the Andersonville monument. In the official records, the author's name is Griffith.

Marshall, Randolph V
An historical sketch of the Twenty-second regiment Indiana volunteers, from its organization to the close of the war, its battles, its marches, and its hardships, its brave officers and its honored dead. Read at the re-union of the Regiment, held at Columbus, Ind., March 7, 1877, by Lieut. R. V. Marshall. Madison, Courier co., printers [1884] 32 p. 19½cm.

           DLC NHi NN          *92*

Mayfield, Leroy S          1841–
A Hoosier invades the Confederacy, letters and diaries of . . . Edited by John D. Barnhart. *InMH* xxxix (1943) 144–91.          *93*

### 23RD INFANTRY

*Mustered in: July 29, 1861.*
*Mustered out: July 23, 1865.*
*Indiana battle flags 177–82.*
*AGR* II 220–8; IV 520–41.

### 24TH INFANTRY

*Mustered in: July 31, 1861.*
*Mustered out: July 19, 1865; November 15, 1865.*
*Indiana battle flags 182–8.*
*AGR* II 229–41; IV 542–62.

Fulfer, Richard J
A history of the trials and hardships of the Twenty-fourth Indiana volunteer infantry. Indianapolis, Indianapolis print. co., 1913. 135 p. 2 illus., 4 ports. 23cm.          DLC          *94*

"Preface" signed: Richard J. Fulfer. Unit roster of Company A included.

Jessup, Lewis B
The 24th Indiana at Shiloh, the long march to get into battle. In National tribune scrap book III 158–9.          *94A*

### 25TH INFANTRY

*Mustered in: August 19, 1861.*
*Mustered out: July 17, 1865.*
*Indiana battle flags 188–93.*
*AGR* II 242–51; IV 563–88.

Foster, John Wells, 1815–1873.
War stories for my grandchildren, by John W. Foster. Washington, Printed for private circulation [by] the Riverside press, Cambridge, 1918. 192 p. front. (2 ports.). plate (illus.). 24cm.          DLC IHi          *95*

Mustered in 25th Indiana, May 1, 1862; promoted Colonel 65th Indiana, August 4, 1862; resigned, March 10, 1864; served as Colonel 100 day 136th Indiana. Copyright by John Foster Dulles.

Snepp, Daniel Webster, 1894–
John W. Foster, soldier and politician. *InMH* xxxII (1936) 207–25.          *96*

### 26TH INFANTRY

*Mustered in: August 31, 1861.*
*Mustered out: January 15, 1866.*
*Indiana battle flags 193–7.*
*AGR* II 252–60; IV 588–612.

Adams, Henry Clay, 1844–1910.
Battle of Prairie Grove, by Lieutenant Henry C. Adams. *Mollus-Ind* 451–64.          *97*

### 27TH INFANTRY

*Mustered in: September 12, 1861.*
*Mustered out: November 4, 1864. Veterans and recruits transferred to 70th regiment of infantry.*
*Indiana battle flags 197–211.*
*AGR* II 261–9; IV 613–29.

Minutes of the eighteenth annual reunion 27th Indiana volunteers infantry association held . . . Indianapolis, Ind., Sept. 17, 1902. 12 p. 1 illus., 17½cm.          NHi          *98*

Title from cover.

Report of the Committee on exchange of compliments (of the 27th Indiana regimental association) with Gen. Geo. H. Gordon. Indianapolis, W. B. Burford, printer, 1886. 8 p. 18½cm.          In NHi          *99*

Bloss, John McKnight, 1839–1905.
Antietam and the lost dispatch, a paper prepared and read before the Kansas commandery of the M.O.L.L.U.S., January 6th, 1892, by John M. Bloss. 14 p. 22cm.          DLC          *100*

On cover: War paper. Also published as *War talks in Kansas*, a series of papers read before the Kansas commandery of the MOLLUS, 77–91.

Brown, Edmund Randolph, 1845–1930.
The Twenty-seventh Indiana volunteer infantry in the War of the rebellion, 1861 to 1865, First division, 12th and 20th corps, a history of its recruiting, organization, camp life, marches and battles, together with a ros-

*27th Infantry, continued*

ter of the men composing it, and the names of all those killed in battle or who died of disease, and, as far as can be known, of those who were wounded. By a member of Company C. [Monticello, 1899] 640, (2) p. illus., plans, ports. 23cm.                DLC NHi    **101**
Unit roster [557]–626. c1899 by E. R. Brown. Coulter 54.

Colgrove, Silas
The finding of Lee's lost order. *BandL* II 603.
                                  **102**

*28th Regiment see 1st Cavalry*

### 29TH INFANTRY

*Mustered in: August 27, 1861.*
*Mustered out: December 2, 1865.*
*Indiana battle flags 213–17.*
*AGR* II 280–8; IV 655–80.

### 30TH INFANTRY

*Mustered in: September 24, 1861.*
*Mustered out: November 25, 1865.*
*Indiana battle flags 217–21.*
*AGR* II 289–300; v 2–32.

Reunion souvenir 30th Indiana regiment consisting of songs, war memories, and etchings of soldier service in the ranks of the 30th regiment Indiana infantry volunteers during the War of the rebellion, with invitation and program for eighth annual reunion to be held at Goshen, Ind., Apr. 7th, 1891. Compiled by J. N. Ohlwine.... Cromwell [Ligonier, Leader steam print, 1891] 35 p. illus. 22½cm.
                                 NHi    **103**

### 31ST INFANTRY

*Mustered in: September 15, 1861.*
*Mustered out: December 8, 1865.*
*Indiana battle flags 221–7.*
*AGR* II 301–10; v 33–55.

Ford, Augustus C       1838–
Midnight on Missionary ridge, by Captain Augustus C. Ford. *MOLLUS-Ind* 239–46.
                                  **104**
Smith, John Thomas
A history of the Thirty-first regiment of Indiana volunteer infantry in the War of the rebellion, by John Thomas Smith, the third Colonel of the Regiment. Cincinnati, Western Methodist Book concern, 1900. 226 p. front. (port.), ports. 24cm. DLC NHi NN    **105**
Unit roster [131]–94. "A soldier's story, the late J. H. Beadle at Fort Donelson" [by J. H. Beadle] 198–213.

Wells, James K
An Indiana volunteer advises his neighbors. Edited by Charles G. Talbert. *InMH* LIII (1957) 175–9.                     **106**

### 32ND INFANTRY

*Mustered in: August 24, 1861.*
*Mustered out: December 4, 1865.*
*Indiana battle flags 227–34.*
*AGR* II 311–22; v 56–82.

Fritsch, William August, 1841–
Oberst-Lieutenant Heinrich Von Treba und das 32. (deutsche) Indiana Infanterie-Regiment, von Dr. W. A. Fritsch. *Deutsch-Amerikanische Geschichtsblätter* x (1910) 31–3.
                                  **107**
Stewart, Charles D
A bachelor General [August Willich] *Wisconsin magazine of history* XVII (1933) 131–54. plate (port.).               **108**
Private 9th Ohio, April 25, 1861; Colonel 32nd Indiana August 25, 1861; Brigadier General, July 17, 1862.

### 33RD INFANTRY

*Mustered in: September 16, 1861.*
*Mustered out: July 21, 1865.*
*Indiana battle flags 234–40.*
*AGR* II 323–33; v 83–111.

Fletcher, Stephen Keyes, 1840–1897.
The Civil war journal of ... Edited by Perry McCandless. *InMH* LIV (1958) 141–90. 2 facs.
                                  **109**
McBride, John Randolph, 1842–
History of the Thirty-third Indiana veteran volunteer infantry during the four years of civil war, from Sept. 16, 1861, to July 21, 1865, and incidentally of Col. John Coburn's Second brigade, Third division, Twentieth army corps, including incidents of the great rebellion, by John R. McBride. Indianapolis, Wm. R. Burford, 1900. 280 p. plates (ports.). 23cm.                   DLC NN    **110**
Unit roster 241–80.

### 34TH INFANTRY

*Mustered in: September 16, 1861.*
*Mustered out: February 3, 1866.*
*Indiana battle flags 241–5.*
*AGR* II 333–43; v 112–31.

Fussell, Joshua L
History of the 34th regiment, Indiana veteran volunteer infantry, "Morton rifles," by Captain I. L. Fussell of Company D. [Marion, Press of the Commercial print. co., n. d.] 55 p. 23cm.
                                 InI    **111**

## 35TH INFANTRY

*Mustered in: December 11, 1861.*
*Mustered out: September 30, 1865.*
*Indiana battle flags 245–54.*
*AGR* II 345–53; v 132–55.

Atlanta campaign, Army of the Cumberland, Easter Sunday, 1864, 1st Irish veteran regt & 35th of Indiana, v. vol. divine service by Rev. P. P. Cooney, C.S.C. Chaplain Gen. of Ind. troops in the field. Milwaukee, Wis., American Oleograph co. lith. [1877] col. illus. broadside, 58 x 70cm.                    InHi      112
c1877 by Louis Kurz.

Cooney, Peter Paul, 1822–
The war letters of Father Peter Paul Cooney of the congregation of Holy Cross. *Records of the American Catholic historical society* XLIV (1933) 47–69, 151–69, 220–37.           113

## 36TH INFANTRY

*Mustered in: September 16, 1861.*
*Transferred to 30th battalion of infantry: July 12, 1865.*
*Indiana battle flags 254–8.*
*AGR* II 355–62; v 156–72.

Ninth annual reunion of the 36th Indiana volunteers, held at Farmland, Indiana, on October 5 and 6, 1892. New Castle, Courier co. print, 1892. 14 p. front. (port.). 23cm.
                            DLC       114
Tenth annual reunion of the 36th Indiana volunteers, held at Indianapolis, Indiana, on September 6 and 7, 1893. New Castle, Courier co. print, 1893. 16 p. 23cm.     NHi       115

Grose, William, 1812–1900.
The story of the marches, battles and incidents of the 36th regiment Indiana volunteer infantry, by a member of the Regiment. New Castle, Courier co. print, 1891. 256 p. plates (ports.). 23cm.         DLC NHi NN      116
Unit roster 14–93. "Preface" signed: William Grose. Coulter 205.

## 37TH INFANTRY

*Mustered in: September 16, 1861.*
*Mustered out: July 25, 1865.*
*Indiana battle flags 262–5.*
*AGR* II 363–70; v 173–96.

Hughes, Frank,          –1864.
Diary of Lieutenant Hugh Frank. Edited by Norman Niccum. *InMH* XLV (1949) 275–84.
                                      117

Lozier, John Hogarth, 1832–1907.
40 rounds from the cartridge box of the fighting Chaplain, embracing the "cream" of the "old war songs" and recitations, and the odes of the W.R.C., G.A.R., S. of V. [Mount Vernon, Iowa, 1887] 53, (1) p. illus. 23½cm.
                            DLC NHi      117A
"Index," (1) p. Cover title: Forty rounds from the cartridge box of the "fighting Chaplain" including "rhymes of tenderfeet and grayback times" and all the old war songs, most popular in camp-fires and re-unions. Together with all the choice recitations used in the entertainments of Chaplain Lozier.

Puntenney, George H
History of the Thirty-seventh regiment of Indiana infantry volunteers, its organization, campaigns, and battles, Sept., '61 – Oct., '64, written by Sergeant George H. Puntenney. Rushville, Jacksonian book and job dept., 1896. 220 p. 1 illus., ports., plates (ports.). 19½cm.            DLC NN      118
Unit roster 140–80.

Shook, Hezekiah
Address delivered on the occasion of the 2nd annual reunion of the 37th Indiana vols. infty. at Greensburg, Ind., Sept. 19, 1878, by Capt. Hezekiah Shook. Indianapolis, Central print. co., 1879. 12 p. 23cm.      NHi      119
Title from cover.

## 38TH INFANTRY

*Mustered in: September 18, 1861.*
*Mustered out: July 15, 1865.*
*Indiana battle flags 258–61.*
*AGR* II 371–81; v 197–221.

Gresham, Matilda (McGrain) 1839–
Life of Walter Quintin Gresham, 1832–1895. Chicago, Rand McNally & co., 1919. 2 v. fronts. (ports.). 23½cm.     NN      119A
Civil war I 146–312. Documents in the effort of Governor Morton to remove Colonel Gresham as Colonel of the 53rd Indiana II 826–35. 38th Indiana, September 18, 1861; 53rd Indiana, March 10, 1862; Brigadier General, August 11, 1863.

Perry, Henry Fales, 1834–
History of the Thirty-eighth regiment Indiana volunteer infantry, one of the three hundred fighting regiments of the Union army, in the War of the rebellion, 1861–1865, by Henry Fales Perry. Palo Alto, Cal., F. A. Stuart, printer, 1906. 385 p. plates (2 illus., ports.). 23½cm.      DLC NN      120
Unit roster 291–385.

Richards, William J          1840–1918.
Rosecrans and the Chickamauga campaign, by Major William J. Richards. *MOLLUS-Ind* 465–75.                                121

*38th Infantry, continued*

Scribner, Benjamin Franklin, 1825–1900.
How soldiers were made; or, the war as I saw it under Buell, Rosecrans, Thomas, Grant and Sherman, by B. F. Scribner, late Colonel Thirty-eighth Indiana. New Albany [Chicago, Donahue & Henneberry, printers] 1887. iv, 5–316 p. 20cm.　　DLC NHi NN　**122**

### 39TH INFANTRY

*Mustered in: August 29, 1861.*
*Designated 8th regiment of cavalry: October 15, 1863.*
*Indiana battle flags 265–9.*

Barnett, John Lympus, 1830–1863.
Some Civil war letters and diary of ... Edited by James Barnett. *InMH* xxxvii (1941) 162–73. port.　　**123**

### 40TH INFANTRY

*Mustered in: December 30, 1861.*
*Mustered out: December 21, 1865.*
*Indiana battle flags 269–75.*
*AGR* ii 392–400; v 251–72.

*41st Regiment see 2nd Cavalry*

### 42ND INFANTRY

*Mustered in: October 9, 1861.*
*Mustered out: July 21, 1865.*
*Indiana battle flags 276–81.*
*AGR* ii 412–21; v 303–29.

Horrall, Spillard F　　1829–
History of the Forty-second Indiana volunteer infantry. Compiled and written at the request of W. M. Cockrum, late Lieutenant-Colonel 42d Indiana regiment, by S. F. Horrall, late Captain of Company G. Published for the author. [Chicago, Donahue & Henneberry, printers] 1892. x, 11–283 p. plates (ports.). 20cm.　　DLC NHi　**124**
Unit roster 28–92. Coulter 240.

### 43RD INFANTRY

*Mustered in: September 27, 1861.*
*Mustered out: June 14, 1865.*
*Indiana battle flags 281–5.*
*AGR* ii 421–30; v 330–59.

Little, Horace B
Reminiscences of the Civil war, escape from Fort Tyler prison. *InMH* xiii (1917) 42–55.　　**125**

McLean, William Edward, 1831–1906.
The Forty-third regiment of Indiana volunteers, an historic sketch of its career and services, prepared by William E. McLean, read at annual reunion of the Regiment, at Indianapolis, Indiana, September, 1902. . . . Terre Haute, C. W. Brown, printer, 1903. 152 p. plates (ports.). 22½cm.　　In　**126**

### 44TH INFANTRY

*Mustered in: November 22, 1861.*
*Mustered out: September 14, 1865.*
*Indiana battle flags 285–8.*
*AGR* ii 430–40; v 360–86.

Butler, Marvin Benjamin, 1834–1914.
My story of the Civil war and the Underground railroad, by M. B. Butler, First Lieutenant Co. A, 44th Ind. Huntington, United Brethren pub. estab., 1914. 390 p. illus., ports. 22½cm.　　DLC IHi　**127**
"Company "A" roll call," [4]–5.

Rerick, John H　　1830–
The Forty-fourth Indiana volunteer infantry, history of its services in the War of the rebellion and a personal record of its members, by John H. Rerick, Surgeon. Lagrange, Published by the author [Ann Arbor, Mich., Courier print. house] 1880. 293 p. plates (illus., fold. map, ports.). 19½cm.
　　DLC NHi NN　**128**
Unit roster [129]–213. "Personal recollections, by Colonel Hugh B. Reed," [215]–72.

*45th Regiment see 3rd Cavalry*

### 46TH INFANTRY

*Mustered in: December 11, 1861.*
*Mustered out: September 4, 1865.*
*Indiana battle flags 288–94.*
*AGR* ii 453–62; v 412–28.

History of the Forty-sixth regiment Indiana volunteer infantry, September, 1861 – September, 1865. Compiled by order of the Regimental association. [Logansport, Press of Wilson, Humphreys & co.] 1888. vi, [9]–220 p. 23½cm.
　　DLC NHi NN　**129**
Unit roster [153]–220. "Preface" signed: Thos. H. Bringhurst [and] Frank Swigart, Committee [to compile the regimental history]

Hartlerode, Lawrence
Out of a Rebel prison during the war, thrilling account of the hairbreadth escapes and life and death struggles of Private Hartlerode of the 46th Indiana. Winamac, J. J. Gorrell, printer [1895] 21 p. illus., 19½cm.　　In　**130**
Title and imprint from cover.

## 47TH INFANTRY

*Mustered in: December 13, 1861.*
*Mustered out: October 23, 1865.*
*Indiana battle flags 294–301.*
*AGR* ii 463–71; v 429–48.

Bert, Henry Lawson, 1845–1910.
Letters of a drummer boy. Edited by Don Russell. *InMh* xxxiv (1938) 324–39.      *131*

## 48TH INFANTRY

*Mustered in: January 28, 1862.*
*Mustered out: July 15, 1865.*
*Indiana battle flags 301–04.*
*AGR* ii 472–81; v 449–70.

Packard, Jasper, 1832–1899.
Four years of camp, march and battle, an address delivered before Post no. 12, G.A.R., Washington, D.C., March 26th, 1870. Washington, D.C., Gibson Brothers, printers, 1870. 15 p. 22cm.        DLC      *133*
Mustered in 48th Indiana, September 12, 1862; promoted 128th Indiana, March 1, 1864; discharged, June 26, 1865.

Schaubel, Gottlob
From Vicksburg, Miss., to Goshen, Ind., reminiscences of incidents and experiences before and after the battle of Champion hill, May 16, 1863. [Logan, Kansas, 1897] 12 p. 14cm.
Caption title.      KHi      *134*

Snure, Samuel E
The Vicksburg campaign as viewed by an Indiana soldier. *Journal of Mississippi history* xix (1957) 263–9.      *134A*

## 49TH INFANTRY

*Mustered in: November 21, 1861.*
*Mustered out: September 13, 1865.*
*Indiana battle flags 304–09.*
*AGR* ii 481–90; v 471–89.

Regimental association of the 49th regiment Indiana vol. infantry, issued to the survivors and the widows and orphans of our dead comrades, by the Association on the 31st anniversary of the organization of the Association. Louisville, Ky., Brewer's print. house [1892] 15, (1) p. 22cm.        In      *135*
Brief history, roster of staff and line officers and roster of survivors of the 49th. Title and imprint from cover.

## 50TH INFANTRY

*Mustered in: September 12, 1861.*
*Consolidated with 52nd regiment of infantry: May 25, 1865.*

*Indiana battle flags 309–13.*
*AGR* ii 490–501; v 490–508.

## 51ST INFANTRY

*Mustered in: December 14, 1861.*
*Mustered out: December 13, 1865.*
*Indiana battle flags 313–17.*
*AGR* ii 501–10; v 509–31.

Hartpence, William Ross
History of the Fifty-first Indiana veteran volunteer infantry, a narrative of its organization, marches, battles and other experiences in camp and prison, from 1861 to 1866, with revised roster, by Wm. R. Hartpence, Sergeant Major. Harrison, Ohio, Published by the author; Cincinnati, Robert Clarke co., printers, 1894. viii, 405 p. plates (1 illus., ports.). 24cm.
        DLC NN      *136*
Unit roster 361–405. Coulter 219.

Richard, Jacob Fraise, 1844–
Brief sketches of the military services, escape from Libby prison, how he won a Medal of honor, and Grand army record of Major Marion T. Anderson, late of the 51st Indiana vet vols. Washington, D.C. Gibson Bros., printers, 1897. 22 p. front. (port.). 23cm.
        InHi NNC      *137*
"Military record," [3]–8 signed: J. Fraise Richard.

Roach, Alva C
The prisoner of war and how treated, containing a history of Colonel Straight's expedition to the rear of Bragg's army, in the Spring of 1863, and a correct account of the treatment and condition of the Union prisoners in the Rebel prisons of the South, in 1863–4, being the actual experience of a Union officer during twenty-two months' imprisonment in Rebeldom. With personal adventures, biographical sketches, and history of Andersonville prison pen, by Lieutenant A. C. Roach. Indianapolis, Railroad City pub. house, 1865. 244 p. 20cm.
Coulter 394.      DLC MiDB NHi      *138*

Russell, Milton
Reminiscences of prison life and escape, by Captain Milton Russell. *MOLLUS-Iowa* i 25–59.      *138A*

Stradling, James M
The lottery of death, two death prizes drawn by Major Henry W. Sawyer, of New Jersey and Captain John M. Flinn, of Indiana, by Lieutenant James M. Stradling. *McClure's magazine* xxvi (1905) 94–101. ports.      *139*

## 52ND INFANTRY

*Mustered in: February 1, 1862.*
*Mustered out: September 10, 1865.*
*Indiana battle flags 317–23.*
*AGR* II 511–23; v 532–62.

Guffin, Ross
A night on the Mississippi. *Putnam's magazine* ns v (1870) 419–24. **140**
The author, a Captain in the regiment, recounts the fate of a detail sent to apprehend smugglers, December 31, 1863.

## 53RD INFANTRY

*Mustered in: March 6, 1862.*
*Mustered out: July 21, 1865.*
*Indiana battle flags 324–7.*
*AGR* II 523–32; v 563–89.

See Title 119A.

## 54TH INFANTRY

*Mustered in: June 10, 1862.* (3 months)
*Mustered out: October 4, 1862.*
*Indiana battle flags 327–30.*
*AGR* II 533–7; v 590–603.
*Mustered in: November 16, 1862.* (1 year)
*Mustered out: December 8, 1863.*
*AGR* II 537–42; v 604–18.

## 55TH INFANTRY

*Mustered in: June 10, 1862.*
*Mustered out: September 6 to October 23, 1862.*
*Indiana battle flags 330.*
*AGR* II 543–7; v 619–27.

## 56TH INFANTRY

*Failed to complete organization.*

## 57TH INFANTRY

*Mustered in: November 18, 1861.*
*Mustered out: December 14, 1865.*
*Indiana battle flags 330–6.*
*AGR* II 548–58; v 628–48.

Kerwood, Asbury L        1842–
Annals of the Fifty-seventh regiment Indiana volunteers, marches, battles, and incidents of army life, by a member of the Regiment. Dayton, Ohio, W. J. Shuey, printer, 1868. 374 p. 19½cm.        DLC NN        **141**
Unit roster [325]–74. "Preface" signed: A. L. K. Coulter 276.

## 58TH INFANTRY

*Mustered in: December 22, 1861.*
*Mustered out: July 25, 1865.*
*Indiana battle flags 336–42.*
*AGR* II 559–68; v 649–72.

Journal of the . . . annual reunion of the Fifty-eighth Indiana regimental association, held at. . . . II–VI 1892–1896.        NHi        **142**
1895–1896 published in one volume.

Organization of the 58th Indiana regimental association, at Oakland city, Indiana, October 22, 1891. Princeton, Clarion job office, 1892. 9 p. 1 illus. 23cm.        MnHi        **143**
Title and imprint from cover.

Patten, James Comfort, 1826–1903.
An Indiana doctor marches with Sherman, the diary of. . . . [Edited by] Robert G. Athearn. *InMH* XLIX (1953) 405–22.        **144**

Stormont, Gilbert R        1843?–1930.
History of the Fifty-eighth regiment of Indiana volunteer infantry, its organization, campaigns and battles, from 1861 to 1865. From the manuscript prepared by the late Chaplain John J. Hight, during his service with the Regiment in the field. Compiled by his friend and comrade, Gilbert R. Stormont, formerly Corporal Co. B. Princeton, Press of the Clarion, 1895. 577 p. illus., 2 maps, ports., plates (ports.). 24cm.        DLC NN        **145**
Running title: Chaplain Hight's history of the Fifty-eighth Indiana regiment. On cover: Height's history 58th Indiana regiment. Stormont's name is used alone on the spine. Coulter 230. For sample pages see Title 142, 1894.

Yaryan, John Lee, 1837–
Stone river, by Adjutant John Lee Yaryan. *MOLLUS-Ind* 157–77.        **146**

## 59TH INFANTRY

*Mustered in: February 11, 1862.*
*Mustered out: June 17, 1865.*
*Indiana battle flags 342–5.*
*AGR* II 569–78; v 673–98.

Lee, Jesse Matlock, 1843–1926.
Address by Gen. Jesse M. Lee, delivered at the 23rd annual reunion of the 59th regiment of Indiana volunteer infantry, held at Hymera, Sullivan county, on the 3rd and 4th of September, 1907. 31 p. 20½cm.        In        **147**
Title from cover.

Mahan, James Curtis, 1840–
Memoirs of James Curtis Mahan. Lincoln, Neb., Franklin press [1919] 176 p. front. (port.). 19cm.        IHi        **148**

## 60TH INFANTRY

*Mustered in: March 21, 1862.*
*Mustered out: March 11, 1865. Veterans and recruits transferred to 26th regiment of infantry, February 24, 1865.*
*Indiana battle flags 346–50.*
AGR II 579–87; VI 2–18.

## 61ST AND 62ND INFANTRY

*Failed to complete organization.*

## 63RD INFANTRY

*Mustered in as a battalion, February 21, 1862. Regimental organization completed, October 1862.*
*Mustered out: Companies A-D, May 3, 1865; remaining companies, June 21, 1865.*
*Indiana battle flags 350–4.*
AGR II 588–97; VI 19–36.

Stiles, Isael Newton, 1833–1895.
On to Richmond in 1862 (read March 10, 1887). *MOLLUS-Ill* III 45–59.        **149**

## 64TH INFANTRY

*Failed to complete organization.*

## 65TH INFANTRY

*Mustered in: August 18, 1862.*
*Mustered out: June 22, 1865.*
*Indiana battle flags 354–8.*
AGR II 598–606; VI 37–53.

Admire, Jacob V
Memoranda Company E, 65th regiment, Indiana infantry volunteers. . . . Osage City, Kansas, Osage City Free press print, 1888. [26] p. front. (port.). 24½cm.
In KHi NHi        **150**
Title and imprint from cover. Unit roster included. "A note to the boys" signed: J. V. Admire.

—— Old army letters, written forty-two years ago, by J. V. Admire. Kingfisher, Okla., 1906. 20 p. 20½cm.        KHi        **150A**
See also Title 95.

## 66TH INFANTRY

*Mustered in: August 19, 1862.*
*Mustered out: June 3, 1865.*
*Indiana battle flags 358–61.*
AGR II 607–13; VI 54–70.

## 67TH INFANTRY

*Mustered in: August 20, 1862.*
*Consolidated with 24th regiment of infantry: December 21, 1864.*
*Indiana battle flags 361–4.*
AGR II 614–20; VI 71–86.

Scott, Reuben B        1839–
The history of the 67th regiment Indiana infantry volunteers, War of the rebellion. Bedford, Herald print, 1892. 140 p. plates (illus.). 20½cm.        DLC NHi        **151**
"Preface" signed: R. B. Scott.

## 68TH INFANTRY

*Mustered in: August 19, 1862.*
*Mustered out: June 20, 1865.*
*Indiana battle flags 364–7.*
AGR II 621–8; VI 87–101.

High, Edwin W        1841–
History of the Sixty-eighth regiment Indiana volunteer infantry, 1862–1865, with a sketch of E. A. King's brigade, Reynold's division, Thomas' corps in the battle of Chickamauga, by Edwin W. High . . . Published by request of the Sixty-eighth Indiana infantry association. [Metamora?] 1902. x, 416 p. map. plates (illus., ports.). 24cm.    DLC NHi NN        **152**
Unit roster [322]–37. "Songs and poetry of the war," [400]–16.

Mauzy, James H        1842–
Historical sketch of the Sixty-eighth regiment Indiana volunteers, with personal recollections by members of Company D, and short biographies of Brigade, Division and Corps commanders. . . . Rushville, Republican co., printers, 1887. 212 p. plates (3 fold. maps, port.). 19½cm.        DLC NHi        **153**
Unit roster [64]–85. On cover: Personal recollections of Company D, 68th Indiana vol. inf. Preface signed: J. H. Mauzy, Capt. Co. D.

## 69TH INFANTRY

*Mustered in: August 19, 1862.*
*Mustered out: July 5, 1865.*
*Indiana battle flags 367–72.*
AGR II 629–39; VI 102–17.

. . . Annual reunion of the Sixty-ninth Indiana regiment. . . . [4]–40, 1888–1924. In        **154**
1888–1892 are not numbered.

Perry, Oran, 1838–1929.
The entering wedge, a paper read before the Indiana commandery of the Military order of the loyal legion of the United States, at Indianapolis, Ind., April 19, 1889. The Ser-

*69th Infantry, continued*

geant of Company F, a sketch from life read at the re-union of the Sixty-ninth Indiana infantry, at Hagerstown, Ind., August 23, 1889. By Oran Perry, late Leuit. [sic]-Colonel 69th Indiana. Indianapolis, Chance-Matthews print. co., 1893. 22 p. 23cm.    In NN   **155**
The title paper was also published in *MOLLUS-Ind* 359–76. See also Title 158.

—— Recollections of the Civil war. 1924. front. (port.). 22½cm.    In   **156**

—— —— Second edition. [Indianapolis] Historical Bureau of the Indiana Library and Historical Department, 1928. 66 p. front. (port.). 22½cm.    MiDB NN   **157**
At head of title: Indiana history bulletin, volume V, extra number 3.

—— The Sergeant of Company F [Solomon J. Harter] [Indianapolis, 1908] [7] p. 16cm.    DLC In   **158**
Caption title. See also Title 155.

### 70TH INFANTRY

*Mustered in: August 8, 1862.*
*Mustered out: June 8, 1865.*
*Indiana battle flags 373–80.*
*AGR II 639–47; VI 118–37.*

Grubbs, George W    1842–
Addresses delivered at 28th annual reunion 70th Ind. regt.: The fortunate regiment, by Geo. W. Grubbs. Flags of 70th Indiana, by F. H. Huron. [n. p., 1902] 34 p. plate (port.). 15½cm.    In   **159**
Title from cover.

Meredith, William Morton, 1835–1917.
A memory of Reseca, by William M. Meredith, Captain. 1912. 8 p. *MOLLUS-DC* no 89.    **160**

Merrill, Samuel, 1831–1924.
Letters from a Civil war officer. Edited by A. T. Volwiler. *Mississippi valley historical review* XIV (1928) 508–29.    **161**

—— The Seventieth Indiana volunteer infantry in the War of the rebellion, by Samuel Merrill. Indianapolis, Bowen-Merrill co. [1900] 372 p. 2 plates (ports.). 23½cm.    DLC NHi NN   **162**
Unit roster 291–372. Coulter 322.

Sievers, Harry Joseph, 1920–
Benjamin Harrison . . . [by] Harry J. Sievers. Introduction by Hilton U. Brown. Chicago, Henry Regnery co., 1952 [v. 2: New York, University publishers, 1959] 2 v. plates (illus., maps, ports.). 24cm.    **162A**
Civil war I 162–317.

### 71ST INFANTRY

*Mustered in: August 18, 1862.*
*Designated 6th regiment of cavalry: February 23, 1863.*
*Indiana battle flags 380–1.*

### 72ND INFANTRY

*Mustered in: August 16, 1862.*
*Mustered out: June 26, 1865.*
*Indiana battle flags 381–8.*
*AGR II 665–73; VI 163–81.*

McGee, Benjamin F    1834–
History of the 72d Indiana volunteer infantry of the Mounted lightning brigade, a faithful record of the life, service, and suffering, of the rank and file of the Regiment, on the march, in camp, in battle, and in prison. Especially devoted to giving the reader a definite knowledge of the service of the common soldier. With an appendix containing a complete roster of officers and men. Written and compiled by B. F. McGee, Sergt. of Co. I, Regimental historian. Edited by Wm. R. Jewell, Lieutenant of Co. G. Lafayette, S. Vater & co., 1882. xviii, 698, 21, (1) p. plates (ports.). 24cm.    DLC NHi NN   **163**
Unit roster, 21 p. "Errata," (1) p.

### 73RD INFANTRY

*Mustered in: August 6, 1862.*
*Mustered out: July 1, 1865.*
*Indiana battle flags 388–91.*
*AGR II 674–82; VI 182–98.*

Fifteenth annual reunion of the 73d regiment Ind. vol. infantry association, held September 5 and 6, 1900, at South Bend, Indiana. Plymouth, Republican press [1900] 29, (1) p. 22cm.    In   **164**
Title and imprint from cover.

History of the Seventy-third Indiana volunteers in the war of 1861–65. Compiled and published by a Committee of the Seventy-third regimental association. Washington, D. C., Carnahan press, 1909. 243 p. illus., map, plates (ports.). 19cm.    IHi   **165**
Unit roster [5]–90.

### 74TH INFANTRY

*Mustered in: August 21, 1862.*
*Mustered out: June 9, 1865.*
*Indiana battle flags 391–5.*
*AGR II 683–91; VI 199–215.*

Peddycord, William F

History of the Seventy-fourth regiment Indiana volunteer infantry, a three years' organization, by Will F. Peddycord. Warsaw, Smith printery, 1913. 144 p. plates (ports.). 23cm.

Unit roster [17]–89. MnHi **166**

## 75TH INFANTRY

*Mustered in: August 19, 1862.*
*Mustered out: June 8, 1865.*
*Indiana battle flags 395–9.*
*AGR III 2–8; VI 216–32.*

Floyd, David Bittle

History of the Seventy-fifth regiment of Indiana infantry volunteers, its organization, campaigns, and battles (1862–65), by Rev. David Bittle Floyd (formerly a Sergeant in Co. I of the Regiment). With an introduction by Major-General J. J. Reynolds. Published for the author. Philadelphia, Lutheran pub. society, 1893. 457 p. illus., maps, ports. 23cm.

DLC NHi NN **167**

Unit roster [407]–49. Coulter 165.

## 76TH INFANTRY

*Mustered in: July 20, 1862.*
*Mustered out: August 20, 1862.*
*Indiana battle flags 399.*
*AGR III 9–11; VI 233–44.*

*77th Regiment see 4th Cavalry*

## 78TH INFANTRY

*Mustered in: August 5, 1862.*
*Mustered out: October 3, 1862.*
*Indiana battle flags 399–400.*
*AGR III 21–2; IV 268–76.*

## 79TH INFANTRY

*Mustered in: September 2, 1862.*
*Mustered out: June 7, 1865.*
*Indiana battle flags 400–03.*
*AGR III 23–9; IV 277–91.*

Constitution and by-laws of the 79th Indiana veterans' association, organized at Indianapolis, Ind., March 7th, 1887 . . . Indianapolis, Hasselman-Journal co. print [1877] 4 p. 15cm.

Title and imprint from cover. In **168**

History of the Seventy-ninth regiment Indiana volunteer infantry in the Civil war of eighteen sixty-one in the United States. Indianapolis, Hollenbeck press, 1899. v, 221 p. 23½cm.

DLC NHi **169**

Unit roster [1]–45. Prepared by a committee of the Regimental association.

Roster of the 79th Indiana veteran association. Indianapolis, Baker & Randolph, printers [1889] [4] p. 24cm. In **170**

Caption title. On cover: Annual reunion of the Seventy-ninth Indiana veteran association, held at Indianapolis, September 25th, 1889 [program]

Dobson, James A C

A historical sketch of Company K of the 79th regiment Indiana volunteers, by James A. C. Dobson, Company historian. Published by the Company association and dedicated to their wives and children. Plainfield, Progress print, 1894. 24 p. 19½cm. In **171**

Title and imprint from cover.

Knefler, Frederick, 1834–1901.

Missionary ridge, by General Fred Knefler. *MOLLUS-Ind* 178–206. **172**

Munhall, Leander Whitcomb, 1843–

The Chattanooga campaign, by L. W. Munhall, Adjutant Seventy-ninth regiment Indiana, delivered before the Loyal legion, Commandery of Pennsylvania . . . May 7, 1902. 16 p. 18½cm. In **173**

Title from cover.

See also Title 43.

## 80TH INFANTRY

*Mustered in: September 8, 1862.*
*Mustered out: June 22, 1865.*
*Indiana battle flags 403–07.*
*AGR III 30–6; VI 292–307.*

## 81ST INFANTRY

*Mustered in: August 29, 1862.*
*Mustered out: June 13, 1865.*
*Indiana battle flags 407–11.*
*AGR III 37–44; VI 308–22.*

Morris, George W

History of the Eighty-first regiment of Indiana volunteer infantry in the great War of the rebellion, 1861 to 1865, telling of its origin and organization, a description of the material of which it was composed, its rapid and severe marches, hard service and fierce conflicts on many bloody fields. Pathetic scenes, amusing incidents and thrilling episodes. A regimental roster. Prison life, adventures, etc. By Corporal Geo. W. Morris. [Louisville, Ky., Franklin print co., 1901] 202 p. 22cm. DLC NHi **174**

Unit roster [159]–202. Coulter 331.

## 82ND INFANTRY

*Mustered in: August 30, 1862.*
*Mustered out: June 9, 1865.*
*Indiana battle flags 411–13.*
AGR III 45–51; VI 323–38.

Hunter, Alfred G
History of the Eighty-second Indiana volunteer infantry, its organization, campaigns and battles. Written at the request of the members, by Alf. G. Hunter, late Adjutant. Indianapolis, Wm. B. Burford, printer, 1893. 255 p. front. (port.), ports. 19½cm.

            DLC NHi NN   *175*
Unit roster 177–255. Coulter 250.

## 83RD INFANTRY

*Mustered in: November 5, 1862.*
*Mustered out: June 3, 1865.*
*Indiana battle flags 414–17.*
AGR III 52–7; VI 339–55.

Grecian, Joseph
History of the Eighty-third regiment, Indiana volunteer infantry, for three years with Sherman, compiled from the Regimental and Company books, and other sources, as well as from the writer's own observations and experience. Written in the "field" and in the "shelter-tent," near Washington, D. C., June 3, 1865, by J. Grecian of Company A. Cincinnati, John F. Uhlhorn, printer, 1865. iv, [5]–163 p. 19½cm.         DLC NN   *176*
Unit roster 101–55.

## 84TH INFANTRY

*Mustered in: September 3, 1862.*
*Mustered out: June 14, 1865.*
*Indiana battle flags 417–20.*
AGR III 58–64; VI 356–71.

## 85TH INFANTRY

*Mustered in: September 2, 1862.*
*Mustered out: June 12, 1865.*
*Indiana battle flags 420–3.*
AGR III 65–71; VI 372–87.

Brant, Jefferson E
History of the Eighty-fifth Indiana volunteer infantry, its organization, campaigns and battles. Written at the request of the members, by Rev. J. E. Brant, late Major and Lieutenant-Colonel. Bloomington, Cravens Bros., 1902. 191, (3) p. plates (ports.). 21cm.
Unit roster 135–91.      DLC NN   *177*

## 86TH INFANTRY

*Mustered in: September 4, 1862.*
*Mustered out: June 6, 1865.*
*Indiana battle flags 423–9.*
AGR III 72–8; VI 388–402.

The Eighty-sixth regiment, Indiana volunteer infantry, a narrative of its services in the Civil war of 1861–1865. Written by a Committee consisting of James A. Barnes, James R. Carnahan and Thomas H. B. McCain. Crawfordsville, Journal co., printers, 1895. viii, 613 (1) p. front. (port.). 23½cm.    DLC NN   *178*
"Errata," (1) p. Unit roster [571]–99.

Carnahan, James Richards, 1840–1905.
    Indiana at Chickamauga, address at dedication of Chickamauga national park, September 19, 1895, by Captain James R. Carnahan. *MOLLUS-Ind* 86–116.     *179*

—— Personal recollections of Chickamauga, a paper read before the Ohio commandery of the Military order of the loyal legion of the United States, by James R. Carnahan, late Captain 86th regiment Indiana. Cincinnati, H. C. Sherrick & co., 1886. 20 p. 21½cm.
              In NHi   *180*
Also published in Sketches of war history . . . Ohio commandery. *MOLLUS* I 401–22.

## 87TH INFANTRY

*Mustered in: August 31, 1862.*
*Mustered out: June 10, 1865.*
*Indiana battle flags 429–34.*
AGR III 79–85; VI 403–20.

First annual reunion, with reports of the meetings, of Society of the Eighty-seventh Indiana volunteer infantry, Laporte, Ind., Sept. 23d and 24th, 1869. . . . South Bend, National Union print. estab., 1870. 51 p. 16½cm.
            In WHi   *181*

Bruce, Foster
    Daniel E. Bruce, Civil war teamster. *InMH* XXXIII (1937) 187–98.     *182*
"This sketch is the joint work of Foster Bruce . . . and the Editor," William O. Lynch. Based on the diary of Daniel E. Bruce, 1836–1920.

Keegan, Peter, 1833–1904.
    The diaries of Peter Keegan, from the original note books, privately printed for his descendants. . . . Indianapolis, 1938. viii, 33 folios. port., 3 plates (2 illus., 3 maps) 30½cm.
              In   *183*
On cover: As transcribed and edited by Dwight Reynolds.

## 88TH INFANTRY

*Mustered in: August 29, 1862.*
*Mustered out: June 7, 1865.*
*Indiana battle flags 434–8.*
*AGR III 86–93; VI 421–37.*

History Eighty-eighth Indiana volunteers infantry, engagements, chronology, roster. Mustered into service, August 29th, 1862; mustered out, June 7; disbanded, June 20th, 1865. Fort Wayne, W. D. Page, printer [1895] 56 p. front. (port.), plates (illus.). 23cm.
DLC NN          **184**
On cover, 1895. Unit roster 9–50. "Reunions of the 88th Indiana," [51]–6.

Dougall, Allan H          1836–1912.
"Bentonville," by Captain Allan H. Dougall.
*MOLLUS-Ind* 212–19.          **185**

## 89TH INFANTRY

*Mustered in: August 28, 1862.*
*Mustered out: July 19, 1865.*
*Indiana battle flags 438–42.*
*AGR III 94–101; VI 438–54.*

Soldiers memorial Sam. Henry's guards, Company B, 89th reg. Indiana volunteers. Cincinnati, Lithogr. & printed in colors by Ehrgott, Forbriger & co. [1862] col. illus. broadside, 55½ x 45½cm.          InHi          **186**
c1862 by J. Wesley Waterman & co.

Craven, Hervey, 1823–
A brief history of the 89th Indiana volunteer infantry, from its organization, August 28, 1862, to the close of its term of service, including official reports, and a list of casualties in actions, by Lieut. Col. Hervey Craven. Wabash, Monson-Corrie co., printers, 1899. 77 p. 21½cm.          DNW          **187**
Unit roster 38–77.

*90th Regiment see 5th Cavalry*

## 91ST INFANTRY

*Mustered in: October 1, 1862.*
*Mustered out: June 26, 1865.*
*Indiana battle flags 442–5.*
*AGR III 112–18; VI 481–500.*

Williams, Benjamin A
Before Atlanta. In National tribune scrap book III 13–15.          **187A**

## 92ND INFANTRY

*Failed to complete organization.*

## 93RD INFANTRY

*Mustered in: October 31, 1862.*
*Mustered out: August 10, 1865.*
*Indiana battle flags 446–8.*
*AGR III 119–24; VI 501–17.*

Devillez, Henry
Reminiscences of the Civil war, Andersonville. *InMH* XI (1915) 144–7.          **188**

Robertson, Melville Cox, 1840–1865.
Journal of. . . . *InMH* XXVIII (1932) 116–37.
**189**

## 94TH, 95TH AND 96TH INFANTRY

*Failed to complete organization.*

## 97TH INFANTRY

*Mustered in: September 20, 1862.*
*Mustered out: June 9, 1865.*
*Indiana battle flags 448–52.*
*AGR III 126–32; VI 518–31.*

Alexander, John David, 1839–1931.
History of the Ninety-seventh regiment of Indiana volunteer infantry, by Captain John D. Alexander. Terre Haute, Moore & Langen, 1891. 34 p. 22cm.          IHi In          **190**

## 98TH INFANTRY

*Failed to complete organization.*

## 99TH INFANTRY

*Mustered in: October 21, 1862.*
*Mustered out: June 6, 1865.*
*Indiana battle flags 452–5.*
*AGR III 133–9; VI 532–46.*

Cook, Charles N
Letters of Privates Cook and [Lafayette] Ball. *InMH* XXVII (1931) 243–68.          **191**

Lucas, Daniel R          1840–1897.
History of the 99th Indiana infantry, containing a diary of marches, incidents, biography of officers and complete rolls, by Chaplain D. R. Lucas. Lafayette, Rosser & Spring, printers, 1865. iv, [5]–179, (1) p. 20½cm.
Unit roster 120–57.          DLC NHi          **192**

—— New history of the 99th Indiana infantry, containing official reports, anecdotes, incidents, biographies and complete rolls, by Chaplain D. R. Lucas. Rockford, Ill., Horner print. co., 1900. 256 p. ports. 23cm.          NHi          **193**
Unit roster 201–36.

*99th Infantry, continued*

Worrell, John
A diamond in the rough, embracing anecdote, biography, romance and history, by Captain John Worrell. Indianapolis, Wm. B. Burford,· printer, 1906. 282 p. front. (port.). 17½cm.                          NN    *194*
Civil war 121–43.

## 100TH INFANTRY

*Mustered in: September 19, 1862.*
*Mustered out: July 8, 1865.*
*Indiana battle flags 455–8.*
*AGR* III 140–7; VI 547–62.

Sherlock, Eli J
Memorabilia of the marches and battles in which the One hundredth regiment of Indiana infantry volunteers took an active part, War of the rebellion, 1861–5, by Captain E. J. Sherlock [Kansas City, Mo., Gerard-Woody print. co., 1896] 432 p. illus., ports. 20cm.
Unit roster 234–423.        DLC NN    *195*

Upson, Theodore Frelinghuysen, 1845–1919.
With Sherman to the sea, the Civil war letters, diaries & reminiscences of Theodore F. Upson. Edited with an introduction, by Oscar Osburn Winther. Baton Rouge, Louisiana State University press, 1943. xxii, 181 p. plates (illus., ports.). 21cm.             NN    *196*
"Map showing the route followed by Theodore F. Upson during the Civil war," end paper. Coulter 457.

—— —— Bloomington, Indiana University press [1958] xxviii, 181 p. plates (illus., map, port.). 22cm.                     NN    *197*
"Preface," by Bell Irvin Wiley, p vii–x. A reprint of Title 196.

Williams, Edward Peet
Extracts from letters to A.B.T., from Edward P. Williams, during his service in the Civil war, 1862–1864. For private distribution. New York, 1903. 122 p. front. (port.). 20cm.
                        DLC NN OHi    *198*
Coulter 477. "These letters were written to Miss Aggy Baldwin Townley of Elizabeth, N. J., who became the wife of Mr. Williams in 1864," manuscript note inserted in NN's copy.

## 101ST INFANTRY

*Mustered in: September 7, 1862.*
*Mustered out: June 24, 1865.*
*Indiana battle flags 458–61.*
*AGR* III 148–54; VI 563–78.

Naus, John A
Yankee letters from Andersonville prison. Edited by Spencer B. King, Jr. *Georgia historical quarterly* XXXVIII (1954) 394–8.    *198A*

## 102ND THROUGH 114TH INFANTRY

*Organized to repel Morgan's raid, July 1863.*
*Indiana battle flags 462–3.*
*AGR* III 155–92; VI 579–699; VII 2–40.

## 115TH INFANTRY

*Mustered in: August 13, 1863.*
*Mustered out: February 25, 1864.*
*Indiana battle flags 463–5.*
*AGR* III 193–6; VII 41–54.

## 116TH INFANTRY

*Mustered in: August 17, 1863.*
*Mustered out: February 29 to March 2, 1864.*
*Indiana battle flags 465–7.*
*AGR* III 197–200; VII 55–69.

## 117TH INFANTRY

*Mustered in: September 17, 1863.*
*Mustered out: February 23–27, 1864.*
*Indiana battle flags 467–8.*
*AGR* III 201–04; VII 70–84.

## 118TH INFANTRY

*Mustered in: September 3, 1863.*
*Mustered out: March 1–4, 1864.*
*Indiana battle flags 469–70.*
*AGR* III 205–08; VII 85–99.

*119th Regiment see 7th Cavalry*

## 120TH INFANTRY

*Organized: December 1863 to March 1864.*
*Mustered out: January 8, 1866.*
*Indiana battle flags 470–2.*
*AGR* III 219–25; VII 131–47.

Benson, William C          –1865.
Civil war diary of. . . . *InMH* XXIII (1927) 333–64.                           *199*

Hudson, David Mitchell, 1837–1864.
Civil war letters of . . . Contributed by Roy D. Hudson. *InMH* XLVII (1951) 191–208. *200*

*121st Regiment see 9th Cavalry*

## 122ND INFANTRY

*Failed to complete organization.*

## 123RD INFANTRY

*Mustered in: March 7, 1864.*
*Mustered out: August 25, 1865.*
*Indiana battle flags 472–5.*
AGR III 233–40; VII 167–82.

Kaler, William S        1835–
Roster and history of the One hundred twenty-third regiment, I.V.I. in the War of the rebellion, compiled by William S. Kaler. . . . Andersonville [Rushville, Press of the American] 1899. 61 p. front. (port.), port. 16cm.
DLC NHi        **201**

Robbins, Irvin, 1838–1911.
War statistics of Indiana, by Major Irvin Robbins. *MOLLUS-Ind* 408–16.        **202**

## 124TH INFANTRY

*Mustered in: March 10, 1864.*
*Mustered out: August 31, 1865.*
*Indiana battle flags 475–7.*
AGR III 241–8; VII 183–97.

Elliott, Joseph Taylor, 1824–1916.
. . . The Sultana disaster, by Joseph Taylor Elliott. Indianapolis, Edward J. Hecker, printer, 1913. p. [163]–99. front. (illus.). 24cm.
In NN        **203**
At head of title: Indiana historical society publications, volume V, number 3.

***125th, 126th and 127th Regiments***
***see 10th, 11th and 12th Cavalry***

## 128TH INFANTRY

*Mustered in: March 18, 1864.*
*Mustered out: April 10, 1866.*
*Indiana battle flags 477–9.*
AGR III 269–75; VII 254–71.

Reunion of the One hundred and twenty-eighth Indiana volunteers, held at Logansport, Indiana, August 6 and 7, 1890. New Albany, Tribune print [1890] 27 p. port. 21½cm.
In        **204**
Title and imprint from cover. The third reunion, minutes of the two proceeding reunions were not published.
See also Title 133.

## 129TH INFANTRY

*Mustered in: March 1, 1864.*
*Mustered out: August 29, 1865.*
*Indiana battle flags 479–81.*
AGR III 276–82; VII 272–87.

## 130TH INFANTRY

*Mustered in: March 12, 1864.*
*Mustered out: December 2, 1865.*

*Indiana battle flags 481–4.*
AGR III 283–9; VII 288–302.

***131st Regiment see 13th Cavalry***

## 132ND INFANTRY

*Mustered in: May 16, 1864.*
*Mustered out: September 7, 1864.*
*Indiana battle flags 484.*
AGR III 297–9; VII 325–37.

## 133RD INFANTRY

*Mustered in: May 17, 1864.*
*Mustered out: September 5, 1864.*
*Indiana battle flags 484–7.*
AGR III 299–302; VII 338–51.

Cox, Jabez Thomas, 1846–
Civil war diary of. . . . *InMH* XXVIII (1932) 40–54.        **205**

## 134TH INFANTRY

*Mustered in: May 25, 1864.*
*Mustered out: September 2, 1864.*
*Indiana battle flags 488–9.*
AGR III 302–04; VII 352–64.

## 135TH INFANTRY

*Mustered in: May 23, 1864.*
*Mustered out: September 29, 1864.*
*Indiana battle flags 489–92.*
AGR III 305–08; VII 365–77.

## 136TH INFANTRY

*Mustered in: May 21, 1864.*
*Mustered out: September 2, 1864.*
*Indiana battle flags 492.*
AGR III 308–11; VII 378–90.
See Title 95.

## 137TH INFANTRY

*Mustered in: May 26, 1864.*
*Mustered out: September 21, 1864.*
*Indiana battle flags 492–4.*
AGR III 311–14; VII 391–403.

Wiley, Harvey Washington, 1844–1930.
Corporal Harvey W. Wiley's Civil war diary [Edited by] William L. Fox. *InMH* LI (1955) 139–62.        **206**

## 138TH INFANTRY

*Mustered in: May 27, 1864.*
*Mustered out: September 22, 1864.*
*Indiana battle flags 494–5.*
AGR III 314–17; VII 404–15.

### 139TH INFANTRY

*Mustered in: June 5, 1864.*
*Mustered out: September 29, 1864.*
*Indiana battle flags 495–6.*
AGR III 317–20; VII 416–27.

### 140TH INFANTRY

*Mustered in: October 24, 1864.*
*Mustered out: July 11, 1865.*
*Indiana battle flags 496–7.*
AGR III 322–6; VII 428–43.

### 141ST INFANTRY

*Failed to complete organization.*

### 142ND INFANTRY

*Mustered in: November 3, 1864.*
*Mustered out: July 14, 1865.*
*Indiana battle flags 497–8.*
AGR III 327–30; VII 444–58.

### 143RD INFANTRY

*Mustered in: February 21, 1865.*
*Mustered out: October 17, 1865.*
*Indiana battle flags 498–9.*
AGR III 331–4; VII 459–73.

### 144TH INFANTRY

*Mustered in: March 6, 1865.*
*Mustered out: August 5, 1865.*
*Indiana battle flags 499.*
AGR III 334–7; VII 474–88.

### 145TH INFANTRY

*Mustered in: February 16, 1865.*
*Mustered out: January 21, 1866.*
*Indiana battle flags 500–01.*
AGR III 337–41; VII 489–503.

### 146TH INFANTRY

*Mustered in: March 9, 1865.*
*Mustered out: August 31, 1865.*
*Indiana battle flags 501–02.*
AGR III 341–3; VII 504–17.

### 147TH INFANTRY

*Mustered in: March 13, 1865.*
*Mustered out: August 4, 1865.*
*Indiana battle flags 502.*
AGR III 344–7; VII 518–33.

### 148TH INFANTRY

*Mustered in: February 25, 1865.*
*Mustered out: September 5, 1865.*
*Indiana battle flags 502–03.*
AGR III 347–50; VII 534–47.

### 149TH INFANTRY

*Mustered in: March 1, 1865.*
*Mustered out: September 27, 1865.*
*Indiana battle flags 503–05.*
AGR III 350–3; VII 548–62.

### 150TH INFANTRY

*Mustered in: March 9, 1865.*
*Mustered out: August 5, 1865.*
*Indiana battle flags 505.*
AGR III 354–6; VII 563–77.

### 151ST INFANTRY

*Mustered in: March 3, 1865.*
*Mustered out: September 19, 1865.*
*Indiana battle flags 505–06.*
AGR III 357–9; VII 578–92.

### 152ND INFANTRY

*Mustered in: March 16, 1865.*
*Mustered out: August 30, 1865.*
*Indiana battle flags 506.*
AGR III 360–2; VII 593–607.

### 153RD INFANTRY

*Mustered in: March 1, 1865.*
*Mustered out: September 4, 1865.*
*Indiana battle flags 506–07.*
AGR III 363–5; VII 608–21.

### 154TH INFANTRY

*Mustered in: April 20, 1865.*
*Mustered out: August 4, 1865.*
*Indiana battle flags 507.*
AGR III 366–8; VII 622–35.

### 155TH INFANTRY

*Mustered in: April 18, 1865.*
*Mustered out: August 4, 1865.*
*Indiana battle flags 508.*
AGR III 369–71; VII 636–49.

### 156TH INFANTRY

*Mustered in: April 12, 1865.*
*Mustered out: August 4, 1865.*
*Indiana battle flags 508.*
AGR III 372; VII 650–7.

OHIO

# Reference Works

Dyer, Frederick Henry, 1849–1917.

A compendium of the War of the rebellion. 1908 (reprinted 1959).

"Regimental index" 200–14; "Regimental histories" 1472–556. The pagination is the same in the 1959 reprint.

Ohio. Roster Commission.

Official roster of the soldiers of the State of Ohio in the War of the rebellion, 1861–1866 . . . Compiled under direction of the Roster commission: Wm. McKinley, Jr., Governor; Samuel M. Taylor, Sec'y of state [and] James C. Howe, Adjutant-General. Published by authority of the General assembly. Akron, Cincinnati, Norwalk, 1886–95. 12 v. 26cm.

The set commenced publication with volume II in 1886. Volume I was published in 1893. The printing was accomplished by four firms:

Werner ptg. & lith. co., Akron, vols I, IV–VI, XI.
Wilstach Baldwin & co., Cincinnati, vol II.
Ohio Valley co., Cincinnati, vol III, VII–X.
Laning co., Norwalk, vol XII.

The names of the printing firms changed during the years in which the volumes were printed. The members of the Roster commission were ex-officio and varied.

Reid, Whitelaw

Ohio in the war: her statesmen, her Generals, and soldiers, by Whitelaw Reid. . . . Cincinnati, Moore, Wilstach & Baldwin, 1868. 2 v. maps, plates (illus., ports.). 24cm.

Contents: I. History of the State during the war and the lives of her Generals; II. The history of her regiments and other military organizations. Volume II cited herein as *Ohio in the war*. Ryan 595.

Ryan, Daniel Joseph

The Civil war literature of Ohio, a bibliography with explanatory and historical notes, by Daniel J. Ryan . . . Cleveland, Burrow Brothers co., 1911. ix, 518 p. 26cm.

The item numbers listed in this work have been added to this checklist.

*The Union army.*

"Record of Ohio regiments," II (1908) 353–483.

United States. Adjutant General's Office.

Official army register of the volunteer force of the United States army for the years 1861, '62, '63, '64, '65. Part V, Ohio, Michigan. Washington, 1865.

A roster of officers by regiments with an alphabetical index for the two states.

# OHIO

## ARTILLERY

### Heavy Artillery

#### 1ST ARTILLERY (HEAVY)

*Organized as 117th regiment of infantry: September 1862.*
*Designated 1st regiment of heavy artillery: August 12, 1863.*
*Mustered out: July 25, 1865.*
*Official roster x 257–308, 678–80.*
*Ohio in the war 608–09.*

First Ohio heavy artillery 22nd reunion minutes and registry, Jackson, Ohio, September 23, 1909. [6] p. 14½cm.    OHi  *1*
Title from cover.

Miller, Hillborn C
First Ohio heavy artillery history. "Our service in East Tennessee," 1864–5, by H. C. Miller, historian. Paper read at reunion at Gallipolis, Ohio, September 21st, 1899. 20 p. 14½ x 17½cm.    DLC  *2*
Title from cover. Ryan 479.

—— Incidents in the history of the First Ohio heavy artillery. Broadside, 52 x 15cm.
"Read at Gallipolis reunion."    OHi  *3*

#### 2ND ARTILLERY (HEAVY)

*Organized: June to September 1863.*
*Mustered out: August 23, 1865.*
*Official roster x 309–61, 681–4.*
*Ohio in the war 909–14.*

Regimental orders of the Second Ohio heavy artillery, from its first organization, September 23, 1863. [n. p., 1864] 137 p. 18½cm.
    OHi  *4*
Through Orders no. 180, dated, Oct. 9, 1864. Ryan 594.

### Light Artillery

#### 1ST REGIMENT, COLONEL JAMES BARNETT COMMANDING

*Mustered in: April 22, 1861.*
*Mustered out: July 27, 1861.*
*Official roster i 711–18.*
*Ohio in the war 891–2.*

Active service: or, campaigning in Western Virginia. *Continental monthly* i (New York, 1862) 330–8.    *5*

Reminiscences of the Cleveland light artillery. Cleveland, Cleveland print. co., 1906. 101 p. front. (illus.). 19cm.    OHi  *6*
Unit roster 94–100.

#### 1ST ARTILLERY (LIGHT)

*For muster in and out information, see the entries of the individual batteries.*
*Official roster x 362–442, 685–92.*
*Ohio in the war 889–90, 892–906.*

##### Battery A

*Mustered in: September 6, 1861.*
*Mustered out: July 31, 1865.*

Report of the . . . annual reunion of Battery "A" association . . . xxv–xxvi 1891–1892; xxviii–xxxii 1894–1898; xxxiv–xliii 1900–1909.    DLC  *7*
Ryan 635–51. Ryan does not list xxvii 1893 and xxxiii 1899.

Davidson, Henry M    –1900.
Experience in Rebel prisons for United States soldiers at Richmond, Danville, Andersonville, Savannah, and Millen. In Prisoners of war and military prisons, personal narratives of experience in the prisons at. . . . (1890) 147–398.    *8*

—— Fourteen months in Southern prisons, being a narrative of the treatment of Federal prisoners of war in the Rebel military prisons of Richmond, Danville, Andersonville, Savannah, and Millen. Describing the author's escape with two comrades, from Andersonville and the blood hounds, his adventures during a fourteen nights' march in the swamps of Western Georgia, and his subsequent re-capture, to which is added a large list of those who have died in various prisons in the Confederacy, by H. M. Davidson, member Battery A, 1st O.V.L.A. Milwaukee, Daily Wisconsin print. house, 1865. viii, [9]–393 p. front. (fold. plan). 20cm.    DLC NHi NN  *9*
Ryan 182. Coulter 114.

—— History of Battery A, First regiment Ohio vol. light artillery. Milwaukee, Daily Wisconsin print. house, 1865. vii, [9]–199 p. 19cm.    DLC NN  *10*
Unit roster [145]–99. "Preface" signed: H. M. Davidson. Ryan 181.

##### Battery B

*Mustered in: October 8, 1861.*
*Mustered out: July 22, 1865.*

*Battery B, continued*

Cutter, Orlando Phelps, 1824–
  Our battery; or, the journal of Company B,
1st O.V.A., by O. P. Cutter. Cleveland, Nevins'
Book and job print, 1864. 152 p. 16½cm.
                                    DLC NN    **11**
  Unit roster [146]–50. Ryan 179.

### *Battery C*

*Mustered in: September 9, 1861.*
*Mustered out: June 15, 1865.*

### *Battery D*

*Mustered in: September 1861.*
*Mustered out: July 15, 1865.*

A military record of Battery D, First Ohio vet-
eran volunteers light artillery, by a committee.
Oil City, Pa., Derrick pub. co., 1908. 221,
(16) p. front. (port.). 21½cm.    NN    **12**
  Unit roster (16) p. Committee on history: Alfred
Sperry, Samuel C. Fry and Perez G. Clark.

### *Battery E*

*Mustered in: October 7, 1861.*
*Mustered out: July 10, 1865.*

### *Battery F*

*Mustered in: December 2, 1861.*
*Mustered out: July 22, 1865.*

### *Battery G*

*Mustered in: December 17, 1861.*
*Mustered out: August 31, 1865.*

### *Battery H*

*Mustered in: November 7, 1861.*
*Mustered out: June 17, 1865.*

Huntington, James Freeman
  The artillery at Hazel grove. *BandL* III 188.
                                              **13**

—— The battle of Chancellorsville, by Brevet
Major James F. Huntington, 1897. *PMHSM* III
150–91.                                         **14**

—— Operations in the Shenandoah valley,
from Winchester to Port Republic, March 10 –
June 9, 1862, by James F. Huntington, Captain, Battery H. First regiment light artillery
Ohio, 1888. *PMHSM* I 301–37.                   **15**

—— Operations in the Shenandoah valley,
from Winchester to Port Republic, 1862.
1888. *PMHSM* VI 1–29.                          **16**

### *Battery I*

*Mustered in: December 3, 1861.*
*Mustered out: June 13, 1865.*

Cody, Darwin, 1838–1924.
  Civil war letters of . . . Edited by Stanley P.
Wasson. *OHQ* LXXIX (1959) 371–407.    **17**

### *Battery K*

*Mustered in: October 22, 1861.*
*Mustered out: July 17, 1865.*

### *Battery L*

*Mustered in: October 8, 1861.*
*Mustered out: July 4, 1865.*

### *Battery M*

*Mustered in: December 3, 1861.*
*Consolidated with Battery I: April 11,
1865.*

## Independent Batteries
## of Light Artillery

### *1st Battery*

*Mustered in: August 6, 1861.*
*Mustered out: June 26, 1865.*
*Official roster x 443–50, 693.*
*Ohio in the war 828–9.*

### *2nd Battery*

*Mustered in: August 7, 1861.*
*Mustered out: August 10, 1865.*
*Official roster x 451–60, 693–4.*
*Ohio in the war 830–1.*

### *3rd Battery*

*Mustered in: November 9, 1861 to March
15, 1862.*
*Mustered out: July 31, 1865.*
*Official roster x 461–8, 694–5.*
*Ohio in the war 832–3.*

### *4th Battery*

*Mustered in: August 17, 1861.*
*Consolidated with 10th battery: March
29, 1865.*
*Official roster x 469–76, 696.*
*Ohio in the war 834–6.*

### 5th Battery

*Mustered in: August 31 to September 20, 1861.*

*Mustered out: July 31, 1865.*

*Official roster x 477–88, 697.*

*Ohio in the war 837–40.*

Hickenlooper, Andrew, 1837–1904.
The battle of Shiloh, by Andrew Hickenlooper, late Lieutenant-Colonel, 1903. MOL-LUS-Ohio v 402–83. 2 plans, plate (illus.). *18*

Contents: Part I, Personal experiences in the battle; Part II, General review of reports of the battle. Ryan 352.

### 6th Battery

*Mustered in: December 10, 1861.*

*Mustered out: September 1, 1865.*

*Official roster x 489–97, 698.*

*Ohio in the war 841–4.*

Hinman, Wilbur F
The story of the Sherman brigade, the camp, the march, the bivouac, the battle, and how "the boys" lived and died during four years of active field service . . . by Wilbur F. Hinman, late Lieutenant-Colonel Sixty-fifth Ohio regiment. Published by the author. [Alliance, Ohio, Press of Daily Review] 1897. xxxii, [33]–1104 p. illus., ports. 23cm.   DLC NN   *19*

Coulter 234. Ryan 357. Unit rosters: 64th Ohio, 935–1003; 65th Ohio, 1004–67; Sixth Ohio battery, 1060–80; McLaughlin's squadron 1081–97.

### 7th Battery

*Mustered in: January 13, 1864, to date, January 1, 1862.*

*Mustered out: August 11, 1865.*

*Official roster x 498–505, 699.*

*Ohio in the war 845–6.*

### 8th Battery

*Mustered in: March 11, 1862.*

*Mustered out: August 7, 1865.*

*Official roster x 506–12; 699–700.*

*Ohio in the war 847–8.*

### 9th Battery

*Mustered in: October 1861.*

*Mustered out: July 25, 1865.*

*Official roster x 513–20, 700–01.*

*Ohio in the war 849–52.*

Record of the 9th independent battery Ohio veteran volunteer artillery, organized at Camp Cleveland, Oct. 11, 1861. Cleveland, Fairbanks, Benedict & co., printers, 1864. 14 p. 19cm.   DLC   *20*

Unit roster 12–14. Ryan 589.

### 10th Battery

*Mustered in: March 3, 1862.*

*Mustered out: July 17, 1865.*

*Official roster x 521–31, 701.*

*Ohio in the war 852–4.*

Owens, Ira S
Tenth Ohio battery. In his Greene county soldiers in the late war (1884) 159–67.   *21*

### 11th Battery

*Mustered in: October 27, 1861.*

*Mustered out: November 5, 1864.*

*Official roster x 532–7, 701–2.*

*Ohio in the war 855–8.*

Neil, Henry Moore, 1832–
A Battery at close quarters, paper read before the Ohio commandery of the Loyal legion, October 6, 1909, by Captain Henry M. Neil, 11th Ohio battery. 15 p. 22½cm.   NN   *22*

"An army experience," by J. B. Sanborn, [13]–15. Title from cover. Ryan 491.

——— ——— Columbus [Champlin press] 1909. 30 p. 21½cm.   NN   *23*

"Captain Twenty-second [sic] Ohio battery."

Sears, Cyrus
The Eleventh Ohio battery at Iuka . . . a paper read by Lieut. Col. Cyrus Sears, late First Lieutenant of the Eleventh Ohio independent battery of light artillery volunteers, read at a reunion of the survivors of that Battery, at Cincinnati, Ohio, Sept. 7, 1898. [Akron, Werner co., 1898] [10] p. front. (port.). 25½cm.   DLC NN RP   *24*

Title from cover. Ryan 733.

### 12th Battery

*Organized as Company D, 25th regiment of infantry: June 8, 1861.*

*Designated 12th battery of light artillery: March 17, 1862.*

*Mustered out: July 10, 1865.*

*Official roster x 538–46, 702–3.*

*Ohio in the war 858–9.*

### 13th Battery

*Battery never fully organized and was discontinued: April 20, 1862.*

*Official roster x 547–52.*

### 14th Battery

Mustered in: September 10, 1861.
Mustered out: August 11, 1865.
Official roster x 553–62, 703–04.
Ohio in the war 860–4.

### 15th Battery

Mustered in: February 1, 1862.
Mustered out: June 20, 1865.
Official roster x 563–70, 704–05.
Ohio in the war 865–7.

### 16th Battery

Mustered in: September 6, 1861.
Mustered out: August 2, 1865.
Official roster x 571–80, 705–06.
Ohio in the war 868–70.

History of the Sixteenth battery of Ohio volunteer light artillery, U.S.A., from enlistment, August 20, 1861, to muster out, August 2, 1865. Compiled from the diaries of comrades, the best recollections of survivors, and official records. [n. p.,] 1906. xiv, 202 (i. e. 220) p. illus., maps, ports. 19cm.                    DLC    25
"Reunions of the Battery survivors," 193–214. Unit roster 106–87.

### 17th Battery

Mustered in: August 21, 1862.
Mustered out: August 16, 1865.
Official roster x 581–8, 706.
Ohio in the war 870–1.

Jackson, Isaac, 1842–1903.
"Some of the boys," the Civil war letters of Isaac Jackson, 1862–1865. Edited by Joseph Orville Jackson, with a foreword by Bell Irvin Wiley. Carbondale, Southern Illinois University press [1960] xx, 264 p. plates (facs., ports.). 22cm.                    NN    26
On the roster of the 83rd Ohio infantry, the author "served in the Seventeenth Ohio battery, first on an attached basis and then on what he thought was a permanent assignment."

Mattox, Absalom H
Response to the toast, "the 17th Ohio volunteer battery, volunteer light artillery," by A. H. Mattox, late 1st Lieutenant, at the first annual re-union of the Battery, Springfield, O., October 1st and 2nd, 1885. Published for the author. Cincinnati, 1885. 24 p. 23cm.
                                        NHi NN    27
On cover: To the "Seventeenth Ohio veteran battery," volunteer light artillery.

—— "What did we fight for?," a response by A. H. Mattox, at the second annual reunion of the Battery, Springfield, Ohio, August 5th, 1886. Cincinnati, Robert Clarke & co., printers, 1886. 12 p. 19½cm.                    OHi    28

### 18th Battery

Mustered in: September 13, 1862.
Mustered out: June 29, 1865.
Official roster x 589–97, 707.
Ohio in the war 872–5.

### 19th Battery

Mustered in: September 10, 1862.
Mustered out: June 28, 1865.
Official roster x 598–602, 707.
Ohio in the war 876–7.

Tracie, Theodore C            1836?–
Annals of the Nineteenth Ohio battery volunteer artillery, including an outline of the operations of the Second division, Twenty-third army corps. Lights and shadows of army life, as seen on the march, bivouac and battlefield, by Theodore C. Tracie. Cleveland, Published for the Battery Committee by J. B. Savage, 1878. xvi, [17]–470 p. 19cm. DLC    29
Unit roster [465]–7. Ryan 830.

### 20th Battery

Mustered in: October 29, 1862.
Mustered out: July 19, 1865.
Official roster x 603–09, 708.
Ohio in the war 878–9.

Peterson, John Stahl.
The issues of the war. Continental monthly v (New York 1864) 274–87.            30

### 21th Battery

Organized: April 29, 1863.
Mustered out: July 21, 1865.
Official roster x 610–14, 708.
Ohio in the war 880.

### 22th Battery

Mustered in: July 14, 1863.
Mustered out: July 13, 1865.
Official roster x 615–21, 709.
Ohio in the war 881.

### 23rd Battery

Organized for three months' service: May 10, 1861.
Reorganized and mustered in for three years' service: June 3, 1861.

*Mustered out: July 10, 1865.*
*Official roster x 622–9, 709.*

### 24th Battery

*Mustered in: August 4, 1863.*
*Mustered out: June 24, 1865.*
*Official roster x 630–4, 710.*
*Ohio in the war 882–3.*

### 25th Battery

*Organized: February 17, 1863.*
*Mustered out: December 12, 1865.*
*Official roster x 635–44, 710.*
*Ohio in the war 884–6.*

See Title 43.

### 26th Battery

*Organized as Company F, 32nd regiment
of infantry: August 1861.*
*Designated 26th battery of light artillery:
December 22, 1863.*
*Mustered out: September 2, 1865.*
*Official roster x 645–52, 711.*
*Ohio in the war 887–8.*

### Charles S. Cotter's Battery

*Organized: April 25, 1861.*
*Mustered out: September 3, 1861.*
*Official roster i 719–21, 772.*

### William S. Williams' Battery

*Organized: June 25, 1861.*
*Mustered out: November 6, 1861.*
*Official roster i 723–5.*

## CAVALRY

### 1ST CAVALRY

*Organized: August 17 to October 5, 1861.*
*Mustered out: September 13 to 26, 1865.*
*Official roster xi 1–50, 753–7.*
*Ohio in the war 745–53.*

Proceedings of the . . . annual reunion First
O.V.V.C. i/ii–xii/xiii, 1880/1881–1891/1892
(OHi); xxiv, 1903 (MnHi); xxxii–xxxvi, 1911–
1915 (MnHi); xxxvii/xxxviii, 1916/1917
(OHi); xxxix–xl, 1918/1919 (MnHi). **31**
1880–1892, 1912–1913, 1916–1919 are published
in biennial volumes. 1904–1915 have cover title:
Roster.

Cappon, Lester Jess, 1900–
"The soldier's creed." *OHQ* lxiv (1955)
320–7. **32**
Text of Minor Millikin's Soldier's creed and comment.

Curry, William Leontes, 1839–1927.
Address of Col. William L. Curry . . . delivered at the reunion of the Washington
county veteran association, held in Marietta,
Ohio, October 13, 14, 15, 1915. [10] p. front.
(port.). 20cm. OHi **33**

—— Four years in the saddle, history of the
First regiment Ohio volunteer cavalry, War of
the rebellion, 1861–1865, by W. L. Curry.
Columbus, Champlin print. co., 1898. iv, iii,
[13]–401, (3) p. plates (illus., maps, ports.).
26cm. DLC NN **34**
With the volume is bound p 1–50 of Official roster
of soldiers of the State of Ohio in the War of the
rebellion, 1861–1866, v. XI. A correction to this roster
of the 1st cavalry is included in (3) p. Ryan 174.

—— Raid of the Confederate cavalry through
Central Tennessee in October, 1863, commanded by General Joseph Wheeler, a paper
read before the Ohio commandery of the Loyal
legion, April 1, 1908, by William L. Curry,
Captain 1st Ohio vol. cavalry. 21 p. map.
23cm. NHi **35**
Ryan 176.

—— —— *JUSCA* xix (1909) 815–42. **36**

—— Raid of the Union cavalry, commanded
by General Judson Kilpatrick, around the Confederate army in Atlanta, August, 1864. [1907]
*MOLLUS-Ohio* vi 252–75. map. **37**

—— —— *JUSCA* xx (1910) 1070–90. map.
**38**

Gillespie, Samuel L
A history of Co. A, First Ohio cavalry, 1861–
1865, a memorial volume, compiled from personal records and living witnesses, by Lovejoy.
Washington Court House [Press of Ohio State
Register] 1898. 298, (1) p. plates (ports.).
23½cm. OHi **39**
"Errata," (1) p. Ryan 276. Portrait facing p [58]
of "Samuel L. Gillespie, 'Lovejoy.' "

McClurg, Alexander Caldwell, 1832–1901.
An American soldier, Minor Millikin (read
June 13, 1890). *MOLLUS-Ill* ii 355–72. **40**

Rea, John P
Four weeks with Long's cavalry in East
Tennessee, by Captain John P. Rea. 1898.
*MOLLUS-Minn* v 17–44. **41**

—— Kilpatrick's raid around Atlanta. 1899.
*MOLLUS-Minn* v 152–74. **42**

Swing, David, 1830–1894.
A discourse in memory of Colonel Minor
Millikin, delivered in the Third Presbyterian

*1st Cavalry, continued*

church, February 8, 1863, by Prof. D. Swing. Oxford, Richard Butler, printer, 1863. 8 p. 20½cm. NB **42A**

## 2ND CAVALRY

*Organized: August – October 1861.*
*Mustered out: September 11, 1865.*
*Official roster* xi 51–116, 757–62.
*Ohio in the war* 754–61.

Report of the reunion of the 2nd Ohio cavalry and 25th Ohio battery. . . . 1903–1906 (DLC); 1907, 1911, 1915 (NN). **43**

Gause, Isaac, 1843–
Four years with five armies, Army of the frontier, Army of the Potomac, Army of the Missouri, Army of the Ohio, Army of the Shenandoah, by Isaac Gause, late of Co. E, Second Ohio cav. New York, Neale pub. co., 1908. 384 p. plates (1 illus., ports.). 21cm.
Coulter 180. Ryan 271. DLC NN **44**

Houghton, Albert C
Reconnaissance of Abraham's creek. The captured Confederate regiment and its battle flag. By Major A. C. Houghton. In Title 43, (1907) 9–35. **44A**

Nettleton, Allured Bayard, 1838–1911.
How the day was saved at the battle of Cedar creek, by Bvt. Brig.-General A. Bayard Nettleton. *MOLLUS-Minn* i 258–75. **45**

—— How the day was saved, a sketch, read by Gen. A. B. Noble, before the Dime sociables of Chelton Hills, Thursday evening, December 17th, 1874. . . . Philadelphia, M'Laughlin Brothers, printers, 1874. 12 p. 18cm. DLC **46**

Polhamus, William Henry Harrison
Appomattox, a poem, by W. H. Polhamus, late of the Second Ohio volunteer cavalry. [n. p., 191–] 8 leaves. 2 illus. 17½cm.
CSmH NN **46A**
"Fifty years ago . . . we were mustered in the service."

Roseboom, Eugene Holloway, 1892–
The mobbing of the Crisis [Columbus, March 5, 1863] *OHQ* lix (1950) 150–3.
A letter of Samuel C. Trescott, Co. C. **47**

Tenney, Luman Harris, 1841–1880.
War diary of Luman Harris Tenney, 1861–1865. Printed for private circulation by Frances Andrews Tenney. Cleveland, Evangelical pub. house, 1914. xix, 195 p. illus., fold. map, ports. 24½cm. NN **48**
"Introductory notes, by A. B. Nettleton, June 10, 1911," ix–xvii.

## 3RD CAVALRY

*Organized: September 4 to December 11, 1861.*
*Mustered out: August 14, 1865.*
*Official roster* xi 117–76, 762–7.
*Ohio in the war* 762–9.

Brown, Charles O
Battle-field revisited. Grant's Chattanooga campaign, a horseback ride from Chattanooga to Atlanta, by C. O. Brown. Kalamazoo, Eaton & Anderson, 1886. 128 p. 18cm.
P WHi **49**
Contents: [1st series] 1880, [5]–74; Second series, 1885, 75–128.

—— The old battle fields revisited after 16 years! A horseback ride from Chattanooga to Atlanta, by comrade C. O. Brown. Sandusky, Register print. house, 1880. 64 p. 16cm.
Title from cover. DLC **50**

Crofts, Thomas
History of the service of the Third Ohio veteran volunteer cavalry in the War for the preservation of the Union from 1861–1865. Compiled from the official records and from diaries of members of the Regiment, by Serg't Thos. Crofts, Company C, Regimental historian. Members of the History committee . . . [4 names] Toledo, Columbus, Stoneman press, 1910. 296, (4) p. plates (1 illus., ports.). 25cm.
DLC **51**
Ruled pages for "Memoranda," (4) p. Unit roster 239–96. Ryan 171.

Marshall, Emogene (Niver)
To the memory of my brother, Edwin W. Niver, compiled by Emogene Niver Marshall. Sandusky [Krewson's printers] 1932. 71, (1) p. illus., ports. 23½cm. DLC **52**
On cover: Reminiscences of the Civil war and Andersonville prison. "Andersonville prison . . . as seen by Corporal H. J. Peters," [126th Ohio infantry] 49–58.

## 4TH CAVALRY

*Organized: November 1861 (Companies L and M, August 15, 1862).*
*Mustered out: July 15, 1865.*
*Official roster* xi 177–238, 767–71.
*Ohio in the war* 770–4.

Adae, Carl Adolph Gottlob
Our military future, a paper read before the Ohio commandery of the Military order of the loyal legion of the United States, by Carl A. G. Adae, late Captain 4th Ohio volunteer cavalry. Cincinnati, Woodruff, Cox & co., 1885. 15 p. 21½cm. DLC WHi **53**
Also published in *MOLLUS-Ohio* i 314–28.

**Crane, William Edmund**
Bugle blasts, read before the Ohio commandery of the Military order of the loyal legion of the United States, by William E. Crane, late Captain 4th O.V.C. Cincinnati, Peter G. Thomson, 1884. 17 p. 21½cm.
         DLC   **54**
Also published in *MOLLUS-Ohio* I 233–51. Ryan 169.

**Kennett, John**
History of the First cavalry division, from November 1, 1862, to January 1, 1863, by John Kennett, Colonel Fourth Ohio cavalry. In G.A.R. war papers, papers read before Fred C. Jones post, no. 401, Department of Ohio, G.A.R. (1891) 337–50.    **55**

**Pike, James, 1834–**
The scout and ranger, being the personal adventures of Corporal Pike of the Fourth Ohio cavalry as a Texan ranger, in the Indian wars, delineating Western adventure. Afterwards a scout and spy, in Tennessee, Alabama, Georgia, and the Carolinas, under Generals Mitchell, Rosecrans, Stanley, Sheridan, Lytle, Thomas, Crook, and Sherman, fully illustrating the secret service. Cincinnati, J. R. Hawley & co., 1865. xi, 19–394, (1) p. front. (port.), illus. 22cm.       CSmH NN  **56**
"Errata," (1) p. Coulter 372. For the points of two issues, see Midland notes, no 80.

**Wulsin, Lucien   –1912.**
Roster of surviving members of the Fourth regiment Ohio volunteer cavalry, 1861–1865, with a brief historical sketch of the Regiment. . . . Cincinnati, Chas. H. Thomson, printer, 1891. 67 p. 22½cm.    NNC  **57**
"Preface" signed: Lucien Wulsin, Secretary 4th O.V.C. ass'n. Ryan 365. Contents: Historical sketch, 5–11; Chasing John Morgan in 1861–62 and the capture of Huntsville, Ala., by Captain W. E. Crane, 12–19; The Fourth Ohio cavalry in Kilpatrick's raid around Atlanta, by Lucien Wulsin, 20–32; A march from Cincinnati to Nashville, by Colonel John Kennett, 32–42; A sketch of the Selma campaign, by Major-General Eli Long, 43–51.

—— The story of the Fourth regiment Ohio veteran volunteer cavalry, from the organization of the Regiment, August, 1861, to its fiftieth anniversary, August, 1911, based on the book of 1890, by Lucien Wulsin. Revised, corrected and edited, by Miss Eleanor N. Adams. . . . Cincinnati, 1912. 216 p. ports., plates (ports.). 25cm.    IHi OHi  **58**
Unit roster [157]–216.

## 5TH CAVALRY

*Organized: September to November 1861.*

*Mustered out: October 30, 1865.*

*Official roster* XI 239–308, 771–5.

*Ohio in the war* 775–87.

**Fanning, Thomas W**
The adventures of a volunteer, by a non-commissioned officer. Cincinnati, P. C. Browne, printer, 1863. 94 p. 18cm.    DLC  **59**
Copyright by T. W. Fanning. Republished in 1865 with the author's later experiences in the 9th Ohio cavalry. (See Title 74).

**Heath, Thomas Tinsley**
Straws, paper read before the Ohio commandery of the Loyal legion, April 7, 1909, by Thomas Tinsley Heath, Colonel 5th O.V. cav. 12 p. 22½cm.    DLC  **60**
Ryan 350.

**Keyes, John R**
An interrupted cavalry charge. *BandG* II (1893) 141–2.    **61**

## 6TH CAVALRY

*Organized: October 7, 1861.*

*Mustered out: August 7, 1865.*

*Official roster* XI 309–66, 775–9.

*Ohio in the war* 788–94.

Report of the . . . annual reunion of the Sixth Ohio veteran volunteer cavalry association. . . . XXXI–XXXIV, 1896–1899 (DLC); XXXV, 1900 (NN); XXXVI, 1901 (DLC); XXXIX, 1904 (DLC); XL, 1905 (IHi); XLI–XLV, 1906–1910 (DLC); XLVI–XLIX, 1911–1914 (IHi); L, 1915 (DLC); LII, 1917 (IHi).    **62**
1915 has title: Souvenir fiftieth annual reunion of the Sixth Ohio veteran volunteer cavalry association . . . 150 p.

**Roberts, John N**
Reminiscences of the Civil war, by Major J. N. Roberts. [1925] 55, (1) p. front. (port.). 21cm.    IHi  **63**

**Rockwell, Alphonso David, 1840–1933.**
Rambling recollections, an autobiography, by A. D. Rockwell, M.D. New York, Paul B. Hober, 1920. 332 p. plates (illus., ports.). 23cm.    NN  **64**
Civil war 112–75. Mustered in 85th Ohio infantry, June 4, 1862; mustered out, September 27, 1862; appointed Assistant surgeon 6th Ohio cavalry, April 18, 1864; mustered out, August 7, 1865.

—— A ride with Sheridan. *Magazine of American history* XIV (New York 1885) 481–500.    **64A**

—— With Sheridan's cavalry. 1901. *MOLLUS-NY* III 228–39.    **65**

## 7TH CAVALRY

*Organized: October 1862.*

*Mustered out: July 4, 1865.*

*Official roster* XI 366–402, 780–5.

*Ohio in the war* 795–803.

*7th Cavalry, continued*

Allen, Theodore Frelinghuysen, 1842–
In pursuit of John Morgan, by Theodore F.
Allen, late Captain Seventh Ohio cavalry. 1901.
*MOLLUS-Ohio* v 223–42. **66**

—— The last battle of the Civil war. *JUSCA*
xviii (1908) 785–6. **67**

—— Six hundred miles of fried chicken.
*JUSCA* xii (1899) 162–75. **68**

—— The "underground railroad" and the
"grapevine telegraph," an escaping prisoner's
experience, 1863. *MOLLUS-Ohio* vi 147–67.
**69**

Mitchell, Charles D
Field notes of the Selma campaign, by
Charles D. Mitchell, First Lieutenant and
Adjutant Seventh Ohio cavalry. *MOLLUS-
Ohio* vi 175–94. **70**

—— The Sanders raid into East Tennessee,
June, 1863. *MOLLUS-Ohio* vi 238–51. **71**

Rankin, Richard C
History of the Seventh Ohio volunteer cav-
alry, written by Captain R. C. Rankin. Ripley,
J. C. Newcomb, printer, 1881. 29 p. 23cm.
DLC NHi NN **72**
Title from cover. Ryan 588.

### 8TH CAVALRY

*44th regiment of infantry designated 8th
regiment of cavalry: January 4, 1864.
Mustered out: July 30, 1865.
Official roster* xi 403–58, 875–8.
*Ohio in the war* 804–07.

### 9TH CAVALRY

*Organized: 1863.
Mustered out: July 20, 1865.
Official roster* xi 459–501, 788–92.
*Ohio in the war* 808–13.

Bates, Ralph Orr, 1847–1909.
Billy and Dick from Andersonville prison to
the White house, by Ralph O. Bates (Billy).
. . . Santa Cruz, Cal., Press Sentinel pub. co.,
1910. 99, (3) p. front. (illus.), illus., plate
(port.). 19½cm. DLC **73**
c1910 by Rozella E. Bates.

Fanning, Thomas W
The hairbreadth escapes and humerous [sic]
adventures of a volunteer in the cavalry serv-
ice, by one of them. . . . Cincinnati, P. C.
Browne, prt., 1865. 200 p. 21½cm.
DLC **74**

Part I was published in 1863 and concerns the
author's experiences in the 5th Ohio cavalry, see Title
59. Ryan 219.

Hamilton, William Douglas, 1832–
In at the death, or the last shot at the Confederacy, by W. D. Hamilton, Brevet Brigadier-General. *MOLLUS-Ohio* vi 287–95. **75**

—— Recollections of a cavalryman of the
Civil war after fifty years, 1861–1865, by William Douglas Hamilton. Columbus, F. J. Heer
print. co., 1915. xvi, 309 p. plates (ports.).
18cm. DLC NN **76**
Roster of officers 9th Ohio cavalry, 69–80.

McKeever, Elliott Bushfield, 1845–1928.
He rode with Sherman from Atlanta to the
sea. Aberdeen, S. D., McKeever press, 1947.
31 p. mounted port. 23cm. OHi **77**
On cover: He rode with Sherman from Atlanta to
the sea, Elliott Bushfield McKeever, 1863–1865.

### 10TH CAVALRY

*Organized: October 1862.
Mustered out: July 24, 1865.
Official roster* xi 503–45, 792–8.
*Ohio in the war* 814–17.

Smith, Frank, 1847–
A Maine boy in the Tenth Ohio cavalry.
*Maine bugle* campaign iv (1897) 11–21. port.
**78**

### 11TH CAVALRY

*Organization commenced as 7th regiment
of cavalry, October 1861.
Consolidated with 6th regiment of cavalry
as a battalion of four companies, December 1, 1861. Battalion permanently detached from 6th regiment of cavalry and
designated 1st independent battalion of
cavalry. Designated 11th regiment of cavalry, July 1863.
Mustered out: 1st battalion, April 1, 1865;
remaining battalions, July 14, 1866.
Official roster* xi 547–82, 798–800.
*Ohio in the war* 818–21.

Crawford, Lewis Fernando, 1870–
Rekindling camp fires, the exploits of Ben
Arnold (Connor) (Wa-si-cu Tam-a-he-ca), an
authentic narrative of sixty years in the old
West . . . by Lewis F. Crawford. Bismarck,
N. D., Capital Book co. [1926] 324 p. front.
(port.), plates (illus., map). 21cm.
NN **78A**
In the narrative, the subject of the biography is
addressed as "Monroe." A Benjamin Monroe was
mustered in the 39th Ohio infantry, August 13, 1861;
discharged for disability, April 5, 1862; mustered in
39th Ohio infantry, August 18, 1862; deserted, No-

vember 5, 1862; mustered in 11th Ohio cavalry, July 18, 1863; deserted——? Civil war 1–77.

Hull, Lewis Byram, 1841–1902.
Soldiering on the high plains, the diary . . . 1864–1866. Edited by Mya E. Hull. *Kansas historical quarterly* vii (1938) 3–53. **79**

Spring, Agnes (Wright), 1894–
Caspar Collins, the life and exploits of an Indian fighter, by Agnes Wright Spring. With a foreword by Maj. Gen. Hugh L. Scott. Together with Caspar Collins' letters and drawings, and various photographs and documents connected with his career. New York, Columbia University press, 1927. 187 p. plates (facs., illus., ports.). 24cm. NN **79A**
The narrative is also concerned with William Oliver Collins, Colonel of the 11th Ohio cavalry.

## 12TH CAVALRY

*Mustered in: November 24, 1863.*

*Mustered out: November 14, 1865.*

*Official roster* xi 583–623, 800–04.

*Ohio in the war* 822–4.

Minutes of the 34th annual reunion of the 12th O.V.C. association, held in Memorial building, Columbus, O., September 9, 1919. 15 p. 17½cm. MnHi **80**
Title from cover.

Banks, Joseph, 1842–1912.
Memorandum of a raid through the Southern states in 1865. *Georgia historical quarterly* xxvi (1942) 291–307. **80A**

Mason, Frank Holcomb, 1840–1916.
General Stoneman's last campaign and the pursuit of Jefferson Davis, by Frank H. Mason, late Captain Twelfth Ohio volunteer cavalry. 1888. *MOLLUS-Ohio* iii 21–43. plate (map). **81**

—— The Twelfth Ohio cavalry, a record of its organization and services in the War of the rebellion, together with a complete roster of the Regiment, by F. H. Mason, late Captain Squadron "L." Cleveland, Nevin's print. house, 1871. 124, (1), 43 p. 22½cm. NHi **82**
Unit roster 43 p. This section has its own title page. The "Note" accompanying the roster, (1) p. Ryan 452.

Thomson, Archibald H
The last blood shed in the Civil war, by Archibald H. Thomson, Captain Twelfth Ohio. *MOLLUS-Ohio* vi 63–70. **83**

## 13TH CAVALRY

*Organized by a consolidation of 4th and 5th battalions of cavalry and mustered in: May 5, 1864.*

*Mustered out: August 10, 1865.*

*Official roster* xi 625–67, 804–06.

*Ohio in the war* 825–7.

Aston, Howard
History and roster of the Fourth and Fifth independent battalions and Thirteenth regiment Ohio cavalry volunteers, their battles and skirmishes, roster of the dead, by Howard Aston, Orderly Sergt. and First Lieut. Co. F. Columbus, Press of Fred J. Heer, 1902. 111, 65 p. plates (ports.). 19½cm.
DLC NN **84**
Unit roster: 5th battalion, 66–72; 13th cavalry (survivors), 73–85: 4th battalion (survivors), 86–91. Ryan 35. "With Sheridan from Petersburg to Appomattox," by Colonel Stephen R. Clark, 1–25, second pagination.

Harvey, Marshall Spencer, 1845–
Recollections of 1864–5 after forty years, written by M. S. Harvey, Co. F, 13th Ohio vol. cav. . . . [Columbus, 1904] 28 p. front. (port.). 23cm. DLC **85**

### 4TH BATTALION OF CAVALRY

*Organized: August 3 to September 21, 1863.*

*Mustered out: February 15 to March 14, 1864.*

*Official roster* xi 669–81, 806–07.

See Title 84.

### 5TH BATTALION OF CAVALRY

*Organized: July 9 to September 2, 1863.*

*Mustered out: February 15, 1864.*

*Official roster* xi 683–93, 807.

See Title 84.

### 3RD COMPANY OF CAVALRY

*Mustered in: State service, July 4, 1861; Federal service, August 16, 1861.*

*Mustered out: May 22, 1865.*

*Official roster* xi 695–700, 807.

### 4TH COMPANY OF CAVALRY

*Mustered in: July 9, 1861.*

*Mustered out: May 28, 1865.*

*Official roster* xi 701–08, 808.

### UNION LIGHT GUARD

*Mustered in: December 17, 1863.*

*Mustered out: September 9, 1865.*

*Official roster* xi 739–43, 811.

*Ohio in the war* 923.

*Union Light Guard, continued*

Ashmun, George C
Recollections of a peculiar service, by
George C. Ashmun, late Second Lieutenant
Seventh independent troop O.V.C. 1888.
*MOLLUS-Ohio* ii 277–92.                **86**

—— —— *Magazine of history* iii (New York
1906) 248–54.                           **86A**

McBride, Robert Wesley, 1842–1926.
. . . Lincoln's body guard, the Union light
guard of Ohio, with some personal recollec-
tions of Abraham Lincoln, by Robert W. Mc-
Bride, late Corporal. Indianapolis, Edward J.
Hecker, printer, 1911. 39 p. 24cm.
                           DLC NHi NN      **87**
At head of title: Indiana historical society publi-
cations, volume V, number 1. Unit roster, 9–14.
Ryan 461.

Stimmel, Smith
Experiences as a member of President Lincoln's body guard, 1863–65. *North Dakota historical quarterly* i No 2 (1926/27) 7–33.
                                         **87A**

### McLAUGHLIN'S SQUADRON OF CAVALRY

*Organized: October to November 1861.*
*Consolidated with Company C, 5th regi-
ment of cavalry: July 28, 1865.*
*Official roster* xi 709–19, 808–10.
*Ohio in the war* 925–6.

See Title 19.

### INFANTRY *

### FULLER'S BRIGADE

**27th, 39th, 43rd, and 63rd regiments
of infantry.**

Fuller's Ohio brigade, 27th 39th, 43rd, and
63rd regiments Ohio volunteer infantry list of
survivors, with post-office addresses so far as
known to the Secretary. January 1, 1891. Oscar
Sheppard, late Sergeant-Major 27th O.V.V.I.,
Secretary. Dayton, Press of United Brethren
pub. house [1891] 26 p. 19cm.      NHi     **88**

Report of proceedings of Ohio brigade reunion,
including addresses, correspondence, etc., held

---

* In the Ohio infantry regiments, numbers 1–22 were
used to designate regiments of three months' enlistment, and used again to designate regiments of three
years' enlistment. *Ohio in the war* reports on the three
month and three year regiments of each number in a
continuous narrative. The page references to *Ohio in
the war* are given under the three month regiments.

at Columbus, Ohio, October 3 and 4, 1878.
Mt. Vernon, Chase & Cassil, 1879. 66 p. 23cm.
                           DLC NHi      **89**

Smith, Charles H        1837–
The history of Fuller's Ohio brigade, its
great march, with roster, portraits, battle maps
and biographies, by Charles H. Smith, Major
27th Ohio regiment. Cleveland [Press of A. J.
Watt] 1909. 623 p. illus., maps, ports. 25cm.
                           DLC NN       **90**
Unit roster: 27th regiment, [451]–86; 39th regiment, [487]–535; 43rd regiment, [537]–82; 63rd regiment, [583]–623. Ryan 775.

For other references on the Ohio brigade,
see the entries under the regiments that formed
the brigade.

### 1ST INFANTRY

*Organized: April 29, 1861.* (3 months)
*Mustered out: August 1 to 16, 1861.*
*Official roster* i 3–18, 747.
*Ohio in the war* 13–20.
*Organized: August 5 to October 30, 1861.*
(3 years)
*Mustered out: September 24 to October
14, 1864.*
*Official roster* ii 1–30, 725–8.

Kern, Albert
History of the First regiment Ohio volunteer
infantry in the Civil war, 1861–1865, compiled
and edited by Albert Kern. Dayton, 1918. 62 p.
2 plates (illus.). 23½cm.        OHi      **91**
Unit roster 35–62.

Mellor, Albert
Experiences in Southern military prisons, by
Albert Mellor, Company H, First Ohio. In
G.A.R. war papers, papers read before Fred C.
Jones post, no. 401, Department of Ohio,
G.A.R. (1891) 264–83.                    **92**

### 2ND INFANTRY

*Organized: April 29, 1861.* (3 months)
*Mustered out: July 31, 1861.*
*Official roster* i 19–36, 747–8.
*Ohio in the war* 21–5.
*Organized: July 17 to September 20, 1861.*
(3 years)
*Mustered out: October 10, 1864.*
*Official roster* ii 31–59, 728–31.

Finch, George Mayhew
The boys of '61, by George M. Finch, late
Lieutenant-Colonel one hundred and thirty-
seventh Ohio. In G.A.R. war papers, papers

read before Fred C. Jones post, no. 401, Department of Ohio, G.A.R. (1891) 237–63.   **93**

The author served as Captain Company A, 2nd Ohio.

—— In the beginning, read before the Ohio commandery of the Loyal legion of the United States, October 1, 1884, by George M. Finch, Cincinnati, Peter G. Thomson, 1884. 14 p. 21½cm.                    DLC   **93A**

Also published as *MOLLUS-Ohio* i 218–32.

McComas, William R.
Ohio troops at Bull run, by Maj. W. R. McComas. G.A.R. war papers, papers read before the Fred C. Jones Post, no. 401, Department of Ohio, G.A.R. (1891) 190–202.       **94**

McCook, Anson George, 1835–1917.
Address before the Society of the Army of the Cumberland at their eleventh reunion, Washington, November 19, 1879, by Anson G. McCook. Cincinnati, Press of Robert Clarke & co., 1879. 16 p. 22½cm. DLC WHi   **95**

## 3RD INFANTRY

*Organized: April 27, 1861.* (3 months)
*Mustered out: August 2, 1861.*
*Official roster* i 37–58, 748.
*Ohio in the war* 26–33.
*Organized: June 20, 1861.* (3 years)
*Mustered out: June 21, 1864.*
*Official roster* ii 60–87, 731–2.

Roster of Third Ohio volunteer infantry, 1889. Independence, Kan., Tribune print. house, 1889. 27 p. 16½cm.            OHi   **96**

A war incident. *BandG* i (1893) 301.   **97**

Beatty, John, 1828–1914.
The citizen-soldier; or, memories of a volunteer, by John Beatty. Cincinnati, Wilstach, Baldwin & co., 1879. vii, [9]–401 p. 19½cm.
NN   **98**

"Capture, imprisonment, and escape, by General Harrison C. Hobart, of Milwaukee, Wisconsin," [375]–98. Ryan 46.

—— Memoirs of a volunteer, 1861–1863, by John Beatty. Edited by Harvey S. Ford. Introduction by Lloyd Lewis. Illustrations by Howard W. Willard. New York, W. W. Norton & co. [1946] 317 p. illus., plate (double map). 23cm.                    DLC NN   **99**

—— A regiment in search of a battle, by John Beatty, late Brigadier-General. *MOLLUS-Ohio* iii 422–52.               **100**

Keifer, Joseph Warren, 1836–1932.
The battle of Rich mountain and some incidents. Paper read before the Ohio command-

ery of the Loyal legion, December 6th, 1911, by J. Warren Keifer, Major General. 24 p. 22cm.                    DLC NN   **101**

"I was then Major of the Third Ohio infantry."

—— Slavery and four years of war, a political history of slavery in the United States, together with a narrative of the campaigns and battles of the Civil war in which the author took part, 1861–1865, by Joseph Warren Keifer. New York, G. P. Putnam's & Sons, 1900. 2 v. plates (illus., maps, ports.). 23½cm.
NN WHi   **101A**

3rd Ohio infantry, April 27, 1861; 110th Ohio infantry, September 30, 1862; Brevet Brigadier General, October 19, 1864; Brevet Major General, April 9, 1865.

## 4TH INFANTRY

*Organized: May 4, 1861.* (3 months)
*Mustered out: August 18–24, 1861.*
*Official roster* i 59–82, 748.
*Ohio in the war* 34–9.
*Organized: June 4, 1861.* (3 years)
*Mustered out: June 21, 1864.*
*Official roster* ii 88–120, 732–4.

Jones, John Sills,        –1903.
From North Ana to Cold harbor, by John S. Jones, late Brevet Brigadier-General. 1893. *MOLLUS-Ohio* iv 147–58.       **102**

Kepler, William, 1841/42–
History of the three months' and three years' service, from April 16th, 1861, to June 22d, 1864, of the Fourth regiment Ohio volunteer infantry in the War for the Union, by Wm. Kepler, Private of Company C. Cleveland, Leader print. co., 1886. 287 p. plates (illus., maps, ports.). 23cm.  DLC NHi NN   **103**

Unit roster: three months' service, [225]–36; three years' service [237]–87. Ryan 414.

## 5TH INFANTRY

*Organized: April 29 to May 9, 1861.*
(3 months)
*Mustered out: August 24 to September 5, 1861.*
*Official roster* i 83–104, 748.
*Ohio in the war* 40–7.
*Organized: June 21, 1861.* (3 years)
*Mustered out: July 26, 1865.*
*Official roster* ii 121–70, 734–5.

Gaul, Joseph L
Personal memorandum of Joseph L. Gaul Co. "C" 5th Ohio vol. infy. *Historical and philosophical society of Ohio publications* (1926) 53–6.               **104**

*5th Infantry, continued*

Kilpatrick, Robert Lang
The Fifth Ohio infantry at Reseca. 1893.
*MOLLUS-Ohio* iv 246–54.                    **105**

Paver, John M          1839–
What I saw from 1861 to 1864, personal
recollections of John M. Paver, 1st Lieutenant
Company C, and R.Q.M. 5th Ohio vol. infantry. [Indianapolis, Scott-Miller co., 1906]
100 p. 2 plates (ports.). 24cm.
    Ryan 548.                DLC NN    **106**

Ray, George B          1838?–
Journal of George B. Ray, Musician, Co.
"H," 5th Ohio vol. infantry. Enlisted April
19th 1861; discharged April 3d 1863. *Historical and philosophical society of Ohio publications* (1926) 57–73.              **107**

### 6TH INFANTRY

*Organized: April 27, 1861.* (3 months)
*Mustered out: August 21, 1861.*
*Official roster* i 105–29, 748.
*Ohio in the war* 48–53.
*Organized: June 18, 1861.* (3 years)
*Mustered out: July 23, 1864.*
*Official roster* ii 171–99, 736–7.

Anderson, Nicholas Longworth, 1838–1892.
The letters and journals of General Nicholas
Longworth Anderson, Harvard, Civil war,
Washington, 1854–1892. Edited by Isabel
Anderson (Mrs. Larz Anderson). New York,
Fleming H. Revell co. [1942] 320 p. front.
(port.). 22½cm.              MnHi NN    **108**

Cist, Henry Martyn, 1839–1902.
Cincinnati with the war fever, 1861. *Magazine of American history* xiv (New York 1885)
138–47.                          **109**

Hannaford, Ebenezer, 1840–
In hospital after Stone river. *Harper's magazine* xxviii (1863/64) 260–5.      **110**

—— In the ranks at Stone river. *Harper's
magazine* xxvii (1863) 809–15.    **110A**

—— The story of a regiment, a history of the
campaigns, and associations in the field, of the
Sixth regiment Ohio volunteer infantry, by E.
Hannaford . . . Published by the author. Cincinnati [Stereotyped at the Franklin type
foundry] 1868. xvi, [17]–622 p. fold. map.
21½cm.                    DLC NN    **110B**
    Unit roster: Independent Guthrie greys, 611–13;
Sixth Ohio (three-years' term), 613–22. Coulter 211.
Ryan 324.

Jones, Frank Johnston, 1838–
Personal recollections and experience of a
soldier during the War of the rebellion, by
Frank J. Jones Brevet Major. *MOLLUS-Ohio*
vi 111–31.                       **111**

—— Personal recollections of some of the
Generals in our army during the Civil war, a
paper read before the Ohio commandery of
the Loyal legion, December 3, 1913. 15 p.
21½cm.                    DLC NN    **112**
    Title from cover.

Russell, Charles Butler
Kindling the fires of war, a paper read before the Ohio commandery of the Loyal legion,
by Captain Charles B. Russell, April 2, 1913.
7 p. 22cm.                DLC NHi    **113**

### 7TH INFANTRY

*Organized: April 22 to 30, 1861.*
(3 months)
*Mustered out: August 18–22, 1861.*
*Official roster* i 131–53, 748.
*Ohio in the war* 54–63.
*Organized: July 16, 1861.* (3 years)
*Mustered out: July 6, 1864.*
*Official roster* ii 200–34, 737–8.

Rooster record, official organ Seventh regiment
O.V.I. association. 1887–92. 23½cm.
    v 1, no 1–6; August 17–23, 1887.  OHi    **114**
    v 2, no 1–6; August 15–21, 1888.
    v 5, no 1: December 1892.

Cross, Judson N
The campaign of West Virginia of 1861, by
Captain Judson N. Cross. *MOLLUS-Minn* ii
146–72.                          **115**

Hopkins, Marcus S
"The days of Sixty-three," poem, by Brevet
Major Marcus S. Hopkins. 1894. 17 p. *MOL-
LUS-DC* no 18.                   **116**

Shurtleff, Giles Waldo
A year with the Rebels, by G. W. Shurtleff,
late Brevet Brigadier-General. 1895. *MOL-
LUS-Ohio* iv 388–410.            **117**

Sterling, James T
Personal experiences of the early days of
1861, a paper read before the Michigan commandery of the Military order of the loyal
legion of the U.S. Detroit, Winn&Hammond,
printers, 1892. 13 p. 21½cm.    DLC    **118**
    Also published as *MOLLUS-Mich* i 18.

Wilder, Theodore
The history of Company C, Seventh regiment, O.V.I., by Theodore Wilder. Oberlin, [. B. T. Marsh, printer, 1866. 83 p. 18½cm.
DLC NN  **119**
Unit roster [44]–82. Ryan 875.

Wilson, Lawrence, 1842–
Itinerary of the Seventh Ohio volunteer infantry, 1861–1864, with roster, portraits and biographies. Edited and compiled by Lawrence Wilson, First Sergeant Company D. Assisted by the Historical committee of the Regimental association. New York, Neale pub. co., 1907. 652 p. plates (illus., maps, ports.). 22½cm.
DLC NN  **120**
Unit roster 521–627. "Biographical sketches, partly compiled by Capt. George A. McKay," [363]–484. Ryan 881.

Wood, George L
The Seventh regiment, a record, by Major George L. Wood. New York, James Miller, 1865. 304 p. 19½cm.
DLC NN  **121**
Coulter 483. Ryan 892. Also published New York, James Miller, 1865, with title Famous deeds by American heroes, a record of events from Sumter to Lookout mountain . . . and printed from the same plates.

## 8TH INFANTRY

*Organized: April 24 to 30, 1861. (3 months)*

*Mustered out: August 18 to 22, 1861.*

*Official roster* i 155–75.

*Ohio in the war* 64–9.

*Organized: June 22, 1861. (3 years)*

*Mustered out: July 13, 1864.*

*Official roster* ii 236–62, 739–40.

Daggett, George Henry
Those whom you left behind you. 1901. MOLLUS-Minn v 332–64.  **122**

Galwey, Thomas Francis De Burgh, 1846–1913.
At the battle of Antietam with the Eighth Ohio infantry, read by First Lieutenant Thomas F. De Burgh Galwey. 1897. MOLLUS-NY iii 70–85.  **123**

—— The valiant hours, by Thomas Francis Galwey, Eighth Ohio volunteer infantry. Narrative of "Captain Brevet," an Irish-American in the Army of the Potomac. Edited by Colonel W. S. Nye. Harrisburg, Stackpole co. [1961] 362 p. maps and plans. 23cm.  NN  **123A**
"Captain Brevet, an honorary title, by Colonel Geoffrey Galway," 238–57.

Dickerson, Azor H
Antietam, a reminiscence. BandG ii (1893) 43–7.  **124**

—— Antietam-Sharpsburg, 1862. *BandG* iv (1894) 125–34. illus.  **125**

Sawyer, Franklin,  –1892.
The Eighth Ohio at Gettysburg, address of General Franklin Sawyer. Re-union at Columbus, Ohio, 1888. Roster of survivors. Published by the Regimental association. Washington, D. C., E. J. Gray, printer, 1889. 15 p. 1 illus., 1 port. 22½cm.  OHi  **126**
Ryan 274.

—— A military history of the 8th regiment Ohio vol. inf'y, its battles, marches and army movements, by Franklin Sawyer, Lieut-Col. of the Regiment. Edited by Geo. A. Groot, Chairman pub. com. Cleveland, Fairbanks & co., printers, 1881. 260 p. front. (port.). 22½cm.  DLC NN  **127**
Unit roster: three months and three years, [185]–240; 3 months men, [241]–60. Ryan 723.

—— Report of the Eighth Ohio regiment. *Firelands pioneer* xii (Norwalk 1876) 77–83.  **128**

## 9TH INFANTRY

*Organized: May 8, 1861. (3 months)*

*Mustered out: August 4, 1861.*

*Official roster* i 177–205.

*Ohio in the war* 70–5.

*Organized: May to June 13, 1861. (3 years)*

*Mustered out: June 7, 1864.*

*Official roster* ii 263–91, 741–2.

Constitution des neunten Regiments Ohio vol. infanterie, von Cincinnati, Ohio, nebst historischen Anhang. Cincinnati, Druck von Geo. Beinert, 1883. 24 p. 14½cm.  NN  **129**
"Anhang. geschichtliche Momente," 11–24, a chronological account of the regiment.

Grebner, Constantin
"Die Neuner," eine Schilderung der Kriegsjahre des 9ten Regiments Ohio vol. Infanterie, vom 17, April 1861 bis 7 June 1864. Mit einer Einleitung von Oberst Gustav Tafel. Cincinnati, Druck von S. Rosenthal & co., 1897. ix, [11]–290, (1) p. front. (5 ports.), illus. 20cm.  DLC NN  **130**
"Der wohlverdiente Dank für seine Arbeit sei dem Verfasser . . . Constantin Grebner." Unit roster 203–46. Coulter 441. On cover: Erstes deutsches Regiment von Ohio. Ryan 796/7.

Wittke, Carl Frederick, 1892–
The Ninth Ohio volunteers, a page from the Civil war record of the German Turners of Ohio, by Carl Wittke. . . . Columbus, F. J. Heer print. co., 1926. 18 p. port. 23cm.  DLC  **132**
"Reprinted from the Ohio archaeological and historical quarterly of April 1926."

See also Title In 108.

## 10TH INFANTRY

*Organized: May 1–12, 1861.* (3 months)
*Mustered out: August 20–23, 1861.*
*Official roster* I 207–33.
*Ohio in the war* 76–80.
*Organized: June 4, 1861.* (3 years)
*Mustered out: June 3, 1864.*
*Official roster* II 292–319, 742–3.

Pirtle, Alfred, 1837–1926.*
Stone river sketches, by Alfred Pirtle, First Lieutenant Tenth Ohio. *MOLLUS-Ohio* VI 95–110.                                    **133**

—— Three memorable days, a letter from Chattanooga, November, 1863. *MOLLUS-Ohio* VI 35–46.                        **134**

## 11TH INFANTRY

*Organized: April 26, 1861.* (3 months)
*Mustered out: August 1–28, 1861.*
*Official roster* I 235–54, 749.
*Ohio in the war* 81–6.
*Organized: June 20, 1861.* (3 years)
*Mustered out: June 11, 1864.*
*Official roster* II 320–50, 743–5.

Proceedings of the . . . annual reunion . . . and roster Eleventh Ohio infantry reunion association. I/II, 1869/1870 (DNW); XII–XIII, 1883, 1885 (NHi); XV/XVI–XXXI/XXXII, 1887/1888– 1903/1904 (NHi); XXXIII/XXXIV–XLVI/XLVIII, 1905/1906–1918/1920 (DLC).          **135**

Horton, Joshua H
A history of the Eleventh regiment (Ohio volunteer infantry), containing the military record, so far as it is possible to obtain it, of each officer and enlisted man of the command, a list of deaths, an account of the veterans, incidents of the field and camp, names of the three months' volunteers, compiled from the official records, by Horton & Teverbaugh. Dayton, W. J. Shuey, printer, 1866. xv, [17]–287, (1) p. 21½cm.          DLC NN   **136**
Unit roster: Three months' service, 279–87; Three years' service, [117]–202. Coulter 241. Ryan 366.

Lyle, William W          1825–
Lights and shadows of army life; or, pen pictures from the battlefield, the camp, and the hospital, by Rev. W. W. Lyle, Chaplain

* Biographical: A glimpse of Alfred Pirtle, 1837–1926, by Otto A. Rother. *Filson club historical quarterly* XI (1937) 211–17. The article includes a letter of Pirtle dated, September 26, 1863.

Eleventh regiment, O.V.I. Cincinnati, R. W. Carroll & co., 1865. xii, [9]–403 p. 19½cm.
                                                    NN   **137**
List of officers and enlisted killed in action, 392– 403. DLC has second edition 1865, a reprint. Ryan 448.

Scott, William Forse, 1843–1933.
Philander P. Lane, Colonel of the volunteers in the Civil war, Eleventh Ohio infantry, by William Forse Scott. Privately printed. [New York] 1920. xx, 296 p. plates (3 fold. maps, 2 ports.). 24cm.                         NN   **138**

## 12TH INFANTRY

*Organized: April 22 to May 4, 1861.*
(3 months)
*Mustered out: July 30 to August 23, 1861.*
*Official roster* I 255–76, 749.
*Ohio in the war* 87–90.
*Organized: June 19–29, 1861.* (3 years)
*Mustered out: July 11, 1864.*
*Official roster* II 351–82, 745–7.

Owens, Ira S
Twelfth regiment O.V.I. In his Greene county soldiers in the late war (1884) 126–39.   **139**

Ward, James E          D
Twelfth Ohio volunteer inf., by J. E. D. Ward. Ripley, 1864. 88 p. 21½cm.
Ryan 861.                                  NHi   **140**

Wilson, Robert Bruce
Bull run bridge, by Robert Bruce Wilson, Lieutenant Twelfth Ohio volunteer infantry. In G.A.R. war papers, papers read before Fred C. Jones post, no. 401, Department of Ohio, G.A.R. (1891) 35–48.                   **141**

—— The Dublin raid, by Capt. R. B. Wilson, Twelfth Ohio. In G.A.R. war papers, papers read before Fred C. Jones post no. 401 Department of Ohio, G.A.R. (1891) 92–120.   **142**

## 13TH INFANTRY

*Organized: April 24 to May 4, 1861.*
(3 months)
*Mustered out: August 14–25, 1861.*
*Official roster* I 277–96, 749.
*Ohio in the war* 91–100.
*Organized: June 12–26, 1861.* (3 years)
*Mustered out: December 5, 1865.*
*Official roster* II 383–413, 747–50.

Leonard, Anthony
With the 13th Ohio. In National tribune scrap book III 120–2.                     **142A**

## 14TH INFANTRY

*Organized: April 25, 1861.* (3 months)
*Mustered out: August 13, 1861.*
*Official roster* I 297–314, 749.
*Ohio in the war* 101–08.
*Organized: August 14 to September 5,*
*1861.* (3 years)
*Mustered out: July 11, 1865.*
*Official roster* II 414–52, 751–7.

Chase, John A        1831/32–
History of the Fourteenth Ohio regiment,
O.V.V.I., from the beginning of the war in
1861 to its close in 1865, compiled and written
by Col. J. A. Chase. Toledo [St. John print.
house] 1881. 130 p. front. (port.). 17½cm.
Unit roster 92–128. Ryan 11. DLC NN   **143**

## 15TH INFANTRY

*Organized: April 27, 1861.* (3 months)
*Mustered out: August 27 to 30, 1861.*
*Official roster* I 315–32, 750.
*Ohio in the war* 109–14.
*Organized: September 1861.* (3 years)
*Mustered out: November 21, 1865.*
*Official roster* II 453–506, 758–64.

Fifteenth Ohio veteran volunteers report of
. . . annual reunion. . . . 1883–1884; XIV–XV,
1890–1891; XXIII, 1898; XXXIV–XXXVII, 1908–
1911.                          OHi    **144**
1883 has title: Constitution of the Fifteenth Ohio
infantry regimental association together with the proceedings of the annual reunion. . . .

Roster of the surviving members of the Fifteenth Ohio veteran volunteer infantry in the
war of 1861–1865. [Columbus, Hann & Adair,
1909] 24 p. 15cm.              OHi    **145**
On cover: Columbus, Ohio, July 20, 1909. Ryan
716.

Cope, Alexis, 1841–1898.
The Fifteenth Ohio volunteers and its campaigns, war of 1861–5, by Alexis Cope. Published by the author. Columbus [Press of the
Edward T. Miller co.] 1916. 796, (1) p. plates
(ports.). 22cm.              DLC NN   **146**
"Corrections," (1) p.

Glover, Amos, 1832–1890.
Diary of Amos Glover. Edited by Harry J.
Carman. *OHQ* XLIV (1935) 258–72.   **147**

McConnell, William
Diary of William McConnell, Private Company I, 15th O.V.V.I., 1st brigade, 3rd div., 4th
army corps, Army of the Cumberland, from
September 16th, 1861, to August 2nd, 1865.

. . . Tiro, Chas. McConnell [1899] 198 p. front.
(port.), ports. 23½cm.        NHi    **148**
On cover: Also a brief record of Auburn township
and Tiro, Ohio, 1899. Soldiers from Auburn township, 151–9.

Ross, Randal
A day's march. *United States service maga-*
*zine* III (1865) 180–3.              **148A**

—— [A letter from San Antonio de Bexar,
October 10, 1865] *United States service maga-*
*zine* V (1866) 172–7.                **148B**

Stewart, Robert B
The battle of Nashville. *BandG* III (1894)
18–20.                                **149**

—— The battle of Stone river, as seen by one
who was there. *BandG* V (1895) 10–14. 1 illus.,
port.                                 **150**

## 16TH INFANTRY

*Organized: May 3, 1861.* (3 months)
*Mustered out: August 18, 1861.*
*Official roster* I 333–50, 750.
*Ohio in the war* 115–19.
*Organized: September 23 to December 2,*
*1861.* (3 years)
*Mustered out: October 31, 1864.*
*Official roster* II 507–34, 765–70.

Proceedings of eleven reunions, held by the
16th regiment, O.V.I., including roll of honor,
roster of the survivors of the Regiment, statistics . . . compiled by Enos Pierson. [Millers-
burg, Republican press] 1887. 172, (2) p.
music, ports. 22½cm.          NN     **151**

Reunion at . . . 16th reg't O.V.I. XII (1887)
[177]–86; XIII (1888) [191]–200 XXII/XXIII
(1897–1898) [313]–24.         NHi    **152**
Pagination continues from Title 151.

Carr, Thomas David, 1846–1879.
Life and confession of Thomas D. Carr, who
was hung at St. Clairsville, Ohio, Thursday,
March 24, 1870, for the murder of Louisa C.
Fox. . . . St. Clairsville, J. H. Heaton & co.,
1870. 46 p. port. on t.p. 21cm. DLC   **152A**

Fleischmann, S       M
The memorial tablet published under the
auspices of Buckley post, No. 12, G.A.R., by
S. M. Fleischmann. [Akron, Beacon pub. co.,
printers] 1883. 66 p. 2 plates (ports.). 15½cm.
                             DLC NHi  **153**
Includes biography of Mrs Catherine Whitacre
Brashear, matron of the 16th Ohio, 1861–1863, and
poems by the author. Ryan 228.

## 17TH INFANTRY

*Organized: April 27, 1861.* (3 months).
*Mustered out: August 15, 1861.*
*Official roster* I 351–68, 750.
*Ohio in the war* 120–5.
*Organized: August 30, 1861.* (3 years)
*Mustered out: July 16, 1865.*
*Official roster* II 535–73, 770–4.

Minutes and roster of the 42nd annual reunion of the 17th O.V.V.I. association, Lancaster, Ohio, September 20th, 1922. [Lancaster, Eagle print, 1922] [15] p. 19½cm.   OHi   **154**

Develling, Charles Theodore
  . . . History of the Seventeenth regiment, First brigade, Third division, Fourteenth corps, Army of the Cumberland, War of the rebellion, compiled by C. T. Develling, Company B. Zanesville, E. R. Sullivan, printer, 1889. 143 p. illus. 26cm.       DLC NN   **155**
  At head of title: 1861   1865. Unit roster [17]–53. Ryan 196.

Hyde, Solon
  A captive of war, by Solon Hyde, hospital steward Seventeenth regiment Ohio volunteer infantry. New York, McClure, Phillips & co., 1900. 389 p. 19½cm.     DLC NHi   **156**
  Ryan 381.

Ward, Durbin, 1819–1886.
  The Army of the Cumberland, oration of.
. . . *Historical magazine* s2 III (Morrisania 1874) 1–6.       **157**

## 18TH INFANTRY

*Organized: May 29, 1861.* (3 months)
*Mustered out: August 28, 1861.*
*Official roster* I 369–87, 750.
*Ohio in the war* 126–31.
*Organized: August 16 to September 28, 1861.* (3 years)
*Mustered out: November 9, 1864.*
*Organized from veterans and recruits of 1st, 2nd, 24th, 35th, and 18th regiments of infantry: October 31, 1864.* (Veteran regiment)
*Mustered out: October 9, 1865.*
*Official roster* II 574–637, 775–80.

Grosvenor, Charles Henry, 1833–1917.
  Oration of General Charles H. Grosvenor before the Society of the Army of the Cumberland at its reunion in Milwaukee, September 20, 1882. Cincinnati, Press of Robert Clarke & co., 1883. 24 p. front. (port.). 22½cm.
                              DLC   **158**
See also Title 152A.

## 19TH INFANTRY

*Organized: May 29, 1861.* (3 months)
*Mustered out: August 18 to 30, 1861.*
*Official roster* I 389–406, 751.
*Ohio in the war* 132–8.
*Organized: September 25, 1861.* (3 years)
*Mustered out: October 24, 1865.*
*Official roster* II 638–82, 781–6.

Erb, William S     S
  Extract from "The battles of the 19th Ohio," by a late acting assistant Adjutant general. . . . Washington, D. C. Judd & Detweiler, printers, 1893. 48 p. 18½cm.     DLC   **159**
  On cover: The valley of death, the battle of Stone river. Ryan 209.

Manderson, Charles Frederick, 1837–1911.
  Address of General Charles F. Manderson, delivered at Chattanooga, Tenn., on September 18th, 1895, before the Society of the Army of the Cumberland. 28 p. 29½cm.
  Title from cover.         NHi   **160**

—— The twin seven-shooters, by Charles F. Manderson, late Colonel 19th Ohio. New York, F. Tennyson Neely [1902] v, [5]–54 p. plates (illus., ports.). 24½cm.     NN   **161**
  Ryan 449.

See also Title 63.

## 20TH INFANTRY

*Organized: May 15–27, 1861.* (3 months)
*Mustered out: August 18, 1861.*
*Official roster* I 407–24, 751.
*Ohio in the war* 139–45.
*Organized: August 19 to September 21, 1861.* (3 years)
*Mustered out: July 15, 1865.*
*Official roster* II 683–722, 786–93.

Adams, Robert Newton, 1835–1914.
  My first company, by Brev. Brig. Gen'l Robert N. Adams. 1905. *MOLLUS-Minn* VI 285–98.                **162**

Brown, Edwin Witherby, 1837–1925.
  Reminiscences of an Ohio volunteer, by Philip D. Jordan and Charles M. Thomas. *OHQ* XLVIII (1939) 304–23.     **163**

Downs, Edward C
  Four years a scout and spy, "General Bunker," one of Lieut. General Grant's most daring and successful scouts, being a narrative of the thrilling adventures, narrow escapes, noble daring, and amusing incidents in the experience of Corporal Ruggles during four years'

service as a scout and spy for the Federal army, embracing his services for twelve of the most distinguished Generals in the U. S. army, by E. C. Downs, Major of the Twentieth Ohio. Zanesville, Hugh Dunne, 1866. xii, 5–404 p. front. (port.), illus. 22½cm.       NHi       *164*
Coulter 131. Ryan 201. The official roster has Ruggles "on detached duty,"

—— The great American scout and spy, "General Bunker," a truthful and thrilling narrative of adventures and narrow escapes in the enemy's country, under orders from Generals Grant, Logan, McPherson, and other leading commanders. Third edition, revised. New York, Olmsted & Welwood, 1868. 400 p. plates (illus., ports.). 21cm.       NHi       *165*

—— —— New York, Olmsted & co., 1870. 400 p. plates (illus., ports.). 21cm.
A reprint of Title 165.       NN       *166*

—— Perils of scout-life; or, exploits and adventures of a government scout, by C. L. Ruggles (of the Twentieth Ohio volunteers). New York, M. L. Byrn, 1875. 399 p. plates (illus., ports.). 22cm.       NHi       *167*
Identical with Titles 165 and 166. An advertisement has been substituted for the "Certificates and endorsements" previously printed on p 400.

Dwight, Henry Otis, 1843–1917.
How we fight at Atlanta. *Harper's magazine* xxix (1864) 663–6.       *167A*

—— Recollections of a recruit, by Kenneth W. Duckett. *Museum echoes Ohio historical society* xxxiv (1961) 35–8. 1 illus.       *167B*
Based on the soldier's sketchbook and diary.

Force, Manning Ferguson, 1824–1899.
Personal recollections of the Vicksburg campaign, a paper read before the Ohio commandery of the Military order of the loyal legion of the United States. Cincinnati, Henry C. Sherick, 1885. 15 p. 21½cm.       DLC       *168*
"Addenda to the . . . " [errata] laid in. Also published in *MOLLUS-Ohio* i 293–309.

Oldroyd, Osborn Hamiltine, 1842–1930.
A soldier's story of the siege of Vicksburg, from the diary of Osborn H. Oldroyd, late Sergeant Co. E, 20th Ohio, with Confederate accounts from authentic sources and an introduction by Brevet Maj.-Gen. M. F. Force. Published for the author. Springfield, Ill. [H. W. Rokker, printer] 1885. viii, 200 p. illus., map, plan, ports. 24½cm. DLC NHi NN       *169*

Whittlesey, Charles, 1808–1886.
An episode of the rebellion. *Magazine of Western history* i (Cleveland 1885) 532–6.       *170*

—— Grant and Lee, an estimate. *Magazine of Western history* ii (Cleveland 1885) 434–40. 2 plates (ports.).       *171*

—— War memoranda. Cheat river to the Tennessee, 1861–1862, by Colonel Charles Whittlesey. Cleveland, W. W. Williams, 1884. 89 p. 5 plates (maps). 23cm.       DLC NN       *171A*
"Errata" slip inserted. "Major [Nathan] Bostwick's experience," 82–7; "Experience of Col. [Conrad] Garis" [168th Ohio] p 87–9.

Wood, David W
History of the 20th O.V.V.I. regiment and proceedings of the first reunion at Mt. Vernon, Ohio, April 6, 1876. Compiled and arranged for publication by D. W. Wood. Columbus, Paul & Thrall, printers, 1876. 70 p. 22½cm.
Ryan 890.       DLC NHi NN       *172*

## 21ST INFANTRY

*Organized: May 20 to 22, 1861.*
(3 months)
*Mustered out: August 12, 1861.*
*Official roster* i 425–42, 751–2.
*Ohio in the war* 146–52.
*Organized: September 19, 1861.* (3 years)
*Mustered out: July 25, 1865.*
*Official roster* iii 1–39, 699–709.

Adams, Jacob, 1842.
Diary of Jacob Adams, Private in Company F, 21st O.V.I. Columbus, F. J. Heer print. co., 1930. 99 p. front. (2 ports.). 23cm.
      DLC       *173*
"Reprinted from the Ohio archaeological and historical quarterly for October, 1929." "Foreword" signed by H. M. Povenmire.

Canfield, Silas S
History of the 21st regiment Ohio volunteer infantry, in the War of the rebellion, by Captain S. S. Canfield. Toledo, Vrooman, Anderson & Bateman, printers, 1893. 192, (1), 47 p. plates (ports.). 23cm.       DLC NN       *174*
"Appendix. Roster Twenty-first regiment . . . " and list of the regiment's battles, (1) p. Unit roster 47 p. Ryan 99.

Vance, William J
On Thomas' right at Chickamauga, by Captain William J. Vance. *BandG* i (1893) 87–99. illus., port.       *175*

Vance, Wilson J
A man and a boy at Stone river, by Wilson Vance. *BandG* i (1893) 347–60.       *175A*
The authorship of Titles 175 and 175A cannot be resolved. The roster of the 21st Ohio carries a 1st Lieutenant William Vance and a 2nd Lieutenant Wilson J. Vance.

## 22ND INFANTRY

*Organized: May 27 to June 10, 1861.*
(3 months)
*Mustered out: August 19, 1861.*
*Official roster* I 443–60, 753.
*Ohio in the war* 153–7.
*Mustered in as the 13th Missouri infantry:*
*November 5, 1861.* (3 years)
*Designated 22nd Ohio regiment of infan-*
*try: March 29, 1862.*
*Mustered out: November 18, 1864.*
*Official roster* III 40–68, 709–13.

## 23RD INFANTRY

*Organized: June 8, 1861 to March 23,*
*1862.*
*Mustered out: July 26, 1865.*
*Official roster* III 69–137, 713–20.
*Ohio in the war* 158–68.

In memoriam James M. Comly. [Columbus?,
1890?] 81 p. front. (port.). 24cm.
CSmH DLC **176**
On cover: In memory of James M. Comly.

Roster of the surviving members of the
Twenty-third regiment O.V.V.I., August, 1896.
Cleveland, Mount & co., printers [1896] 14 p.
15cm. OHi **177**

Conwell, Russell Herman, 1843–1925.
Life and public services of Rutherford B.
Hayes, President of the United States, by Rus-
sell B. Conwell. Boston, R. B. Russell & co.,
1877. 344 p. illus., 2 plates (ports.). 19cm.
Civil war 69–128. NHi **178**

Hayes, Rutherford Birchard, 1822–1893.
Incidents at the battle of Cedar creek, by
Rutherford B. Hayes, late Brigadier-General.
1889. *MOLLUS-Ohio* IV 235–45. **179**

—— Remarks of General R. B. Hayes at the
reunion of the 23d Ohio veterans, Canton,
Ohio, September 1, 1880. 4 p. 24cm.
Caption title. Ryan 338. OHi **180**

—— Remarks of Gen. Rutherford B. Hayes,
at the annual reunion of the Twenty-third regiment, Ohio vet. vol. inf., at Youngstown, Ohio,
September 17, 1879. 11 p. 23½cm.
Ryan 337. NHi **181**

McKinley, William, 1843–1901.
A Civil war diary of William McKinley.
Edited by H. Wayne Morgan. *OHQ* LXIX
(1960) 272–90. **182**

Watkins, H    K
President McKinley's visit to Fremont, Ohio.
Reunion of the 23rd O.V.V., the regiment of

two Presidents, Toledo Critic, v. VIII, no. 8,
Saturday, August 28, 1897. Reunion souvenir
number. 32 p. illus., ports. 31cm. OHi **183**
Title from cover. "This souvenir number designed
and compiled by H. K. Watkins.

## 24TH INFANTRY

*Organized: May 29 to June 17, 1861.*
*Mustered out: July 17–24, 1864.*
*Official roster* III 138–65, 720–3.
*Ohio in the war* 169–73.

Cockerill, John A
A boy at Shiloh. *MOLLUS-Ohio* VI 14–34.
**184**

—— —— *BandG* I (1893) 9–19. **185**

## 25TH INFANTRY

*Organized: June to July 1861.*
*Mustered out: June 18, 1866.*
*Official roster* III 166–226, 724–9.
*Ohio in the war* 174–81.

Hollis correspondence. *InMH* XXXVI (1940)
275–94. **186**
Joseph H. Hollis.

Culp, Edward C
The 25th Ohio vet. vol. infantry in the War
for the Union, by Edward C. Culp, late Lieut.
Colonel. Topeka, Kan., Geo. W. Crane & co.,
printers, 1885. 168, (1) p. 19cm.
DLC NN **187**
Battles of the regiment, (1) p. Ryan 172.

Hunt, David R
Restoring the flag at Fort Sumter, by David
R. Hunt, late Captain Twenty-fifth Ohio. 1898.
*MOLLUS-Ohio* V 522–30. **188**

## 26TH INFANTRY

*Organized: June 8 to July 24, 1861.*
*Mustered out: October 21, 1865.*
*Official roster* III 227–62, 730–5.
*Ohio in the war* 182–6.

Gist, William Wesley,    –1923.
The battle of Franklin. *Tennessee historical*
*magazine* VI (1920/21) 213–65. 2 plates
(maps, 1 fold.). **188A**

Kelly, Walden
A historic sketch, lest we forget, Company
"E," 26th Ohio infantry in the War for the
Union, by Captain Welden [sic] Kelly. [Os-
born, Mo., 1909] 45 p. 24½cm. DLC **189**
Signed: Walden Kelly. Ryan 407.

## 27TH INFANTRY

*Organized: July 15 to August 18, 1861.*
*Mustered out: July 11, 1865.*
*Official roster* III 263–300, 735–9.
*Ohio in the war* 187–91.

Adkins, Charles I
Service observations from the standpoint of
a private soldier, a glimpse of Sedalia in the
first winter of the war. In National tribune
scrap book I 54–62.                          *189A*

Smith, Charles H
Fuller's Ohio brigade at Atlanta. In National
tribune scrapbook I 155–7.                   *189B*

Sweet, Benjamin F
Civil war experiences. Edited by Vivian
Kirkpatrick McLarty. *Missouri historical review*
XLIII (1948/49) 237–50.                      *189C*

## 28TH INFANTRY

*Organized: June 10, 1861.*
*Mustered out: July 23, 1864.*
*Official roster* III 301–50, 739–42.
*Ohio in the war* 192–6.

## 29TH INFANTRY

*Organized: August 26, 1861.*
*Mustered out: July 13, 1865.*
*Official roster* III 351–93, 742–7.
*Ohio in the war* 197–9.

The Twenty-ninth Ohio at Gettysburg, 1863–
1887. [7] p. 2 illus. 22½cm.        OHi    *190*
Title from cover. Ryan 832.

SeCheverall, John Hamilton
Journal history of the Twenty-ninth Ohio
veteran volunteers, 1861–1865, its victories
and its reverses, and the campaigns and battles
of Winchester, Port Republic, Cedar mountain, Chancellorsville, Gettysburg, Lookout
mountain, Atlanta, the march to the sea, and
the campaign of the Carolinas, in which it bore
an honorable part, by J. Hamp SeCheverell
(late Company B). Cleveland, 1883. 284 p.
front. (port.). 18½cm.       DLC NN    *191*
Unit roster 159–232. Coulter 409. Ryan 735.

## 30TH INFANTRY

*Organized: August 28, 1861.*
*Mustered out: August 13, 1865.*
*Official roster* III 394–425, 747–53.
*Ohio in the war* 200–06.

Brinkerhoff, Henry R
History of the Thirtieth regiment Ohio volunteer infantry, from its organization, to the
fall of Vicksburg, Miss., by Lieut. Henry R.
Brinkerhoff. Columbus, James W. Osgood,
printer, 1863. 112 p. 17½cm.    NN    *192*

## 31ST INFANTRY

*Organized: August to September 1861.*
*Mustered out: July 20, 1865.*
*Official roster* III 426–68, 753–7.
*Ohio in the war* 207–10.

McNeil, Samuel A
Personal recollections of service in the Army
of the Cumberland and Sherman's army, from
August 17, 1861, to July 20, 1865, by S. A.
McNeil, Company F, 31st Ohio. [Richwood,
1910?] 76 p. 21cm.     DLC MB OHi    *193*

Putnam, John H
A journalistic history of the Thirty-first regiment, Ohio volunteer infantry, with its lights
and shadows. Volume 1, embracing the first
years of its existence, by Capt. J. H. Putnam.
Louisville, Ky., Printed by John P. Morton &
co., 1862. 114 p. 23½cm.     IHi NN    *194*
Unit roster [7]–25. The author resigned his commission, February 2, 1863.

## 32ND INFANTRY

*Organized: August 20 to September 7,*
*1861.*
*Mustered out: July 20, 1865.*
*Official roster* III 469–516, 757–61.
*Ohio in the war* 211–16.

Minutes of the 30th annual reunion, held at
Columbus, O., Sept. 5, 1906, Regimental association 32nd regt. O.V.V.I. Minutes of the 31st
annual reunion, held at Columbus, O., Sept. 4,
1907. [Bridgeport, Press of Sprague print. co.,
1908] 23 p. 1 illus., 2 ports. 16½cm.
Title from cover.                   OHi    *195*

Roster of the Regimental association 32nd
regt. O.V.V.I. [1900] 19 p. port. 16cm.
Title from cover. Ryan 713.         OHi    *196*

Burson, William, 1833–
A race for liberty; or, my capture, imprisonment, and escape, by William Burson, of Company A, 32d reg't O.V.I. With an introduction
by W. B. Derrick. . . . Wellsville, W. G. Foster, printer, 1867. xii, [5]–135 p. 16½cm.
Coulter 60. Ryan 96. DLC NN OHi    *197*

Hays, Ebenezer Z
History of the Thirty-second regiment Ohio
veteran volunteer infantry. Edited by E. Z.

*32nd Infantry, continued*

Hays, Chairman of the Regimental historical committee, and examined and approved by Warner Mills, George Knofflock [and] W. G. Snodgrass, Historical committee. Columbus, Cott & Evans, printers, 1896. 279 p. plates (ports.). 23½cm.     DLC OHi NN     **198**
Unit roster included. Company histories are signed by their author. Ryan 345.

See also Title 76.

### 33RD INFANTRY

*Organized: August 27 to October 11, 1861.*
*Mustered out: July 12, 1865.*
*Official roster* III 517–52, 761–7.
*Ohio in the war* 217–20.

Constitution and roster of the 33d Ohio volunteer infantry association, adopted September 12th, 1888. Chillicothe, Daily News, 1889. 8, xiv p. 15cm.     OHi     **199**

Johnson, Warren L
Diary of Sergeant W. L. Jackson, of Company C, 33d regiment, Ohio volunteer infantry. In Fifth annual report of the New York state Bureau of military statistics (1868) 682–714.     **199A**

Waddle, Angus L     1826?–
Three years with the Armies of the Ohio and the Cumberland, by Angus L. Waddle, late Adjutant 33d, O.V.V.I. Chillicothe, Scioto Gazette, 1889. iv, [7]–81 p. 23½cm.
DLC NN     **200**
Coulter 460. "Originally published in the 'Ohio soldier,' over the signature of 'Adjutant,' in a period running from January 21st, 1888, to October 13th of the same year."

### 34TH INFANTRY

*Organized: July 27 to September 14, 1861.*
*Consolidated with 136th regiment of infantry: February 24, 1865.*
*Official roster* III 553–98, 768–71.
*Ohio in the war* 221–7.

Hawkins, Morton Lytle
Sketch of the battle of Winchester, September 19, 1864, a paper read before the Ohio commandery of the Loyal legion of the United States, by First Lieutenant M. L. Hawkins. Cincinnati, Peter G. Thomson, 1884. 17 p. 21½cm.     DLC     **201**
Also published as *MOLLUS-Ohio* I 142–59. Ryan 333.

Merry, Lemuel E
Company "D," Thirty-fourth O.V.I. regiment. *Firelands pioneer* XII (Norwalk 1876) 83–6.     **202**

Owens, Ira S
Thirty-fourth regiment O.V.I. In his Greene county soldiers in the late war (1884) 175–85.     **203**

Smith, George T
Prison experience of a North soldier, by Rev. George T. Smith. *Southern historical society papers* XI (1883) 330–5.     **204**

Thomson, James A
The Lynchburg campaign, June, 1864, by James A. Thomson, Company F, Thirty-fourth Ohio. In G.A.R. war papers, papers read before Fred C. Jones post, no. 401, Department of Ohio, G.A.R. (1891) 121–47.     **205**

### 35TH INFANTRY

*Organized: August to September 1861.*
*Mustered out: August 26 to September 28, 1864.*
*Official roster* III 599–634, 771–6.
*Ohio in the war* 228–30.

Boynton, Henry Van Ness, 1835–1905.
The annual address delivered at the twenty-third reunion of the Society of the Army of the Cumberland, held at Chickamauga, Georgia, September 14 and 15, 1892, by Henry V. Boynton. Cincinnati, Robert Clarke & co., 1892. 37 p. 22½cm.     DLC NB     **206**

—— The battles about Chattanooga, Lookout mountain, and Missionary ridge, by H. V. Boynton, Lieutenant-Colonel 35th Ohio. 1892. *PMHSM* VII 373–407.     **206A**

—— The Chickamauga campaign. 1906. *PMHSM* VII 321–72.     **207**

—— Was General Thomas slow at Nashville? With a description of the greatest cavalry movement of the war and General James H. Wilson's cavalry operations in Tennessee, Alabama, and Georgia, by Henry V. Boynton. New York, Francis P. Harper, 1896. 95 p. front. (port.). 17cm.     NHi NN     **207A**

Keil, Frederick W
Thirty-fifth Ohio, a narrative of service from August, 1861, to 1864, by F. W. Keil, formerly commanding Company C. With an introductory by General H. V. Boynton. The original Persimmon regiment. Fort Wayne, Indiana, Archer, Housh & co., printers, 1894. xii, 272 p. plates (illus., 2 maps, ports.). 20cm.
DLC NN OHi     **208**
Unit roster [251]–72. Ryan 405.

### 36TH INFANTRY

*Organized: July 30 to August 31, 1861.*
*Mustered out: July 27, 1865.*

*Official roster* III 635–95, 776–82.
*Ohio in the war* 231–7.

Palmer, Jewett
Roster survivors 36th Ohio infantry, 1908, prepared by Jewett Palmer. Marietta [1908] 18 p. port. 14½cm.                OHi    **209**
—— —— 1916. [Marietta, 1916] 27, (2) p. 15½cm.                        OHi    **209A**

### 37TH INFANTRY

*Organized: September 9, 1861 to March 1, 1862.*
*Mustered out: August 7, 1865.*
*Official roster* IV 1–34, 709–14.
*Ohio in the war* 238–44.

Ninth reunion of the 37th regiment O.V.V.I., St. Marys, Ohio, Tuesday and Wednesday, September 10 and 11, 1889. Toledo, Montgomery & Vrooman, printers, 1890. 89, (1) p. 23cm.                       NHi OHi    **210**
Partial contents: From Camp Brown to Mission ridge, by John S. Kountz, 10–41; Atlanta campaign, by John H. Puck, 45–54; From Atlanta to the sea, through the Carolinas to Washington and home, by Cap. Louis E. Lambert, 55–61; Reply to toast, Die ersten Rekruten des 37.(3. deutschen Regiments), by Wm. H. Birkenhauer, 68–73; Eine Erinnerung an den Tag der Schlacht von Atlanta, 73–82; Eight months a prisoner in Andersonville, by John A. Melcher, 83–9. On cover: History of the 37th regiment O.V.V.I. furnished by comrades at the ninth reunion. . . . Ryan 360.

### 38TH INFANTRY

*Organized: July 24, 1861 to April 12, 1862.*
*Mustered out: July 12, 1865.*
*Official roster* IV 35–80, 714–24.
*Ohio in the war* 245–9.

### 39TH INFANTRY

*Organized: August 3–13, 1861.*
*Mustered out: July 9, 1865.*
*Official roster* IV 81–131, 724–30.
*Ohio in the war* 250–5.

Cadman, George Hovey, 1823–1864.
Johnny Bull — Billy Yank, by Carrol H. Quenzel. *Tennessee historical quarterly* XIV (1955) 120–41.                        **212**
"An excerpt-buttressed summary of 105 letters written by . . . from August 22, 1862, until his death in September 1864.

Chidlaw, Benjamin Williams, 1811–1892.
A thanksgiving sermon preached before the Thirty-ninth O.V.U.S.A., at Camp Todd, Macon, Missouri, Nov. 28, 1861, and a sketch of the Regiment, by Rev. B. W. Chidlaw,

Chaplain. Cincinnati, George Crosby, 1861. 24 p. 19cm.                   DLC OHi    **213**
Ryan 115.

Gilbert, Alfred West, 1816–1900.
Colonel A. W. Gilbert, citizen soldier of Cincinnati. Edited by William E. Smith and Ophia D. Smith. Cincinnati, Historical and Philosophical Society of Ohio, 1934. 122 p. plates (fold. map, ports.). 23½cm.
                              DLC MB NN    **214**
"Diary of events connected with the 39th O.V.I. in the campaign of 1861–2," 50–117.

Hurd, Ethan O
The battle of Collierville [sic] by E. O. Hurd, late Captain Thirty-ninth Ohio. 1900. *MOLLUS-Ohio* v 243–54.                    **215**

Nixon, Oliver Woodson, 1825–1905.
Reminiscences of the first year of the war in Missouri (read May 5, 1886). *MOLLUS-Ill* III 413–36.                          **216**

See also Title 78A.

### 40TH INFANTRY

*Organized: September to November 1861.*
*Mustered out: October to December 1864.*
*Official roster* IV 132–66, 730–8.
*Ohio in the war* 256–8.

Beach, John N
History of the Fortieth Ohio volunteer infantry, by John N. Beach, late Surgeon of the Regiment. London, Shepherd & Craig, printers, 1884. viii, [9]–243, (1) p. 19cm.
                              DLC NN OHi    **217**
Unit roster [145]–243. Ryan 44.

Doan, Isaac C
Reminiscences of the Chatanooga campaign, a paper read at the reunion of Company B, Fortieth Ohio volunteer infantry, at Xenia, O., August 22, 1894, by Sergeant Isaac C. Doan. Richmond, Ind., Printed at J. M. Coe's printery, 1894. 16 p. 22½cm.
                              DLC NHi OHi    **218**

### 41ST INFANTRY

*Organized: August 26 to October 29, 1861.*
*Mustered out: November 27, 1865.*
*Official roster* IV 167–208, 738–46.
*Ohio in the war* 259–65.

Roster of surviving members of the Forty-first regiment Ohio veteran volunteer infantry in the War of the rebellion, 1861–1865, giving name, company, rank and P.O. address. Cleve-

*41st Infantry, continued*

land, W. R. Smellie, printer, 1903. 18 p.
14½cm.                                    OHi    *219*
Ryan 714.

Hart, Albert Gaillard
The surgeon and the hospital in the Civil
war, by Major Albert Gaillard Hart Surgeon
41st regiment Ohio. 1902. *PMHSM* xiii 229–
85.                                               *220*

Hazen, William Babcock, 1830–1887.
A narrative of military service, by General
W. B. Hazen. Boston, Ticknor and co., 1885.
x, 450 p. plates (illus., maps, partly fold.,
plans, ports.). 21½cm.            NN    *221*
"The Forty-first Ohio," 1–14.

Kimberly, Robert L
The Forty-first Ohio veteran volunteer infantry in the War of the rebellion, 1861–1865,
by Robert L. Kimberly and Ephraim S. Holloway, with the co-operation of the Committee
of the Regimental association. Cleveland, W.
R. Smellie, 1897. 292, (2) p. plates (1 illus.,
ports.). 22½cm.        DLC NN OHi    *222*
Unit roster 137–263. Ryan 416.

### 42ND INFANTRY

*Organized: September to November 1861.*
*Mustered out: September 30 to December
30, 1864.*
*Official roster* iv 209–43, 746–52.
*Ohio in the war* 266–70.

Garfield, James Abraham, 1831–1881.
My campaign in East Kentucky. *North
American review* cxliii (1886) 525–35. *222A*

Hopkins, Owen Johnston, 1844–1902.
Under the flag of the Nation, diaries and
letters of a Yankee volunteer in the Civil war.
Edited by Otto F. Bond. Columbus, Ohio State
University press for the Ohio Historical Society
[1961] xi, 308 p. 3 plates (ports.). 22cm.
                                    DLC NHi    *222B*
Unit roster Company K, 296–301. Enlisted 42nd
Ohio, September 28, 1861; mustered out, October 18,
1864; enlisted 182nd Ohio, October 25, 1864; discharged, March 2, 1865. Half-title: Publications of
the Ohio Civil war centennial commission, number 1.

Mason, Frank Holcomb, 1840–1916.
The Forty-second Ohio infantry, a history of
the organization of that Regiment in the War
of the rebellion, with biographical sketches of
its field officers and a full roster of the Regiment. Compiled and written for the Veteran's
association of the Forty-second Ohio, by F. H.
Mason, Private of Company "A." Cleveland,

Cobb, Andrews & co., 1876. 306, (1) p. front.
(port.), map. 22cm.    DLC NN OHi    *223*
Unit roster 259–306. "Errata," (1) p. Two errata
slips inserted in the roster. Coulter 317. Ryan 453.

—— The life and public services of James A.
Garfield, twentieth President of the United
States, a biographical sketch, by Captain F. H.
Mason, late of the Forty-second [Ohio] regi-
ment, U.S.A. With a preface by Bret Harte.
London, Trübner & co., 1881. vi, [9]–134 p.
front. (port.). 18½cm.
                                DLC NB NN    *223A*
"General Garfield as a soldier," 46–72.

Petty, Edward T
The Cumberland gap campaign. In National
tribune scrap book i 119–21.                *223B*

Rudolph, Joseph, 1841–1934.
. . . Early life and Civil war reminiscences of
Captain Joseph Rudolph. Hiram, Hiram Historical Society, Hiram College, 1941. 36 p.
23cm.                            IHi NN    *224*
At head of title: Pickups from the "American way"
[series II, no. 1]

### 43RD INFANTRY

*Organized: September 28, 1861 to Feb-
ruary 1, 1862.*
*Mustered out: July 13, 1865.*
*Official roster* iv 244–92, 752–7.
*Ohio in the war* 271–6.

Fuller, John Wallace, 1827–1891.
"Our Kirby Smith," a paper read before the
Ohio commandery of the Military order of the
loyal legion of the United States, March 2,
1887, by John W. Fuller. Cincinnati, H. C.
Sherick & co., 1887. 21 p. 21½cm.
                                    DLC OHi    *225*
Also published in *MOLLUS-Ohio* ii 161–79.

Lybarger, Edwin L
Leaves from my diary, being a transcript of
the daily record I kept during Sherman's
march to the sea and to the end of the war,
now compiled for the 17th army corps, by Edwin L. Lybarger. [Coshocton, 1910] [13] p.
Ryan 447.                               OHi    *226*

—— Leaves from my diary, being verbatim
excerpts from the journal I kept while marching through Georgia with Sherman and here
assembled that they may recall days of peril
and yet of happiness to my comrades of the
grand army, by Edwin Lybarger. [Coshocton,
n. d.] [14] p. port. 23cm.            OHi    *227*
The type of Title 226 has been used.

Wise, George M          1841–1923.
Civil war letters of . . . Edited by Wilfred
W. Black. *OHQ* lxv (1956) 53–81.        *228*

—— Marching through South Carolina, another Civil war letter of Lieutenant George M. Wise. Edited by Wilfred W. Black. *OHQ* LXVI (1957) 187–95. **229**

### 44TH INFANTRY

*Organized: September 12 to October 14, 1861.*

*Designation changed to 8th Regiment of cavalry: January 4, 1864.*

*Official roster* IV 293–319, 757–9.

*Ohio in the war* 277–9.

Owens, Ira S
Forty-fourth regiment O.V.I. In his Greene county soldiers in the late war (1844) 154–8. **230**

### 45TH INFANTRY

*Organized: August 19, 1862.*

*Mustered out: June 12, 1865.*

*Official roster* IV 320–53, 759–69.

*Ohio in the war* 280–3.

Wilshire, Joseph W
A reminiscence of Burnside's Knoxville campaign, paper read before the Ohio commandery of the Loyal legion, April 3rd, 1912, by Joseph Wilshire, Captain 45th O.V.I. 22 p. 22cm. DLC NN **231**

### 46TH INFANTRY

*Organized: October 23 to January 28, 1862.*

*Mustered out: July 22, 1865.*

*Official roster* IV 354–87, 769–76.

*Ohio in the war* 284–9.

Worthington, Thomas, 1807–1884.
Abstract of evidence, &c, in the proceedings of the Court martial for the trial of Col. T. Worthington, at Memphis, August 14th, 1862. 8 p. 22½cm. OHi **232**
Caption title. Ryan 885.

—— Address of Col. Thomas Worthington, 46th Ohio, to the Union volunteers, August 10, 1880. Morrow, Warren County Free Press print, 1880. [4] p. 20cm. OHi **233**

—— Ballads of the rebellion, with a sketch of his service in the Civil war, and evidence of treachery by Union commanders at Shiloh; only to be obtained by a Court-martial, after all efforts for an inquiry had failed, August, 1862, by Gen. Tom Worthington, late Col. 46th Ohio vols. [n. p., 1878?] p [33]–39, 3, 4, p. 23cm. OHi **234**
Title from cover. "Brief record of Colonel Worthington's service during the Civil war," (3) p. "'Facts developed as to the battle of Shiloh by Colonel Worthington's Court-martial, August, 1862,'" (4) p.

—— The blunders of the rebellion and their Dead-sea fruit, in six numbers, being a general review of the causes which protracted the war, quadrupled its expense, in waste of life, money, and national credit . . . by T. Worthington. Washington, D. C., 1869. 15 p. 23cm. At head of title: No. 1. OHi **235**

—— Brief history of the 46th Ohio volunteers, by Col. T. Worthington. [Washington, D. C.? 1880?] 24 p. front. (port.), illus. t.p. 22cm. DLC NN **236**
Running title: History of the 46th Ohio while under Colonel Worthington's command. Ryan 884.

—— Col. Worthington vindicated. Sherman's discreditable record at Shiloh on his own and better evidence. Washington, D. C., Thomas McGill & co., printers, 1878. 18 p. 21cm. NN **236A**

—— A correct history, Grant at the battle of Shiloh . . . by T. Worthington. Washington, D. C., Thomas McGill & co., printers, 1880. 44 p. 22½cm. NN **237**
"Grant at the" of title on paster.

—— A correct history of Pope, McDowell, and Fitz John Porter, at the second battle of Bull run, August 29, 1862, by T. Worthington. Washington, D. C., Thomas McGill & co., printers, 1880. 15, (1) p. plate (plan). 23cm. DLC In **238**
Title and imprint from cover, p [1]

—— Extracts from a diary of the Tennessee expedition, 1862, by T. Worthington, Col 46th reg't Ohio [n. p., n. d.] 8 p. 23cm. Caption title. OHi **239**

—— Report of the right flank march to join McClernand's right at 9 a.m., and operations of the 46th reg't Ohio vols., 1st brigade, 5th division, on the extreme Union right, at Shiloh, April 6, 1862 . . . Col. Worthington, commanding. Washington, D. C., 1880. 39 p. 22cm. DLC NHi NN **240**
A second report, The march to Corinth, is included. Both reports are signed by Worthington. Unit roster of the 46th regiment, 6th April, 1862, at noon, [22]–7.

—— Shiloh; or, the Tennessee campaign of 1862, written especially for the Army of the Tennessee in 1862, and for the friends and relatives of those patriot soldiers, who sank into their graves on Shiloh's field . . . by a comrade on the battlefield and a West-Point graduate of 1827. Washington, D.C., McGill & Witherow, printers, 1872. 164 p. plates (facs., 2 maps). 23cm. NHi OHi **241**
On cover: Shiloh, the only correct military history of U. S. Grant and of the missing army records, for which he is alone responsible, to conceal his organized defeat of the Union army at Shiloh, April 6, 1862, by T. Worthington. Ryan 887.

## 47TH INFANTRY

*Organized: August 27, 1861.*
*Mustered out: August 11, 1865.*
*Official roster* iv 388–431, 776–80.
*Ohio in the war* 290–5.

Roesler, J    Nep
[The Civil war in West Virginia, as sketched
by J. Nep Roesler. Cincinnati, Printed by
Ehrgott, Forbriger & co., 1862]. Volume of 20
plates with guard sheets. 32½ x 43cm.
WvU    **242**
"Sketched fr. nature & drawn on stone, by J. Nep.
Roesler, Corp. of col., 47th regt. O.V." On cover:
Camp Anderson, W. Va.

Saunier, Joseph A
A history of the Forty-seventh Ohio veteran
volunteer infantry, Second brigade, Second
division, Fifteenth army corps, Army of the
Tennessee. Edited by Joseph A. Saunier, Regimental historian, assisted by diaries and manuscripts furnished by . . . [11 names] and many
others, and official reports of War department.
From June 15th, 1861, to August 24th, 1885.
[Hillsboro, Lyle print. co., 1903] 576 p. 22cm.
Unit roster [483]–574. DLC NHi OHi    **243**

Taylor, Thomas A
A sketch of the operations of the Forty-
seventh Ohio volunteer infantry, from May 3,
1864, to September 8, 1864. Cincinnati, Press
of George P. Huston, 1885. 15 p. 22cm.
GEU NN(P)    **243A**
An official report signed: Thos. A. Taylor, Major
commanding. Ryan 800.

## 48TH INFANTRY

*Organized: September to December 1861.*
*Consolidated with 83rd regiment of infan-
try: January 17, 1865.*
*Official roster* iv 432–88, 781–5.
*Ohio in the war* 296–8.

Bering, John A    1839–
History of the Forty-eighth Ohio vet. vol.
inf., giving a complete account of the Regiment, from its organization at Camp Dennison,
O., in October, 1861, to the close of the war,
and its final muster-out, May 10, 1866 . . . by
John A. Bering, late Major, and Thomas Montgomery, late Captain. Hillsboro, Printed at the
Highland News office, 1880. xv, 290 p.
17½cm.    DLC NN OHi    **244**
Ryan 50.

—— Reminiscences of a Federal prisoner.
*Publications of the Arkansas historical associa-
tion* ii (1908) 372–8.    **245**

Geer, John James, 1833–
Beyond the lines; or, a Yankee prisoner loose
in Dixie, by Captain J. J. Geer, late of General
Buckland's staff, with an introduction, by Rev.
Alexander Clark. . . . Philadelphia, J. W.
Daughaday, 1863. 285 p. front. (port.), plates
(illus.). 18cm.    DLC OHi    **246**
Ryan 272. Coulter 181.

## 49TH INFANTRY

*Organized: August 15 to September 22,
1861.*
*Mustered out: November 30, 1865.*
*Official roster* iv 488–545, 785–95.
*Ohio in the war* 299–304.

Souvenir sixty-first reunion Forty-ninth regiment O.V.V.I. [1926] [24] p. ports. 21cm.
OHi    **247**
Title from cover. Held at Fostoria, September,
"last annual reunion."

Bigger, David Dwight
Ohio's silver-tongued orator, life and speeches
of General William M. Gibson, by David
Dwight Bigger. Sold only on subscription.
Dayton, Press of United Brethren pub. house,
1901. xvii, 19–558 p. illus., ports. 21cm.
DLC NN    **248**
Civil war experiences as Colonel of the 49th Ohio,
311–430.

## 50TH INFANTRY

*Organzied: August 1862.*
*Mustered out: June 26, 1865.*
*Official roster* iv 546–84, 795–800.
*Ohio in the war* 305–07.

Winters, Erastus, 1843–
In the 50th Ohio serving Uncle Sam, mem-
oirs of one who wore the Blue . . . by Erastus
Winters, Corporal Company "K," 50 O.V.I.
[East Walnut Hills, 1905] 188 p. front. (port.).
23cm.    NN (M)    **249**
Unit roster Company K, 186–8.

## 51ST INFANTRY

*Organized: September 9 to October 12,
1861.*
*Mustered out: October 3, 1865.*
*Official roster* iv 585–644, 800–08.
*Ohio in the war* 308–12.

Gentsch, Charles
Instantaneous rigor-mortis occasionally oc-
curing and observed upon the battlefield, a
paper read before the Ohio commandery of the
Loyal legion, December 4, 1907. Cincinnati,
1907. 16 p.    NHi    **250**
Ryan 273.

Helwig, Simon
The capture and prison life in Rebeldom for fourteen months of Simon Helwig, late Private, Co. F, 51st O.V.I. [Canal Dover, Bixley print. co., n. d.] 50 p. 14½cm.     OHi    **251**
Ryan 349. Title from cover.

## 52ND INFANTRY

*Organized: August 1862.*
*Mustered out: June 3, 1865.*
*Official roster* iv 645–72, 808–13.
*Ohio in the war* 313–19.

Roster of the survivors of Col. Dan McCook's 52d regiment, Ohio volunteer infantry. . . . Scio, 1907. [8] p. 2 fronts. (ports.). 21½cm.
Ryan 715.     OHi    **252**

Anderson, Edward Lowell, 1842–
Colonel Archibald Gracie's The truth about Chickamauga, paper read before the Ohio commandery of the Loyal legion, February 7th, 1912, by Edward L. Anderson, Captain 52nd O.V.I. 27 p. double plate (plan). 22cm.
Title from cover.     DLC NHi    **253**

—— —— *JUSCA* xxiii (1912) 185–206.
    **254**

Barnes, Philander Y
War reminiscences, by P. Y. Barnes, late of 52nd O.V.I. Shiloh, S. F. Rose, printer, 1925. 26 p. 15½cm.     CtY    **254A**

Holmes, James Taylor
52d O.V.I., then and now, by J. T. Holmes, late Bv't Lieut. Colonel. Volume 1. Columbus, Berlin print. co., 1898. 285 p. 23½cm.
    DLC NN    **255**
Contents: The war journal, 1–38; Camps and battle-fields revisited, 41–277, c1922 by Lawrence A. Holmes. "Printed, not published." "Errata" slip inserted. No further volumes published. "That the printing of the text of the said book was completed in 1898; that the said book was published on the 12th day of Nov., 1921." — copyright application.

James, Frank Bakewell,
McCook's brigade at the assault upon Kenesaw mountain, Georgia, June 27, 1864, by F. B. James, late Captain Fifty-second Ohio. 1895. *MOLLUS-Ohio* iv 255–77. fold. map.
    **256**

—— Perryville and the Kentucky campaign of 1862. 1897. *MOLLUS-Ohio* v 130–66. **257**

Stewart, Nixon B
Dan. McCook's regiment, 52nd O.V.I., a history of the Regiment, its campaigns and battles, from 1862 to 1865, by Rev. Nixon B. Stewart, Sergt. Co. E. Published by the author. [Alliance, Review print] 1900. 225 p. ports. 20½cm.     DLC NN    **258**
Ryan 787.

## 53RD INFANTRY

*Organized: October 5, 1861 to February 5, 1862.*
*Mustered out: August 11, 1865.*
*Official roster* iv 673–706, 814–20.
*Ohio in the war* 320–4.

Dawes, Ephraim Cutler, 1840–1895.
The Army of the Tennessee, by E. C. Dawes, late Brevet Lieutenant-Colonel. 1892. *MOLLUS-Ohio* iv 411–17. plate (port.).    **259**

—— The battle of Shiloh, by Ephraim C. Dawes, Major 53d Ohio. 1893. *PMHSM* vii 101–71.     **260**

—— The Confederate strength in the Atlanta campaign. *BandL* iv 281–3.     **261**

—— Strength of the Confederate army at Gettysburg. *Century magazine* xxxviii (1889) 309–10.     **262**

—— A hero of the war, by Maj. E. C. Dawes, Fifty-third Ohio. In G.A.R. war papers, papers read before Fred C. Jones post, no. 401, Department of Ohio (G.A.R.) 293–8.    **263**
Eulogy of Captain James H. Percy 53d Ohio.

—— My first day under fire at Shiloh. 1896. *MOLLUS-Ohio* iv 1–22. plate (port.).    **264**

Duke, John K     1844–
History of the Fifty-third regiment Ohio volunteer infantry, during the War of the rebellion, 1861 to 1865, together with more than thirty personal sketches of officers and men, by John K. Duke, Company F. Portsmouth, Blade print. co., 1900. 303 p. col. front. (illus.), plates (illus., ports.). 22cm.
    DLC NN OHi    **265**
Unit roster 224–35. "Personal sketches and reminiscences," [237]–95. Coulter 137. Ryan 205.

## 54TH INFANTRY

*Organized: October 1861.*
*Mustered out: August 15, 1865.*
*Official roster* v 1–35, 709–14.
*Ohio in the war* 325–8.

Neff, Cornelius
Neal Neff's new national poems, composed by a Captain of line belonging to the 54th O.V.V.I. . . . Cincinnati, Moore, Wilstach & Baldwin, 1866. 159, (1) p. 19½cm.
    DLC OHi    **266**
Copyright Neal Neff. Ryan 490.

Owens, Ira S
Fifty-fourth regiment O.V.I. In his Greene county soldiers in the late war (1884) 170–3.
    **267**

*54th Infantry, continued*

Smith, Walter George, 1854–1924.
Life and letters of Thomas Kilby Smith, 1820–1887, by his son, Walter George Smith. New York, G. P. Putnam's Sons, 1898. vii, 487 p. plates (ports.). 23½cm.
DLC NHi NN    **268**
Civil war 10–147, 169–408.

## 55TH INFANTRY

*Organized: September to December 1861.*
*Mustered out: July 11, 1865.*
*Official roster v 37–81, 714–20.*
*Ohio in the war 329–34.*

Keesy, William Allen
War as viewed from the ranks, by Rev. W. A. Keesy. Personal recollections of the War of the rebellion by a private soldier. Norwalk, Experiment and News co., c1898. xvi, 240 p. illus., port., 2 plates (ports.). 25cm.
DLC NN    **269**
Ryan 397. "Regimental officers and company rosters," 171–6.

Osborn, Hartwell, 1840–1914.
The Eleventh army corps. *Western Reserve university bulletin* xvi (1913) 12–42.    **270**

—— The Eleventh corps in East Tennessee, by Captain Hartwell Osborn (read Nov. 1, 1900). *MOLLUS-Ill* iv 348–78.    **271**

—— The Fifty-fifth regiment Ohio volunteer infantry, its forty-eighth annual reunion. *Firelands pioneer* ns xviii (Norwalk 1915) 1677–80.    **272**

—— On the right at Chancellorsville (read February 1, 1900). *MOLLUS-Ill* iv 171–92.    **273**

—— Sherman's Atlanta campaign. *Western Reserve university bulletin* xiv (1911) 116–31.    **274**

—— Sherman's Carolina campaign. *Western Reserve university bulletin* xv (1912) 101–19. map.    **275**

—— Some relics and reminiscences of the Fifty-fifth Ohio infantry. *Firelands pioneer* ns xvi (Newark 1907) 1359–94.    **276**

—— Trials and triumphs, the record of the Fifty-fifth Ohio volunteer infantry, by Captain Hartwell Osborn and others. Chicago, A. C. McClurg & co., 1904. 364 p. plates (illus., maps, ports.). 22½cm.
DLC NN OHi    **277**
Unit roster 284–364. "The chapters in this book not credited to other writers are from his [Hartwell Osborn's] pen." Coulter 354. Ryan 542.

54th – 59th Ohio Infantry

—— The Twentieth army corps on the march to the sea. *Western Reserve university bulletin* xv (1912) 1–19. 2 maps.    **278**

## 56TH INFANTRY

*Organized: October to December 1861.*
*Mustered out: November to December 1864.*
*Official roster v 83–125, 720–6.*
*Ohio in the war 335–9.*

Williams, Thomas J
The battle of Champion's hill, by T. J. Williams, late First Lieutenant Fifty-sixth Ohio. 1896. *MOLLUS-Ohio* v 204–12.    **279**

—— An historical sketch of the 56th Ohio volunteer infantry during the great Civil war, from 1861 to 1866, by Thos. J. Williams. [Columbus, Lawrence press co., 1899] 191 p. plates (1 col. illus., ports.). 23cm.
Unit roster 145–91. Ryan 879.    OHi    **280**

## 57TH INFANTRY

*Organized: October 1861.*
*Mustered out: August 15, 1865.*
*Official roster v 127–64, 726–33.*
*Ohio in the war 340–7.*

## 58TH INFANTRY

*Organized: October 1 to January 28, 1862.*
*Mustered out: January 14, 1865. Veterans and recruits consolidated to a battalion and mustered out: September 16, 1865.*
*Official roster v 165–209, 734–41.*
*Ohio in the war 348–51.*

Stuber, Johann, 1838?–1895?
Mein Tagebuch über die Erlebnisse im Revolutions-Kriege von 1861 bis 1865, von Johann Stuber. In ehrender und liebvoller Erinnerung herausgegeben von seiner Wittwe, Frau Rosa Stuber. Cincinnati, Druck von S. Rosenthal & co., 1896. 206 p. 24cm.
Roster of officers 10–13.    DLC    **281**

## 59TH INFANTRY

*Organized: September 12, 1861 to September 23, 1862.*
*Mustered out: November 1, 1864. Veterans and recruits consolidated to a battalion and mustered out: June 28 to July 16, 1865.*
*Official roster v 210–41, 741–4.*
*Ohio in the war 352–5.*

## 60TH INFANTRY

*Organized: February 25–28, 1862.*
*Mustered out: November 10, 1862.*
*Official roster v 243–64, 744–5.*
*Ohio in the war 356, 358–60.*
*Organized: February to May, November
to December 1864.* (Reorganized)
*Mustered out: July 28, 1865.*
*Official roster v 265–92, 745–50.*
*Ohio in the war 356–7, 361.*

Campbell, George Warren
  The genealogy and actual experience of an
Ohio soldier during the Civil war, by George
Warren Campbell. [Columbus, 1924] [13] p.
14½cm.                                OHi    *282*
  Title from cover.

## 61ST INFANTRY

*Organized: March to May 1862.*
*Consolidated with 83rd regiment of in-
fantry: March 31, 1865.*
*Official roster v 293–322, 750–4.*
*Ohio in the war 362–5.*

Jewett, Leonidas M
  The boys in Blue at Missionary ridge, by
Brevet Major Leonidas M. Jewett. *MOLLUS-
Ohio* vi 89–94.                             *283*
—— From Stafford heights to Gettysburg in
1863. 1902. *MOLLUS-Ohio* v 213–22.    *284*

Peabody, James H
  Battle of Chancellorsville, reminiscences of
J. H. Peabody, First Sergeant Company B,
Sixty-first Ohio. In G.A.R. war papers, papers
read before Fred C. Jones post, no. 401, De-
partment of Ohio G.A.R. (1891) 49–75.  *285*

Wallace, Frederick Stephen
  The Sixty-first Ohio volunteers, 1861–1865.
Written and compiled by Frederick Stephen
Wallace. Marysville, Published for private cir-
culation by Theodore Mullen, 1902. 37 p.
19½cm.                            DLC OHi   *286*
  Ryan 859.

## 62ND INFANTRY

*Organized: September 17 to December
24, 1861.*
*Consolidated with 67th regiment of infan-
try: September 1, 1865.*
*Official roster v 323–79, 754–60.*
*Ohio in the war 366–70.*

Proceedings of the 62d Ohio infantry association . . . [Marietta, E. R. Alderman & Sons,
1884] 27 p. 19½cm.                    NHi    *287*
  Zanesville, Sept. 19, 1878; Cambridge, Aug. 27,
1879; Columbus, July 26, 1883; Zanesville, Sept. 10–
11, 1884.

Reunion of the 62nd O.V.I. regimental association. . . . v–xii 1888–1895 (NHi); 1915
(OHi); xxxviii 1921 (OHi).             *288*

Moore, Francis Marion, 1846–
  "Ghosts or devils," I'm done, by Francis M.
Moore, the startling adventures of two officers
of the 62nd Ohio infantry on Polly island, S.C.,
during General Gilmore's siege of Fort Sump-
ter in the War of the rebellion and the story
which incited their adventure. Deadwood,
S.D., Press of O. C. Cole & Son [1908] 72 p.
21½cm.                               DLC NN   *289*

## 63RD INFANTRY

*Organized by consolidation of battalions
from the 22nd and 63rd regiments of in-
fantry: January 25, 1862.*
*Mustered out: July 8, 1865.*
*Official roster v 381–430, 760–8.*
*Ohio in the war 371–5.*

Roster of the 63rd regiment O.V.V.I., and
"Sixty-third regiment," a poem, by Jennie
Shrader. [Beverly] Beverly Dispatch print,
1893. 30 p. 15cm.                     OHi    *290*

Jackson, Oscar Lawrence, 1840–1920.
  The Colonel's diary, journals kept before
and during the Civil war, by the late Colonel
Oscar L. Jackson of New Castle, Pennsylvania,
sometime commander of the 63rd regiment
O.V.I. [Sharon, Penn., 1922] 262 p. plates
(ports.). 22½cm.                     DLC NN   *291*
  Coulter 255.

## 64TH INFANTRY

*Organized: November 6 to December 14,
1861.*
*Mustered out: December 3, 1865.*
*Official roster v 431–76, 769–76.*
*Ohio in the war 376–80.*

Shellenberger, John K          1843?–
  The battle of Franklin, Tennessee, November 30, 1864, a statement of the erroneous
claims made by General Schofield, and an ex-
position of the blunder which opened the battle, by Captain John K. Shellenberger. Cleveland, Printed for the author by Arthur H. Clark
co., 1916. 42 p. 24cm. DLC NHi NN    *292*

*64th Infantry, continued*

—— The battle of Franklin, paper read before the Minnesota commandery of the Loyal legion U.S., December 9th, 1902. 29 p. 23cm.
DLC NHi     **293**
Title from cover. Also published as *MOLLUS-Minn* v 496–521.

—— The battle of Spring hill, Tennessee, read after the stated meeting held February 2d, 1907. 26 p. 24cm.    DLC NHi    **294**
At head of title: Military order of the Loyal legion of the United States. Commandery of the State of Missouri.

—— The battle of Spring hill, Tennessee, November 29, 1864, a refutation of the erroneous statements made by Captain Scofield in his paper entitled "The retreat from Pulaski to Nashville. Cleveland, Printed for the author by Arthur H. Clark co., 1913. 49 p. map. 24cm.
DLC NHi NN    **295**

—— With Sheridan's division at Missionary ridge. 1893. *MOLLUS-Ohio* iv 52–67.   **295A**

See also Titles 19, 269.

### 65TH INFANTRY

*Organized: October 13 to December 14, 1861.*
*Mustered out: November 30, 1865.*
*Official roster v 477–515, 776–83.*
*Ohio in the war 381–4.*

Gardner, Washington, 1845–1928.
Civil war letters. *Michigan history magazine* i no 2 (1917) 3–18. plate (port.).    **296**

Hinman, Wilbur F
Camp and field, sketches of army life, written by those who followed the flag, '61–'65, compiled by W. F. Hinman. Cleveland, N. G. Hamilton pub. co. [1892] 704 p. illus., plates, ports. 23½cm.      DLC    **297**

—— Corporal Si Klegg and his "Pard." How they lived and talked and what they did and suffered, while fighting for the Flag, by Wilbur F. Hinman, late Lieutenant-Colonel Sixty-fifth regiment, Ohio veteran volunteer infantry, with 193 original illustrations, drawn by George Y. Coffin. Cleveland, N. G. Hamilton & co., 1889. xix, 706 p. illus., music. 22cm.
OHi    **298**
Ryan 355. Later numbered editions are reprints. NN has 10th, 1895, and 12th, 1900. Si Klegg also appears by in the writings of John McElroy of the 16th Illinois cavalry.

See Title 19.

### 66TH INFANTRY

*Organized: December 1861.*
*Mustered out: July 15, 1865.*
*Official roster v 516–62, 783–9.*
*Ohio in the war 385–9.*

Powell, Eugene, 1838–
An incident of the capture of Lookout mountain, by Brevet Brig. Genl. Eugene Powell, Lt. Col. 66th O.V.I. *Historical and philosophical society of Ohio publications* (1926) 44–52.
   **299**

### 67TH INFANTRY

*Organized: October 1861 to January 1862.*
*Mustered out: December 7, 1865.*
*Official roster v 563–630, 789–95.*
*Ohio in the war 390–3.*

The West in the War of the rebellion, as told in the sketches of some of its Generals. A. C. Voris. *Magazine of Western history* iv (1886) 507–15.    **300**

The Sixty-seventh Ohio veteran volunteer infantry, a brief record of its four years of service in the Civil war, 1861–1865. [Massillon, Ohio print. and pub. co., 1922] 24 p. 23 x 10cm.
OHi    **301**
"Foreword" signed: Wm. H. Handy. Title from cover.

Voris, Alvin Coe
The battle [Winchester, March 23, 1862] of the boys, by A. C. Voris Brevet Major-General. 1891. *MOLLUS-Ohio* iv 87–100.    **302**

—— Charleston in the rebellion, a paper read before the Ohio commandery of the Military order of the loyal legion of the United States, March 7, 1888. Cincinnati, Robert Clarke & co., 1888. 49 p. front. (map). 23cm.
NHi    **303**
Also published as *MOLLUS-Ohio* ii 293–341. Ryan 850.

Wheeler, Xenophon
The experiences of an enlisted man in the hospital in the early part of the war. Paper read before the Ohio commandery of the Loyal legion, December 2, 1908, by Xenophon Wheeler, Sergeant 67th O.V.I. 8 p. 23cm.
Title from cover. Ryan 868.      DLC    **304**

### 68TH INFANTRY

*Organized: October to December 1861.*
*Mustered out: July 10, 1865.*
*Official roster v 631–68, 796–803.*
*Ohio in the war 394–8.*

Reynolds, Charles E

Thirteen months at Andersonville prison and what I saw there, a paper delivered before the N. L. association, Napoleon, Ohio, April 24, 1869. *Northwest Ohio quarterly* xxvii (1955) 94–113.                                    *305*

## 69TH INFANTRY

*Organized: October 1861 to April 1862.*

*Mustered out: July 17, 1865.*

*Official roster* v 669–705, 803–08.

*Ohio in the war* 399–402.

## 70TH INFANTRY

*Organized: November 1861 to February 1862.*

*Mustered out: August 14, 1865.*

*Official roster* vi 1–39, 697–703.

*Ohio in the war* 403–06.

Connelly, Thomas W          1840–

History of the Seventieth Ohio regiment, from its organization to its mustering out, by T. W. Connelly, of Company G. Cincinnati, Peak Bors [1902] 182, v p. ports. 22cm.

DLC NHi OHi          *306*

Unit roster [169]–82. "Appendix. Resolutions on death of President Loudon. In memory of President Heaton," v p. Ryan 133.

## 71ST INFANTRY

*Organized: September 1861 to January 1862.*

*Mustered out: November 30, 1865.*

*Official roster* vi 41–79, 704–08.

*Ohio in the war* 407–10.

Sixth annual re-union of the Seventy-first Ohio veteran infantry, held at Celina, Ohio, August 29, 1873. 8 p. 22cm.

Caption title.          NHi OHi          *307*

Mason, Rodney

Testimony submitted to the President of the United States, by Rodney Mason, late Colonel of the 71st Ohio volunteer infantry, with his application for the appointment of a Court of inquiry or Court martial to investigate charges against him. [Springfield, 1863] 32 p. 19½cm.

Caption title.          OHi          *308*

## 72ND INFANTRY

*Organized: October 1861 to February 1862.*

*Mustered out: September 11, 1865.*

*Official roster* vi 81–121, 708–17.

*Ohio in the war* 411–16.

Lemmon, John M

Speech of Captain John M. Lemmon, delivered at the reunion of the Seventy-second reg't O.V.I., held in Fremont, O., June 17, 1875. [Fremont, I. M. Keeler & Son, printer, 1875] 17 p. 22½cm.          DLC NHi          *309*

Caption title. Ryan 432.

—— Address of Capt. John M. Lemon [sic] of Clyde, O., delivered at the reunion of the 72d O.V.I., held at Fremont, O., June 17th, 1875. 11 p. 21cm.          CSmH          *310*

Caption title.

Woolverton, William B          1843–1894.

A sketch of prison life at Andersonville . . . *Firelands pioneer* vii (Newark 1894) 63–71.          *311*

## 73RD INFANTRY

*Organized: December 30, 1861.*

*Mustered out: July 20, 1865.*

*Official roster* vi 123–68, 717–26.

*Ohio in the war* 417–25.

Hurst, Samuel H

Journal-history of the Seventy-third Ohio volunteer infantry, by Samuel H. Hurst, late commander of the Regiment. Chillicothe, 1866. viii, [9]–253, (1) p. 20cm.

DLC NN          *312*

Unit roster [184]–253. Coulter 251. Ryan 376.

## 74TH INFANTRY

*Organized: October 5, 1861 to March 27, 1862.*

*Mustered out: July 10, 1865.*

*Official roster* vi 169–204, 726–9.

*Ohio in the war* 426–31.

Findley, Robert P

A story of a march, by R. P. Findley, late Lieutenant-Colonel Seventy-fourth Ohio. In G.A.R. war papers, papers read before Fred C. Jones post, no. 401, Department of Ohio, G.A.R. (1891) 351–66.          *313*

Owens, Ira S

Greene county in the war, being a history of the Seventy fourth regiment, with sketches of the Twelfth, Ninety fourth, One hundred and tenth, Forty fourth, and One hundred and fifty fourth regiments, and the Tenth Ohio battery, embracing anecdotes, incidents and narratives of the camp, march and battlefield, and the author's experience while in the army, by Ira S. Owens, Torchlight job rooms, 1872. xii, [13]–196 p. 17½cm.          DLC NN          *314*

Unit roster of the 74th, 141–53. Ryan 545.

*74th Infantry, continued*

—— Greene county soldiers in the late war, being a history of the Seventy-fourth O.V.I., with sketches of the Twelfth, Ninety-fourth, One hundred and tenth, Forty-fourth, Tenth Ohio battery, One hundred and fifty-fourth, Fifty-fourth, Seventeenth, Thirty-fourth, One hundred and eighty-fourth, together with a list of Greene county's soldiers, by Ira S. Owens, Company C, Seventy-fourth O.V.I. Dayton, Christian pub. house print., 1884. 294 p. 19cm.                    NN      *315*

Unit roster of the 74th, 188–212 [248]. Roster of Greene county soldiers arranged by regiments, 213–47. Ryan 546.

### 75TH INFANTRY

*Organized: November 17, 1861 to January 8, 1862.*

*Mustered out: November 16, 1864 to January 17, 1865. Veterans and recruits consolidated to a battalion and mustered out: July 27, 1865.*

*Official roster vi 205–54, 729–34.*

*Ohio in the war 432–8.*

Monfort, Elias R
"From Grafton to McDowell through Tygart's valley," a paper read before the Ohio commandery of the Military order of the loyal legion of the United States, by E. R. Monfort, late Capt. 75th Ohio. Cincinnati, H. C. Sherick co., 1886. 20 p. 21½cm.    DLC NN    *316*

Also published as *MOLLUS-Ohio* ii 1–23. Ryan 482.

### 76TH INFANTRY

*Organized: October 5, 1861 to February 3, 1862.*

*Mustered out: July 15, 1865.*

*Official roster vi 255–96, 735–52.*

*Ohio in the war 439–43.*

The crisis and its demands, by a Private in the 76th regiment Ohio volunteer infantry. [n. p., n. d.] 15 p. 22cm.        OHi    *317*

Caption title.

Herndon, Charles Frederick, 1929–
Some comments concerning Civil war letters of an Ohio family, by Charles F. Herndon. Fresno, Cal., 1959. v, (1), 100 folios. 28cm. mimeographed.              DLC    *318*

Letters of Lieutenant John Henry Hardgrove of the 76th Ohio.

Willison, Charles A        1846?–
Reminiscences of a boy's service with the 76th Ohio in the Fifteenth army corps, under General Sherman, during the Civil war, by

that "boy" at three score [by] Charles A. Willison, private soldier. [Menasha, Wis., Press of George Banta pub. co., 1908] 127 p. 19½cm.
                                 DLC NHi    *319*

### 77TH INFANTRY

*Organized: September 28, 1861 to January 5, 1862.*

*Mustered out: December 10, 1864. Veterans and recruits consolidated to a battalion and mustered out: March 8, 1866.*

*Official roster vi 297–347, 743–9.*

*Ohio in the war 444–8.*

Fearing, Benjamin Dana
The 77th Ohio volunteer regiment at Shiloh, by Gen. B. D. Fearing. *The College olio* xiii (Marietta 1885) 49–52.        *319A*

Flemming, Robert H
The battle of Shiloh as a Private saw it, by Robert H. Flemming, Captain, Seventy-seventh Ohio. *MOLLUS-Ohio* vi 132–46. *320*

McCormick, Andrew W
Battles and campaigns in Arkansas, by Andrew W. McCormick Brevet Lieutenant Colonel. *MOLLUS-Ohio* vi 1–13.        *321*

—— Sixteen months a prisoner of war. 1899. *MOLLUS-Ohio* v 69–87.        *322*

Thomas, James W
An Ohio Corporal's testament. *BandG* i (1893) 307–09.        *323*

### 78TH INFANTRY

*Organized: October 24, 1861 to January 16, 1862.*

*Mustered out: July 11, 1865.*

*Official roster vi 349–96, 750–8.*

*Ohio in the war 449–53.*

Official report Col. M. D. Leggett of the engagement near Bolivar, Aug. 30th, 1862 . . . M. D. Leggett, Col. 78th O.V.I., commanding 1st brigade. broadside, 34 x 24½cm.
                                      DLC    *323A*

Roster of the Regimental association 78th O.V.V.I. [1901] 44 p. 16cm.    OHi    *324*

Title from cover. "Diary" of William P. Gault, [2]–22. Ryan 710.

Munson, Gilbert D
Battle of Atlanta, by Gilbert D. Munson, late Lieutenant-Colonel Seventy-eighth Ohio. *MOLLUS-Ohio* iii 212–30.        *325*

Stevenson, Thomas M
History of the 78th regiment O.V.V.I., from its "muster-in" to its "muster-out," comprising

its organization, marches, campaigns, battles and skirmishes, by Rev. Thomas M. Stevenson, Chaplain of the Regiment. (Sold only by subscription.) Zanesville, Hugh Dunne, 1865. vii, [9]–349, (2) p. 22½cm.        DLC NN        **326**

Unit roster [22]–94. Index, "Errata," (2) p. Coulter 433. Ryan 786.

## 79TH INFANTRY

*Organized: August 20 to October 21, 1862.*
*Mustered out: June 9, 1865.*
*Official roster vi 397–427, 758–62.*
*Ohio in the war 454–7.*

By-laws of the 79th Ohio vol. inf'y assoc'n to which is appended the proceedings at the annual reunion of 1885 together with a roll of survivors, James M. Ayers, Secretary. Cincinnati, Henry Siebel print. co., 1885. 24 p. 17cm.        **327**

On cover: 79th Ohio vol. infantry association. 1885. In private collection of G. D. McDonald.

## 80TH INFANTRY

*Organized: October 1861 to January 1862.*
*Mustered out: August 13, 1865.*
*Official roster vi 429–66, 762–7.*
*Ohio in the war 458–62.*

Fryer, David F        –1924.
History of the Eightieth Ohio veteran volunteer infantry, from 1861 to 1865, written and compiled by D. H. Fryer, Sergeant of Company "D." Newcomerstown, 1904. 43 p. plates (illus., ports.). 24cm.        OHi        **328**

Unit roster 27–35.

—— Record and roster of the Eightieth O.V. V.I., 1861–1865, compiled by Comrade J. R. Fryer. New Philadelphia, 1917. 104 p. front. (port.). 23cm.        NN OHi        **329**

Title and imprint from cover. Unit roster 91–100. Blank pages for "Memorandum," 101–04.

Pepper, George Whitefield, 1833–1899.
Personal recollections of Sherman's campaigns in Georgia and Carolinas, by Capt. George W. Pepper. Zanesville, Hugh Dunne, 1866. 522 p. 21½cm.        NHi NN        **330**

Coulter 369. Ryan 556.

—— Under three flags; or, the story of my life as preacher, Captain in the army, Chaplain, Consul, with speeches and interviews, by the Reverend George W. Pepper. Cincinnati, Printed for the author by Curts & Jennings, 1899. 542, (1) p. plates (illus., ports.). 23½cm.        MB NHi        **331**

Civil war 83–113.

## 81ST INFANTRY

*Organized: August to September 1861.*
*Mustered out: July 13, 1865.*
*Official roster vi 467–506, 767–72.*
*Ohio in the war 463–9.*

. . . In memoriam companion Robert Newton Adams, died at St. Paul, Minnesota, March 24, 1914. [5] p. front. (port.). 23½cm.
DNW        **331A**

At head of title: Military order of the loyal legion of the United States Commandery of the State of Minnesota.

Adams, Robert Newton, 1835–1914.
The battle and capture of Atlanta, by Brevet-Brigadier-General Robert N. Adams. 1893. *MOLLUS-Minn* iv 144–63.        **332**

—— Campaign for Atlanta. 1894. *MOLLUS-Minn* iv 176–87.        **333**

Chamberlin, William Henry
History of the Eighty-first regiment Ohio infantry volunteers, during the War of the rebellion, by W. H. Chamberlin, late Major. Cincinnati, Gazette steam-print. house, 1865. 198, (1) p. 2. front. (12 ports.). 18½cm.

Unit roster 169–97. Ryan 110. DLC NN        **334**

—— Hood's second sortie at Atlanta. *BandL* iv 326–31.        **335**

—— Recollections of the battle of Atlanta. *MOLLUS-Ohio* vi 276–86.        **336**

—— The skirmish line in the Atlanta campaign. 1889. *MOLLUS-Ohio* iii 182–96.        **337**

Wright, Charles
A Corporal's story, experiences in the ranks of Company G, 81st Ohio vol. infantry, during the War for the maintenance of the Union, 1861–1864, by Charles Wright, with an introduction by Major W. H. Chamberlin. Philadelphia [James Beale, printer] 1887. 143, viii p. front. (port.). 23cm. DLC NN        **338**

Ryan 896.

## 82ND INFANTRY

*Organized: October to December 1861.*
*Mustered out: July 24, 1865.*
*Official roster vi 507–67, 772–8.*
*Ohio in the war 470–8.*

Lee, Alfred Emory, 1838–
The battle of Gettysburg. In Report of the Ohio Gettysburg memorial commission (1888) 95–142.        NHi        **339**

Also appears separately without change in pagination.

*82nd Infantry, continued*

—— Campaigning in the Mountain department. *Magazine of American history* xv (1885) 391–6, 483–91, 590–5.                     *340*

Contents: Our first battle, Bull Pasture mountain; The battle of Cross Keys; Battles of Port Republic and Lewiston.

—— Cedar mountain. *Magazine of American history* xvi (1886) 81–8, 159–67.     *341*

—— From Cedar mountain to Chantilly. *Magazine of American history* xvi (1886) 266–82, 370–86, 467–82, 574–85.               *342*

## 83RD INFANTRY

*Organized: August to September 1862.*
*Consolidated with 48th regiment of infantry: January 17, 1865.*
*Official roster* vi 569–619, 779–83.
*Ohio in the war* 479–83.

Gerard, Clinton W
A diary, the Eighty-third Ohio vol. inf. in the war, 1862–1865, by C. W. Gerard. [Cincinnati, 1889] 76 p. 23½cm.     IHi     *343*
Ryan 274.

Marshall, Thomas B
History of the Eighty-third Ohio volunteer infantry, the Greyhound regiment, by T. B. Marshall, First Sergeant, Co. K. Published by the Eighty-third Ohio volunteer infantry association. . . . [Cincinnati, Gibson & Perin co. print.] 1912. 227 p. plates (ports.). 23½cm.
Unit roster 190–227.  DLC NHi OHi   *344*

See also Title 26.

Page, Thomas Manning
Bohemian life; or, autobiography of a tramp. . . . San Francisco, J. Dewing & co., 1884. x, 451 p. illus., plates (illus.). 22cm.
                                    DLC NN   *344A*
The author served as a junior drummer.

See 17th Ohio Battery, p 46.

## 84TH INFANTRY

*Organized: May to June 1862.*
*Mustered out: September 20, 1862.*
*Official roster* vi 621–38, 784.
*Ohio in the war* 484.

Howbert, Abraham R
Reminiscences of the war [by] A. R. Howbert. [Springfield, 1888] 388 p. front. (port.). 17½cm.                          DLC   *345*

Woodward, Henry D
Letters from Henry D. Woodward to his mother. [Toledo, 1874] 19 p. front. (mounted port.). 22½cm.                        NHi   *346*
"Preface to his comrades of the 84th regiment" signed: Martha C. Woodward.

## 85TH INFANTRY

*Organized: May to June 1862.*
*Mustered out: September 23, 1862.*
*Official roster* vi 639–58, 784.
*Ohio in the war* 485.

See Title 64.

## 86TH INFANTRY

*Organized: June 10, 1862.* (3 months)
*Mustered out: September 25, 1862.*
*Official roster* vi 659–75, 784.
*Ohio in the war* 486, 488–9.

*Organized: July 14, 1863.* (6 months)
*Mustered out: February 10, 1864.*
*Official roster* vi 677–94, 785–6.
*Ohio in the war* 486–8.

Ashburn, Joseph Nelson, 1838–
History of the Eighty-sixth regiment Ohio volunteer infantry, by Joseph Nelson Ashburn, late Private of Company A. Cleveland [A. S. Gilman print. co.] 1909. 149, (1) p. illus., ports. 23½cm.          DLC NN OHi   *347*
Unit roster 105–44. Ryan 24.

McFarland, Robert White, 1825–1910.
The surrender of Cumberland gap, September 9, 1863, by R. W. McFarland, late Lieutenant Colonel 86th O.V.I. Columbus, Press of Nitschke Brothers, 1898. 32 p. 2 plates (illus.). 22cm.                              NN   *348*
Ryan 468.

## 87TH INFANTRY

*Organized: June 10, 1862.*
*Mustered out: October 1 to 4, 1862.*
*Official roster* vii 1–23, 687.
*Ohio in the war* 490.

Arpe, R     N
The Army of the Potomac, a page of history corrected. *Magazine of history* ii (1905) 127–44, 171–80, 249–58.                  *349*
Contents: i. Halleck and Fitz John Porter; ii. Pope and Porter; iii. Halleck and Pope. "A veteran of the 87th Ohio," a statement not confirmed by the roster.

## 88TH INFANTRY

*Organized: June 1862.* (3 months service)
*Mustered out: September 26, 1862.*

*Official roster* VII 24–38, 687.

*Ohio in the war* 491–3.

*Organized: September 24 to October 27, 1862, and designated: 1st battalion, Governor's guards.* (3 years service)

*Six new companies organized, July 24 to August 3, 1863, and designated: 88th regiment of infantry.*

*Mustered out: July 3, 1865.*

*Official roster* VII 39–64, 687–8.

*Ohio in the war* 494–8.

## 89TH INFANTRY

*Organized: August 22, 26, 1862.*

*Mustered out: June 7, 1865.*

*Official roster* VII 65–94, 689–94.

Foraker, Joseph Benson, 1846–1917.
Speech of Captain J. B. Foraker at the first reunion of the Eighty-ninth regiment, O.V.I., Fair grounds, Hillsboro, Ohio, September 20th, 1869. [Cincinnati, 1910] 11 p. 23cm.
Ryan 230. Caption title.     OHi    **350**

Johnson, William C
The march to the sea, by W. C. Johnson, Company F, Eighty-ninth Ohio. In G.A.R. war papers, papers read before Fred C. Jones post, no. 401, Department of Ohio, G.A.R. (1891) 309–36.     **351**

McKell, William James     –1864.
The journal of Sergt. Wm. J. McKell. *Civil war history* III (1957) 315–39.    **352**
"Editor's foreword" signed: Watt P. Marchman. "Notes added by a companion, Robert S. Brown," 335–9.

## 90TH INFANTRY

*Organized: August 29, 1862.*

*Mustered out: June 13, 1865.*

*Official roster* VII 95–124, 694–9.

*Ohio in the war* 499–503.

Harden, Henry O
History of the 90th Ohio volunteer infantry in the War of the great rebellion in the United States, 1861 to 1865, by H. O. Harden. Stoutsville, Press of Fairfield-Pickaway News, 1902. 337 p. plates (illus., ports.). 20cm.
Unit roster 234–304. Ryan 327. NN OHi    **353**

Walker, Robert, 1841–1865.
Letters of Robert Walker, a soldier in the Civil war of 1861–1865. Biography by Mrs. Hugh Henry West. Edited by Clara A. Glenn. Viroqua, Wis., Vernon County Censor, 1917. 32 p. front. (port.). 21cm.    DLC    **354**

## 91ST INFANTRY

*Organized: September 7, 1862.*

*Mustered out: June 24, 1865.*

*Official roster* VII 125–55, 699–702.

*Ohio in the war* 504–10.

Ewing, Elmore Ellis, 1840–1900.
Bugles and bells; or, stories told again. Including the story of the Ninety-first Ohio volunteer infantry. Reunion poems and social tributes, by E. E. Ewing. Cincinnati, Press of Curtis & Jennings, 1899. 322 p. front. (ports.). 19cm.     DLC OHi    **355**
Ryan 212.

—— The story of the Ninety-first, read at a re-union of the Ninety-first regiment Ohio volunteer infantry, held at Portsmouth, Ohio, April 8, 1868, in response to the toast, "Our bond of union," by E. E. Ewing. Portsmouth, Printed by the Republican print. co., 1868. 25 p. 14½cm.     DLC NHi OHi    **356**
Poetry. Ryan 211.

Wilson, Edward Stansbury, 1841–
The Lynchburg campaign, by Edward S. Wilson, late Lieutenant Ninety-first Ohio. 1893. *MOLLUS-Ohio* IV 133–46.    **357**

Windsor, Anthony H
History of the Ninety-first regiment, O.V.I., by A. H. Windsor, Chaplain. Cincinnati, Gazette print. house, 1865. 68 p. 19½cm.
Ryan 882. Unit roster 5–39.     OHi    **358**

## 92ND INFANTRY

*Organized: September 7–17, 1862.*

*Mustered out: June 14, 1865.*

*Official roster* VII 156–83, 703–7.

*Ohio in the war* 511–16.

Loring, Francis F
General George A [sic] Thomas, by Major F. H. Loring. *MOLLUS-Iowa* I 279–95.    **359**

## 93RD INFANTRY

*Organized: August 20, 1862.*

*Mustered out: June 8, 1865.*

*Official roster* VII 184–212, 707–12.

*Ohio in the war* 517–21.

Anderson, Charles, 1814–1895.
A paper read before the Cincinnati society of ex-army and navy officers, January 3d, 1884, by Charles Anderson, late Colonel Ninety-third Ohio. Cincinnati, Peter G. Thomson, 1884. 51 p. 21cm.     WHi    **360**

*93rd Infantry, continued*

Demoret, Alfred
A brief history of the Ninety-third regiment
Ohio volunteer infantry, recollections of a Private, by A. Demoret, Private in Co. F. [Ross,
Graphic print., 1898] 54 p. 19½cm.
Ryan 188.           DLC OHi    *361*

Kumler, Jeremiah Prophet Elias
A discourse on the death of Charles C. Barrows, of Co. C, Ninety-third O.V.I., died at
Murfreesboro, April 15, 1863, by Rev. J. P. E.
Kumler. Oxford, Richard Butler, printer, 1863.
8 p. 22cm.            DLC    *362*
Title and imprint from cover.

Patton, Joseph T
Personal recollections of four years in Dixie,
a paper read before the Commandery of the
State of Michigan, Military order of the loyal
legion of the United States, by J. T. Patton,
late Captain Co. A 93d regiment Ohio. . . .
Detroit, Winn & Hammond, printers, 1892.
31 p. 21½cm.           DLC    *363*
Also published as War papers I no 20. Ryan 547.

Richards, Henry
Letters of Captain Henry Richards of the
Ninety-third Ohio infantry. Cincinnati, Press of
Wrightson & co., 1883. 48 p. front. (mounted
port.). 21½cm.          NHi NN    *364*

### 94TH INFANTRY

*Organized: August 24, 1862.*
*Mustered out: June 5, 1865.*
*Official roster* VII 213–44, 713–17.
*Ohio in the war* 522–5.

Record of the Ninety-fourth regiment Ohio
volunteer infantry in the War of the rebellion.
Cincinnati, Valley press [189–] 166 p. 23½cm.
                  DLC NN OHi    *365*
On cover: "The gallant Ninety-fourth." Unit roster
103–68. Ryan 590.

Owens, Ira S
Ninety-fourth regiment O.V.I. In his Greene
county soldiers in the late war (1884) 140–5.
                          *366*

### 95TH INFANTRY

*Organized: August 19, 1862.*
*Mustered out: August 14, 1865.*
*Official roster* VII 245–80, 717–23.
*Ohio in the war* 526–30.

Roster surviving members of the 95th regiment
O.V.I., October 17th, 1916. . . . [Columbus,
Champlin press, 1916] 10 p. 23cm.
Title from cover.        DLC OHi    *367*

—— August 16th, 1922. [5] p. 23cm.
Caption title.          OHi    *367A*

### 96TH INFANTRY

*Organized: August 19, 22, 1862.*
*Mustered out: July 7, 1865.*
*Official roster* VII 281–320, 724–30.
*Ohio in the war* 531–3.

Bartlett, Robert Franklin, 1840–
Roster of the Ninety-sixth regiment, Ohio
volunteer infantry, 1862 to 1865, compiled by
Robt. F. Bartlett. Souvenir edition. Columbus,
Press of Hann & Adair, 1895. 179, (2) p.
18½cm.            DLC NN OU    *368*
"Comrades of the 96th Ohio," by A. H. Brown,
173–9. "Errata," "Additional errata and addenda,"
(2) p. Ryan 42.

Woods, Joseph Thatcher, 1828–1911.
Services of the Ninety-sixth Ohio volunteers,
by J. T. Woods, late Surgeon 99th Ohio vols.
Toledo, Blade print. and paper co., 1874. viii,
[9]–247 p. plan, plates (2 plans, 3 ports.).
21cm.             DLC NN    *369*
Unit roster [157]–244. Ryan 894.

—— Steedman and his men at Chickamauga,
by J. T. Woods. Toledo, Blade print co., 1876.
iv, [9]–133 p. 2 double maps. 20cm.
Ryan 895.            DLC NHi    *370*

### 97TH INFANTRY

*Organized: September 2, 1862.*
*Mustered out: June 10, 1865.*
*Official roster* VII 321–51, 731–7.
*Ohio in the war* 534–8.

Constitution, by-laws and roster of the 97th
O.V.I. regimental association. [Zanesville, H.
M. Dickson, print., n. d.] 34 p. 14½cm.
                          OHi    *371*

Constitution, by-laws, roster and history of the
97th O.V.I. regimental association. [n. p., n. d.]
60 p. 15cm.            OHi    *372*
Ryan 134.

Roster, history, constitution and by-laws of the
97th O.V.I. regimental association. [Columbus,
Hann and Adair] 1909. 58 p. 15½cm.
Ryan 712.            OHi    *373*

### 98TH INFANTRY

*Organized: August 20–21, 1862.*
*Mustered out: June 1, 1865.*
*Official roster* VII 352–80, 737–43.
*Ohio in the war* 539–41.

Branum, John Marshall, –1865.
Letters of Lieut. J. M. Branum from the 98th Ohio vol. inf. [New Castle, Penn., Press of Warnock Brothers, 1897] 48 p. 22½cm.
OU    374

### 99TH INFANTRY

*Organized: August 26, 1862.*
*Consolidated with 50th regiment of infantry: December 31, 1864.*
*Official roster* VII 381–408, 743–9.
*Ohio in the war* 542–5.

### 100TH INFANTRY

*Organized: July – September 1862.*
*Mustered out: June 20, 1865.*
*Official roster* VII 409–44, 750–6.
*Ohio in the war* 546–7.

### 101ST INFANTRY

*Organized: August 30, 1862.*
*Mustered out: June 12, 1865.*
*Official roster* VII 445–78, 756–61.
*Ohio in the war* 548–51.

Roster and historical sketch of the 101st regiment Ohio volunteer infantry. . . . Tiffin, Russel L. Knapp, printer, 1897. 41 p. port. 15cm.
DNW    375

"Historical (from Whitelaw Reid's Ohio in the war)," [1]–10. Brief biographies of Colonel Leander Stem and Lieut. Colonel Moses F. Wooster, 11–13.

Butler, Jay Caldwell, 1844–1885.
Letters home [by] Jay Caldwell Butler, Captain, 101st Ohio volunteer infantry, arranged by his son, Watson Hubbard Butler. . . . [Binghamton, N.Y.] Privately printed, 1930. x, 153 p. 21½cm.
DLC    376

Coulter 62.

Day, Lewis W
Story of the One hundred and first Ohio infantry, a memorial volume, by L. W. Day. Cleveland, W. M. Bayne print. co., 1894. xiv, [17]–463 p. illus., ports. 20½cm.
DLC NN    377

Unit roster [360]–463. "Errata" slip inserted. Coulter 119. Ryan 184.

Green, Charles Ransley, 1845–1915.
Volunteer service in Army of Cumberland . . . all these several pieces written up and published by C. R. Green. . . . Olathe, Kansas, 1913–14. 1 v. plates (1 illus., ports.).
DLC NHi NN    378

Contents: Part first, History of the volunteers from Clarksfield, Huron co., Ohio in the 101st O.V.I., 8–23;

Part second, List of the volunteers from Wakeman, O. the whole war. [10] p.; Part third, Sergeant Benj. T. Strong's biography, and history of the Chickamauga campaign. [24] p; Part fourth, Descendants of Justus Minor, who moved from Conn. in 1821 to Wakeman, O. [14] p. On cover: The part we took in the great rebellion. Or, some history 50 years after, by a Buckeye. 1914.

Read, Ira Beman, 1841–1897.
The campaign from Chattanooga to Atlanta as seen by a Federal soldier. Edited by Richard B. Harwell. *Georgia historical quarterly* xxv (1941) 262–78.    379

Strong, Benjamin Thomas
3 years or during the war. Sergeant Benj. T. Strong's biography, reminiscences of his service in Co. A 101st O.V.I., Gen'l Davis' division, Army of the Cumberland. Prefaced by his short story of the battle of Chicamauga, casualties of Co. A, subsequent prison life and return home. Edited and some additions made by his comrade, C. R. Green. . . . An appendix giving C. R. Green's experiences Sept. and Oct. '63 on the Chicamauga campaign and getting back to Nashville. Olathe, Kansas, C. R. Green, 1913. [25] p. plates (2 ports.). 21cm.
NN    380

### 102ND INFANTRY

*Organized: August to September 1862.*
*Mustered out: June 30, 1865.*
*Official roster* VII 479–510, 762–7.
*Ohio in the war* 552–5.

Schmutz, George S    1846?–
History of the 102d regiment, O.V.I. Published and compiled by Geo. S. Schmutz, Co. I, 1907. 285 p. plates (illus., ports.). 22½cm.
Unit roster 17–72.    DLC    381

### 103RD INFANTRY

*Organized: August to September 1862.*
*Mustered out: June 12, 1865.*
*Official roster* VII 511–40, 768–70.
*Ohio in the war* 556–9.

Personal reminiscences and experiences, by members of the One hundred and third Ohio volunteer infantry, campaign life in the Union army, from 1862 to 1865. [Oberlin, News print. co., 1900] 441 p. 19½cm. OHi    382

Contributions are signed by their authors. Unit roster 390–444. Ryan 559.

Soldiers record Medina Union boys, Company I, 103d Ohio vol. inf. regiment. Chicago, Kellog, Groner & Smith, c1862. col. illus. broadside, 56 x 45cm.    NHi    382A

"Lith. Chas. Shober, Chicago, Ills." Hyatt & Calhoun, printers, Chicago.

*103rd Infantry, continued*

Hayes, Philip Cornelius, 1833–
Campaigning in East Tennessee, by General P. C. Hayes (read May 1, 1902). *MOLLUS-Ill* IV 318–47.  **383**

—— Journal-history of the One hundred & third Ohio volunteer infantry, by Philip C. Hayes, late Lieutenant-Colonel of the Regiment. Bryan [Toledo, Commercial steam print. house] 1872. viii, [9]–148, iv p. 20cm.
NN  **384**
"Individual memorial," form to enter individual record, iv p. Ryan 336.

Scofield, Levi Tucker, 1842–
"The retreat from Pulaski to Nashville," a paper read before the Ohio commandery of the Military order of the Loyal legion of the United States, December 1, 1886, by Levi T. Scofield. Cincinnati, H. C. Sherick & co., 1886. 28 p. fold. map. 23cm. DLC NHi NN  **385**
Also published as *MOLLUS-Ohio* II 121–52.

—— The retreat from Pulaski to Nashville, Tenn. Battle of Franklin, Tennessee, November 30, 1864, by Levi T. Scofield. Cleveland, Press of the Caxton co., 1909. 67 p. illus., maps, ports. 23½cm.  DLC OHi  **386**
Ryan 730.

Vought, John E
An incident in the last Nashville campaign, by Lieutenant John E. Vought. *MOLLUS-Ind* 382–92.  **387**

## 104TH INFANTRY

*Organized: August 30, 1862.*
*Mustered out: June 17, 1865.*
*Official roster* VII 541–69, 771–4.
*Ohio in the war* 560–4.

Gaskill, Joseph W
Footprints through Dixie, life of the man under a musket, on the firing line and in the trenches, 1862–1865, by J. W. Gaskill. Alliance [Bradshaw print. co.] 1919. 186 p. 23½cm.  DLC NN OHi  **388**
On cover: From diary of 1862–1865. "Errata" slip mounted on front-fly-leaf.

Pinney, Nelson A  1844–
History the 104th regiment Ohio volunteer infantry, 1862 to 1865, by N. A. Pinney. Akron, Printed by Werner & Lohmann, 1886. 148 p. front. (port.). 23cm.
DLC NHi OHi  **389**
Unit roster 95–148. Ryan 563.

Ricks, Augustus J  1843–1906.
Carrying the news of Lee's surrender to the Army of the Ohio, a paper read before the Ohio commandery of the Military order of the loyal legion of the United States, November 2, 1887, by Augustus J. Ricks, late 1st Lieutenant 104th O.V.I. Cincinnati, H. C. Sherick & co., 1887. 15 p. 23cm. DLC NHi NN OHi  **390**
Also published as *MOLLUS-Ohio* II 234–46.

## 105TH INFANTRY

*Organized: August 20–21, 1862.*
*Mustered out: June 3, 1865.*
*Official roster* VII 570–98, 774–80.
*Ohio in the war* 565–71.

Fradenburgh, Jason Nelson, 1843–
In memoriam Henry Harrison Cumings, Charlotte J. Cumings, by Rev. J. N. Fradenburgh. Oil City, Penn., Derrick pub. co., 1913. 236 p. front. (port.), illus., ports. 24½cm.
DLC  **391**
Includes extracts from Cuming's diary while serving in the 105th Ohio, [35]–163.

Tourgée, Albion Winegar, 1838–1905.
The story of a thousand, being a history of the service of the 105th Ohio volunteer infantry, in the War for the Union, from August 21, 1862, to June 6, 1865, by Albion W. Tourgée. Buffalo, McGerald & Son, 1896. 409, XLIV p. 3 maps, ports., plate (double map). 22cm.
DLC NN  **392**
Unit roster x–xliv. Coulter 451. Ryan 829.

—— —— *Cosmopolitan* XVIII (1894/95) 69–80, 223–34, 341–55, 491–6, 608–19, 728–38. illus., maps, ports.  **392A**
Illustrated by Frederic Remington.

## 106TH INFANTRY

*Organized: August 26 to October 25, 1862.*
*Mustered out: June 29, 1865.*
*Official roster* VII 599–626, 780–1.
*Ohio in the war* 572–5.

## 107TH INFANTRY

*Organized: September 9, 1862.*
*Mustered out: July 10, 1865.*
*Official roster* VII 627–61, 781–4.
*Ohio in the war* 576–8.

Cooper, John Snyder,  –1907.
The Shenandoah valley in Eighteen hundred and sixty-two, by Col. John S. Cooper (read December 9, 1886). *MOLLUS-Ill* IV 36–60.  **393**

Smith, Jacob
Camps and campaigns of the 107th regiment Ohio volunteer infantry, from August,

1862, to July, 1865. Compiled and written by Jacob Smith, Company D. . . . [1910?] 314 p. plates (1 illus., map, ports.). 19cm.
Unit roster 240–314.    DLC OHi    **394**

## 108TH INFANTRY

*Organized: August 21 to December 19, 1862.*
*Mustered out: June 9, July 22, 1865.*
*Official roster* vii 662–83, 784–6.
*Ohio in the war* 579–83.

## 109TH INFANTRY

*Failed to complete organization.*

## 110TH INFANTRY

*Organized: October 3, 1862.*
*Mustered out: June 25, 1865.*
*Official roster* viii 1–43, 709–13.
*Ohio in the war* 584–8.

Owens, Ira S
One hundred and tenth O.V.I. In his Greene county soldiers in the late war (1884) 146–53.    **395**
See also Title 101A.

## 111TH INFANTRY

*Organized: September 5 to 6, 1862.*
*Mustered out: June 27, 1865.*
*Official roster* viii 44–74, 714–19.
*Ohio in the war* 589–93.

Sherwood, Isaac Ruth, 1835–1925.*
The army grayback, a reminiscence, by Isaac R. Sherwood. Illustrations by Alfred Gillam, Coffin and Klemroth. Canton, Published by the author, 1889. 48 p. illus. 19cm.
Poetry.    WHi    **396**

—— The heroic literature of the war period, a paper read before the Ohio commandery of the Loyal legion, October 2, 1907, by Brevet Brigadier General Isaac R. Sherwood, Colonel 11th O.V.I. 11 p. 23cm.    DLC NHi    **397**
Ryan 763.

—— Memories of the war, by Gen. Isaac R. Sherwood. Toledo, H. J. Chittenden co., 1923. 238 p. plates (ports.). 20½cm.
DLC NN    **398**

—— Souvenir One hundred eleventh O.V.I. in memory of the old war days. [Toledo, B. F.

Wade & Sons co., printers, 1907] 20 p. mounted port. 23½cm.    MnHi OHi    **399**
On cover: Annual reunion, October 1st, 1907. "Issued as a tribute to the surviving soldiers of the 111th O.V.I. by their old comrade and commander, Isaac R. Sherwood."

Smith, Gustavus F
Battle of Franklin, by Gus F. Smith 1st Lieut. 111th Ohio infantry (read April 7, 1898). *MOLLUS-Mich* ii 249–63.    **400**

## 112TH INFANTRY

*Failed to complete organization.*

## 113TH INFANTRY

*Organized: October 10 to December 12, 1862.*
*Mustered out: July 6, 1865.*
*Official roster* viii 75–105, 719–25.
*Ohio in the war* 594–6.

The twenty-ninth annual reunion of the 113th regiment O.V.I., held at Worthington, Ohio, September 2, 1902. . . . 27 p. 14½cm.
Title from cover. Ryan 676.    OHi    **401**

McAdams, Francis Marion
Every-day soldier life; or, a history of the One hundred and thirteenth Ohio volunteer infantry, by F. M. McAdams, Sergeant of Co. E. Columbus, Chas. M. Cott & co., printers, 1884. 400 p. 2 plates (ports.). 23cm.
DLC NN    **402**
"Our knapsack . . . anecdotes [etc.] . . . contributed by members of the command," [265]–400. Unit roster 175–264. Ryan 460.

—— Our knapsack, sketches for the boys in Blue, compiled and published by F. M. McAdams, late Sergeant 113th O.V.I. Columbus, Chas. M. Cott & co., printers. 1884. 136 p. plates (ports.). 22cm.    DLC WHi    **403**
Title and imprint from cover. Signed contributions by members of the Regiment.

## 114TH INFANTRY

*Organized: September 1862.*
*Mustered out: July 31, 1865.*
*Official roster* viii 106–45, 725–32.
*Ohio in the war* 597–600.

Moore, John Henry, 1828–1869.
The horizon and zenith of the great rebellion; or, the Kansas troubles, and the taking of Vicksburg, personal adventures and observations, by John Henry Moore, late of the 114th

---

* Biographical: General Isaac R. Sherwood, by Francis P. Weisenburger. *Northwest Ohio quarterly* xiv (1942) 42–54.

*114th Infantry, continued*

regiment O.V.I. . . . Cincinnati, Elm Street print. co., 1870. ix, [15]–409 p. plates (illus.). 21cm.                                    NN   *404*
"In memoriam" signed: Wm. C. Gray.

### 115TH INFANTRY

*Organized: August to September 1862.*
*Mustered out: June 22, 1865.*
*Official roster* viii 146–78, 732–6.
*Ohio in the war* 601–03.

Proceedings of the first annual re-union of the 115th reg't O.V.I., together with the address of Lieut. James J. Clark, at Salem, Ohio, on Friday, September 13th, 1872. Canton, Hartzell & Saxton, printers, 1872. 14 p. 22cm.
                                         DLC   *405*
"Address of Lieut. James J. Clark," [7]–14 has running title: History of the 115th O.V.I.

### 116TH INFANTRY

*Organized: September to October 1862.*
*Mustered out: June 14, 1865.*
*Official roster* viii 179–214, 736–4.
*Ohio in the war* 604–07.

Brown, LeRoy D
Address of L. D. Brown at the re-union of the 116th Ohio volunteers, held at Caldwell, Ohio, September 17, 1884. Caldwell, Press print, 1884. 10 p. 19cm.          OHi   *406*

Dalzell, James McCormick, 1838–1924.
Private Dalzell, his autobiography, poems and comic war papers. . . . Cincinnati, Robert Clarke & co., 1888. 242, (1) p. plates (facs., illus., ports.). 20cm.   DLC NN   *407*

Wildes, Thomas Francis, 1834–1883.
Record of the One hundred and sixteenth regiment, Ohio infantry volunteers in the War of the rebellion, by Thos. F. Wildes, late Lieutenant-Colonel of the Regiment. Sandusky, O. I. F. Mack & Bro., printers, 1884. xxiv, 364 p. 24cm.                  DLC NN   *408*
Unit roster 322–64. Ryan 876.

### 117TH INFANTRY

*Organized: September 1862.*
*Designated 1st regiment of heavy artillery: August 12, 1863.*

### 118TH INFANTRY

*Organized: September 12 to November 7, 1862.*
*Mustered out: June 24, 1865.*

---

# 114th – 123rd Ohio Infantry

*Official roster* viii 215–39, 741–4.
*Ohio in the war* 610–12.

### 119TH INFANTRY

*Failed to complete organization.*

### 120TH INFANTRY

*Organized: October 7 to 17, 1862.*
*Consolidated with 114th regiment of infantry: November 27, 1864.*
*Official roster* viii 240–72, 744–50.
*Ohio in the war* 613–17.

### 121ST INFANTRY

*Organized: September 11, 1862.*
*Mustered out: June 8, 1865.*
*Official roster* viii 273–306, 750–5.
*Ohio in the war* 618–23.

### 122ND INFANTRY

*Organized: September 30 to October 8, 1862.*
*Mustered out: June 26, 1865.*
*Official roster* viii 307–46, 755–60.
*Ohio in the war* 624–7.

Bristol, Frank Milton, 1851–1932.
The life of Chaplain McCabe, Bishop of the Methodist Episcopal church, by Frank Milton Bristol. New York, Fleming H. Revell co. [1908] 416 p. plates (2 facs., 1 double and 1 fold.; ports.). 21cm.     DLC OHi   *409*
Civil war 70–216.

Granger, Moses Moorhead, 1831–1913.
The battle of Cedar creek, by Moses M. Granger, late Lieutenant-Colonel One hundred and twenty-second O.V.I. 1888. *MOLLUS-Ohio* iii 100–43.                    *410*

—— The official war record of the 122nd regiment of Ohio volunteer infantry, from October 8, 1862, to June 26, 1865. Copied from volumes 25 . . . 46, series I, U.S. war records, and from volumes 3 and 5 of Series III. By Moses Moorhead Granger. Zanesville, George Lilienthal, printer, 1912. 146 p. 23cm.
                                         DLC   *411*

### 123RD INFANTRY

*Organized: August to October 1862.*
*Mustered out: June 12, 1865.*
*Official roster* viii 347–85, 760–4.
*Ohio in the war* 628–33.

Caldwell, David S
Incidents of war; or, Southern prison life, by Capt. D. S. Caldwell, 123d, O.V.I. Published for the author. Dayton, United Brethren print. estab., 1864. 61 p. 21½cm.
IHi OHi    **412**

Chamberlin, John W
Scenes in Libby prison, by J. W. Chamberlain [sic] late Captain One hundred and twenty-third O.V.I. 1888. *MOLLUS-Ohio* II 342–70.
**413**

Clapp, Henry Seymour
Sketches of army life in the sixties and "The mansion by the spring," a Civil war story of the Shenandoah, by Henry S. Clapp, 123rd Ohio volunteer infantry and 19th colored troops, U.S.A. [Newark, 191–] 61 p. 2 plates (ports.). 19½cm.
NN    **414**
Originally published in the Norwalk reflector, 1908–09, and republished by his daughters, Mary Belle Clapp Cline and Katharine B. Clapp Horton, who signed the "Preface."

Keyes, Charles M
The military history of the 123d regiment of Ohio volunteer infantry. Edited by C. M. Keyes, 1st Lieutenant 123d reg. Sandusky, Register press, 1874. 196 p. 20cm.
DLC NN    **415**
Unit roster: Muster in, 6–28; muster out, 139–62. Coulter 277. Ryan 415.

Snyder, Edwin, 1840–
Adventures and misadventures, civil and military of a Union veteran of the Civil war, by Edwin Snyder, Sergeant Company E, 123 O.V.I. [Topeka, Cavanaugh print. co., 1909] 48 p. plates (ports.). 21cm. IHi KHi    **416**
Title from cover.

Spetnagel, Frederick K
The sword, a Civil war story, by Frederick K. Spetnagel . . . Chillicothe, Ohio Valley Folk Research Project, Ross County Historical Society, 1959. 7 folios. 28cm. mimeographed. (Ohio valley folk publications, ns no. 36).
NN    **417**
"Introduction" signed: John E. Wissler.

## 124TH INFANTRY

*Organized: August to September 1862.*
*Mustered out: July 9, 1865.*
*Official roster* VIII 386–416, 764–8.
*Ohio in the war* 634–9.

Lewis, George W    1837–
The campaigns of the 124th regiment Ohio volunteer infantry, with roster and roll of honor, by G. W. Lewis. Akron, Manufactured by the Werner co. [1894] 285 p. plates (ports.). 22½cm.    DLC NHi    **418**
Unit roster 217–74. Ryan 434.

Price, Peter
124th Ohio at Pickett's Mills. In National tribune scrap book III 156–8.    **418A**

Smith, Frank W
Smith "knapsack" of facts and figures, '61 to '65. Toledo, Spear, Johnson & co., printers, 1884. 111, (1) p. 15½cm. DLC NHi    **419**
"Preface" signed: Frank W. Smith, late co. "D," 124th O.V.I. Ryan 774.

## 125TH INFANTRY

*Organized: September 16, 1862 to December 5, 1863.*
*Mustered out: September 25, 1865.*
*Official roster* VIII 417–49, 768–74.
*Ohio in the war* 640–6.

Clark, Charles T    1845–
Opdycke tigers, 125th O.V.I., a history of the regiment and the campaigns and battles of the Army of the Cumberland, by Charles T. Clark, Capt. Co. F. Published by direction of the 125th O.V.I. association. Columbus, Spahr & Glenn, 1895. 472, (4) p. illus., plans, ports., plates (ports.). 23cm.    DLC NN    **420**
Unit roster 451–72. Ryan 119.

Moore, David Hastings, 1838–1915.
An escape that did not set me free, a by-product of Morgan's raid, a paper read before the Ohio commandery of the Loyal legion, April 7, 1915, by Lieut.-Col. David Hastings Moore, 125th O.V.I. 16 p. 21½cm.
NHi NN    **421**

Opdycke, Emerson,    –1884.
Notes on the Chickamauga campaign. *BandL* III 668–71.    **422**

## 126TH INFANTRY

*Organized: September 4 to October 11, 1862.*
*Mustered out: June 25, 1865.*
*Official roster* VIII 450–91, 774–80.
*Ohio in the war* 647–51.

Gilson, John H
Concise history of the One hundred and twenty-sixth regiment, Ohio volunteer infantry, from the date of organization to the end of the rebellion, with a complete roster of each company, from date of muster, battles and skirmishes participated in, lists of the killed, wounded and missing, and other incidents of the camp and field. Compiled by comrade J. H. Gilson of Company D. Salem, Walton, printer, 1883. 272 p. plates (ports.). 20½cm.
Ryan 279. Unit roster 130–211.    OHi    **423**

*126th Infantry, continued*

Hyatt, Thomas Jefferson, 1830–1864.

Captain Hyatt, being the letters written during the years 1863–1864, to his wife, Mary, by Captain T. J. Hyatt, 126th Ohio. Edited by Hudson Hyatt. *OHQ* LIII (1944) 166–83. **424**

## 127th Infantry
see *5th United States Colored Troops*

## 128TH INFANTRY

*Organized: December 7, 1861 to January 8, 1864.*
*Mustered out: July 13, 1865.*
*Official roster* VIII 492–524, 780–1.
*Ohio in the war* 652–6.

Mitchell, Eugene O

Johnson's island, military prison for Confederate prisoners, by E. O. Mitchell, late First Lieutenant 128th Ohio. 1896. *MOLLUS-Ohio* v 118–29. **425**

Phillips, George M

Johnson's island and the Lake Erie raid of 1864, by Lieutenant George M. Phillips. *MOLLUS-Minn* III 242–61. **426**

## 129TH INFANTRY

*Organized: August 10, 1863.*
*Mustered out: March 4–10, 1864.*
*Official roster* VIII 525–42, 781–2.
*Ohio in the war* 657–8.

## 130TH INFANTRY

*Organized: May 3 to 31, 1864.*
*Mustered out: September 22, 1864.*
*Official roster* VIII 543–57, 782.
*Ohio in the war* 659.

## 131ST INFANTRY

*Organized: May 14, 1864.*
*Mustered out: August 25, 1864.*
*Official roster* VIII 558–71, 782.
*Ohio in the war* 660.

Vail, Henry Hobart, 1839–1925.

What I saw of the Civil war, privately printed for the family. Woodstock, Vt., 1915. 37 p. 23cm. NN **427**

"Of this pamphlet there have been printed fifty copies." NN has signed letter of Vail acknowledging authorship.

## 132ND INFANTRY

*Organized: May 15, 1864.*
*Mustered out: September 10, 1864.*
*Official roster* VIII 572–85, 783.
*Ohio in the war* 661.

## 133RD INFANTRY

*Organized: May 6, 1864.*
*Mustered out: August 20, 1864.*
*Official roster* VIII 586–600, 784.
*Ohio in the war* 662.

Sherman, Sylvester M

History of the 133d regiment, O.V.I. and incidents connected with its service during the "War of the rebellion," by the Historian of the Association of its survivors, S. M. Sherman, M.D. Columbus, Champlin print. co., 1896. 163, (1) p. 20cm. DLC NN **428**

"Roll of honor," (1) p. Unit roster [153]–63. Ryan 759.

## 134TH INFANTRY

*Organized: May 6, 1864.*
*Mustered out: August 31, 1864.*
*Official roster* VIII 601–16, 784–5.
*Ohio in the war* 663.

McDonald, Colin

Personal notes, by Colin McDonald, 1864–1877. [Columbus, 1928] 47 p. front. (port.). 23cm. DLC **428A**

Civil war 4–6. "An apology" dated: Columbus, Ohio, August, 1928.

## 135TH INFANTRY

*Organized: May 11, 1864.*
*Mustered out: September 1, 1864.*
*Official roster* VIII 617–35, 785–6.
*Ohio in the war* 664.

Gatch, Conduce H

General O. M. Mitchel, and his brilliant march into the heart of the Southern Confederacy, by Lieutenant-Colonel C. H. Gatch. *MOLLUS-Iowa* II 110–28. **429**

## 136TH INFANTRY

*Organized: May 13, 1864.*
*Mustered out: August 30, 1864.*
*Official roster* VIII 636–49, 787.
*Ohio in the war* 665.

## 137TH INFANTRY

*Organized: May 10, 1864.*
*Mustered out: August 19, 1864.*
*Official roster* VIII 650–62, 787.
*Ohio in the war 666.*

## 138TH INFANTRY

*Organized: May 15, 1864.*
*Mustered out: September 1, 1864.*
*Official roster* VIII 663–77, 788.
*Ohio in the war 667.*

In memoriam Samuel S. Fisher. Cincinnati, Robert Clarke & co., print, 1874. 92 p. front. (port.). 23cm.   CSmH DLC NN   **430**

Chadwick, Wallace W
    Into the breach, Civil war letters of . . . Edited by Mabel Watkins Mayer. *OHQ* LII (1943) 158–80.   **431**

## 139TH INFANTRY

*Organized: May 10, 1864.*
*Mustered out: September 13, 1864.*
*Official roster* VIII 692–706, 788.
*Ohio in the war 668.*

## 140TH INFANTRY

*Organized: May 10, 1864.*
*Mustered out: August 30, 1864.*
*Official roster* VIII 636–49, 787.
*Ohio in the war 669.*

## 141ST INFANTRY

*Organized: May 11 to 14, 1864.*
*Mustered out: September 3, 1864.*
*Official roster* IX 1–15, 749.
*Ohio in the war 670.*

## 142ND INFANTRY

*Organized: May 13, 1864.*
*Mustered out: September 2, 1864.*
*Official roster* IX 16–29, 749–50.
*Ohio in the war 671–2.*

## 143RD INFANTRY

*Organized: May 12–13, 1864.*
*Mustered out: September 13, 1864.*
*Official roster* IX 30–44, 750–1.
*Ohio in the war 673.*

## 144TH INFANTRY

*Organized: May 11, 1864.*
*Mustered out: August 24, 31, 1864.*
*Official roster* IX 45–61, 751–2.
*Ohio in the war 674.*

## 145TH INFANTRY

*Organized: May 12, 1864.*
*Mustered out: August 24, 1864.*
*Official roster* IX 62–75, 753.
*Ohio in the war 675.*

## 146TH INFANTRY

*Organized: May 9–12, 1864.*
*Mustered out: September 7, 1864.*
*Official roster* IX 76–90, 753.
*Ohio in the war 676.*

## 147TH INFANTRY

*Organized: May 16, 1864.*
*Mustered out: August 30, 1864.*
*Official roster* IX 91–105, 753.
*Ohio in the war 677.*

Roster of the 147th regiment Ohio volunteer infantry, with age at enlistment, post office address and deaths as far as could be ascertained, August 1899, T. C. Schilling, Secretary. Revised, August 1913, M. C. Pierce, Secretary. West Milton, Radabaugh Bros., printers [1913] 46, (2) p. ports. 17½cm.
Title and imprint from cover.   OHi   **432**

## 148TH INFANTRY

*Organized: May 17–18, 1864.*
*Mustered out: September 14, 1864.*
*Official roster* IX 106–20, 754.
*Ohio in the war 678–9.*

## 149TH INFANTRY

*Organized: May 8–11, 1864.*
*Mustered out: August 30, 1864.*
*Official roster* IX 121–38, 755.
*Ohio in the war 680.*

Perkins, George, 1844?–
    A summer in Maryland and Virginia; or, campaigning with the 149th Ohio volunteer infantry, a sketch of events connected with the service of the Regiment in Maryland and the Shenandoah valley, Virginia. Written by

*149th Infantry, continued*

George Perkins, a member of Company A, at the request of his comrades of the Regiment. Chillicothe [School print. co.] 1911. 106 p. ports. 19½cm.          DLC NN OHi     **433**
Unit roster 69–106.

## 150TH INFANTRY

*Organized: May 5, 1864.*

*Mustered out: August 23, 1864.*

*Official roster* ix 139–54, 756.

*Ohio in the war* 681.

Cannon, James Calkins
Memorial — 150th Ohio — Company K. [Lakewood, 1907] 18 p. 2 plates (illus., port.). 23½cm.          DLC OHi     **434**
"Introductory" signed: J. C. Cannon. Report of exercises at the placing of Company K memorial in Battleground cemetery, Washington, D. C., July 11, 1907, with reminiscences of the battle of Fort Stevens, July–11–12, 1864. Ryan 101.

—— Record of service of Company K, 150th O.V.I. 1864. By James C. Cannon, reunion secretary for Co. K. 1903. 23cm.
                                     DLC OHi     **435**
P 20–1 and 24–5 are blank for additional information. Ryan 100.

Gleason, William J
Historical sketch of the 150th regiment Ohio volunteer infantry, by William J. Gleason, delivered at the 5th annual reunion, Scenic park, Rocky river, July 12th, 1899. Roster of the Regiment. Published by order of the Association. 30 p. 23cm.          OHi     **436**
Ryan 282. Unit roster [20]–30.

## 151ST INFANTRY

*Organized: May 13, 1864.*

*Mustered out: August 27, 1864.*

*Official roster* ix 155–69, 756.

*Ohio in the war* 682.

## 152ND INFANTRY

*Organized: May 8–11, 1864.*

*Mustered out: September 2, 1864.*

*Official roster* ix 170–83, 756.

*Ohio in the war* 683.

Nichols, Clifton Melvin, 1830–1903.
The "Nickliffe" correspondence, one hundred days of soldier life with the 152d regiment, Ohio national guards, and the 35th battalion, from Clarke co., by Clifton M. Nichols

of the Springfield (O.) news. Springfield, Hastings and Nichols, 1864. 62 p. 19½cm.
                                     NHi     **438**
"Originally appeared in the columns of the Springfield (O.) news."

—— A summer campaign in the Shenandoah valley in 1864, "one hundred days" (four months and two days) of soldier life with the 152d regiment Ohio volunteer infantry, by Clifton M. Nichols. Springfield, New Era printers, 1899. 172 p. 3 plates (ports.). 19½cm.          OHi     **439**

## 153RD INFANTRY

*Organized: May 10, 1864.*

*Mustered out: September 9, 1864.*

*Official roster* ix 184–99, 757.

*Ohio in the war* 684.

## 154TH INFANTRY

*Organized: May 9, 1864.*

*Mustered out: September 1, 1864.*

*Official roster* ix 200–12, 757.

*Ohio in the war* 685.

Owens, Ira S
One hundred and fifty-fourth regiment O.V.I. In his Greene county soldiers in the late war (1884) 168–9.          **440**

Stipp, Joseph A
The history and service of the 154th Ohio volunteer infantry, by Joseph A. Stipp. Toledo, Hadley & Fullagar, printers, 1896. 73 p. plates (fold. plan, 2 ports.). 23cm. NN OHi     **441**
Unit roster [65]–73. Ryan 788.

## 155TH INFANTRY

*Organized: May 8, 1864.*

*Mustered out: August 27, 1864.*

*Official roster* ix 213–28, 758.

*Ohio in the war* 686.

## 156TH INFANTRY

*Organized: May 15 to 17, 1864.*

*Mustered out: September 1, 1864.*

*Official roster* ix 229–43, 758.

*Ohio in the war* 687.

## 157TH INFANTRY

*Organized: May 15, 1864.*

*Mustered out: September 10, 1864.*

*Official roster* ix 244–56, 759.

*Ohio in the war* 688.

## 158TH INFANTRY

*Organization not completed.*

## 159TH INFANTRY

*Organized: May 9 and 10, 1864.*
*Mustered out: August 22, 24, 1864.*
*Official roster* ix 257–72, 759.
*Ohio in the war* 689.

## 160TH INFANTRY

*Organized: May 12–14, 1864.*
*Mustered out: September 7, 1864.*
*Official roster* ix 273–87, 759–60.
*Ohio in the war* 690.

## 161ST INFANTRY

*Organized: May 9, 1864.*
*Mustered out: September 2, 1864.*
*Official roster* ix 288–301, 760.
*Ohio in the war* 691.

## 162ND INFANTRY

*Organized: May 20, 1864.*
*Mustered out: September 4, 1864.*
*Official roster* ix 302–15, 760–1.
*Ohio in the war* 692.

## 163RD INFANTRY

*Organized: May 12, 1864.*
*Mustered out: September 10, 1864.*
*Official roster* iv 316–29, 761–2.
*Ohio in the war* 693.

## 164TH INFANTRY

*Organized: May 11, 1864.*
*Mustered out: August 27, 1864.*
*Official roster* ix 330–43, 762.
*Ohio in the war* 694.

*165th Infantry see 165th Battalion*

## 166TH INFANTRY

*Organized: May 13, 15, 1864.*
*Mustered out: September 9, 1864.*
*Official roster* ix 355–70, 763.
*Ohio in the war* 696.

## 167TH INFANTRY

*Organized: May 14 to 17, 1864.*
*Mustered out: September 8, 1864.*
*Official roster* ix 371–84, 763.
*Ohio in the war* 697.

## 168TH INFANTRY

*Organized: May 12 to 19, 1864.*
*Mustered out: September 8, 1864.*
*Official roster* ix 385–99, 764.
*Ohio in the war* 698.

See Title 171A.

## 169TH INFANTRY

*Organized: May 13 to 15, 1864.*
*Mustered out: September 4, 1864.*
*Official roster* ix 400–14, 764–5.
*Ohio in the war* 699.

## 170TH INFANTRY

*Organized: May 13 to 14, 1864.*
*Mustered out: September 10, 1864.*
*Official roster* ix 415–30, 765.
*Ohio in the war* 700.

## 171ST INFANTRY

*Organized: May 7, 1864.*
*Mustered out: August 20, 1864.*
*Official roster* ix 431–46, 766.
*Ohio in the war* 701–02.

## 172ND INFANTRY

*Organized: May 14, 1864.*
*Mustered out: September 3, 1864.*
*Official roster* ix 447–61, 767.
*Ohio in the war* 703.

## 173RD INFANTRY

*Organized: September 1864.*
*Mustered out: June 26, 1865.*
*Official roster* ix 462–81, 768–9.
*Ohio in the war* 704–05.

## 174TH INFANTRY

*Organized: August 18 to September 21, 1864.*
*Mustered out: June 28, 1865.*
*Official roster* ix 482–504, 769–72.
*Ohio in the war* 706–08.

*174th Infantry, continued*

Jones, John Sills,       –1903.
History of the 174th O.V.I., address delivered by Gen. J. S. Jones, at the reunion of
the 174th O.V.I., August 30, 1894, at Marysville, Ohio. [Marysville, Journal print, 1894]
35 p. 21cm.                            OHi      **442**
On cover: History of the 174th O.V.I. and roster
of the Regiment. Caption title. Ryan 391.

### 175TH INFANTRY

*Organized: October 1864.*
*Mustered out: June 27, 1865.*
*Official roster* ix 505–28, 772–6.
*Ohio in the war* 709–10.

### 176TH INFANTRY

*Organized: August 21 to September 21,*
*1864.*
*Mustered out: June 14, 1865.*
*Official roster* ix 529–53, 776–8.
*Ohio in the war* 711–12.

### 177TH INFANTRY

*Organized: September 23 to October 14,*
*1864.*
*Mustered out: June 24, 1865.*
*Official roster* ix 554–75, 778–9.
*Ohio in the war* 713–14.

### 178TH INFANTRY

*Organized: September 26, 1864.*
*Mustered out: June 29, 1865.*
*Official roster* ix 576–96, 780–1.
*Ohio in the war* 715–16.

Munk, Joseph Amasa, 1847–1927.
Activities of a lifetime, by Joseph Amas
Munk. Los Angeles, Times-Mirror press, 1924.
221 p. plates (illus., ports.). 20cm.
"Army days," 35–65.    DLC KHi NN      **443**

### 179TH INFANTRY

*Organized: September 1864.*
*Mustered out: July 12, 1865.*
*Official roster* ix 619–40, 783–4.
*Ohio in the war* 717.

### 180TH INFANTRY

*Organized: September to October 1864.*
*Mustered out: July 12, 1865.*
*Official roster* ix 619–40, 783–4.
*Ohio in the war* 718–19.

Abbott, Horace R
. . . My escape from Belle isle, a paper pre-
pared and read before Michigan commandery
of the Military order of the loyal legion of the
United States, December 5, 1889, by Lieut.
Horace R. Abbott. Detroit, Winn & Hammond,
printers, 1889. 39 p. 21½cm.    DLC      **444**
At head of title: War paper no. 13.

### 181ST INFANTRY

*Organized: September 29 to October 10,*
*1864.*
*Mustered out: July 14, 1865.*
*Official roster* ix 641–66, 784–5.
*Ohio in the war* 720–1.

### 182ND INFANTRY

*Organized: August 4 to October 27, 1864.*
*Mustered out: July 7, 1865.*
*Official roster* ix 667–91, 785–6.
*Ohio in the war* 722–3.

See Title 222B.

### 183RD INFANTRY

*Organized: September to October 1864.*
*Mustered out: July 17, 1865.*
*Official roster* ix 692–724, 787–9.
*Ohio in the war* 724–5.

### 184TH INFANTRY

*Organized: February 1865.*
*Mustered out: September 20, 1865.*
*Official roster* ix 725–45, 789–90.
*Ohio in the war* 726.

Owens, Ira S
One hundred and eighty-fourth regiment
O.V.I. In his Greene county soldiers in the late
war (1884) 186–7.                              **445**

### 185TH INFANTRY

*Organized: February 25, 1865.*
*Mustered out: September 26, 1865.*
*Official roster* x 1–19, 665–6.
*Ohio in the war* 727.

### 186TH INFANTRY

*Organized: February 1865.*
*Mustered out: September 18, 1865.*
*Official roster* x 20–39, 666–7.
*Ohio in the war* 728–9.

## 187TH INFANTRY

*Organized: March 2, 1865.*
*Mustered out: January 20, 1866.*
*Official roster* x 40–59, 668.
*Ohio in the war* 730–1.

## 188TH INFANTRY

*Organized: March 2–4, 1865.*
*Mustered out: September 21, 1865.*
*Official roster* x 60–83, 669.
*Ohio in the war* 732.

## 189TH INFANTRY

*Organized: January 12 to March 6, 1865.*
*Mustered out: September 28, 1865.*
*Official roster* x 84–107, 670–1.
*Ohio in the war* 733.

## 190TH INFANTRY

*Failed to complete organization.*

## 191ST INFANTRY

*Organized: January to February 1865.*
*Mustered out: August 27, 1865.*
*Official roster* x 108–25, 672.
*Ohio in the war* 734–5.

## 192ND INFANTRY

*Organized: March 9, 1865.*
*Mustered out: September 1, 1865.*
*Official roster* x 126–45, 672.
*Ohio in the war* 736–7.

## 193RD INFANTRY

*Organized: March 1865.*
*Mustered out: August 4, 1865.*
*Official roster* x 146–64, 673.
*Ohio in the war* 738.

## 194TH INFANTRY

*Organized: March 1865.*
*Mustered out: October 24, 1865.*
*Official roster* x 165–84, 674–5.
*Ohio in the war* 739.

## 195TH INFANTRY

*Organized: March 14 to 20, 1865.*
*Mustered out: December 18, 1865.*
*Official roster* x 185–203, 675.
*Ohio in the war* 740–1.

## 196TH INFANTRY

*Organized: March 25, 1865.*
*Mustered out: September 11, 1865.*
*Official roster* x 204–20, 676.
*Ohio in the war* 742.

## 197TH INFANTRY

*Organized: January 8 to April 11, 1865.*
*Mustered out: July 31, 1865.*
*Official roster* x 221–40, 677.
*Ohio in the war* 743–4.

## 198TH INFANTRY

*Organized: April 17–27, 1865.*
*Mustered out: May 8, 1865.*
*Official roster* x 241, 677.
*Ohio in the war* 744.

# *Battalions*

## 4TH BATTALION

*Formed from veterans and recruits of the
4th and 8th regiments of infantry: June
26, 1864.*
*Mustered out: July 12, 1865.*
*Official roster* i 681–94, 771–2.

## 11TH BATTALION

*Formed from veterans and recruits of the
11th regiment: June 1864.*
*Mustered out: June 11, 1865.*
*Official roster* i 695–709, 772.

## 48TH BATTALION

*Organized by consolidation of 48th, 83rd,
and 114th regiments of infantry: July 24,
1865.*
*Mustered out: May 1866.*

## 165TH BATTALION

*Organized: May 14, 19, 1864.*
*Mustered out: August 31, 1864.*
*Official roster* ix 344–54, 762.
*Ohio in the war* 695.

# SHARPSHOOTERS

## 1ST COMPANY

( *Company G, 66th Illinois Infantry* )

*Mustered in: November 23, 1861.*
*Mustered out: July 7, 1865.*
*Official roster* i 539–46, 753–5.

## 2ND COMPANY

(*Company H, 66th Illinois Infantry*)

*Mustered in: November 30, 1861.*
*Mustered out: July 7, 1865.*
*Official roster* I 539–42, 547–50, 753–5.

## 3RD COMPANY

(*Company K, 66th Illinois Infantry*)

*Mustered in: April 7, 1862.*
*Mustered out: April 26, 1865.*
*Official roster* I 539–42, 550–2, 735–5.

## 4TH COMPANY

(*Co. K, 79th Ohio*)

*Mustered in: September 29, 1862.*
*Assigned to 79th Ohio regiment of infantry.*
*Official roster* I 553–7, 755.

## 5TH COMPANY

*Mustered in: December 5, 1862.*
*Mustered out: July 19, 1865.*
*Official roster* I 559–64, 756.

## 6TH COMPANY

*Mustered in December 20, 1862.*
*Mustered out: July 19, 1865.*
*Official roster* I 565–9, 757.

## 7TH COMPANY

*Mustered in: January 27, 1863.*
*Mustered out: July 28, 1865.*
*Official roster* I 571–6, 757–8.

McCrory, William
    Early life and personal reminiscences of General William T. Sherman, by Captain W. McCrory. 1891. *MOLLUS-Minn* III 310–46. **446**

## 8TH COMPANY

*Mustered in: March 9, August 22, 1863.*
*Mustered out: July 19, 1865.*
*Official roster* I 577–81, 758.

## 9TH AND 10TH COMPANIES

*Mustered in: 9th, February 26, 1864; 10th, April 1, 1864.*
*Transferred to 60th regiment of infantry: February 24, 1865.*
*Official roster* I 583–90.

# Regimental Publications
# & Personal Narratives
# of the Civil War

## A Checklist

*Compiled by* C. E. DORNBUSCH

Volume One   Northern States

PART VI   IOWA, KANSAS, MICHIGAN,
MINNESOTA, AND WISCONSIN

New York

The New York Public Library

1962

THIS VOLUME HAS BEEN PUBLISHED WITH HELP
FROM THE EMILY ELLSWORTH FORD SKEEL FUND

# Preface

THIS CHECKLIST of regimental histories, publications of regimental associations, and personal narratives of participants in the Civil War is a revision of and supplement to the section on "Military Organizations" in the third edition of the *Bibliography of State Participation in the Civil War*, prepared and published by the War Department Library, Washington, D. C. in 1913 as its Subject Catalogue No 6.\*

The present checklist is to be published in seven Parts. The first six will cover the batteries and regiments of seventeen Northern states: I Illinois; II New York; III New England states; IV New Jersey and Pennsylvania; V Indiana and Ohio; and VI Iowa, Kansas, Michigan, Minnesota, and Wisconsin. A final section will provide an index of authors and, where required, titles of the publications listed for these seventeen states.

No subject index to the checklist is contemplated. Besides supplying references for the history of a battery or regiment, the checklist does the same for battles and engagements. To locate references on a battle or engagement, however, the user must determine from the order of battle available in Dyer's *Compendium of the War of the Rebellion* which units were involved and then turn to their entries in the checklist. It is also useful to know the other regiments of a brigade as a means of obtaining from the checklist additional narratives of an incident or battle.

The compiler has followed the arrangement of the 1913 work. Within each state military units are arranged numerically by arm of service — Artillery, Cavalry, and Infantry. While the earlier work entered only units for which publications were known, the present compilation has recorded all units which were organized. Again, while rosters and compilations of regimental histories were reported in one section headed "State Publication" in *BSP*, the present work has indexed these publications under the individual military units.

The compiler has located and personally examined each work entered in this checklist. Some entries which were listed in *BSP* have been omitted —

\* The Bibliography (hereafter referred to as *BSP*) was prepared as a catalogue and index of a major Civil War collection, now part of the National War College Library, Washington.

entries based on titles taken from bibliographies, correspondence, dealers'
catalogues, and other sources but not in the War Department Library. Such
"ghosts" as have remained have been omitted here. The present checklist
also omits the *BSP* references to the *National Tribune*, and a group of articles
by George L. Kilmer which are cited in *BSP* not by original publication but
as mounted clippings in ten volumes in the War Department Library collections.

Although a monumental work, some errors found their way into the *BSP*.
For instance, Douglas Putnam's *Recollections of the battle of Shiloh* was
entered under the 92nd Ohio Regiment, the regiment to which he belonged.
But that regiment was formed some months after the battle was fought, and
Putnam could write of it not as a member but as a civilian observer. Similarly
Eagan's *Battle of Birch Coolie* is entered under the 1st Minnesota Heavy
Artillery, although that unit did not participate in the battle.

The seventeen states covered by this checklist had a total of 2,202 batteries
and regiments which took part in the Civil War. Each of these units has been
listed with a brief statement of its service, i. e. muster in and muster out
dates. Where the same number has been assigned to two regiments, they
have been distinguished by the term of original enlistments, i. e. three
months or three years. Changes in a unit's designation or arm of service
as well as amalgamations have been reported. Although some units mustered
out before the close of the war and transferred their recruits and veterans to
other units, the checklist has not reported this movement of personnel. Reference is made to regimental rosters and narratives of a unit's service where
this information may be found.

The compiler has included any articles and publications which could be
associated with a particular battery or regiment. The bulk of these are the
regimental histories, reunion proceedings, and unit rosters. Publications of
sermons preached at soldiers' funerals have been reported. Though their
size did not lend to preservation, a surprising number of soldiers' memorials
has been located. Broadsides of company rosters, often illustrated in color,
were soldiers' souvenirs of the war. The inclusion of all these types of
material has here resulted in the broadest possible bibliographical coverage
of Civil War materials. All prison narratives have been entered under the

regiment in which the author was serving at the time of his capture. Newspapers printed in the field by army units have not been included.

The value of this checklist is primarily in the listing of the personal narratives of Civil War participants, the rank and file as well as officers, from Lieutenant to Colonel. (By reason of the honorary Brevet rank, the Colonel of a regiment could be appointed Brigadier General at the close of the war, and in this case later reference to his rank is as General.) Usually the publication identifies the battery or regiment of the author. Occasionally, however, he may have served in two or more units, and the later service (often at a higher rank) is used on the title-page. Such items are entered in the checklist under the unit in which the author served at the time the events narrated took place.

Narratives which reflect service in two or more units are entered under the unit of first service, with cross references from other units in which the author served. When an author's service crossed state lines or when it was with the United States Colored Troops, his narrative has been fully entered under each unit.

The compiler has made extensive search of American journals and periodicals published since the close of hostilities. The very magnitude of this undertaking precludes even the hope of a definitive checklist. One assumes that obscure imprints with limited distribution have tended to disappear. In many cases only single surviving copies have been located. The search is continuing while other sections of the list are in preparation, and it is hoped that publication will bring new additions to light.

Following the statement of unit service, entries are given in two groups, anonymous publications followed by author entries. At least one location of each title is reported by means of the *Symbols Used in the National Union Catalogue of The Library of Congress*, seventh edition revised, 1959. Standard works such as the papers of the Military Order of the Loyal Legion and periodicals are not located in the checklist. The user is referred for these to the *Union List of Serials* and its supplements. Title-pages have been transcribed in full, including author statements which supply rank and unit. Distinction is made between illustrations which appear in the body of the text and illustrations which appear on unpaginated plates. Plates that are

paged have been considered as text illustrations. The place of publication is not identified when within same state as checklist is describing. The collation of reunion proceedings has been limited to their numbering and date.

Economy of effort deferred until the preparation of the Index the research necessary for completing names and supplying birth and death years. The user of this Checklist will find in the Index (Part VII) additional information not only for authors, joint-authors, and editors but also for individuals mentioned in notes. The age on enlistment as given in the Rosters is responsible for any questioned or doubled years of birth.

The very size of the compiler's undertaking has meant assistance from many sources. In his inspection of collections throughout the country, the compiler has been helped by many librarians, and their contributions have been acknowledged in the appropriate sections of the checklist. Above all the compiler is indebted to the administrators of The Emily E. F. Skeel Fund of The New York Public Library for making the compilation of this checklist possible and for freedom in developing it.

# Table of Contents

# IOWA, KANSAS, MICHIGAN, MINNESOTA,
# AND WISCONSIN

# Acknowledgments

IOWA

It is fitting to mention here Dr James I. Robertson, Jr. From the inception of this bibliographical undertaking when he was Editor of *Civil War History* at Iowa City and now in his present post, Executive Director of the Civil War Centennial Commission, Dr Robertson has actively supported the compiler with encouragement and assistance.

Dr William J. Petersen, Superintendent, Iowa State Historical Society

Much help has also been given by Mr Fleming Fraker, Editor, Annals of Iowa

KANSAS

Miss Alberta Pantle, Librarian, Kansas State Historical Society

MICHIGAN

Dr George S. May, Research Archivist, Michigan Historical Commission

Mrs E. B. Loughin, Michigan State Library

MINNESOTA

Mr James Taylor Dunn, Librarian, Minnesota Historical Society

WISCONSIN

Mr Benton Wilcox, Librarian, The State Historical Society of Wisconsin

# Abbreviations

| | |
|---|---|
| *AG's report* | Report of the Adjutant general of the State of Kansas, 1861–'65, (1896) |
| *AI* | Annals of Iowa |
| *BandL* | Battles and leaders, New York, 1887–88. 4 v. |
| *BandG* | Blue and Gray, Philadelphia |
| *CHSW* | Collections of the State historical society of Wisconsin |
| *Coulter* | Travels in the Southern states, a bibliography, by E. Merle Coulter, 1948 |
| *IHR* | Iowa historical record |
| *IJH* | Iowa journal of history |
| *Iowa colonels* | Iowa colonels and regiments, by A. A. Stuart, 1865 |
| *Iowa and the rebellion* | Iowa and the rebellion, by L. D. Ingersoll, 1867 |
| *JUSCA* | Journal of the United States cavalry association |
| *KHQ* | Kansas historical quarterly |
| *Michigan in the war* | Michigan in the war, compiled by Jno. Robertson, Adjutant general |
| *Military history* | A separately paged section of the Report of the Adjutant general of the State of Kansas, 1861–'65 |
| ------------ | The military history of Wisconsin, by E. B. Quiner, 1866 |
| *MOLLUS* | Military order of the loyal legion of the United States |
| *DC* | War papers District of Columbia commandery |
| *Ill* | Military essays and recollections Illinois commandery |
| *Ind* | War papers Indiana commandery |
| *Iowa* | War sketches and incidents Iowa commandery |
| *Mass* | Civil war papers Massachusetts commandery |
| *Mich* | War papers Michigan commandery |
| *Minn* | Glimpses of the Nation's struggle Minnesota commandery |
| *Mo* | War papers and personal reminiscences Missouri commandery |
| *Neb* | Civil war sketches and incidents Nebraska commandery |

[ 13 ]

| | |
|---|---|
| *MOLLUS, continued* | |
| NY | Personal recollections of the War of the rebellion New York commandery |
| *Ohio* | Sketches of War history Ohio commandery |
| *Wis* | War papers Wisconsin commandery |
| *MiH* | Michigan history |
| *MiHC* | Michigan historical collections |
| *MiHM* | Michigan history magazine |
| *Minnesota in the Civil and Indian wars* | Minnesota in the Civil and Indian wars, 1861–1865, (1890–93) |
| *MH* | Minnesota history |
| *MHB* | Minnesota history bulletin |
| *P* | Palimpsest |
| *PMHSM* | Papers of the Military historical society of Massachusetts |
| *Roster* | Roster and record of Iowa soldiers in the War of the rebellion . . . 1908–11. 5 v. |
| ------------ | Roster of Wisconsin volunteers, War of the rebellion . . . 1886 |
| *TKHS* | Transactions Kansas historical society |
| *Wisconsin in the war* | Wisconsin in the War of the rebellion, by Wm. DeLoss Love, 1866 |
| *WMH* | Wisconsin magazine of history |

# IOWA

# Reference Works

Dyer, Frederick Henry, 1849–1917.

A compendium of the War of the rebellion, 1908 (reprinted 1959).

"Regimental index" 140–4; "Regimental histories" 1158–81. The pagination is the same in the 1959 reprint.

Ingersoll, Lurton Dunham.

Iowa and the rebellion, a history of the troops furnished by the State of Iowa to the volunteer armies of the Union, which conquered the great Southern rebellion of 1861–5, by Lurton Dunham Ingersoll. Third edition. Philadelphia, J. B. Lippincott & co., 1867. 743 p. maps. 23cm.

Iowa.  Adjutant-General.

Roster and record of Iowa soldiers in the War of the rebellion, together with historical sketches of volunteer organizations, 1861–1866 . . . Published by authority of the General assembly, under the direction of Brig. Gen. Wm. H. Thrift [v. 3–6, Brig. Gen. Guy E. Logan] Adjutant general. Des Moines, E. H. English, State printer, 1908–11. 6 v. 23cm.

Volume 6 has title: Roster and record of Iowa soldiers in miscellaneous organizations of the Mexican war, Indian campaigns, War of the rebellion and the Spanish-American and Philippine wars, together with historical sketches of volunteer organizations.

Petersen, William J.

Iowa history reference guide, compiled by William J. Petersen. Iowa City, State Historical Society of Iowa, 1952. 192 p. 24½cm.

"Iowa and the Civil war," 95–104.

Stuart, Addison A.

Iowa colonels and regiments, being a history of Iowa regiments in the War of the rebellion, and containing a description of the battles in which they fought, by Captain A. A. Stuart, Seventeenth Iowa infantry. Des Moines, Mills & co., 1865. 656 p. plates (ports.). 22½cm.

*The Union army.*

"Record of Iowa regiments," iv (1908) 134–86.

United States.  Adjutant General's Office.

Official army register of the volunteers of the United States army for the years 1861, '62, '63, '64, '65. Part VII. Washington, 1867.

A roster of Iowa officers by regiments, p 227–301, 402–04, with an alphabetical index to the eight states in this volume.

# IOWA

## ARTILLERY

### Batteries (Light)

#### 1ST BATTERY

*Mustered in: August 17, 1861.*
*Mustered out: July 5, 1865.*
*Roster v 1689–1722.*

Black, Samuel, 1840?–
A soldier's recollections of the Civil war, by S. Black, member of the First Iowa battery, with supplemental chapters by comrades. . . . Minco, Okla., Printed by the Minco Minstrel, 1912. 117 p. plates (ports.). 21cm.
DLC    *1*

Dilts, William G
Record of the First Iowa battery with the autobiography of Captain W. H. Gay and letters and documents, 1861–1865. [n. p., 1905] 40 p. plates (ports.). 22cm.    Ia-HA    *2*
"Prefatory" signed: W. G. Dilts.

#### 2ND BATTERY

*Mustered in: August 8, 31, 1861.*
*Mustered out: August 7, 1865.*
*Roster v 1723–46.*

Dodge, Grenville Mellen, 1831–1916.
. . . Fiftieth anniversary Fourth Iowa veteran infantry, Dodge's Second Iowa battery [and] Dodge's band as guests, Society of the Army of the Tennessee, Council Bluffs, Iowa, October 10 and 11, 1911. [Council Bluffs, Monarch print. co., 1911] 81 p. 4 fronts. (ports.). 23cm.    NN    *3*
"Compiled by Major General Grenville M. Dodge."
At head of title: 1861 1911.

Reed, Joseph Rea, 1835–1925.
Guntown and Tupelo, by Joseph R. Reed, late Captain Second battery Iowa volunteers. *MOLLUS-Iowa* II 300–24.    *4*

#### 3RD BATTERY

*Mustered in: September 24, 1861.*
*Mustered out: October 23, 1865.*
*Roster v 1747–82.*

#### 4TH BATTERY

*Mustered in: November 23, 1863.*
*Mustered out: July 14, 1865.*
*Roster v 1783–99.*

## CAVALRY

### 1ST CAVALRY

*Mustered in: July 30–31, August 17, September 12, 1861.*
*Mustered out: February 15, 1866.*
*Roster IV 1–211.*
*Iowa and the rebellion 358–73.*
*Iowa Colonels 541–64.*

Historical society of the First regiment Iowa cavalry volunteers. *IHR* II (1886) 272–3.    *5*
Announcement of formation, officers and purposes signed by the Secretary, Dr. Chas. H. Lothrop.

Proceedings of the first reunion of the First Iowa cavalry, held at Davenport, September 19, 20, and 21, 1883. Historical sketch, by Surgeon M. B. Cochran. Davenport, Egbert, Fidlar, & Chambers, 1884. 67 p. 23cm. IaHi    *6*
"Historical sketch," 9–33.

Proceedings of the second reunion of the First Iowa veteran volunteer cavalry, held at Cedar Rapids, Iowa, September 21st, 22d and 23d, 1886. Compiled by the Secretary of the Association. With Historical sketch, by Surgeon M. B. Cochran. Cedar Rapids, Daily Republican print. house, 1886. front. (port.), ports. 24cm.    Ia-HA    *6A*

Allen, William P
Three frontier battles, 1897. *MOLLUS-Minn* IV 478–93.    *7*
Wilsons Creek, Pea Ridge and Prairie Grove.

Andrews, Malcomb S
Civil war diary of M. S. Andrews. . . . Seymour [n. d.] 82 folios. 28cm. Mimeographed.
IaHi    *8*

Gulick, William O    1843?–1863.
The journal and letters of Corporal William O. Gulick. *IJH* XXVIII (1930) 194–267, 390–455, 543–603.    *9*
Editor, Max Hendricks Guyer.

Iowa. House of Representatives.
First Iowa cavalry [report of Committee on incident of flogging in the Army] [Des Moines, 1865] 5 p. 22cm.    Ia-HA    *10*
Caption title.

Lothrop, Charles Henry, 1831–1890.
A brief history of the First regiment Iowa cavalry veteran volunteers, by Chas. H. Lothrop. [Lyons, 1887] 36 p. 22½cm.
Caption title.    Ia-HA    *11*

*1st Cavalry, continued*

—— A history of the First regiment Iowa cavalry veteran volunteers, from its organization in 1861, to its muster out of the United States service in 1866. Also, a complete roster of the Regiment. By Charles H. Lothrop, Surgeon. Lyons, Beers & Eaton, printers, 1890. x, [13]–422, v, (1) p. plates (ports.). 23cm.

NHi NN    12

Unit roster [385]–422. "Index," v p. "Names of portraits," (1) p. Work was completed and seen through the press by the author's wife, Sarah Virginia Lothrop.

## 2ND CAVALRY

*Mustered in: August 30 to September 28, 1861.*

*Mustered out: September 19, 1865.*

*Roster iv 213–416.*

*Iowa and the rebellion 374–95.*

*Iowa colonels 565–82.*

. . . Biennial reunion Second Iowa veteran cavalry association. iii 1887 (NHi); iv–v 1889, 1891 (IaHi); vii 1895 (Ia-HA); ix–xv 1899–1911 (Ia-HA); xvii 1915 (Ia-HA).    13

Burnap, Willard A    1840–1923.
What happened during one man's lifetime, 1840–1920, a review of some great, near great and little events, by Willard A. Burnap. Fergus Falls, Minn., Burnap Estate, 1923. 461 p. illus., plans, double plate (map). 20½cm.

DLC NN OU    14

Horton, Charles Cummins, 1839–1916.
Col. Edward Hatch's great charge at Farmington, Mississippi. *AI* s3 vi (1904) 444–6. 15

Pierce, Lyman B
History of the Second Iowa cavalry, containing a detailed account of its organization, marches, and the battles in which it has participated; also, a complete roster of each company, by Sergeant Lyman B. Pierce, Regimental Color-bearer. Burlington, Hawk-Eye print. estab., 1865. viii, [9]–237 p. 22cm.

Unit roster 169–237.    DLC NHi NN    16

## 3RD CAVALRY

*Mustered in: August 30 to September 14, 1861.*

*Mustered out: August 9, 1865.*

*Roster iv 417–635.*

*Iowa and the rebellion 396–416.*

*Iowa colonels 583–606.*

Bryant, Thomas Julian
The capture of General Marmaduke by James Dunlavy, an Iowa private cavalryman. *IJH* xi (1913) 248–57.    17

Bussey, Cyrus, 1833–1915.
The Pea ridge campaign considered, by Brevet Major-General Cyrus Bussey. 1905. 24 p. *MOLLUS-DC* no 60.    18

—— The battle of Athens, Missouri. *AI* s3 v (1901) 81–92. plate (port.).    19

Calkin, Homer L
Life in the army. *P* xxiii (1942) 1–15.    20
Based on the diary of Benjamin Keller, 1833–

Gilpin, Ebenezer Nelson
The last campaign, cavalryman's journal. *JUSCA* xviii (1908) 617–75. ports.    21

Gilpin, Thomas C
History of the 3rd Iowa volunteer cavalry, from August, 1861, to September, 1865, by Brevt. Major T. C. Gilpin. Winterset, Winterset News [189–?] 61 p. 20cm.    Ia-HA    22
Title and imprint from cover.

Noble, John Willock, 1831–1912.
Battle of Pea ridge, or Elk Horn tavern, by Brevet Brig.-Gen. John W. Noble. *MOLLUS-Mo* i 211–42.    23

## 4TH CAVALRY

*Mustered in: November 23, 1861 to January 1, 1862.*

*Mustered out: August 8, 1865.*

*Roster iv 637–841.*

*Iowa and the rebellion 417–40.*

*Iowa colonels 607–20.*

Thomas Drummond. *AI* s3 xxx (1950) 315–42. 2 plates (illus., port.).    24
Partial contents: Thomas Drummond, by Emory H. English, 315–27; Military service conspicuous, by A. N. Harbert, 328–32.

Scott, William Forse, 1843–1933.
The last fight for Missouri, a paper read by Adjutant Wm. Forse Scott, 1904. *MOLLUS-NY* iii 292–328.    25

—— The story of a cavalry regiment, the career of the Fourth Iowa veteran volunteers, from Kansas to Georgia, 1861–1865, by Wm. Forse Scott, late Adjutant. New York, G. P. Putnam's Sons, 1893. xxii, 602 p. front. (port.), plates (maps, partly fold.). 23cm.

DLC NHi NN    26

—— Roster of the Fourth Iowa cavalry veteran volunteers, 1861–1865, an appendix to "The story of a cavalry regiment," by Wm. Forse Scott. New York, J. J. Little & co., 1902. 243 p. plates (ports.). 23½cm.

DLC NHi NN    27

Vanorsdol, James O        1840–
Four years for the Union, by James O. Vanorsdol. [Springfield, Col., n. d.] 80 p. plates
(1 illus., ports.). 23cm.                    KHi    28
"Errata" slip inserted.

White, John H
Forgotten cavalrymen, General Edward
Francis Winslow. *JUSCA* xxv (1915) 375–89.
                                                    29
Whiting, Frederick
Diary and personal recollections of the sec-
ond Grierson raid through Tennessee and Mis-
sissippi, December, 1864, and January, 1865,
and the General Wilson raid through Alabama
and Georgia during the months of March and
April, 1865, by Captain F. S. Whiting. *MOL-
LUS-Iowa* I 89–104.                                  30

### 5TH CAVALRY

*Organized as Curtis horse: December 20,
1861. Companies A, B, C, D, the Nebraska
battalion; Companies E, F, G, H, the Minnesota battalion; Companies I, K, L, M,
the Osage mounted rifles, and Captains
Brackett's, West's and Naughton's companies.*

*Assigned to the State of Iowa as 5th regi-
ment of cavalry: June 25, 1862.*

*Consolidated with 15th regiment of infan-
try: August 8, 1864.*

*Roster* IV 843–1013. 5th veteran cavalry
consolidated, IV 1015–1112.

*Iowa and the rebellion* 441–56.

*Iowa colonels* 621–30.

Alley, Charles
Excerpts from the Civil war diary of Lieu-
tenant Charles Alley, Company "C," Fifth
Iowa cavalry. Edited by John S. Ezell. *IJH*
XLIX (1951) 241–56.                                  31

Garland, John Lewis
The Irish dragoons in the American Civil
war. *Irish sword* I Dublin (1949) 37–9.     32

Lightcap, William Henry
The horrors of Southern prisons during the
War of the rebellion, from 1861 to 1865, by
W. H. Lightcap. Lancaster, Wis. [Platteville,
Wis., Journal job rooms, c1902] 95 p. front.
(port.). 22cm.                   DLC NN     33
Captured at Newnan, Georgia, July 31, 1864.

Nott, Charles Cooper, 1827–1916.
Kriegs-Scenen, von Karl C. Nott, Ritter-
meister im 5. Kavallerie-Regiment Iowa. Uber-
setzt von Hermann von Hoff. Berlin, Wilhelm
Baensch, 1884. viii, 154 p. 20½cm.
                                     MB    34

—— Sketches of the war, a series of letters to
the North Moore street school of New York, by
Charles C. Nott, Captain in the Fifth Iowa
cavalry. New York, Charles T. Evans, 1863.
174 p. 18½cm.                          NN    35
Coulter 350.

—— —— Second edition. New York, Anson
D. F. Randolph, 1865. 174 p. 18½cm.
Printed from the plates of Title 35. NN    36

—— —— Third edition. New York, Anson
D. F. Randolph, 1865. 184 p. 18½cm.
                                       NN    37
Printed from the plates of Title 35 with the addi-
tion of an Appendix, 175–84.

—— —— Fourth edition. New York, Anson
D. F. Randolph, 1865. 184 p. 18cm.
For note see that of Title 37.        NN    38

—— —— Revised and enlarged edition.
New York, William Abbatt, 1911. xviii, 201 p.
19½cm.                              NN    38A
A reprint with a change in the order of chapters
I–V. New matter are the Publisher's introduction and
two appendixes.

Seavey, Webber S
Personal recollections, 1862–1865. In National tribune scrap book III 16–18.      38B

### 6TH CAVALRY

*Mustered in: January 31 to March 5, 1863.*

*Mustered out: October 17, 1865.*

*Roster* IV 1015–1249.

*Iowa and the rebellion* 680–9.

*Iowa colonels* 631–2.

Drips, Joseph H        1843?–
Three years among the Indians in Dakota,
by J. H. Drips, Sergeant in Company L, Sixth
Iowa cavalry. Kimball, S. D., Brule Index,
1894. 139 p. 4 ports. 19cm.
                            DLC NHi NN    39
Myers, Frank
Soldiering in Dakota, among the Indians, in
1863-4-5, by Private Frank Myers, Co. B, 6th
Iowa cavalry. Huron, Huronite print. house,
1888. 60 p. 21cm.                      NN    40

—— —— Reprinted by State historical society. Pierre, S. Dakota, 1936. 48 p. 23cm.
                                       WHi    41

### 7TH CAVALRY

*Mustered in: April 7 to July 13, 1863.*

*Mustered out: June 22, 1866.*

*Roster* IV 1251–1392; 7th cavalry reorganized, IV 1393–1503.

*Iowa and the rebellion* 690–3.

*Iowa colonels* 633–8.

*7th Cavalry, continued*

Iowa troops in the Sully campaigns. *IJH* xx (1922) 364–443.                                **42**

Contents: The narrative of Henry J. Wieneke, 14th Iowa, 366–74; The manuscripts of Amos R. Cherry, 14th Iowa, 374–440; Letter of Josiah F. Hill, 7th Iowa cavalry, 440–3.

Pattison, John J
With the U.S. army along the Oregon trail, 1863–66, diary by. . . . *Nebraska history magazine* xv (1934) 79–93. illus.                                **42A**

Ware, Eugene Fitch, 1841–1911.
The Indian war of 1864, being a fragment of the early history of Kansas, Nebraska, Colorado and Wyoming. Topeka, Kansas, Crane & co., 1911. xi, 601 p. illus. 19½cm. NN    **43**
Includes unit roster of Co. F.

—— The Indian war of 1864. With an introduction and notes by Clyde C. Walton. New York, St. Martin's press [1960] xix, 483 p. facs., plans. 24cm.                NB NN    **43A**

Wieneke, Henry J            1837–1923.
Iowa troops in Dakota territory, 1861–86, based on the diaries and letters of Henry J. Wieneke. Edited by Mildred Throne. *IJH* lvii (1959) 97–120. map.                **43B**
"Consists of diaries and letters of Henry J. Wieneke . . . and of numerous letters from various members of the regiment published in Iowa city newspapers."

## 8TH CAVALRY

*Mustered in: September 30, 1863.*

*Mustered out: August 13, 1865.*

*Roster* iv 1505–1639.

*Iowa and the rebellion* 694–703.

*Iowa colonels* 639–50.

Belfield, Henry Holmes, 1837–1912.
My sixty days in Hades, paper read by Henry H. Belfield, formerly First Lieutenant and Adjutant Eighth Iowa cavalry volunteers, before the Commandery of the State of Illinois, Military order of the loyal legion, January 14, 1907. Chicago, Dial press, 1899. p [44]–64. 22cm.                NB    **44**
Also published as *MOLLUS-Ill* iii 447–64.

—— The Wilson raid, by Adjutant Henry Holmes Belfield (read January 3, 1905). *MOLLUS-Ill* iv 503–21.         **45**

Bird, Hiram Thornton, 1846?–
Memories of the Civil war, by Hiram Thornton Bird, 8th Iowa cavalry. [n. p., 1925?] 67 p. ports. 22½cm.                DLC NN    **46**

Mead, Homer, 1847–1926.
The Eighth Iowa cavalry in the Civil war, autobiography and personal recollections of

Homer Mead. Carthage, Ill., S. C. Davdison [1925] 27 p. ports. 22½cm.       DLC    **47**
On cover: In the Union cavalry, a reminiscence, by Homer Mead.

—— —— Augusta, Illinois. Carthage, Ill., S. C. Davidson [1927] 118, (2) p. 2 illus., ports. 24cm.                NN    **48**
Mary Davidson, editor.

Monlux, George, 1843–
To my comrades of Company "I," Eighth Iowa cavalry living and to the memory of those who are dead, I dedicate these lines — George Monlux. [Rock Rapids?, 193–] 105, (1) folios. port. 27½cm. mimeographed.
Ia-HA    **49**

Walden, Madison M            1836–
A brief history of the Eighth Iowa volunteer cavalry, prepared and read by Captain M. M. Walden, at the reunion of said Regiment held at Fairfield, Iowa, September 12 and 13, 1889. Des Moines, Register and Leader co., 1909. 15 p. 3 ports. 19½ x 11cm.    Ia-HA    **50**
Title and imprint from cover, p [1]

## 9TH CAVALRY

*Mustered in: November 30, 1863.*

*Mustered out: February 3 to March 23, 1866.*

*Roster* iv 1641–1767.

*Iowa and the rebellion* 708–13.

*Iowa colonels* 651.

Herriott, Frank I
Judge Orlando C. Howe, somewhat of his life and letters, Part III, Correspondence, 1863–1865. *AI* s3 xix (1934) 323–51, 406–43.
**51**

## INFANTRY

## *Brigades*

### *Crocker's Iowa Brigade*

*11th, 13th, 15th and 16th infantry regiments.*

Proceedings of Crocker's Iowa brigade at the . . . biennial reunion. [i]–ii 1881–1883 (DLC); iii–vi 1885–1891 (NHi); vii–xvi 1894–1911 (DLC); xvii–xix 1913/1917 (Ia-HA).    **52**
The proceedings of 1889–1911 were published with two biennial meetings covered in each volume. The proceedings of 1889 and 1891 were separately paged in the volume; other years the two meetings were continuously paged.

Belknap, William Worth, 1829–1890.
Song of Crocker's Iowa brigade. Air: "Benny havens, O!" Sung first at their third

reunion. . . . Washington, D.C., Gibson Bros., printers, 1889. 11 p. music. 23cm.

DLC NHi    **53**

"The words with the exception of verses six and seven, by General Belknap. Verses six and seven, by Major H. C. McArthur of the 15th Iowa."

Dodge, Grenville Mellen, 1831–1916.
Gen. G. M. Dodge's historical address. *AI* s3 iv (1901) 577–94. plate (port.).    **54**

Before the reunion of the Crocker brigade reviewing the operations of that command.

For other references on Crocker's Iowa brigade, see the entries under the regiments that formed the Brigade.

### Hornet's Nest Brigade

*2nd, 7th, 8th, 12th and 14th infantry regiments.*

. . . Reunion of Iowa Hornets' nest brigade, Second, Seventh, Eighth, Twelfth and Fourteenth Iowa infantry, U.S.V. . . . i 1887 (DLC); iii 1895 (IaHi); viii 1911 (IaHi); ix 1912 (IaHi).    **55**

For other references on the Hornet's nest brigade, see the entries under the regiments that formed the Brigade.

### Union Brigade

*Included detachments from the 8th, 12th and 14th infantry regiments.*
*Roster* v 1575–81.

### Northern Border Brigade (Militia)

*Roster* vi 171–207.

Ingham, William H
The Iowa Northern border brigade of 1862–63, by Capt. William H. Ingham. *AI* s3 v (1901–03) 481–523.    **55A**

### Southern Border Brigade (Militia)

*Roster* vi 209–72.

### 1ST INFANTRY

*Mustered in: May 14, 1861.*
*Mustered out: August 21, 1861.*
*Roster* i 3–88.
*Iowa and the rebellion 17–32.*
*Iowa colonels 22–34.*

Flag day reunion of the First Iowa infantry veterans association, Aug. 10th, 1894. 23rd [sic] anniversary of Wilson's creek, Des Moines, Iowa. 8 p. 20½cm.    DNW    **56**

Caption title.

Carlson, Gretchen
Francis Jay Herron. *P* xi (1930) 141–50. plate (port.).    **57**

Clark, James Samuel, 1841–
General Lyon and the fight for Missouri, by Captain J. S. Clark. *MOLLUS-Iowa* ii 274–92.    **58**

—— Life in the Middle West. Reminiscences of J. S. Clark. Chicago, Advance pub. co. [1916] 226 p. front. (port.), ports. 20cm.

DLC    **58A**

Civil war 44–127. Served in the 1st Iowa infantry; appointed 2nd Lieutenant 34th Iowa infantry, August 13, 1862; mustered out, August 15, 1865.

McDonald, Arthur Young, 1834–1891.
Personal Civil war diary of Andrew Young McDonald, April 23, 1861, to September 12, 1861. [Dubuque, 1956] 24 p. 1 illus., port. 20½cm.    NN    **59**

Title from cover. "1856–1956. This diary is published in observance of the centennial of A. Y. McDonald manufacturing co . . . which was founded by A. Y. McDonald."

Matson, Daniel, 1842–1920.
Life experiences of Daniel Matson. [Fowler, Col., Tribune print., 1924] 144 p. front. (mounted port.). 23½cm.    DLC    **60**

Copyright by Mrs Bessie M. Higbee who signed the "Foreword." Author served in 1st Iowa infantry; mustered in 14th Iowa infantry, November 6, 1861; discharged to accept promotion in 2nd Tennessee heavy artillery (colored), October 29, 1863.

O'Connor, Henry, 1820–1900.
History of the First regiment of Iowa volunteers, by Henry O'Connor, a Private in Company "A," Originally prepared for the Iowa state historical society. Muscatine, Printed at the Faust print. house, 1862. 24 p. 22cm.
Unit roster [14]–28.    DLC NHi    **61**

—— With the First Iowa infantry. *P* iii (1922) 53–61.    **62**

A letter dated, July 16, 1861, originally published in the Muscatine weekly journal, August 2, 1861, and republished in Title 61.

Price, Hiram
Paying the First Iowa. *P* iii (1922) 62–5. **63**

Ware, Eugene Fitch, 1841–1911.
The Lyon campaign in Missouri, being a history of the First Iowa infantry, and of the causes which led up to its organization and how it earned the thanks of Congress, which it got, together with a birdseye view of the conditions in Iowa preceding the great Civil war of 1861, by E. F. Ware, a private soldier in Company E of said regiment. Topeka, Kan., Crane & co., 1907. xi, 377 p. front. (facs.), plates (2 maps, 2 ports.). 20cm.

DLC NN    **64**

Unit roster 357–77. Coulter 464.

*1st Infantry, continued*

White, Edgar
The first soldier newspaper. *Missouri historical review* VIII (1913/14) 223-6.   **64A**
Our whole Union, printed at the plant of the Macon, Mo. Register, June 15, 1861, by C. M. Fowler of the 1st Iowa infantry.

Wilkie, Franc Bangs, 1832-1892.
The Iowa First, letters from the war, by Franc. B. Wilkie. Dubuque, Printed at the Herald book and job estab., 1861. 114 p. 22cm.
NHi   **65**

*1st Regiment of Infantry (African Descent)*

see *60th United States Colored Troops*

## 2ND INFANTRY

*Mustered in: May 27-28, 1861.*
*Mustered out: July 12, 1865.*
*Roster* I 89-226; 2nd veteran infantry I 227-79.
*Iowa and the rebellion* 33-51.
*Iowa colonels* 35-82.

Company E, Second regiment, Iowa infantry [roster] Davenport, Lithographed and printed by A. Hageboeck [1863] illus. broadside, 45½ x 56cm.   DLC   **65A**

Second reunion of the Second Iowa infantry at Fairfield, Iowa, Thursday and Friday, October 1st and 2d, 1885. Des Moines, Brewster & co., printers, 1886. 28 p. 25½cm.   Ia-HA   **66**

Minutes of the third annual reunion of the Second Iowa infantry, held at Ottumwa, Iowa, Oct. 5 and 6, 1886, with a history of the Regiment in blank verse, by Levi Neiswanger of Co. H. Ottumwa, Press of J. S. McCleland & co., 1887. 31 p. 22cm.   IaHi   **67**
"Poetical history of the Second Iowa infantry," 24-31.

Proceedings of Flag day reunion of the Second Iowa infantry veteran volunteers, held at State capitol, August 9-10, 1894. Also, addresses delivered at the reunion of Company D, at the Fort Donelson anniversary, held at Des Moines, February 15, 1892, which go to make up history. Des Moines, Carter & Hussey, printers, 1895. 19 p. 23cm.   Ia-HA   **68**

Bell, John Thomas, 1842-1918.
Chattanooga to Washington afoot, by Lieut. John T. Bell, 1901. *MOLLUS-Neb* I 232-5. **70**

—— Civil war stories, compiled from official records, Union and Confederate, by John T. Bell (formerly of Second Iowa infantry). San Francisco, Whitaker and Ray co., 1903. 189 p. front. (port.). 20½cm.   DLC NHi   **71**

—— Tramps and triumphs of the Second Iowa infantry, briefly sketched, by John T. Bell, Lieut. Co. "C." Omaha, Neb., Gibson, Miller & Richardson, printers, 1886. 32 p. 21½cm.
Coulter 25.   DLC NHi   **72**

—— —— Original text unaltered, reprinted with footnotes and drawings, by the Valley bank and trust company, Des Moines, Iowa, in cooperation with the Iowa State historical department as a contribution to the Civil war centennial observance. [Des Moines] 1961. 54, (1) p. illus., ports. 22½cm. NN   **72A**
"Introduction" signed: Fleming Fraker, State department of history & archives.

Callender, William
Thrilling adventures of William Callender, a Union spy from Des Moines. Des Moines, Mills & co., printers, 1881. 116 p. 22cm.
NN   **73**
"Note by the editor" signed: J. M. Dixon.

Cate, Wirt Armistead, editor, 1900-
Two soldiers, the campaign diaries of Thomas J. Key, C.S.A., December 7, 1863 — May 17, 1865; and Robert J. Campbell, U.S.A., January 1, 1864 — July 21, 1864. Edited with an introduction, notes and maps, by Wirt Armistead Cate. Chapel Hill, University of North Carolina press, 1938. xiii, 277 p. maps, plates (facs., ports.). 22½cm.   NN   **74**
Robert J. Campbell, 1837-1927, served with 2nd Iowa.

Curtis, Samuel Ryan, 1807-1866.
"The irrepressible conflict of 1861," the letters of . . . Edited by Kenneth E. Colton. *AI* s3 XXIV (1942) 14-58.   **75**

—— With Fremont in Missouri, letter of . . . Edited by Kenneth E. Colton. *AI* s3 XXIV 104-67.   **76**

Greenawalt, John G        1840?-
The capture of Fort Henry and Fort Donaldson, February, 1862. 1912. 26 p. *MOLLUS-DC* no 87.   **77**

—— A charge at Fort Donelson, February 15, 1862, prepared by First Lieutenant John G. Greenawalt. 1902. 16 p. *MOLLUS-DC* no 41.   **78**

Heaton, Hiram
A soldier saint [Lyman Steadwell] *IHR* XIII (1899) 180-7.   **79**

Howe, Samuel Storrs, 1808-1888.
Obituary of Capt. Jonathan S. Slaymaker of Davenport, Iowa, who fell at Fort Donelson, Feb. 15, 1862, in the famous charge of the Second Iowa infantry, by the former Editor of the Annals. *AI* II (1864) 283-5.   **79A**
Text signed: S. S. H.

McCoid, Moses A
The charge of the Second Iowa at Fort Donelson!, by Lieut. Moses A. McCoid. Fairfield, 1899. 4 leaves. 22cm.    Ia-HA    *80*
Title from cover.

Mackley, John
The Civil war diary of . . . Edited by Mildred Throne. *IJH* xlviii (1950) 141–68.    *81*

Mills, Frank M
Colonel N. W. Mills of the Second Iowa infantry. *AI* s3 xiii (1922) 375–81. port.    *82*

Parker, Leonard Fletcher, 1825–1911.
Fort Donelson, the Second Iowa infantry. *IHR* ii (1886) 344–50.    *83*

Sharp, John, 1819–1901.
The Sharp family Civil war letters. Edited by George Mills. *AI* s3 xxxiv (1959) 481–532. plate (2 ports.).    *84*
Author mustered in 2nd Iowa infantry, November 20, 1861; discharged for disability, November 1862; mustered in 10th Iowa infantry, January 16, 1865; mustered out, August 15, 1865.

Throne, Mildred, editor.
Letters from Shiloh. *IJH* lii (1954) 235–80.    *85*
Accounts from the battlefield published in the press. Includes letters of William Harris, 6th Iowa; Adolphus G. Studer, 15th Iowa; Addison H. Sanders, 16th Iowa; Harold M. White, 11th Iowa; William Swan, 3rd Iowa; Noah W. Mills, 2nd Iowa.

Turner, William H
Diary of W. H. Turner, M.D., 1863. Edited by Mildred Throne. *IJH* xlviii (1950) 267–82.    *85A*

Tuttle, James Madison,    –1892.
Personal recollections of 1861, by General J. M. Tuttle. *MOLLUS-Iowa* i 18–24.    *86*

Twombly, Voltaire P    1842–1918.
The Second Iowa infantry at Fort Donelson, February 15, 1862, together with an outline history of the Regiment from its organization at Keokuk, Iowa, May 27, 1861, to final discharge at Davenport, Iowa, July 20, 1865, by Capt. V. P. Twombly. Des Moines, Plain Talk print. house [189–] 27 p. front. (port.). 23cm.
Title and imprint from cover.    IaHi    *87*

### 3RD INFANTRY

*Mustered in: June 8 to 10, 1861.*

*Veterans consolidated in a battalion, July 1864.*

*Battalion consolidated with 2nd regiment of infantry, November 4, 1864.*

*Roster* i 281–389; 3rd veteran infantry i 391–433; 2nd and 3rd veteran infantry consolidated i 435–524.

*Iowa and the rebellion* 52–74.
*Iowa colonels* 83–108.

Crosley, George W    1839–1913.
"Charge of the Light brigade" [Jackson, Miss., July 12, 1863] by Colonel George W. Crosley. *MOLLUS-Iowa* i 380–92.    *88*
With title, Lauman's charge at Jackson, *AI* s3 i (1894) 371–81.

—— Some reminiscences of an Iowa soldier. *AI* s3 x (1911) 119–36.    *88A*

Garden, Robert I    1840–
History of Scott township, Mahaska county, Iowa. War reminiscences. Did the Buffalo ever inhabit Iowa? By Robert I. Garden. Oskaloosa, Globe presses, 1907. 291 p. front. (port.), 2 plates (illus.). 20cm.    DLC MB    *89*
"War reminiscences," 93–205. "Preface" signed: Geo. W. Shockley.

Iowa Park and Forestry Association.
Major John F. Lacey memorial volume. [Cedar Rapids] Iowa Park and Forestry Association [1915] xix, 454 p. front. (port.). 2 plates (illus.) 25cm.    DLC NN    *89A*
"Excerpts from the autobiography of John F. Lacey," 392–415: With the Third Iowa infantry; My second service in the war. Mustered in 3rd Iowa infantry, June 8, 1861; discharged, November 1, 1861; mustered in 33rd Iowa infantry, September 6, 1862. Prepared by L. H. Pammel.

Lacey, John Fletcher, 1841–1913.
Address of Major John F. Lacey, April 7th, 1912, at Shiloh battle ground, Tennessee, on fiftieth anniversary of battle. . . . 13 p. port, on p. 4 of cover. 14 x 7½cm.    DLC    *89B*
Title from cover, p [1]. For service record see Title 89A.

Olney, Warren, 1841–1921.
The battle of Shiloh with some personal reminiscences. *Overland monthly,* ns v (1885) 577–89.    *90*

—— "Shiloh" as seen by a private soldier, a paper read before California commandery of the Military order of the loyal legion of the United States, May 31, 1889. 26 p. 22cm.
On cover: War paper no. 5. . . .    DLC    *91*

Patrick, Joseph M    –1921.
Civil war memoirs written by a participant in it, by Joseph M. Patrick, Bedford, Iowa. Enid, Okla., Drummond & Patrick [191–] 52 p. 19½cm.    IaHa NN(M)    *91A*
Running title: The battle of Shiloh.

Richards, Arthur Wherry, 1832–
Progress of life and thought; or, "Papa's scrap book." Sixty years' experience . . . by A. W. Richards, author and publisher. Des Moines, Iowa print. co., 1892. 363 p. plates (illus., ports.). 24cm.    DLC NN    *91B*
Civil war 97–113. Discharged, December 23, 1861, for disability.

### 3rd Infantry, continued

Thompson, Seymour Dwight, 1842–1904.
Recollections with the Third Iowa regiment,
by Lieut. S. D. Thompson. Cincinnati, Published for the author, 1864. xi, [13]–396 p.
19cm.                              DLC NN    92

Wright, Luella M
The pioneer greys. *P* xxii (1941) 1–32.    93
Contents: The call to arms, Filling the quota, The
community gift, Farewell assemblies, The departure.

See also Title 85.

### 4TH INFANTRY

*Mustered in: August 8–31, 1861.*
*Mustered out: July 24, 1865.*
*Roster* i 525–672.
*Iowa and the rebellion* 75–93.
*Iowa colonels* 109–24.

Arbuckle, John C
Civil war experiences of a foot soldier who
marched with Sherman, causes preliminary to
the war, battles, campaigns, marches with
Sherman, by John (C) Arbuckle, a Private in
Company K, Fourth Iowa. Columbus, Ohio,
1930. 188 p. 3 plates (ports.). 19½cm.
                             NNC OHi    94
On cover: Marching with Sherman.

Compton, James R
Andersonville, the story of man's inhumanity to man, by James R. Compton, Private in
Company "F," Fourth Iowa. Des Moines, Iowa
print. co., 1887. 100 p. 16½cm.
                               IHi NN    95

Dodge Grenville Mellen, 1831–1916.
Gen. James A. Williamson [Colonel 4th
Iowa] *AI* s3 vi (1903) 161–84. plate (port.).
                                       96

—— Colonel William H. Kinsman. *AI* s3 v
(1902) 241–5. plate (port.).            97
Kinsman 2nd Lieutenant 4th Iowa infantry, October
1, 1861; Lieutenant-Colonel 23rd Iowa infantry, September 19, 1862; died of wounds, May 18, 1863.

Ingersoll, Lurton Dunham
General James A. Williamson. *AI* viii (1870)
170–84. plate (port.).                97A

See also Title 3.

### 5TH INFANTRY

*Mustered in: August 8 to 31, 1861.*
*Mustered out: July 30, 1864. Veterans
transferred to 5th regiment of infantry.*
*Roster* i 673–782.
*Iowa and the rebellion* 94–111.
*Iowa colonels* 125–46.

Proceedings of the third annual reunion of the
Fifth Iowa infantry veteran association, held
at Newton, Iowa, Sept. 14 and 15, 1887. Keota,
Eagle print. co. [1887] 35 p. 18½cm.
                                  Ia-HA    98

[Roster. Cedar Rapids, 1891] 41 p. 18cm.
                                  Ia-HA    99
Includes Secretary's report, Aug. 9, 1891; and a
list of regimental personnel who have died. Cover
missing from copy examined.

Statistical roster of the Fifth Iowa volunteer
infantry . . . George T. Ditto, Secretary. Sigourney, Smith's Iowa Times print., 1897. 173 p.
plates (ports.). 22cm.           Ia-HA    100
"Story of prisoners' escape, by Michael Hoffman,"
[159]–73.

Byers, Samuel Hawkins Marshall, 1838–1933.
The battle of Iuka. *IHR* iii (1887) 543–52.
                                       100A

—— The burning of Columbia. *Lippincott's
magazine* xxix (1882) 255–61.           101

—— A historic war song, how and where I
wrote "Sherman's march to the sea." *MOL-
LUS-Iowa* i 393–400.                    102

—— How men feel in battle, recollections of
a Private at Champion hills. *AI* s3 ii 438–49.
plate (port.).                          103

—— The march to the sea. *North American
review* cxliv (1887) 235–45.            104

—— The march to the sea, a poem. . . . Boston, Arena pub. co., 1896. 149 p. front. (port.),
plates (illus.). 19½cm          NN    104A

—— Poems of S. H. M. Byers, selected. . . .
New York, Neale pub. co., 1914. 216, 149 p.
front. (port.), 2 plates (illus.). 18cm.
"The march to the sea," 149 p.    NN    105

—— Sherman's attack at the tunnel. *BandL*
iii 712–3.                              106

—— Ten days in the Rebel army. *Atlantic
monthly* xlv (1880) 617–24.             107

—— —— *IHR* vi (1890) 467–77.         108

—— What I saw in Dixie; or, sixteen months
in Rebel prisons, by Adjutant S. H. M. Byers.
Dansville, N.Y., Robbins & Poore, printers,
1868. 126 p. 17½cm.              NHi    109
"List of officers of the United States army and
navy, confined at Columbia, South Carolina," [95]–
128. Coulter 64.

—— With fire and sword, by Major S. H. M.
Byers. New York, Neale pub. co., 1911. 203 p.
2 fronts. (ports.). 19cm.         NN    110
Coulter 64.

Fosdick, Charles
Five hundred days in Rebel prisons, by Chas. Fosdick, formerly of Co. K, 5th Iowa vols. Bethany, Mo., Printed at the Clipper office, 1887. 132 p. front. (port.). 19cm.
Coulter 168.                           NB    *111*

—— —— Blythdale, Mo. [Chicago, Chicago Electrotype and Stereotype co.] 1887. 118 p. 2 ports. 18½cm.                    NHi    *112*

—— —— Blythe Dale, Mo., 1887. 118, (1) p. illus., 2 ports. 19½cm.    DLC IaHi    *112A*
"Roll of honor Fifth Iowa infantry," (1) p.

## 6TH INFANTRY

*Mustered in: June 17–18, 1861.*
*Mustered out: July 21, 1865.*
*Roster* i 783–908
*Iowa and the rebellion* 112–27.
*Iowa colonels* 147–62.

Roster 6th Iowa vol. inft. arranged by companies, name and P.O. address of all surviving comrades so far as known. . . . Des Moines, Advocate pub. co. [1888] 16 p. 14½cm.
Title and imprint from cover.    DNW    *113*

Ingersoll, Lurton Dunham
Sixth Iowa infantry. (Republished by Daniel R. Kinley, Marion, Iowa, formerly Sergeant of Co. A, Sixth Iowa veteran volunteer infantry, from "Iowa in the rebellion," by L. D. Ingersol). [n. p., n. d.] 16 p. 21cm.
NHi    *114*
On cover: Sixth Iowa infantry, 1861–1865, from muster in to muster out. Caption title.

Kremer, Wesley Potter, 1841–
Roster of Co. I, 6th Iowa infantry, War of the rebellion, recruited and organized at Burlington, Springtime of 1861 . . . by W. P. Kremer. Rutherford, N.J. [190–] [13] folios plate (port.). 27 x 15½cm. DLC NN    *115*
Title from cover.

Sweney, Joseph H
Nursed a wounded brother [Charles Sweney]. *AI* s3 xxxi (1952) 177–99.    *116*

Wright, Henry Haviland, 1840–1905.
A history of the Sixth Iowa infantry, by Henry H. Wright. Iowa City, State Historical Society of Iowa, 1923. xii, 539 p. 23cm.
DLC NN    *117*
"The editing, verification, and preparation of General Wright's manuscript for the press is largely the work of Dr. Erik McKinley Eriksson." Coulter 488.

See also Title 85.

## 7TH INFANTRY

*Mustered in: July 23 to August 2, 1861.*
*Mustered out: July 12, 1865.*
*Roster* i 909–1057.
*Iowa and the rebellion* 128–45.
*Iowa colonels* 163–78.

Carpenter, C        C        and George W. Crossley
Seventh Iowa volunteers in Civil war gave valiant service. *AI* s3 xxxiv (1957) 100–11.
*118*

Frank, Malcolm, 1834–1884.
"Such is war:" the letters of an Orderly in the 7th Iowa infantry. Edited by James I. Robertson, Jr. *IJH* lviii (1960) 321–56.    *119*

Mahon, Samuel, 1840–
The Civil war letters of Samuel Mahon, Seventh Iowa infantry. Edited by John K. Mahon. *IJH* li (1953) 233–66.    *120*

—— The forager in Sherman's last campaign. *MOLLUS-Iowa* ii 188–200.    *121*

Rutherford, George S
The poetic history of the Seventh Iowa regiment, containing all its principal marches and all the battles they have engaged in, from the day of their entering service to the present time. Composed and written by one of their number who has passed through, or borne his part in, nearly all the scenes he has described. Muscatine, Journal office, 1863. 30 p. 18½cm.
DLC    *122*
Author's preface signed: George S. Rutherford.

Smith, Henry I
History of the Seventh Iowa veteran volunteer infantry during the Civil war, by H. I. Smith. Mason City, E. Hitchcock, printer, 1903. 313 p. plates (illus., ports.). 22cm.
DLC NN    *123*

—— The sad war experiences of two Iowa brothers [Henry I, and Peter D. Smith]. *AI* s3 i (1895) 621–8. plate (port.).    *124*

## 8TH INFANTRY

*Mustered in: August 31 to September 4, 1861.*
*Mustered out: April 20, 1866.*
*Roster* i 1059–1222.
*Iowa and the rebellion* 731–6.
*Iowa colonels* 179–94.

Roster and proceedings of the Eighth Iowa infantry association, held at Sigourney, Iowa, September 24 and 25, 1884. Oskaloosa, Saturday Globe print. house, 1884. 29 p. 17cm.
Ia-HA    *125*

8th Infantry, continued

Fourteenth reunion of the Eighth Iowa infantry, Sigourney, Iowa, October 2–3, 1907. [Oskaloosa] Globe presses [1907] 12, (1) p. 15½cm. Ia-HA **126**

A roster of survivors. Title from cover, p [1]

Huff, Samuel W
The Eighth regiment Iowa infantry and its Colonel, James L. Geddes, at Spanish fort, Alabama. *AI* v (1867) 947–53. **127**

Palmer, David
Recollections of war times. *AI* s3 x (1909) 134–42. **128**

Searle, Charles P
Personal reminiscences of Shiloh, by Captain C. P. Searle. *MOLLUS-Iowa* I 326–39. **129**

## 9TH INFANTRY

*Mustered in: September 2 to 24, 1861.*
*Mustered out: July 18, 1865.*
*Roster* II 1–141.
*Iowa and the rebellion* 146–65.
*Iowa colonels* 195–214.

An address on the presentation of a stand of colors to the 9th Iowa volunteers by the ladies of Boston [July 10, 1862] [3] p. 20cm. Ia-HA **130**

Caption title. Includes "Colonel Vandever's reply," dated: Aug. 3, 1862, camp near Helena, Arkansas.

First reunion of the Ninth Iowa infantry regiment veteran volunteers, held at Independence on the anniversary of the battle of Pea Ridge, March 6th, 7th and 8th, 1883. Independence, "Bulletin" print. house, 1883. 65 p. 22cm. Ia-HA **131**

Abernethy, Alonzo, 1836–1915.
Incidents of an Iowa soldier's life; or, four years in Dixie. *AI* s3 XII (1920) 401–28. plate (port.). **132**

Adams, John, 1836–1918.
Letters of . . . to Catherine Varner, 1864–1865. *North Dakota historical quarterly* IV (1929/30) 266–70. **132A**

Harwood, Nathan S
The Pea Ridge campaign, a paper read before the Nebraska commandery of the Military order of the loyal legion of the United States, by Nathan S. Harwood, late Lieutenant 46 Iowa vol. inf., June 1st, 1887. [Omaha, Neb., Ackermann Bros. & Heintze, printers, 1887] 22 p. 23cm. NHi **133**

"Fourth Corporal in Company "G," 9th Iowa infantry." Also published in *MOLLUS-Neb* I 110–21.

## 10TH INFANTRY

*Mustered in: September 6–7, 1861.*
*Mustered out: August 15, 1865.*
*Roster* II 143–271.
*Iowa in the rebellion* 166–80.
*Iowa colonels* 215–34.

Macy, Jesse, 1842–1919.
Jesse Macy, an autobiography. Edited and arranged by his daughter Katharine Macy Noyes. Springfield, Ill., Charles C. Thomas, 1933. xix, 192 p. plates (facs., ports.). 24½cm. "The Civil war," 36–72. NN **133A**

See also Title 84.

## 11TH INFANTRY

*Mustered in: September 14 to October 19, 1861.*
*Mustered out: July 15, 1865.*
*Roster* II 273–404.
*Iowa in the rebellion* 211–28.
*Iowa colonels* 235–42.

Burge, William, 1842–
Through the Civil war and Western adventures, by William Burge, Co. K, 11th Iowa. Lisbon [190–] 81, (4) p. 20½cm. IaHi **134**

"Roll of Co. 'K,' 11th regular Iowa infantry," (4) p.

Caddle, Cornelius
An Adjutant's recollections. 1899. *MOLLUS-Ohio* v 384–401. **134A**

Downing, Alexander G 1842–
Downing's Civil war diary, by Sergeant Alexander G. Downing, Company E, Eleventh Iowa infantry, Third brigade, "Crocker's brigade," Sixth division of the Seventeenth corps, Army of the Tennessee, August 15, 1861 — July 31, 1865. Edited by Olynthus B. Clark. Des Moines, Historical Department of Iowa, 1916. vi, 325 p. plates (facs., ports.). 23½cm. Company E roster, 303–09. DLC NHi **135**

Fultz, William Stroup, 1836–1915.
A history of Company D, Eleventh Iowa infantry, 1861–1865. Edited by Mildred Throne. *IJH* LV (1957) 35–90. **136**

Lloyd, Frederick
War memories. *IHR* IV–XV (1888–99). For page references, consult the annual indexes of the Iowa historical record. **137**

Author Assistant Surgeon 11th Iowa, October 21, 1861; Surgeon 16th Iowa, June 14, 1862; Assistant Surgeon U.S. vols., August 15, 1862; Surgeon U.S. vols., November 14, 1863.

Martin, William, 1836–1919.
"Out and forward;" or, recollections of the war of 1861 to 1865, by William Martin, Company C, 11th Iowa. [Manhattan, Kansas, Art Craft print., 1941] 48 p. front. (port.), illus., plans, port. 19½cm.     DLC NN     *138*
Copyright by Ann Eliza Martin. "Foreword" signed: Charles M. Sheldon.

Michael, William Henry, 1845–1916.
Address of William H. Michael, Iowa soldiers and sailors in the War of the rebellion, before the biennial meeting of the Association of Crocker's Iowa brigade at Waterloo, Iowa, September 14, 1904. 40 p. 23½cm.
DLC WHi     *139*

—— Address of Ensign William H. Michael . . . Cooperation between General Grant and Commodore Foote and between General Grant and Admiral Porter, delivered at the biennial meeting, nineteen hundred and four, of Crocker's Iowa brigade. [n. p., 1904?] 29 p. 23cm.
DLC     *140*
Title from cover. Considerably altered and abridged from Title 139.

Smith, Charles Alphonso
Recollections of prison life at Andersonville, Ga., and Florence, S.C., by C. A. Smith, Co. G, 11th Iowa. Muscatine, R. A. Holmes, printer [n. d.] 56 p. front. (port.). 15½cm.
IaHi     *141*
Text is dated: July 14, 1875. The volume was probably printed at a later date.

See also Title 85.

## 12TH INFANTRY

*Mustered in: October 17 to November 25, 1861.*
*Mustered out: January 20, 1866.*
*Roster* II 405–550.
*Iowa and the rebellion* 181–94.
*Iowa colonels* 243–54.

. . . Reunion of Twelfth Iowa vet. vol. infantry. I–VIII 1880, 1884, 1888, 1892, 1894, 1896, 1901, 1903.     DLC     *142*
Eighth reunion has sub-title: Dedication Lincoln monument and Col. Henderson statue, Claremont, June 19–20, '03.

Revised roster Company D Twelfth regiment Iowa infantry volunteers. [1908] [4] p. 23cm.
IaHi     *143*

—— Supplement to. . . . [1911] [3] p. 18cm.
IaHi     *144*
Dunham, Abner, 1841–1910.
Civil war letters of . . . Edited by Mildred Throne. *IJH* LIII (1955) 303–40.     *145*

Duzee, Edward M
Incidents of prison life in 1862. *AI* VI (1868) 54–64, 92–104, 220–33.     *146*

Reed, David Wilson, 1841–
Campaigns and battles of the Twelfth regiment Iowa veteran volunteer infantry, from organization, September, 1861, to muster-out, January 20, 1866, by Major David W. Reed. [Evanston, Ill., 1903] 319, (1) p. 2 fold. maps in pocket, plates (illus.). 21½cm.
DLC NHi NN     *147*
"Errata," (1) p. Unit roster, 258–319.

—— "University recruits" Company C, 12th Iowa infantry [by] D. W. Reed. [Evanston, Ill., 1903] 28 p. 20½cm.     DLC NHi     *148*
Also issued as an appendix to Title 147.

Rich, Joseph Warford, 1838–1920.
The battle of Shiloh. *IJH* VII (1909) 503–81. plans.     *149*

—— The battle of Shiloh. Iowa City, State Historical Society of Iowa, 1911. 134 p. front. (port.), maps. 23½cm.     NHi NN     *150*
"Editor's introduction," signed: Benj. F. Shambaugh.

—— —— *JUSCA* XXII (1911) 428–36.     *151*
A reply to Stephen H. Elliott's review of Title 150 published in *JUSCA* XXII (1911) 157–66.

—— The color bearer [Henry J. Grannis] of the Twelfth Iowa volunteer infantry. *IJH* VI (1908) 96–102.     *152*

—— The death of General Albert Sidney Johnston on the battlefield of Shiloh. *IJH* XVI (1918) 275–81.     *153*
Publishes a letter of Major D. W. Reed to General Duke describing the visit of Senator Harris to Shiloh park for the purpose of identifying the spot where General Johnston fell.

—— General Lew. Wallace at Shiloh, how he was convinced of an error after forty years. *IJH* XVIII (1920) 301–08.     *154*

Soper, Erastus B     1841–1917.
A chapter from the history of Company D, Twelfth Iowa infantry volunteers, by Captain E. B. Soper. *MOLLUS-Iowa* II 129–42.     *155*

Stibbs, John Howard, 1840–
Andersonville and the trial of Henry Wirz, by John Howard Stibbs, sole survivor of the commission that tried Henry Wirz. . . . [Iowa City, Clio press, 1911] 30 p. front. (port.). 28cm.     DLC     *156*
"Reprinted from the January 1911 number of the Iowa journal of history and politics for the George H. Thomas post number five of the City of Chicago, the Department of Illinois Grand army of the republic."

—— —— *IJH* XI (1911) 33–56.     *157*

—— McArthur's division at Nashville as seen by a regimental commander (read February 12, 1906). *MOLLUS-Ill* IV 485–502.     *158*

*12th Infantry, continued*

Sumbardo, Charles L
Incidents of prison life, with causes of Confederate cruelty, by Captain C. L. Sumbardo. *MOLLUS-Minn* III 347–77.                    **159**

—— Some facts about the battle of Shiloh, 1889. *MOLLUS-Minn* III 26–41.          **160**

Zuver, Byron Plympton
Iowans in Southern prisons, 1862, edited by Mildred Throne. *IJH* LIV (1956) 67–88.   **161**

Two accounts: Prisoner of war, by B. P. Zuver; and Officers as prisoners of war, by Capt. J. H. Stibbs, taken from the manuscript history of Company D, 12th Iowa, written by Erastus B. Soper.

### 13TH INFANTRY

*Mustered in: October 15 to November 2, 1861.*

*Mustered out: July 21, 1865.*

*Roster* II 551–717.

*Iowa and the rebellion* 229–45.

*Iowa colonels* 255–70.

Eyestone, John Wesley, 1837–
Our family history and father's war experiences, written by himself, John Wesley Eyestone. Mount Vernon, 1910. 106 p. plates (1 illus., ports.). 21½cm.       IHi   **162**

Lloyd, Frederick
Gen. James Wilson, late Provost marshal, Army of the Tennessee. *IHR* III (1887) 481–96. plate (port.).          **163**

Rood, Henry H
History of Compny "A," Thirteenth Iowa veteran infantry, from September 12, 1861, to July 21, 1865. Cedar Rapids, Daily Republican print, 1889. 34 p. 21cm.        NHi   **164**
"Introductory" signed: H. H. Rood.

—— Iowa's record, a sketch of Iowa's record during the War for the preservation of the Union, 1861–1865, by Adjutant H. H. Rood. *MOLLUS-Iowa* I 369–79.       **165**

—— Sketches of the Thirteenth Iowa. *MOLLUS-Iowa* I 115–56.          **166**

Thrall, Seneca Brown, 1832–1888.
Letters of Dr. Seneca B. Thrall, September 19, 1862 – May 5, 1864, and miscellaneous correspondence of Civil war era. [n. p., n. d.] 1 vol. 36cm. mimeographed.   NNC   **167**
Text on rectos.

—— An Iowa doctor in Blue, the letters of Seneca E. Thrall, 1862–1864. Edited by Mildred Throne. *IJH* LVIII (1960) 97–188. **167A**

Townsend, Francis Torrey, 1829–
Autobiography of Francis Torrey Townsend, and genealogy of the Townsends. White River Junction, Vt., 1905. 102, (1) p. front. (port.). 23½cm.               DLC   **167B**
Civil war 37–43. "Errata," (1) p.

Williams, Ora
The sword of General Crocker. *AI* s3 XXVIII (1946) 61–8. plate (illus.).       **168**

### 14TH INFANTRY

*Mustered in: October 23 to November 6, 1861.*

*Mustered out: November 16, 1864.*

*Roster* II 719–879.

*Iowa and the rebellion* 195–210.

*Iowa colonels* 271–80.

Leaves from a soldier's diary, random recollections of an Iowa volunteer. *BandG* III (1894) 93–7.                    **169**
"To be continued."

Elarton, John W      1844–
Andersonville prison and National cemetery, Andersonville, Georgia. [Aurora, Neb., Printed by Burr pub. co., c1913] [40] p. illus., ports. 17 x 24cm.            DLC NB   **169A**
Caption title.

Garretson, Owen Albright
A famous war horse. *P* XII (1931) 354–8.    **170**

Hazlett, Andrew H
Prison life, east and west, by Lieutenant A. H. Hazlett. *MOLLUS-Iowa* II 375–88.  **171**

Kiner, Frederick F
One year's soldiering, embracing the battles of Fort Donelson and Shiloh, and the capture of two hundred officers and men of the Fourteenth Iowa infantry, and their confinement six months and a half in Rebel prisons, by F. F. Kiner, Chaplain, Fourteenth Iowa. Lancaster, Penn., E. H. Thomas, printer, 1863. 219, (1) p. 15½cm.     IHi Ia-HA IaU   **172**
"Errata," (1) p.

Rhodes, Milton I
Captives in Dixie. *P* x (1929) 243–66.   **173**

Shaw, William T      1822–1909.
The battle of Pleasant hill. *AI* s3 III (1897–99) 401–23. 2 plans, 2 plates (ports.).   **174**

—— The battle of Shiloh, by Colonel Wm. T. Shaw. *MOLLUS-Iowa* I 183–207.    **174A**

Spawr, Valentine L
A diary of the late rebellion (from June 28 until Sept. 15, 1863), written by Valentine L.

Spawr, a member of Company C, 14th regiment Iowa inft. vols. Lexington, Ill., Unit pub. co., printers, 1892. port. 17cm.    IHi    **175**

Thomas, Benjamin F
Off to the war. *P* xxii (1941) 161–77.    **176**
Adapted from his Recollections of soldier life, privately published in 1907.

Williams, Ora
College student and soldier boy [Charles W. Hadley]. *AI* s3 xxvi (1944) 45–54.    **177**

Wilson, Peter
Peter Wilson in the Civil war. *IJH* xl (1942) 153–203, 261–320, 339–414.    **178**

See also Titles 42 and 60.

## 15TH INFANTRY

*Mustered in: November 1, 1861 to February 22, 1862.*
*Mustered out: July 24, 1865.*
*Roster* ii 881–1055.
*Iowa and the rebellion* 246–68.
*Iowa colonels* 281–302.

Belknap, William Worth, 1829–1890.
History of the Fifteenth regiment, Iowa veteran volunteer infantry, from October, 1861, to August, 1865, when disbanded at end of the war. Keokuk, R. B. Ogden & Son, 1887. 644 p. plates (ports.). 22½cm.
DLC NHi NN    **179**
Muster in roster, 118–73; the veteran roll, 287–99; additional enlistments, 426–43. "Preface" signed by Wm. W. Belknap who writes, "the labor of the work has been done by Mr. Loren S. Tyler."

—— The obedience and courage of the private soldier, and the fortitude of officers and men in field, in hospital, and in prison, with some incidents of the war, by Brevet Major-General William W. Belknap. *MOLLUS-Iowa* i 157–71.    **180**

Bosworth, John S
The battle of Atlanta. *BandG* ii (1893) 236–8.    **181**

Boyd, Cyrus F
The Civil war diary of C. F. Boyd, Fifteenth Iowa infantry. Edited by Mildred Throne. *IJH* l (1952) 47–82, 155–84, 239–70, 345–78. map.    **182**

—— —— Iowa City, State Historical Society of Iowa, 1953. 135 p. map, plates (illus., ports.). 23cm.    WHi    **183**

Day, James G
The Fifteenth Iowa at Shiloh, by Captain James G. Day. *MOLLUS-Iowa* ii 173–87. **184**

Goodrell, William H
The burning of Columbia, S.C. *IHR* iv (1888) 125–8.    **185**

McArthur, Henry Clay, 1838–
The capture and destruction of Columbia, South Carolina, February 17, 1865. Personal experiences and recollections of Major H. C. McArthur, Fifteenth Iowa infantry. [Washington, 1911] 16 p. 2 illus. 22½cm. NN    **186**
Title from cover.

Tyler, Loren S    1845–1914.
The Tyler photographs of Iowa military men. *AI* s3 x (1912) 408–30.    **187**

See also Title 85.

## 16TH INFANTRY

*Mustered in: December 10, 1861 to March 12, 1862.*
*Mustered out: July 19, 1865.*
*Roster* ii 1056–1199.
*Iowa and the rebellion* 269–87.
*Iowa colonels* 303–12.

Sixteenth regiment Iowa volunteers, 1861–1865 [roster] Red Oak, Express ptg. co. [190–] 47 p. 15½cm.    Ia-HA    **188**

Lloyd, Frederick
General Alexander Chambers. *IHR* ix (1893) 385–93. plate (port.).    **189**

—— Recollections of Crocker's Iowa brigade. *IHR* i (1885) 129–32.    **190**

Parkhurst, Clinton Henry, 1844–1933.
The attack on Corinth. *P* iii (1922) 169–91.    **191**

—— A few martial memories. *P* i (1920) 111–28.    **192**

—— Our first view of Vicksburg. *P* iii (1922) 69–83.    **193**

—— The siege of Corinth. *P* iv (1923) 1–13.    **194**
For biographical notice of the author, see Clint Parkhurst, by August P. Richter, *P* i (1920) 183–92.

Pray, Gilbert B
Crocker's brigade in war and peace, at the fifth biennial reunion . . . 18th September 1889. *IHR* v (1889) 374–83.    **195**

—— A tribute to the 16th Iowa. *IHR* v (1889) 225–30.    **196**

Smith, John Henry, 1827–1919.
The Civil war diary of Colonel John Henry Smith. Edited by David M. Smith. *IJH* xlvii (1949) 140–70.    **197**

*16th Infantry, continued*

Stallcop, James
Letters of . . . to Catherine Varner, Charlotte, Iowa, 1863–1865. *North Dakota historical quarterly* IV (1929/30) 116–42.      **197A**

See also Titles 85 and 137.

## 17TH INFANTRY

*Mustered in: March 21 to April 16, 1862.*
*Mustered out: July 25, 1865.*
*Roster* III 1–114.
*Iowa and the rebellion* 288–306.
*Iowa colonels* 313–42.

## 18TH INFANTRY

*Mustered in: August 5 to 7, 1862.*
*Mustered out: July 20, 1865.*
*Roster* III 115–222.
*Iowa and the rebellion* 307–18.
*Iowa colonels* 343–50.

## 19TH INFANTRY

*Mustered in: August 17–23, 1862.*
*Mustered out: July 10, 1865.*
*Roster* III 223–338.
*Iowa and the rebellion* 319–39.
*Iowa colonels* 351–60.

Diary of an unknown soldier. Edited with foreword and closing by Elsa Vaught (Mrs. W. W.). *Arkansas historical quarterly* XVIII (1959) 50–89. plates (facs., maps).      **198**
"Covers the Territory of Northwest Arkansas and Southwest Missouri, from September 5, 1862, to December 7, 1862, as the 19th Iowa infantry regiment of volunteers maneuvered."

—— [Van Buren, Ark., Press-Argus print. co., 1959] 45 p. facs., maps. 23cm.   DLC   **199**
Title from cover.

Dungan, J      Irvine
History of the Nineteenth regiment Iowa volunteer infantry, by J. Irvine Dungan. Davenport, Luse & Griggs, 1865. viii, [9]–187 p. fold. plan. 19½cm.      IaHi   **200**
Unit roster [9]–40.

Houghland, James E
The 19th Iowa in battle and in prison. In National tribune scrap book I 63–82.   **200A**

## 20TH INFANTRY

*Mustered in: August 22–27, 1862.*
*Mustered out: July 8, 1865.*
*Roster* III 339–438.

*Iowa and the rebellion* 340–57.
*Iowa colonels* 361–6.

Barnes, Joseph D
What I saw you do, a brief history of the battles, marches, and sieges of the Twentieth Iowa volunteer infantry, during their three years' of active service in the War of the rebellion, by J. D. Barnes, late Lieutenant Co. K. Port Byron, Ill., Owen & Hall [1896] 48 p. front. (port.). 17cm.      MBLL   **201**

Barney, Chester
Recollections of field service with the Twentieth Iowa infantry volunteers; or, what I saw in the army, embracing accounts of marches, battles, sieges and skirmishes, in Missouri, Arkansas, Mississippi, Louisiana, Alabama, Florida, Texas, and along the northern border of New Mexico, by Capt. C. Barney. Printed for the author. Davenport, Gazette job rooms, 1865. viii, [9]–323 p. 19cm.   NN RP   **202**
Coulter 16.

Eberhart, Uriah, 1821–
History of the Eberharts in Germany and in the United States from A.D. 1265 to A.D. 1890 — 625 years, by Rev. Uriah Eberhart, with an autobiographical sketch by the author, including many reminiscences of his ministerial and army life. [Chicago] Donohue & Henneberry, 1891. iv, (2), [5]–263 p. front. (port.). 20½cm.      DLC NN   **202A**
Civil war 231–54.

Leake, Joseph Bloomfield, 1828–1913.
Campaign of the Army of the frontier (read October 1, 1884). *MOLLUS-Ill* II 269–87. **203**

—— Some recollections of a Southern prison (read March 3, 1886). *MOLLUS-Ill* I 345–68.
    **204**

## 21ST INFANTRY

*Mustered in: June 4, 1862.*
*Mustered out: July 18, 1865.*
*Roster* III 439–555.
*Iowa and the rebellion* 457–71.
*Iowa colonels* 367–74.

Crooke, George
The Twenty-first regiment of Iowa volunteer infantry, a narrative of its experience in active service, including a military record of each officer, non-commissioned officer, and private soldier of the organization. Compiled by George Crooke, late Adjutant. For private distribution only. Milwaukee, King, Fowle & co., 1891. 232 p. illus., maps, plate (fold. map). 23½cm.      DLC NN   **205**
"Memoranda," ruled blank leaves, 221–32. Unit roster 166–220.

Crooke, William D
Address to surviving members of the Twenty-first regiment Iowa volunteer infantry, on occasion of their fourth reunion, at Strawberry point, Iowa, September 3d, 1889, by William D. Crooke, late Major of the Regiment. Printed for private distribution by request of comrades. Chicago, Pettibone, Wells & co., printers, 1889. 56 p. plans. 23½cm. Ia-HA **206**
On cover: Twenty-first reg't Iowa volunteer infantry. Fourth reunion, September 3d, 1889. . . .

## 22ND INFANTRY

*Mustered in: September 7–10, 1862.*
*Mustered out: July 20, 1865.*
*Roster* III 556–668.
*Iowa and the rebellion* 472–89.
*Iowa colonels* 7–15, 375–80.

First reunion Twenty-second Iowa regiment at Iowa City, Sept. 22 and 23. [Iowa City, 1886] 12 p. 22cm.      DLC **207**
Caption title. Dated August 13, 1886, the publication is a prospectus and includes a roster of survivors.

Proceedings of the Twenty-second regiment Iowa volunteers at its first reunion, held at Iowa City, Wednesday and Thursday, Sept. 22d and 23d, 1886. . . . Iowa City, Republican pub. co., 1887. 79, (2) p. front. (port.). 23cm.
IaHi **208**
"Autobiographical, the frontispiece," a notice of the Colonel, John C. Shrader, (2) p.

List of names and addresses of surviving members of the Twenty-second Iowa vol. inf., corrected up to Sept. 15, 1903. 19 p. 15½cm.
Title from cover, p [1]      IaHi **209**

Barnett, Simeon
History of the Twenty-second regiment Iowa volunteer infantry, from the date of enlistment to muster out of the service of the United States, giving all the important events in its campaigns in Missouri, in the siege and capture of Vicksburg, in the Texas expedition and in the Shenandoah valley, by Simeon Barnett, Drum major. Iowa City, N. H. Brainerd, 1865. 36 p. 19½cm.      NHi **210**
Title and imprint from cover.

Booth, Benjamin F      1837?–
Dark days of the rebellion; or, life in Southern military prisons, giving a correct and thrilling history of unparalled suffering, narrow escapes, heroic encounters, bold achievements, cold blooded murders, severe tests of loyalty and patriotism. Written from a diary kept while in Libby and Salisbury prisons in 1864–5, and now in possession of the author, by B. F. Booth, late Co. I, 22d Ia. vol. inft. Indianola,

Booth pub. co., 1897. 375 p. illus., ports. 19½cm.      DLC NHi **211**

Griffith, Joseph Evan
The Twenty-second Iowa infantry at Vicksburg. *AI* VI (1868) 215–19.      **212**

Jones, Samuel Calvin, 1838–
Reminiscences of the Twenty-second Iowa volunteer infantry, giving its organization, marches, skirmishes, battles, and sieges, as taken from the diary of Lieutenant S. C. Jones of Company A. Iowa City, 1907. 164, (2) p. plates, 2 double (1 illus., ports.). 23½cm.
DLC NN **213**
"Index," "Errata," (2) p. Coulter 267.

Switzer, Jacob Carroll, 1843–1914.
Reminiscences of Jacob Carroll Switzer of the 22nd Iowa. Edited by Mildred Throne. *IJH* LV (1957) 319–50; LVI (1958) 37–76.
**214**

Turner, Job B
Collecting the soldier vote. *P* XXIII (1942) 282–6.      **215**

## 23RD INFANTRY

*Mustered in: September 19, 1862.*
*Mustered out: July 26, 1865.*
*Roster* III 669–778.
*Iowa and the rebellion* 491–500.
*Iowa colonels* 381–96.

See Title 97.

## 24TH INFANTRY

*Mustered in: September 18, 1862.*
*Mustered out: July 17, 1865.*
*Roster* III 779–899.
*Iowa and the rebellion* 501–14.
*Iowa colonels* 397–406.

Proceedings and roster of the second reunion of the Twenty-fourth Iowa volunteers, held at Cedar Rapids, Thursday, December 17th, 1885. Compiled by the Secretary. Tipton, Chas. L. Longley, printer, 1886. 38, (1) p. 22cm.      NHi **216**
"Appendix C, official roster 24th Iowa [officers]. . . .," (1) p.

Ely, John F
First year's medical history of the Twenty-fourth Iowa, by Surgeon John F. Ely. *MOLLUS-Iowa* I 105–14.      **217**

Ford, Orrin B      1845–
Biography of O. B. Ford, "written by himself." [Yale, Okla., Yale Record print, 191–] 64 p. port. 19½cm. NN (M) OkHi **217A**
"The Civil war from 1861 to 1866," 4–23.

*24th Infantry, continued*

Longley, Charles L
Champion's hill, by Sergeant Charles L.
Longley. *MOLLUS-Iowa* I 208–14.          **218**

—— The Twenty-fourth Iowa volunteers. *AI*
s3 I (1894) 446–54, 553–65; s3 II (1895) 44–
56. 2 plates (ports.).          **219**

Lucas, Charles Alexander
A soldier's letters from the field. *IHR* xvI/
xvIII (1900–02) 126–57, 172–96, 217–53,
293–304, 348–51, 371–96, 438–48, 463–96,
511–51. 2 plans, 2 ports.          **220**
Translated for publication from the French by the
author.

Lyon, Bessie L
Christian soldier [Amasa O. Allen] *P* xxv
(1944) 50–64.          **221**

Rigby, William Titus, 1841–
Lincoln and McClellan, by Captain William
T. Rigby. *MOLLUS-Iowa* I 232–55.          **222**

Scott, Robert Graham, 1845–1935.
Memoirs and poetic sketches, Col. R. G.
Scott, author. [Camden, Mo.] Reveille print.
[191–] [26] p. front. (port.), double map.
21½cm.          IaHa NN (M)          **222A**

Smith, Thaddeus L
The Twenty-fourth Iowa volunteers. *AI* s3 I
(1893) 15–37, 111–28, 180–96.          **223**

### 25TH INFANTRY

*Mustered in: September 27, 1862.*
*Mustered out: June 6, 1865.*
*Roster* III 901–1014.
*Iowa and the rebellion* 515–27.
*Iowa colonels* 407–14.

### 26TH INFANTRY

*Mustered in: August 30, September 30 to*
*October 1, 1862.*
*Mustered out: June 6, 1865.*
*Roster* III 1015–1112.
*Iowa and the rebellion* 528–38.
*Iowa colonels* 415–20.

Frank, Elijah H
E. H. Frank to Catherine Varner, Charlotte,
Iowa, 1862–1863. *North Dakota historical*
*quarterly* IV (1929/30) 186–96.          **223A**

### 27TH INFANTRY

*Mustered in: September 1 to October 3,*
*1862.*
*Mustered out: August 8, 1865.*
*Roster* III 1113–1225.
*Iowa and the rebellion* 539–51.
*Iowa colonels* 421–8.

Donnan, William G          1834–1908.
A reminiscence of the last battle of the Red
river expedition. *AI* s3 vI (1904) 241–57.
plate (port.).          **224**

### 28TH INFANTRY

*Mustered in: October 10, 1862.*
*Mustered out: July 31, 1865.*
*Roster* III 1227–1340.
*Iowa and the rebellion* 552–65.
*Iowa colonels* 429–44.

Blake, Ephraim, 1842–
A succinct history of the 28th Iowa volun-
teer infantry, from date of muster into service,
October 10th, 1862, at Iowa city, Iowa, to its
final muster out, August 13th, 1865, at Daven-
port, Iowa, by E. E. Blake, Private, Co. G.
Covering every march, skirmish and battle
throughout the sieges of Vicksburg, Jackson,
Teche and Red river expeditions, the Shenan-
doah valley campaign, 1864, and the trip to
Savannah, New Berne and Augusta. Belle
Plain, Union press, 1896. 143, (1) p. 19½cm.
          MBLL          **225**
Unit roster [90]–143. "Erratum," (1) p.
NHi has copy lacking p 123–143.

Simmons, John T
History of the Twenty-eighth Iowa volunteer infantry, from the date of enlistment down
to January 1st, 1865, covering all the principal
scenes of its eventful history throughout the
sieges of Vicksburg, Red river expedition and
the Shenandoah valley, by Chaplain J. T. Simmons. Washington, Printed by Wm. H. Moore,
1865. 40 p. 21½cm.          IaHi          **226**
"List of the dead of the 28th Iowa vol. infantry,"
[35]–9.

### 29TH INFANTRY

*Mustered in: December 1, 1862.*
*Mustered out: August 10, 1865.*
*Roster* III 1341–1471.
*Iowa and the rebellion* 566–73.
*Iowa colonels* 445–52.

Nicholson, William L          1832–1890.
The engagement at Jenkin's ferry. *AI* s3 xI
(1914) 505–19.          **227**

Wright, John P
Diary of John P. Wright, U.S.A., 1864–65.
Edited by Ralph R. Rea. *Arkansas historical*
*quarterly* xvI (1957) 304–18.          **228**

### 30TH INFANTRY

*Mustered in: September 23, 1862.*
*Mustered out: June 5, 1865.*
*Roster* III 1473–1577.
*Iowa and the rebellion* 574–86.
*Iowa colonels* 453–66.

Fowler, James A          1843–
History of the Thirtieth Iowa infantry volunteers, giving a complete record of the movements of the Regiment, from its organization until mustered out. Written and compiled by James A. Fowler and Miles M. Miller, by authority of the Regimental association. Mediapolis, T. A. Merrill, printer, 1908. 184 p. 24cm.                    IaHi    **229**
Unit roster 144–84.

### 31ST INFANTRY

*Mustered in: September 15 to October 13, 1862.*
*Mustered out: June 27, 1865.*
*Roster* III 1579–1683.
*Iowa and the rebellion* 587–96.
*Iowa colonels* 467–74.

### 32ND INFANTRY

*Mustered in: September 8, 1862.*
*Mustered out: August 24, 1865.*
*Roster* v 1–133.
*Iowa and the rebellion* 597–612.
*Iowa colonels* 475–86.

Ackerman, Michael
After the battle of Pleasant Hill, La. *AI* s3 XI (1913) 218–24.                    **230**

Aldrich, Charles, 1828–1908.
Incidents connected with the history of the Thirty-second Iowa infantry, by Charles Aldrich. Iowa City, State Historical Society of Iowa [1906] 18 p. 26½cm.    DLC    **231**
Title from cover. "Reprinted from the January 1906 number of the Iowa journal of history and politics."

—— The song "Sherman's march to the sea." *AI* s3 XI (1913) 215–17.          **232**

Benson, Solon F          1839–
The Battle of Pleasant Hill, Louisiana. *AI* s3 VII (1906) 481–522. 4 plates (3 fold. maps, 3 ports.).          **233**

Scott, John, 1824–
Story of the Thirty second Iowa infantry volunteers. Compiled and published by John Scott. Nevada, 1896. 526 p. front. (illus.), ports, plates (fold. map, ports.). 24cm.
                    DLC NN    **234**
"Approximate roster of companies," 410–501.

Tod, George A          1846–
Adventures of Geo. A. Tod, an Iowa drummer boy in Rebel prisons at Cahawba and Andersonville. *IJH* XLIX (1951) 339–51.    **235**

### 33RD INFANTRY

*Mustered in: October 1, 1862.*
*Mustered out: July 17, 1865.*

*Roster* v 135–252.
*Iowa and the rebellion* 613–23.
*Iowa colonels* 487–500.

Ingersoll, Lurton Dunham
Brigadier General Samuel A. Rice. *AI* III (1865) 384–403.          **236**

Morgan, John S          1841–1874.
Diary of . . . Company G, Thirty-third Iowa infantry. *AI* s3 XIII (1923) 483–508, 570–610. facs., port.          **237**

Newman, James A          1840–
The autobiography of an old fashioned boy, by J. A. Newman. [Oklahoma City, Okla.] 1923. 100 p. illus., ports. 21cm.    In    **238**

Sperry, Andrew F
History of the 33d Iowa infantry volunteer regiment, 1863–6, by A. F. Sperry. Des Moines, Mills & co., 1866. viii, 237 p. front. (port.). 23cm.                    DLC NN    **239**
Unit roster 197–215.

Thompson, Thomas M
Roster of living and dead comrades, members of Co. H, 33rd Iowa infantry, revised to Aug. 1, 1899. Prepared by T. M. Thompson, Historian. White Pigeon, 1899. [5] p. 17½cm.
Title from cover.          Ia-HA    **240**
See also Title 89A.

### 34TH INFANTRY

*Mustered in: October 15, 1862.*
*Mustered out: August 15, 1865.*
*Roster* v 253–399; 34th and 38th regiments consolidated, v 401–505.
*Iowa and the rebellion* 624–39.
*Iowa colonels* 501–06.

Clark, James Samuel, 1841–
The Thirty-fourth Iowa regiment brief history. Des Moines, Watters-Talbott print. co., 1892. 59 p. 17cm.          DLC NHi    **241**
Unit roster 34–52. Copyright by J. S. Clark, Historian.
See also Title 58A.

### 35TH INFANTRY

*Mustered in: September 18, 1862.*
*Mustered out: August 10, 1865.*
*Roster* v 507–612.
*Iowa and the rebellion* 640–50.
*Iowa colonels* 507–12.

First and second re-unions of the Thirty-fifth Iowa infantry, held at Muscatine, Iowa. First re-union, September 29, 1886. Second re-union, October 2 and 3, 1889. Muscatine, Journal print. co., 1889–90. 57 p. plates (ports.). 22½cm.                    DLC NHi    **242**

## 36TH INFANTRY

*Mustered in: October 4, 1862.*
*Mustered out: August 24, 1865.*
*Roster v 613–737.*
*Iowa and the rebellion 651–60.*
*Iowa colonels 513–20.*

Drake, Francis Marion
Campaign of General Steele, by Brevet Brigadier-General F. M. Drake. *MOLLUS-Iowa* I 60–73. **243**

Pearson, Benjamin Franklin, 1815–1883.
. . . War diary. *AI* s3 xv (1925–26) 83–129, 194–222, 281–305, 377–89, 433–63, 507–63. 1 illus., port., plate (facs.). **244**

Swiggett, Samuel A
The bright side of prison life, experiences, in prison and out, of an involuntary sojourner in Rebeldom, by Captain S. A. Swiggett. Baltimore, Press of Fleet, McGinley & co. [1897] 254 p. plates (ports.). 19½cm.   NN   **245**

## 37TH INFANTRY

*Mustered in: December 15, 1862.*
*Mustered out: May 24, 1865.*
*Roster v 739–832.*
*Iowa and the rebellion 661–3.*
*Iowa colonels 521–2.*

## 38TH INFANTRY

*Mustered in: November 4, 1862.*
*Consolidated with the 34th regiment of infantry: January 1, 1865.*
*Roster v 833–936; 34th and 38th regiments consolidated, v 401–505.*
*Iowa and the rebellion 664–8.*
*Iowa colonels 523–4.*

## 39TH INFANTRY

*Mustered in: November 24, 1862.*
*Mustered out: June 5, 1865.*
*Roster v 937–1043.*
*Iowa and the rebellion 717–30.*
*Iowa colonels 525–32.*

Johnson, William Benjamin, 1846–1908.
Union to the hub and twice around the tire, reminiscences of the Civil war, by William Benjamin Johnson. [Balboa, Cal., 1950] vi, 119 folios. 28cm.   CSmH DLC   **246**
Title from cover. "Foreword" signed: Wm. A. Johnson.

## 40TH INFANTRY

*Mustered in: November 15, 1862.*
*Mustered out: August 2, 1865.*
*Roster v 1045–1156.*
*Iowa and the rebellion 669–79.*
*Iowa Colonels 533–8.*

Campbell, Angus K
Col. John A. Garrett. *AI* viii/ix (1870/71) 429–45. plate (port.). **246A**

## 42ND AND 43RD INFANTRY

*Regiments failed to complete organization.*

## 44TH INFANTRY

*Mustered in: June 1, 1864.*
*Mustered out: September 15, 1864.*
*Roster v 1201–84.*

Davis, Carlyle Channing
Olden times in Colorado, by Carlyle Channing Davis. Los Angeles, Phillips pub. co., 1916. 448 p. plates (illus., ports.). 23cm.
Civil war 19–36.   DLC NN   **246B**

Horack, Frank E
The flag of the University company. *IHR* xv (1899) 517–20. **247**

## 45TH INFANTRY

*Mustered in: May 25, 1864.*
*Mustered out: September 16, 1864.*
*Roster v 1285–1369.*

## 46TH INFANTRY

*Mustered in: June 10, 1864.*
*Mustered out: September 23, 1864.*
*Roster v 1371–1454.*

## 47TH INFANTRY

*Mustered in: June 4, 1864.*
*Mustered out: September 28, 1864.*
*Roster v 1455–1537.*

### 41st Battalion

*Detached from 14th regiment of infantry: September 18, 1862.*
*Consolidated with 7th regiment of cavalry: April 25, 1863.*
*Roster v 1157–91.*

### 48th Battalion

*Mustered in: July 13, 1864.*
*Mustered out: October 21, 1864.*
*Roster v 1539–73.*

# KANSAS

# Reference Works

Dyer, Frederick Henry, 1849–1917.

A compendium of the War of the rebellion, 1908 (reprinted 1959).

"Regimental index" 144–6; "Regimental histories" 1181–9. The pagination is the same in the 1959 reprint.

Kansas. Adjutant General.

Report of the Adjutant general of the State of Kansas, 1861–'65. Vol. I[–II] (reprinted by authority). Topeka, Kansas State print. co., 1896. 654, 294 p. 23cm.

"Military history of Kansas regiments" 1–281, 294 of second pagination.

*The Union army.*

"Record of Kansas regiments," IV 202–25.

United States. Adjutant General's Office.

Official army register of the volunteers of the United States army for the years 1861, '62, '63, '64, 65. Part VII. Washington, 1867.

A roster of Kansas officers by regiments, 345–75, 405, with an alphabetical index to the eight states in this volume.

# KANSAS

## ARTILLERY

### 1ST BATTERY LIGHT ARTILLERY

*Organized: July 24, 1861.*
*Mustered out: July 17, 1865.*
*AG's report 623–7.*
*Military history 263.*

Life of Capt. Marcus D. Tenney. *TKHS* xi (1910) 291–5.                                        **1**

Muster-out roll of First Kansas battery volunteers, commanded by Capt. Marcus D. Tenney. . . . Ottawa, Newman Waring, printer, 1896. 23 p. 23½cm.                               KHi   **2**

Gardner, Theodore, 1844–1929.
An address delivered before the Fire insurance men's "Monday lunch club," at the Chamber of commerce, Topeka, Kansas, February 18, 1918, by Theodore Gardner, late Sergeant, First Kansas battery. [Topeka, H. Clarkson print., 1918] 12 p. 20½ x 9½cm.
Title from cover, p [1]                      KHi   **3**

—— The First Kansas battery, an historical sketch, with personal reminiscences of army life, 1861–'65. *TKHS* xiv (1918) 235–82. 3 fold. maps, port.                                        **4**

### 2ND BATTERY LIGHT ARTILLERY

*Mustered in: September 10, 1862.*
*Mustered out: August 11, 1865.*
*AG's report 628–32.*
*Military history 263–7.*

### 3RD BATTERY LIGHT ARTILLERY

*Organized as Company B, 2nd regiment of cavalry: December 9, 1861.*
*Organized as Battery with designation Hopkin's battery: October 27, 1862.*
*Designated 3rd battery of light artillery: October 1, 1863.*
*Mustered out: January 19, 1865.*
*AG's report 633–6.*
*Military history 268–72.*

## CAVALRY

### 2ND CAVALRY *

*Organized as 12th regiment of infantry. Designated 9th regiment of infantry: February 4, 1862. Designated 2nd regiment of cavalry: March 5, 1862.*

*Mustered out: August 17, 1865.*
*AG's report 78–124.*
*Military history 15–65.*

Britton, Wiley, 1842–1930.
A day with Colonel W. F. Cloud. *Chronicles of Oklahoma* v (1927) 311–21.            **4A**
Cloud served also in the 10th infantry and the 15th cavalry.

Crawford, Samuel Johnson, 1835–1913.
Kansas in the sixties, by Samuel J. Crawford, war Governor of Kansas. Chicago, A. C. McClurg & co., 1911. xv, 441 p. plates (ports.). 20½cm.                                         NN   **5**
Author served with 2nd Kansas infantry, June 20 – October 31, 1861; with 2nd Kansas cavalry, March 27, 1862 – December 6, 1863; with 2nd Kansas colored infantry, December 6, 1863 – December 2, 1864. Roster of regimental officers: 2nd Kansas infantry, May 1861, 389–90; 2nd Kansas cavalry, 390–1; 2nd Kansas colored infantry, 392–3.

Lines, Charles Burrill, 1807–1889.
Memorial of Edward C. D. Lines, late Captain of Co. C, 2d reg't Kansas cavalry. New Haven, Tuttle, Morehouse & Taylor, printers, 1867. 34 p. front. (port.). 22cm.
                                          DLC NHi   **6**
On cover: Tribute to the memory of a Kansas soldier. Foreword signed: C. B. L.

Manning, Edwin Cassander, 1838–1915.
Biographical, historical and miscellaneous, by Edwin Cassander Manning, March 7, 1838 – January 1, 1911. Privately printed. Cedar Rapids, Iowa [Torch press] 1911. 194, (1) p. plates (illus., facs., ports.). 23½cm.
                                          DLC NN   **6A**
Civil war 42–52. "My supplication," (1) p.

—— A Kansas soldier [Samuel J. Crawford] *TKHS* x (1908) 421–8. port.                    **7**

Osborne, Vincent B        1839–1879.
Vincent B. Osborne's Civil war experiences. Edited by Joyce Farlow and Louise Barry. *KHQ* xx (1952) 108–33, 187–223.        **8**
Mustered in 2nd Kansas infantry, July 10, 1861; mustered out, October 31, 1861; mustered in 2nd Kansas cavalry, February 19, 1862; discharged for disability, May 8, 1865.

Rechow, Theodore G        1846–
Autobiography Theodore G. Rechow. Bolivar, Mo., 1929. 29 p. 22cm.
"Civil war record," 5–15.   MoHi NNC   **8A**

---

* Kansas regiments are numbered continuously without reference to arm of service.

## 5TH CAVALRY

*Organized: July 12, 1861 to January 22, 1862.*

*Mustered out: Companies A — H, August 11 to December 8, 1864; Companies I — K, June 22, 1865; Companies L — M consolidated with 15th regiment of cavalry, August 22, 1865.*

*AG's report 125–63.*

*Military history 66–72.*

Fifth Kansas cavalry association regimental roster. . . . [Mound City, 1896] [23] p. 15cm.
Title from cover.                      WHi    9

—— [n. p.,] 1911. [27] p. front. (port.). port on p 4 of cover. 17cm.                KHi    10
Title from cover.

A plea for justice for one [Daniel W. Boutwell] court-martialed, sentenced and shot, reported as a deserter, and afterward, as a private citizen, through bravery and heroism in time of danger to the Federal forces saved millions of stores for the United States government. [Topeka, 1909] 39 p. 1 illus., plates (facs., ports.). 19cm.                      KHi WHi    11
Title from cover.

Proceedings of the members of the Fifth Kansas volunteer cavalry who were present at the soldiers' reunion, at Leavenworth, Kan., October 10, 11 and 12, 1883, and the subsequent doings of the officers chosen at that meeting. Valley Falls, Register print, 1884. 14 p. 17cm.
Title from cover.                       KHi    12

Bondi, August, 1833–1907.
Autobiography of August Bondi, 1833–1907. Published by his sons and daughters for its preservation. Galesburg, Ill., Wagoner print. co., 1910. 177, (1) p. plates (illus., ports.). 24cm.                              KHi    13
"Civil war" 73–122.

Boutwell, Daniel Webster, 1831–1912.
A veteran's history of his unrequited service to the Republic, sworn statement of Daniel W. Boutwell. [Topeka, 190–] 8 p. 20cm.
Caption title.                          WHi    13A

Fisher, Hugh Dunn, 1824–1905.
The gun and the gospel, early Kansas and Chaplain Fisher, by Rev. H. D. Fisher. . . . Chicago, Kenwood press, 1896. 317 p. plates (illus., ports.). 20cm.        DLC KHi    14

—— Second edition. Chicago, Medical Century co., 1897. xi, [9]–344 p. plates (illus., ports.). 20½cm.                    DLC    15
The plates of Title 14 have been used in part. KHi and NN have an 1899 reprint.

Jenkins, Wilton A
Address of Col. W. A. Jenkins, at the seventh annual reunion of the Fifth Kansas cavalry veterans at Fort Leavenworth, Kansas, October 14, 1897. [4] p. port. on cover. 23cm.
Title from cover.                       KHi    16

—— A leaf from army life (read December 8, 1887). MOLLUS-Ill III 437–45.    17

—— Rubaiyat of the Fifth Kansas. Topeka [Chicago, C. M. Staiger, printer] 1898. 22 p. ports. on p. 1 and 4 of cover. 17cm.
Title from cover.                       KHi    18

## 6TH CAVALRY

*Organized: July 1861.*

*Mustered out: August 27, 1865.*

*AG's report 164–213.*

*Military history 73–92.*

Britton, Wiley, 1842–1930.
The Civil war on the border, a narrative of operations in Missouri, Kansas, Arkansas and the Indian territory during the years, 1861–62, based upon the official reports of the Federal commanders, Lyon, Sigel, Sturgis, Fremont, Halleck, Curtis, Schofield, Blunt, Herron and Totten, and of the Confederate commanders, McCulloch, Price, Van Doren, Hindman, Marmaduke, and Shelby, by Wiley Britton, 1861–62. New York, G. P. Putnam's Sons, 1890. xvii, 465 p. plates (2 fold. maps, 2 ports.). 23½cm.                         DLC NN    19

—— Second edition, revised. New York, G. P. Putnam's Sons, 1891. xix, 473 p. plates (3 maps, 2 fold.; 2 ports.). 23½cm. DLC    20
Printed from plates of Title 19. The additional matter, p 467–73, is an Index.

—— Third edition, revised. New York, G. P. Putnam's Sons, 1899. xix, 473 p. plates (3 maps, 2 fold.; 3 ports.). 23½cm. NN    21
Printed from plates of Title 19.

—— The Civil war on the border, a narrative of military operations in Missouri, Kansas, Arkansas, and the Indian territory, during the years, 1863–65, based upon official reports and observations of the author, by Wiley Britton. Volume II. New York, G. P. Putnam's Sons, 1899. xxiii, 546 p. 22cm.    DLC NN    22
"Preface" dated 1898.

—— —— Another printing 1904.
                                        DLC    23

—— Memoirs of the rebellion on the border, 1863, by Wiley Britton, late Sixth Kansas cavalry. Chicago, Cushing, Thomas & co., 1882. 458 p. 19½cm.              DLC NN    24
Coulter 52.

—— Pioneer life in Southwest Missouri. *Missouri historical review* xvi (1921/22) 42–85, 263–88, 388–421; xvii (1922/23) 62–76, 198–211, 358–75.                                **24A**

Partial contents: A reconnaissance into Southwest Missouri; Preparing for active service.

—— Resume of military operations in Missouri and Arkansas, 1864–65. *BandL* iv 374–7.                                **25**

—— Union and Confederate Indians in the Civil war. *BandL* 335–6.                **25A**

—— The Union Indian brigade in the Civil war, by Wiley Britton. Kansas City, Mo., Franklin Hudson pub. co., 1922. 474 p. plates (1 illus., maps, ports.). 19cm.
                            DLC NN     **26**

Cory, Charles Estabrook, 1852–
The soldiers of Kansas. The Sixth Kansas cavalry and its commander, an address by Charles E. Cory. [Topeka, 1910] 24 p. plan. 23cm.                     DLC NN     **27**

"Reprinted from Collections Kansas historical society, vol. XI, 1909–'10."

Martin, George Washington, 1841–1914.
A Kansas soldier's [Robert Henderson] escape from Camp Ford, Texas. *TKHS* viii (1904) 405–15.                         **28**

### 7TH CAVALRY

*Organized: October 28, 1861.*

*Mustered out: September 29, 1865.*

*AG's report 214–56.*

*Military history 93–7.*

[Spinning, George L      ]
Old Glory, the army mule and other sketches. Cincinnati, Elm Street print. co. [1893] 39 p. illus. 18cm.                      DLC NHi     **29**

"Dedicated to the Grand army of the Republic by G. L. S. of the Seventh Kansas cavalry." On the cover: "Just the thing for Post camp-fires." A campfire madrigal including a song to Old glory and an ode to the grand army mule.

Songs of camp and field, new and original, by Curly Q., esq., 7th Kansas cavalry. Memphis, Bulletin job office print. [1863] broadside, 45 x 33cm.                         KHi     **30**

Contents: Jeff Davis' dream; The soldier's evening song: My meerschaum pipe; My father's Sharpe's rifle; I want to be a veteran; Letters from home.

Cody, William Frederick, 1846–1917.
Autobiography of Buffalo Bill (Colonel W. F. Cody). Illustrated by N. C. Wyeth. New York, Cosmopolitan Book corp., 1920. 328 p. front. (port.), plates (illus.). 19½cm.
                            DLC NN     **30A**

Enlisted 7th Kansas cavalry, February 19, 1864; discharged, September 29, 1865. Also served as guide

and scout in the Spring of 1862 for the 9th Kansas cavalry on an expedition to the Kiowa and Comanche country on the Arkansas river.

Fox, Simeon M      1841–1938.
The early history of the Seventh Kansas cavalry, written by S. M. Fox, late Adjutant Seventh Kansas cavalry, for the Kansas state historical society. [Topeka, 1910] 16 p. 23cm.
                                NN     **31**

Caption title. Advance issue of article to appear in v. 11 of Transactions of Kansas state historical society.

—— The Seventh Kansas cavalry, its service in the Civil war, an address before the State historical society, December 2, 1902, by S. M. Fox, First Lieutenant and Adjutant. Also, a brief narration of the first eight Kansas regiments. Topeka, State print. office, 1908. 59 p. 23cm.                             NN     **32**

"Reprinted from eighth volume of the Kansas historical collections."

—— Story of the Seventh Kansas. [Topeka, 1902] 36, (1) p. 23cm.        DLC     **33**

Coulter 171. Identical with Title 32.

### 9TH CAVALRY

*Organized: March 27, 1862.*

*Mustered out: July 17, 1865.*

*AG's report 296–346.*

*Military history 166–77.*

Bartles, William Lewis, 1842–
Massacre of Confederates [command of Colonel Charles Harrison] by Osage Indians in 1863. *TKHS* viii (1904) 62–6.        **33A**

Without author credit, the article was republished in *The Osage magazine* (February 1910) 49–52.

Greene, Albert Robinson, 1842–
Campaigning in the army of the frontier. *TKHS* xiv (1918) 283–310.         **34**

—— On the battle of Wilson creek, an address delivered. . . . *TKHS* v (1896) 116–27.                                **35**

—— What I saw of the Quantrill raid. *TKHS* xiii (1915) 430–51. port.        **36**

Phillips, Charles J
Alvin Woods' retreat from Prairie Grove. *Chronicles of Oklahoma* vii (1929) 170–1. plate (port.).                        **36A**

Woods was a member of a contingent of over 100 Osage braves that were attached to the 9th Kansas cavalry.

Pike, Joshua
Statement of Capt. J. A. Pike concerning the Quantrill raid. *TKHS* xiv (1918) 311–18.    **37**

See also Title 30A.

**11TH CAVALRY**

*Organized: August 1862.*
*Mustered out: September 26, 1865.*
*AG's report 382–419.*
*Military history 198–220.*

. . . Annual reunion of the surviving comrades of Companies C and E Eleventh Kansas cavalry. . . . xvii–xviii 1907–1908; xxii–xxiii 1911–1912.                                    KHi    **38**
A program and a menu.

Connelley, William Elsey, 1855–1930.
The life of Preston B. Plumb, 1837–1891 . . . by William Elsey Connelley. Chicago, Browne & Howell co., 1913. vi, (3), 475 p. front. (port.), fold. maps. 23cm.
Civil war 98–208.                    DLC NN    **39**

Fairfield, Stephen Henry, 1833–1915.
The Eleventh Kansas regiment at Platte bridge. *TKHS* viii (1904) 352–62. 2 illus., plate (illus.).                                **40**

Hamilton, Clad, 1867–
A Colonel of Kansas [Henry C. Lindsey] *TKHS* xii (1912) 282–92. port.    **41**

Hannahs, Harrison, 1832–1911.
Address given at a meeting of the Colorado commandery, Military order of the loyal legion of the United States, Denver, Colorado, September 7, 1909, by Major Harrison Hannahs. Published by order of the Commandery. . . . [Denver, Paradis' print, 1909] 68, (1) p. 22½cm.                        DLC    **42**
Caption title: War's cruelty on the Border.

—— General Thomas Ewing, Jr. *TKHS* xii (1912) 276–82. port.                **42A**

Kitts, John Howard, 1842–1870.
The Civil war diary of. . . . *TKHS* xiv (1918) 318–32.                            **43**

Nichols, William F
The 11th Kan. cav. after Price and the Indians. In National tribune scrap book i 113–18.
**43A**
Palmer, Henry Emerson, 1841–1911.
The Border war, when, where, by Capt. H. E. Palmer, 1898. *MOLLUS-Neb* i 173–89. **44**

—— Company A, Eleventh Kansas regiment in the Price raid. *TKHS* ix (1906) 431–43. **45**

—— The Lawrence raid, 1898. *MOLLUS-Neb* i 190–204.                        **46**

—— An outing in Arkansas; or, forty days and a week in the wilderness, 1899. *MOLLUS-Neb* i 213–25.                        **47**

—— Powder river Indian expedition of 1865, with a few incidents preceeding the same,

read February 2, 1887, and revised February 2, 1900. *MOLLUS-Neb* i 59–109.    **48**

—— History of the Powder river Indian expedition of 1865. *Transactions and reports of the Nebraska state historical society* ii (1887) 197–229.                        **49**
"Read before the Nebraska commandery of the MOLLUS, February 2, 1887."

—— The Powder river expedition of 1865, the first Indian campaign after the Civil war . . . edited and illustrations supplied by Robert Bruce. *U.S. army recruiting news*, August 15 – October 1, 1928. illus., maps, ports.    **50**

Pennock, Isaac B
Diary of Jake Pennock [May–September 1865]. *Annals of Wyoming* xxiii (1951) 4–29.
**50A**
Walker, George Morton, 1830–
Eleventh Kansas cavalry, 1865, and the battle of Platte bridge. *TKHS* xiv (1918) 332–40. fold. map, port.                        **51**

**14TH CAVALRY**

*Organized: April 1863.*
*Mustered out: June 25, 1865.*
*AG's report 471–99.*
*Military history 228–32.*

**15TH CAVALRY**

*Organized: September to October 1863.*
*Mustered out: December 7, 1865.*
*AG's report 500–33.*
*Military history 232–43.*

Hunt, Robert Henry, 1839–1908.
General orders no. 11, by Lieut. Col. R. H Hunt, 15th Kansas cavalry. Kansas commandery of the Military order of the loyal legion of the United States. [Topeka] 1908. 7 p. 23½cm.
DLC NHi    **52**

**16TH CAVALRY**

*Organized: November 1863 to May 1864.*
*Mustered out: December 6, 1865.*
*AG's report 534–64.*
*Military history 243–4.*

**INFANTRY**

**1ST INFANTRY**

*Organized: May 20 to June 3, 1861.*
*Mustered out: August 30, 1865.*
*AG's report 22–66.*
*Military history 3–11, 275–81.*

*1st Regiment Colored Troops Infantry*
*see 79th United States Colored Troops*

McGonigle, James Andrew, 1834–1925.
First Kansas infantry in the battle of Wilson's creek. *TKHS* XII (1912) 292–5.     **53**

## 2ND INFANTRY

*Mustered in: June 20, 1861.*
*Mustered out: October 31, 1861.*
*AG's report 67–77.*
*Military history 11–15.*

Brant, Randolph C
Campaign of Gen. Lyon in Missouri, its value to the Union cause, a paper read before the Oregon commandery of the Military order of the loyal legion of the United States, November 7, 1894, by Randolph C. Brant, late Chaplain 2nd Kan. vol. inft. Portland, Ore., Schwab Bros. print. co., 1895. 14 p. 23cm.
On cover: War paper no. 3. . . .     DLC     **54**

See also Titles 5 and 8.

*2nd Regiment Colored Troops Infantry*
*see 83rd United States Colored Troops*

## 2ND INFANTRY (MILITIA)

*Called into service, October 9, 1864, to resist Price's invasion.*
*Disbanded, October 29, 1864.*

[Steele, James W        ]
The battle of the Blue of the Second regiment, K.S.M., October 22, 1864, the fight, the captivity, the escape, as remembered by survivors and commemorated by the Gage monument at Topeka, Kansas. Printed under the direction of D. H. Christophel. Chicago, W[omen's] T[emperance] P[ub.] A[ssoc.] [1896] 157 p. plates (illus.). 23½cm.     KHi NN     **55**
Dedication signed: G. G. Gage. Unit roster 101–07.

## 4TH INFANTRY (MILITIA)

*Called into service to resist Price's invasion: October 9, 1864.*
*Disbanded: October 29, 1864.*

McClure, William T        1845–
The Fourth Kansas militia in the Price raid. *TKHS* VIII (1904) 149–51.     **55A**

## 8TH INFANTRY

*Organized: August 1861.*
*Mustered out: November 29, 1865.*
*AG's report 257–95.*
*Military history 98–166.*

Reunion proceedings of the Eighth Kansas veteran vol. infantry, Ft. Leavenworth, Kansas, October 10th, 11th and 12th, 1883, with the address of Colonel John A. Martin. . . . Atchison, Haskell & Son, printers, 1883. 7, (1) p. 21½cm.     NHi NN     **56**
Title and imprint from cover.

Roster of the Eighth Kansas infantry . . . September 1, 1888. Topeka, Geo. W. Crane pub. co., printers, 1888. 39 p. 13½cm.
                                    DLC KHi     **57**
"Introduction" signed: S. M. Lanham, Secretary. Address of Colonel John A. Martin, 7–16.

Cain, William Stephen, 1836–
Autobiography of Captain W. S. Cain, biographical sketches of relatives, reminiscences of 1861–1865. . . . Topeka, Printed by Crane & co., 1908. 126 p. front. (port.), 1 illus., ports., fold. chart. 20½cm. CtY DLC     **57A**
Mustered in 8th Kansas infantry, September 19, 1861; discharged for promotion to 12th U.S. colored infantry, September 30, 1863.

Love, James Edwin, 1830–
The autobiography of James E. Love. *Missouri historical society bulletin* VI (1950) 124–38, 400–11.     **58**

Martin, John Alexander, 1839–1889.
Addresses, by John A. Martin, delivered in Kansas. For private circulation. Topeka, Kansas pub. house, 1888. 248 p. 23½cm.
                                    KHi NN     **58A**
Partial contents: The First Kansas; Eighth Kansas veteran volunteers; The Grand army of the Republic; A wartime picture; General Grant — memorial address; Our duty to the Union soldier; In memoriam; Memories of the march.

—— Military history of the Eighth Kansas veteran volunteer infantry, by Col. John A. Martin. Leavenworth, Printed at the Daily Bulletin print. house, 1869. 112 p. 21cm.
                                    NN     **59**

—— Some notes on the Eighth Kansas infantry and the battle of Chickamauga, letters of Col. John A. Martin. Edited by Martha B. Caldwell. *KHQ* XIII (1944) 139–45.     **60**

## 10TH INFANTRY

*Organized: April 3, 1862.*
*Mustered out: August 30, 1865.*
*AG's report 347–81.*
*Military history 177–97.*

Hills, Charles S
The last battle of the war, recollections of the Mobile campaign, by Brevet Colonel Chas. S. Hills. *MOLLUS-Mo* I 177–90.     **61**

## 12TH INFANTRY

*Organized: September 1862.*
*Mustered out: June 3, 1865.*
*AG's report 420–44.*
*Military history 220–3.*

Twelfth Kansas infantry association regimental rosters. . . . [189–] 31 p. 15½ x 8cm.
KHi    **62**
"A brief history of the 12th Kansas regiment volunteer infantry," by William E. Kibbe, [1]–6.

Cone, John Philip
   Told out of school, by one of the pupils. [1910] 25 p. 22cm.   KHi NN(M)   **62A**

## 13TH INFANTRY

*Mustered in: September 20, 1862.*
*Mustered out: June 26, 1865.*
*AG's report 445–70.*
*Military history 223–7.*

## 17TH INFANTRY

*Organized: July 28, 1864.*
*Mustered out: November 16, 1864.*
*AG's report 565–73.*
*Military history 244–6.*

Drake, Samuel Adams, 1833–1905.
   The old army in Kansas, by Lieutenant Colonel Samuel Adams Drake. *MOLLUS-Mass* 1 141–52.   **63**

# MICHIGAN

# Reference Works

Dyer, Frederick Henry, 1849–1917.

A compendium of the War of the rebellion, 1908 (reprinted 1959).

"Regimental index" 160–5; "Regimental histories" 1269–93. The pagination is the same in the 1959 reprint.

Michigan. Adjutant General.

Michigan in the war, compiled by Jno. Robertson, Adjutant general. Revised edition. By authority. Lansing, W. S. George & co., State printers, 1882. 1039 p. 3 plates (ports.). 23cm.

Contents: Part I. In the State; Part II. In the field; Part III. Register of commissioned officers.

Michigan. Adjutant General.

Record of service of Michigan volunteers in the Civil war, 1861–1865. Published by authority of the Senate and House of representatives of the Michigan Legislature under the direction of Brig. Gen. Geo. H. Brown, Adjutant general. [Kalamazoo, Ihling Bros. & Everard, printers, 1905] 46 v. 24cm.

In each of the 46 volumes, the frontispiece and "Introductory" text of viii pages are identical. Volume numbering appears only on the spine. The title for each individual volume appears on the front cover. In this Checklist each volume of the Record of service of Michigan volunteers has been given a separate entry.

Because of its miscellaneous content the following volume has not been analyzed and is cited here:

Record: Merrill horse; 23rd, 37th, 44th Illinois; Co. C, 70th New York infantry; Co. K, 1st New York cavalry; 47th Ohio infantry; 1st Michigan lancers; Chandler horse guards; Provost guard; miscellaneous: Civil war, 1861–1865. [Kalamazoo, Ihling Bros. & Everard, printers, 1905] 324 p. 24cm. (Record of service of Michigan volunteers in the Civil war, 1861–1865, v 45).

Other volumes in this series are cited and described under the appropriate regiments.

Michigan. State Secretary.

Alphabetical general index to public library sets of 85,271 names of Michigan soldiers and sailors individual records . . . under supervision and direction of Coleman C. Vaughan, Secretary of state. Lansing, Wynkoop Hallenbeck Crawford co., State printers, 1915. 1097 p. 22½cm.

*The Union army.*

"Record of Michigan regiments," III (1908) 390–433.

United States. Adjutant General's Office.

Official army register of the volunteer force of the United States army for the years 1861, '62, '63, '64, '65. Part V. Ohio, Michigan. Washington, 1865.

A roster of officers by regiments with an alphabetical index to the two states.

# MICHIGAN

## 1ST ARTILLERY (LIGHT)

Michigan. Adjutant General.
Record First Michigan light artillery Civil war, 1861–1865. [Kalamazoo, Ihling Bros. & Everard, printers, 1905] 274 p. 24cm. (Record of service of Michigan volunteers in the Civil war, 1861–1865, v 42).

### Battery A

Mustered in: May 28, 1861.
Mustered out: July 28, 1865.
Michigan in the war 509–20.

### Battery B

Mustered in: November 26, 1861.
Mustered out: June 14, 1865.
Michigan in the war 521–4.

Arndt, Albert F    R    1830–
Reminiscences of an artillery officer, a paper read before the Michigan commandery of the Military order of the loyal legion of the U.S., by A. F. R. Arndt, Major First Michigan light artillery.... Detroit, Winn & Hammond, printers, 1890. 15 p. 21½cm.        DLC    **1**
Also published as War papers I no 13.

### Battery C

Mustered in: November 28, 1861.
Mustered out: June 22, 1865.
Michigan in the war 524–6.

### Battery D

Mustered in: September 17, 1861.
Mustered out: August 3, 1865.
Michigan in the war 526–8.

See Title 94.

### Battery E

Mustered in: December 6, 1861.
Mustered out: July 30, 1865.
Michigan in the war 528–9.

### Battery F

Mustered in: January 9, 1862.
Mustered out: July 1, 1865.
Michigan in the war 529–32.

### Battery G

Mustered in: January 17, 1862.
Mustered out: August 6, 1865.
Michigan in the war 532–4.

### Battery H

Mustered in: March 6, 1862.
Mustered out: July 22, 1865.
Michigan in the war 534–6.

Tuthill, Richard Stanley, 1841–1920.
An artilleryman's recollections of the battle of Atlanta (read April 7, 1886). MOLLUS-Ill I 293–309.        **2**

### Battery I

Mustered in: August 29, 1862.
Mustered out: July 14, 1865.
Michigan in the war 536–7.

### Battery K

Mustered in: February 20, 1863.
Mustered out: July 22, 1865.
Michigan in the war 537–8.

### Battery L

Mustered in: April 16, 1863.
Mustered out: August 22, 1865.
Michigan in the war 538–9.

### Battery M

Mustered in: June 30, 1863.
Mustered out: August 1, 1865.
Michigan in the war 540–1.

## 13TH BATTERY

Mustered in: January 28, 1864.
Mustered out: July 1, 1865.
Michigan in the war 541.

Richards, David Allen, 1820–1893.
The Civil war diary of . . . Edited with an introduction by Frederick D. Williams. MiH XXXIX (1955) 183–220.        **3**

## 14TH BATTERY

Mustered in: January 5, 1864.
Mustered out: July 1, 1865.
Michigan in the war 541–2.

*6th Regiment of Heavy Artillery* see
*6th Regiment of Infantry*

## CAVALRY

### 1ST CAVALRY

*Mustered in: September 13, 1861.*
*Mustered out: March 10, 1866.*
*Michigan in the war 553–66, 573–613.*

Michigan. Adjutant General.
Record First Michigan cavalry Civil war,
1861–1865. [Kalamazoo, Ihling Bros & Everard, printers, 1905] 109 p. 24cm. (Record of
service of Michigan volunteers in the Civil
war, v 31). 3

Articles of association and roster of survivors
of "Gen'l Custer's" Michigan cavalry brigade
association, meeting, September 10, 1903, Detroit, Michigan. 48 p. illus., music, ports. 19cm.
NB 3A

Roster of the survivors of the 1st, 5th, 6th
and 7th cavalry regiments of Michigan, January 1, 1912, constituting the Custer Michigan
cavalry brigade, 1863–1865. 38 p. ports.
20½cm. MiU 3B
Title from cover. Port. p 2 of cover; illus. p 3–4
of cover.

Edwards, Arthur, 1834–1901.
Those who fought without guns (read June
2, 1886). *MOLLUS-Ill* I 441–52. 4

Johnson, George Kinney, 1822–1908.
The battle of Kernstown, March 23, 1862, a
paper prepared and read before the Michigan
commandery of the Military order of the loyal
legion of the U.S., by Bvt.-Col. Geo. K. Johnson. . . . Detroit, Winn & Hammond, 1890.
10 p. 21½cm. DLC NHi 5
Also published as War papers I no 16.

### 2ND CAVALRY

*Mustered in: October 2, 1861.*
*Mustered out: August 17, 1865.*
*Michigan in the war 614–27.*

Michigan. Adjutant General.
Record Second Michigan cavalry Civil war,
1861–1865. [Kalamazoo, Ihling Bros & Everard, printers, 1905] 178 p. 24cm. (Record of
service of Michigan volunteers in the Civil
war, 1861–1865, v 32).

Souvenir Grand army of the Republic, banquet and social evening of the veterans of the
Second Michigan cavalry association and their
friends at the thirty-fifth annual grand encampment, held at Lansing, Michigan, June
seventeenth, nineteen hundred thirteen. 20 p.
23cm. Mi 6
Title from cover.

Alger, Russell Alexander, 1836–1907.
Eulogy on the late Philip H. Sheridan, by
Gen. R. A. Alger, delivered at the reunion of
the Army of the Cumberland, Chicago, September 19, 1888. Detroit, John F. Eby & co.,
printers, 1888. 15 p. 20cm. DLC Mi 7

Anderson, David D
The Second Michigan cavalry under Philip
H. Sheridan. *MiH* XLV (1961) 210–18. 7A

Ranney, George Emery, 1839–1915.
Reminiscences of an army surgeon, by Dr.
Geo E. Ranney, Surgeon 2d Michigan cavalry
(read December 2, 1897). *MOLLUS-Mich* II
172–90. 8

Thatcher, Marshall P
A hundred battles in the West, St. Louis to
Atlanta, 1861–65, the Second Michigan cavalry, with the Armies of the Mississippi, Ohio,
Kentucky and Cumberland, under Generals
Halleck, Sherman, Pope, Rosecrans, Thomas
and others, with mention of a few of the famous regiments and brigades of the West, by
Captain Marshall P. Thatcher, Co. "B." Published by the author. Detroit [L. F. Kilroy,
printer] 1884. xiv, [17]–416, 15, (63) p. illus.,
maps, ports., plates (illus., maps, ports.).
23½cm. DLC NN 9
Unit roster (63) p. Coulter 446.

Vogel, John, 1839–1907.
Memoir of John Vogel, immigrant and pioneer. Translated by B. G. Oosterbaan and
edited by H. S. Lucas. *MiHM* xxx (1946) 546–
60. 10

### 3RD CAVALRY

*Mustered in: November 1, 1861.*
*Mustered out: February 12, 1866.*
*Michigan in the war 628–38.*

Michigan. Adjutant General.
Record Third Michigan cavalry Civil war,
1861–1865. [Kalamazoo, Ihling Bros. & Everard, printers, 1905] 188 p. 24cm. (Record of
service of Michigan volunteers in the Civil
war, 1861–1865, v 33).

Gillet, Orville
Diary of Lieutenant Orville Gillet, U.S.A.,
1864–1865. Edited by Ted R. Worley. *Arkansas historical quarterly* XVII (1958) 164–204.
illus. 11

Wilcox, Lyman G          1831–1918.
At the front with the Third Michigan cavalry, by Major Lyman G. Wilcox. Chicago, Samuel Harris [1918] 16 p. 15½cm.  P     *12*
Title from cover.

—— The South in war times (read April 5, 1894). *MOLLUS-Mich* II 12–38.          *13*

## 4TH CAVALRY

*Mustered in: August 29, 1862.*
*Mustered out: July 1, 1865.*
*Michigan in the war 639–87.*

Michigan. Adjutant General.
Record Fourth Michigan cavalry Civil war, 1861–1865. [Kalamazoo, Ihling Bros & Everard, printers, 1905] 165 p. 24cm. (Record of service of Michigan volunteers in the Civil war, 1861–1865, v 34).

Dickinson, Julian George,          –1916.
The capture of Jeff. Davis, a paper read before Michigan commandery of the Military order of the loyal legion of the United States, January 9th, 1889, by Julian G. Dickinson, late Adjutant 4th Michigan cavalry. Detroit, Ostler print. co., 1888. 15 p. illus. 21½cm.
                              DLC NHi     *14*
Also published as War papers I no 9.

## 5TH CAVALRY

*Mustered in: August 30, 1862.*
*Mustered out: June 22, 1865.*
*Michigan in the war 567–8, 573–613.*

Michigan. Adjutant General.
Record Fifth Michigan cavalry Civil war, 1861–1865. [Kalamazoo, Ihling Bros & Everard, printers, 1905] 157 p. 24cm. (Record of service of Michigan volunteers in the Civil war, 1861–1865, v 35).

Martin's soldiers record Captain Purdy's company, Company "H" First Michigan mounted rifles. Milwaukee, Samuel W. Martin, 1862. col. illus. broadside, 50½ x 50cm.
                                   MiDB     *15*
Unit roster. The space for "Memoranda" has not been used. Samuel W. Martin "inventor of the first ornamental soldiers record in the U.S. made legal in the State of Wis. by an Act of the Legislature approved April 7th 1862." "Lith. by L. Lipman, Milwaukee."

Soldier's memorial Company H, 5th regt. Michigan cavalry. Baltimore, J. C. Fuller & co., 1864. illus. broadside, 57 x 48cm.
                                   MiDB     *16*
"Lith. of Major & Knapp, 449 Broadway, New York." Unit roster with list of the Company's engagements.

Bigelow, Edwin Burnham, 1838–1916.
Edwin B. Bigelow, a Michigan Sergeant in the Civil war. Edited by Frank L. Klement. *MH* XXXVIII (1954) 193–252. plate (port.). *17*

Cooper, David Mack, 1827–1908.
Obituary discourse on occasion of the death of Noah Henry Ferry, Major of the Fifth Michigan cavalry, killed at Gettysburg, July 3, 1863, by Rev. David M. Cooper. Published by request. New York, John F. Trow, printer, 1863. 46 p. front. (port.). 22½cm.
On cover: Our hero.          DLC NHi     *18*

Harris, Samuel, 1836–1920.
A curious way of getting rid of a cowardly Captain. French girls. By Samuel Harris. Chicago, Samuel Harris & co. [Press of Adolph Selz, 191–] 8 p. port. 15½cm.     P     *19*
Title from cover.

—— Michigan brigade of cavalry at the battle of Gettysburg, July 3, 1863, under command of Brig.-Gen. Geo. A. Custer, by Samuel Harris, 1st Lieut. Co. A 5th Michigan cavalry, delivered at the annual reunion of Co. A, 5th Michigan cavalry, held at Cass city, Michigan, June 14, 1894. [Chicago, 1894] 16 p. front. (illus.). 16½cm.          Mi MiDB     *20*

—— Personal reminiscences of Samuel Harris. Chicago, Rogerson press, 1897. 172 p. plates (illus., ports.). 20cm.          DLC NN     *21*

—— A story of the War of the rebellion, why I was not hung, by Samuel Harris. . . . [Chicago, Henneberry press [189–] 31 p. 16½cm.
                                        WHi     *22*
"With compliments of Samuel Harris & co."

Hastings, Smith H
The cavalry service, and recollections of the late war. *Magazine of Western history* XI (1890) 259–66.          *23*
"A paper read before the Colorado commandery of the MOLLUS."

Hickox, George Hunn, 1822–
Remarks at the funeral of Lieut. Percival S. Leggett, of Company I, Fifth regt. Michigan cavalry, by G. H. Hickox. Detroit, O. S. Gulley's presses, 1863. 7 p. 22cm.     MiDB     *24*
On cover: In memoriam.

Murden, B      F
A sermon preached at Milford on the funeral occasion of Lieut. Henry K. Foote of the Fifth Michigan cavalry, who died at Poolesville, Md., February 8, 1863, by Rev. B. F. Murden. . . . Pontiac, Beardsley & Turner, printers, 1863. 16 p. 20cm.          Mi     *25*

5th Cavalry, continued

Wallace, Robert C
A few memories of a long life [by] R. C. Wallace. [Helena, Mont., 1916] 66, (1) p. port. 23cm.                              IHi    26
Also served in 1st Michigan infantry (three months' service).

See also Titles 3A and 3B.

## 6TH CAVALRY

*Mustered in: October 13, 1862.*
*Mustered out: November 24, 1865.*
*Michigan in the war 569–70, 573–613.*

Michigan. Adjutant General.
Record Sixth Michigan cavalry Civil war, 1861–1865. [Kalamazoo, Ihling Bros. & Everard, printers, 1905] 155 p. 24cm. (Record of service of Michigan volunteers in the Civil war, 1861–1865, v 36).

Kidd, James Harvey, 1840–1913.
Address of Gen. James H. Kidd at the dedication of Michigan monuments upon the battlefield of Gettysburg, June 12th, 1889. 25 p. front. (port.). 24cm.       NB    27
Also published with plates (3 maps, ports.) in JUSCA iv (1891) 41–63.

—— The Michigan cavalry brigade in the Wilderness, a paper read before the Michigan commandery of the Loyal legion. Detroit, Winn & Hammond, printers, 1889. 17 p. 21½cm.                              DLC    28
Also published as War paper i no 11.

—— Personal recollections of a cavalryman with Custer's Michigan cavalry brigade in the Civil war, by J. H. Kidd, formerly Colonel, Sixth Michigan cavalry. Ionia, Sentinel print. co., 1908. xiv, 476 p. plates (3 maps, ports.). 21½cm.                         DLC NN    29
Coulter 278. "List of those killed in action, or died of wounds received in action in the four regiments which constituted the Michigan cavalry brigade, commanded by General George Armstrong Custer, in the Civil war," 1st, 5th-7th regiments, [453]-76.

Page, James Madison, 1839–
The true story of Andersonville prison, a defense of Major Henry Wirz, by James Madison Page, late 2d Lieut. Company A, Sixth Michigan cavalry, in collaboration with M. J. Haley. New York, Neale pub. co., 1908. 248 p. front. (port.), plate (port.). 21½cm.    30
Coulter 360.

See also Titles 3A and 3B.

## 7TH CAVALRY

*Mustered in: January 16, 1863.*
*Mustered out: December 15, 1865.*
*Michigan in the war 571–613.*

Michigan. Adjutant General.
Record Seventh Michigan cavalry Civil war, 1861–1865. [Kalamazoo, Ihling Bros & Everard, printers, 1905] 146 p. 24cm. (Record of service of Michigan volunteers in the Civil war, 1861–1865, v 37).

Roster of survivors of the Seventh Michigan cavalry and muster out rolls of the Regiment. [Ann Arbor] Register pub. co. [1895] 65 p. 15cm.                              DNW    31
Title from cover.

Clark, John A
The final push to Appomattox, Captain Clark's account of the Seventh Michigan cavalry in action. Edited by Frances R. Reece. MiHM xxviii (1944) 456–64.    32

Havens, Edwin R          1842–
How Mosby destroyed our train. MiHM xiv (1930) 294–8.    33
"Reprinted from Personal and historical sketches, 1902," Title 41.

Isham, Asa Brainard, 1844–
Care of prisoners of war, North and South, a paper read before the Ohio commandery of the Military order of the loyal legion of the United States, October 5, 1887, by A. B. Isham, late 1st Lieutenant Co. F, 7th Michigan cavalry. Cincinnati, H. C. Sherrick & co., 1887. 25 p. 21½cm.                        NHi    34
Also published as MOLLUS-Ohio ii 205–33.

—— The cavalry of the Army of the Potomac, 1900. MOLLUS-Ohio v 301–27.    35

—— Experience in Rebel prisons for United States officers at Richmond, Macon, Savannah, Charleston and Columbia, 1890. In Prisoners of war and military prisons, personal narratives of experiences in the prisons. . . . (1890) 1–146.    36

—— An historical sketch of the Seventh regiment Michigan volunteer cavalry, from its organization, in 1862, to its muster out, in 1865, by Asa B. Isham, Historian of the Regiment. New York, Town Topics pub. co. [1893] 118 p. front. (port.), ports. 20½cm.
DLC NN    37
"Officers' register," [89]–98. Killed in action, [99]–118.

—— The story of a gunshot wound, 1896. MOLLUS-Ohio iv 429–43.    38

—— Through the Wilderness to Richmond, a paper read before the Ohio commandery of the

Loyal legion of the United States. Cincinnati, Peter G. Thomson, 1884. 18 p. 21½cm.
NHi **39**
Also published as *MOLLUS-Ohio* I 198–217.

Lee, William O   1844–1924.
Michigan cavalry brigade at Gettysburg. *Gateway* III 2 (Detroit 1904) 45–50. **40**

—— Personal and historical sketches and facial history of and by members of the Seventh regiment Michigan volunteer cavalry, 1862–1865. Compiled by William O. Lee, late Q.M. Sergeant Co. "M." Published by 7th Michigan cavalry association. Detroit [Ralston-Stroup print. co., 1901] ix, [10]–313 p. facs., 1 illus., ports. 21cm.   DLC NHi **41**
"Corrected personal, Major James L. Carpenter, Blissfield, Mich," inserted slip.

See also Titles 3A and 3B.

## 8TH CAVALRY

*Mustered in: May 2, 1863.*

*Mustered out: September 22, 1865.*

*Michigan in the war 688–704.*

Michigan. Adjutant General.
Record Eighth Michigan cavalry Civil war, 1861–1865. [Kalamazoo, Ihling Bros. & Everard, printers, 1905] 173 p. 24cm. (Record of service of Michigan volunteers in the Civil war, v 38).

Wells, James Munroe, 1838–
Tunneling out of Libby prison, a Michigan Lieutenant's account of his own imprisonment and daring escape. *McClure's magazine* XXII (1903/04) 317–26. illus. **42**

—— "With touch of elbow;" or, death before dishonor, a thrilling narrative of adventure on land and sea, by Captain James M. Wells. Philadelphia, John C. Winston co., 1909. iii, (3), 362 p. plates (facs., illus., ports.). 19½cm.   DLC **42A**

Wormer, Grover Salman
The Morgan raid (read January 6, 1898). *MOLLUS-Mich* II 190–216. **42B**

## 9TH CAVALRY

*Mustered in: May 19, 1863.*

*Mustered out: July 21, 1865.*

*Michigan in the war 705–15.*

Michigan. Adjutant General.
Record Ninth Michigan cavalry Civil war, 1861–1865. [Kalamazoo, Ihling Bros. & Everard, printers, 1905] 112 p. 24cm. (Record of service of Michigan volunteers in the Civil war, 1861–1865, v 39).

History of the Ninth Mich. cavalry. **42C**
Published in the January – May 1890 issues of the Coffee cooler, Sturgis, Michigan. The January installment "by Lt. W. W. Cook"; the February – May installments "by Geo. H. Turner and W. A. Blye." Mounted clips of the text from the John P. Nicholson collection are in CSmH.

Ransom, John L
Andersonville diary, escape, and list of the dead, with name, Co., regiment, date of death and no. of grave in cemetery [by] John L. Ransom, late First Sergeant Ninth Mich. cav., author and publisher. Auburn, N.Y., 1881. 304 p. ports. 19cm.   DLC NHi NN **43**
Coulter 398.

—— —— Philadelphia, Douglass Brothers, 1883. 381 p. illus., ports. 18½cm. NN **44**

—— The story of the Libby prison tunnel escape. [Chicago, 188–] 10, (2) p. illus., port. 21½cm.   IHi **45**
Caption title.

## 10TH CAVALRY

*Mustered in: November 18, 1863.*

*Mustered out: November 11, 1865.*

*Michigan in the war 716–28.*

Michigan. Adjutant General.
Record Tenth Michigan cavalry Civil war, 1861–1865. [Kalamazoo, Ihling Bros. & Everard, printers, 1905] 155 p. 24cm. (Record of service of Michigan volunteers in the Civil war, v 40).

Trowbridge, Luther Stephen, 1836–1911.
. . . A brief history of the Tenth Michigan cavalry, by General L. S. Trowbridge, late Colonel of the Regiment. . . . [Detroit, Friesema Bros. print. co., 1905] 44, (1) p. plates (ports.), fold. map at end. 20½cm. NN **46**
At head of title: Prepared at the request of the Adjutant general of Michigan.

—— Lights and shadows of the Civil war (read Feb. 6, 1896). *MOLLUS-Mich* II 101–09. **47**

—— . . . Michigan at Gettysburg, address of Gen. L. S. Trowbridge, July 1st, 2nd and 3rd. June 12th, 1889. Detroit, Winn & Hammond, printers [1889] 12 p. front. (port.), plates (illus.). 23½cm.   DLC NHi **48**
At head of title: "Michigan troops in the battle of Gettysburg." Title and imprint from cover.

—— The Stoneman raid of 1865. *JUSCA* IV (1891) 188–96. **49**

—— —— a paper prepared and read before Michigan commandery of the Military order of the loyal legion of the United States, January 8th, 1888. Detroit, Ostler print. co., 1888. 15 p. 21½cm.   DLC **50**
Also published as War papers I no 6.

## 11TH CAVALRY

*Mustered in: December 10, 1863.*
*Mustered out: July 20, 1865.*
*Michigan in the war 729–39.*

Michigan. Adjutant General.
Record Eleventh Michigan cavalry Civil war, 1861–1865. [Kalamazoo, Ihling Bros. & Everard, printers, 1905] 109 p. 24cm. (Record of service of Michigan volunteers in the Civil war, 1861–1865, v 41).

Reynolds, Daniel N      1848–1925.
Memories of Libby prison. Edited by Paul H. Giddens. *MiHM* xxiii (1939) 391–8.   **51**

## Engineers and Mechanics

### 1ST REGIMENT

*Mustered in: October 29, 1861.*
*Mustered out: September 22, 1865.*
*Michigan in the war 494–508.*

Michigan. Adjutant General.
Record First Michigan engineers and mechanics Civil war, 1861–1865. [Kalamazoo, Ihling Bros. & Everard, printers, 1905] 232 p. 24cm. (Record of service of Michigan volunteers in the Civil war, 1861–1865, v 43).

Chapin, Samuel S      1819–
The three campaigns, sermon preached before the First regiment Michigan fusiliers at Camp Owen. Marshall, Michigan, October 20, 1861, by Rev. S. S. Chapin. Marshall, Printed by Mann and Noyes, 1861. 12 p. 17cm.
                            MiU    **52**

Greenalch, James      –1892.
Letters of James Greenalch. Edited with an introduction by Knox Mellon, Jr. *MiH* xliv (1960) 188–240.   **53**

McKinney, Francis F      1891–
. . . The First regiment of Michigan engineers and mechanics. *Michigan alumnus quarterly review* lxii (1955/56) 140–50.   **53A**
At head of title: Roads and railways for the Army of the Cumberland.

Sligh, Charles Robert, 1850–
History of the services of the First regiment Michigan engineers and mechanics during the Civil war, 1861–1865, by Charles R. Sligh. Grand Rapids [White print. co.] 1921. 112 p. front. (port.), illus., ports. 26½cm.
                            DLC    **54**
Unit roster 91–112. The author's father was killed in action with the Regiment.

## Infantry

### 1ST INFANTRY

*Mustered in: May 1, 1861.* (3 months' service)
*Mustered out: August 7, 1861.*
*Michigan in the war 165–73.*
*Mustered in: September 16, 1861.* (3 years' service)
*Mustered out: July 9, 1865.*
*Michigan in the war 174–86.*

Michigan. Adjutant General.
Record First Michigan infantry Civil war, 1861–1865. [Kalamazoo, Ihling Bros. & Everard, printers, 1905] 151 p. 24cm. (Record of service of Michigan volunteers in the Civil war, 1861–1865, v 1).

*1st Regiment of Colored Infantry see*
*102nd Regiment United States Colored Troops*

[Two Orders of Headquarters, Alexandria, Va., dated May 26, 1861: Special orders no. 1, Captain Whittelsey of the 1st Michigan is detailed as Provost marshal; Orders no. 2, Colonel O. B. Willcox assumes command of the Union forces in and about Alexandria] [Alexandria] Galloway & O'Donnell, printers, First reg. Mich. vol. [1861] broadside, 43½ x 29½cm.
                            DLC    **54A**

Clowes, Walter F
The Detroit light guard, a complete record of this organization from its foundation to the present day, by Walter F. Clowes. . . . Detroit, John F. Eby & co., 1900. 566 p. facs., plates (illus., ports.). 24½cm.   DLC NN  **55**
Service as Company A, 1st Michigan infantry, 1861, 30–56. Unit roster 48–50.

Elderkin, James D      1820–
Biographical sketches and anecdotes of a soldier of three wars, as written by himself, the Florida, the Mexican war and the great rebellion, together with sketches of travel, also of service in a militia company and a member of the Detroit light guard band for over thirty years, by James D. Elderkin. Detroit, 1899. 202 p. 4 plates (illus., 3 ports.). 17½cm.
                            DLC    **56**

Hopper, George C      1831–
The battle of Groveton; or, second Bull run, a paper read before the Commandery of the State of Michigan, Military order of the loyal legion of the United States, by Geo. C. Hopper, late Major 1st regiment Michigan. . . . Detroit, Winn & Hammond, printers, 1893. 15 p. 21½cm.   DLC  **57**
Also published as War papers i no 21.

—— First Michigan infantry, three months and three years, proceedings of 1891 reunion at Detroit. Brief history of the Regiment, by Major Geo. C. Hopper. Roster of living members. Coldwater, Courier print [1891] 41 p. 14cm.      CSmH DLC    **57A**

Isham, Frederic Stewart, 1866–1902.
History of the Detroit light guard, its records and achievements, compiled by Frederick S. Isham and Purcell & Hogan. Published by the Detroit light guard. Detroit [Wm. Graham print. co.] 1896. 104, (2) p. facs., ports. 28cm.
Civil war 24–66.      DLC NHi    **58**

Kells, David
"The ways of the world," being a history of the life of David Kells, the hero of seven battles, written by himself. Adrian, Printed for the author, 1867. 24 p. 20½cm.   DLC   **59**
The author served in the 1st Michigan infantry, the 4th Rhode Island battery and the 3rd Massachusetts battery.

Owen, Charles W
The First Michigan infantry, three months and three years, brief history of the Regiment from its organization in May, 1861, until its muster out in July, 1865, together with personal experiences of the writer. [Quincy] Quincy Herald print [1903] [73] p. front. (port.). 16cm.      Mi   **60**
Title and imprint from cover.

Paddock, Benjamin H
"Our cause, our confidence, and our consequent duty, a sermon preached in Christ church, Detroit, Sunday after Ascension, May 12th, 1861, before Company A, First regiment Mich. volunteers, by Benj. H. Paddock. Detroit, Daily Advertiser print, 1861. 15 p. 21cm.      Mi   **61**

Petersen, Eugene Thor, 1920–
The Civil war comes to Detroit. *Detroit historical society bulletin* xvii 9 (Summer 1961) 4–11. illus.      **61A**

Pittman, Samuel Emlen
The operations of General Alpheus S. Williams, and his command in the Chancellorsville campaign, as witnessed by a member of his staff, a paper read before Michigan commandery of the Military order of the loyal legion of the United States, April 6th, 1887, by Col. Sam'l E. Pittman. 18 p. col. fold. map. 21½cm.      DLC   **61B**
Also published as War papers i no 5.

Williams, Newton H
Michigan's First regiment. Incidents, marches, battles and camp life and the adventures of the author, known as the Indiana banker, who was Fifer in Company "F," and made such remark-

able time in leaving Bull run — time: first mile, 2 minutes 38 seconds. Printed for the author. Detroit, 1861. iv, [5]–19 p. 22½cm.      Mi RP   **61C**

Withington, William Herbert, 1835–1903.
The first call of the Civil war, personal recollections of Michigan's response, a paper read by Gen. W. H. Withington, before Edward Pomeroy Post, G.A.R., at Jackson, Michigan, in 1897. 32 p. 21cm.      Mi   **61D**
Dedication dated: February 6, 1901. "Printed by Mrs. Withington and dedicated to the classes in American history of Jackson High school."

—— Michigan in the opening of the war, a paper read before Michigan commandery of the Military order of the loyal legion of the United States, March 2nd, 1887. Detroit, Ostler print. co., 1889. 17 p. 21½cm.      DLC NHi   **61E**
Also published as War papers i no 4.

## 2ND INFANTRY

*Mustered in: May 25, 1861.*
*Mustered out: July 28, 1865.*
*Michigan in the war 185–205.*

Michigan. Adjutant General.
Record Second Michigan infantry Civil war, 1861–1865. [Kalamazoo, Ihling Bros. & Everard, printers, 1905] 189 p. 24cm. (Record of service of Michigan volunteers in the Civil war, 1861–1865, v 2).

Reunion of the 2d Mich. infantry at Lansing, October 11, 1883. *Veteran* i (Lansing 1883) 129–52.      **61F**

Dannett, Sylvia G      Liebowitz, 1909–
She rode with the Generals, the true and incredible story of Sarah Emma Seelye, alias Franklin Thompson [by] Sylvia G. L. Dannett. New York, Thomas Nelson and Sons [1960] 326 p. 2 plates (illus., ports.). 21½cm.      NN   **61G**

Edmonds, Sarah Emma Evelyn, 1841–1898.
Nurse and spy in the Union army: comprising the adventures and experiences of a woman in hospitals, camps, and battlefields, by S. Emma E. Edmunds. Hartford, W. S. Williams & co., 1864. 384 p. front. (port.), plates (illus.). 20cm.      NN   **62**
Text in ruled border. NN has an 1865 reprint. Author enlisted as Franklin Thompson Company F and is thus carried on the roster with an explanation of her correct name and sex.

—— Unsexed: or, the female soldier, the thrilling adventures, experiences and escapes of a woman, as nurse, spy and scout, in hospitals, camps and battle-fields, by S. Emma E.

*2nd Infantry, continued*

Edmonds. Philadelphia, Philadelphia pub. co. [c1864] 384 p. front. (port.), plates (illus.). 18½cm.　　　　　　　　　NN　　62A
A reprint of Title 62. The ruled border is omitted.

Fladeland, Betty
"Alias Franklin Thompson." *MiH* xlii (1958) 435–62. plate (port.).　　　　　　62B

Gallup, Philo H　　–1862
The Second Michigan volunteer infantry joins the Army of the Potomac. Edited with an introduction by Chester McArthur Destler. *MiH* xli (1957) 385–412.　　　62C

Hardy, John C
The final effort, last assault of the Confederates at Petersburg, by John C. Hardy, Captain 2d Michigan infantry (read Feb. 3, 1898). *MOLLUS-Mich* ii 217–28.　　　63

Lyster, Henry Francis Le Hunte, 1837–1894.
Recollections of the Bull run campaign after twenty-seven years, a paper read before the Michigan commandery of the Military order of the loyal legion of the United States, February 1st, 1887. Detroit, Wm. S. Ostler, printer, 1888. 18 p. 21½cm.　　　DLC NHi　64
Also published in War papers i no 7.

Petzold, Herman
Memoirs of the Second Michigan infantry, by Herman Petzold. [n. p., 1897] 62 p. 24cm.　　　　　　　　　　　　MiDB　65

Robinson, Charles
My experiences in the Civil war. *MiHM* xxiv (1940) 23–50.　　　　　　　66
Originally published in the Battle creek enquirer and news, 1928.

Schneider, Frederick, 1840–
Incidental history of the flags and color guard of the Second Michigan veteran volunteer infantry, 1861–5, by Col. Frederick Schneider. . . . Lansing, Winfield S. Sly [M. E. Gardner, printer, 1905] 28 p. 1 illus., ports. 21cm.　　　　　　　　　　Mi　67

### 3RD INFANTRY

*Mustered in: June 10, 1861.*
*Mustered out: June 20, 1864.*
*Michigan in the war 206–19.*
*Mustered in: October 15, 1864.*
(reorganized)
*Mustered out: May 25, 1866.*

Michigan. Adjutant General.
Record Third Michigan infantry Civil war, 1861–1865. [Kalamazoo, Ihling Bros. & Ever-

ard, printers, 1905] 211 p. 24cm. (Record of service of Michigan volunteers in the Civil war, 1861–1865, v 3).

Crotty, Daniel G
Four years campaigning in the Army of the Potomac, by Color Sergeant, D. G. Crotty, Third Michigan. Grand Rapids, Dygert Bros. & co., printers, 1874. 207 p. 22cm.
　　　　　　　　　　　　　　DLC　68

### 4TH INFANTRY

*Mustered in: June 10, 1861.*
*Mustered out: June 30, 1864.*
*Michigan in the war 220–35.*
*Mustered in: October 14, 1864.*
(reorganized)
*Mustered out: May 26, 1866.*

Michigan. Adjutant General.
Record Fourth Michigan infantry Civil war, 1861–1865. [Kalamazoo, Ihling Bros. & Everard, printers, 1905] 197 p. 24cm. (Record of service of Michigan volunteers in the Civil war, 1861–1865, v 4).

Barrett, Orvey S
Reminiscences, incidents, battles, marches and camp life of the old 4th Michigan infantry in the War of the rebellion, 1861 to 1864, by O. S. Barrett, late Lieut. Co. B, 4th Michigan infantry. Dedicated to the survivors of the Regiment. . . . Detroit, W. S. Ostler, 1888. 44, (1) p. illus. 22½cm.　　DLC NHi　69
"Appendix," (1) p.

Campbell, Robert, 1836–
Pioneer memories of the war days in 1861–1865. *MiHC* xxx (1906) 567–72.　　70

Tuttle, James Gilmore, 1839–1906.
Recollections of the Civil war. *MiH* xxxi (1947) 287–300. plate (port.).　　71

### 5TH INFANTRY

*Mustered in: August 28, 1861.*
*Mustered out: July 5, 1865.*
*Michigan in the war 236–58.*

Michigan. Adjutant General.
Record Fifth Michigan infantry Civil war, 1861–1865. [Kalamazoo, Ihling Bros. & Everard, printers, 1905] 136 p. 24cm. (Record of service of Michigan volunteers in the Civil war, v 5).

Cavendish, C. U. T. [pseud.]
[Contributions to the *Veteran*, Lansing and Detroit, August 1883 – July 15, 1884]:
Fun on picket duty. ii 248–9, 264–5, 280–2, 294–6, 326–8, 342–4, 358–60.　　72

General Philip Kearny. I 362–4.          73
Scout duty on the Peninsula. II 388–90, 406–
07.                                      74
A slight acquaintance with "Stonewall" Jackson. I 348–50.                          74A

Gunn, Jane Augusta (Terry)
Memorial sketches of Doctor Moses Gunn,
by his wife. With extracts from his letters and
eulogistic tributes from his colleagues and
friends. Chicago, W. T. Keener, 1889. xx,
380 p. front. (port.). 20cm.      DLC    75
Civil war 69–168.

Sweet, Albern K
Reminiscences, an interesting historical
resume given by A. K. Sweet, at the golden
anniversary Fifth Michigan v. v. infantry,
Flint, Mich., August 30, 1911. [8] p. 20 x 10cm.
                        Mi NN (P)        75A

## 6TH INFANTRY

*Mustered in: August 20, 1861.*

*Converted to heavy artillery retaining its
infantry number.*

*Mustered out: August 20, 1865.*

*Michigan in the war 259–69.*

Michigan. Adjutant General.
Record Sixth Michigan infantry Civil war,
1861–1865. [Kalamazoo, Ihling Bros. & Everard, printers, 1905] 158 p. 24cm. (Record of
service of Michigan volunteers in the Civil
war, 1861–1865, v 6).

Bacon, Edward, 1830–1901.
Among the cotton thieves, by Edward
Bacon, Colonel of Sixth Michigan volunteers.
Detroit, Free Press print. house, 1867. 298,
(1) p. 23cm.                       NHi    76
"Errata," (1) p. Coulter 14.

Chase, Milton, 1837–1924.
How a '61 man went into the army. *Michigan alumnus* IX (1902) 12–13.           77

Fowler, Smith W          1829–1894.
Autobiographical sketch of Capt. S. W.
Fowler, late of the 6th Mich. inft'y. Together
with an appendix containing his speeches on
the state of the Union, "reconstruction" etc.,
also his report on the "soldiers' voting bill"
made in the Michigan Senate, etc. Manistee,
Times and Standard print., 1877. 37, 61 p.
19½cm.                    MiDB MiUH      78
The title leaf has been inserted. The autobiographical sketch, 37 p., may have been issued separately but
does not have a separate title page in this volume.
The appendix, 61 p, has a separate title page and
was also issued as a separate publication: The soldiers'
voting bill. Reconstruction, a speech on the state of
the Union during the darkest days of the war, by

S. W. Fowler. Manistee, Times and Standard print.,
1876. A leaf with a portrait has been tipped to the
front end paper.

—— Autobiographical sketch of Capt. S. W.
Fowler, late of the 6th Michigan infantry.
Manistee, 1878. 24 p. 20cm.      Mi      78A
Title and imprint from cover. Crude portrait on
cover. A reprint of Title 78.

Johnson, Benjamin C
Sketches of the Sixth regiment Michigan infantry. *Veteran* I 171–3, 188–91, 204–05,
237–8, 253–4, 268–9, 288–90, 302–04, 321–2,
338–40, 354–6, 399–401; II 182–5, 229–31,
250–2, 261–4, 277–80.                     79

Soule, Harrison
From the Gulf to Vicksburg, by Harrison
Soule, Major 6th Michigan infantry (read De-
cember 6, 1894). *MOLLUS-Mich* II 51–71. 80

## 7TH INFANTRY

*Mustered in: August 22, 1861.*

*Mustered out: July 5, 1865.*

*Michigan in the war 270–80.*

Michigan. Adjutant General.
Record Seventh Michigan infantry Civil
war, 1861–1865. [Kalamazoo, Ihling Bros. &
Everard, printers, 1905] 117 p. 24cm. (Record
of service of Michigan volunteers in the Civil
war, 1861–1865, v 7).

Tivy, Joseph Albert, 1840–
Souvenir of the Seventh, containing a brief
history of it, prefaced with a view front and
rear of the "late unpleasantness," embellished
with cuts representing three phases of the soldier and other appropriate illustrations, by
Sergeant J. A. Tivy. Detroit [190–] 78 p. col.
front. (illus.), illus., music. 17½cm.
                            DLC NN        81

## 8TH INFANTRY

*Mustered in: September 23, 1861.*

*Mustered out: July 30, 1865.*

*Michigan in the war 281–92.*

Michigan. Adjutant General.
Record Eighth Michigan infantry Civil war,
1861–1865. [Kalamazoo, Ihling Bros. & Everard, printers, 1905] 148 p. 24cm. (Record of
service of Michigan volunteers in the Civil
war, 1861–1865, v 8).

Rebellion memorial Company B, 8th reg.
Michigan vol. [1863] illus. broadside, 54 x
42½cm.                           MiDB     82
Unit roster with a brief history of the Company.

*8th Infantry, continued*

Dodge, William Sumner
Robert Henry Hendershot; or, the brave
drummer boy of the Rappahannock, by William Sumner Dodge. . . . Chicago, Church and
Goodman, 1867. vi, [7]-202 p. front. (port.).
22½cm.           DLC NHi    82A

Fox, Wells B
What I remember of the great rebellion, by
Wells B. Fox, late Surgeon Eighth Michigan
infantry. Lansing, Darius D. Thorpe, printer,
1892. 278 p. plates (ports.). 22cm. NN    83

Maile, John Levi, 1844–
"Prison life in Andersonville," with special
reference to the opening of Providence spring,
by John L. Maile. . . . Los Angeles, Grafton
pub. co. [c1912] 152 p. 2 illus., plates (illus.,
plan, ports.). 18cm.       DLC NN    84

## 9TH INFANTRY

*Mustered in: October 15, 1861.*

*Mustered out: September 15, 1865.*

*Michigan in the war 293–301.*

Michigan. Adjutant General.
Record Ninth Michigan infantry Civil war,
1861–1865. [Kalamazoo, Ihling Bros. & Everard, printers, 1905] 164 p. 24cm. (Record of
Michigan volunteers in the Civil war, 1861–
1865, v 9).

Report of the semi-centennial of the Ninth
Michigan infantry at Fort Wayne, 1861–1911.
Ypsilanti, 1911. [4] p. port. 22½cm.
    Caption title.             MiDB    85

Bennett, Charles Wilkes, 1838–
Historical sketches of the Ninth Michigan infantry (General Thomas' headquarters guards),
with an account of the battle of Murfreesboro,
Tennessee, Sunday, July 13, 1862. Four years
campaigning in the Army of the Cumberland,
by Charles W. Bennett of Company C. Regimental meetings since the war, by Henry C.
Rankin. Regimental and company organizations, by Frank A. Lester, Jr. Coldwater, Daily
Courier print, 1913. 75, (1) p. 2 illus., 2 ports.,
plates (illus.; ports., 1 fold.). 22cm.
                     DLC NHi    86

Duffield, Henry Martin, 1842–1912.
Address at the dedication of the monuments
erected by the State of Michigan to her regiments and batteries on the battlefields of
Chickamauga and Missionary ridge, September 18th, 1895, delivered on the battlefield of
Chickamauga, by Henry M. Duffield, 17 p.
23cm.                      NN    87

—— Chickamauga, a paper read before Michigan commandery of the Military order of the
loyal legion of the United States, February
2nd, 1887. Detroit, Ostler print. co., 1888.
15 p. 21½cm.               DLC    88
Also published as War papers 1 no 3.

Lester, Frank A
Society of the Ninth Michigan infantry veteran volunteers [semi-centennial roster] [Lan-
sing, Ripley & Gray print. co.] 1911. [104] p.
illus., ports. 15 x 22cm.         Mi    89
"Preface" signed: Frank A. Lester.

Parkhurst, John Gibson, 1824–1906.
Recollections of Stone's river, a paper read
before the Michigan commandery of the Mili-
tary order of the loyal legion of the U. S., by
John G. Parkhurst, Col. 9th reg't Mich. . . .
Detroit, Winn & Hammond, 1890. 15 p.
21½cm.                 DLC    90
Also published as War papers 1 no 14.

Richardson, John E
Muldrough's hill; or, the soldier's complaint,
song by John E. Richardson, Company F, 9th
Michigan infantry. [n. p., n. d.] [4] p. 25½cm.
    Caption title. "Tune, Hard times." MiDB    91

## 10TH INFANTRY

*Mustered in: February 6, 1862*

*Mustered out: July 19, 1865.*

*Michigan in the war 302–12.*

Michigan. Adjutant General.
Record Tenth Michigan infantry Civil war,
1861–1865. [Kalamazoo, Ihling Bros. & Everard, printers, 1905] 126 p. 24cm. (Record of
Michigan volunteers in the Civil war, v 10).

Foote, Corydon Edward, 1849–1944.
With Sherman to the sea, a drummer's story
of the Civil war, as related by Corydon Edward Foote to Olive Deane Hormel. With a
foreword by Elizabeth Yates. New York, John
Day co. [1960] 255 p. front. (2 ports.), 2
maps. 21cm.            DLC NN    92

Hewes, Fletcher Willis
History of the formation, movements, camps,
scouts and battles of the Tenth regiment Michigan volunteer infantry, containing a short historical sketch of every officer connected with
the Regiment. Also, the names, dates of enlistments, nativity, occupation, etc. of every member of the organization, together with dates
and places of discharge, deaths, etc., from the
first enlistment to date of re-enlistment. Written and compiled by F. W. H., a member of
the Regiment. Detroit, John Slater's book print.
estab., 1864. 229, (1) p. front. (port.). 22cm.
    Unit roster included.           DNW    93

—— Outline of the veteran service of the Tenth regiment of Michigan veteran volunteer infantry, February 6, 1864 – July 19, 1865 [by] F. W. H. [Bloomfield, N. J., 1891] 31, (1) p. 21cm.     DNW   **93A**
Statement of his appointment as historian and outlining a program for achieving a regimental history, (1) p, signed: F. W. Hewes.

## 11TH INFANTRY

*Mustered in: September 24, 1861.*
*Mustered out: September 30, 1864.*
*Michigan in the war 313–23.*
*Mustered in: March 16, 1865.*
*(reorganized)*
*Mustered out: September 16, 1865.*

Michigan. Adjutant General.
Record Eleventh Michigan infantry Civil war, 1861–1865. [Kalamazoo, Ihling Bros. & Everard, printers, 1905] 177 p. 24cm. (Record of Michigan volunteers in the Civil war, 1861–1865, v 11).

Proceedings of the Eighth annual reunion of the Eleventh Michigan infantry and Fourth Michigan battery, held at Centreville, Mich., August 24, 1875. Three Rivers, W. H. Clute & co., printers [1875] 20 p. 21½cm. Mi   **94**
Title and imprint from cover, p [1]

Hicks, Borden M
Personal recollections of the War of the rebellion, by Captain Borden M. Hicks, 1907. *MOLLUS-Minn* vi 519–44.   **95**

## 12TH INFANTRY

*Mustered in: March 5, 1862.*
*Mustered out: February 15, 1866.*
*Michigan in the war 324–30.*

Michigan. Adjutant General.
Record Twelfth Michigan infantry Civil war, 1861–1865. [Kalamazoo, Ihling Bros. & Everard, printers, 1905] 178 p. 24cm. (Record of Michigan volunteers in the Civil war, 1861–1865, v 12).

Ruff, Joseph   –1921.
Civil war experiences of a German emigrant as told by Joseph Ruff. *MiHM* xxvii (1923) 271–301, 442–62.   **96**

## 13TH INFANTRY

*Mustered in: January 17, 1862.*
*Mustered out: July 25, 1865.*
*Michigan in the war 331–41.*

Michigan. Adjutant General.
Record Thirteenth Michigan infantry Civil war, 1861–1865. [Kalamazoo, Ihling Bros. & Everard, printers, 1905] 163 p. 24cm. (Record of Michigan volunteers in the Civil war, 1861–1865, v 13).

Sketch of the life of Col. Michael Shoemaker. [n. p., 1890] 93 p. 20½cm.   Mi   **97**
Pages 52–93 are reprinted from Title 100.

Keen, Joseph S
Experiences in Rebel military prisons at Richmond, Danville, Andersonville, and escape from Andersonville, a paper prepared and read, June 24th, 1890, before Detroit post no. 384, G.A.R., by Joseph S. Keen. Detroit, Detroit Free Press print. co., 1890. 67 p. 20cm.   In   **98**

Shoemaker, Michael, 1818–1895.
The Michigan Thirteenth, narrative of the occupation, fortification, attack upon, defense of, and retreat from Stevenson, Alabama, in 1862, by the Thirteenth regiment of Michigan volunteer infantry under command of Colonel Michael Shoemaker. *MiHC* iv (1881) 133–68.   **99**

—— Narrative of Colonel Michael Shoemaker, of the part taken by the Thirteenth regiment Michigan volunteer infantry in the battle of Stone river or Murfreesboro, in Tennessee, on the 29th, 30th and 31st December, 1862, and the 1st, 2d and 3d January, 1863. *MiHC* ii (1880) 612–37.   **100**

—— War sketch by Col. Shoemaker, narrative of the capture of Colonel Michael Shoemaker of the Thirteenth regiment of Michigan volunteer infantry, his journey to Richmond, Virginia, his experience in Libby prison, his exchange and return . . . [Lansing, 1881] 25 p. 22½cm.   NHi   **101**
"From volume III, Michigan pioneer collections."

## 14TH INFANTRY

*Mustered in: February 13, 1862.*
*Mustered out: July 18, 1865.*
*Michigan in the war 342–53.*

Michigan. Adjutant General.
Record Fourteenth Michigan infantry Civil war, 1861–1865. [Kalamazoo, Ihling Bros. & Everard, printers, 1905] 130 p. 24cm. (Record of service of Michigan volunteers in the Civil war, 1861–1865, v 14).

Mizner, Henry R
Reminiscences (read January 2, 1895). *MOLLUS-Mich* ii 72–82.   **102**

## 15TH INFANTRY

*Mustered in: March 20, 1862.*
*Mustered out: August 13, 1865.*
*Michigan in the war 354–8.*

Michigan. Adjutant General.
Record Fifteenth Michigan infantry Civil war, 1861–1865. [Kalamazoo, Ihling Bros. & Everard, printers, 1905] 181 p. 24cm. (Record of service of Michigan volunteers in the Civil war, 1861–1865, v 15).

McBride, George W
My recollections of Shiloh. *BandG* iii (1894) 8–12. **103**

—— Shiloh, after thirty-two years. *BandG* iii (1894) 303–10. **104**

—— With Ewing at Tunnel hill. *BandG* iv (1894) 221–6. **105**

## 16TH INFANTRY

*Mustered in: September 8, 1861.*
*Mustered out: July 8, 1865.*
*Michigan in the war 359–73.*

Michigan. Adjutant General.
Record Sixteenth Michigan infantry Civil war, 1861–1865. [Kalamazoo, Ihling Bros. & Everard, printers, 1905] 180 p. 24cm. (Record of service of Michigan volunteers in the Civil war, v 16).

Apted, Alfred M
Roster of survivors 16th Michigan veteran volunteer infantry, compiled by A. M. Apted, Secretary. . . . Grand Rapids, 1895. 21, (1) p. 14½cm. MiG NN(E) **105A**

Breakey, William F 1835–1915.
Recollections and incidents of medical military service, by Dr. Wm. F. Breakey, Ass't Surgeon 16th Michigan (read February 4, 1897). *MOLLUS-Mich* ii 120–52. **106**

Graham, Ziba B
On to Gettysburg, ten days from my diary of 1863, a paper read before the commandery of the State of Michigan, Military order of the loyal legion of the U. S., by Ziba B. Graham, late 1st Lieut. 16th regt. Mich. . . . Detroit, Winn & Hammond, printers, 1893. 16 p. 21½cm. DLC **107**
Also published as War papers i no 23.

Jacklin, Rufus W 1842–
The famous old Third brigade, by Rufus W. Jacklin, Major 16th Michigan infantry (read November 1, 1894). *MOLLUS-Mich* ii 39–50. **108**

Keeler, Francis D 1842–
War letters, written during the rebellion, by Francis D. Keeler, Second Lieutenant Co. E, Sixteenth Michigan. Saginaw, Julian A. Keeler, 1895. vi, 101 p. 15½cm. MiDB **109**
"Printed a single page at a time from a small amateur printer's outfit by the son of the author," from a newspaper clipping inserted in MiDB's copy. In the "Preface" of MiDB's copy the author's birth date has been corrected in ms to 1841.

Petersen, Marcus
The 16th at Owosso [by] Marcus Petersen. [Lansing, Printed by Robert Smith co., 1893] [4] folios. 16 plates (ports.). 17½cm.
Mi **110**
On cover: Thirteenth reunion 16th Michigan infantry at Owosso, October 18, 1893. Souvenir. Compliments of comrade John G. Berry. Poetry.

## 17TH INFANTRY

*Mustered in: August 21, 1862.*
*Mustered out: June 3, 1865.*
*Michigan in the war 374–83.*

Michigan. Adjutant General.
Record Seventeenth Michigan infantry Civil war, 1861–1865. [Kalamazoo, Ihling Bros. & Everard, printers, 1905] 116 p. 24cm. (Record of service of Michigan volunteers in the Civil war, 1861–1865, v 17).

Comrades 17th Michigan infantry [communication from the Secretary, Chas. D. Cowles, including a roster of survivors] Lansing, 1885. [3] p. 21½cm. WHi **111**
Title and imprint from caption.

. . . Roster 17th Michigan infantry, 1862–1865. [Kalamazoo, 1892] [12] p. 14 x 8cm.
Title from cover. MiDB **112**

Roster of Seventeenth regiment, Michigan infantry association. [Detroit] 1901. 49 p. 17½cm. IHi Mi **113**

The West in the War of the rebellion, as told in the sketches of some of its Generals. W. H. Withington. *Magazine of Western history* iv (1886) 493–507. **114**

Brearley, William Henry, 1846–1909.
Recollections of the East Tennessee campaign, battle of Campbell Station, 16th Nov., 1863, siege of Knoxville, 17th Nov.–5th Dec. 1863, by Will H. Brearley, Co. E, 17 Mich. vols. Detroit, Tribune book and job office, 1871. 48 p. 22½cm. DLC NHi NN RP **115**

Campbell, Gabriel, 1838–
Charge of the Stonewall regiment. *Dartmouth magazine* xvii (Hanover, 1903) 241–4.
Poetry. **116**

—— War pictures, a poem, by Gabriel Campbell, Captain Seventeenth Michigan. Ann Arbor, Press of Dr. A. W. Chase, 1865. 18 p. 23½cm.                          DLC MiU    *117*

Dowling, Morgan E          1845–1896.
Southern prisons; or, Josie, the heroine of Florence. Four years of battle and imprisonment . . . a complete history of all Southern prisons, embracing a thrilling episode of romance and love, by Morgan E. Dowling. . . . Detroit, William Graham, 1870. xii, [13]–506 p. plates (illus., ports.). 22cm.
                            DLC MiDB   *118*
George, Austin
The Michigan State normal school in the Civil war. In A history of the Michigan State normal school . . . by Daniel Putnam (1899) 255–94.                              *119*
Also published separately.

Lane, David
A soldier's diary, the story of a volunteer. [Jackson?, 1905] 270 p. 19½cm.
On cover: By David Lane.  DLC NN    *120*

Orcutt, William Dana, 1870–1953.
Burrows of Michigan and the Republican party, a biography and a history, by William Dana Orcutt. New York, Longmans, Green and co., 1917. 2 v. plates (illus., ports.). 23cm.
"The soldier husband," I 37–115. NN    *120A*

Swift, Frederick W
My experiences as a prisoner of war, a paper prepared and read before Michigan commandery of the Military order of the loyal legion of the United States, December 1st, 1886, by Lt. Col. F. W. Swift. Detroit, Wm. S. Ostler, printer, 1888. 24 p. 21½cm.  DLC    *121*
Also published as War papers I no 2.

## 18TH INFANTRY

*Mustered in: August 26, 1862.*
*Mustered out: June 26, 1865.*
*Michigan in the war 384–91.*

Michigan. Adjutant General.
Record Eighteenth Michigan infantry Civil war, 1861–1865. [Kalamazoo, Ihling Bros. & Everard, printers, 1905] 109 p. 24cm. (Record of service of Michigan volunteers in the Civil war, 1861–1865, v 18).

Aldrich, Hosea C          1837–
Cahawba prison, a glimpse of life in a Rebel prison; also, the explosion and burning of the steamer Sultana on the Mississippi river, 1,700 lives lost, by H. C. Aldrich. [Jerome, n. d.] 20 p. 17½cm.                      MiU    *124*
Title from cover. Caption title adds: . . . in a Rebel prison in 1864.

Doolittle, Charles Camp, 1832–1903.
The defense of Decatur, Alabama, by Charles C. Doolittle, late Brigadier-General, 1889. *MOLLUS-Ohio* III 265–77.    *125*

Pomeroy, Randolph C
The Civil war diary of. . . . *Northwest Ohio quarterly* XIX (1947) 129–56.    *126*

## 19TH INFANTRY

*Mustered in: September 25, 1862.*
*Mustered out: June 10, 1865.*
*Michigan in the war 392–6.*

Michigan. Adjutant General.
Record Nineteenth Michigan infantry Civil war, 1861–1865. [Kalamazoo, Ihling Bros. & Everard, printers, 1905] 102 p. 24cm. (Record of Michigan volunteers in the Civil war, 1861–1865, v 19).

Baldwin, Alice (Blackwood), 1845–
Memoir of the late Frank D. Baldwin, Major General, U.S.A., by Alice Blackwood Baldwin (Mrs. Frank D. Baldwin). With a foreword by Hunter Liggett. Edited by Brigadier General W. C. Brown, Colonel C. C. Smith and E. A. Brininstool. Los Angeles, Wetzel pub. co., 1929. xv, 204 p. plates (1 illus., ports.). 23½cm.                          DLC Mi    *127*

Baughman, Theodore, 1845–
Baughman, the Oklahoma scout, personal reminiscences, by Theodore Baughman. Chicago, Belford, Clarke & co., 1886. 215 p. front. (port.), plates (illus.). 18cm.  DLC    *128*

Cogshall, Israel
Journal of Israel Cogshall, 1862–1863. Edited by Cecil K. Byrd. *Indiana magazine of history* XLII (1946) 69–87.    *129*

Lincoln, Charles Perey, 1843–1911.
"Engagement at Thompson station, Tennessee," prepared by Captain Charles P. Lincoln. 1893. 17 p. *MOLLUS-DC* no 14.    *130*

Rice, Franklin G
Diary of 19th Michigan volunteer infantry during their three years service in the War of the rebellion, by Franklin G. Rice. [Big Rapids, n. d.] 55 p. 22cm.              Mi    *131*
Title from cover. Caption title: A journal of events that occurred while a member of Co. "E," 19th Mich. infantry volunteers.

## 20TH INFANTRY

*Mustered in: August 19, 1862.*
*Mustered out: May 30, 1865.*
*Michigan in the war 397–411.*

*20th Infantry, continued*

Michigan. Adjutant General.
Record Twentieth Michigan infantry Civil war, 1861–1865. [Kalamazoo, Ihling Bros. & Everard, printers, 1905] 104 p. 24cm. (Record of service of Michigan volunteers in the Civil war, 1861–1865, v 20).

Roster of the 20th Michigan infantry, including also a list of deceased and honorary members. [Ann Arbor, Courier, printers, 1899] 36 p. 14½cm.                          Mi     132

Roster of the Twentieth Michigan infantry. . . . [Chelsea, Standard, printers, 1914] [2] p, [14] folios. 15cm.                    MiDB    133
Text printed on rectos.

Berry, Chester D                     1844–
Loss of the Sultana and reminiscences of survivors, history of a disaster where over one thousand five hundred human beings were lost, most of them being exchanged prisoners of war on their way home after privation and suffering from one to twenty-three months in Cahaba and Andersonville prisons, by Rev. Chester D. Berry. Lansing, Darious D. Thorp, printer, 1892. 426 p. front. (illus.), ports. 19cm.                         DLC NHi    134
"Official list of exchanged prisoners on the boat," 383–417. Supplementary roster of those not in official list, 418–19.

Boston, William, 1837–1915
The Civil war diary of William Boston, a Union soldier of Company H, Twentieth Michigan volunteer infantry, Ninth corps, August 19, 1862 – July 4, 1865. [Ann Arbor, 1937] 96 folios. 2 plates (mounted facs. and mounted port.). 22cm. Mimeographed.
                                       DLC    135
"Foreword" signed: Orlan W. Boston. Two National park service publications on the National military parks of Fredericksburg & Spotsylvania and Petersburg are inserted and not included in the collation.

Cutcheon, Byron Mac, 1836–1908.
Recollections of Burnside's East Tennessee campaign of 1863, prepared by Brevet Brigadier-General Byron M. Cutcheon. 1902. 19 p. *MOLLUS-DC* no 39.                      136

—— East Tennessee campaign and siege of Knoxville. *MiHC* xxxii (1902) 410–18.    137
Also appears in Title 138 as Chapters 12–13.

—— The story of the Twentieth Michigan infantry, July 15th, 1862, to May 30th, 1865, embracing official documents on file in the records of the State of Michigan and of the United States referring to or relative to the Regiment. Compiled by Byron M. Cutcheon, formerly Colonel of the Regiment. Lansing,

Robert Smith print. co., 1904. 271, (1) p. plates (1 illus., ports.). 24cm.
                                       DLC NN    138
With this is bound Record Twentieth Michigan infantry Civil War, 1861–1865. On cover: History of the Twentieth Michigan infantry Civil war.

—— The Twentieth Michigan regiment in the assault on Petersburg, July, 1864. *MiHC* xxx (1905) 127–39.                         139

### 21ST INFANTRY

*Mustered in: September 4, 1862.*
*Mustered out: June 8, 1865.*
*Michigan in the war 412–19.*

Michigan. Adjutant General.
Record Twenty-first Michigan infantry Civil war, 1861–1865. [Kalamazoo, Ihling Bros. & Everard, printers, 1905] 127 p. 24cm. (Record of service of Michigan volunteers in the Civil war, 1861–1865, v 21).

The battle of Murfreesboro, by a Private of the Twenty-first Michigan infantry. Detroit, J. A. Roys [1863] broadside, 28 x 21½cm.
                                       MiDB    140

Bates, Marcus Whitman, 1840–
The battle of Bentonville, by Lieutenant Marcus W. Bates, 1899. *MOLLUS-Minn* v 136–51.                                141

—— From Michigan to Chattanooga in 1862, 1894. *MOLLUS-Minn* iv 215–26.      142

Belknap, Charles Eugene, 1846–1929.
Bentonville, what a bummer knows about it, prepared by Brevet Major Charles E. Belknap. 1893. 10 p. *MOLLUS-DC* no 12.     143

—— Christmas day near Savannah in wartime. *MiH* vi (1922) 591–6. plate (port.).
                                              143A

—— Recollections of a bummer. 1898. 16 p. *MOLLUS-DC* no 28.                 144

Foote, Allen Ripley, 1842–1921.
Some of my war stories, a paper read before the Ohio commandery of the Loyal legion, October 1, 1913. 12 p. 21½cm.
Title from cover.             DLC NN    145

McCreery, William B             1836–1896.
"My experience as a prisoner of war, and escape from Libby prison," a paper read before the Commandery of the State of Michigan, Military order of the loyal legion of the U. S., by Wm. B. McCreery, late Colonel of the 21st regt. Mich. Detroit, Winn & Hammond, printers, 1893. 29 p. 21½cm.         DLC    146
Also published as War papers i no 10.

—— —— Grand Rapids, West Michigan print. co. [189–] 40 p. 3 plates (ports.). 23½cm. MiU **147**

Petersen, Eugene Thor, 1920–
. . . The grand escape. *Michigan alumnus quarterly* LXIV (1957/58) 258–67. 1 illus., port. **147A**
At head of title: Through "rat hell" to freedom.

Taylor, John C
Lights and shadows in the recollections of a youthful volunteer in the Civil war, by J. C. Taylor. Ionia, Sentinel-Standard [n. d.] 32 p. ports., fold. plate (illus.). 23½cm.
NHi **148**

## 22ND INFANTRY

*Mustered in: August 29, 1862.*

*Mustered out: June 26, 1865.*

*Michigan in the war 420–8.*

Michigan. Adjutant General.
Record Twenty-second Michigan infantry Civil war, 1861–1865. [Kalamazoo, Ihling Bros. & Everard, printers, 1905] 160 p. 24cm. (Record of service of Michigan volunteers in the Civil war, 1861–1865, v 22).

Atkinson, John
The story of Lookout mountain and Missionary ridge, by John Atkinson Lt.-Colonel 3rd Michigan infantry (read May 3, 1894). *MOLLUS-Mich* II 277–96. **149**

Atkinson, William F 1841–
The Rock of Chickamauga, by Wm. F. Atkinson, Captain 3rd Michigan infantry (read December 7, 1893). *MOLLUS-Mich* II 5–11. **150**

Dean, Henry S 1830–
The relief of Chatanooga, a paper read before the Commandery of the State of Michigan, Military order of the loyal legion of the United States, by Captain Henry S. Dean, late Lieutenant-Colonel 22d Michigan infantry, at Detroit, Mich. May 4, 1893. Detroit, Winn & Hammond, 1893. 14 p. 22½cm. DLC **151**

Foote, Charles E
Only a button, by Charles E. Foote, 1st Lieut. 22d Michigan infantry (read Feb. 6, 1895). *MOLLUS-Mich* II 83–8. **152**

Graecen, James
Fifteen months in Rebel prisons. In National tribune scrap book III 134–44. **152A**

Snook, John H
Governor Wisner and the Twenty-second Michigan volunteer infantry. *MiH* XXXI (1947) 12–20. **153**

## 23RD INFANTRY

*Mustered in: September 13, 1862.*

*Mustered out: June 28, 1865.*

*Michigan in the war 429–37.*

Michigan. Adjutant General.
Record Twenty-third Michigan infantry Civil war, 1861–1865. [Kalamazoo, Ihling Bros. & Everard, printers, 1905] 118 p. 24cm. (Record of service of Michigan volunteers in the Civil war, 1861–1865, v 23).

## 24TH INFANTRY

*Mustered in: August 15, 1862.*

*Mustered out: June 30, 1865.*

*Michigan in the war 438–49.*

Michigan. Adjutant General.
Record Twenty-fourth Michigan infantry Civil war, 1861–1865. [Kalamazoo, Ihling Bros. & Everard, printers, 1905] 164 p. 24cm. (Record of Michigan volunteers in the Civil war, 1861–1865, v 24).

Curtis, Orson Blair, 1841?–1901.
History of the Twenty-fourth Michigan of the Iron brigade, known as the Detroit and Wayne county regiment, by O. B. Curtis. Detroit, Winn & Hammond, 1891. 483 p. illus., maps and plans, ports., plates (2 illus., 1 col.; ports.). 24½cm. DLC NN **154**
Unit roster 321–70. Coulter 107.

## 25TH INFANTRY

*Mustered in: September 22, 1862.*

*Mustered out: June 24, 1865.*

*Michigan in the war 450–61.*

Michigan. Adjutant General
Record Twenty-fifth Michigan infantry Civil war, 1861–1865. [Kalamazoo, Ihling Bros. & Everard, printers, 1905] 82 p. 24cm. (Record of service of Michigan volunteers in the Civil war, 1861–1865, v 25).

Travis, Benjamin F
The story of the Twenty-fifth Michigan, by B. F. Travis, Lieutenant. Kalamazoo, Kalamazoo pub. co., 1897. 400 p. front. (port.), map, ports. 23½cm. DLC **155**
Unit roster 377–99.

## 26TH INFANTRY

*Mustered in: December 12, 1862.*

*Mustered out: June 4, 1865.*

*Michigan in the war 462–9.*

*26th Infantry, continued*

Michigan. Adjutant General.
Record Twenty-sixth Michigan infantry Civil war, 1861–1865. [Kalamazoo, Ihling Bros. & Everard, printers, 1905] 83 p. 24cm. (Record of service of Michigan volunteers in the Civil war, 1861–1865, v 26).

Twenty-sixth Michigan infantry volunteers fourth annual re-union at Alma, November 14th, 1883. Reed City, "People" print, 1883. [20] p. 20½cm.          Mi    **156**

### 27TH INFANTRY

*Mustered in: April 10, 1863.*
*Mustered out: July 26, 1865.*
*Michigan in the war 470–8.*

Michigan. Adjutant General.
Record Twenty-seventh Michigan infantry Civil war, 1861–1865. [Kalamazoo, Ihling Bros. & Everard, printers, 1905] 148 p. 24cm. (Record of service of Michigan volunteers in the Civil war, 1861–1865, v 27).

### 28TH INFANTRY

*Mustered in: November 10, 1864.*
*Mustered out: June 5, 1865.*
*Michigan in the war 479–81.*

Michigan. Adjutant General.
Record Twenty-eighth Michigan infantry Civil war, 1861–1865. [Kalamazoo, Ihling Bros. & Everard, printers, 1905] 70 p. 24cm. (Record of service of Michigan volunteers in the Civil war, 1861–1865, v 28).

Cummings, Charles L      1848–
All about it for ten cents, to which is appended Geo. E. Reed's poetical description of the campaigns of the Sixth army corps during the year 1863, together with the following humorous and patriotic recitations . . . Compiled by Chas. L. Cummings, late Private Co. E, 28th Mich. infantry. . . . Harrisburg, "Field and Post-room" print [1886] 32 p. 23cm.
              NHi    **157**
Advertising matter 31–2. Title and imprint from cover.\*

---

\* In citing the editions of this popular publication (Titles 157–60), the compiler has not attempted to establish their order of appearance. In Title 160 a list of "Editions of this pamphlet" does afford some information. Cummings lists the editions with their pagination, press run and publication date as follows:
First, 32 pages, 5,000 copies, issued January, 1886.
Second, 40 pages, 5,000 copies, issued May, 1886.
Third, 40 pages, 10,000 copies, issued September, 1886.
Fourth, 48 pages, 10,000 copies, issued April, 1887.
Fifth, 48 pages, 5,000 copies, issued November, 1887.

—— The great war relic, valuable as a curiosity of the rebellion, together with a sketch of my life, service in the army, and how I lost my feet since the war. Also, many interesting incidents illustrative of the life of a soldier. Compiled and sold by Chas. L. Cummings. [Harrisburg, Penn., 188–] 48 p. 1 port. 23cm.
Title from cover.        MiDB    **157A**

—— The great war relic, together with a sketch of my life, service in the army, and how I lost my feet since the war, also, many interesting incidents illustrative of the life of a soldier, respectfully dedicated to my comrade George E. Reed, Post 58, Dept. Penn'a, G.A.R., Harrisburg, Pa., for his valuable war relic, "The campaign of the Sixth army corps," thereby assisting me to compile this work. Valuable as a curiosity of the rebellion. Compiled and sold by Chas. L. Cummings. [Harrisburg, Penn., 188–] 48 p. 1 port. 22½cm.
            MiDB    **158**
Title from cover. Printed in double columns. Portrait of author on p 1 and 3 of cover.

—— A poetical description of the Sixth army corps campaign during the year 1863, by George E. Reed, while a Private in Co. A, 95th regt. Pa. Together with a sketch of my life and service in the army, how I lost my feet seven years after I was mustered out of service, and a number of other articles relating to the rebellion. Compiled by Charles L. Cummings. Harrisburg, Penn., Meyers print. house [188–] 48 p. 23½cm.      MiDB    **159**
—— —— Harrisburg, Penn., S. E. Shade, printer [1887] 48 p. 23cm.    NN    **160**
Advertising matter 46–8.

### 29TH INFANTRY

*Mustered in: October 3, 1864.*
*Mustered out: September 6, 1865.*
*Michigan in the war 482–4.*

Michigan. Adjutant General.
Record Twenty-ninth Michigan infantry Civil war, 1861–1865. [Kalamazoo, Ihling Bros. & Everard, printers, 1905] 71 p. 24cm. (Record of service of Michigan volunteers in the Civil war, 1861–1865, v 29).

### 30TH INFANTRY

*Mustered in: January 9, 1865.*
*Mustered out: June 30, 1865.*
*Michigan in the war 485–7.*

Michigan. Adjutant General.
Record Thirtieth Michigan infantry Civil war, 1861–1865. [Kalamazoo, Ihling Bros. & Everard, printers, 1905] 64 p. 24cm. (Record of service of Michigan volunteers in the Civil war, 1861–1865, v 30).

## SHARPSHOOTERS

### 1ST REGIMENT

*Mustered in: July 7, 1863.*
*Mustered out: July 28, 1865.*
*Michigan in the war 543–52.*

Farling, Amos
Life in the army, containing historical and biographical sketches, incidents, adventures and narratives of the late war. Also a history of the war with the Indians of the Far West, giving a description of the lives, habits and customs of the different Indian tribes. Amos Farling, author and publisher. Buchanan, 1874. 43 p.     NN (M)    *161*

Unit roster of Company G, 25–6. The author enlisted in the 27th U.S. infantry, March 18, 1866, and relates his experiences, 31–43. The examined copy did not include information on the Indian tribes.

Michigan. Adjutant General.
Record: First Michigan sharpshooters; First and Second U. S. sharpshooters: Company D, Western sharpshooters; Civil war, 1861–1865. [Kalamazoo, Ihling Bros. & Everard, printers 1905]. 182 p. 24cm. (Record of service of Michigan volunteers in the Civil war, 1861–1865, v 44).

First regiment Michigan sharpshooters soldiers record Company "D" Michigan vols. Chicago, Lith. & printed in colors by Chas. Shober [1863] col. illus. broadside, 56 x 43cm.
        MiDB    *162*

A unit roster with a brief history of the company.

Four companies were raised in Michigan for service with the United States sharpshooters: Company B, 1st regiment U. S. sharpshooters Companies C, I, and K, 2nd regiment U. S. sharpshooters.

# MINNESOTA

# Reference Works

Dyer, Frederick Henry, 1849–1917.

A compendium of the War of the rebellion, 1908 (reprinted 1959).

"Regimental index" 164–5; "Regimental histories" 1293–1301. The pagination is the same in the 1959 reprint.

Minnesota, Civil and Indian Wars Commissioners.

Minnesota in the Civil and Indian wars, 1861–1865. Prepared and published under the supervision of the Board of commissioners,, appointed by the Act of the Legislature of Minnesota of April 6, 1889. St. Paul, Printed for the State by the Pioneer press co., 1890–93. 2 v. 25½cm.

Contents: v. [1] [Narratives and rosters of the regiments] v. 2, Official reports and correspondence.

Minnesota. Historical Society.

Minnesotans in the Civil and Indian wars, an index to the rosters in Minnesota in the Civil and Indian wars, 1861–1865. Compiled as W.P.A. project for the Minnesota historical society under the direction of Irene B. Warming, Reference assistant. Saint Paul, Minnesota Historical Society, 1936. 488 folios. 28½ × 22½cm.

"An original typed copy and five carbons have been prepared."

*The Union army.*

"Record of Minnesota regiments," IV (1908) 98–114.

United States. Adjutant General's Office.

Official army register of the volunteers of the United States army for the years 1861, '62, '63, '64, '65. Part VII. . . . Washington, 1867.

A roster of officers by regiments with an alphabetical index to the eight states in this volume.

# MINNESOTA

## ARTILLERY

### 1ST REGIMENT (HEAVY)

*Organized: September 1864 to February 1865.*

*Mustered out: September 27, 1865.*

*Minnesota in the Civil and Indian wars* 612–39. Narrative by Lieutenant James J. Egan.

Cline, Cullen E
Comparison of the two sides when the struggle began, by Lieutenant C. E. Cline. *MOL-LUS-Iowa* II 143–53.                                  **1**

## Batteries

### 1st Battery (Light)

*Organized: November 21, 1861.*

*Mustered out: July 1, 1865.*

*Minnesota in the Civil and Indian wars* 640–53. Narrative by Lieutenant Henry S. Tucker.

### 2nd Battery (Light)

*Organized: March 21, 1862.*

*Mustered out: August 16, 1865.*

*Minnesota in the  Civil and Indian wars* 654–67.

### 3rd Battery (Light)

*Organized: February 2 to May 1, 1863.*

*Mustered out: February 27, 1866.*

*Minnesota in the Civil and Indian wars* 668–80. Narrative by Lieutenant G. Merrill Dwelle.

## CAVALRY

### 1ST CAVALRY

*Organized: October 9 to December 30, 1862.*

*Mustered out: October 20 to December 7, 1863.*

*Minnesota in the Civil and Indian wars* 519–52. Narrative by Captain Eugene M. Wilson.

Austin, Horace, 1831–1905.
The frontier of Southwestern Minnesota in 1857, the Ink-Pa-Doota outbreak, the campaign of 1863 against the Sioux, by Captain Horace Austin, 1893. *MOLLUS-Minn* IV 124–43.                                              **2**

Potter, Theodore Edgar, 1832–1910.
The autobiography of Theodore Edgar Potter. [Concord, N.H., Rumford press, 1913] ix, 228 p. 3 plates (ports.). 21½cm.

DLC MnHi NN     **3**

Partial contents: The Sioux war, 161–86; The Dakota campaign, 187–201; Under Thomas in Tennessee 203–20. The author served in the 1st Minn cavalry and the 11th Minn infantry mustering in and out with the Regiments.

—— Captain Potter's recollections of Minnesota experiences. *MH* I (1916) 419–521. plate (port.).                                              **4**

Civil war 465–90.

Starkey, James, 1818–1892.
Reminiscences of Indian depredations in Minnesota, by Captain James Starkey, 1891. *MOLLUS-Minn* III 262–86.                             **5**

## 2ND CAVALRY

*Organized: December 5, 1863 to January 5, 1864.*

*Mustered out: November 17, 1865 to May 4, 1866.*

*Minnesota in the Civil and Indian wars* 543–71. Narrative by Lieutenant Martin Williams.

### Brackett's Battalion

*Organized as 1st, 2nd and 3rd companies, Minnesota light cavalry and assigned to Curtis horse, later 5th Iowa cavalry: September to November 1861. Three Minnesota companies detached and organized as Brackett's battalion of cavalry: January 1864.*

*Mustered out: June 1, 1866.*

*Minnesota in the Civil and Indian wars* 572–93. Narrative by Sergeant Isaac Botsford.

### Hatch's Independent Battalion

*Organized: July 25 to September 1863.*

*Mustered out: April 26 to June 22, 1866.*

*Minnesota in the Civil and Indian wars* 594–611. Narrative by Major C. W. Nash.

## INFANTRY

### 1ST INFANTRY

*Mustered in: April 29, 1861.*

*Mustered out: July 15, 1865.*

*Minnesota in the Civil and Indian wars* 1–78, 681–2. Narrative by Lieutenant William Lochren.

*1st Infantry, continued*

History of the First regiment Minnesota volunteer infantry, 1861–1864. Stillwater, Easton & Masterman, printers, 1916. 508 p. plates (illus., fold. maps, ports.). 21½cm.

         DLC MnHi NN    **6**

"The body of this text was originally prepared by Mr. R. I. Holcombe." Unit roster 455–500.

Roster of the First Minnesota regiment volunteer infantry, enlisted at Fort Snelling, April 29, 1861, for three years. Stillwater, "Journal" print [1910] 31, (1) p. 21½cm.  MnHi  **7**

"Compiled by Adolphus C. Hospes, Sec'y First Minnesota regimental association, October 29, 1910"

Roster of survivors First Minnesota volunteer infantry, 1861–1864. 1893–1930. 8 nos. 13cm. (1893, 14½cm.).         MnHi  **8**

Collation: 1893, [1897] 1902, 1914, 1917, 1922, 1926, 1930. Volumes for 1922, 1926, and 1930 have on cover 56th [60th, Sixty fourth] annual reunion.

A soldier's [Samuel Bloomer] Christmas, 1861. *MH* xxxvii (1961) 334.         **8A**

Caukin, Gavin B

From Cold Harbor to Petersburg with the Second army corps (read January 8, 1896). Portland, Ore., 1896. 16 p. *MOLLUS-Oregon* no 4.         MnHi  **8B**

Coolidge, Calvin, 1872–1933.

Address of President Coolidge dedicating a memorial to Colonel William Colvill at Cannon Falls, Minnesota, July 29, 1928. Washington, Govt. print. office, 1928. 5 p. 23½cm.

Title and imprint from cover.  DLC NN  **8C**

Davis, Cushman Kellogg, 1838–1900.

Address before the Society of the Army of the Tennessee, August 13, 1884, by C. K. Davis. St. Paul, West pub. co. [1884] 24 p. 23½cm.         MnHi  **9**

Title from cover.

—— An address by Cushman K. Davis at Gettysburg, July 24, 1897, at the unveiling of the statue erected by the State of Minnesota to commemorate the charge made by the First regiment Minnesota infantry volunteers on the second day of July, 1863. 10 p. 24cm.

         MnHi NN  **10**

Gordon, Hanford Lennox, 1836–1920.

Gettysburg: charge of the First Minnesota, by H. L. Gordon. Written for the camp-fire of the G.A.R., Department of Minnesota, National encampment of the Grand army of the Republic at Minneapolis, July 22, 1884. [Minneapolis, 1884] 2 leaves. 24cm.  NN  **11**

Poetry. Eagle at head of title, text bordered in red on three unnumbered pages, last page is blank.

Heffelfinger, Christopher B    1834–1915.

Memoirs of Christopher B. Heffelfinger, by Lucia L. Peavey Heffelfinger, Santa Barbara, California, nineteen hundred fifteen. Minneapolis, 1922. 101 p. plates (ports.). 24cm.

"Forty copies published."    MnHi  **12**

King, Josias Ridgate, 1832–1916.

The battle of Bull run, a Confederate victory obtained but not achieved, by Lieut. Colonel Josias R. King, 1907. *MOLLUS-Minn* vi 497–510.         **13**

Lee, Aaron, 1832–

From the Atlantic to the Pacific, reminiscences of pioneer life and travels across the continent . . . also a graphic account of his army experiences in the Civil war, by Aaron Lee, member of First Minnesota infantry. Seattle, Metropolitan press [1915] 190 p. front. (port.), illus., plate (illus.). 20cm.

Civil war 136–88.    DLC MB  **14**

Lochren, William, 1832–1912.

The First Minnesota at Gettysburg, by Lieutenant William Lochren. 1890. *MOLLUS-Minn* iii 42–56.         **15**

Maginnis, Martin, 1841–1919.

The Army of the Potomac. "Rally on Washington!" — "On to Richmond." Address of Martin Maginnis before the Society of the Army of the Potomac at its fourteenth annual reunion, delivered in National theatre at Washington, Wednesday, May 16, 1883. Washington, D.C., Rufus H. Darby, printer, 1883. 24 p. 22cm.         WHi  **16**

Neill, Edward Duffield, 1823–1893.

Incidents of the battles of Fair Oaks and Malvern hill, by Chaplain Edward D. Neill, 1892. *MOLLUS-Minn* iii 454–94.  **17**

Also published as Macalester college contributions: Department of history, literature and political science, 2nd ser, no 1.

Searles, Jasper Newton, 1840–1927.

The First Minnesota volunteer infantry, by Captain J. N. Searles. *MOLLUS-Minn* ii 80–113. plate (map).         **18**

Swisshelm, Jane Grey (Cannon), 1815–1884.

Crusader and feminist, letters of Jane Grey Swisshelm, 1858–1865. Edited with an introduction and notes by Arthur J. Larsen. Saint Paul, Minnesota Historical Society, 1934. ix, 327 p. plates (fold. facs., illus., ports.). 20½cm.    DLC MnHi NN  **19**

Half-title: Publications of the Minnesota historical society. Narrative and documents, volume II. "The First Minnesota," 104–25.

Taylor, Isaac Lyman, 1837–1863.

Campaigning with the First Minnesota, a Civil war diary. Edited by Hazel C. Wolf.

*MH* xxv (1944) 11–39, 117–52, 224–57, 342–
61.  **20**
Caption title: The diary of Isaac Lyman Taylor,
January 1, 1862 – July 2, 1863.

## 2ND INFANTRY

*Mustered in: June 26 to August 23, 1861.*
*Mustered out: July 11, 1865.*
*Minnesota in the Civil and Indian wars*
79–146, 682–6. Narrative by General J.
W. Bishop.

In the matter of the request for removal of the
Second Minnesota monument from De Long
point to Strock knob before the Chickamauga
and Chattanooga park commission. Brief of
the survivors of the Minnesota monument commission. [1911] 19 p. 23cm.  MnHi  **21**
Title from cover: MnHi's copy dated in ms, Feby.
10, 1911. Brief signed: J. W. Bishop, A. H. Reed and
J. C. Donahower.

The Second Minnesota regiment veteran volunteer infantry, 1861–1865, roster of surviving
members, May 1909. 12 p. 17cm. MnHi  **22**
Title from cover.

Bircher, William
A drummer-boy's diary, comprising four
years of service with the Second regiment Minnesota veteran volunteers, 1861 to 1865, by
William Bircher. St. Paul, St. Paul book and
stationery co., 1889. 199 p. plates (illus.).
19½cm.  DLC MnHi NHi  **23**

Bishop, Judson Wade, 1831–1917.
The Mill springs campaign, some observa-
tions and experiences of a company officer, by
Brevet Brigadier-General J. W. Bishop. *MOL-
LUS-Minn* ii 52–79.  **24**

—— Official records concerning the Second
Minnesota veteran volunteer infantry, 1887.
Saint Paul, H. M. Smythe print. co., 1887.
61 p. 21½cm.  MnHi  **25**
At head of title: 1861. 1865. "To my comrades
. . ." signed: J. W. Bishop.

—— The story of a regiment, being a narrative of the service of the Second regiment,
Minnesota veteran volunteer infantry, in the
Civil war of 1861–1865, by Judson W. Bishop,
late Colonel. . . . St. Paul 1890. 256 p. 3 plates
(ports.). 20½cm.  DLC MnHi NN  **26**

—— Van Derveer's brigade at Chickamauga.
. . . [St. Paul?, 1903] 24 p. 22½cm.
MnHi  **28**
Title from cover. Also published as: *MOLLUS-Minn*
vi 53–74; *US* s3 iv (1903) 448–64.

Donahower, Jeremiah C  1837–1921.
Lookout mountain and 'Missionary ridge.
. . . [St. Paul?, 1898] 29 p. 23cm. MnHi  **29**
Title from cover. Also published in *MOLLUS-Minn*
v 74–102.

Foot, Samuel Alfred, 1790–1878.
Memorial of John Foot, late Captain in Sec-
ond regiment of Minnesota volunteers. [New
York, Francis & Loutrel, printers, 1862] 24 p.
front. (port.). 23½cm.  DLC  **30**
Title from cover.

Gleason, Levi
The experiences and observations of a
drafted man in the Civil war, by Chaplain Levi
Gleason, 1907. *MOLLUS-Minn* vi 545–56. **31**

Imm, Ivan Earl
The Civil war as seen by Colonel James
George Second Minnesota volunteer regiment.
*Olmstead county, Minn., historical society
monthly bulletin* ii (1960) 33–9. port.  **31A**

Reed, Axel Hayford, 1835–1917.
[Diary and army record of Axel H. Reed]
In Genealogical record of the Reads, Reeds,
the Bisbees, the Bradfords (1915) 103–63.
2 ports.  **32**

Stone, Sylvanus Whipple
[Civil war letter] to Mrs. Elizabeth Knight
Stone, December 24, 1864. *North Dakota historical quarterly* i 2 (January 1927) 64–6.
**32A**

## 3RD INFANTRY

*Organized: October 2 to November 14,
1861.*
*Mustered out: September 2, 1865.*
*Minnesota in the Civil and Indian wars*
147–97, 686–8. Narrative by General C.
C. Andrews.

. . . Reunion Third Minnesota veterans. . . .
iii–xii, xiv–xlvii (1886–1896, 1898–1931).
MnHi  **33**
1930–1931 are not numbered. "The old Third, their
first annual reunion," 23–7 of 1889 reunion volume.

History of the Third regiment infantry Minnesota vols. [n. p., 186–] [15] p. 22cm.
Caption title. Includes a roster.  MnHi  **34**

Andrews, Christopher Columbus, 1829–1922.
Christopher C. Andrews . . . General in the
Civil war. Recollections, 1829–1922, edited by
his daughter, Alice E. Andrews, with Introduction by William Watts Folwell. Cleveland,
Arthur H. Clark co., 1928. 327 p. plates (illus.,
ports.).  DLC NN  **35**
"Civil war service and imprisonment in Confederate
prisons," 147–73.

—— My experience in Rebel prisons, 1893.
*MOLLUS-Minn* iv 24–40.  **36**

—— Report of the military services of C. C.
Andrews, Brigadier General and Brevet Major
General U.S. volunteers, in the War of the re-

*3rd Infantry, continued*

bellion, furnished in compliance with the request from the Adjutant general's office, U.S. army, dated April 10, 1872. 21 p. 20½cm.
Caption title.                     DLC MnHi    **37**

——— The surrender of the Third regiment Minnesota volunteer infantry. *MOLLUS-Minn* I 337–68.                                          **38**

——— The Third Minnesota in the battle of Fitzhugh's woods, by Brig. Gen'l C. C. Andrews, 1907. *MOLLUS-Minn* VI 511–18.    **39**

Hoyt, James B
Reminiscences of my confinement as a prisoner of war, by James B. Hoyt, Lieut. Col. *MOLLUS-Minn* VI 75–81.             **40**

Lombard, Charles W
History of the Third regiment infantry Minnesota volunteers with the final record of the original regiment, compiled by C. W. Lombard. Faribault, Printed by C. W. Lombard at Central Republican office, 1869. 4, (11) p. 23cm.                         MnHi NHi    **41**
"Summary of the history of the Third regiment," 4 p. Unit roster (11) p. Title and imprint from cover.

Morse, William F
The Indian campaign in Minnesota in 1862, read by Brevet-Major William F. Morse, 1910. *MOLLUS-NY* IV 184–96.             **42**

### 4TH INFANTRY

*Mustered in: October 4 to December 23, 1861.*

*Mustered out: July 19, 1865.*

*Minnesota in the Civil and Indian wars* 198–242, 689–91. Narrative by Captain Alonzo L. Brown.

Brown, Alonzo Leighton, 1838–1904.
History of the Fourth regiment of Minnesota infantry volunteers during the great rebellion, 1861–1865, by Alonzo L. Brown of Company B. St. Paul, Pioneer press co., 1892. 594 p. plates (illus.; maps and plans, 1 fold.; ports.). 23½cm.                   DLC MnHi NN    **43**
Unit roster 469–556. "Reunions since the war," 1884–1891, 557–81.

### 5TH INFANTRY

*Organized: March 15 to April 30, 1862.*

*Mustered out: September 6, 1865.*

*Minnesota in the Civil and Indian wars* 243–99. Narrative by General L. F. Hubbard.

Flag presentation to the Fifth Minnesota regiment, at Fort Snelling, May 11, 1862. Ad-

dresses of Gov. Ramsey and Col. Borgersrode. broadside, 43 x 20½cm.             MnHi    **44**

Pocket register of the 5th Minnesota vol. infantry association. Published by order of the Association, September, 1891. Albert Lea, McCulloch & Whitcomb, printers [1891] 15 p. 10½cm.                          MnHi    **45**

——— Correction sheet to accompany Pocket register. . . . [Albert Lea, n. d.] 5 nos. 10½cm.
Caption title.                      MnHi    **46**

Bishop, John F
The Yellow Medicine massacre, by First-Lieutenant John F. Bishop, 1889. *MOLLUS-Minn* IV 17–25.                        **47**

Carr, Levi
[Civil war letters written to Richard Carr by his brother, Levi Carr] *North Dakota historical quarterly* I 1 (1926/27) 62–4.    **47A**

Hubbard, Lucius Frederick, 1836–1913.
Civil war papers. *Collections of the Minnesota historical society* XII (1908) 531–638. plates (illus., maps, port.).             **48**

——— Minnesota in the battle of Corinth, by Brevet Brig. Gen'l Lucius F. Hubbard, 1907. *MOLLUS-Minn* VI 479–96.               **49**

——— Minnesota in the battle of Nashville, December 15–16, 1864, 1905. *MOLLUS-Minn* VI 259–84.                          **50**

——— The Red river expedition. *MOLLUS-Minn* II 267–79.                        **51**

Johnson, Roy P
The siege of Fort Abercrombie. *North Dakota history* XXIV (1957) 5–79. illus., map, plan, ports.                        **51A**
Originally published with title, Abercrombie siege, bloody chapters in Valley history, in the Sunday edition of the Fargo forum, issues, July 19 to August 16, 1953.

Martin, N    B
Letters of a Union officer, L. F. Hubbard and the Civil war. *MH* XXXV (1957) 313–19. 2 illus., port.                       **52**

Wall, Oscar Garrett, 1844–1911.
Recollections of the Sioux massacre, an authentic history of the Yellow Medicine incident, of the fate of Marsh and his men, of the siege and battles of Fort Ridgely, and of other important battles and experiences. Together with a historical sketch of the Sibley expedition of 1863. By Oscar Garrett Wall. [Lake City, Printed at "the Home printery"] 1909. 282, iii p. front. (port.), illus., 2 plans. 20cm.
"Index," iii p.            DLC MnHi NN    **53**

## 6TH INFANTRY

*Organized: September 29 to November 20, 1862.*

*Mustered out: August 29, 1865.*

*Minnesota in the Civil and Indian wars* 300–46, 691–2. Narrative by Charles W. Johnson.

[Reunion proceedings] 1929–37. 8 nos. 28cm. Mimeographed.                MnHi    **54**

MnHi's file includes circular letter signed by the Secretary, Grace M. Longfellow, reporting that the 47th reunion, 1938, would not be held.

Egan, James Joseph, 1842–1911.
The battle of Birch Coolie, by Lieutenant James J. Egan, 1889. *MOLLUS-Minn* III 7–16.
**55**

The author participated as a civilian. He was mustered in the 1st Minnesota regiment of heavy artillery, October 13, 1864.

Hill, Alfred James, 1833–1895.
History of Company E of the Sixth Minnesota regiment of volunteer infantry, by Alfred J. Hill, with an appendix by Capt. Charles J. Stees. Published by Prof. T. H. Lewis. St. Paul, Pioneer press co., 1899. 45 p. front. (port.). 24cm.    DLC MnHi NHi NN    **56**

"Appendix, Lieut. Col. Marshall's raid into Dakota, 1862, by Capt. Charles J. Stees," [40]–5. Unit roster 8–10.

## 7TH INFANTRY

*Organized: August 16 to October 30, 1862.*

*Mustered out: August 16, 1865.*

*Minnesota in the Civil and Indian wars* 347–85, 692–5.

Hasting guards, Company F, 7th regiment, Minn. vols [n. p., 1863] col. illus. broadside, 54½ x 42½cm.                MnHi    **57**

A roster and brief history of the Company. c1864 by Joseph Miller in the Clerk's office, District court for the Northern district of Illinois.

Carter, Theodore George, 1832–
The Tupelo campaign as noted at the time by a line officer in the Union army. *Publications of the Mississippi historical society* x (1909) 91–113.                **58**

Collins, Loren Warren, 1838–1912.
The expedition against the Sioux Indians in 1863, under General Henry H. Sibley, by Captain L. W. Collins. *MOLLUS-Minn* II 173–203.                **59**

Hagadorn, Henry J        1832–1903.
On the march with Sibley in 1863, the diary of Private Henry J. Hagadorn. *North Dakota historical quarterly* v (1930/31) 103–29. **59A**

Marshall, William Rainey, 1825–1896.
Reminiscences of General U. S. Grant, by Brevet Brigadier-General W. R. Marshall. *MOLLUS-Minn* I 89–106.                **60**

——— Some letters by General W. T. Sherman, U.S.A., chiefly relating to Shiloh, 1892. *MOLLUS-Minn* IV 605–14.                **61**

Pritchett, John Perry, 1902–
Sidelights on the Sibley expedition from the diary of a Private. *MH* VII (1926) 326–35. **62**

Scantlebury, Thomas, 1832?–1864.
Wanderings in Minnesota during the Indian troubles of 1862. Chicago, F. C. S. Calhoun, printer, 1867. 32 p. 21½cm.    MnHi    **63**

Title and imprint from cover. "Appendix," [29]–32 supply biographical information on the author and notices and testimonials occasioned by his death.

## 8TH INFANTRY

*Mustered in: August 13 to November 17, 1862.*

*Mustered out: July 11, 1865.*

*Minnesota in the Civil and Indian wars* 386–415. Narrative by William H. Houlton.

Brunson, Benjamin Wetherell, 1823–1898.
Reminiscences of service with the Eighth Minn. infantry, 1901. *MOLLUS-Minn* v 365–81.                **64**

Kingsbury, David Lansing, 1842–1912.
General Alfred Sully's Indian campaign of 1864, by Lieutenant David L. Kingsbury, 1896. *MOLLUS-Minn* IV 401–19.    **65**

——— Sully's expedition against the Sioux in 1864, by Lieut. David L. Kingsbury. *Collections of the Minnesota historical society* VIII (1895/98) 449–62. fold. map.    **65A**

Paxson, Lewis C        1836–
Diary of Lewis C. Paxson, Stockton, N.J., 1862–1865. Bismarck, N.D., 1908. 64 p. 23½cm.                NNC    **65B**

"Reprinted from vol. 2 Collections State historical society of North Dakota."

## 9TH INFANTRY

*Organized: August 15 to October 31, 1862.*

*Mustered out: August 24, 1865.*

*Minnesota in the Civil and Indian wars* 416–54, 695. Narrative by C. F. MacDonald.

Surviving members of the Ninth regiment Minnesota volunteers in the War of the rebel-

*9th Infantry, continued*

lion with rank and postoffice address, prepared June 10, 1885. 26 p. 23½cm.

MnHi        **66**

Blank unnumbered pages at the end of each Company's roster. Title from cover.

Aslakson, Burns, 1835?–1889.
Ti maaneders fangenskab i Andersonville, Savannah, Millen, Blackshear og Thomasville, af B. Aslaksen. [Minneapolis, Augsburg pub. co., 1887?] 32 p. 18½cm.        MnHi        **67**

Caption title from p 2. Preceding text is an introduction by the editor of Folkebladet.

Lyon, William Franklin, 1842–
In and out of Andersonville prison, by W. F. Lyon, Comp'y G, 9th reg't Minn. Detroit, Geo. Harland co., 1905. 121 p. 4 plates (2 illus., 2 ports.). 18cm.        NHi        **68**

MacDonald, Colin Francis, 1843–1919.
The battle of Brice's cross roads, 1906. *MOLLUS-Minn* vi 443–62.        **69**

## 10TH INFANTRY

*Organized: August 12 to November 15, 1862.*

*Mustered out: August 18, 1865.*

*Minnesota in the Civil and Indian wars* 455–87. Narrative by General J. H. Baker.

Baker, James Heaton, 1829–1913.
General U. S. Grant, his military character and position in history, 1896. *MOLLUS-Minn* iv 379–400.        **70**

Jennison, Samuel Pearce, 1830–1909.
The illusions of a soldier, by Brevet Brigadier-General S. P. Jennison. *MOLLUS-Minn* i 369–80.        **71**

Kinney, Newcombe, 1842–
Reminiscences of the Sioux Indian and Civil wars, by veteran Newcombe Kinney, transcribed by Mrs. John Mahon. [n. p.,] 1916. 9, (1) p. 2 ports. 23½cm.        MnHi        **72**

## 11TH INFANTRY

*Organized: August to September 1864.*

*Mustered out: June 26, 1865.*

*Minnesota in the Civil and Indian wars* 488–506. Narrative by Rufus Davenport.

See Title 3.

## SHARPSHOOTERS

### 1ST COMPANY

See 1st United States Sharpshooters Company A.

### 2ND COMPANY

*Mustered in: March 20, 1862.*

*Mustered out: March 19, 1865.*

*Minnesota in the Civil and Indian wars* 513–18. Narrative by J. B. Chaney.

*The company was attached for a period to the 1st United States Sharpshooters as Company I.*

WISCONSIN

# Reference Works

Bradley, Isaac Samuel.

. . . A bibliography of Wisconsin's participation in the War between the States, based upon material contained in the Wisconsin historical library, compiled by Isaac Samuel Bradley. [Madison] Wisconsin History Commission, 1911. ix, 42 p. 23½ cm.

At head of title: Wisconsin history commission: Original papers no. 5.

Dyer, Frederick Henry, 1849–1917.

A compendium of the War of the rebellion, 1908 (reprinted 1959).

"Regimental index" 236–40; "Regimental histories" 1666–89. The pagination is the same in the 1959 reprint.

Love, William DeLoss, 1819–1898.

Wisconsin in the War of the rebellion, a history of all regiments and batteries the State has sent to the field, and deeds of her citizens, Governors and other military officers, and State and National legislators to suppress the rebellion, by Wm. DeLoss Love. Chicago, Church and Goodman, 1866. xxi, [17]–1144 p. maps, plates (ports.). 23cm.

Quiner, Edwin B    1816–1868.

The military history of Wisconsin, a record of the civil and military patriotism of the State in the War for the Union, with a history of the campaigns in which Wisconsin soldiers have been conspicuous, regimental histories, sketches of distinguished officers, the roll of the illustrious dead, movements of the Legislature and State officers, etc., by E. B. Quiner. Chicago, Clarke & co., 1866. 1022 p. plates (ports.). 23½ cm.

The Union army.

"Record of Wisconsin regiments," iv (1908) 44–86.

United States. Adjutant General's Office.

Official army register of the volunteers for the years 1861, '62, '63, '64, '65. Part VII. Washington, 1867.

A roster of Wisconsin officers by regiments with an alphabetical index to the eight states in this volume.

Wisconsin.   Adjutant General.

Roster of Wisconsin volunteers, War of the rebellion, 1861–
1865 . . . Compiled by authority of the Legislature, under the
direction of Jeremiah M. Rusk, Governor, and Chandler P. Chapman, Adjutant General. Madison, Democrat print. co., 1886. 2 v.
21½ cm.

Wisconsin.   Adjutant General.

Wisconsin volunteers War of the rebellion, 1861–1865, arranged
alphabetically. Compiled under the direction of the Adjutants
general during the years 1895–1899. Published by the State.
Madison, Democrat print. co., 1914. 1137 p. 21½ cm.

"Preface" signed: Charles E. Estabrook, Chairman History commission;
Duncan McGregor, Private secretary to the Governor; Orlando Holway the
Adjutant general.

# WISCONSIN

## ARTILLERY

### 1ST REGIMENT (HEAVY)

*Battery A organized as Company K, 2nd regiment of infantry and performed duty as heavy artillery. The Company was permanently detached and organized as Battery A, December 9, 1861. The other batteries of the Regiment were organized, September 1863 to October 1864.*

*Mustered out: June 26 to September 21, 1865.*

*Roster* I 254–93.

*Wisconsin in the war* 1015–19.

*Military history* 970–3.

Powers, William Penn, 1842–1928.
Some annals of the Powers family, compiled by W. Powers. Los Angeles, 1924. 304 p. illus., ports., fold. plate (port.). 21cm.     NN     **1**
Civil war 19–75.

## Batteries of Light Artillery

### 1st Battery

*Mustered in: October 10, 1861.*

*Mustered out: July 18, 1865.*

*Roster* I 202–06.

*Wisconsin in the war* 912–15.

*Military history* 928–32.

Butterfield, Ira, 1836–1891.
The [Civil war] correspondence of. . . .
*North Dakota historical quarterly* III (1928/29) 129–44.     **1A**

Webster, Daniel, 1833?–
History of the First Wisconsin battery light artillery, by Dan Webster and Don C. Cameron. [Washington, D.C., National Tribune co.] 1907. 263, vi p. plates (ports.). 24½cm.
Unit roster vi p.     NN     **1B**

### 2nd Battery

*Mustered in: October 10, 1861.*

*Mustered out: July 10, 1865.*

*Roster* I 207–10.

*Wisconsin in the war* 1019–20.

*Military history* 933.

### 3rd Battery

*Mustered in: October 10, 1861.*

*Mustered out: July 20, 1865.*

*Roster* I 210–14.

*Wisconsin in the war* 915–17.

*Military history* 934–7.

Roster Third Wisconsin battery, light artillery. Compiled from reunion at Milwaukee, August 28, 1889. [Milwaukee, Cramer, Aikens & Cramer, printers, 1889] 16 p. 16cm.
     DLC     **2**
"Compiled by Esau Beaumont . . . and E. D. Case." "History of the Battery," [3]–5.

Bradt, Hiram Henry Gillespie, 1826–
History of the services of the Third battery Wisconsin light artillery in the Civil war of the United States, 1861–1865, compiled from all sources possible, but principally from members themselves. Berlin, Courant press [1902] 102, (2) p. 1 illus. 15½cm.     DLC NHi     **3**
"Addendum. Errata," (2) p. "Preface" signed: H. H. G. Bradt, Secretary. Unit roster [71–9]

### 4th Battery

*Mustered in: October 1, 1861.*

*Mustered out: July 3, 1865.*

*Roster* I 214–18.

*Wisconsin in the war* 1020–2, 463.

*Military history* 937–9.

See Title 1.

### 5th Battery

*Mustered in: October 10, 1861.*

*Mustered out: June 6, 1865.*

*Roster* I 219–22.

*Wisconsin in the war* 463–4, 1022–3.

*Military history* 940–5.

Gardner, George Q
"The 5th Wisconsin battery" (response to above toast, by Geo. Q. Gardner . . . ). In Episodes of the Civil war, by G. W. Heer (1890) 407–13.     **4**

—— Souvenir of the first reunion of the Fifth Wisconsin battery, held at Monroe, Wis., September 9th, 1886. Response of Geo. Q. Gardner, Decorah, Iowa, to the toast, "The Fifth Wisconsin battery." [Decorah, Iowa, Republican print, 1886] 12 p. photograph mounted on p 4 of cover. 22½cm.     IHi     **5**
Title from cover.

Worick, Samuel R
Organization of the 5th Wisconsin battery, with summary of service. In Episodes of the Civil war, by George W. Heer (1890) 406.     **6**

[ 75 ]

## 6th Battery

Mustered in: October 2, 1861.
Mustered out: July 3, 1865.
Roster I 223–7.
Wisconsin in the war 463–4, 917–19.
Military history 945–50.

Jones, Jenkin Lloyd, 1843–1918.
. . . An artilleryman's diary, by Jenkin Lloyd
Jones, Private Sixth Wisconsin battery. [Madison] Wisconsin history Commission, 1914.
xviii, 395 p. front. (port.). 23½cm.
                                DLC NN      7
At head of title. Wisconsin history commission.
Original papers, no. 8. Coulter 266.

Keene, Harry S
History of the 6th Wisconsin battery, with
roster of officers and members, also proceedings of Battery reunions, speeches, &c. Lancaster, Herald book and job rooms, 1879. 65 p.
19cm.                           DLC NHi      8
"Preface" signed: H. S. Keene. Unit roster 57–64.

## 7th Battery

Mustered in: October 4, 1861.
Mustered out: July 6, 1865.
Roster I 227–31.
Wisconsin in the war 464, 919–21.
Military history 950–3.

## 8th Battery

Mustered in: January 8, 1862.
Mustered out: August 10, 1865.
Roster I 232–6.
Wisconsin in the war 921–3.
Military history 953–6.

## 9th Battery

Mustered in: January 27, 1862.
Mustered out: September 30, 1865.
Roster I 236–9.
Wisconsin in the war 923–6.
Military history 956–8.

Dodge, James H
"Across the Plains with the Ninth Wisconsin
battery in 1862," prepared by Captain James
H. Dodge. 1896. 14 p. MOLLUS-DC no 23.  9

Stulken, Gerhard E
My experiences on the Plains. Wichita, Kansas, Grit printery, 1913. 36 p. front. (port.).
20½cm.                          CoD NNC     9A

## 10th Battery

Mustered in: February 10, 1862.
Mustered out: April 26, 1865.
Roster I 240–3.
Wisconsin in the war 501–02, 1023–5.
Military history 958–61.

## 11th Battery

Mustered in as 17th regiment of infantry:
March 15, 1862.
Transferred to 1st Illinois light artillery as
Battery L: February 1862.
Roster I 244–5.
Wisconsin in the war 1026–7.
Military history 961–3.

## 12th Battery

Recruited, February to March 1862, as a
company for the 1st Missouri light artillery.
Mustered out: June 26, 1865.
Roster I 246–50.
Wisconsin in the war 464–5, 1028–9.
Military history 964–8.

## 13th Battery

Mustered in: December 29, 1863.
Mustered out: July 20, 1865.
Roster I 250–3.
Wisconsin in the war 926–7.
Military history 968–9.

Bristoll, William M
Excerpts from the diary of William M. Bristoll, 1864–65. Transcribed by Elen Jones
Carleton. [1945?] [10] p. 17cm. MnHi     10
A facsimile reproduction of selections from a diary
written in 1908.

## CAVALRY

## 1ST CAVALRY

Mustered in: March 10, 1862.
Mustered out: July 19, 1865.
Roster I 1–49.
Wisconsin in the war 553–66, 879–91.
Military history 881–99.

. . . Annual reunion of the First Wisconsin cavalry association. . . . [xxix]–xxxiv 1913–1918;
xxxviii 1921.                   WiHi      11
1913 not numbered. "History of the First Wisconsin
cavalry," 1917, 48–56, "To be continued."

Harnden, Henry, 1823–1900.
The capture of Jefferson Davis, a narrative of the part taken by Wisconsin troops, by Henry Harnden, late commander of the First Wisconsin cavalry. Madison [Tracy, Gibbs & co., printers] 1898. 105 p. plates (ports.). 16½cm.     DLC NHi NN   **12**

—— "The capture of Jefferson Davis," 1896. *MOLLUS-Wis* III 102–21.   **13**

—— The First Wisconsin cavalry at the capture of Jefferson Davis. *CHSW* XIV (1898) 516–32.   **14**

Westover, Carlos S     1843–1925.
The capture of Butt McGuire, an unrecorded incident of the Civil war, by Carlos S. Westover, First Wis. cavalry, Company A. [Whitewater, Whitewater Register print, 191–] 30, (1) p. facs., 1 illus., 2 ports. 24½cm.     WHi   **15**

Williamson, Peter J
With the First Wisconsin cavalry, the letters of . . . Edited by Henry Lee Swint. *WMH* XXVI (1943) 333–45, 433–49.   **16**

## 2ND CAVALRY

*Organized: December 30, 1861 to March 10, 1862.*

*Mustered out: November 15, 1865.*

*Roster* I 50–90.

*Wisconsin in the war* 567–73, 891–7.

*Military history* 900–08.

Ferris, Antoinette (Barnum), 1843–
A soldier's souvenir; or, the terrible experiences of Lieut. L. L. Lancaster, of the Second Wisconsin cavalry, a martyr to the cause of truth and justice. Comprising short biographical sketches, with the story of his death sentence, reprieve, banishment, hardship and final release. To which is added "The song of the veterans." By Antoinette Barnum Ferris. . . . Eau Claire, Pauly Brothers, printers, 1896. vi, [9]–61 p. front. (port.). 16cm.   DLC   **17**

Grigsby, Melvin, 1845–
The smoked Yank, by Melvin Grigsby. Sioux Falls, Dakota Terr., Bell pub. co., 1888. ix, [10]–227 p. 24cm.     DLC   **18**

—— —— Second edition. Chicago, Regan print. co., 1891. 238 p. plates (illus.). 23cm.     In   **19**

—— —— Revised edition. [Sioux Falls, S. D., M. Grigsby, 1911] 251 p. 2 ports., plates (illus.). 23cm.     NN   **20**

West Emmet C
History and reminiscences of the Second Wisconsin cavalry regiment, by Emmet C.

West, Q.M. Sergt. Co. E. Portage, State Register print, 1904. 32 p. front. (port.). 22½cm.     WHi   **21**

## 3RD CAVALRY

*Mustered in: January 28, 1862.*

*Mustered out: September 29 to October 26, 1865.*

*Roster* I 91–155.

*Wisconsin in the war* 574–8, 897–900.

*Military history* 909–20.

Calkins, Elias A     1828–1914.
History of the Loyal legion, by E. A. Calkins, Lieutenant Colonel, 3d Wisconsin cavalry, 1899. *MOLLUS-Wis* III 343–52.   **22**

—— —— US 3rd ser III (1903) 951–8.   **23**

—— Sketch of Col. Wm. A. Barstow's military services. *CHSW* VI (1872) 110–22.   **24**

—— The Wisconsin cavalry regiments, 1893. *MOLLUS-Wis* II 173–93.   **25**

## 4TH CAVALRY

*Mustered in as 4th regiment of infantry: July 2, 1861.*

*Designated 4th regiment of cavalry: August 22, 1863.*

*Mustered out: May 28, 1866.*

*Roster* I 156–201.

*Wisconsin in the war* 527–52, 900–11.

*Military history* 921–7.

Pocket register 4th Wisconsin cavalry association. Published by order of the Association, November, 1889. [Milwaukee] Burdick, Armitage & Allen, printers, 1889. 27 p. 10½cm.     WHi   **26**

Carter, George W
The Fourth Wisconsin at Port Hudson, by George W. Carter, Captain 4th Wisconsin, 1898. *MOLLUS-Wis* III 226–40.   **27**

Chittenden, Newton H
History and catalogue of the Fourth regiment Wisconsin volunteers, from June 1861, to March 1864. Baton Rouge, La., Printed at the "Gazette & Comet" book and job office, 1864. 71, (1) p. 20½cm.   WHi   **28**
"Errata," (1) p. Introduction signed: N. H. Chittenden, Adj't 4th Wis. cavalry. Unit roster 20–67.

Culver, Newton H
Brevet Major Isaac N. Earl, a noted scout of the Department of the Gulf. . . . [Madison, State Historical Society, 1917] [307]–38. plate (4 ports.). 24cm.   DLC NN   **29**
"Separate no. 178 from the Proceedings of the Society for 1916."

*4th Cavalry, continued*

Mason, William H
W. H. Mason's personal memoirs of the great
Civil war (from 1861 to 1865). Hancock,
Mich., W. H. Mason [Finnish Lutheran book
concern] 1915. 72 p. port. on cover. 19cm.
                    IHi      **29A**

Nelson, Knute, 1843–1923.
Three Christmas days in the Civil war.
[Minneapolis, Augsburg pub. house, 1920]
facs., 2 ports. (Yuletide VI). MnHi     **29B**

Rankin, George William
William Dempster Hoard, by George William Rankin. Fort Atkinson, W. D. Hoard &
Sons co. [1925] 261 p. plates (facs., illus.,
port.). 21cm.          NN     **29C**
"Civil war record," 31–51. Brief reference to his
later service of a year in Battery A, 1st New York
light artillery.

## INFANTRY

### Iron Brigade *

*2nd, 6th and 7th Wisconsin Infantry.*
*19th Indiana Infantry.*
*24th Michigan Infantry.*
*Wisconsin in the war 288–318.*
*Military history 438–82.*

A roster of the surviving members of the Iron
brigade of the War of the great rebellion or
American Civil war, 1861 to 1865. [n. p., 1923]
32 p. Mimeographed, cover title and date
printed.          NN     **29D**

Aubery, Cullen Bullard, 1845–1928.
Echoes from the marches of the famous Iron
brigade, 1861–1865, unwritten stories of that
famous organization. . . . [1900] 68 p. facs.,
illus., ports. 18cm.      WHi   **29E**
WHi's copy autographed: Compliments of the
author, Doc Aubery.

—— Recollections of a newsboy in the Army
of the Potomac, 1861–1865. His capture and
confinement in Libby prison. After being
paroled sharing the fortunes of the famous
Iron brigade, by Doc Aubery. [Milwaukee,
1904] 166, (1) p. facs., 1 illus., ports. 19½cm.
                    NN     **29F**

—— Twenty-five years on the streets of Milwaukee after dark. Together with sketches of
experiences as newsboy in the army, capture
and imprisonment in Libby prison, and other
war-time notes and incidents. By C. B. (Doc)
Aubery. Milwaukee, J. H. Yewdale & Sons co.,
printers, 1897. 112 p. illus. 19cm.
                DLC   **29G**

---

* For other references on the Iron brigade, see the entries under the regiments that formed the Brigade.

The author was not a soldier but ran away with
his three brothers who were enrolled in the 2nd
Vermont infantry.

Nolan, Alan T
The Iron brigade, a military history [by]
Alan T. Nolan. With maps by Wilson K. Hoyt
III. New York, Macmillan co., 1961. xvi, (1),
412 p. maps and plans, plates (illus., ports.).
21½cm.          DLC NN   **29H**
End paper maps: Where they came from, the Iron
brigade states of the old Northwest, 1861–1865, the
Iron brigade counties; Where they went, the Iron
brigade's theater of operations. . . .

## 1ST INFANTRY

*Mustered in: May 17, 1861 (State service,
April 27th). (3 months)*
*Mustered out: August 21, 1861.*
*Roster I 294–311.*
*Wisconsin in the war 211–27.*
*Military history 423–5.*
*Mustered in: October 19, 1861. (3 years)*
*Mustered out: October 13, 1864.*
*Roster I 312–44.*
*Wisconsin in the war 448–55, 761–5.*
*Military history 425–37.*

General Patterson's campaign in Virginia. *Con-*
*tinental monthly* I (1862) 257–63.   **30**

Anderson, Thomas, 1836–1904.
Rebel prison life, 1863–1865, a graphic story
of the capture, imprisonment and escape of a
Union soldier, by Corp. Thomas Anderson.
Lawrence, Kansas, Press of Lawrence Journal
co., 1906. 92 p. plates (1 illus., ports.).
20½cm.          KHi   **31**

Damon, Herbert C
History of the Milwaukee light guard, by
Herbert C. Damon. Organized, July 16, 1855.
Milwaukee, Printed by the Sentinel co., 1875.
319 p. plates (ports.). 24cm.
"War record," 156–70. DLC NHi NN   **32**

Ferguson, Edward, 1843–1901.
The Army of the Cumberland under Buell,
by Lieut. Edward Ferguson, 1888. *MOLLUS-*
*Wis* I 424–32.          **33**

Keyes, Dwight W
1861, the First Wisconsin infantry, its organization and move to the front, by Dwight W.
Keyes, First Lieutenant 1st Wis. inf. *MOL-*
*LUS-Wis* III 90–101.         **34**

Kingman, Newton Hawes, 1837–1937.
. . . Life story of Captain Newton H. Kingman, 90th birthday revelations. Second edi-

tion, 91st birthday greetings. [Eugene, Ore., 1928] 39 p. plates (1 illus., ports.). 22cm.

IHi     **35**

Title from cover. At head of title: 1837, May 20, 1898. There was no published first edition, says a statement from Mr. Kingman's son. His explanation is that "second" refers to the manuscript held by the family.

Pierce, James Oscar, 1836–1907.
The skirmish at Falling Waters [July 2, 1861] *MOLLUS-Minn* II 289–313.     **36**

Starkweather, John Converse, 1830–1890.
Statement of military services of Brigadier General John C. Starkweather of Wisconsin, since the 4th of March, 1861. By request of the War department. Milwaukee, Daily Sentinel print [1864] 14 p. 22½cm.  WHi     **36A**
Title and imprint from cover. Colonel 1st Wisconsin, May 17, 1861; Brigadier General, July 17, 1863.

Stone, Henry      –1898.
The battle of Shiloh. 1895. *PMHSM* VII 31–99.     **36B**

## 2ND INFANTRY

*Mustered in: June 11, 1861.*
*Mustered out: July 2, 1864. Veterans and recruits consolidated to a battalion which merged with the 6th regiment of infantry, November 30, 1864.*
*Roster* I 345–84.
*Wisconsin in the war* 228–41, 969–70.
*Military history* 438–43.

Allen, Thomas Scott, 1825–1905.
The Second Wisconsin at the first battle of Bull run, by Bvt. Brig. Gen. Thomas S. Allen, 1890. *MOLLUS-Wis* I 374–93.     **37**

Beecham, Robert K      1838–
Gettysburg, the pivotal battle of the Civil war, by Captain R. K. Beecham. Chicago, A. C. McClurg & co., 1911. 298 p. plates (illus., fold. map, ports.). 21cm.     NN     **37A**

Harries, William Henry, 1843–1921.
Gainesville, Virginia, Aug. 28, 1862, by Captain William H. Harries, 1904. *MOLLUS-Minn* VI 157–68.     **38**

—— In the ranks at Antietam, 1897. *MOLLUS-Minn* IV 550–66.     **39**

—— The Iron brigade in the first day's battle at Gettysburg, 1895. *MOLLUS-Minn* IV 337–50.     **40**

Jackson, Heman B      1837–1924.
From Washington to Bull run and back again, by Lieutenant H. B. Jackson 2nd Wis., 1910. *MOLLUS-Wis* IV 233–50.     **41**

—— A reminiscence, by Captain H. B. Jackson, 1892. *MOLLUS-Wis* II 137–44.     **42**

Wheeler, Cornelius, 1840–1915.
Reminiscences of the battle of Gettysburg, by First Lieutenant Cornelius Wheeler, 1893. *MOLLUS-Wis* II 207–20.     **43**

—— A roster of the surviving members of the Iron brigade of the War of the great rebellion; or, American Civil war, 1861 to 1865. 1904. 56 p. port. 20½cm.     WHi     **44**
Title from cover. "Compiled by Cornelius Wheeler, late 2d Wis. infty., National home, Wisconsin."

## 3RD INFANTRY

*Mustered in: June 19, 1861.*
*Mustered out: July 18, 1865.*
*Roster* I 385–436.
*Wisconsin in the war* 242–9, 976–8.
*Military history* 483–97.

Proceedings of the . . . annual reunion of the Association of the Third regiment Wisconsin infantry veteran volunteers. . . . [I]–xx 1890–1910.     WHi     **45**
1890 is not numbered. At head of title, 1900: The Chaplain Springer memorial.

Bryant, Edwin Eustace, 1835–1903.
The battle of Gettysburg, by Colonel Edwin E. Bryant, 1893. *MOLLUS-Wis* II 231–75. maps.     **46**

—— History of the Third regiment of Wisconsin veteran volunteer infantry, 1861–1865, by Edwin E. Bryant, late Adjutant, with maps, compiled by Wm. F. Goodhue, and a complete roster of all who were members of the Regiment. Published by the Veteran association of the Regiment. Madison [Democrat print. co.] 1891. xvii, 445, (1) p. plates (fold. maps, ports.). 23½cm.     DLC NN     **47**
Unit roster [401]–45. "Errata" (1) p.

Crane, Louis H      D      1826–1862.
Ball's bluff, from the diary of the late Major L. H. D. Crane, Third Wisconsin volunteers. *US* XVII (1897) 8–16.     **48**
Text signed: William R. Hamilton.

Hinkley, Julian Wisner, 1838–1916.
. . . A narrative of service with the Third Wisconsin infantry, by Julian Wisner Hinkley, Captain of Company E. [Madison] Wisconsin History Commission, 1912. xi, 197 p. front. (port.). 23½cm.     NN     **49**
"Editor's preface" signed: R. G. T. [Reuben G. Thwaites] At head of title: Wisconsin history commission: Original papers no. 7. Coulter 233.

—— Some experiences of a veteran in the rear, 1893. *MOLLUS-Minn* IV 112–23.     **50**

*3rd Infantry, continued*

**Meffert, William C**
An incident of the battle of Chancellorsville, by W. C. Meffert. [Janesville, E. O. Kimberly, 1908] [7] p. 2 plates (ports.). 15cm.
NN    **50A**
At the Regimental reunion of 1904, the author relates the experience of Lieut. R. H. Williams and Lee McMurtrey. Imprint from NN's entry. Caption title. On cover: An incident of Chancellorsville, 1863. Meffert.

### 4TH INFANTRY

*Mustered in: July 2, 1861.*

*Designated 4th regiment of cavalry: August 22, 1863.*

### 5TH INFANTRY

*Mustered in: July 12, 1861.*

*Mustered out: June 24 to July 11, 1865.*

*Roster* i 437–93.

*Wisconsin in the war* 260–87, 978–81.

*Military history* 508–25.

Report of the proceedings of the 5th Wisconsin vol. infantry . . . annual reunion. 1897/1898 (DNW); 1899 (NHi); xiv–xviii 1900–1904 (WHi).    **51**

**Anderson, James Sibru,** 1841–1927.
The march of the Sixth corps to Gettysburg. *MOLLUS-Wis* iv 77–84.    **52**

**Butterfield, Miles L**    1837–
Personal reminiscences with the Sixth corps, 1864–5, by M. L. Butterfield, Bvt. Lieutenant Colonel, 1905. *MOLLUS-Wis* iv 85–93.    **53**

**Castleman, Alfred Lewis,** 1808–1877.
The Army of the Potomac. Behind the scenes. A diary of unwritten history, from the organization of the army by General George B. McClellan, to the close of the campaign in Virginia, about the first day of January, 1863, by Alfred L. Castleman, Surgeon of the Fifth regiment of Wisconsin volunteers. . . . Milwaukee, Strickland & co., 1863. 288 p. 18½cm.
DLC NN WHi    **54**

**Cobb, Amasa,** 1823–1905.
Williamsburg, Virginia, by Brig. Gen. Amasa Cobb, 1893. *MOLLUS-Neb* i 152–62.    **55**

**Holbrook, Arthur,** 1842–1917.
With the Fifth Wisconsin at Williamsburg, by First Lieutenant Arthur Holbrook, 1902. *MOLLUS-Wis* iii 525–45.    **56**

**Jones, Evan Rowland,** 1840–1920.
Four years in the Army of the Potomac, a soldier's recollections, by Major Jones. Lon-

don, Tyne pub. co. [1881] 246 p. front. (port.), double plate (map). 22cm.    DLC    **57**

—— Personal recollections of the American war, by Evan R. Jones, late Captain 5th regiment Wisconsin v. i. . . . Newcastle-on-Tyne, M. and M. W. Lambert [1872] 18 p. 21½cm.
NN    **58**
"Reprinted from the "Newcastle chronicle" of Saturday, February 10th, 1872."

**Leonard, James H**    1843–1901.
Letters of a Fifth Wisconsin volunteer. Edited by R. G. Plumb. *WMH* iii (1919) 52–83.    **59**

**Manitowoc County Historical Society.**
The flag of Company A, Fifth Wisconsin volunteer infantry, 1861–1925. [Manitowoc] Manitowoc County Historical Society [1925] [46] p. plates (col. illus., ports.). 18cm.
WHi    **60**

### 6TH INFANTRY

*Mustered in: July 16, 1861.*

*Mustered out: July 2, 1865.*

*Roster* i 494–537.

*Wisconsin in the war* 290–3, 971–4.

*Military history* 438–82, as a regiment of the Iron brigade.

In memoriam Amasa A. Davis, Company "K," 6th Wisconsin infantry, died April 16th, 1894, aged 62 years. This tribute is published by Arkansas city post, no. 158, Department of Kansas, G.A.R. [4] p. 17½cm. DNW    **60A**
Text signed: B. F. Childs, J. D. Guthrie [and] R. A. Gilmer, Committee.

**Bragg, Edward Stuyvesant,** 1827–1912.
Address of Gen. Edward S. Bragg, before the Society of the Army of the Potomac, at Detroit, Michigan, June 14, 1882. Washington, D. C., E. W. Oyster, 1882. 19 p. 23cm.
DLC    **60B**

—— Address of Edward S. Bragg on occasion of decorating soldiers' graves at Antietam, Maryland, May 30th, 1879. Washington, D. C. Rufus H. Darby, printer, 1879. 18 p. 22½cm.
NN    **60C**

—— General Edward S. Bragg's reminiscences [by] J. G. Hardgrove. *WMH* xxxiii (1950) 281–309, plate (port.).    **61**

**Cheek, Philip,** 1841–1911.
History of the Sauk county riflemen, known as Company "A," Sixth Wisconsin veteran volunteer infantry, 1861–1865, written and compiled by Philip Cheek [and] Mair Pointon. [Madison, Democrat print. co.] 1909. 220 p. plates (1 illus., fold. plan, ports.). 21½cm.
DLC NN    **62**
Unit roster 191–203. Coulter 77.

Dawes, Rufus Robinson, 1838–1899.
On the right at Antietam, by Rufus R. Dawes, Brevet Brigadier-General, 1889. *MOLLUS-Ohio* III 252–63. **63**

—— Service with the Sixth Wisconsin volunteers. . . . Marietta, Ohio, E. R. Alderman & Sons, 1890. vi, [5]–330 p. illus., plates (ports.). 21½cm. DLC NN **64**
Coulter 117.

—— With the Sixth Wisconsin at Gettysburg, 1890. *MOLLUS-Ohio* III 364–88. illus., plans. **65**

Fitch, Michael Henrick, 1837–1930.
Echoes of the Civil war as I hear them, by Michael H. Fitch, Brevet Colonel of volunteers. New York, R. F. Fenno & co., 1905. 368 p. front. (port.). 19½cm.
DLC NHi **66**
Author mustered in 6th Wisconsin, October 23, 1861; resigned, July 17, 1862; Colonel 21st Wisconsin, July 18, 1862; mustered out, June 8, 1865.

Harris, Loyd G
Army music, by First Lieut. Loyd D. Harris. *MOLLUS-Mo* I 287–94. **67**

Haskell, Franklin Aretas, 1828–1864.
The battle of Gettysburg, by Frank A. Haskell. [n. p., 187–] 72 p. 21½cm. WHi **68**
Title from cover. "To H. M. Haskell."

—— In A History of the Class of 1854 in Dartmouth college, including Col. Haskell's narrative of the battle of Gettysburg, (1898) 69–131. plate (map). **69**
"Eliminating criticism of General Sickles," Catalogue of the John P. Nicholson library, 1914.

—— Published under the auspices of the Commandery of the State of Massachusetts, Military order of the loyal legion of the United States. Boston [Mudge press, 1908] vi, 94 p. 2 plates (plan, port.). 23½cm.
NN **70**

—— Reply of the Philadelphia brigade association to the foolish and absurd narrative of Lieutenant Frank A. Haskell, which appears to be endorsed by the Military order of the loyal legion Commandery of Massachusetts and the Wisconsin history commission. . . . [Philadelphia, Bowers print. co.] 1910. 42 p. 23cm. NHi NN **71**
On cover: The battle of Gettysburg, how General Meade turned the Army of the Potomac over to Lieutenant Haskell, see page 10.

—— [Madison] Wisconsin History Commission [Democrat print. co.] 1908. xxiii, 185 p. front. (port.), 2 plates (plans). 23½cm.
NN **72**

At head of title: Wisconsin history commission: Reprints, No. 1. "Preface" signed: R. G. T. [Reuben G. Thwaites]

—— —— *JUSCA* xx (1909) 203–38, 415–67. **73**

—— —— In *Harvard classics* XLIII (1910) 347–440. **74**

—— —— Second edition. [Madison] Wisconsin History Commission [Democrat print. co.] 1910. xxviii, 192 p. front. (port.), 3 plates (plans, port.). 23½cm. WHi **74A**
For notes see those of Title 72.

—— An eye-witness account of the decisive battle of the Civil war. Titusville, Penn., Titusville Herald, 1937. 95 p. plate (map). 24cm. WHi **75**
"Words of explanation" signed and dated: Wisconsin historical library, December, 1908.

—— The battle of Gettysburg, by Frank A. Haskell. Edited by Bruce Catton. Cambridge, Houghton Mifflin co. [1958] xviii, 169 p. 3 maps. 22cm. NN **76**

Kellogg, John Azor, 1828–1883.
. . . Capture and escape, a narrative of army and prison life, by John Azor Kellogg, Colonel of the Sixth Wisconsin. [Madison] Wisconsin History Commission, 1908. xvi, 201 p. front. (port.). 23½cm. NN **77**
At head of title: Wisconsin history commission: Original papers no. 2. Coulter 270. "Preface" signed R. G. T. [Reuben G. Thwaites]

Watrous, Jerome Anthony, 1840–1922.
Mosby and his men, by Captain J. A. Watrous, 1887. *MOLLUS-Wis* II 303–7. **78**

### 7TH INFANTRY

*Mustered in: September 2, 1861.*
*Mustered out: July 2, 1865.*
*Roster* I 538–76.
*Wisconsin in the war* 290–3, 974–6.
*Military history* 438–82, as a regiment of the Iron brigade.

Kelley, Margaret (Ryan), 1858–
A soldier [William W. Ryan, 1827–] of the Iron brigade. *WMH* XXII (1939) 286–311. **79**

Monteith, Robert, 1840–1904.
Battle of the Wilderness and death of General Wadsworth, by Captain Robert Monteith, 1886. *MOLLUS-Wis* I 410–15. **80**

Prutsman, Christian Miller
A soldier's experience in Southern prisons, by C. M. Prutsman, Lieut. in Seventh regiment, Wisconsin volunteers, a graphic description of the author's experiences in various Southern prisons. New York, Andrew H. Kellogg, 1901. 80 p. front. (port.). 18½cm.
DLC NHi **81**

## 8TH INFANTRY

*Mustered in: September 13, 1861.*
*Mustered out: September 5, 1865.*
*Roster* i 577–603.
*Wisconsin in the war* 456–61, 765–70.
*Military history* 526–39.

Army life and stray shots, by a staff officer of the 8th regiment Wis. vols., 15th army corps, Third division. Memphis, Argus print. estab., 1863. 2 nos. (32 p.). 20½cm.   WHi    *81A*
   Preface signed: Germantown, Tenn., March 8th, 1863. "To be continued." [Number I] 16 p; Number II, p [17]–32.

The new picture of the Eagle. (From a photograph taken in March, 1865). Album portrait of "Old Abe" the live eagle which was carried by . . . the 8th Wisconsin regiment. . . . Chicago, Dunlop, Sewell & Spaulding. 1865. card, 10 x 6cm.           DLC    *81B*
   Colored illus. of eagle, text on verso. "Sold for the benefit of the Great sanitary fair in Chicago, which opens May 30, 1865."

Baker, Charlotte Alice, 1833–1909.
Old Abe, the war eagle of Wisconsin, by C. Alice Baker. Printed for the benefit of the Deerfield academy and Dickinson high school. Deerfield, Mass., 1904. vi, 22 p. plate (illus.). 25½cm          NB WHi    *81C*
   Presented as a lecture at the Old South meeting house, Boston, February 22, 1879.

Barrett, Joseph O
History of "Old Abe," the live war eagle of the Eighth regiment Wisconsin volunteers, by Joseph O. Barrett . . . Published by Alfred L. Sewell. Chicago, Dunlop, Sewell & Spalding, printers, 1865. 71 p. map, 2 col. plates (illus., port.). 23½cm.      DLC NN    *82*
   At head of cover title: The soldier bird!

—— The soldier bird, "Old Abe," the live war-eagle of Wisconsin, that served a three years' campaign in the great rebellion, by J. O. Barrett . . . Fifth edition. Madison, Atwood & Culver, 1876. 128 p. front. (map). 19½cm.
                         NHi    *83*

—— —— Sixth edition. Madison, Atwood & Culver, 1876. 128 p. 2 front. (illus., map). 19cm.            DLC NHi    *84*

Dodge, Marguerite Cottingham
Old Abe, the Wisconsin war eagle. Second edition. [n. p., 1930] 8 p. illus. 23½cm.
                         WHi    *85*

Farley, Edwin
Experiences of a soldier, 1861–1865 [by] Farley. Paducah, Ky., Printed by Billings print. co. [1918] 111 p. front. (port.). 19½cm.
                         IHi    *86*

Flower, Frank Abial, 1854–1911.
Old Abe, the Eighth Wisconsin war eagle, a full account of his capture and enlistment, exploits in war and honorable as well as useful career in peace. With an appendix. By F. A. F. Madison, Curran and Bowen, 1885. 173 p. front. (illus.), 3 ports. 17½cm.  DLC    *87*

Griggs, George W
Opening of the Mississippi; or, two years' campaigning in the South-west, a record of the campaigns, sieges, actions and marches in which the 8th Wisconsin volunteers have participated, together with correspondence, by a non-commissioned officer. Madison, Wm. J. Park & co., printers, 1864. vi, [7]–149, (1) p. 20cm.               DLC NN    *88*
   "Errata," (1) p. "Preface" signed: G. W. D. Coulter 133.

Greene, James H
Reminiscences of the war, bivouacs, marches, skirmishes and battles. Extracts from letters written home from 1861 to 1865, by J. H. Greene, Capt. Co. F, 8th 'Eagle' Wis. regt. inft. [Medina, Ohio] Gazette print, 1886. 87 p. 22cm.                 MB    *89*
   Printed in an edition of fifty copies in double columns from the type of the original publication in the Medina county gazette, 1885–86.

Heimstreet, Edward Burton
The history of old Abe, the war eagle and a condensed record of the Eighth Wisconsin infantry, better known as the Eagle regiment, as told to me by Captain Charles H. Henry. Compiled by E. B. Heimstreet. Lake Mills [193–] [8] p. illus. 16cm.      WHi    *90*
   Title and imprint from cover.

Hobart, Ella E    G    1821–
The soldier's gift. The dangers and temptations of army life, by Ella E. G. Hobart. Chicago, Tribune press, 1863. 32 p. 14½cm.
                   DLC WHi    *91*
   "To my husband, Chaplain of the live eagle regiment, Eighth Wis. vol., this work is affectionately dedicated."

Lyon, William Penn, 1822–1913.
Reminiscences of the Civil war, compiled from the war correspondence of Colonel William P. Lyon and from personal letters and diary of Mrs. Adalia C. Lyon. Published by William P. Lyon, Jr. [San Jose, Cal., Press of Muirson & Wright] 1907. 274 p. plans, plates (ports.). 24cm.       DLC NN    *92*
   Coulter 303. Mustered in 8th Wisconsin, August 7, 1861; Colonel 13th Wisconsin, August 5, 1862; mustered out, September 11, 1865

McLain, David
The story of Old Abe. *WMH* viii (1925) 407–14.                       *93*

Miles, Selim C
The eagle of the Regiment, a complete history of that famous bird, "Old Abe," the war eagle, with thrilling battle scenes, and incidents of fighting Joe Mowers' "invincible" Second brigade, and all the different phases of the soldier's life in the great Civil war of the United States, by Selin C. S. . . . [Stetsonville] War Eagle Book Association, 1894. 56 p. front. (port.). 23cm.                              WHi      94
A prospectus?

Miller, Charles D
"Old Abe" the war eagle. In his Report of the great re-union of the veteran soldiers and sailors of Ohio (1878) 111–16.                    95

Nelson, C          P
Abe, the war eagle. To the veterans of the Civil war, this story is respectfully dedicated. . . . [Lynn, Mass.] c1903. 31, (1) p. illus. 17cm.                                  WHi      96
Copyright by C. P. Nelson.

Sherwood, Lorraine
"Old Abe," American eagle [by] Lorraine Sherwood. Illustrated by K. Milhous. New York, Charles Scribner's Sons, 1946. 60, (3) p. illus. (partly col.). 20cm.    DLC NN      97

—— Old Abe, the American eagle, by Lorraine Sherwood. [n. p., c1954] 47, (1) p. front. (port.), illus. 21½cm.                   DLC      98
"Revised edition."

Smith, Albert E          1836–1932.
A few days with the Eighth regiment, Wisconsin volunteers at Iuka and Corinth, by Albert E. Smith, Captain 8th Wisconsin, 1908. MOLLUS-Wis iv 61–7.                        99

Todd, Maria P
"Old Abe," war eagle of the 8th Wisconsin. Military collector & historian iv (1952) 72–3. illus.                                      100

Williams, John Melvin, 1843–
"The Eagle regiment," 8th Wis. inf'ty vols., a sketch of its marches, battles and campaigns, from 1861 to 1865, with a complete regimental and company roster, and a few portraits and sketches of its officers and commanders, by a "non-vet" of Co. "H." Belleville, "Recorder" print, 1890. 166 p. ports. 23½cm.
                                    DLC NN      101
Unit roster 99–135. "Preface" signed: J. M. Williams.

### 9TH INFANTRY

*Mustered in: October 26, 1861.*

*Mustered out: January 30, 1866.*

*Roster* i 604–43.

*Wisconsin in the war* 578–81, 770–2.

*Military history* 540–7.

Ruegger, Edward          –1916.
Five weeks of my army life . . . Introductory note by Lilian Krueger. WMH xxxvii (1954) 163–8. port.                              102

### 10TH INFANTRY

*Mustered in: October 14, 1861.*

*Mustered out: October 25, 1864.*

*Roster* i 644–67.

*Wisconsin in the war* 601–4, 772–4.

*Military history* 548–58.

. . . Annual reunion of the Tenth Wisconsin infantry. . . . iv 1898 (WHi); v–vii 1899–1902 (NHi); viii–xxi 1903–1921 (WHi). 103
"Reprints of reports of earlier reunions," 1899, 1–19.
No meeting was held in 1900.

Day, William W
Fifteen months in Dixie; or, my personal experience in Rebel prisons. A story of the hardships, privations and sufferings of the "boys in Blue" during the late War of the rebellion. Owatonna, Minn., People's press, 1889. 80 p. 21cm.                 DLC      104
Coulter 121.

Hinckley, Lucius D
A few months in a Rebel prison, by Lucius D. Hinckley, 1st Lieut. 10th Wisconsin, 1901. MOLLUS-Wis iii 436–52.                    105

McMynn, John Gibson (Mrs.)
Sketch of the military career of John Gibson McMynn, Colonel 10th Wisconsin infantry, prepared by Mrs. J. C. McMynn, and read by his son, John Clarke McMynn. MOLLUS-Wis iv 1–20.                                106

Marks, Solon, 1827–1914.
Experiences at the battle of Stone river, by Surgeon Solon Marks, 1895. MOLLUS-Wis ii 385–98.                              107

—— Experiences with the Ninth brigade, Rousseau's division, Army of Ohio, 1892. MOLLUS-Wis ii 102–9.                       108

### 11TH INFANTRY

*Mustered in: October 18, 1861.*

*Mustered out: September 5, 1865.*

*Roster* i 668–701.

*Wisconsin in the war* 592–6, 774–80.

*Military history* 559–73.

Reunion of the Eleventh and Twenty-third regiments of Wisconsin volunteer infantry, 1886. 40 p. 23½cm.          DLC      109
Title from cover.

*11th Infantry, continued*

**McMyler, James J**
History of the 11th Wisconsin veteran vol.
inf., giving a reliable account of its marches,
hardships and battles, from its organization to
October, 1864. Compiled and published by
James J. McMyler. New Orleans, 1865. 32,
61 p. 23cm.                        WHi     *110*
Unit roster, 61 p. County recruited and muster in
dates of companies; Statistics by companies of recruits;
deceased, discharged, transfer and deserted, (2) p.

## 12TH INFANTRY

*Organized: October 18 to December 13,*
*1861.*
*Mustered out: July 20, 1865.*
*Roster I 702–38.*
*Wisconsin in the war 596–600, 981–3.*
*Military history 574–89.*

Reunion story of Company E of the Twelfth
Wisconsin infantry. . . . 1894 (DLC), 1899–
1906 (DLC), 1907 (NHi), 1908–1912 (DLC).
No meeting held 1903. Not published 1909. *111*

Reunion story of the Twelfth Wisconsin infantry. . . . 1895 (NHi), 1896–1897 (WHi),
1902–1903 (DLC), 1904–1905 (NHi), 1907
(NHi), 1908–1910 (DLC), 1913–1920 (DLC),
1921–1927 (WHi).                          *112*
Not published 1898–1901. A joint reunion with the
16th Wisconsin, 1903–1904.

A tribute of loving respect to the memory of
comrade Samuel Glyde Swain of Company E,
Twelfth Wisconsin regiment veteran volunteer
infantry. Died at Winona, Minnesota, April 6,
1904. Published by the Company E association. [Milton, Milton Journal] 1904. 79 p.
front. (port.). 16cm.                DLC     *113*

**Higbee, Chester G**
Personal recollections of a line officer, by
Captain Chester G. Higbee, 1895. *MOLLUS-*
*Minn* IV 313–28.                          *114*

**Miller, Alonzo**
Diaries and letters written by Pvt. Alonzo
Miller, Co. 'A,' 12th Wisconsin infantry,
Force's brigade, Leggett's division, Blair's 17th
army corps, 1864–1865. . . . [Marietta, Ga?,
1958] 122 folios. 27cm. Mimeographed.
                                   DLC NN     *115*
Copyright by John Paul Cullen and Clarence J.
Stolt.
At head of section "Annotations," f 2–5, . . .
National Park service, Kennesaw mountain national
battlefield park, Marietta, Georgia.

**Putney, Frank H          1841–1914.**
Incidents of Sherman's .march through the
Carolinas, by Frank H. Putney, 2d Lieut. 12th
Wisconsin, 1900. *MOLLUS-Wis* III 381–7.
                                             *116*

**Rood, Hosea Whitford, 1845–1933.**
The Grand army of the republic and the
Wisconsin department. *WMH* VI 280–94, 403–
13.                                          *117*

——— Story of the service of Company E, and
of the Twelfth Wisconsin regiment, veteran
volunteer infantry in the War of the rebellion,
beginning with September 7th, 1861, and ending with July 21st, 1865. Written by one of the
boys. Milwaukee, Swain & Tate co., printers,
1893. 547 p. illus., plates (ports.). 23cm.
                                   DLC NN     *118*
Unit roster 36–8. "Rendered in their behalf by
comrade Hosea W. Rood, the author of the preceding
history."

——— ——— [with additional matter] [Milwau-
kee? 1898] 1 v. 23½cm.            DLC     *119*
"When this History of Company E was printed,
ninety-three copies were left unbound. Those who had
the work in charge thought that within two or three
years additions to the book might be suggested, and
that when these could be made and printed the
remaining copies thus completed could be bound."
The (96) pages include proceedings of Company and
Regimental reunions, 1894–1897; Memorial service in
honor of Captain Gillespie at Delton, Wisconsin, Feb.
11, 1871; and additional personal sketches.

**Strong, William Emerson, 1840–1891.**
The campaign against Vicksburg (read
April 7, 1880). *MOLLUS-Ill* II 313–54.   *120*

——— The death of General James E. Mc-
Pherson (read October 13, 1887). *MOLLUS-*
*Ill* II 311–43.                          *121*

## 13TH INFANTRY

*Mustered in: October 17, 1861.*
*Mustered out: November 24, 1865.*
*Roster I 739–69.*
*Wisconsin in the war 781–7.*
*Military history 590–7.*

**Lovejoy, Daniel B**
From youth to age, adventures in a varied
life, by D. B. Lovejoy. Chicago, American
Authors' Protective pub. so. [1894] 272 p.
front. (port.). 19½cm.        DLC WHi     *122*
Civil war 90–161.

**Woodman, Edwin Ellis, 1838–1915.**
Death and dishonor, by Captain Edwin E.
Woodman, 1901. *MOLLUS-Minn* V 303–13.
                                             *123*
See also Title 92.

## 14TH INFANTRY

*Mustered in: January 30, 1862.*
*Mustered out: October 9, 1865.*
*Roster I 770–803.*
*Wisconsin in the war 475–7, 787–90.*
*Military history 598–611.*

Engle, Francis E
Worden's battalion and Company E of the Fourteenth Wisconsin veteran volunteer infantry, paper prepared for reunion of Regiment, Fond du Lac, June 8, 9 and 10, 1904, by Lieutenant Francis E. Engle. Indianapolis, Ind., 1904. 68 p. 22cm.                WHi    *124*
Title and imprint from cover. "Unaccounted for. Corrections and additions," inserted leaf.

Hancock, John, 1830–
The Fourteenth Wisconsin, Corinth and Shiloh, 1862–1895, paper on battle of Shiloh, by Colonel Hancock. Pilgrimage of Engle and Tucker to battle fields of Corinth and Shiloh, 1895. [Indianapolis, Ind., Printed by F. E. Engle & Son, 1895] 40 p. illus., plates (ports.). 23cm.                WHi    *125*

Houghton, Edgar P        1845–1926.
History of Company I, Fourteenth Wisconsin infantry, from October 19, 1861, to October 9, 1865. *WMH* xi (1927) 26–49.        *126*

Magdeburg, Frederick H        1841–1916.
Capture of Fort Donelson, by Captain F. H. Magdeburg, 14th Wis., 1899. *MOLLUS-Wis* iii 284–95.        *127*

—— The Fourteenth Wisconsin infantry at the battle of Shiloh, 1897. *MOLLUS-Wis* iii 176–87.        *128*

—— General W. T. Sherman, 1891. *MOLLUS-Wis* ii 1–51.        *129*

—— Worden's battalion, paper read by Capt. F. H. Magdeburg, at the first annual reunion of the 14th Wisconsin veteran vol. infantry, held at Fond du Lac, Wis., Wednesday and Thursday, June 16–17, 1886. [10] p. 22cm.                WHi    *129A*

Newton, James K        –1892.
A Wisconsin boy in Dixie, the selected letters of James K. Newton. Edited by Stephen E. Ambrose. Madison, University of Wisconsin press, 1961. xviii, 188 p. 3 maps, plates (facs., illus., port.). 22cm.        NN    *129B*
Roster of Company F, 173–82.

—— A Wisconsin boy at Vicksburg, the letters of James K. Newton. Edited by Stephen E. Ambrose. *Journal of Mississippi history* xxiii (1961) 1–14.        *129C*

Rogers, James B
War pictures, experiences and observations of a Chaplain in the U. S. army in the War of the Southern rebellion, by Rev. J. B. Rogers, Chaplain of the 14th Wis. . . . Chicago, Church & Goodman, 1863. xi, [13]–258 p. front. (port.), plates (illus.). 19cm. DLC NHi NN    *130*

Spink, Richard A
Diary jottings of march from Nashville to Eastport, Miss., morning after the battle, Dec. 17, 1864. In National tribune scrap book iii 116–19.        *130A*

Stockwell, Elisha, 1846–1935.
Private Elisha Stockwell, Jr. sees the Civil war. Edited by Byron Abernethy. Norman, University of Oklahoma press [1958] xiii, 210 p. plates (illus., port.). 21cm.
DLC NN    *131*

Tucker, William H
The Fourteenth Wisconsin vet. vol. infantry (General A. J. Smith's command) in the expedition and battle of Tupelo. Also, wanderings through the wilds of Missouri and Arkansas in pursuit of Price, by W. H. Tucker. [Indianapolis, Ind., Printed by F. E. Engle & Son, 1892] 30, (2) p. illus., plates (fold. map, ports.). 23cm.                WHi    *132*

—— The Fourteenth Wisconsin vet. vol. infantry, October 1st, 2d, 3d, and 4th, 1862, at the battle of Corinth, by Sergeant W. H. Tucker, Company D. Read at regimental reunion, Fond du Lac, Wis., June 13th, 14th and 15th, 1893. [Indianapolis, Ind., F. E. Engle & Son, printers, 1893] 23 p. illus., port. 23cm.
WHi    *133*

## 15TH INFANTRY

*Mustered in: February 14, 1862.*
*Mustered out: December 1, 1864 to February 13, 1865.*
*Roster* i 804–29.
*Wisconsin in the war* 461–3, 790–3.
*Military history* 612–31.

Ager, Waldemar Theodor, 1869–1941.
Oberst Heg og hans gutter, ved Waldemar Ager. Eau Claire, Fremad pub. co., 1916. 326, (1) p. illus., map, ports., fold. map. 22½cm.        *134*
"Indhold," (1) p. Unit roster 289–320. "Det Norske Ko. H i 27 de Wis regiment," 320–2.

Blegen, Theodore Christian, 1891–
Colonel Hans Christian Heg, by Theodore C. Blegen. . . . [Madison, 1920] 28 p. front. (port.). 26cm.        DLC    *135*
"Reprinted from the Wisconsin magazine of history, v. IV, no. 2, December, 1920."

Brunsted, George H        1841–1864.
Letters from a Canadian recruit in the Union army. Edited by Doris Fleming. *Tennessee historical quarterly* xvi (1957) 159–66.        *136*

*15th Infantry, continued*

Buslett, Ole Amundson, 1855–1924.

Det Femtende regiment Wisconsin frivillige, samlet og bearbeidet af O. A. Buslett, Tilegnet det Norske folk i Amerika. Decorah, Iowa, Paa forfatterens forlag trykt hos B. Amundsen [1894] 696 p. ports. 20cm. DLC WHi **137**

Unit roster with biographies [293]–649.

Dietrichson, Peter Gabriel, 1844–1901.

The Fifteenth Wisconsin infantry during the late war. *Scandanavia* I (1883/84) 297–300.

**138**

—— En kortfattet skildring af det femtende Wisconsin regiments, historie og virksomhed under Borgerkrigen, samt nogle korte troek af fangernes ophold i Andersonville, af P. G. Dietrichson. Chicago, Trykt hos John Anderson & co., 1884. 32 p. front. (port.). 15½cm.

DLC NHi NN **138A**

Enander, Johan Alfred, 1842–1910.

Borgerkrigen i de forenede stater i Nord Amerika, udarbeidet af Joh. A. Enander, med en kortfattet beretning om det 15de Wis regiments deltagelse i krigen. La Crosse, Trykt i "Faedrelandet og Emigrantens" officin, 1881. 128 p. 2 plates (ports.). 19½cm.

NHi NN **139**

Heg, E    Biddle

Stephen O. Himoe, Civil war physician, by E. Biddle Heg. *Norwegian American studies and records* XI (1940) 30–56. **140**

Heg, Hans Christian, 1829–1863.

The Civil war letters of Colonel Hans Christian Heg. Edited by Theodore C. Blegen. Northfield, Minn., Norwegian-American Historical Association, 1936. ix, 260 p. plates (facs., 1 fold.; illus.; ports.). 23cm.

DLC NN **141**

Coulter 226. "Colonel Hans Christian Heg, a biographical essay," by Theodore C. Blegen, 1–45.

Johnson, John Anders, 1832–1901.

Det Skandinavske regiments historie (15de Wisconsin regiment), en kortfattet historie om dets organisation og de feldt-toge, hvori det tog del, samlet af J. A. Johnson. La Crosse, Trykt i "Faedrelandet og Emigranten's" trykkeri, 1869. 134, 27 p. 23cm. NHi **142**

Unit roster 27 p.

Kuhns, Lester M

An army surgeon's letters to his wife. *Proceedings of the Mississippi valley historical association* VII (1914) 306–20. **143**

Excerpts from the letters of Stephen Oliver Himoe, 1832–1904, Surgeon of the 15th Wisconsin.

## 16TH INFANTRY

*Mustered in: January 31, 1862.*

*Mustered out: July 12, 1865.*

*Roster* II 1–48.

*Wisconsin in the war* 477–8, 983–4.

*Military history* 632–43.

Sixth annual reunion of Company "F," 16th Wis. vols., held near Evansville, Wis., June 18, 1890. Maryville, Mo., Printed by H. E. Robinson, 1890. 8 p. front. (port.). 17½cm.

DLC NHi **144**

DLC's copy has inserted leaf with caption: At St. Paul in 1896.

Jones, D    Lloyd

The battle of Shiloh, reminiscences, by D. Lloyd Jones, First Lieutenant 16th Wisconsin, 1903. *MOLLUS-Wis* IV 51–60. **145**

Porter, Daniel R

The Colonel and the private go to war. *WMH* XLII (1958/59) 124–7. 1 illus. **145A**

Vail, David Franklin, 1838?–

Company K, of the 16th Wisconsin, at the battle of Shiloh, recollections of Lieut. D. F. Vail. [n. p.] 1897. 7 p. 20½cm. WHi **146**

Title and imprint date from cover. "Suggested by a series of contributions to a local paper by a recruit, that appeared in 1896 and 1897, devoted principally to the criticising of the military record of officers of the 16th regiment," inserted slip.

See also Title 112.

## 17TH INFANTRY

*Mustered in: March 15, 1862.*

*Mustered out: July 14, 1865.*

*Roster* II 49–82.

*Wisconsin in the war* 493–5, 984–6.

*Military history* 644–55.

Wescott, Morgan Ebenezer, 1844–

Civil war letters, 1861 to 1865, written by a boy in Blue to his mother, by M. Ebenezer Westcott. [Mora, Minn.] c1909. [32] p. 2 ports. on cover. 19cm. DLC **147**

On cover: Co. E, 17th Wis vol. infty.

## 18TH INFANTRY

*Mustered in: March 15, 1862.*

*Mustered out: July 18, 1865.*

*Roster* II 83–111.

*Wisconsin in the war* 479–80, 986–8.

*Military history* 656–67.

## 19TH INFANTRY

*Mustered in: April 30, 1862.*
*Mustered out: August 9, 1865.*
*Roster* II 112–39.
*Wisconsin in the war* 389–95, 988–90.
*Military history* 668–74.

Strong, Rollin M
A prisoner of war, by Lieut. Col. Rollin M.
Strong, 1894. *MOLLUS-Neb* I 163–6.    **148**

## 20TH INFANTRY

*Mustered in: August 23, 1862.*
*Mustered out: July 14, 1865.*
*Roster* II 140–64.
*Wisconsin in the war* 581–4, 794–800.
*Military history* 675–85.

Miller, Edward Gee, 1840–1906.
. . . Captain Edward Gee Miller of the 20th
Wisconsin, his war, 1862–1865. Edited by W.
J. Lemke. Fayetteville, Ark., 1960. 42 p.
(port.). 28cm. Mimeographed. NN    **148A**
"No. 37 in the Booklet series of the Washington
county historical society." Unit roster Company G,
35–7.

## 21ST INFANTRY

*Mustered in: September 5, 1862.*
*Mustered out: June 8, 1865.*
*Roster* II 164–200.
*Wisconsin in the war* 604–05, 991–3.
*Military history* 686–96.

Proceedings of the Twenty-first regiment association at its . . . annual reunion. v–x 1891–
1897 (WHi); xi–xiii 1898–1900 (NHi); xiv–
xxix 1901–1916 (DLC); xxx–xli 1917–1928
(WHi).                                    **149**
1–4 were not published. "No later meetings held,"
note in WHi's copy of 1928.

Fitch, Michael Hendrick, 1837–1930.
. . . The Chattanooga campaign, with espe-
cial reference to Wisconsin's participation
therein, by Michael Hendrick Fitch. Lieu-
tenant-Colonel of the Twenty-first Wisconsin.
[Madison] Wisconsin History Commission,
1911. xiii, 255 p. plates (maps). 23½cm.
                                    NN    **150**
At head of title: Wisconsin history commission:
Original papers, no. 4. Introduction signed: R. G. T.
[Reuben G. Thwaites]

Hobart, Harrison Carroll, 1815–1902.
Capture, imprisonment and escape, by General Harrison C. Hobart. In The citizen-soldier;
or, memoirs of a volunteer, by John Beatty,
(1879) [375]–98.                          **151**

—— Libby prison, the escape, 1891. *MOL-
LUS-Wis* I 394–409.                       **152**

Holmes, Mead
A soldier of the Cumberland, memoir of
Mead Holmes, Jr., Sergeant of Company K,
21st regiment Wisconsin volunteers, by his
father, with an introduction by John S. Hart.
Boston, American Tract Society [1864] xiv,
[15]–240 p. front. (port.), plates (illus.).
17cm.                          DLC NN    **153**

See also Title 66.

## 22ND INFANTRY

*Mustered in: September 2, 1862.*
*Mustered out: June 12, 1865.*
*Roster* II 201–30.
*Wisconsin in the war* 993–5.
*Military history* 697–706.

Bradley, George S
The Star corps; or, notes of an Army Chap-
lain, during Sherman's famous "march to the
sea" [by] Rev. G. S. Bradley, Chaplain 22d
Wisconsin. Milwaukee, Jermain & Brightman,
printers, 1865. xi, [13]–304 p. front. (port.).
19cm.                          DLC NN    **154**
Partial contents: The Thirty-third Indiana, by
Joseph R. Shelton, [13]–21; The Twenty-second Wis-
consin, 21–31; The Nineteenth Michigan, 31–3; The
Eighty-fifth Indiana, by Lt. Col. J. E. Brant, 33–6.
Coulter 49.

Cansdell, Henry W
Journal of. . . . *Vineland historical magazine*
VII (Vineland, N. J. 1922) 55–60; VIII (1923)
72–6, 92–7, 111–14, 135–8.               **155**
"To be continued."

## 23RD INFANTRY

*Mustered in: August 30, 1862.*
*Mustered out: July 4, 1865.*
*Roster* II 231–55.
*Wisconsin in the war* 800–06.
*Military history* 707–19.

Reunion of the Twenty-third regiment Wisconsin infantry volunteers at. . . . 1898 (WHi),
1907 (WHi), 1912 (DLC).                 **155A**
1886 held with the Eleventh Wisconsin, see Title
109.

Roster of the survivors of the Twenty third
regiment Wisconsin volunteer infantry. Nee-
nah, Blair & Huie, printers, 1889. [34] p. 17cm.
                                 DLC    **156**
Title and imprint from cover. "Historical sketch
(abridged from report of Capt. Duncan)" included.
A roster of surviving members published with 1907,
Title 155A.

23rd Infantry, continued

Acker, Henry J
Gulf spy, Sgt. Henry J. Acker 23rd Wisconsin
vol. inf. Tall Timbers, Md., Headquarters press
[1961] 24 p. 23cm.                    NN     **156A**
"The story is printed here as Sergeant Henry J.
Acker wrote it."

Vilas, William Freeman, 1840–1908.
    . . . A view of the Vicksburg campaign, a
paper read before the Madison literary club,
October 14, 1907, by William Freeman Vilas,
Lieutenant-Colonel of the Twenty-third Wis-
consin. [Madison] Wisconsin History Commis-
sion, 1908. xii, 104 p. front. (port.), fold. map.
23½cm.                                NN     **157**
    At head of title: Wisconsin history commission:
Original papers, no. 1. "Selected bibliography of the
Vicksburg campaign, compiled by Minnie Myrtle
Oakley," 85–104.

### 24TH INFANTRY

Mustered in: August 15, 1862.
Mustered out: June 10, 1865.
Roster II 256–81.
Wisconsin in the war 605–06, 806–13.
Military history 720–33.

Ford, Thomas J
With the rank and file, incidents and anecdotes during the War of the rebellion, as remembered by one of the non-commissioned
officers, by Thomas J. Ford, Sergeant Company H, Twenty-fourth Wisconsin infantry.
Milwaukee, Press of the Evening Wisconsin
co., 1898. 95 p. front. (port.). 14½cm.
                                DLC NHi     **158**

Furness, Henry B
A general account of prison life and prisons
in the South during the War of the rebellion,
including statistical information relating to
prisoners of war. In Prisoners of war and military prisons, personal narratives of experience
. . . (1890) 399–487.                        **159**

Hickman, Charles
A statistical record of the 24th Wisconsin
volunteer infantry, compiled from the Adjutant general's report of the State of Wisconsin,
by Charles Hickman, of Co. "D." Milwaukee
[Burdick & Allen, printers] 1900. 44, (1) p.
22cm.                                MnHi     **160**

Ingraham, John Phillips Thurston, 1817–1906.
A sermon in memory of Captain F. A. Root
and Lieutenant R. J. Chevas of the 24th regt.
Wisconsin vol. infantry, by their pastor, the
Revd. J. P. T. Ingraham, delivered December
20th, 1864. Milwaukee, Presses of Starr & Son,
1864. 14 p. 21cm.                    WHi     **161**

Jones, Adoniram J
A Private of the Cumberland, memoirs and
reminiscences of the Civil war, by A. P. Jones,
Company B, 24th Wisconsin volunteers. [n. p.,
190–] 68 p. facs., plates (facs., double map,
ports.). 18cm.                        NN     **161A**
    "I have compiled these extracts from letters written
home by my father," "Appendix" signed: A. P. J. The
volume publishes a facsimile of Arthur MacArthur's
letter dated January 25, 1907, to Mr. A. P. Jones
which includes the statement "am glad to know that
you intend to prepare a memorial that will commemorate his [A. J. Jones] valuable services."

Parsons, Edwin B            1836–1920.
Chickamauga, by Captain E. B. Parsons,
1895. MOLLUS-Wis II 438–43.            **162**

—— Missionary ridge, 1888. MOLLUS-Wis I
189–200.                                **163**

—— Sheridan, 1888. MOLLUS-Wis I 275–
84.                                    **164**

### 25TH INFANTRY

Mustered in: September 14, 1862.
Mustered out: June 7, 1865.
Roster II 282–311.
Wisconsin in the war 996–8.
Military history 734–45.

Reunion of the Twenty-fifth regiment of Wisconsin volunteer infantry [Sparta, June 8–9]
1887. 36 p. 22½cm.                    WHi     **165**
    Title from cover. "Only reunion that was published.
I have the record of two more but the proceedings
were not put in print," autograph letter of James I. Dunlap, dated Oct. 13, 1896, inserted in WHi's copy.

Brobst, John F            1838/39–1917.
Well Mary, Civil war letters of a Wisconsin
volunteer. Edited by Margaret Brobst Roth.
Madison, University of Wisconsin press, 1960.
ix, 165 p. plates (facs., illus., ports.). 22½cm.
                            DLC NN NNC     **165A**
    "Itinerary of Private John F. Brobst during the
Civil war," map facing p 3.

Clark, James Ira, 1924–
The Civil war of Private Cooke, a Wisconsin
boy in the Union army, by James I. Clarke.
Madison, State Historical Society of Wisconsin, 1955. 20 p. illus., plan, port. 23cm.
                                DLC     **166**

Cooke, Chauncey Herbert, 1846–1919.
A Badger boy in Blue, the letters of Chauncey
H. Cooke. WMH IV (1920) 75–100, 208–17,
321–44; v (1921) 63–98. plate (illus.).     **167**

—— Soldier boy's letters to his father and
mother, 1861–5. [Independence, News-office,
c1915] 97 p. 22cm.                    DLC     **168**
Title from cover.

Lamb, Alfred
My march with Sherman to the sea, a diary
of Sgt. Alfred Lamb, owned by Lester Bennett, Arlington Heights, and published in serial
form in Paddock publications' newspapers.
Printed in pamphlet form for the benefit of
chapters of the Daughters of American revolu-
tion and interested public libraries [n. p.]
Paddock Publications, 1961. [6] leaves. 28cm.
                                    IHi        **169**

Rusk, Jeremiah McLain, 1830–1893.
Address of J. M. Rusk to the survivors of the
Twenty-fifth regiment of Wisconsin volunteers
[at Sparta, June 9, 1887] 11 p. 22cm.
Caption title.                      WHi        **170**

Shaw, John M
The life and services of General John A.
Rawlins, by Captain John M. Shaw. *MOL-
LUS-Minn* III 381–403.                         **171**

## 26TH INFANTRY

*Mustered in: September 17, 1862.*

*Mustered out: June 17, 1865.*

*Roster* II 312–29.

*Wisconsin in the war* 395–403, 998–9.

*Military history* 746–59.

Domschcke, Bernhard, 1827–1869.
Zwanzig Monate in Kriegs-Gefangenschaft,
Erinnerungen, von Bernhard Domschcke. . . .
Milwaukee, Druck und Verlag von W. W.
Coleman, 1865. 247 p. 17½cm.
                              DLC NN      **172**
"Verzeichnis der Deutschen Officiere, welche in der
Zeit vom 1. Mai 1863 bis 1. März 1865 in den Ge-
fangnissen zu Richmond, Danville, Macon, Savannah,
Charleston und Columbia sich befanden," 241–7. Bio-
graphical: Bernhard Domschcke, by J. J. Schlicher,
*WMH* XXIX (1945/46) 319–32, 435–56. plate
(port.).

Wallber, Albert, 1842–1911.
From Gettysburg to Libby prison, by Albert
Wallber, 1st Lieutenant 26th regiment Wis-
consin, 1909. *MOLLUS-Wis* IV 191–200.  **173**

## 27TH INFANTRY

*Mustered in: March 7, 1863.*

*Mustered out: August 5, 1865.*

*Roster* II 340–65.

*Wisconsin in the war* 814–17.

*Military history* 760–6.

See Title 134.

## 28TH INFANTRY

*Mustered in: October 14, 1862.*

*Mustered out: August 23, 1865.*

*Roster* II 366–89.

*Wisconsin in the war* 817–26.

*Military history* 767–73.

Proceedings of the . . . annual reunion of the
Society of the 28th regt. . . . I/III 1882–1883,
1885 (WHi); IV–VII 1886–1889 (NHi); VIII
1890 (WHi); IX 1891 (DLC); X 1892 (WHi);
XI 1893 (DLC); XII–XIII 1894–1895 (WHi);
XIV–XVII 1896–1899 (DLC); XVIII 1900
(DNW); XIX 1901 (WHi); XX 1902 (DNW);
XXI 1903 (WHi); XXII–XXIII 1904–1905 (DNW);
XXIV 1906 (WHi); XXV–XXIX 1907–1911 (DNW);
XXX–XXXVI 1912–1918 (WHi).            **174**
1/3 published 1904.

Davidson, John Nelson, 1848–1945.
The beginning of the march from Atlanta to
the sea, a diary by Alonzo B. [sic H.] Lothrop
and Frank B. Lothrop. With a letter written
by Joseph Nelson during Sherman's advance
on Atlanta. Edited and published by J. N.
Davidson. Madison, Forward press [192–]
[8] p. 23cm.                         WHi   **175**
Title and imprint from cover. Text on p 2–3 of
cover.

—— —— Revised. Letter by Henry Jackson
Houston. Madison, Forward press [192–]
[12] p. 22cm.                        WHi   **176**
Title and imprint from cover. Text on p 2–4 of
cover.

## 29TH INFANTRY

*Mustered in: September 27, 1862.*

*Mustered out: June 22, 1865.*

*Roster* II 390–415.

*Wisconsin in the war* 826–32.

*Military history* 774–88.

Col. Bradford Hancock. Born January 18,
1831, at Sackett's harbor, N. Y. Died May 15,
1887, at Chicago, Ill. [11] p. 23½cm.
                                     WHi  **176A**
On cover: In memoriam. Address of Rev. Arthur
Little and resolutions of the survivors of the 29th
Wisconsin.

Report of the proceedings of the . . . annual
reunion of the 29th Wisconsin infantry, held
at. . . . V–X 1890–1895; XIII–XIV 1898–1899.
                                     WHi   **177**
French, Frank F
The lost detachment . . . by F. F. French,
29th Wisconsin. [Humboldt, Iowa, 1907] 24 p.
19½cm.                               WHi   **178**
Title from cover.

Whipple, Henry P        1838–1921.
The diary of a private soldier, the exact copy
of a record kept day by day during the Civil
war, by Henry P. Whipple, late a Private in
the Twenty-ninth Wisconsin volunteer infantry. Transcribed in 1906. Waterloo, 1906. 80 p.
port. 23cm.                          WHi   **179**

## 30TH INFANTRY

*Mustered in: October 21, 1862.*
*Mustered out: September 20, 1865.*
*Roster* II 416–43.
*Wisconsin in the war* 833–9.
*Military history* 789–92.

A diary of the 30th regiment, Wisconsin volunteers, a history of the Regiment since its organization, compiled from reliable sources and statistics. Madison, Printed, published and sold, by Martin & Judson, 1864. 110 p. front. (illus.). 17cm.                    WHi    *180*
A unit roster.

Roster of the Thirtieth Wisconsin infantry volunteers. Mustered in, October 18, 1862, Madison, Wis., mustered out, September 20, 1865, Louisville, Ky. Printed for the Association. Madison, M. J. Cantwell, printer, 1896. 71, (1) p. 20cm.                    DLC    *181*

Hastings, Samuel Dexter, 1816–1903.
Address by Samuel D. Hastings before the Hastings invincibles, Company "C," 30th reg. Wis. volunteers, on Sunday evening, November 9th, 1862, in the Congregational chapel, Madison, Wisconsin. Madison, Willard G. Roberts, printer, 1862. 22 p. 22½cm.
                        WHi    *182*

## 31ST INFANTRY

*Mustered in: October 9 to December 24, 1862.*
*Mustered out: July 8, 1865.*
*Roster* II 444–70.
*Wisconsin in the war* 1000–02.
*Military history* 793–9.

Peck, George Record, 1843–1923.
Major-General George H. Thomas (read November 12, 1896). *MOLLUS-Ill* III 289–302.                        *183*

Stelle, Abel Clarkson, 1842–
1861 to 1865, memoirs of the Civil war, the 31st regiment Wisconsin volunteer infantry, by Abel C. Stelle. [New Albany, Ind., 1904] 87 p. front. (port.). 19cm.          IHi WHi    *184*

## 32ND INFANTRY

*Mustered in: September 25, 1862.*
*Mustered out: June 12, 1865.*
*Roster* II 471–500.
*Wisconsin in the war* 1002–06.
*Military history* 800–07.

. . . Annual reunion Thirty-second Wisconsin regiment survivors' association XVII–XLII 1894–1920.                        WHi    *185*
1897–1898 were not printed.

Hodges, William Romaine, 1840–
. . . "Lest we forget," by Captain William R. Hodges. Saint Louis, Woodward & Tiernan print. co. [1912] 14 p. 23cm.    WHi    *186*
Title and imprint from cover, p [1].

—— The Western sanitary commission and what it did for the sick and wounded of the Union armies from 1861 to 1865, with mention of the services of Companion James E. Yeatman therewith. Read before the Commandery of the State of Missouri Military order of the loyal legion of the United States, February 3, 1906, by Captain W. R. Hodges. [St. Louis, 1906] 16 p. 22½cm.    CSmH DLC    *186A*

## 33RD INFANTRY

*Mustered in: October 18, 1862.*
*Mustered out: August 8, 1865.*
*Roster* II 501–24.
*Wisconsin in the war* 839–849.
*Military history* 808–19.

Robinson, Arthur J        1845–
Memorandum and anecdotes of the Civil war, 1862 to 1865, by Arthur J. Robinson, a Private, Co. E, 33d reg. Wis. vols. Portland, Ore., Printed by Glass & Prudhomme co., c1910. 38, (2) p. facs., port. 18½cm.
                        DLC    *187*
On cover: In remembrance of the boys who fought to maintain, one flag, one country and one people, 1861 to 1865. . . .

—— —— [St. Paul, Minn., Printed by the Webb pub. co.] c1910. 48 p. facs., 1 illus., port. 19cm.                    DLC    *188*
On cover: c1912.

—— [n. p.] c1912. 48 p. facs., illus., map, ports. 19cm.                    IaHi    *189*
Title and imprint date from cover.

—— A private soldier's Christmas dinner, December 25, 1863. Milwaukee, 1913. [12] p. facs., port. 19cm.            DLC    *190*
Title and imprint from cover.

## 34TH INFANTRY

*Organized: December 1862.*
*Mustered out: September 8, 1863.*
*Roster* II 525–49.
*Wisconsin in the war* 849–50.
*Military history* 820.

## 35TH INFANTRY

*Mustered in: February 27, 1864.*
*Mustered out: March 15, 1866.*
*Roster* II 550–77.
*Wisconsin in the war* 850–4.
*Military history* 821–3.

## 36TH INFANTRY

*Mustered in: March 23, 1864.*
*Mustered out: July 12, 1865.*
*Roster* II 578–603.
*Wisconsin in the war* 1006–09.
*Military history* 824–34.

Aubery, James Madison, 1843–

The Thirty-sixth Wisconsin volunteer infantry, 1st brigade, 2d division, 2d army corps, Army of the Potomac, an authentic record of the Regiment, from its organization to its muster out. A complete roster of its officers and men with their record. A full list of casualties, in detail, dates and places. Maps showing its movements. A copy of every official paper in the War department pertaining to the Regiment, and others pertaining indirectly to the command . . . with reminiscences from the author's private journal [by] James M. Aubery, Lt. Co. G. [Milwaukee, Evening Wisconsin co., 1900] 430 p. illus., maps, ports. 24½cm.

Unit roster 293–319.     DLC NN    **191**

Coon, David,     –1864.

Civil war letters of. . . . *North Dakota historical quarterly* VIII (1941) 191–218.    **192**

"Foreword" signed by the author's son, John W. Coon.

Warner, Clement Edson, 1836–1916.

Appomattox and Lee's surrender, by Clement E. Warner, Lieutenant-Colonel 36th regiment Wisconsin volunteer infantry, 1902. *MOLLUS-Wis* IV 21–9.    **193**

## 37TH INFANTRY

*Organized: April 9, 1864.*
*Mustered out: July 26, 1865.*
*Roster* II 604–31.
*Wisconsin in the war* 1009–11.
*Military history* 835–44.

Eden, Robert C     –1907.

The sword and the gun, a history of the 37th Wis. volunteer infantry, from its first organization to its final muster out, by Major R. C.

Eden. Madison, Atwood & Rublee, printers, 1865. 120 p. 16cm.     DLC NN    **194**

Unit roster [70]–109. Coulter 145.

## 38TH INFANTRY

*Mustered in: Companies A, B, C and D, April 15, 1864. Other Companies joined the Regiment later in the year.*
*Mustered out: July 26, 1865.*
*Roster* II 632–55.
*Wisconsin in the war* 1011–13.
*Military history* 845–53.

Pierce, Solon Wesley, 1831–1903.

Battle fields and camp fires of the Thirty-eighth, an authentic narrative and record of the organization of the Thirty-eighth regiment of Wis. vol. inf'y, and the part taken by it in the late war, a short biographical sketch of each commissioned officer, and the name, age at time of enlistment, nativity, residence and occupation of every enlisted man, with notes of incidents relating to them, by Lieut. S. W. Pierce. Milwaukee, Daily Wisconsin print. house, 1866. viii, [9]–254, (1) p. 19½cm.

                NN    **195**

"Errata," p (1). Biographical sketches of the officers, [143]–202. "Record of enlisted men," [203]–54.

## 39TH INFANTRY

*Mustered in: June 3, 1864.*
*Mustered out: September 22, 1864.*
*Roster* II 656–72.
*Wisconsin in the war* 855–8.
*Military history* 854.

## 40TH INFANTRY

*Mustered in: June 14, 1864.*
*Mustered out: September 16, 1864.*
*Roster* 673–89.
*Wisconsin in the war* 858–60.
*Military history* 855.

Annals of the Fortieth. Sundry proceedings, sayings, doings and "undoings" of the 40th reg. Wis. vol. inf. are herein chronicled. [4] p. 56cm.     WHi    **195A**

Caption title. From A bibliography of Wisconsin's participation in the War between the States, by I. S. Bradley: "By Julius Converse Chandler, familiarly known as "Shanghai Chandler." Newspaper form, 15 x 21 inches. Reprinted in same form by C. A. Libby of Evansville enterprise about 1890.

Roster of the Fortieth Wisconsin infantry. [Madison, Frank S. Horner, printer] 1893. 31 p. 14½cm.     WHi    **196**

## 41ST INFANTRY

*Mustered in: June 8, 1864.*
*Mustered out: September 24, 1864.*
*Roster 690–702.*
*Wisconsin in the war 860–1.*
*Military history 855–7.*

## 42ND INFANTRY

*Mustered in: September 7, 1864.*
*Mustered out: June 20, 1865.*
*Roster II 703–22.*
*Wisconsin in the war 861–3.*
*Military history 858–9.*

McGregor, Duncan, 1836–1921.
Incidents in army life, by Duncan Mc-Gregor, Captain 42nd Wisconsin, 1913. *MOL-LUS-Wis* IV 377–86.                **197**

## 43RD INFANTRY

*Mustered in: August 8 to September 30, 1864.*
*Mustered out: June 24, 1865.*
*Roster II 723–42.*
*Wisconsin in the war 863–6.*
*Military history 859–60.*

Report of the meeting of 43d Wis. inf. vols., in Milwaukee, Aug. 28 and 29, 1889. [4] p. 22cm.                            WHi    **198**
Caption title.

Re-union of the 43rd Wisconsin volunteer infantry in Chicago, August 29th, 1900. [4] p. 24cm.                            WHi    **199**
Caption title.

Cobb, Amasa, 1823–1905.
Johnsonville, an address read at a re-union of 43d Wisconsin vol. inf., at the encampment of the G.A.R., at Chicago, August 29, 1900, by Gen. Amasa Cobb. [Milwaukee] Published by the Regimental Association [1900] 26 p. 23½cm.                          WHi    **200**

Mockett, Richard H        1838–1935.
The Richard H. Mockett diary. Edited by James L. Sellers. *Mississippi valley historical review* XXVI (1939) 233–40.          **201**

## 44TH INFANTRY

*Organized: October – November 1864.*
*Mustered out: August 28, 1865.*
*Roster II 743–65.*
*Wisconsin in the war 866–7.*
*Military history 860–1.*

## 45TH INFANTRY

*Organized: November 8, 1864.*
*Mustered out: July 17, 1865.*
*Roster II 766–86.*
*Wisconsin in the war 868.*
*Military history 862.*

## 46TH INFANTRY

*Mustered in: March 2, 1865.*
*Mustered out: September 27, 1865.*
*Roster II 787–806.*
*Wisconsin in the war 868–9.*
*Military history 862–3.*

## 47TH INFANTRY

*Mustered in: February 27, 1865.*
*Mustered out: September 4, 1865.*
*Roster II 807–27.*
*Wisconsin in the war 869–70.*
*Military history 863–4.*

## 48TH INFANTRY

*Organized: February to March 1865.*
*Mustered out: December 20, 1865 to March 24, 1866.*
*Roster II 828–45.*
*Wisconsin in the war 870–2.*
*Military history 864–6.*

Herrick, William, 1848–
. . . Life and deeds of William Herrick, hermit of Minnehaha falls. A tale of the wild West in early days, a true story. Edited by Samuel A. Hatch. [Minneapolis, University press, 1903]. 56 p. illus., ports. 23cm.
                             DLC    **201A**
At head of title: Souvenir. Pages with illus. and accompanying text are not paged. Civil war 7–12.

Pearsall, Uri B
The official reports of the building the "Red river dam," at Alexandria, La., May, 1864, which saved the Mississippi flotilla under Admiral Porter, from destruction. Compiled by U. B. Pearsall, late Col. 48th Wis. infty., from volume 34, series 61, of the "History of the Union and Confederate armies," published by the War department. [Lansing, Kansas, 1896] 14, (2) p. 21¼cm.                NHi NN    **202**
Title from cover. Illustrations: Building the "Red river dam" and Gunboats passing through the "Red river dam," p 2 and 3 of cover.

## 49TH INFANTRY

*Organized: December 24, 1864 to March 5, 1865.*
*Mustered out: November 8, 1865.*
*Roster* II 846–67.
*Wisconsin in the war 872–4.*
*Military history 866–7.*
High, James Lambert, 1844–1898.
My hero (General William F. Bartlett) (read January 12, 1893). *MOLLUS-Ill* III 155–71.                *203*

## 50TH INFANTRY

*Organized: March to April 1865.*
*Mustered out: April 19 to June 12, 1866.*
*Roster* II 868–89.
*Wisconsin in the war 875.*
*Military history 867–8.*

## 51ST INFANTRY

*Organized: March 20 to April 29, 1865.*
*Mustered out: August 16–30, 1865.*
*Roster* II 890–908.
*Wisconsin in the war 876.*
*Military history 868–9.*

## 52ND INFANTRY

*Organized: April 1865.*
*Mustered out: July 28, 1865.*
*Roster* II 909–20.
*Wisconsin in the war 877.*
*Military history 869.*

## 53RD INFANTRY

*Organized: March to April 1865.*
*Transferred to 51st regiment of infantry: June 10, 1865.*
*Roster* II 921–30.
*Wisconsin in the war 877–8.*
*Military history 870.*

## SHARPSHOOTERS

*A company was raised in Wisconsin for service with the United States sharpshooters, Company G, 1st regiment U. S. sharpshooters.*

# Regimental Publications
# & Personal Narratives
# of the Civil War

## A Checklist

*Compiled by* C. E. DORNBUSCH

Volume One    Northern States

PART VII   INDEX OF NAMES

New York

The New York Public Library

1962

THIS VOLUME HAS BEEN PUBLISHED WITH HELP
FROM THE EMILY ELLSWORTH FORD SKEEL FUND

# Foreword

ALL authors, editors, illustrators, and individuals mentioned in the text of this checklist of *Regimental Publications & Personal Narratives of the Civil War* are entered in this Index. Apart from entries for individuals, no subject indexing has been attempted. For anonymous works some title entries have been included. Citations in italics are subject entries for individuals.

In this checklist separate series of entry numbers have been given for each state. Index references consist of the state abbreviation (as used by the *National Union Catalog* of The Library of Congress) followed by the citation number within that state. The state abbreviations are as follows:

| | | | |
|---|---|---|---|
| Ct | Connecticut | Mn | Minnesota |
| I | Illinois | N | New York |
| In | Indiana | Nh | New Hampshire |
| Ia | Iowa | Nj | New Jersey |
| K | Kansas | O | Ohio |
| Me | Maine | P | Pennsylvania |
| M | Massachusetts | R | Rhode Island |
| Mi | Michigan | Vt | Vermont |
| | W | Wisconsin | |

Effort has been made to make the information in this Index as complete as possible. In many instances it has been impossible to determine the full names of individuals and their birth and death years. The compiler would welcome any additional information which readers of this checklist might bring to his attention.

C. E. D.

# INDEX OF NAMES

# Index

18

Index of Names